CH

Works by Amiri Baraka

Poetry

Preface to a 20 Vol Suicide Note
  (1961)
The Dead Lecturer (1964)
Black Art (1967)
In Our Terribleness (1968)
It's Nation Time (1968)
Black Magic Poetry (1969)
Spirit Reach (1971)
Afrikan Revolution (1973)
Hard Facts (1976)
Selected Poetry (1979)
Reggae or Not (1981)

Fiction

Blues People (1961)
The System of Dante's Hell (1963)
Home (1965)
Black Music (1967)
Tales (1968)
A Black Value System (1970)
Raise Race Rays Raze (1971)
Selected Prose and Drama (1979)
Daggers & Javelins, Essays 74–79
  (1982)

Anthologies

The Moderns (1963)
Afrikan Congress (1971)
Black Fire (1972)
Confirmation: An Anthology of
  African American Women
  (with Amina Baraka, 1982)

Drama

The Baptism (1964)
Dutchman (1964)
A Black Mass (1965)
Experimental Death Unit #1 (1965)
J-E-L-L-O (1965)
The Slave (1965)
The Toilet (1965)
The Death of Malcolm X (1966)
Great Goodness of Life (1966)
Home on the Range (1966)
Madheart (1966)
Arm Yrself or Harm Yrself (1967)
Police (1967)
Slave Ship (1967)
Four Black Revolutionary Plays (1969)
The Sidnee Poet Heroical (pub 1980)
  (1970)
Junkies Are Full of Shhh (1972)
Columbia The Gem of The Ocean
  (1972)
S-1 (1976)
The Motion of History (1977)
What Was the Relationship of the Lone
  Ranger to the Means of Production
  (1979)
Money (Jazz Opera) (1979), Production,
  New York City, January 1982,
  Workshop, LaMama Theater
Boy & Tarzan Appear in a Clearing
  (1980), Production, October 1981,
  New York City, Henry Street Theater
Dim'Crackr Party Convention (1980),
  Production, July 1980,
  Columbia University

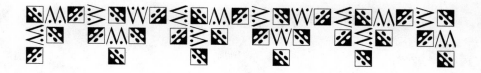

THE AUTOBIOGRAPHY OF LEROI JONES

AMIRI BARAKA

LAWRENCE HILL BOOKS

Library of Congress Cataloging-in-Publication Data

Baraka, Imamu Amiri, 1934–
   The autobiography of LeRoi Jones.
     p. cm.
   ISBN 1-55652-231-2
   1. Baraka, Imamu Amiri, 1934– —Biography.   2. Authors, American—20th century
—Biography.   3. Revolutionists—United States—Biography.   4. Afro-Americans—
Politics and suffrage.   I. Title
PS3552.A583Z463   1997
818'.5409 [B]   83-20576
                                               CIP

The author is grateful to the following for permission to reprint material:
From THE TRACKS OF MY TEARS, words and music by William "Smokey" Robinson,
Warren Moore, and Marv Tarplin, © 1965, Jobete Music Company, Inc.
Cover photo courtesy of Frederick Ohringer

Published by Lawrence Hill Books
An imprint of Chicago Review Press, Incorporated
814 N. Franklin Street
Chicago, Illinois 60610

ISBN 1-55652-231-2

10 9 8 7 6 5 4 3 2 1

For my wife, Amina
who is responsible
for any
truth
in this,
or in the chapters
to come!

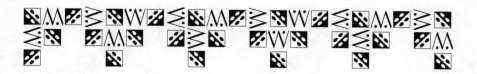

Contents

A Note to the Reader from Lawrence Hill Books

When Amiri Baraka's *The Autobiography of LeRoi Jones* was first published, by Freundlich Books in January, 1984, the publisher made substantial cuts to the text of the original manuscript. This new Lawrence Hill Books edition has reinstated all the excised material under the careful direction of the author. What you will read here is in effect the first complete edition of *The Autobiography of LeRoi Jones*.

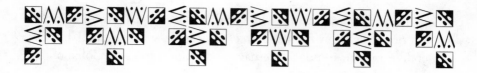

Introduction

The last writing of this stopped somewhere in 1974, when we had become Communists finally, Amina and I. From there, there has been a whole whirl and world of changes and contradictions, unions and struggles until we gets into 1996.

The politics is the underlying catalyst, though. And it always is in all of our lives, were we conscious of it. The fact that I became a Communist is not startling to me, as much of a stompdown cultural nationalist as I at one time was. I was sincere, but I usually always am. The abject racism and economic superexploitation, denial of rights and national oppression, and the imperialist overbeing was pressed upon me even in the eastern city of LaLa Land, "The Village." It grew, this sense of it, as I grew, intellectually, experientially, ideologically . . . whatever. I had seen a pattern, social, aesthetic, and ideological, that had worked on me, among those who spose' to be the whatever of the whatitis. And that was cold funky, spaced out above the real, which got to be corny or wrong, since laying in the cloud of ain't-I-hip here in the capital of anything goes, how could the who-ain't-here be anything but not?

Then the rush that Malcolm's murder pulled the trigger on. What Malcolm was saying, what he was for me, was a trigger, a maximum weapon of legitimate resistance to the whole bullshit of the place from its whole-ass America to its corny EVillage streets. It was the same, after all, however you code it in your mind. Supremacy and Oppression and Collaboration and Double Consciousness.

The vows I made from the streets of Chicago, as a young smart-ass just got put out of Howard University that I "would learn something new every day," till ejecting out of the error farce, to the eventual "shot out of guns" into Harlem and the Dangs and crazies there, but it was still the deep commitment I had made, not just with my intellectual self, but with everything that kept me alive and sane. That we would raise this fight to the highest intensity, we would not be slaves like this. No!

So then Newark, and the way I came, and what I wanted to do, and what I did, and my meeting Sylvia Robinson, who became my wife, Amina Baraka, and all we did together in tune or in opposition, was who I would become, certainly, but there is always the shadow that being and doing makes. The "Other," like my mad phenomenologist friend, Peter Schwartzburg, used to say. What it all had dragging behind it, what it, my being, being and doing caused, is the question.

The question is important because everybody knows the answer . . . that there is a specific question, the same folk are less clear. The question that tracked me was about my other former life, everybody had a hold on it, every body, but fewer minds.

I mean all the mad speculation and rumors and total lies. Plus, remember, for all the mix-and-serve hype of the now, then, was another story. Oh, yes, it was. What amazes me is that the stories pile up behind you like cities you have escaped clutching your sanity like a naive virgin.

Certainly, as my wife is fond of saying, my writing tells much of the story. Who I was, who I wanted to become, and what became of all that. Yet it is not wholly there, and for the many who knew LeRoi Jones and his works, and even might have dug them or not, there are many fewer, as of yet, who know this Baraka chap. The bosses aim to keep it that way. Like the good doctor, DuBois, when he finally put on his Red Star and proclaimed it to the world, he understood, as he expressed it: "Now the little children will no longer know my name." But, dig, Doc, we gonna make sure that don't last.

Anyway, as the book out and inlines, escaping from the place or places I had journeyed to and travailed in was much more difficult than I thought. Like Dr. DuBois I proclaimed it, all right, but the megatons of flying bullshit that flew back at me in return was more than I expected.

Looking back, the organizations that I had helped create were absolutely necessary. What they attempted to accomplish still must be done. And that is the real odor of Beelzebub that still won't let me rest. Through CAP, which was basically an alliance of local organizations centered nationally around the principles of Maulana Karenga's Kawaida (Swahili for tradition) doctrine. At first, armed with this nationalist fuel, we did some positive things.

It is still my contention that we were revolutionaries, albeit saddled with the weight of nationalism, which does not even serve the people. In fact, in the U.S., since White nationalism is the dominant social ideology, reactionary Black nationalism merely reinforces the segregation and discrimination of the oppressors.

I mean we were anti-imperialists, even as nationalists, which is what should be meant by the often-abused term "revolutionary nationalist." We were fighting our national oppression as we understood it. That was manifest as "White people" to us for obvious reasons. That is the nature of the Big Bourgeois is the U.S. And indeed, the very development of imperialism divides the world into a tiny group of industrialized, mostly European nations, which feed on the rest of the nations of the world in the name of "supremacy" or progress or straight-out as money!

I was always anti-imperialist in essence; the works, the previous organizations show that. And I was not always a Black cultural nationalist. The book makes that obvious. But the fact that I had been so much a part of the liberal "integrated" Village scene, including marriage to a White woman, and a kind of growing recognition as a writer, &c., I guess created a whirlpool of tempest and shock among the people I had known in those islands of abstract intoxication, when I finally "changed up" and decided to "book."

One thing must be understood, that all the people who benefited, or appreciated or whatever, from that Village scene were generally drugged at me for splitting—Blacks and Whites. Many have still not forgiven me! And certainly now, with the deadly plummet of the imperialist God's rock back down the mountain on Black Sisyphus's head, to try to obliterate the gains that the sixties' revolutionary democratic struggle produced, some of these same folks are guffawing in stereo that, "Hey, shit, Roy, I told you that shit wasn't happening. That you should have stayed down here with all us liberals and cryptofascists and anarchists and opportunists and got over like a big dog!"

The truth of this is that, yes, the Bigs do not want you to cry out, make known how to kill them. They understand that Black nationalism is a form of bourgeois ideology, and that they will be able to negotiate with these darker bourgeois to keep the rest of us in our place (Dig Newark! &c.).

But once you start talking about (WHAT?) socialism and multinational unity, you is definitely (a la DuBois) not to be seen or heard "enty" (as Al Hibber would say) more! This has happened to me with a vengeance. It is with a strict kind of exclusion, except to damn, that these wheels and heels deal with anything I (or even my post-Village Black family) do.

But this is one of the insistent points I draw in what I say and write. Why should you expect the cirtter you are trying desperately to waste to help you do that? So that the publishing and producing and distribution of revolutionary works must be the concern of these activists themselves. To whine about how Rocky ain't helping you kill him is, at the least, a sign of extreme naiveté cuddling with neon streaks of opportunism.

The transition to socialism was inevitable in my case because, in essence and emotional concern, I had been hovering around that open stance for a long time. But the rise of Black nationalism in the sixties with Malcolm X set me to contemplating myself with another kind of misunderstanding, though there was, at base, a road laid out that I could hit when I had reached a certain level of understanding and move to an emotional and ideological clarity I had not been able to achieve before. What remains important right this minute is what this transition has wrought, not only philosophically and psychologically, but what changes it has brought to my real life.

When I first assumed chairmanship of CAP in 1972, I began by putting out the slogans of Nationalism, Pan-Africanism, and Ujamaa. This moved, with my readings of Nyerere and Toure, to African scientific socialism. I had begun to conceive in my head by that time that I was moving even further to the Left. Not only my obsessive reading and peeping of this and that, but the experience of working in Black bourgeois politics as part of the whole democratic struggle, gave me an up close and very negative experience with them and their petty bourgeois managers.

Part of the burning union of my marriage to Silvia had been a yearning to be completely whole. To be able to struggle with my whole heart and soul, with my whole being, for what was deepest in me, which I took, then, as Blackness. The nationalist groupings I had been part of could never even concrete a consistent ideological illumination of what that meant. Though it should mean, at its most revolutionary, the possession of national consciousness that not only arises from the blunt patriotism of nationality but the fierce determination not to submit to evil in this racist and oppressive dungeon of Dis.

But as I hoped I laid out, coming from where I was with that tendency to extremes that Lenin characterizes as petty bourgeois and that Fanon confirms (where before I had been, in my own estimation, absorbed within an inch of my senses with the EuroAmerican aesthetic and intellectual traditions, by school, by the negrossity of my socialization, super-White), now I turned furiously around and vowed to be BLACK, I guess like DuBois's "Smoke King." We would prove our right to exist and be respected by hating these oppressors more openly and more violently than anyone else.

Yet the struggle in Newark had shown me, along with tireless work within the Black liberation movement and all political and intellectual work that went with that, that nationalism, no matter how justified, was not justifiable. The middle passage cannot justify nationalism just as the ovens of Auschwitz cannot justify the imperialist nature of Israel.

When I was about to come straight out and declare Marxism, I talked to Amina and told her how this move would have many of the Uberschwartzes saying, "See, I told you that dude would jump back White again." But I had passed all that mindless Blackbaiting and was ready to make the step.

This struggle within the Communist movement has been continuous and rugged. Now I was attacked often not only for the Black nationalist I had been but the Communist I would become. This was not all. The organization split, but even worse my marriage was on the verge of it as well.

Even today, Amina and I have a level of constant polemic that rises and sets like time and the beat. And it is rooted most clearly in ideological and class struggle. For we are both Communists.

Throughout CAP's history, the cultural nationalist ideology and politics of that movement had a social expression, too. Chauvinism for most men — if expressed to them as part of their psychological patois of thought and practice — can be denied hotly or jokingly, or received legitimately or falsely, whatever. But for the cultural nationalism of our organization, this male chauvinism was glorified as a form of African culture.

We had followed the Karenga doctrine, which said that women were not equal but complementary to men (which could be called sophistry), and that their role in the struggle was to "Inspire the Men, Educate the Children, and Participate in Social Development," which is almost "Kinder, Kirche, and Kuche." Same base as cultural nationalism in H's Deutschland.

So as we entered into the antirevisionist Communist movement, moving away from the Black cultural nationalism movement, the criticism we received from the misguided that we had abandoned Black people for a White ideology was now matched by the Left, which not only criticized us for our cultural nationalism but staunchly tried to beat us up about our not having the correct Marxist line.

The fact that most of the these Leftists were themselves out of the box and not near correct made it a swirling, finally destructive polemic that saw that movement, aided by the Fascist Bureau of Intimidation, all but disappear! Within these organizations (and this must be finally summed up and documented) during the middle and late seventies, the entire Left press was given over more to polemics against each other than against imperialism. Plus many of us still thought that revolution would be here in a few days, based on the fierceness of our rhetoric and posturing. Though, to be sure, there were a great many staunch, serious, capable, actual revolutionaries among our crowd. But the internal contradictions were such that with the external forces (e.g., Crazed Imperialist Assassins, Operation KAOS), the young forces of that movement were thrown apart, screaming defiance at each other, off into the wherever.

Many reasons can be cited in the specific example of our own organization; my leadership, of course. All are agreed to that, even me. Also the fact that we were still mostly nationalists. Remember, it was the very struggle we were involved in that helped free up the productive forces. Black capitalism in the nineties is much more developed than in the sixties and seventies; on the real side, not a figment of Nixon's imagination. The development of capitalism is contingent upon the broadening of democracy! And these developments are not only obvious; there is a positive aspect to them as well as the deadly negative. For one thing, until a certain level of productive forces (education of the workers and level of the tools they use, &c.) is reached, through the extension of democracy (what that is under capitalism), certain struggles will not be of a mass nature. The internal class struggle, for instance, inside the national Black community is muted by the struggle against the oppressor nation, White America.

For Amina, the shattering impact of our move to socialism brought a self-awareness of this intense and formal male chauvinism disguised as African traditionalism that disfigured our movement. The more we saw the atavism and cultural nationalism as backward, so the male chauvinism, in all of its ugly disguises and pretenses, the more—she will tell you this—she felt used and made silly by the whole of our ideological trend.

I tried to transform the organization. We read Engels's *Origin of the Family, Private Property, and the State*; we studied the woman question

together, once a week. Each morning I had the men reading and discussing the Marxist texts. On the oppression of women, the overthrow of
motherright as the denouement of the first class struggle, male against
female. I thought this was critical, if we were to advance in our understanding and reform both organizationally and ideologically.

But the Marxist teaching outraged many of us, some openly. The national organization flew apart, and each local did, too. The "dizzy
imbecility" of dialectical and historical materialism as a "White ideology"
(I'd said it myself, even in print, a bunch of times) was all around us, inside
and outside. Plus we did not understand completely what we were reading. We could not yet translate the theories into real-life understanding.
We were dogmatic or liberal. Book worshippers or insufficiently critical of
ourselves. We were also made deeply defensive by the rounds of criticism,
some accurate, some F.O.S., that kept being poured at us.

I was called an opportunist, a traitor, a disguised nationalist, a police
agent, a White-minded Negro, &c. The Left, in their frenzy of sectarian
dogmatism and liberal empiricism, offered us no help. But the altered
environs of the intraorganizational struggle among the Lefts was new to
us. Not only the incessant call of socialist revolution and the much-talked-
about struggle against opportunism and war against nationalism and cultural
nationalism that rang around us, but even the personal and organizational
style of the Lefts was new. A few of the cultural nationalist women including my wife embraced this because as the original practice changed and
women were drawn more directly into day-to-day organizing, the long African clothes became a less central part, or at least a less obsessive part, of
our thinking. Particularly when we began to come into contact with the
young African students, many of them Marxists who denounced traditional
feudal women-oppressing Africa with all their might. The Ethiopian students were especially strident in this regard, urging CAP women to fight
against the male chauvinism and African atavism they were fighting at
home.

There were so many strains of Marxist-Leninist, revisionist, Trot, and
social democratic trends bent in the wind around us that it would take
some time for us to accurately distinguish, so we were pushed from there
to there in unpredictable currents. The advocates we sent to various meetings would likewise come back perhaps influenced by this line or that line
and proceed to pump them into our superstructure without a peep.

The organization did change, on the topside. I made the structural
changes Marxism and its democratic centralism called for. We were heavy

on the centralist side, as cultural nationalists. So that when the struggles arose within the organization they would reflect the various lines that whipped around us with surprising turbulence. It was a turbulent time for the whole movement, for the entire anti-imperialist movement. There was a sharp lurch to the Left, but also there was a pitiless retrenchment and overturning of solid anti-imperialist values as well. (An extreme or infantile Left position always comes back around to embrace the Right, in essence.) We were headed for the time when the sabotage and undermining and murders and buyouts and internal disruption caused by our enemies would take a qualitative leap and the period when Revolution Is The Main Trend would come, at least temporarily, to a halt.

I could no longer, as the leader, be seen as invincible and all-correct. The conference in D.C., "Which Way the Black Liberation Movement?" sponsored by the Left-leaning ALSC leadership, saw our last threads of cultural nationalist cant thrashed publicly by an outright socialist line. But under scientific scrutiny it was still an incorrect old CP line that in a few months I had penetrated and easily dispatched. As for our other leading attackers, likewise, in a relatively short period of time, I had brought enough genuine analysis into our studies to point out their flaws and ideological deviations. At least it seemed and still does seem that way to me.

But the top-down nature of our organization and the genuine disorder the introduction of the socialist line had caused by challenging and attacking deeply held nationalist lines meant that for many of our advocates real understanding of what we were doing and where we were going came too late, or not at all.

Amina took the new socialist learning to be a truly liberating factor. So that with the catalyst of now having the ultimate tool against male chauvinism, she was drawn to those political lines that seemed most at variance with the old CAP teachings. When I was under all kinds of attacks from organizations and sources from Left to Right, she took my furious response to be resistance to change, and often tried to point out the correctness of the critics, even though they might, at the same time, be saying I was some kind of collaborator with the police.

I took this as a kind of betrayal, chafing at the loss of the official male domination, which had never really taken root in our house in the first place. Still, I could not accept the public criticism of our line by someone I felt should always be in my corner. For instance, I upheld the new leadership in China after Mao's death and their attacks on the ultra-Left "Gang of Four." Amina never did, and this caused deep conflict.

The call for the Proletarian Party by forces like RWL and WVO and the so-called "Revolutionary Wing" brought us into conflicts characterized by screaming rage, since she agreed with their premises, which I thought, and still think, were infantile Leftist, and since they were also relentlessly attacking me, personally and by name.

We were all ideologically confused, but I was struggling day and night for clarity, trying to keep the organization together the best I could. This is a book in itself. Finally, Amina resigned from CAP. Though she was now a member of our reorganized central committee, along with a few other women, she declared that she could no longer uphold the "bogus" cultural nationalist line and chauvinism of CAP.

She said that not only could she not uphold our "backward male chauvinist political lines," but that as the last days of CAP rolled toward us, she was more and more openly attacked by both the women and the men in the organization. The women, because their men had left the organization and they blamed it on Amina. Often, rather than blame the men who were runaways (which many of them soon became as well), they began to point at Amina, not as the main spearhead of the anti-male chauvinist, anti-Kawaida line, but as a splitter of marriages.

But also, now that the socialist mode of organization had been brought to CAP, some of her erstwhile closest comrades felt that the context was what they needed to struggle openly (more or less) with her for leadership. One line that crept up from the swamp was that just because a woman was married to the chairman of a local CAP branch she should not automatically be made chairwoman of that local women's division. Purportedly, this line had arisen about local CAPs, but Amina perceived that this was really aimed at her, though she was intellectually and ideologically qualified for leadership if she had never met me. But the introduction of the socialist line had broken down all the old leadership structure of CAP, and before it was over there were even physical blows struck.

Her resignation was very public, and she even got up in public forums to let people know that she didn't agree with me, that she was seeking unity with the true Bolshevik wing of the movement. The fact that later it would be proven, at least to me, that these people were incorrect and went on to prove themselves not even long-lived as Marxists, gave me some satisfaction, but it did not then. All I knew is that I had been betrayed. How could I be less capable theoretically than these people? How could she just throw our marriage out the window (my own chauvinistic, opportunistic b.s.) in exchange for "political correctness" that wasn't even correct? How could she dismiss and belittle my work and study for some two-bit soi-disant "Bolsheviks" who turned out not even to be that?

There was in this a deeper contradiction than either of us understood. For me, I felt I was being belittled in the sense that I had spent my adult life in intellectual pursuits, and for the last decade in clearly political struggle, albeit in a mainly literary and arts context. And now it was being dismissed by someone who claimed to love me.

Whatever someone might think, I knew I was no fool. I knew I could finally grasp the depth of Marxist theory and I could not believe that Amina would feel that there were other forces out there who would have a superior understanding of "the science" or anything else.

How could this be true? Didn't she know that however incorrect I was in whatever juncture of this travail that ultimately I would find the clarity and correct political direction? How could our relationship be dismantled by some political disagreement? No matter how much we might differ, I thought that if we worked together, as husband and wife and as committed revolutionaries, we would come up with the correct political focus, together. But also, I could not understand how our being together could not be the result of a single underlying political unity of focus and commitment; I guess, like the bourgeoisie who think democracy is a form of competition.

But Amina's disconnection with the organization I took as a dismissal of me as relevant to the revolutionary struggle itself. How could you be married to somebody whose ideas you did not even respect? As well, cries were thrown at us that CAP had built a cult of personality around us and that this cult had negated whatever political errors I made for the sake of some metaphysical elevation of "Imamu." And even though many of the features that seemed to do this—buttons with my picture, organizational celebrations of my birthday—had been advanced by Amina, she now felt that Marxist organization demanded the vocalizing of this anti-cult of personality line, which I felt was just an attempt to disrupt the organization and alienate the advocates from leadership.

The male chauvinist public image of CAP was another alienating factor. Many of the CAP women felt that unless they now were outspoken in their rejection of such atavistic male domination, in the new context of our public embrace of Marxism, they would be made ridiculous and pitiful, ignorant figures. Amina felt this. Always sensitive to what she measured as the opinions of the advanced, she felt doubly compromised by our cultural nationalist past.

In addition, the women's division was exactly that. Amina had taken the cultural nationalist division of men and women and created a women's group that in many ways always resisted the male chauvinist and opportunist aspects of the CAP leadership, including Karenga.

There was always a spray of negatives about me, surrounding us. As I said, I had never been forgiven by the Village denizens and their replicas internationally. Many of them, as they drifted into more contact with us after the partial inaccessibility the cultural nationalist organization had given us, now had more access to all of us. So that the many contradictions and oppositions that these people and I had had were now transformed into background stories that "Newark people" didn't know. Their continuing disagreements were given as simple statements of fact. And the resentment at my sudden swoop into hyper-Blackness and disappearance into Harlem and Newark would be represented as measures of my character by "old friends."

My characterization as "wrong" and "always alienated from the people" and a "Johnny-come-lately" in the Black thing were represented as tales of insiders trying to inform the uninformed about my pre-Black days, but they were also attempts to legitimize their opposition or refusal to participate in the struggle in the mode I had chosen.

The predictable co-optation of the political movement I had helped give leadership to, by the petty bourgeois Negro politicians, or the resurgence of the Beat movement, which now used me to give it some connection to the Black Arts Movement, could be part of the explanation of why I had acted the way I had, and why I had thought the things I did, and why eventually I would be reabsorbed by the totally backward and betray all those who trusted me.

My first wife was one spearhead of continuous rancor and bullshit, both privately and publicly. Her strategy for harassment and undermining was that she would ingratiate herself with my parents (and many of the people I had disconnected from) and thus create a hookup to undermine and disrupt my public life, my marriage, and alienate my parents.

I knew this from the beginning and knew, as well, that the deviousness of the petty oppressor is as damaging, in a specific context, as the Bigs'. For one thing, she created an entire revisionist version of our life together for herself so she could fill our children's heads and everyone else's within wordshot with lies and self-legitimizing martyr stories. She created a lying picture of herself as a dedicated political activist who could not understand why I had left in the first place since she was always high up in the movement. She said, as well, that she was a writer, but she had sacrificed her writing, even hidden it from me, because of the crushing weight of my male chauvinism and her selfless desire to forward my career.

In this endeavor of lie mongering, she has been helped by other empty-headed cryptoracists, whose statements printed or reported did have the positive aspect of eliminating the "crypto" from their description, and by the big superstructure of bourgeois untruth itself, particularly the literary sector. The woman herself published a book twenty-five years later explaining how she got to be my wife! Still using my last name as hers, since she never really liked her last name in the first place.

So for all the years since that organization's emphatic marking of my own life's changes, the shadow, the "Other," the dead past, has not been dead at all, but an animated agent of straight-out lies and harassment, from the shabby little autobiography full of plain untruths and opportunistic misdirection running into the willful distortions of White America that I really ceased to exist once I left the White folks! Like all opportunists, she now claims a "feminism" nowhere visible during our connection. But the open, racist dismissal of what I went on to do, with a sickening glorification of her cottage-industry martyrdom and self-effacing support of me, at least let more discerning people check her out in a way that explained the very shallow yet pompous nature of that Village life from another angle, as well as highlighting the sick and hardly subliminal national chauvinism of those masquerading as radicals and liberals. The underlying motif of all the exes in my life, even those of blood, and the various sycophants, revenge-filled guilty bystanders, racists, charming ignoramuses and weak liberals who waved, and will always wave, bye-bye at any real human upsurge, is that they have given a good portion of their energy and consciousness to being the subjective yet part of the objective (No for every Yes), the fake knowers like witches and devils, spreading delusion that passes as real life. Living human propaganda that serves as identity as part of the system's loyal opposition.

White America has been only too glad to help in this endeavor, because once I became a Marxist, they were not interested in publishing my opinion "enty way." The struggles and transformations during this Marxist phase of my life were not documented at all. I had more and more problems getting published, while everyone associated with the "Other" was ubiquitous—both the Blacks who resisted Baraka's "Black Fascism" and refused to leave the Village, and the onetime radicals who more and more could be projected as they grew openly less radical. An entire revisionist account of those times and their meaning grew up around us, which in bitter irony was actually believed by many of the people it was intended to hurt. And so it has hurt them even worse.

The fact that now I could not get published as easily, that the infrastructure of militant resistance I had built had dissipated and not only the old Village Black and White intellectuals could testify to my incorrectness, in bold print, but the political types around us, whether nationalists or on the Left, also "Amen!"-ed the same opinion about my "hopeless, self-deluded irrelevance," left me, for a time, disoriented to a degree.

As CAP disintegrated I accepted a job at Yale as visiting professor. And using the subjective and chauvinist feeling that I had been betrayed and isolated, I took up with a wholly reactionary woman in the program I was teaching and had an affair, justifying it with my outrage at being "politically rejected" since I would say to myself that Amina must not care about our marriage any more if she is willing to publicly denounce me as some kind of political swindler and charlatan. But, alas, wasn't that proof?

When the first printing of this book appeared she was furious that I seemed to pay more attention to the Village and first wife than our lives or the lives of the people with whom I had worked and lived since. She began to say after a while that I had wasted her life by pretending to be a revolutionary and that the cultural nationalist CAP had finally not done much but empower the petty bourgeoisie. Plus, people, "old friends of mine," had told her how sick I was in the first place. If she had only listened, she would lament.

Amina also feels this autobiography hides my abuse and betrayal of her and seems to paint the White woman, first wife, as a martyr while implying, when I speak of her at all, that Amina's life with me has been glorious fun and games—that I have hidden the many affairs I have been accused of and the cruel male chauvinism and covering of her life and work, which have locked her in a jail of nonrecognition by the world.

One clear expression of our embrace of Marxism has been Amina's emphatic identification with the working class, since that is her own class origin and her feeling that this in itself is reason to believe that she is correct about things I could not possibly understand. Though I have tried to convince her that twenty-nine years of marriage to a petty bourgeois intellectual means that the objective social context is petty bourgeois, and that working class now only refers to her class origins. But she still rejects that. And the fact of my own pitiful petty bourgeois origins, that class's social and cultural mores, the Howard University socialization, and most importantly, my socialization in the White-dominated Village and marriage to a White woman, means that as a working-class woman there will always be obvious contradictions between us.

So her sharpened opposition to male chauvinism, with a yeast of guilt at having been publicly "taken in," I feel—at having been in a cultural nationalist organization that preached the subjugation of women—has seen her move to a kind of social feminist position (I feel), where feminism has replaced Black nationalism, except that manifests itself now as an intense mistrust of petty bourgeois women, most of whom are White. (We are probably struggling about this right now!)

She also feels that she must take positions as publicly as possible in contradiction to mine since the petty bourgeois origin, White Village socialization (the Beat thing), the White-woman marriage, her longtime belief that my family (these "classic petty bourgeois Negroes") is not only hostile to her but consciously undermining her and our marriage, plus the celebration of my first wife by the media and the children of that first marriage (and by me, she insists) as a conscious harassment of her, make her stance, to her, as necessary as it is consistent.

She also feels that I have always neglected her and our children, and that she cannot be petty bourgeois, nor can they, because they have never lived like that, just me. And in sharp contrast to the children of my first marriage and two others outside that marriage who have "gotten over," our children have been locked up, shot, harassed (for being ours, but particularly because their mother is Black), and dismissed by me and the world.

What the affair did was convince her that she does not even have to seriously consider the relevance of much of anything "political" I say. She feels that the only way she can express her own individual feelings is to put them in sharp relief to my own. Amina still maintains that my autobiography is a book full of lies and attempts to denigrate and belittle her and give her accomplishments to other women. As much as I dispute this and say that the reader can be the judge, she refutes, saying, "How would the reader really know the truth?" What is true is that the development of political organization that came out of the Spirit House would never have happened in the ways that it did without her. This is one reason that her Left public alienation and what I felt as abandonment angered me so thoroughly. Whatever our disagreements, and like everyone else, we have always had them, I thought they could be worked out within the context of our private and political and organizational life. I did not expect to be denounced as politically incorrect as the public polemic of an opposing political trend.

The initial internal organization of CAP owes a great deal to Amina's insight and hard work. Certainly any growth and development of the women's division is her work. The African Free School, which at one time was our crowning achievement, was brought about largely through her efforts, organizational and theoretical. The insidious characterization of her as some silent, male-dominated anonymity has continuously outraged her, and her political declaration of independence was obviously meant to fly publicly into the face of that lie. And she has constantly accused me of collaborating with this characterization and characterizers, which include my first wife and the children we had, and through her influence, my family as a whole, which she feels has never been reconciled to our marriage. That is, she thinks they have tried to split us up because they didn't dig me being married to a working-class woman.

All of this, as far as I'm concerned, is untrue or at most overstated and distorted. But our enemies go to great lengths to make these absurdities seem palpable. For instance, Amina feels that her own background as dancer, painter and sculptor, actress, political activist, and cultural organizer are hidden not only by the hostile system, but with even greater injury, by me as well. Again, I am collaborating with our enemies to attack, belittle, and falsely characterize her. One reason for this, as a certain assembled opinion will confirm, is my historical alienation from Black women.

This is a strange introduction to the reprinting of this book. I am still not ready to write the autobiography past the years circa 1974–75 where this book leaves off. I have no doubt I will. These comments, I suppose, are an attempt to sum up partially where my mind, as least, is now and why it is there.

Amina and I are still married and chances are we will be for the rest of our lives. Why? Because we love each other. Despite the sharpness and continuity of our struggles, nothing but love could have held us together under the force of such opposition, though I do not, and nor does she, I think, claim invincibility, either in our public or personal lives. But we do claim the emotional, psychological, and intellectual strength to withstand our enemies' designs and learn to live with our own contradictions as a visible confirmation that with all them disagreements, it must be love, like the song says.

—AB 1996

Stages
Memoirs

Stages here are Steps and attempts at evaluation (essays, assays). These are summings up, if only partially, of various steps, processes, beginnings, middles, endings in my life. These stages are also places whereupon acts occur and also those acts themselves, as part of one overall act, really *process* my life. And so these stages are like essays trying to help us understand and illuminate a portion of the American experience.

Within that American experience is the history and life of the African American Nation; a piece of the whole, yet *unintegrated* into that whole, black noncitizens whose only forward direction must be toward Self-Determination!

For me, being here has always been a condition of struggle and, hopefully, growth. These could be called *Essays on the Stages of My Life*. To essay is also to attempt! So these are attempts to sum up that life, before having lived it all. Attempts to "make sense" where it has been difficult to see any sense.

> *Step*
> *of a life*
> *turns*

under the sun
& the sun
turns &
burns &
finally one last day
goes
out
Its history
is a tail
Tales for
remembering
words for
understanding
A long way (opens)
Back then &
there
we see now
again
To know
Seeing
& understand
Our
Being.

Why these "Memoirs"? Because it seems my life plagues a few people. They want to "know" how I got wherever they perceive I am. Why I would leave where they "thought" I was in the first place. But was I ever there, where they thunk? And where was they?

But it is, has been, a path. From the beginning. And these "findings" are meant as darkness-altering mechanisms, small lights for seeing what a person will do and maybe why.

But even so (just to put a little doo doo in the contest), who knows if this is the real stuff, the *lowdown*. Perhaps I'm distorting for my own reasons, hiding various things. Who can say? The lies officials will put out about me (even the unofficial officials) will be bad enough to make these memoirs of mine at least a relief. At least that's what I say.

—AB 1981

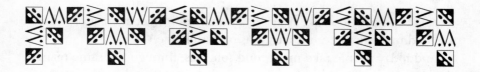

One

Young

Growing up was a maze of light and darkness to me. I never fully understood the purpose of childhood. Baby pictures nonplussed me. It looks like me a little, I thought. But what the hell, I didn't know nuthin'. It ain't that cute. Falling back like that, toothless grimace, mouth bare, legs bent, fat with diapers. And them probably wet.

Growing has obsessed me, maybe because I reached a certain point and stopped. My feeling is that I was always short. Maybe that's why people like those baby pictures, because you couldn't tell I was short then. Later, it became obvious and people started to rub it in.

I was not only short, little, a runt. But skinny too. Short and skinny. But as a laughing contrast I got these big bulbous eyes. Big eyes. And it was no secret where they came from: my old man. Actually, you could say I got my whole "built" from him (Coyette Leroy Jones). But I don't want to slander him, because he is my father and I love him.

But people always would be sliding up to me saying, "You look just like your father," or to him, "Roy, he look just like you," or to my mother or some other hopeless "responsible" in whose charge I was placed, "Hey, he look just like Roy"—"He look just like his father." It made you wonder (even then) why they put so much insistence on this. Was this a miracle?

Wasn't I spose' to look like him? What was this wonder at creation? (Later, I would make up other implications of this charge.)

And today people take my second son, Ras, through the same bizness. And to a lesser extent his three brothers and sister. But this was a stamp or some stamps of Young: that I was short and skinny with big eyes and looked just like my father. These were the most indelible. My earliest identity.

I knew, too, rather early, that I was brown. Brown with a round face and sometimes wavy hair. These were later dissociations. Brown, round, and wavy. OK.

I thought I looked OK. Sometimes better than other times. When I had on what I wanted and wasn't too sparkly from my brown mom's Vaseline aspirations, I didn't look bad. Shit, I was just short! That's all. (Even the "skinny" shit was a secondary harassment.)

Another thing is that we were always in motion. It seemed that way. But why or how or even the supposed chaos of such a situation never registered. It certainly was never explained to me by anyone. Though I guess you could get some word from these Johnny-come-lately sociologists, if you got the time to be bored with their chauvinism. But it was our way, is what etched itself somewhere.

From Barclay Street, a "luxury" project we had to move out of, $24 a month was too much even though my ol' man had just got a good job at the Post Office. But he couldn't cut those prices, so we had to space. But I have some early memories of that place. Its park, its fire escapes (I nearly fell off and ended the saga right here), its red bricks and some light browns and yellows flittin' round.

Earlier than this is a blank, though I have "memories" produced by later conversations. Like being hit by a car—banged in the head (or do I remember the steel grille smacking my face, trying to wake me up!?).

A dude hit me in the head with a big rock. And I still carry the scar. I think I remember that sharp pain. A cold blue day. A brown corduroy jacket. And the whiz of wind as I broke round the corner to our crib.

I pulled a big brown radio down, also on my head. (Ah, these multiple head injuries—is something beginning to occur to you? Spit it out!) Another scar, still there. The radio had a knob missing and the metal rod sunk into my skull just left of my eye.

Tolchinskie's Pickle Works across the street. A smell and taste so wonderful I been hooked ever since (every sense). Hey, man, in a wooden barrel, with them big green pimples on 'em. And good shit floatin' around in the barrel with 'em.

A guy who flashed around and tried to teach us to play tennis. That's how "horizontal" our community was then. Almost all of us right there, flattened out by the big NO. Later, more would "escape," rise up a trifle by our collective push. PUSHy niggers. That's later a verticality rises, so we know. The vicissitudes of NO.

But I never learned how to play tennis. That yellowness never got in. But it was different in my house than out in the street. Different conventions. Like gatherings—of folks and their histories. Different accumulations of life. So those references and their *enforcement*.

You see, I come from brown niggers from way back. Yeh. But some yellow niggers—let's say color notwithstanding—some yellow and even some factual, *a* factual, white motherfucker or fatherfucker in there.

I was secure in most ways. My father and mother I knew and related to every which way I can remember. They were the definers of my world. My guides. My standards. (So any "nut-outs" y'all claim got to begin there!)

I was a little brown boy on my mother's hand. A little brown big-eyed boy with my father. With a blue watch cap with Nordic design. At the World's Fair (1939) eyes stretched trying to soak up the days and their lessons.

But the motion was constant. And that is a standard as well. From Barclay to Boston (Street) and the halfdark of my grandmother's oil lamp across the street. They had me stretched out one night, buddeeee, and this red-freckle-face nigger was pickin' glass outta my knee. There were shadows everywhere. And mystery.

My grandfather had had a grocery store on that same street earlier, but that was washed away in the '30s with a bunch of other stuff. My grandfather didn't shoot himself, or jump off a building. But after that, we was brown for sure!

And so for that branch of the family, there was a steep descent. My mother's folks, the Russes. In Alabama the old man owned two grocery stores and a funeral parlor. First grocery stores burned down by "jealous crackers" (my grandmother's explanation). After the second arson, they had to hat. First, to Pennsylvania (Beaver Falls) and then finally to Newark.

My father was running from dee white folkz too. He had bopped some dude side the head in a movie he ushered in. The dude was an ofay. (Naturlich!) And so, again, the hat was called for.

To arrive, out of breath, in a place you thought was The Apple but turned out to be the *prune* (Newark) or the raisin. Jobless, detached from the yellow streak of the Jones's (nee Johns's) upward mobility, even there inside the brown. A part-time barber, for mostly white folks, with a high school diploma—though three of his sisters were bound for college. Projected from a teeny brown white-haired widow lady, daughter of another teeny brown white-haired widow lady, who shot the distaffs through on sewing for white folks and a blissful irony that smiled the bittersweet recognition of the place and its inhabitants. Its mores and morons.

So that's where we was coming from. The church of specific reality. Inside the general (flight) our Johns-Jones/Russ lives merging. But see, they had sent my mother to Tuskegee (when it was a high school) and then to Fisk. I used to look at both yearbooks full of brown and yellow folks. She had one flick poised at the starting line, butt up, large eyes catching the whole world, about to take off. Her name then was "Woco-Pep," a Southern gasoline. She was that fast.

Where she was going to in her parents' heads, I ain't exactly hip. Except it's safe to say it was *up*. Storekeeper father, mother and brother assistants in the joint, and whatnot. But somehow she ran into this big-eyed skinny dude. (MF) My father. A tipsy part-time barber or a barber who occasionally got deep in his cups. The story goes he flipped his little Ford on top of his drunk self on 13th Avenue and come out from under swearing off.

You see an irony here? No? A split-off from the upwardly mobile somehow molests (with permission) the scioness of the nigger rich. Except by 1929 all them fireworks was put out by Ugly Sissy's fatal flaw—capitalismus. And so the new day dawned with a pregnant coed who did not get to go to the Olympics and a new member of the family who didn't come from "bad stock" (!aagh hopeless!) but what the hell was his thoroughly brown ass going to do now?

Marrying your mama, Jim. What else? And so flow the streams together. (But wasn't one of the first Negroes to read in South Carolina, complete with plaque and multiple modest legend, your old man's Uncle Enoch? Yaas—that's affirmative—over. And them slender and fat sisters of his, wasn't they all got to be teachers and shit? Affirmative—J.A.M.F. So couldink you say they was all in the same shit—anyway?)

You see, you doesink understand colored people or color peepas either. My mother's folks was in business. Them funeral parlor dudes was and is the actual colored rich guys. The bourgeoisie, dig? Them teachers and shit (his old man [MF's] was a preacher part-time and chef, also bricklayed a taste. Got the flu and it took him off), they just the petty bourgeoisie. And hell, they even had food smells and brick dust on 'em and some sew-for-white-ladies thread on 'em. Whew!

Later, it really cracked up. They was drug down! That's what the scuttle-butt was. Arguments in our weird orange house years later. My uncle called my father a "nincompoop." What is that? Because these Russes had been drug down, Jim! Outta they funeral parlors, outta they stores, Granddaddy to be a night watchman, his wife on the bus to Essex Fells to curl up some white ladies' hairs, and wouldn't ya know it, MF "had" MM in a dusty-ass Jew factory doing piecework. (But he did make a breakthrough, you got to admit. He wasn't jes' a dum' nigger. He did get in the Post Office!) Thass rumblings all up in there as part of the collective psyche. On the X spot of the altar. The forebodings and nigger history. All stuffed into me gourd unrapped on arrival. But ye gets used to hearing tumblings in the wind and words the leaves make spinning in the air like that.

But would ya tell from me mischievous ways the stuffings inside me round peapicker knot? A trained eye, ye say? Oh?

So, Boston Street. And "Bunny" and "Princess" across the street. His mother tortured him in the bathtub with green water. I couldn't help him—he was weeping and shit. I was froze and puzzled, standing there. What was in that water? Or was it just he didn't want no bath?

Boston Street.

Ellie the painter raved in them parts. Crawling over the fences in spotted coveralls, drunk as the social system. We lived in two houses on that street—at one address I tumbled off the stone porch and busted my collarbone. And a preacher blew his wife to smithereens around the corner. It was a spooky house with a narrow path. And Miss Rhapsody across the street gettin' ready for evening so she could put on her purple flower and go out and sing the blues. (She had a fine-ass daughter. Blue, stiff, and beautiful!)

But all that soon was in the wind. We moved, ya see? Looked up and we were way cross town near the Italian border. I was born in the center of the city (New Ark) in a hospital named for a yellow doctor, Kinney Memorial. But by age five or six we'd spaced—dot-dot-dash-dot, communications—going somewhere. Wound up on a little street the other side of nowhere.

And we were all in there. Mama Daddy Nana Granddaddy Uncle Elaine and me. On Dey Street. The niggers were so cynical they called it *die*—the white folks so full of shit they called it *day*. Take your pick!

Orange house with a porch you sit on, or crawl under and plot shit. Living room, dining room, kitchen, left turn, bathroom. Back door and little yard, edged by cement and a two-car garage. Second floor: narrow bedroom (Uncle), middle bedroom with big oak bed with a back tall as a man and footpost taller than a six-year-old (Nana and Granddaddy). Front bedroom (Mama and Daddy and little kids, us).

A red-nosed Irishman (Ol' Man Doyle) and his wife on one side next to a vacant lot and right next door Angel Domenica Cordasca (female), a little nonromantic Italian playmate. Next to Doyle, the playground at the edge of which sat Central Avenue School. Next to Angel, a factory. Across the street from Central Avenue School, a row of brown houses. Clarence P. (funny), his older brother (weird), his mother (church stalker). Danny W., a confederate, short and curly-haired. Fast but plump. Another lot for an auto parts store. (They got the whole block now.) Then Pooky, a little Italian troublemaker, his twin sisters, snotty-nosed midgets. The Davises next, eight black curly-headed all-sized colored kids—actually light brown in color, black in socio-eco terms. Who knew Mr. D.? Mrs. D. was always called Ms. as far as I know. And she ran that bunch, literally, up and down the street. Frank, big and away soon to the army, never to return. Evelyn, big and fine with that wavy, straightish hair them kinda folks had, but way outta my generation. Sam called Lon-nell. It was Lionel. Orlando called "Board," meaning Bud. Algernon called "Algy." Jerome, real name "Fat." "Rookie," given name unknown, and Will, the pee wee. The D's always seemed like more than they were. At least ten or twelve. They were a standard of measure around those parts. Their name called by my mother meant "many" or "dirty" or "wild" or something like that. Algy and Board were running buddies of ours. Board was a desperado. And my mother didn't dig us running together. Nutty as he was, I didn't dig it too much. Algy was wild too, but cooler. Lon-nell you liked to have on your team as one of the "big boys."

Next to the Davises, Dominick, an Italian iceman, and his brood. Some more Italians, a couple, next to him, with a red and white very clean house. Dominick's house was yellow and brown. The red and white house had cherries in the back of it and you know we hit on them whenever our ass stopped aching from the last hit reported to the mama authorities. But those cherries, and I think some hard green knot peaches, like that cause we never let 'em stay there long enough to ripen, were cause for much adventure and repeated instruction in cause and effect.

There was also contrast in that and all along this one-block center (Central Avenue to Sussex Avenue) there was a similar contrast from a similar dissimilarity—mixture. For now we'd (Jones/Russ) flashed into a *mixed* neighborhood. I was about six now. And already a veteran of three different abodes. This made the fourth. (Barclay Street, two on Boston Street, and now Dey.) But all those other places had been the Central Ward—or at that time the Third Ward—near round "The Hill," center of black life. But this last move took us into the West (literally the West Ward) and a place where the black community trailed off in a sputter of Italians. Or likewise where the Italian community thinned and more and more blacks had moved in. So that in our block and all around in that area, there was a kind of standoff. Central Avenue School, it seems to me, was heavier black. The life there more controlled in the playground, in the hallways, by the black students. And the year the Warren Street contingent came in it was "The Hill" for sure pouring in. So that even in that part of the West headed North, the ambassadors from Central and even South brought those places to us. And so the Black Belt South—and so Africa.

But that mixture carried contradictions in it far beyond we youth, hey— even beyond many of the grown folks. We were friends and enemies in the non-final cauldron of growing up. We said things—did things—were things—and even became some other things that maybe could be understood on those streets, ca. 1940s.

So next to the red and white clean cherry and peach house, a lot with brown-grey gravel. A useless rusty lot that ended with a brick wall to nowhere. The back of some factory. And like a miniature boundary line, that twenty feet of lot separated the lower-middle-class Italian Cleaney from Eddie Clay's brown and tan rundown clapboard shack.

And in that shack, like a ghost of the black South—a drunken building—it had some living ghosts, poverty struck and mad. Old toothless snuff-chumping ladies. Staring old men. People with hard rusty hands. A woman named Miss Ada (I always thought it was ATOR, a weird radio drama monster name) who wandered and staggered and stared and got outrageous drunk and cursed out history.

We made up stories about Eddie and teased Eddie. A veil hung over the house. A food like musk—an oldness strangeness. Yet Eddie was one of The Secret Seven (the kids who hung with us sometimes, my sister and I, Board, Algy, Norman, Danny, Eddie). We were The Secret Seven, which met under our porch at 19 Dey Street to plot the destruction of packs of Kits and jars of Kool-Aid.

And we'd all tease Eddie about his weird house. It was old and poor-looking, full of old country Negroes usually drunk. And sometimes Eddie'd chase one or a bunch of us when we talked about his creepy old house. Yet across the hard gravel were the anonymous cherry-growing Italians in their white, spotless, red-trimmed number. The best-looking house on the block.

Our orangish brown clapboard number seemed merely like "headquarters." It seemed like it sagged a bit or leaned. Especially after a hurricane blew a big tree down on the bathroom and tore off the bathroom roof. It was on the street doing something, looking like something (to others), but what that was I really can't say. It was headquarters. Where I came out of and had to go back to—after school—after playground—after sneaking off—or after any stuff I'd got into—that leaning orangish brown house was my center, and my fate.

Next to Eddie's was my fake cousin Lorraine's red job. Red shingles and short brick steps. Her name was Jones so we could play cousins, though I liked her, from time to time, as a girlfriend, but that never went anywhere. But some older dudes thought she was my cousin on the real side and they would be trying to program me to drop their names on her. Some really vulgar types would tease me about what they was going to do to my cousin, like it mattered to me. (Though it did in the sense that I was jealous—not outraged like a relative, but the whole thing was so unreal that it was a very minor thing.)

Lorraine's house was short and squat, though it was three stories. Lorraine's mother looked just like her, chain smoking. A factory worker going back and forth during the war years like Rosie the Riveter. When we all had house keys tied on strings around our necks.

Then Mattie's narrow tall porched brown joint. I guess like Mattie herself. Tall narrow brown with glasses she'd be peering through. In street-wide gatherings when young and old kids big and little were together for some reason. Some summers, happenings or chance gatherings, Mattie would be there, a big stringbean girl (no matter what age). She had a kind of horsiness to her face that set the boys to razzing her about it when they were in that frame of mind. Sometimes they'd be saying some other things and Mattie'd turn on her long narrow heel.

A fence next to Mattie's, then Joycee's yard (her family shared it with the New Hope Baptist church). And that was the end of the block. On my side, across the street, after Angel's house, there was a factory that made boxes. They took up the rest of the block. The loading platform was the only interest, otherwise I remember wondering why they wanted to make our block dull with their grey building business.

And the block was, it seemed to me, fairly quiet. The scrambles of kids ran up and down and around the corner and around the other corner. I guess since Central Avenue School and playground sat on the block, it obviously couldn't have been quiet on school days, when those children ran screaming up and down the street. But Dey Street and, on either side, Newark Street to the west and Lock Street to the east, were like a swath of mixtures. Black heavy but still mixed, Italian and black. In fact, all the way to Orange Street, this mixture persisted. On the north side of Orange, you jumped into the Italian neighborhood. The old First Ward, now North Ward.

There was a mixture at the little-kid level which we carried most times successfully and at the tops of our voices. Adults fed us various poisons that pushed us apart as we grew, naturally. And by high school, almost miraculously, the relationships we'd had on the street level and in grammar school had disappeared. So quickly, I was startled. And I remember consciously taking note that this is what had happened. When I was a sophomore in high school I could see very clearly what had happened. That we had reached another stage, and those previous relationships were ended. And that while nobody spoke openly about this, we all, from our opposite sides of the nationality wall, knew what it meant, and acted accordingly. But that was a later stage; the open door onto it.

You wonder thinking back to Young, reflecting on memories of all that passed. What is left that coheres and brings it back, what does it mean now really? What it did mean then I guess is beyond us or we can glimpse occasionally an actual relationship, an actuality of that earlier life that gives deep recognition. I guess we understand ourselves better for today's steps and pauses.

So much does come back, flicks and flitting images. Faces and voices. A walk, a way of turning, a laugh, a silhouette just before darkness. We remember games, gangs, houses people lived in, general relationships and tales about all these. And from this we try to get an outline of we then. We try to understand who we're talking about. We're like snakes with billions of skins falling off like the blinks of an eye. And each skin a sensitivity that makes a certain specific identity. Though generally we're who we are, we're even who we were, though we learn different things, some of us go different places. Some of us don't go anywhere. We can be screamed at, locked up, beaten, almost killed. We can read books or look at plays and films. We can be talked to a long time by people who shape us in some ways. In a school, an outfit, a bar—some *place*. Mostly factories—cold in winter, hot in summer. And we *do* change. Sometimes we grow. On the real side.

For me the slow whiz of my life is full of sparkling pictures, glittering sequin images that speak of times and places, people and feeling. I register these impressions in the polymedium of my life and now try to recall a pattern, an overview without overviewer (except myself, years later).

Of earlier historical family scuttlebutt ya knows what I tolt ya. The three previous places we lived, that is, a we that included me, we had left by the time I was about six. At six we were on Dey, Russes and Joneses together. (It seemed normal to me but maybe it wasn't. In the end there was loudness and tension—it seemed bad feeling and we went our separate ways.) But it seemed normal to me. What dry types call "the extended family" and whatnot.

Those were the war years, so my youth has one told-to-me background of the Depression and another background that I was conscious of, World War Two. The Dey Street years are the World War Two years—the Joe Louis years, the Franklin Delano Roosevelt years (those were my maximum heroes!).

So I think I remember the Sunday the news of Pearl Harbor came. I didn't fully understand, then. But everything was heightened. There was excitement and fast talking. And I began to see obvious changes and as I understood more (reading the daily news everyday) I could see how the war moved things and changed things.

For one thing my mother, who'd been a college dropout because of my birth, now got a better, a college-type, job. Where before she had done piecework in various sweatshops she used to describe—on Beacon Street and Rankin Street—where there were sewing machines and dress patterns. A kind of Newark garment district. When the war came she got a job with the ODB (Office of Dependency Benefits) doing some of the administrative work that had to be done to see that the GIs' allotment checks got sent home to wives, parents, or whoever. And my mother got a job downtown, in a big flat red building they built in the center of town very swiftly. (Prudential insurance uses it as one of their ripoff points nowadays.)

So now she could dress up as an office worker and go off to do office work. It was better money, better surroundings, easier work, my mother said. Plus, you know, she could dig it with her background. My father was still on the mail truck then, delivering packages. He'd come home winter

times and stand on the grating the hot air came up through from the fur-
nace, the "registers" we called them, and stand there trying to get warm.
He was almost frozen stiff. (Before I got to high school he'd got inside the
P.O., and by time of college he was a supervisor.)

So the war brought that change to us as it probably brought some kind
of change to a great many people. One thing it meant now was that my
grandmother was raising my sister and me almost exclusively. And sometimes when my grandmother was taking that long ride up to Essex Fells,
where the rich white folks lived, to curl up somebody's hair or cook or
clean for the Fortes, my sister and I went real wartime and had to get our
own lunches in a lunchroom across the street from the school. My mother
paid in advance and we'd come in and get our sandwich and milk. Tuna
fish salad or bacon lettuce and tomato or bologna and cheese. We used to
crack up over this one big four-eyed white boy—Ralphie—who everyday,
without fail, got the same sandwich, grilled cheese. Somehow I thought
he was being tortured or something. (Just like my friend Bunny, who I saw
bathing in green smoking water and crying. I thought his mother was torturing him or something, it looked so out to me.) God-Lee, Ralphie is
having to eat grilled cheese sandwiches everyday. Ga-uhd-Lee, and my
sister and I laughed at him, but still I suspected some grimmer motivation.

But the war against the Germanies and the Japaneses, the Germans and
the Japs we came to call them, took up much of my time, and was the
background panorama of my young life. At one point some genius on our
block had offered the hypothesis that since the Japanese were "yellow" the
Germans must be green. (Was it me?) But that was quickly disproven.
We'd go to movies and see Germans doing they evil shit. They looked like
white people to us, though that didn't register as such, what with those
wild uniforms.

The difference between Germans and Nazis was not outlined for us. It
was just Germans that was doing the shit—all of 'em. Somehow the Italian
fascist participation in the war was muted and muffled in that neighborhood. But we never connected our Italian running partners with Mussolini
and Co. They had different uniforms. Plus we weren't clear on what an
"Italian" was. The kids we knew were Augie, Anthony, Thomas, Angel,
Pookie, Dolores, Marian, and they were white kids first but even that was
muted. We ran with some and didn't run with others, that was final enough
for us then.

But they were the contrasting shape of our environment. Augie D. was
my closest white friend. Him and Anthony Arlotta. Anthony, a school friend,

lived over in Baxter Terrace, the white side. Augie D. was around the corner on Newark Street. And while The Secret Seven was the main force of my daily young life of shaping, the whites like dots and dashes or points of contrast doing what they did completed the whole. They were not "us" though they were close enough to us—we lived on the same streets, went to the same schools. But the adult world held us apart in ways we didn't even understand.

Actually we most times were in different groups, gangs, had different white and black friends we were most intimate with, but then we crisscrossed at points, came together at times around whatever. I often wonder what those guys and girls carried away from that experience with us and what they make of it. (I know one guy, Tommy R., a pretty advanced white dude, an engineer, who comes back to Newark to see his mother, who still lives in Baxter Terrace, though there's no more white side; it, like most other things in town, is very very black. But I've yet to talk to him and try to find out what he got, what he found out about all that, and what it means to him.)

I'm not totally clear what I got out of all that. All those experiences and impressions. All that touching and going. For instance, what was elementary school? Then? Now it's, as I mentioned, a shuffling of shadows and images. Odd textures and fragments. Names and the lies memory tells.

But what was it then? What did I think it was? School was what? I knew I went because that's why my mother waked me up and got me dressed. Going to Central Avenue School, I could hear the first bell from my house and still get there on time, so close we lived. A vacant lot and one house, the playground (you could go through there) or the green door on the Dey Street side.

I went to school because I was supposed to go. Nothing in grammar school was hard (to me). Except keeping quiet. Otherwise it was just something you did because, well, you did it. I didn't think I was "learning" or anything like that. I just went cause I was supposed to go. In fact I never had any pretensions ever about "learning" till I'd gotten run out of college and was in the air force. Then I started to appreciate the "learning" process. And actually did, then, become attached to that activity. I mean it was then I fell in love with learning. But only after I'd come out of school.

School was classes and faces and teachers. And sometimes trouble. School was as much the playground as the classroom. For me it was more the playground than the classroom. One grew, one had major confrontations with real life in the playground, only rarely in the classroom. Though

I had some terrible confrontations in the classroom I can remember. Around discipline and whatnot. The only black teacher in the school at that time, Mrs. Powell, a tall statuesque powder brown lady with glasses, beat me damn near to death in full view of her and my 7B class because I was acting the fool and she went off on me (which apparently was sanctioned by my mother—it probably had something to do with conflicting with the *only* black teacher in the whole school and that had to be revenged full blood flowingly at once as an example to any other interlopers). But Mrs. Powell was one of the only teachers to take us on frequent trips to New York. And she had us publish a monthly newspaper that I was one of the cartoonists for. But apparently I did something "out" and she took me "out."

But in school when I was in kindergarten I got sick (went off with the whooping cough, then the measles). And I learned to read away from school—my first text Targeteer Comics—and when I came back I was reading—and haven't stopped since.

I skipped 3B a few years later—I can't tell you why. But the 3A teacher was drugged for some reason or more likely I drugged her with my perpetual motion mouth and she made me *skip* around the room. (For some reason it makes me think of my son, Amiri!)

I have distorted in various books and stories and plays and whatnot iron confrontations in the school with the various aspects recalled at various different times. The seventh grade beating by Mrs. Powell. The weird comic strip I created/semiplagiarized, called *The Crime Wave*, which consisted of a hand with a gun sticking out of strange places holding people up. For instance, as a dude dived off the diving board the ubiquitous hand would be thrust up out of the water holding a gun and in the conversation balloon the words "Your money!" A series of those all over the goddam place and only "Your money!"

I think I saw the concept somewhere else but I was attracted to it and borrowed it and changed it to fit my head. But why "Your money!"? No cabeesh.

When the curious old Miss Day, the white-haired liberal of my early youth, shuffled off into retirement as principal there came Mr. Van Ness, hair parted down the middle and sometimes seeming about to smile but sterner seeming than Miss Day. We loved Miss Day, we seemed to fear Mr. Van Ness, probably because he seemed so dressed up and stiff. (The irony of this is that I just had drinks with old man Van Ness two months ago, up at his apartment with my wife and a lady friend of his—a black woman!—and we went over some of these things. Because, as it turns out,

Van Ness was an open investigating sort, actually a rather progressive person!)

Van Ness even took some interest in the fact that my mother had been to Fisk and Tuskegee. And based on these startling credentials he could ask me what was proper, "Negro" or "Colored." I said "Negro" and Van Ness told the students, "Remember, there's a right and a wrong way of saying that." You bet!

In the eighth grade we had a race riot. Not in the eighth grade but in Newark. And in them days race riot meant that black and white "citizens" fought each other. And that's exactly what happened in Newark. It was supposed to have jumped off when two white boys stopped a guy in my class named Haley (big for his age, one of the Southern blacks put back in school when he reached "Norf") and asked him if he was one of the niggers who'd won the races. He answered yes and they shot him. They were sixteen, Haley about the same age even though he was only in 8B and most of us in our earlier teens—I was about twelve.

The races they'd talked about were part of the citywide elementary school track meet. The black-majority schools had won most of those races and this was the apparent payoff. So rumbles raged for a couple weeks on and off. Especially in my neighborhood, which confronted the Italian section. The Black Stompers confronted the Romans—a black girl was stripped naked and made to walk home through Branch Brook Park (rumor had it). A white girl got the same treatment (the same playground rumor said). But two loud stone and bottle throwing groups of Americans did meet on the bridge overpassing the railroad tracks near Orange Street. The RR tracks separating the sho-nuff Italian streets from the last thrust of then black Newark. The big boys said preachers tried to break it up and got run off with stones. It was the battle of the bridge.

Beneath that fabric of rumor and movement, the bright lights of adventure flashing in my young eyes and the actual tension I could see, the same tensions had rose up cross this land now the war was over and blacks expected the wartime gains to be maintained and this was resisted. Probably what came up on the streets of Newark was merely a reflection of the Dixiecrats who declared that year for the separation of the races. But whatever, New Jersey became the first state to declare that year a statute against all discrimination—(I just found that out a few seconds ago, you see a cold vector from out my past illuminating itself and the present where I sit) so maybe it was connected and it's all connected to me. I to it.

But the whys of any life propel it, the hows it forms and means. We want to know why we got to here, why we was where we was (our parents), why we thought and think the way we did and do now. Why we changed our thinking, if we did. When we did.

As a child the world was mysterious, wondrous, terrible, dangerous, sweet in so many ways. I loved to run. Short bursts, medium cruises, even long stretched-out rhythm-smooth trips. I'd get it in my head to run somewhere — a few blocks, a mile or so, a few miles through the city streets. Maybe I'd be going somewhere, I wouldn't take the bus, I'd just suddenly get it in my head and take off. And I dug that, the way running made you feel. And it was a prestigious activity around my way, if you was fast you had some note. The street consensus.

I only knew what was in my parents' minds through their practice. And children can't ever sufficiently "sum that up," that's why or because they're children. You deal with them on a perceptual level — later you know what they'll do in given situations (but many of their constant activities you know absolutely nothing about). Later, maybe, deadhead intellectuals will try to look back and sum their parents up, sometimes pay them back for them having been that, one's parents. Now that we are old we know so much. But we never know what it was like to have ourselves to put up with.

My family, as I've tried to tell, was a lower-middle-class family finally. For all the bourgeois underpinnings on my mother's side, the Depression settled the hash of this one black bourgeois family. And those tensions were always with us. My mother always had one view, based on being conscious and taking advantage of any opening. I cannot even begin to describe the love factor in my mother and father's relationship, what brought them together aside from their bodies and some kind of conversation.

My father from the widowed wing of the lower middle class, a handsome high school graduate from the South, a barber, a postal worker, who tells the old traditional black lie that he thought Newark was New York and it wasn't until much later that. His family was upwardly mobile, of course, that's the ideological characteristic of the class. But what if the ruined sector of the black bourgeoisie and the bottom shadow of the petty bourgeois come together? The feudings in that, the fumings, the I-used-to-be's and We-woulda-been's and the many many If-it-wasn't-for's oh boy oh boy all such as that. The damaged aristocracy of ruined dreams. The open barn door of monopoly capitalism. What a laugh. I mean, if some big-eyed dude was to step in and give a lecture, no, if suddenly there in the darkness of my bedroom I (or whoever could pull this off sleeping in my bed) could have stepped forward into the back and forth of sharp voices trying to deal with their lives, in our accepted confusion of what life is, and say, "Look, the bourgeoisie of the oppressed nation always faces a tenuous existence, the petty bourgeoisie of any nation is always shaky. And yeh they can get thrown down, like in a fixed rasslin match, thrown down among that black bubbling mass. Yeh, they can get thrown down and all lit-up fantasies of Sunday School picnics in the light-skinned church of yellow dreams could get thrown down, by the short trip home, to the vacant lots and thousands of dirty Davises, and what you-all is doin' is class struggle of a sort, yeh, it's only that, translated as it has to be through the specifics of your life, the particular paths, crossroads and barricades, but that's all it is ya know?"

I guess their, my parents, eyes would've lit up, for a second, and then a terrible hard loss would've settled there, because they would've figured the goddam kid is crazy, he's babbling outta his wits. What? And they'd look at each other in the halfdark, and exchange looks about what to do. I'm glad I wasn't that smashed up. What I did do, with a taste of Krueger's beer in my mouth my mother had let me sip out of her glass earlier that night when they had friends over, I just opened my eyes so they glowed softly bigly in the dark and said nothing. I heard my sister's slow deep breathing in the bed under mine.

I went through school because I had to. Going where? I didn't know. I don't know if my parents did either. At one point later I pretended they wanted me to be a doctor. But my mother claims this wasn't true. My father says, "Hey, we didn't care what you did. You could do what you wanted." Graduating from grammar school, I was the third or fourth from the shortest of the boys. And it was a two-way track, I guess, the actuality of being a black kid in Newark in a public school in the West Ward in the 1940s United States. Son of a postal worker and an office worker. (My mother had got away from the piecework in the dress factories and her smart turned-down fedora and neat-cut suit let you know she wasn't thinking about going back. Though we were always back in the sense of the flatness, the horizontal character of our community and nationality—we were not laid back, we were held back. Black. I think we were colored and Negroes then.) But also remember the flashy zoom projection of the inside black bourgeois mind, the lockstep black middle class frantic not to be totally connected with the flat-out black majority. Brain sweat and soul shivers would come, my mother's waking nightmare, perhaps, that you would be only invisible, only connected to the mass pain, an atom of suffering, that you would not *amount* to anything. Whew! (How much??)

We were we surrounded by the world. A world I thought I knew better than I did. The playground taught me. The black running masses there. Even the poetic line of speech comes from my heart is theirs, so purely, the cutting edge of life description, was once simple dozens. The cynicism, the echoing blues, hollow laughter, bright and distance-filled, kids around my way would hear everyday, from a little big-eyed dude in short pants and a blue shirt, cutting across the playground.

I had the sense of a Jones-Russ life/universe that was an extension of everybody's. All the bloods mostly. The others I didn't understand, except as I could describe them and make some differentiation or make some similarity. As for instance when I went to my mother and asked, because Anthony Ar and I got picked out of Miss Hill (a terrible old bitch)'s art class to go down to Bamberger's and build the boat we'd put together out of clay and painted. I asked if Catholics was the same as Baptists. Anthony had said they were. My mother disagreed. I kept this to myself. Shit, it didn't really matter to me.

It didn't really matter that the whites lived in the white part of Baxter Terrace. Where else would whites live? It didn't matter at the top that the Davises lived like they lived or Eddie or Norman or the Hills or the colored people on Newark Street, which was our metaphor then for very poor. It didn't matter to me on the top, they was just people, phenomena to my wheeling big space-eating image-making eyes.

But the Jones-Russ orangish brown house was one *secure* reality and the scrambling moving changing colors and smells and sounds and emotions world at my eye and fingertips was something connected but something else. I knew that many of the kids I ran with did not have the same bulk of bodies and history and words and *articulation* to deal with what kept coming up every morning when I'd rise. There was a security to my home life. That's the only way I can describe it. A security that let me know that all, finally, was well. That I'd be all right, if I could just survive the crazy shit I thought up to do. And the wild shit some wildass people thought up to drop on you.

It never occurred to me that my mother and father would be anything or anywhere but where they were and who they were. For that matter, it never occurred to me that my grandmother (my mother's mother, *Nana*) could be anywhere or do anything but what I depended on for my understanding of life and reality. My uncle and grandfather were the most questionable parts of my household. My uncle because he was always on the road. A big tall brawny Pullman porter on the Pennsylvania Railroad. And my grandfather because I never knew much about him except what came from my mother or grandmother's mouth. He was big and distinguished looking. A black businessman in a boater hat and three-piece suit and cane. He was a Republican, the legacy of Lincoln, and known as a "race man," i.e., something of a Nationalist. I found *One Hundred Amazing Facts about the Negro, with Complete Proof* by J. A. Rogers in his drawer, while "plundering," as my grandmother would say. I also found Krafft-Ebing's *Psychopathia Sexualis*, a book on the Masonic mysteries, and a revolver. All of them were beyond me, at the time. Though the Rogers made some impact, I couldn't figure out the point Rogers was making hooking up black people with so many wild things. Plus I didn't think I could really use an idea like "Beethoven was black." I wasn't sure he was, but then even if he was, so what? I was very young.

My grandfather was big in black Republican politics and after his grocery store folded in the Depression he got a patronage job as night watchman in the election machine warehouse for Essex County, on Wilsey Street in Newark. It was within walking distance of our house, right down the street from the Newark Street Jail. There was a big vacant lot across from the jail and I played baseball when I got up into high school as part of the Newark Cubs, complete with uniforms. A hundred years later I was locked up in that same jail during the Newark Rebellions and saw the National Guard shoot up a black couple's car from that same vacant lot.

My sister and I would accompany my grandmother with her slow rocking stride over to the warehouse where she would go with my grandfather's dinner packed in a picnic hamper with big folding handles. The food was hot, complete with a thermos of coffee and cornbread or biscuits. And while "Old Miss" and "E'rett" talked back and forth as he ate, my sister and I would range up and down the long rows of election machines in a virtual frenzy of ecstasy. We could run down down the rows, in and out. We could flash as hard and fast as we could. We could hide, we could catch each other. And the best treat of all, we could climb up on top of the machines and run from one end of the warehouse, which ran an entire city block, to the other, streaking on top of the padded machines, leaping from one machine to the other, without stopping, playing war games and hero games and simply using up some of our boundless energy.

As I said, my grandfather was a big important man in that community or in middle-class black Newark. He was president of the Sunday School at the yellow and brown folks' Bethany Baptist Church and a trustee. The trustees, after those collections, would rise up and file into the back. It was a kind of dignified swagger. It was as important as any position in our world, it was at least as heavy as a civil service job. And I could go through there and see them counting that money, the respected elder gents of the church. And a preacher white as God himself!

But Tom Russ was a name to conjure with in those times. Important in the church, politically connected, but the failed business could not help but have lowered him in those folks' eyes. Those yellow and browns he was ranked among. But he was the *head* of that house, in those early days. No doubt about it. And I think its stabilizing center.

One night there was terror in our house, there was pain on everyone's face, weeping and shouted unknown words—negative passion flaring. And then it was said my grandfather had been hurt, he had got struck down on a street corner—where Springfield meets South Orange just down from the Essex theater. They told me a streetlight dropped out of the fixture onto his head! They did. That's what they said. I repeated it but somehow never (to this day) believed it. A streetlight? From way up at the top of the pole with perfect random accidental accuracy smashing him right in the center of the head? Yeh, that's what they said.

And it all but destroyed Tom Russ. From the tall striding dignified family patriarch who swept my lil' plump grandma up when she was fifteen (his second bride) and left a trail of funeral parlors, general stores, and colored productive force, he finally came home paralyzed and silent. In fact I never heard him utter another sentence. He merely sat in a chair, smoking his cigars and spitting, spitting, into a tin can. There was some money in a pension, but I never understood why the city wasn't sued if that's what had happened, an accident. They even took him up to Overbrook for a minute, a hospital for the insane and mentally incompetent. But they brought him back in a little while. Perhaps my grandmother just wouldn't go for that. And she tended him the rest of his life. Frustration now shot out all the way into tragedy! And the pain in those stopped eyes, stopped from vision and transformation, was horrible, like death alive and sitting in a chair completely dominated by reality.

My grandfather's last years were all like that. Stopped motion, frustration turned all the way to tragedy. And the old image of Tom Russ slowly evaporated from our young minds and we cruel kids, my sister and I, would whisper to each other like savages about "Spitto" sitting there. We mocked him. But why could we create such ugliness in ourselves? How did it come to replace the awe and respect? Was it just the grossness and crudity of children or was there some impulse we picked up from the adults around us?

But it didn't come from my grandmother. His "Old Miss." She was with him, close by him, waiting on him, even to her own detriment, until he died. Until they cut down one of his black coats so I could wear it to his funeral.

Now my grandmother was my heart and soul. She carried sunshine around with her, almost in her smile. She'd have some little hat cocked to one side and she strutted when she walked. Rocked when she was a little weary. But full of fun, her eyes sparkled. You cross her, you were gonna get at least pinched. Like mess up in church, be talking, or fidgeting, she'd cop your flesh between her fingers and rival the inquisition with their more complicated shit. And she had to do that to me quite often in church because I would go completely out, like some kind of menace. A little big eyed monster, yapping, running up and down stairs, giggling and laughing. One time I turned off the electricity down in the basement for the whole church and the organist (another Miss Ada) was pushing on the keys and people rushed to her thinking she was having another stroke. They caught me just as I came up out of the basement. Even the special policeman, Mr. Butler, wanted to smash me. But I got ate up when I got home.

My grandmother was deeply and completely religious. Her life was defined by Jesus and the holy ghost. Every aspect of her life either had God in it or she hooked him up in some way. And the church was her world. She was head of the Ladies Aid Society, an usherette, and a teacher in the Sunday School. And now and again she'd get "happy" in church and start fanning and weeping, rocking back and forth, but most times she'd just sing and listen and amen, under her little flat-top hat trying to see God from behind her rimless glasses.

It was my grandmother who most times fed us and kept us, and her spirit is always with us as part of our own personality (I hope). I loved my grandmother so much because she was Good. If that had any meaning in the world. She'd tell you, "Do Unto Others as You'd Have Them Do Unto You," and you knew that's what she believed and that's what she practiced. She'd tell me when I was doing something she approved of, "Practice makes perfect!" Maybe it was being polite, emptying the garbage like I was supposed to, or having shined shoes, or even getting good grades in grammar school. "Practice Makes Perfect."

And she was funny, really. Like all those various "teams" on radio and later television whose names she'd turn around. I'm not sure why—was it intentional or why she had to twist it up—but it always cracked my sister and me up. Like she'd talk about Abner and Lum or Costello and Abbott. And when she came out with Andy and Amos I thought she was putting us on, but she would pull it with a straight sincere look and it cracked us up.

And she dug *The Road of Life*, *Life Can Be Beautiful*, *Ma Perkins*, *Young Widder Brown*, *Our Gal Sunday*, *Stella Dallas*, *Lorenzo Jones* (and his wife, Belle). She'd be listening when we came in and then the kid adventure stuff would come on and she'd fade to do her dinner, preparing stuff, though sometimes she listened with me. Hop Harrigan, Jack Armstrong, Captainnnnnnn Midnight, Tom Mix (and Wash White). And then later she'd be into Beulah, Andy and Amos, and them. When I was sick and had to stay in bed I heard all those soaps along with her while I sprawled. All had organ music and a voice-over telling you what was up. It was a crazy world of villains in civilian clothes.

Plus when my grandmother was working up at those Fortes' house and the other rich white folks', when she'd come back, Jim, she'd have a bundle of goodies. Clothes, books, I got the collected works of Dickens, H. Rider Haggard, and random books of Pooh Bear, Sherlock Holmes, and even an almost whole set of Rudyard Kipling, if you can get to that! They were gifts, is what she told us. The white folks was just giving stuff away. I guess they had better stuff, or they needed room. Some of the stuff she brought my sister would have "Anna Marie Forte" sewn on labels in the collars. I always wondered about those goddam Fortes, how they could have all that stuff up there in Essex Fells, how they looked and what they had to say. But I never found out.

My grandmother also had gone to Poro beauty school and she talked about that. She was a hairdresser. The shop she worked in in Newark still sits there on Norfolk Street. So sometimes Elaine and I would be out in front of the beauty parlor, weekends, running around, but connected to the hot curling irons and pressing combs of Ora's beauty parlor and our grandmother sitting there talking and straightening hair with that hunk of grease on the back of her hand.

If I have ever thought seriously about "Heaven" it was when my grandmother died because I wanted her to have that since she believed so strongly. I wrote a poem saying that. I'd been writing for a while when she died, mostly poems in magazines, and I always regretted that she never got to see a book of mine. I had the dust jacket of *Blues People* in my hand around the time she died, a few weeks later it came out. And I wanted her to see that all the dreams and words she'd known me by had some reality, but it was too late. She'd already gone.

I wrote a story about my grandfather in a magazine my first wife and I published called *Zazen*. It was called "Suppose Sorrow Was a Time Machine?" She'd seen that and my mother told me she'd liked it. But it wasn't a book. I wanted my Nana to see that I'd learned Practice Makes Perfect. But she was gone.

My uncle was the exotic personality in our house. On the road, and when he came home in checked sports coats. He was a man about town, like they say. And once he took me downtown Newark to a quality restaurant on Market Street, the Novelty Bar & Grill (so you see how long ago this was). And I felt slick and knowledgeable walking with him, and with that pastrami sandwich on the plate, I was dressed up myself, that was a new high in my life.

G.L. was my uncle's name, he didn't have any other. But pressure from Americans made my grandfather come up with George as a name to cool out various institutions who defied Southern mores with their chrome-plated cold shit.

They tell me my uncle got married once, to some light-skinned babe, but I don't know anything about that. But, whatever, it didn't hold and he was a bachelor when I started knowin' him. Uncle had his own stuff and it had a certain aura to it, of strangeness and sophistication. He had some quality things he had and he was no stranger to money, he just didn't believe he could take it with him.

The railroad job let him travel and gave him that air of urbanity and sophistication. He had a porkpie hat he wore sometimes with the brim snapped down. He went to New York and did his shopping and spent a lot of time over there. Plus he thought up a scam that seemed like a hip idea the more I got to understand it. G.L. sold the sandwiches on the Pullman, those flat, dry sandwiches the railroad sold. But G.L. figured that *he* could sell some sandwiches too, for G.L., since it was free enterprise and whatnot. So he had my grandmother (and we helped too) make spiced ham sandwiches with cheese and mayonnaise, modest but colored-good. The whole kitchen table would be laid out with "G.L.'s sandwiches." My grandmother turned it into a real cottage industry, and it was the focus of many family discussions. As to what and why I ain't entirely clear, sometimes there seemed like there was some conflict about "G.L.'s sandwiches" but I can't say. I just ate some. And figured as I got older that it was a hell of a good idea. Cause when the dry old RR sammiches give out (or before they give out) G.L. would slide Nana's sammiches in there and take down the bux. I thought it was hip.

One day much later there was a heated argument, evening to late evening, and stomping around and actual bad words. And my uncle was calling my father "a nincompoop." It shocked me. "A nincompoop." Goddam. Why he have to be all that? And not much later we had broke up, the Russ-Jones family connection had broke up and for a while we went different ways. That really turned me around, but that was later.

Mao points out how we move from perception to rational knowledge to changing our practice, like the three levels of knowledge. And for much of our lives we are at the mostly perceptual level. We see and react, are touched by, moved, cry, scream, pout, taste, but that is all. So much moves just above us and we might call it anything. A lotta stuff go by we don't even comment on, just turn our head or miss it as it moves, we are fundamentally baffled or it's just too much too much what with the other stuff we got to walk with and be practically responsible for.

But then we try to make theories out of our perception. We try to explain what was or is making repeated indents upon our senses, life. We rationalize and give something a name, a number, try to recognize a persistent quality to some element of sorrow, distance, feeling.

Then we do something if we can. Based on that step up opening into higher consciousness, when this does come. Quiet desperation could sum up far too many in this sliver of world this sliver of time, passing, this dot of organism, part of the immensity of coming into being, development, going out of being, transformation. Ah well. From time to time we do reorder our lives.

The world has changed so much since my youth, and I could lay it out to what degree in many surface ways. Even some important fundamental ways. And I want, more than anything, to chart this change within myself. This constant mutability in the face of the changing world.

Childhood is like a mist in so many ways. A mist in which a you is moving to become another you.

What the school says you learned and were responsible for is way off far away from what came away with in a practical sense. The reading, writing, arithmetic, geography, social studies, shop, history, penmanship, gym we got was one thing. But learning about dicks and pussies and fags and bulldaggers. Seeing the reaction to cocksuckers and motherfuckers and sonafabitches and bastards. Understanding what fucking was and what it had to do with sucking. All these things and such as that.

The games and sports of the playground and streets was one registration carried with us as long as we live. Our conduct, strategies, and tactics, our ranking and comradeship. Our wins and losses. (Like I was a terrible terrible loser and still am.) I would fight, do anything to stop losing. I would play superhard, attacking, with endless energy to stop a loss. I would shout and drive my team on. Stick my hands in the opponents' faces, guard them chest to chest, or slash through the line from the backfield and catch them as they got the pass back from center. Or take the passes and cut around end and streak for the goal. Or double step, skip, stop, leap, jump back, ram, twist, hop, back up, duck, get away, hustle, and rush into the end zone. I could leap and catch passes one-handed, backwards, on my back, on the run, over someone's shoulders, and take it in. And mostly I never got hurt. I had a fearlessness in games and sports. A feeling that I could win, that I could outrun or outhustle or outscramble or rassel or whatever to pull it out. I would slide head first into home, even first. On tar and cement. I would turn bunts into homeruns, by just putting my head down and raging around the bases.

And we learned in our own gatherings, like The Secret Seven, our youngest collective, led, I guess, by me, with Board as the official outlaw. We'd roam those streets getting into things, climbing over roofs, "exploring," going around the corner two or three blocks—strange places. Confronting mysteries daily and giving childish explanations or shrugging our shoulders and pulling off the leaves of a "poverty tree" to play "sord fighting" like Tyrone Power in *The Black Swan*. Our thing was roaming and registering, laughing and eating candy when we were lucky. Board, the bad one, Algy, his younger skinny brother, fast and usually snotty-nosed, who got my baseball suit cause I went off and stayed in the movies all day till dark and said the devil made me do it.

Norman, long-head colored Norman was our designation so as to distinguish him from white Norman. Norman was fast, a good ring-a-leerio man, and would go off with you anytime you wanted to do some serious exploring. Eddie, of the tilted old smelly house, was strong and fast and very recent. Like so many of us he had just come up from the black belt a few minutes ago.

My sister, a tomboy, dogged my tracks. I was always looking over my shoulder as I scaled another fence, when we took it in our minds to try and "duck" her. I would get furious when we couldn't and she would get furious when we could. I know we had begun to get older when I began to be able to beat her running, I guess from the added weight of hips and breasts. But in them early days it was hell getting loose. Her job, it seemed to me, in The Secret Seven was to see that I didn't get too far out.

Board liked to fight and steal. He was a little bit of a bully, a big bit on the real side. And people at one age were afraid of him. But he lived across the street, so we got tight in a standoffish kind of way. (I think he liked my sister.) Running with him finally got me in trouble cause we started lifting stuff out of cars. I watched him get popped in a trap set up by the local company. He'd got the stuff out the car window (simple shit glove compartment stuff). But this time they were waiting for him/us and they caught him as he climbed on his bicycle and tried to pull away. I was standing in S's yard in back of the playground watching it from behind a billboard. It scared me as much as anything in my life.

Also we'd gone into the school a couple of times and lifted silly shit. Pitch pipes, school materials, but then played vandal and threw shit every which way. I was deeply paranoid after that and thought any minute we were sure to get busted. But Board must've squealed when they got him at the car because in a few weeks I had to go down to police headquarters. My father and mother sat by my side and the white man gave me some vague lecture. Afterwards my father said that he and my mother had "decided to stick by me." (I'd figured that, it surprised me to hear him say that and it sounded a little artificial to me. So I wondered why had he said that. But sometimes my father could be curiously formal. My mother would usually just bop me in the head.)

And Danny whose brother was gay in those days when we called them "sissies." And that carried a weight then, Jim. "He's a sissy." Wow. And the dude did pitch and switch when he walked and his hair was done up rococo and curled up, his eyes and mouth were pornography. Danny was dusty and slightly off speed, a little plump. He was kept by his grandmother, a lowdown church lady. She was always dragging Danny off to church and since it was sanctified they went every other day, it seemed to us, and we giggled and teased him to distraction. One great cap on Danny was imitating his speech, as for instance he would tell us he was going to his sister's "wettin'." He had a cousin just a little older than us who also was "funny," who fanned up and down the street like he was on his way to mind the seraglio. So Dan had to hear about that. But there was calmness and loyalty in Danny and a quiet palship you always counted on. But he was a great source of merriment, as for instance when his grandmother had him by the ear pulling him toward Sanctified Heaven. We fell off the stairs and rolled on the sidewalk.

The radio, I've told over and again, was always another school for my mind. I listened to the radio all my young life, seriously and continuously, changing my focus, I guess, as I changed. The TV must serve the same purpose now for kids. The daily adventure stories after school and before dinner. And the later night shows like *The Lone Ranger* and *Inner Sanctum* (the creaking door), *Mr. Keen, Tracer of Lost Persons*, *I Love a Mystery*, *Mr. District Attorney*. The weekend shows like *Sam Spade* and *Gangbusters*. But two of the most meaningful to me were *The Shadow* and *Escape*. My father even took me to see *The Shadow* over there in Radio City. I got to see the actors, with scripts in their hands, saw them make the sound effects, and saw the guy who played the Shadow go into a booth when he "became invisible" (so his voice sounded weird and spooky). "The Hypnotic Power to Cloud Men's Minds So They Cannot See Him." That seemed deep. Or "The Weed of Crime Bears Bitter Fruit!" Wow. Or the laugh. "Eh-eh-eh-eh-eheh-eh The Shadow Knows" was deep.

Escape came on later after we had left Dey Street. They did more literary stories. Tales by H. Rider Haggard, H. G. Wells, F. Scott Fitzgerald, tales of the fantastic, the strange, science fiction. It came on late at night but I would play the radio soft in my room in the dark and listen, fantasizing the most strange and spooky world that could fit in that room and my head. One night I heard Fitzgerald's "A Diamond as Big as the Ritz." Another time "Leiningen and the Ants." Wells's "The Valley of the Blind" and "The Man Who Would Be King." And one strange story about people who lived in department stores after closing who buried their dead by turning them into display dummies. They were changed by people in the store called the Dark Men and the story was found on a note outside a department store left by a guy who had been trapped in there and grabbed by the Dark Men because he wanted to leave and give away their secret. The guy reading the note looked up as he finished reading and a dummy in the window fitting the writer's description stared out from behind the glass with unseeing horror-fixed eyes! Scared the shit out of me!

Saturday stories from the little kids' *Land of the Lost*, with Red Lantern, a fish who led kids down below the sea to find their lost toys. (He was not to be confused with Green Lantern, a caped crusader from the comic books I also dug. I put his incantatory dedication to fight against evil in my book *The Dead Lecturer*. To wit: "In Blackest Day/In Blackest Night/No Evil Shall Escape My Sight!/Let Those Who Worship Evil's Might/Beware My

Power/Green Lantern's Light." A green ring he recharged in front of a green lantern which gave him all kinds of powers. Powers, I guess, to reach the absolute.)

I heard *Let's Pretend*, when younger, the Grimms' fairy tales dramatized for radio. And later *Grand Central Station*, which came on when it was "high noon on Broadway." That was exciting and somehow even then described New York to me with its anonymous dramas in a way that I wanted to check out. And *Junior Miss* with Peggy Ann Garner, who lived in the story in an apartment high up, on West 87th Street or nearabouts, and lived the life of the bright middle-class New York kid in those days before white flight.

I heard heroes and saw them in my mind and imagined what evil was and cheered at its destruction. In the movies too, in film after film, evil could be destroyed. By Errol Flynn—*Robin Hood* will probably be ruled subversive by Strom Thurmond in a minute—and Tyrone Power, and Douglas Fairbanks, Jr., Gregory Peck, Jimmy Stewart, John Garfield, Humphrey Bogart, Gene Kelly, Stewart Granger, John Wayne, Alan Ladd, Gary Cooper, Henry Fonda. They taught us that evil needed to be destroyed. I saw it every weekend. I heard it on almost every radio show I listened to. That evil needed to be destroyed. And I believed that—impressionable as I was at those young ages—but the trick is that I still believe it! (And this, I was later to find out, can get you killed!)

In ring-a-leerio, I was always with the little guys and I actually liked that. There was always more of us allowed on the team, cause we were little. But our secret was that we were fast and shifty. I had one move where just as the big boy would be about to snatch me after the run, I'd stop short very suddenly and duck down, and this would send this big dude literally flying over my shoulders. Me, Johnny Boy Holmes, Skippy, and a few others patented that move. So they had to be wary and not run so hard after us and instead try to hem us in and get a couple or three of them to run us down. So we were the dangerous ringy players. And sometimes we'd even break loose and slide into the box and free the others already caught. Streaking into the box, which was marked on the ground, and against the fence of one side of the playground, "RINGALEERIO," we'd scream, whoever got that honor of charging through the ring of big boys to free the others. Sometimes we'd form a kind of flying wedge and come barreling in. But some other times them big dudes would smash us, block us, knock us down. Or if we didn't have our thing together, some of the really fast and shifty dudes wasn't playing for instance, they'd chop us off one by one and you had a hell of a time if it was the big boys' time to run out to stop those dudes. But we could and did. If there was enough of us we'd roam in twos and threes and tackle them suckers and sit on them. But you also had to get them back to the box, and they'd be struggling and pulling and that could be worse than just catching them.

But ringy was the top game for my money. It involved all the senses and all the skills and might and main of little-boydom. We played everything, baseball, basketball, football, all day every day, according to what season it was (though we'd play basketball all the time, regardless of what the big leagues was doing) but ringy was something else again. I'd like to see a big league ringy game and league. It's just war pursuit and liberation without weapons. Imagine a ringy game in Yankee Stadium, with karate, boxing, wrestling, great speed, evasion tactics, plus the overall military strategy and tactics that would have to be used, that would really be something.

Ringy got you so you could get away from any assault and at the same time fear no one in terms of running directly against big odds trying to free your brothers in the box. And sometimes if you were the only one left, and could keep the bigs darting and running and twisting, and outspeeding them, with the whole playground watching, that was really something, really gratifying.

Another teaching experience I had was the game Morning. It had its variations, Afternoon, and perhaps there was also an Evening, though I don't think so. Morning happened in the mornings. The first time we came in contact with each other the first one to see the other could hit him, saying, Morning. And though the other variations probably could be played, Morning was most happening I guess because at that time it was the first confrontation of the day and folks just getting up could be unawares and thus bashed.

And these suckers who most liked to play Morning were not kidding. When they hit they was trying to tear your shoulder off. The shoulder was the place most often hit. The real killers like this dude Big Shot would sneak up on you and hit you in the small of the back and that would take most people down and rolling on the ground in pain. Sometimes actual tears.

Close friends wouldn't actually play it or they wouldn't actually hit each other and if they did it wouldn't be a crushing blow. They'd just make believe they were playing it to keep you on your toes. But killers like Shot and some other dudes, little ugly Diddy and dudes like that, would actually try to take you off the planet.

If there was a slight tension, an outdoing or competitive thing, between dudes they would use Morning as an excuse to get off. But then the only thing that meant is that the other guy would come creeping around looking for an opening to bash the other one. I got hit a couple times, most times not hard—these were my main men who did it, cause I'd be watching, Jim. I was not going to get Morninged too often. And I caught a couple of them terrible snake-ass niggers a couple times and tried to tear 'em up, though they were taller and huskier, so my mashing punch was more embarrassment and aggravation than physical wipeout. I got Shot one time and jumped off my feet punching this sucker in his back and he got mad (which was supposed to be against the "rules") and he started chasing me around the playground. But then he really got embarrassed, because his ass was too heavy to catch me. I motored away from him, ducking and twisting, just like in ringy. And finally he got tired and people was laid out on the fence of the playground laughing at his sorry ass.

But then he runs over to my main man Love and catches him. You see, you were supposed to say, "Morning," then the other dude couldn't hit you. So Shot zooms over and catches Love right between the shoulder blades and damn near kills him. Love and Shot were always on the verge of going around anyway. Love had a close-cut haircut and a funny, bony-looking head, according to us. And we called him Bonehead or Saddlehead or some such. But it was the usual joke time. With Shot it was some kind of bitter rebuke, cause Love could play ball—any kind of ball—Shot couldn't do nothing but terrorize people with his ugly-ass self.

Love was hurt but when he come up a fight almost started, and then goddam Shot wanted to talk about the "rules." "Like how come Love wanna fight he just don't know how to play the goddam game. If you a sissie you can't play."

"How come you can play then, Shot?" And people cracked up, knowing he could not catch me. But from then on I had to watch Shot very close.

The "rules." And he had just broke 'em himself. People like that I knew about early. And also I learned how to terrorize the terrorizers.

The Dozens. You know the African Recrimination Songs!! Yeh yeh, see, I gotta anthropological tip for you as well. But Dozens always floated around every whichaway, around my way, when you was small. Or with close friends, half lit, when you got big. But that was either fun, for fun connected folks, or the sign that soon somebody's blood would be spilt.

The lesson? The importance of language and invention. The place of innovation. The heaviness of "high speech" and rhythm. And their USE.

Not in abstract literary intaglios but on the sidewalk (or tar) in the playground, with everything at stake, even your ass. How to rhyme. How to reach in your head to its outermost reaches. How to invent and create. Your mother's a man—Your father's a woman. Your mother drink her own bathwater—Your mother drink other people's. Your mother wear combat boots—Your mother don't wear no shoes at all with her country ass. She just come up here last week playin' a goddam harmonica. Or the rhymed variations. I fucked your mama under a tree, she told everybody she wanted to marry me. I fucked your mama in the corner saloon, people want to know was I fucking a baboon. Or Your mother got a dick—Your mother got a dick bigger than your father's! Point and Counterpoint. Shot and Countershot. Up and One Up.

(In the late '60s when I was going through some usual state harassment—to wit, I had supposedly cussed out a policeman in a bank. The truth being that this dude had been harassing us every few evenings, riding by the house, making remarks to the women, creep gestures at us, etc. So he comes in this bank with a shotgun out on "bank patrol" and starts talking loudly about George Wallace, who was running for president. Hooking him up with some local creep, Imperiale, and saying he was voting for Wallace. I said, "You should, it's your brother!" Or something like that. There was an ensuing baiting, a scuffle, more cops summoned, and three of us who'd been in this bank talking bad to the cop, then cops, got taken away. But it was later thrown out because the prosecution said I'd baited the cop by talking about his father. My attorney and I pointed out that while that might be the mores of Irish Americans (the prosecutor) African Americans focused on de mama, so it was an obvious frame. The judge blinked, hmmm, case dismissed. Some street anthropology. And if you coulda been there, judge, in them playgrounds, and heard it, you'd see my point. But, miraculously, he did.)

I learned that you could keep people off you if you were mouth-dangerous as well as physically capable. But being Ebony Streak also helped just in case you had to express some physical adroitness. Cause your mouth might get your ass into a situation it could not handle! In which case it was the best thing to rapidly change your landscape.

Fighting, avoiding fights, observing fights, knowing when and when not to fight, were all part of our open-air playground street-side education. And fights were so constant, a kind of staged event of varying seriousness. Sometimes very serious. Sometimes just a diversion, for everyone. Like two dudes or girls woofing. Woof woof woof woof woof. They'd be standing somewhere, maybe the hands on the hips, the chicks especially, hands on hips. Maybe one hand gesturing. Or each with one hand on the hip and one hand gesturing. Or they'd get closer and closer. In the purely jive fights the audience would get drugged and push the would-be combatants into each other and that could either start a real fight or it would reveal the totally jive nature of the contest.

And these girls, the black ones, in Central would really get down. There were a couple, Edna, Charlene, plus Laverne and some others, who was so bad that dudes seriously didn't want to get into nothing with them. (Last time I saw Edna years later she was giving some white folks hell in Irvington about them trying to jack her kids up in that school near the Newark city line which was now heavy black so the concocted tensions of the racist system were provoking. I thought, when I saw her, shit, these motherfuckers just do not know what they are about to get into. I saw Edna kick so many little girls' asses when she was a not so little girl—she wasn't never really little when I was knowin' her! She even jumped on some dudes and run 'em up Central Avenue with they eyes rollin'.)

And they would fight. After school every day. The famous ones every other day. The corner of Newark Street and Central Avenue, a rumble. And when it was female, hey man, skirts rolling up, drawers in the wind. Dudes would press close up on that just to peep the flesh. But there were some terrible rumbles—clash and noise and conflict—eyes on fire. And the gathering of kids in motion to see, themselves a wild event. But we never got to the outer edge with the chicks' struggles. We thought they were serious, some even scary—as to the violence—but none we perceived as *deadly*, as when the dudes would get down. And then when a couple of famous knucklers and especially when they were representing some clear faction in the broader community, yeh, then that would seem deadly, deadly, like indeed death was easing close to our faces and our eyes would be propped open like at a horror movie with our favorites sounded loud, only if we were with one of the factions.

Yet, compared to today's constant communications of outright death in the streets every day, especially from the gangs, our clashes of yesterday seem tame. But then, death in those times was mostly unthinkable, though it happened. But when you fought you did not expect anybody to have a knife, let alone a piece. When today the pulling of shanks is normal, and guns, just about.

There were the gang clashes later that I knew about and almost got mashed up in several times. The story "The Screamers" talks about this, and in *The System of Dante's Hell*. I was caught between a small war inside a party between The Dukes (and I capitalize their names from leftover respect, not just grammar shit) and The North Newark Dudes. Hey, there was meat cleavers flying around in that one (during my teenage hip blue-light party roamings), the thing smacked my green Tyrolean lid off my head and sent me scrambling into the prone bodies. And there was a gang named The Geeks, uh uhm uhmp, the name itself could freeze you in your thirteen-year-old pimples. And those were titanic to us then, but the memory gets blunted by today's horrific reality, the projection of the dying monster trying to kill all life as it books.

But we had more experience day by day with individual confrontations. Gangs rose up in my experience more directly in my later teenage times.

Matthew Holden of the Central Avenues vs. Baxter Terrace's color bearer, Larry Thomas, was one standout of fixed tension and underlying terror. Matthew was known around Central Avenue as about the baddest of the big boys. He'd been kept back in school because he came up out of the South, so he was sixteen and in the eighth grade, just like the dead Haley. Matthew was big lean fast and strong. He excelled at all sports and was a likable kind of guy but took absolutely no shit. We littler ones laughed with him sometimes and he might get upset if we said some off the wall stuff, like made mock of his Southern speech, and what's more, if you did you'd take two or three steps and he'd have your ass by the collar and punch you in your shoulder paralyzing you. But he didn't "take tech" as some of the monsters like Shot or Diddy might. He was a straight-ahead dude, only you couldn't mess with him.

Thomas I knew only vaguely by rep. He was from Baxter Terrace, and about the same age as Matthew, only he had been born, I guess, up North, so he was already in high school. He was shorter than Matthew, stocky, built up, already playing high school football. And the Baxters relied on him as their baddest dude.

Baxter Terrace was actually in our neighborhood and most of the younger kids went to Central Avenue with us. But they had a Baxter Terrace playground in those projects where they played after school. And they had teams in another league, so there was some distance, though they played with us and around us often enough.

The fight was almost like some passion play. It happened in the middle of the playground, a crowd had formed and the two moved around inside that thick crowd armed and slowed with tension. The crowd itself had ranged around like two halves of some giant organic creature, with much leering and balling of fists and the shouting somehow strained and shallow. Each half connected itself from the inside with its champion. For one thing, I didn't understand how this dude Larry expected he could seriously take on Matthew. That seemed dumb, but the fact that he did do that seemed to breach something important, it seemed a nasty corny affront and I thought he should be made to disappear.

Actually not much went on, there was much scrambling and twisting. Some blows got struck, none decisive. I think before it went too far both sides had somehow intervened. Perhaps neither the Baxter Terraces nor we Central Avenues wanted this conflict to go full up. It would have been too damaging. There was such fire in the preliminaries, and the feeling that this was it. That an Armageddon lurked in this conflict for us. Perhaps the world would blow up or split into pieces.

But for all that playground diplomacy, that tiff was deep. I know I kept some tension and distance with regards to Baxter Terrace after that, though I certainly had friends, even a couple girlfriends, over there. But the feeling that the place and the people were *other* remained. And when we played their teams baseball or basketball that tension and resentment always partially surfaced.

So despite our various lives somehow there was a collective passion, a collective life, generated by our presence together on those streets, in that playground, and in that school. A collective description of us (whatever it was) that we had internalized. There were no real gangs at my age group (turning thirteen) but under that generalized dome of our youth there were indeed factions that could be mobilized more tightly by some threatened hostility. And that existed as a loose collage of sees and dos.

I did belong to a basketball team, actually it was an ASC (Athletic Social Club)—most of the clubs and teams were termed such. Ours was the Cavaliers. This was junior high and early high school, when we were tightest. Really from late grammar school to middle high school, I guess. We won trophies in the junior league inside Central Avenue (which was an elementary school). Some of us had been in school together for some time. There was Love, Hines, Johnny Boy, Snooky, Skippy, Barry, J.D., and me at one time. Later, Johnny Boy, Skippy, and J.D. dropped out and Bob and Earl Early came in, then Leon and Dick plus Sess and Ray and toward the end even big Sleepy, who coulda been a pro. We gave a couple dances through the years. When we got into high school we gave a few sets at Club Harold and made a little money. (Also most of us were on a baseball team called the Newark Cubs and with our country manager with big ideas we thought we were semipro and still in high school.)

But we could play ball and we had a good reputation, as ballplayers. We never came on like fighters. We were ballplayers and a couple dudes thought they was lovers.

We got our name from a group of older boys, also athletes, that we admired, called the Caballeros. And we picked out Cavaliers because it sounded like Caballeros, and now I know it's the same word. And that was our sense of ourselves, Knights, gentlemen of a certain kind. Later we even got some way-out jackets—red, white, and blue—reversible jackets with a white satin side and a blue wool side, both with the head of a Cavalier, slightly cross-eyed and staring off into space. I wanted hoods on the jacket, but that was voted down in some strange manner I have never been able to fathom. I thought we had decided to get hoods but when we got to the store that Saturday afternoon after we had paid all our money and the guy brought out the jackets, there were no hoods. I said, "Where's the hoods?" And everybody laughed. I was embarrassed and dropped the subject, but I never understood what happened to the hoods. But probably somebody undermined that idea behind my back.

I treasured that jacket, and would probably wear it today if it didn't get lost or stolen. I spilt ink on the satin side (which I am still doing today). But otherwise, until I got deep into high school and got a letter jacket, my Cavalier jacket was me in my high street style.

Basketball was our maximum game. In elementary school I was number 6 man, in junior high I got moved down, by high school I was about 8, definitely not a starter. But I almost never minded because we had a great team within our limitations (which we occasionally were well exposed to) and a great street rep that made you strut just to be a Cavalier, Jim. I was a playmaker, a guard, me and Barry would bring the ball down and set up the plays. I was never a great shooter, but I could move the ball and connect with those passes. I got big off assists. But if I got matched with a small man I would go into my scoring act—such as it was.

Sometimes, in those games, in those various leagues we played in, even in some neighboring towns, as we got older, there was some element of violence, like we thought we might have to fight. And we would if pressed but we was, like gentlemen, athletes and lovers, not no head beaters.

We'd even tease each other after such encounters about how we knew we was going to fade. Especially we'd get on Love, everybody always teased him, because he was such a great player but so totally unsophisticated and country-like off the court. We'd say, "Love's ass was already down the street when this other dude was looking to fight. He'd have to be Rocket Man to catch Love's ass." But, in reality, we would do whatever the moment called for but we never fancied ourselves pugs.

I had the most mouth on the court. Constantly talking to the other team, harassing them, face-guarding them, stealing the ball. I guess to make up for my light shot. And that could stir up the other team where they wanted to "kick that little nigger's ass" but that never happened. Once we did get run out of this "country" town just west of Newark called Vaux Hall. We played baseball up there in what looked like a cow pasture. And we always had stories about the Negroes in Vaux Hall. But one night we played basketball up there and at the end of the game, because of some kind of encounter, we had to motor on down Springfield Avenue for several blocks until we got out of harm's way. We blamed that on Love, too.

The focus of that club changed as we got older. Love and Hines, who were best friends, both went on to Central High School, and they were the emotional and spiritual center of our group, especially as an athletic team. And they began to gather dudes from Central High onto the squad. There was a heavy social underpinning to the club/team and when we were all in Central Avenue that was the focus. I went off to McKinley Junior High and later Barringer, which was almost all Italian, so I couldn't bring too many onto the squad or into the social circle that formed the basis for our team. So my influence, such as it was, lessened. Though Sess, who was a high school star, did come in from Barringer and he brought Ray, who went to South Side (now Malcolm X Shabazz), because they lived in the same project on Waverly Avenue cross town. Later I moved back cross town, onto The Hill again, around my junior year in high school, so Sess and Ray and I got tight. But Leon, Bobby, Earl, Dick, Barry (plus Love, Hines, and Snooky) were all Central High dudes, so that was the social and athletic center of the team when we were in our early high school days.

From time to time I see some of the old Cavaliers, and there is still that bond of fondness held high by memory. I know now that the club/team was a mixture of the lower middle class and the workers (and a couple of peasants turned workers just a couple minutes ago). But by high school the winnowing process had seriously begun. Central was a technical and commercial high school, Barringer supposedly college prep. And we had a couple dudes from West Side and South Side (a mixture of both, plus business) and so we got sprayed out into auto plants, utilities, electronic tube factories, mechanics, white-collar paper shuffling, teachers, small businessmen, security guards, commercial artists, and even a goddam poet.

For us, athletics was art, a high expression of culture. And as athletes the only expression of that, within the other framework of society, was as cool, dignified, profilin' dudes, self-sustaining and collective, but individually distinctive. That was at our best. At our worst, wow, we would mess with people. Especially egged on by one dude Love and Hines hooked up with later. Although we was all mischievous and even at times, from the narrow perch of that limited collectivity, somewhat arbitrary and cruel. I mean sometimes we would tap old dudes on the shoulder walking down the street, or say out of the way things to women minding their business, or flip somebody's hat off they head, and shoot up the street laughing. We were great agitators. And mostly we agitated among ourselves. We would throw each other's hats and bags, flip each other's sneakers and run off with them. Talk about each other like dogs and about each other's mamas even worse. But we were comrades most of us—as it went on, some gaps grew in that fabric, because of the different social situations we got into, but at its strongest it was something to be treasured and now looked back at with great feeling.

By high school I'd gotten into several different sectors of community or social life that complicated my life somewhat, even more than I knew. But that was a constant in my life I recognized, change. And though sometimes it saddened me and I regretted it, I saw after a while that that was what was happening.

So there was a mist-life while very young on Barclay Street in the Douglass-Harrison apartments (And I always, for a long time, dug those small red buildings and park in the back with green slat benches. And even the people that seemed to live there. Sometimes I longed for those people, in some not totally explained to me way), but we had to cut out. And then Boston Street, two sites, one near South Orange Avenue and then for a minute in my grandparents' house up the street, near West Market. (I had a late-night knee operation in the last house. Under oil lamps my knee formed a silhouette against the greenish wall and a baldhead doctor with a red wig—a blood with red freckles—meticulously picked the glass out of my messed up knee while the family stood in one corner and watched.) That was right down the street from my grandfather's store which had closed in the Depression, though the tale persisted in our family that it was because my grandfather gave out too much credit—it was implied—to ungrateful niggers. Which meant simply that that is the myth they wanted to invest their lives with, not understanding the actual political economy of this United Snakes. And how depression always kills off the petty and small bourgeoisie rat away!

But the bias of that description is to put down both Tom Russ and black people, but not the ugly thang that actual did de damage! And so the twist you inherit of seeing from who teaches you to see. I guess I carried the obvious putdown, of the bloods, on the top, cause that is what was most directly given. I carried less consciously the putdown of Tom which could then come full out when he was stricken and sat dying staring off into space. But the whole I came only much later to see and only now to sum up.

From there we went to Dey Street and the orange-red casa of my coming to little-boy consciousness. That was the center of my little-boy life. Central Avenue School, the playground, the evening recreation program we called "the Court" for some reason, The Secret Seven, wild fights, my athletic training, the Cavaliers, some of the remembered paths and lessons and teachers of whatever style, and even my first full-up meeting with white folks, though on my turf.

There was some other heavy stuff I found out and got into in them Dey Street days, a little romance, the church, and the Newark Eagles, and they need to be talked about. Why? Because they had something to do with it—the shaping, the answering—of the question How did you get to be you?

For one thing, the whites, almost all Italians and a few Irish and a German or two around somewhere, were definitely at the fringe, as I said before, of most of the Dey Street world. Not that they were sealed off by us in any way. It was just how we related, the deep cultural connects and the invisible and not so invisible antecedents in all directions even then. And our West Ward thrust was some kind of frontier. We were aware that a few blocks away the world changed and Italians lived in growing numbers.

And though they were on the fringe of the Dey Street life there were some distinct and concrete effects of their existence among us, and out beyond us. A couple of them could play ball, like Augie D., for instance, but we thought in the main their game was baseball. As little boys we played mixed teams, but at another point the teams were mostly black, and then you could get a black vs. white game, which was still not much until we got older and it began to reflect and take on the tension of the whole society.

By the time we were teenagers we were playing all-white baseball teams and those games were for something other than little-boy note. The baseball team we put together always talked about playing the white teams for cases of beer, but most of us were teetotalers and that didn't mean much to us.

Then there was the weird situation in which we actually by time of seventh grade or so began to take certain liberties with the white girls that we did not would not had better not take with the black ones. Like a couple big ol' (for seventh grade) white girls I knew, we would "feel up" in the cloakroom. (I remember a couple of names but will graciously refrain.) It never dawned on me to delve into why, or maybe it did and I couldn't. But we certainly liked quite a few of the little black girls we went to school with but we would no more think of feeling any of them except certain rogues I'm told did feel on certain of the wilder-repped sisters and that would cause a small shooting war in most cases. Maybe the other cases where that meant something else were kept from me young gourd by the benevolent moralists of me age. But some dudes later as we got into junior high would brag about women. What they did. But none of that was too clear to me anyway. That was real mystery. And there were a couple of these white girls who'd giggle and push you away, like they dug it. My god, what would they Italian fathers and brothers have said at seeing that. Wow, it makes me shudder even now.

And Augie was the first in the neighborhood I knew about to get a TV. (I remember clear as a bell when we got our first telephone—on Dey Street. MI2-5921. Our first electric refrigerator—a Kelvinator, and we called it that, exchanging the brand name for the genre. We had to put quarters in it to keep it going. We didn't get our first TV until I was about thirteen or fourteen, one year I came back from summer boy scout camp and walked into the house and there was a 14-inch Motorola, later we got a 17-inch, we never had a really big screen when it was hip to brag about that.) But we would, some of us, pile up in Augie's house to watch the TV. Augie's father was some kind of worker, a medium-sized guy with black hair grey at the edges. He never said much, just nodded to us. I wonder what he thought about the crowd of colored kids that would push in there to watch that early tube.

But later I could tell that something was happening in the whole of that Dey Street/Newark Street/Lock Street world, bounded by Central and Sussex Avenues, when Augie began to say certain things. Like one time we were sitting on the auditorium steps in the playground bullshitting about something and he was combing his hair. Augie loved to comb his goddam hair, and I think his little brother was with him and fat (white) Norman and maybe staring Johnny, who had the weird disease that made him go into trances at odd times. So I says to Augie to lemme use the comb. My hair was always cut very close, we called them "Germans" the way our hair was cut. And later a little longer on the top and front was called a "German bush." But Augie nixes me and says, "Don't mix the breeds."

I didn't know what the fuck he was talking about, "Don't mix the breeds." Huh? I said. Huh? Whatta you talking about, ol' bean, don't mix the breeds? (Not exactly in those words, ya know?) But he says it again. And I did get the meaning. I got it the first fucking time, not literally but generally and emotionally and psychologically I understood exactly what he meant. And hey, I didn't even get mad. It didn't even faze me. Actually it confirmed some upside-down shit I had in my head. That we were white and black. And I knew the abstract social history of that. I also knew what I saw every-day in various ways that manifested some meaning and connection with what Augie was saying.

Shit, I saw Mantan Moreland and *Amos 'n' Andy* and *Beulah* and Stepin Fetchit. I knew what "Feets, don't fail me now" meant. And who Birming-ham really was. And why Ellic in the Bob Hope picture *Ghost Breakers* had got so scared in the clock that when it opened he stood there shivering and turned completely white. I had seen Butterfly McQueen and Hattie McDaniel and Louise Beavers. I had seen the wild-eyed woogies in Tarzan and how knowledgeable Tarzan was. I had seen Al Jolson do his bullshit—hey and most of that *was* funny. HaHaHaHaHaHaHaHaHaHaHaHaHaHa HaHaHaHaHaHa (except Al Jolson, he wasn't shit). But still, anyway, down beneath that actual laughter there was something else. Besides the embar-rassment and even shame for the feeble-minded, beneath all that, boys and girls, there was something else that it took me a long time to fully dig. (I'll tell you about it later!)

Sure, I knew exactly what my best white friend Augie was saying, and I knew instinctively that his mother had probably put that shit in his head. What could have been the expression on my little round brown face with the big comical eyes? But what does it mean then, on the actual sidewalks and playgrounds of our lives? Whatever I said, it could only have been an acknowledgment of the time, the place, the condition. Like a fucking flag salute.

Another time, I'm hiking Augie, like his mother had all this grey hair and I'm calling her the Grey Terror, like we did. But Augie, then, pauses and asks me what color my mother's hair is. And I, like a sap, say black, which it was. And Augie looks half-eyed at I donno who, Normie or somebody, and says, "The Black Terror." It was a good hike, I guess. I ain't gonna be an objectivity freak—it's my funking memoirs—but more than the hike qua hike was the thing it really raised, that Augie really was putting into the game that which could not have been kept out in any real take on the world. But it let you know that all that was abstract to you, about black and white and all that, was not really abstract, that it all could not be waved away, or laughed away, or forgot or not known about. It meant to me that there was real shit over which I did not have total control, that I did not even properly understand. And I could be, on such occasions, quietly stunned. Turned inward and set adrift in a world of my feelings I couldn't yet deal with.

Those were some of the steps, the paths, of our divergence. And I told you how in high school (at least for me) the old relationships completely fell apart. For one thing, it was an Italian high school and junior high I went to. (Heading for college prep in my jumbled-up but crystal-clear head.) And so all things were openly reversed. The Italians now sat in center stage and controlled the social life of those two institutions. And year after year (only four, really), I went through various kinds of bullshit and humiliation that actually made me feel at one point that I hated Italians straight out.

(Earlier, in the seventh grade, we'd gone to the Bronx Zoo, and I'm lagging behind in the elephant house, holding my nose but wanting to check close up on the elephants. So I see this guy, he's cleaning up or something in there, and I ask him, "Wow, how do you stand it in here?" Meaning the terrible odor of elephant shit. So he says to me, "I don't mind it. I live in Harlem." Yeh, a white guy said this, and it went through me like a frozen knife. And I knew exactly what he meant. Except I also wondered, even right then at that ugly moment, why he wanted to drop that kind of shit on me. I knew he was attacking me, saying a bad thing to me, my big eyes must have wheeled and caught his face for a second, then dropped down into the zoo dirt, and carried the rest of me out of there. But what did that do, I wonder, for Mr. Elephant Shit Shoveler to say that? Did it make him feel good or heroic or like he wasn't really shoveling elephant shit? And all that was nestled tightly in me gourd by time I got out of grammar school. And Augie's words and news of "race riots" and even a couple runins my mother had with cut-rate racists, one in a candy store downtown— the lady wanted to sell her some "nigger toes" and my mother says, "Those are Brazil nuts, lady," grabs my hand, and stalks out. Later she had a near-rumble with a bus driver who wanted to talk to her funny. I took all that in, and carried it, carried it with me—who knows when you need such experiences? I felt subconsciously.)

But I was totally unprepared for the McKinley and Barringer experiences in which the whites ran the social and going to school/academic part of that institutional life. And I put up with many nigger callings and off the wall comments and intimidations, even getting cussed out regularly in Italian. I even learned Italian curse words (though not many precise meanings) and would fling them back sometimes. But I tried to hold my own. For instance, when a big schizophrenic white boy—a blond dude named Joe S.—threw a ball at me in the McKinley playground not long after I got there, I flung the bat at his head. The other white dudes kept him off me.

And later in school I developed an interior life that was split obviously like the exterior life. One half-tied to Dey Street while we still lived there and the black life of the playground and streets. And the other tied to the school experiences of McKinley and Barringer. It must be true, maybe obvious, that the schizophrenic tenor of some of my life gets fueled from these initial sources (and farther back with words whispered into the little boy's ear, from mouths and radios). But the white thing was only periphery in me young days, a fringe thing I didn't even recognize. And then to go into McKinley and then Barringer and be in a white world ruled by white Italians whose most consistent emotion regarding me was unconcern, that took me up by the ankles and dangled me in *no* space and put *not*'s in my head and not *me*'s.

The life of emotion, which is historical, like anything else, gets warped in high school I'm certain now. And to understand I must go back now several years to give a picture of one side of my life, feelings, mind, head, and then come back to this threshold of pain, then we can draw conclusions together!

One emotional center of my earlier life was my special relationship with my father. My father loved sports, and playing sports was the prerequisite for being part of the community of youth I ran with. I'd read the *Daily News* sports pages from way back in grammar school. And he'd take me to football games, baseball games, I mean the pros.

And, as I've said, there was a special *grandeur* to going someplace with my father and having all the "you look just like your father" folks identify us as such. There was a pride in that, I mean for the persons saying that, not just for my old man and me. But in the people it seemed to be a kind of high joy that such a genetic miracle could be produced. And that it was a sleek brown kid that had been produced—Eureka!—down to the sky-drinking eyes.

But the specialest feeling was when my father took me down to Ruppert Stadium some Sundays to see the Newark Eagles, the black pro team. Very little in my life was as heightened (in anticipation and reward) for me as that. What was that? Some black men playing baseball? No, but beyond that, so deep in fact it carried and carries memories and even a *politics* with it that still makes me shudder.

Ruppert Stadium was "Down 'Eck," down below the station, in the heavy industrial section, and then mostly whites, including the Portuguese, lived down there. But we were never really thinking about that when we went there. The smell or smells, and I always associate them with Newark, could be any wild thing. Sometimes straight-out rotten eggs, fart odor, or stuff for which there was no known identification. Just terrible Newark Down Neck smell.

But coming down through that would heighten my sense because I could dig I would soon be standing in that line to get in, with my old man. But lines of all black people! Dressed up like they would for going to the game, in those bright lost summers. Full of noise and identification slapped greetings over and around folks. Cause after all in that town of 300,000 that 20 to 30 percent of the population (then) had a high recognition rate for each other. They worked together, lived in the same neighborhoods, went to church (if they did) together, and all the rest of it, even played together.

The Newark Eagles would have your heart there on the field, from what they was doing. From how they looked. But these were professional ballplayers. Legitimate black heroes. And we were intimate with them in a way and they were extensions of all of us, there, in a way that the Yankees and Dodgers and whatnot could never be!

We knew that they *were* us—raised up to another, higher degree. Shit, and the Eagles, people knew, talked to us before and after the game. That fabulous year they were World Champs of the black leagues (two years later they were gone!). The Negro National League. We was there opening day, Jim, and Leon Day pitched a no-hitter! Opening Day! And the bloods threw those seat cushions all over Ruppert Stadium and the white folks (also owners of the New York Yankees) who owned that stadium wouldn't let us have the things after that. We noted it (I know I did) but it didn't stop nothin'.

That was the year they had Doby and Irvin and Pearson and Harvey and Pat Patterson, a schoolteacher, on third base, and Leon Day was the star pitcher, and he showed out Opening Day! But coming into that stadium those Sunday afternoons carried a sweetness with it. The hot dogs and root beers! (They have never tasted that good again.) A little big-eyed boy holding his father's hand.

There was a sense of completion in all that. The black men (and the women) sitting there all participated in those games at a much higher level than anything else I knew. In the sense that they were not excluded from either identification with or knowledge of what the Eagles did and were. It was like we all communicated with each other and possessed ourselves at a more human level than was usually possible out in cold whitey land.

Coming in that stadium with dudes and ladies calling out, "Hey, Roy, boy he look just like you." Or "You look just like your father." Besides that note and attention, the Eagles there were something *we* possessed. It was not us as George Washington Carver or Marian Anderson, some figment of white people's lack of imagination, it was us as we wanted to be and how we wanted to be seen being looked at by ourselves in some kind of loud communion.

And we *knew*, despite the newspapers, radios, Babe Ruth candy bars, who that was tearing around those bases. When we saw Mule Suttles or Josh Gibson or Buck Leonard or Satchel Paige and dug the Homestead Grays, Philadelphia Stars, New York Black Yankees (yes!), Baltimore Elite (pronounced E-Light) Giants, Kansas City Monarchs, Birmingham Black Barons, and even the Indianapolis Clowns! We knew who that was and what they (we) could do. Those other Yankees and Giants and Dodgers we followed just to keep up with being in America. We had our likes and our dislikes. "Our" teams. But for the black teams, and for us Newarkers, the Newark Eagles was pure *love*.

We were wilder and calmer there. Louder and happier, without hysteria. Just digging ourselves stretch out is what, and all that love and noise and color and excitement surrounded me like a garment of feeling. I know I thought that's the way life was supposed to be.

And my father was a part of that in a way that he was part of nothing else I knew. The easy comradeship among the spectators, but he even knew some of the players. And sometimes after the games he'd take me around to the Grand Hotel (used to be on West Market Street), right down the street from our church. Right next to the barbershop my father took me to.

(And going to that barbershop was almost as hip as going to the Grand or the games. Them niggers was arguin' in there one day about something and one guy mentions something that MacArthur had said and another dude, some old black man, said there wasn't no such thing as MacArthur! That has *always* blown my mind, what that meant!)

At the Grand Hotel, the ballplayers and the slick people could meet. (That was when Baba, Russell Bingham, was in his high-up thing with the digits and whatnot—clean as the Board of Health.) Everybody super-clean and highlifin', glasses jingling with ice, black people's eyes sparklin' and showin' their teeth in the hippest way possible.

You could see Doby and Lennie Pearson and Pat Patterson or somebody there and I'd be wearin' my eyes and ears out drinking a co-cola, checking everything out.

The movies I dearly dug but you never got to go behind the screen and shake hands with the heroes. But at the Grand Hotel you could and my old man saw that I did.

It was black life that was celebrated by being itself at its most unencumbered. Mrs. Effa Manley, who owned the team, would even come through and Baba or somebody would buy her a drink. Or my father would push me forward for an introduction and Monte Irvin would bend down and take my little hand in his and, Jim, I'd be all the way out.

In the laughter and noise and colors and easy hot dogs there was something of us celebrating ourselves. In the flying around the bases and sliding and home runs and arguments and *triumphs* there was more of ourselves in celebration than we were normally ever permitted. It was *ours*. (Not just the ownership of the teams, the Negro National League, though that had to be in it too.) But our expression unleashed for our and its own sake. It made us know that the Mantans and Birminghams were clowns—funny, but obviously used against us for some reason. Was it a big creep in a white hood somewhere in charge of trying to make black people feel bad? I thought so. But the clowns we knew were scarecrows, cardboard figures somebody was putting out trying to make us feel bad. Cause we knew, and we knew, that they wasn't us. Just clowns. Somebody got hooked up. We was out on the field at Ruppert Stadium, Jim. And we was even up in the stands diggin' it. Laid back in a yellow shirt with the collar open and white pencil-stripe pants. We was in the sun with a hot dog and a root beer having our hands shook by one of our father's friends. We was cheering for Mule Suttles or seeing Larry Doby make a double play. We was *not* clowns and the Newark Eagles laid that out clear for anyone to see!

But you know, they can slip in on you another way, Bro. Sell you some hand magic, or not sell *you*, but sell somebody somewhere some. And you be standin' there and all of a sudden you hear about—what?—Jeckie Rawbeanson. I could tell right away, really, that the dude in the hood had been at work. No, really, it was like I heard the wheels and metal wires in his voice, the imperfected humanoid, his first words "Moy nayhme is Jeckie Rawbeanson." Some Ray Bradbury shit they had mashed on us. I knew it. A skin-covered humanoid to bust up our shit.

I don want to get political and talk bad about "integration." Like what a straight-out trick it was. To rip off what you had in the name of what you ain't never gonna get. So the destruction of the Negro National League. The destruction of the Eagles, Grays, Black Yankees, Elite Giants, Cuban Stars, Clowns, Monarchs, Black Barons, to what must we attribute that? We're going to the big leagues. Is that what the cry was on those Afric' shores when the European capitalists and African feudal lords got together and palmed our future? "We're going to the big leagues!"

So out of the California laboratories of USC, a synthetic colored guy was imperfected and soon we would be trooping back into the holy see of racist approbation. So that we could sit next to drunken racists by and by. And watch our heroes put down by slimy cocksuckers who are so stupid they would uphold Henry and his Ford and be put in chains by both while helping to tighten ours.

Can you dig that red-faced backwardness that would question whether Satchel Paige could pitch in the same league with who?

The Dodgers could take out some of the sting for those who thought it really meant we was getting in America. (But that cooled out. A definition of pathology in blackface would be exactly that, someone, some Nigra, who thunk they was *in* this! Owow!) But the scarecrow J.R. for all his ersatz "blackness" could represent the shadow world of the Negro integrating into America. A farce. But many of us fell for that and felt for him, really. Even though a lot of us knew the wholly artificial disconnected thing that Jackie Robinson was. Still when the backward crackers would drop black cats on the field or idiots like Dixie Walker (who wouldn't even a made the team if Josh Gibson or Buck Leonard was on the scene) would mumble some of his unpatented ku klux dumbness, we got uptight, for us, not just for J.R.

I remained a Giant "fan," cause me fadder was, even when J.R. came on the scene. I resisted that First shit (though in secret, you know, I had to uphold my own face, alone among a sea of hostile jerks!).

(So what? So Jackie came on down to D.C. town and they got his ass to put Paul Robeson down!! I remember that, out of the side of my head I checked that. I wondered. What did it mean? What was he saying? And was it supposed to represent me? And who was that other guy—Paul Robeson? I heard that name somewhere.)

The Negro League's like a light somewhere. Back over your shoulder. As you go away. A warmth still, connected to laughter and self-love. The collective black aura that can only be duplicated with black conversation or *music*.

The road, the path, now I'm graduated out of grammar school (in the photograph the fourth from the end, next to Bruce Miller and little Sylvester who said quite accurately, "You'll never be no doctor"). And I'm in McKinley, with all these white dudes. When we Cavaliers came down there for one a those street carnivals, we didn't even know what they was. A big fat 400-pound dude, a nasty motherfucker I never really met but saw quite a bit in high school. A team manager. Water boy, really. He says to us out the side of his mouth—hissing it like a fat snake—"Get out! Get out!" But there was seven or eight of us, so we looked around a little while longer then we got out. But I had to come back to those parts to school in a day or two. And so it goes. So it went!

The Russ-Jones combine broke up about then as well. As I said, accompanied by loud declarations of still unclear resentment and perhaps rage. Certainly I heard frustration in that too, as you must whenever you are listening to African Americans.

The Jones section moved even further north, away from Dey Street, across the invisible borders down all the way into Italian land. That was short-lived and boy was I glad about that. But for a minute we lived on 8th Avenue, with some other strange person. We were boarders in her little house, down below Broad Street. So I went right up the hill to McKinley and even went to this nearly all-Italian Boys Club. Egad, they even had metal chains instead of nets on the baskets. I'd never seen that. So that instead of "swish" as the term of success it was "ching." So much for cultural pluralism.

It was all spread out and vague and alien for me now. The old Dey Street/Newark Street/Lock Street breakdown had broke down. The Central Avenue playground crowd had vanished as far as I was concerned. And certainly some of that was subjective. You feel once you leave a place it's literally "not there" anymore. But "the fates" had sent large sectors of my own age group scattering to the winds of high school.

I felt totally alone and isolated living down there on 8th Avenue. I felt totally alone and isolated going to McKinley Junior High. And I was contemptuous, frightened, and awed by the tons of white students I had to see everyday. But this was not a fancy private school, this was a largely Italian public school in the old First Ward (somebody could give you a list of the people that came out of there and some of them would be some well-known gangsters as well as movie stars, singers, boxers, police, businessmen, etc.). A lot of these same kinds of students today would be in Catholic school way out in the suburbs. But quite a few would still be there—dealing with those Mean Streets.

In McKinley and in the 8th Avenue Boys Club I related only to what was inside my head. You want to know what alienation is? That was it. I had Italian teachers who told inside jokes to the Italian students and even knew them after school. One teacher even had the kids bring him Hershey bars, and they loved to do it. But it was intimidation to me. Especially since this dude one time denounced me—I mean made a class-stopping pronouncement—for having my sneakers sitting on top of the desk. Like they were some all-time PeeUuus! That was more than just funny, at least for me.

I was "Jones" then, to the teachers and to the students. And from a familiar figure appreciated and denigrated for my actualities, as had been the case on Dey Street, I was now all but invisible, and when not that, the butt of something unpleasant. Plus I was completely contemptuous of them as far as athletics, though for certain there were some good players there, in all the sports. But part of my defense, the defense of my psyche, was found in silently denouncing these dudes for their lack of athletic skill and art. I mean, even if a dude could shoot, most of 'em looked funny to me (I said) and it cracked me up.

And I would get out in the playground and wear some unsuspecting turkeys out, though if I ran into some quality players, which I did, I would get cooled out. But the sense in myself was of some wall—some dull and wholly uninteresting wall—between myself and the life and persons of the place. And I wondered often what I was doing there. Except there had come into my head and out of my mouth some vague "decision" to go to Barringer.

At the beginning of the tenth grade I did go on to Barringer. They had some junior high school system consisting of the ninth grade for some of the high schools and that's what my sojourn at McKinley had been. (These days, the '80s, McKinley, now named 7th Avenue, is like a New York City school jammed up with blacks and Latinos in the advanced stages of ghettofication.)

Barringer was larger and if possible an even more foreign place. It was larger and on the other side of Branch Brook Park. There was less of the narrow ghetto First Ward feeling to it because it was larger and up toward the more middle-class Italian areas. But that was another world. McKinley was ugly and baroque and teeming and narrow and ghetto Italian. Barringer was larger and more open but it seemed even more completely separated from my Dey Street life.

And we had moved again, around this time of my life. We had moved all the way back across town into the Central Ward. The old Third Ward. And right on top of The Hill. So this meant that I had to take a bus every-day all the way crosstown to school. Coming out of the geographical look-out post of the growing black ghetto, on Belmont Avenue and Spruce Street. What they called the Four Corners. And during them days everybody and everything black passed across or under or over or around those streets either day or night. It was like X marked the spot of another kind of black life. Back over not far from where I was born and spent my earliest days, down the hill in Douglass-Harrison, but underneath my Belmont Avenue windows I began to be aware of the Fast Life.

It was like a sociologist's joke. Up in the morning, come down from our third-floor apartment. (My grandmother and uncle were with us again, but in much smaller space.) Down into the street, to the corner of Belmont (beautiful mountain?) to wait for the 9 Clifton bus. Hey, and there were quite a few other refugees and cutouts from the mostly black (and a trifle Jewish) high school at the edge of the Central Ward, South Side. It was in my head, as well, to flee South Side. (How did that get in my head? The talk among friends? Overhearing adults? I donno. But it came out of my mouth, "I don't wanna go to South Side. I wanna go to Barringer.") And there were kids on that wild 9 Clifton. Some coming from even further south going to West Side and Central, even Vo-Tech, and the last stop, way cross town in another world, Barringer. There were a few of us made that long trip every day, back and forth, from the Central Ward and even the South Ward, all the way to Rome. (And yes, just below the school sat the Vatican. The still unfinished Sacred Heart Cathedral, that towers now, and towered then with a useless romanticism wasted on most of us black kids who went to Barringer who saw it simply as a hated landmark.)

The joke? From the Four Corners to Rome and back. And now I was completely disoriented (though calmer now, at home, because of less hostile surroundings). Because I didn't know anybody at Barringer and I didn't know anybody on Belmont Avenue. My friends, at that time, still lived around Central Avenue School, Baxter Terrace, on Norfolk and Sussex and Lock and Jay and Hudson and Warren. And for a time it was a drag at both ends.

At Barringer it was the amazingly dull process of being an outsider that I was involved with. Though there were a few black students there I got tight with. At least to joke with in school and release some of the tension built up by our being black in Italian Antarctica. (Of the two closest joke-time buddies in my homeroom in Barringer—that is, we would jive and put each other down and bump each other and grin in the hallways and maybe the lunchroom—one, Ken, is a detective lieutenant, the other a career navy man. And even these dudes, black though they was, called me "Jones.")

Two of my other friends for other kinds of talk, they were in some of my other classes, the college-prep-oriented ones, were white. And they were outsiders too. We must a made a weird trio, Jim. One guy, J., was tall and skinny and talked incessantly of sports. But he wasn't Italian, could not play any sports worth a damn, plus when he was in grammar school (he went to Central Avenue too!) he had a kind of strange odor about him— oh, look, it was urine—that set him off from most of us then. I talked to him in Central but with another relationship. In Barringer we got tight and the pee smell had mostly gone, but he had pimples all over his face and his lack of coordination made him the brunt of much bullshit (as it had in Central—but that was a mostly black school). I didn't really like the way people acted toward J. in high school, though I guess I had heaped plenty of bullshit on him myself in grammar school. But now there was, I guess, some kind of half kinship. Since now I was on the outside, on the fringe of this social focus, and so was J., as usual. And hell, we both liked sports. And every morning he'd come to high school with the local newspaper and we'd discuss whatever was going down in the pros or high school or college, it made no difference to us. We rapped on it.

V., my other walking buddy, was also completely uncoordinated and a silent (though super-opinionated, egoistic, and talky with us) shy loner-type figure. He had a potbelly and looked middle-aged at sixteen and thought about smoking a pipe. V. fancied himself an intellectual and he was. But that was his defense against the mainstream life of Barringer. That he was other because his head was somewhere else.

He was Italian but totally disconnected from the Italian life of that place. Plus he wanted to be a writer and it was with V. that I first exchanged young vague ideas about writing. V. had read some books. He liked *The Red Badge of Courage* (I think because he lived in a place named after Stephen Crane) and he wrote short stories and poems like Crane's.

J., I think because of V.'s influence, later began to say that he wanted to be a sportswriter. All three of us went to a writing class in Barringer our senior year given by a hard-faced unsmiling teacher named Miss Stewart (but she turned out to be a caring human being).

So in my homeroom I swung with two bloods and in my other classes with two white intellectuals. Maybe all three of us were and came on like intellectuals. I know I didn't feel like no goddam intellectual. I just felt drugged being isolated and alienated and surrounded by such bullshit in white Barringer.

Swinging down off that 9 Clifton, on the other side, at the Four Corners, I faced an entirely different reality. On the corner a liquor store (still there), the Foxes, and next to that, coming toward my house, a black frozen custard and hot dog place; next was a black cleaner's, a Polish tinsmith, a house, then our house, 154 Belmont Avenue. On the top floor, the Joneses and Russes, and on the second floor, Dr. Bell, a young black dentist who had just got out of school. (He lived there a hot minute but this was his office mostly. He was also the building's landlord.) On the first floor, a Polish oil stove place run by this Polish man and woman who must have been a hundred.

When we got to Belmont there were still a few Poles there, mostly stores. And you could get some good kielbasy—Polish sausage. And down the street in the other direction there was still a good sprinkling of Jews, probably Polish, too. But the Poles lived mostly in that one block between Spruce and 17th Avenue. The remains of a larger community, just as was the sprinkling of Jews, but centered by a huge church, which is still there, for the Polish Catholics. I went to boy scout camp with some of the Polish kids because even though most of them had moved out of Newark their troop was located at St. Stanislaus on Belmont Avenue and so they belonged to the Robert Treat Council, which covered Newark. One of the funniest dudes from that Polish troop who regularly used to crack us up at camp was Sigmund Pilch, who was like a nonstop wisecracking slapstick artist, who I never saw once we came back into Newark after camp.

Across the street, on the corner, was the Four Kegs, where you could stand outside and peep into and see the highlife going on thick and fast on the weekends but happening at top speed any night. And down Spruce Street the straight-out ghetto, which I still had to investigate with my teenage legs and eyes and ears. And that came in on time. But early in my Barringer days and the horrible incarceration at McKinley I was stretched out like some despairing quiet animal not even sure what was wrong. But I knew.

I grew up on one side of town and part of my head was shaped by that ice and alienation, that hostility and silence in the face of adversity. And I grew up on the other side of town too and that is something else.

I was run home a few times from Barringer by the warring white boys. Tricked and insulted any number of times. Looked at funny by teachers (one of whom now in black Newark is trying to grin and skin his way past that old arrogance—whoa!). I looked at the white girls and their boyfriends and tried to see through the wall of our separation at what that would be like. But I never went with a white girl in high school (shit, that couldn't happen in Barringer). But I didn't go with any black girl either who went to the school. I just looked and fantasized about all of 'em.

The awards and the honors, the straight-out teenage joys, the simple concern, was never mine and I thought that I existed in that place in a separate piece of space where I thought my thoughts and had my resentments. And I openly did not like it. That separation and white-out. I did not like it. And it did not like me. I think it did something to me too. Like how could some nonstop sardonic-mouthed joker and quick-start artist like me be banned to an island of noninterest and overlook and uncomprehending babble. Perhaps I lusted after the life of the real inhabitants of that place. In my weakest moments I must have. But most of the time I was just passing through, even as words were coming out of my mouth or doing whatever I was doing. I was not wholly there, I felt, but the part of me that was, suffered.

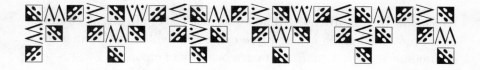

Two

Black Brown
Yellow White

These are some basic colors of my life, in my life. A kind of personal, yet fairly objective class analysis that corresponds (check it) to some real shit out in the streets in these houses and in some people's heads.

Belmont and Spruce was a corner in (of) black life. The people moving back and forth on Belmont, Livingston, 18th Avenue, and down the street on Broome and Prince and Morton and Charlton, or up the street on Waverly or round the corner on Hillside Place or over on West Kinney. That was black life full and open, bent under its history, yet that bend sometimes would seem like blue streamlining—hey, especially on the weekend with everything in front of you but absolute reality.

I had come back from the West, which was black life too, but on The Hill a different kind of thing went down. Like on Newark Street, yeh, but The Hill was more open and spread out, blacker in its spread and magnitude. The blues was our black footsteps, our basic reality, the ideological material of our lives. The mashed down flat social geography of the African American community put all kinds of dents and strokes and twists and turns in that black and blue base. There was the fundamental horizontal quality of an oppressed nationality—yet we were not all completely at the same level of being bent. Some of us did have more money, and in those

53

days before the suburbs opened up for blacks to a certain extent, almost all of us were piled along in one place or another within the same general community though sections of it were better than others.

There were people who lived in East Orange, even Orange and Montclair. And we did look at them different—though they were part of a basic *yellow* reality, that had some presence in official white world as black, but that was meaningless to us in our day-to-day lives.

The black was fundamental black life, the life of blues people, the real and the solid and the strong and the beautiful. But I developed these understandings as I went. And The Hill was the laboratory in which they developed.

The brown was my family and me, half real and half lodged in dream and shadow. The connected to reality by emotion (and logic). The walking through the streets and ambushes of that harshest reality unscathed except psychologically. The house with hidden insides and unknown wild projections. Not us exclusively, but personally, from my inside looking out, in those days.

The yellow, the artificial, the well-to-do, the middle class really. Described by a term like petty bourgeoisie with steel precision, but something else of caste was what my definition came to mean even without me understanding or saying that. The high-up over the streets avoiding disaster by several hundred thousand feet and some straight hair.

The browns had to weave in betwixt and between the harshest disasters, getting cut in the street, locked up by police, living in places with smelly halls, having hair "standing all over your head," being "Blue" (a nickname) or "Liverlips" or having a drunk father or mother or a falling-down house, or a tiny apartment decorated with rotogravure covers. Or failing in school, being left back, put back for being from the South, dropping out to go to work, having parents that couldn't speak "good English." Browns barely escaped all this and actually had to be tested by yellows and whites or yellow and white "reality" to see if they passed.

Because the black was also the damned, the left behind, the left out, the disregarded, the abandoned, the drunk and disorderly, the babbling and the staggering, the put down and the laughed at, the heir of the harshest of lives I could see.

But the brown, while caught between the black and the yellow, did not, in spite of themselves, like the yellow. They hated it, them, even worse than white, even worse than white folks (normally) because white folks didn't exist with the same day-to-day common reality. The yellow would be around bugging you, having a haircut neatly parted with well-greased legs and knees. The yellow would be sitting with new moccasins and striped tee shirts and newly creased shorts. They would be laughing and having always good exclusive times, usually at your expense, even if it didn't have nothing to do with you.

Brown sensitive to this even unable to speak of it, sensitive to it watching it. Touched by both streams of life and consciousness yet being its own being shaped by both and the white other. I mean I could come out of my brown house (no matter its color) into the streets and be facing a black reality. A blue shimmer pushing off the streets and twisting round the corner catching me, caressing me, and being a background for everything, the motion behind the motion which is itself's full dimension.

Or you could come out of your house (be brought out by your brown (and yellow) mama) and find yourself at the Y being laughed at by the yellow for having your hair cut close or being brown or not having a mother who was a "fashion model."

Or you could come running out of your brown (and orange) crib and head for the Court and dash smack into the lovely brown E., whose long curly hair like a blood version of Shirley Temple and old man who sang on television (with *Your Show of Shows*) made them remote and yellow despite your secret protests of love and fantasies and stopped phone calls ("She's not here. Don't call here anymore!"), despite the fact they lived in Baxter Terrace, where, hey, some straight-out black was obviously lodged and a corresponding brown you would have sworn prepared them to love you.

(That was a long "alas" of my young life, one of the pitiful unrequiteds youth seems filled with.)

You'd sit looking at a yearbook of your mom's Tuskegee Normal High School days or of those slim tiny Woco Pep Fisk days (stopped by your appearance) and wander outside dead into a drunk man with wine-red lips threatening you with his existence.

Saturday afternoons the whole of The Hill was music. Up top the blues, all kinds, country and city, guitars and saxophones, screamers and moaners. I dug the Ravens, the Orioles, Amos Milburn, Dinah Washington, Little Esther, Ruth Brown was our heartbeat, Larry Darnell, Louis Jordan and His Tympany Five, Earl Bostic, Tab Smith. It was everywhere everywhere in that space, in the air, on the walls, in the halls, in the laundromats, whistled and sung and stomped to. It colored the vacant lots where barbecue was being perfected, it zoomed out of the bars and lit up our mouths, it bluesed us along through those grey streets and carried the message and feeling of black life.

'Cause Newark was iron grey for me then and it is still but now ripped apart by piled-up despair. But in those days grey and steel were its thrusts into me, its dominant unwavering tone. And the strongest, the deepest, the basic construction element of its design was the black of its bottom of the lives whose majority it held and spoke for. Such an ugly place, so hard so unyielding it seemed—grey industrial city. But black life made it blue. Its beating heart was blue therefore rooted in black life and its streets strummed my head like a guitar.

Inside our house my sister and I were readied for brown stars that flickered in the yellow logic of my mother's prose like white twinkling distance we'd cover as easily as an amendment is written in the constitution. "Guaranteeing" you something you could only be guaranteed with power. Readied you in brown for white to be yellow. Is that the exact psychology of such beings as what was meing? Yet outside under the invisible white tarpaulin of held-down obstructed life called oppression there was black life and it was strongest everyday where we lived. And no matter the brown inside game plan your mama hammered out with piano lessons, drum lessons, art lessons, singing and dancing in summer school and at the Y in choruses of yellow and brown folks. Or ballet and tap lessons for my sister and pink toe shoes and boubous or our trips down South where we lived out in the suburbs of Columbia, S.C., between two rich yellow doctors (one housed my maximum passion of that time)—when you came out that house it was black people whose lives spelled out the direction and tenor of our day-to-day being.

The brown was like a reserve, an exit or quick passage to somewhere else. You look up you could be getting a scholarship somewhere or shaking Joe Louis's and Sandy Saddler's hand or being introduced by Willie Bryant as a bright Negro child, or reciting the Gettysburg Address in a boy scout suit down at the Old First Church, where George Washington was and most black people wasn't.

But I ran the streets and walked the streets everyday hooked up to black life. And it builded, however, despite the cold white shot of my daily Barringer trip that taught me to lust after abstract white life abstractly. Really, to be concerned with it in some abstract yet intimate way. While even as I moved, Larry Darnell would light up my insides and I could walk down the halls of that cold-ass place and be reciting with cool solemnity his blue tragic ballad:

You're right Up on top now
You want To be free
Why you're Afraid to be seen
With somebody like me
You're afraid to present me
To the friends of your set
Oh well, I guess
We'll forgive and forget.

But you come back from white Barringer, bam, it was blues and black people everywhere I see. And that church my mother and grandmother took us to was classic in that regard. It was a yellow church, a yellow folks' church. In fact someone told me that they used to sing, "Only the yellow, only the yellow, will see God." Some blunt agitprop.

Yet within it there was the brown and the black. The black folks would scream and fall out. The brown would fan themselves and fall out from time to time, but not regular like the black, who would "get happy" at the drop of a note or a word.

The preacher in that church (I mean the *minister*, only the black got preachers, the yellow got ministers and the browns be strung out as usual somewhere twixt the two, over here with it, over there without). The minister, Rev. H., was white as snow. His hair was white as snow. Rev. H. was whiter (in complexion) than white folks ever thought about being. And, to me, if he wasn't exactly what God would look like, from my training, then I couldn't picture what God would look like. God had to look exactly like Rev. H. Tall, slender, solemn, cold blue eyes (or green?), and white as air. Or snow.

But dig, the struggle in that church was classic too. Class and Classic and Class-sick struggle. The browns vs. the yellows and the blacks with the browns vs. the yellows. Under the huge tarpaulin of the white. (Amen!) Like it would be very clear most times around the music. The yellow wanted Handel and Schumann and Lieder with some switching flit with a dull crokinole to conduct while trying to point his hiney at some protein projectile.

Easter and Xmas, Jim, you was took down and off. HALLELUIA it was spelled in gold leaf on the hymnal with white cherubim straight from heaven. The stark raving corny nongrandeur of those stiff shows would make great films for our archive of torture and cultural aggression. You thought you was being moved (those chills through you) but that was rigor mortis on your ass with hobnailed boots.

And the black and the brown who they rescued from yellow death as plastic persons would be agitating for some heat, some feeling and description of themselves, not going to white heaven so much as crossing that Jordan and escaping finally from the horrible pain. They wanted the old warm hymns, the sorrow songs, and gospel, some modern stuff. Me grandma and Sarah Vaughan's mother was part of that cadre—they sang in the group called the William P. Sims Gospel Chorus, whose obvious aim was to bring some life and some warmth, some word of black Jesus and black God and black heaven translated to mean some good that included them, some life after death in which they would be much more than silent servants on the fringe of reality.

So struggle would be going down in there. (Known to me only recently as class struggle.) But I did perceive it as struggle. I knew, for instance, that my sweet grandmother for whom I would have done anything and the actually yellow-colored Mrs. B. did not like each other. My grandmother as head of the Ladies Aid with her faint smile and glasses going to sleep in the "front room" of our house making believe she was watching television.

Mrs. B. was head of the Flower Committee. The symbolism was clear— some flowers or some aid. They had different ways (and different things) they wanted to worship. And it was manifest all over if you would pick up the words and looks. Ultimately, I guess, that struggle was really between those who wanted to eliminate a "black church" and those who wanted Xtian worship to be a form of African American culture. Simple now? (I remember throwing out, even before writing *Blues People*, how you could tell much about black people by what church they went to. And under investigation the concreteness and correctness of that staggered me.) The "purest" African Xtian church in the U.S. is the sanctified—with drums, horns, tambourines, dance, and song. The poorest too—in storefronts, little halls off alleyways, over delicatessens. I'd like to list all the black churches in Newark one day—their names are so weird—take pictures of some— living mythology, dreams housed in despair. The big ol' churches, stone and steel and huge stained glass, are more European. White. More bourgeois. Less emotional. A church based on money and spurious rationalism. Like Pascal's cold pensées—"Hey, we better believe in god, along with Money. First: Suppose there is a god after all, we'll really be up shit's creek!" But the passion of the black church, which even some white peasants go to in the black belt South, is very different!

My mother dropped it several times how Nana and Mrs. B. didn't get on. I figured it was because Mrs. B. was out of her mind. Nana liked most people. I could not penetrate to the actuality of their dispute, but my perception confirmed that the little Minnie Mouse-looking Mrs. B., who put layers of pink and white powder on her pale pink face and "put on airs" as even my mother pointed out, was frantic with corniness.

The S's were hooked up with Mrs. B. The S. clan's mama B.S. wore pince nez, yeh yeh yeh whew! Really. I didn't know what the fuck they were. A couple dizzy bitches in Bethany wore them. Yes. White bourgeois apes in yellow. It was a weird church.

And just as in any class struggle, much undermining and jockeying for positions and rear actions and frontal assaults went on. For one thing, Mrs. B. was always trying to get note. She was the senior yellow lady rep, Mrs. S. her junior minister. Invariably, they'd appear, after the services when announcements were made, to rah rah for the Flower Committee and get people to wave their fans back and forth (applause wasn't dignified).

My grandmother made announcements most times to mention the next regular meeting of the Ladies Aid. She was an usherette too, on special church occasions and she wore those white church uniforms with white shoes.

One reason the Flower Committee could get over is that one member of the family, F., worked for a florist. Later he became an apprentice undertaker for Beckett's. F. was the loudest (the most human, actually) of the clan—a brown Mickey Rooney tied by everything to yellow life.

But flowers, flowers. Look—hey—we've arranged you see, for flowers flowers.

Snide remarks, grimaced conversations. My mother would drop it about "Mrs. Banks and them." My grandmother never said anything. She just met with the Ladies Aid and kept aiding, doing her work.

B., the junior partner in the yellow flower line, had other illustrious posts in the church. Plus her husband was a supervisor with the P.O. while my father still drove a truck. The son, W., was a prototype, neat haircut and clothes and Vaselined yellow kid. He was as famous at church picnics as Andrew Young. Actually, if there was any stereotype of yellow, as kid, it was W. Bland, glasses, grinning, goofy, "sissified." The kind of thing your mother would beat you in the head with. A yellow brownjack to pop you with. "W. got W. did " and on and on, a razz for your disconnection from her program of upward and forward to where? The yellowest part of brown? (A question?)

But the real life of where we lived what I perceived as strongest was not any of that but *black*. That was the life I was tied to—even "shot from guns," like famous (brown) toasted cereal, the connection I made was with black life.

So that the yellow church was dry and boring at one side—yellow and artificial at another. And even if I'd wanted to (which I never did) there was no way you could bring no yellow shit in the streets or walk with that in no playground without gettin' laughed at minimally, chased if you pushed it and beat the hell out of if you blew altogether.

No matter the browns and the yellows could collect minusculely—in the streets of our lives, black life shaped us. We were judged by it and defined (to ourselves by ourselves) by it.

W. was a "sissy-punk" where I was most comfortable. That East Orange shit was another world. You saw its products on Sundays. One dude, H., a yellow comedian with glasses, called me "Gloom" every Sunday in honor of my seriousness (?) and the black life he peeped had grown me a blue soul.

At some point I envied yellow its neat haircuts (wavy) and new moccasins. Its cars and exotic addresses. The pretty little girls that grinned at you accidentally or never. I might fantasize about these in some way (depending upon the chronological maturity of my genitals) but that never seemed real.

Except down South there was a girl who lived next door to my folks with a high hill-like lawn at the top of which was her red and white house and a lawn chair you could swing in. The group of us, my two cousins, my sister and I, and her, S.J., would swing there and scramble across and up that high hill lawn. That was a terrible knife in my young heart that she should be forever and always out of my reach. It was so pitiful because I never told her how I felt. It was too ridiculous. She was too distant, haughty, light-skinned gorgeous. With a doctor father. I could not even pretend to mention my passion. But sometimes if strange waves pushed through me, a physical dazzle to my head turned awry staring past a blurred bird at his wind, I'd think, "These are my S.J. moments," and sigh.

Another girl, in Newark, I went to see down on Waverly Avenue. Another light-skinned—off to the side—kind of pretty girl. Was so proper and quiet and grinned little quiet jokes. I'd go to see her in my late high school days. She had a very old light father who I never talked to, only saw a few times before he passed. Her mother was young, in her thirties, and tall dark brown and lovely. She always seemed, I guess in contrast to her husband, athletic and vigorous, like she was on her way to a dance or tennis match. Her stepdaughter had much of her father in her, quiet and old even as a teenager. And I made her house a pilgrimage of sorts, consciously to sit, clean and smiling and pressing my suit, which was no suit at all. It was just that I felt good sitting there nice and all like a good boy but I never took it seriously though I might have thought I did. But I never even thought that. She was too quiet and yellow. I could not have told anybody she was my girlfriend. Even when I was fairly sure that I was the only one seeing her. And certain people did think our thing together was somewhat serious. Still I never thought she thought it was other than a mild surface pastime. I was too brown. Too gross. Too bounded by malevolent experience. Too grimy. My hands were dirty (another little brown chubby girl said). I could never talk to her about some things, that wiggled and screamed and bluesed my head up. I could never tell her my feelings, even about her. Which were dry enough for a "big-time" marriage with pictures in the Afro. "Dr. Jones, I presume," neither bone nor contention. But it was all like something I saw walk past. Pretty girl. Quiet little yellow girl. Sitting there across from me in her quiet father's home. Her mother and she, she told me always, were like sisters. And her mother was sleek and brown and it was she—sad confession—who really turned me on, on the real side. (Is this Oedipal and shit?) So did I think—my other sister? No, not flat-out like that. But something like that, cool and quiet and on your best behavior—a quiet almost like in a photograph or five-and-ten repro. I was gone from that no matter what postures I made, I was gone from that, just walking.

But none of this can be totally separated from Music. Because that was the great definer and link, the extension chord of blackness in me. And so everything (else) had a music to it. A shimmer of sound you heard as you saw it, or you saw as you heard it. The blues hugged me close to the streets and the people. That was what we breathed and Saturdays was when we breathed (full out).

But the brown yellow white tip was a constant too, by contrast, so you knew the real did exist more totally and in you more completely as the informant, creator, and disperser of mystery. Barringer and McKinley were certainly white—and the newspaper—and voices on the radio. Though I transformed the radio in my transmutating mind so it told brown tales somehow. (Yet you understand the term brainwash and must acknowledge certain brain damage. Yet I claim the transduction of certain impulses, so that the output was not just white noise, but a heroic grimace when I smile that contains absolute desire for the destruction of evil.)

My terror was white, and racists (who I knew since the Elephant House, and Augie's slaps and Birmingham's rolling eyes, etc., and tales my grandmother told. And when I was thirteen I read *Black Boy*, the alternate selection of Book-of-the-Month Club, and I feared for R.W.'s life and wondered how he dared say such things and still walk around. Yeh, I knew in my young life about "crackers" as my grandfather called them) yes, they were white, and scrunched up dudes and ugly ladies arguing with my mother in buses and Fanny Farmer candy stores. They were most assuredly white. And the unknown monsters my grandmother told me had cut off a young boy's "privates" near Dothan, stuck 'em in his mouth, then gathered the young black girls to see, so a lesson would be taught. They were definitely white. And the killers of Emmett Till, whose ruptured swollen horrible body I saw in *Jet*, swallowing hard and being actually afraid. No, they were very very white. But mostly it was the outside limits of our world. In the distance, and cold, like the end of the world, beyond which you fell off (?). Who knew?

There were teachers, interesting that they were all rec teachers, who were white and who were real enough to talk to. They would even throw me out of the playground for "cursing." Mr. F., Mr. R. were the main dudes. I had a bad mouth, Jim, a bad mouth. Withering in its obscene intensity. But the white was merely distance or, close up, terror. And even the Italian dudes that I knew when I was young were somewhat removed and that was the definition.

The yellow was always a combatant. Distant (somehow) colored people, whom you did not know well. Made up shit, painted up shit. Stiffness— corniness. Sissified, dull shit. Stuff in church. The Y where they made you sing. Lessons. Picnics your mama carried you off to when there was real baseball games to be played—shit to be explored. The Secret Seven to be hung around with. Or, later, just the blues streets to be walked and the big-assed black girls to be stared at from within the brown recesses.

The yellow was a promise you could never keep. A challenge you did not want. A frustrating distant thing some mama threw up in your face that you did not care about but just did not want to be compared with. The so 'n' so's or little So 'n' So or Master So 'n' So, against which your mama would rank you and you knew you could never measure up. (I could make the sound of a madman at this point ahhhhhddggggggggggggg to show my frustration!)

Cotillions and Mrs. B. found them and drug a few selected (mostly brown) ghetto kids outta the hopeless muck of their lives and shot them off upward and onward (fake style) into the bull's-eye of yellow enterprise. Now that was banana yellow. In tuck-see-dose and evening gowns, we lidda brown and yellow chilruns were readied for our entrance into the waiting warren of slaughter. Where our brains would be took out and placed in a safety deposit box for Mister Big Guy, one day, to make use of.

The cotillion, which I approached as a high school youth, was designed so that brown and yellow ladies could be presented to society. (There was also the Debutantes' Ball, which surfaced at the same time but had less note.) And we practiced our bows and turns and went to practice week nights, walking home in groups afterwards. Chubby brown Betty was my partner and we went together for three or four years on and off.

I was awarded scholarships, and the four of us, mother, father, sister and I, sat downtown at the Terrace Ballroom and watched the proceedings. There was a real effort to include the brown folks in this. But somehow we sat just outside of the connected up "human" thrust of that (was there any?) and the animating stream of yellow life made that run like an escalator to nowhere.

And see there was one group of "friends," acquaintances, from rehearsal that you took up with on one level. You want to know the complexity of my young life? Well, I still knew the Cavaliers but by late high school we'd drifted in a real sense. I'd see S. and R., they were even in the cotillion and they lived on The Hill and were fairly tight. But the others, the boys I'd known earlier, had mostly faded except at odd times around odd occasions. Games we played in together were getting fewer and fewer and by the time I got out of high school and started going to the Newark branch of Rutgers I did not see them at all nor play any ball with them.

At the same time, for several years I'd taken up with some brothers around the corner on Hillside Place. The Cavaliers were brown compared to the Hillside Place brothers, who were definitely black. And for most of my high school years, after white school, black Hillside Place was who I ran with. (Though I had a brown band I put together, R. on alto, D. on drums, me on trumpet, and we played upstairs in my house on Belmont Avenue, "Tenderly," "September in the Rain" [the same song], "Perdido," etc.) Yellow church shit and Y stuff and Jones Street Y stuff, which was much browner, were all shot in there.

But the black was the constant. The people, the life, the rules, the mores, the on-the-street definitions of what was beautiful or hip. The constant background of our breathing, the blues, was always everywhere. And Saturdays raised up like a great space mural (blues as) companionship of thought and feeling; it was feeling. The real good-looking girls and tough dudes, who you wanted to make laugh and impress, the style you had to perfect was black—black and blue.

And though I came striding out of a brown house with plenty of bullshit packed between my eyes. There was nowhere to go but the black streets and the people who ran those streets and set the standards of our being were black. And no matter where we would go and what we would get into, when we were true to ourselves, when we were actually pleasing our deepest selves, being the thing we most admired and loved, we were black (and blue).

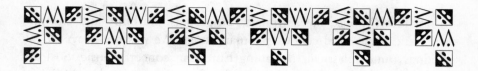

Three

Music

I've said that one constant for me from the time of any consciousness in helping to define the world has been music. The various kinds of music, of course, gave dimension to the world. There was/is not just one music. There are many. (Though when I talk with black jazz musicians we say, sometimes, *The Music*, meaning African American improvised music. What we've called, in our deeper moments, Jazz. Directly from the African, *jassm*, *orgasm*, i.e., "come music." I guess that stuck because that's where white folks first heard the music, in New Orleans whorehouses, and that's what they were doing when they heard it, jassing, or trying to jass. The word first means sexual intercourse.)

Music is the term for this chapter because I want to lay out an entirety of my feelings about The Music and Music and connect them precisely to the growth of my perception and its history. Because music is both an emotional experience and a philosophical one. It is also an aesthetic experience and the history of my moving from one music to another, the history of being drawn most directly to one music or another, is another kind of path and direction in my life. Part of the answer to the question How did you get to be you?

In our brown house was spirituals and gospels and blues and jazz and white and brown and yellow "popular" songs. We was not heavy (thank goodness) into "classical" (meaning European concert) music. So I did not have to do too much shedding of that from the inside when I thought I needed to shed that. I picked up that stuff much later.

At the yellow church I told you they would pile Handel and Bach and Mozart on our ass but that was lightweight on the real side except for the Hallelujah Chorus and stuff mashed on you around Xmas. Even in that yellow fortress, spirituals mostly dominated and my grandmother and them tried to ease the gospel number in on them but that was limited.

The school, you know, had some white stiff shit to mash on you when they could. I was in the All-City Chorus and they had us singing something called "The Song of Man," a mixture of idealism and straight-out metaphysics that identified Humanism. In my music lessons or in the school auditorium we would have snatches of The Classics bounced off us but that was not my main diet.

We also had the radio jugging with you (and later on television in some small way) and movie background music I would use to "sord fight" around and across people's cars parked unsuspectingly on our street, or as the mouthed background music for our playground and vacant-lot shootouts.

The radio carried the *Make Believe Ballroom*, turned on when I was younger by my parents. Somehow I connect it up with my father. Martin Block with that sinuous voice. On the weekends they had the *Hit Parade*, and I remember as an early high school baseballer hanging my portable radio over the handlebars and listening between innings to Ezio Pinza sing songs from *South Pacific* — "Some Enchanted Evening," "This Nearly Was Mine," also Mary Martin. Plus songs from *The King and I* or *Wish You Were Here* or *Guys and Dolls* as well as the other crazy stuff like "Rag Mop, R-A-G-G-M-O-P-P" (a black song in whiteface), almost as crazy as the "Mairzy Doats" and "Hut Sut Ralston" of earlier times when I was small before I had my own radio.

Sometimes Nat King Cole would come on, like with "Nature Boy" or once in a while the hip "Straighten Up and Fly Right." But that *Hit Parade*, though it had some tunes I did like, for the most part I thought of as composed of lace glass lemon peels — some bounce for the ounce but something to be looked at, waved at, as it passed. Though I liked the show tunes.

I liked Bing Crosby better than Frank Sinatra (that was a raging controversy in junior high school, though the Hershey bar receiving teacher told us in his high wisdom that the best voice of all was Perry Como!). And stuff like Rosemary Clooney and Vaughn Monroe and Johnnie Ray and Frankie Laine ("Mule Train"). Even my father told me he was a "Jew boy singing like a colored fellow." That was what the *Hit Parade* pumped at us.

But how strange is the human mind that it can receive all kinds of things from all kinds of places. Be put in weird situations (like at the end of the 9 Clifton run), yet retain some connection with its richest sources. Like the African slaves worshiping Catholic saints, yet St. Michael and St. Stephen, when you get up close on the slave converts renderings of them, have tiny cuts etched in their alabaster faces. These cuts speak of another world, another culture and language and life. You could hear some deadbeat in a turned around collar who's been jerking off for thirty-five years scream, "Why these are tribal marks, Father Noel. Tribal marks! These heathen have been deceiving us all along!"

So that I was stretched between two lives and perceptions. (I've told you it was four—BlackBrownYellowWhite—but actually it's two on the realest side, the two extremes, the black and the white, with the middle two but their boxing gloves.) And when I returned on that bus ride from Barringer and swung down onto Belmont Avenue, blues took me. Black people surrounded me. And that was the element I felt easiest in.

Even inside my brown house, as secure as it was (and that was its most carryable beauty, its security, that I never once had to wonder who and what was going on or where my next anything was coming from. My father and mother and grandmother, Jim, were solid as a rock), there was a certain posture you had to take on, after all, whatever yo mama wanted you to be, you was gon' be that, to some extent, or get yo ass turned into a neon artifact. The casual lectures, casual in that they were constant and could accompany any other activity—combing your hair, washing your face, putting on your clothes, doing your homework (or having not done it), coming in late, wanting to take drawing lessons instead of piano lessons, you could be the recipient of an instant lecture on why you better do something other than you was doing or look or be better than you were, with immediate reference to somebody who was, were constant.

It was the normal guidance of what one assumes is the normal parent-to-child relationship, yet it is turned wherever the parent is turned and its specifics shaped by whatever the parent is and has been shaped by.

Moving in the blue/black streets there was a freedom, a possibility of becoming anything I could imagine. I was completely on my own (and even more so once I realized it), and everything in that world began and was defined by me, in me, by music. The blues heaviest and most constant. The quartets like the Orioles and the Ravens are Belmont Avenue near Spruce Street. I could look out my back window Saturday mornings and watch a young black girl hanging up clothes singing "The Glory of Love." And she was just accompanying the jukebox or record player from somewhere. (In those days black radio was not as widespread, so most of the sounds were on 78s or jukeboxes or out of people's mouths.)

And as I got older I could move in those streets with more ease and direction and go to hear specifically what I wanted to hear. In the house, from the beginning Amos Milburn might be playing "Bad Bad Whiskey" or "Let Me Go Home, Whiskey" or "One Scotch, One Bourbon, One Beer." Louis Jordan, our main man, and His Tympany Five had me steppin' from before I could even read. "Knock Me a Kiss," "Don't Worry about That Mule," "Caledonia, Caledonia, What Makes Your Big Head So Hard? Mop!" The drama of "Saturday Night Fish Fry." We was rocking till the break of dawn. And even later when he went calypso with Ella Fitzgerald and did "Run, Joe" and "Stone Cold Dead in de Market," he was our man. He was cookin' in our language. That's what "jive" was. And why jive was jive? Well, it had to be for us to stay alive.

The lyrics of the blues instructed me. Explained what the world was and even how men and women related to each other, and the problems inherent in that. Even later so basic a communication as "Work with Me, Annie," then "Annie Had a Baby (Annie Can't Work No More)," could just about sum up some aspects of life in the black ghetto part of the western hemisphere.

But the blues singers were oldest and most basic. My grandfather even dug Lonnie Johnson, Amos Milburn, and Louis Jordan singing "Don't Worry about That Mule." The blues was old and basic, and everywhere, for us. There was people sitting on the fender of somebody's car singing something. And you might stop or laugh as you went by. But it spilled out of windows and soon even out of car windows. It was the party and the party goers. It was old people and young slick-haired dudes.

Duke and Count and Jimmie Lunceford I associated with my parents. Those songs like "Don't Get Around Much Anymore" (Hibbler sang it "enty-moooore") or "Move to the Outskirts of Town" or "One o'Clock Jump" or "Jumping at the Woodside," I heard from them or with them or at their social events. That was more sophisticated to me, like highballs and the wartime upsweeps my mother wore. But we all liked Louis Jordan, everybody. It made me think of all of us, laughing at his jive.

Erskine Hawkins and Lucky Millinder were on the posters of the public dances where my folks would go with Ritz crackers, chicken, and whiskey on the table. Down at the Terrace or Wideway Hall or wherever they went in those early days.

When I first came back into the Central Ward I went to the frozen custard bar and two guys came up and checked me out. One a big barrel-chested guy who looked like he had a two-by-four shoved up his ass that also resulted in a grin approaching cretinous proportions. The other a dark squat husky dude with a homburg pushed back on his head. He looked absolutely serious but in the long run he had the most humor. "What's your name?" the grinning one said, in a way that suggested he thought there was a leer on his face. Maybe he thought he looked terrifying. "Leroy," I said, without saying much.

"You live around here?" the same one said.

"Yeh, up the street." I was looking for the woman to get my order, talking tight-lipped with real tension.

"You gonna give us your money?" the barrel-chested guy said.

"No," I said, so direct it frightened me. "Not a chance." And stuck out my chest. Dinah Washington was playing in the background and her wide arching penetrating notes musta gave me something. Maybe I knew with Dinah in the background I couldn't turn to stone and I couldn't melt anyway. I stuck out my chest and ordered my hot dog. Not frightened but frozen.

"This guy thinks he's tough," the stiff one kept on. Now the bass-voiced singer with the Ravens was talking and singing "Ol' Man River" and I wondered what they'd do next.

"I am tough," I said. Why? Who's to say? Maybe Jimmy Ricks's heavy notes had aided me, and after him on the box, a stream of them. "Sixty Minute Man," "Charles Brown," or some of the Honkers. Finally, the grinning one acknowledged his grin and Pigfoot, the other one, a real sweet guy, started laughing and stuck out his hand. "You just moved around here, didn't you? I seen your sister. Man, you got a fine sister." And that friendship lasted until I went away to college to duke with the white and the yellow.

"This is The Poet," he said of the other guy, whose hand was also pushed out. Poet was his street name, given because he had an elaborate exaggerated way of speaking and being. And later, as my own pretensions toward poetry emerged, I thought of this Poet so natural in his outpouring it was acknowledged as part of the scene. My own poetry was more difficult to come by because it began much less naturally.

But that transition, from outsider to through the door anyway, was accompanied by the sounds in the frozen custard store, as was every other event in our time, by the sounds. Just a few doors from my house, across the street, music came out of the Four Corners. Where the Fly and the Swift sped in and out. I could watch late nights sometimes from my window which looked right out on Belmont. (Though the window to my room looked out on the backyard and all the way to Livingston Street, where the more intimate life of The Hill would go on.)

At all the parties we went to the slow drag was the premier sound and the rhythm "fast tunes" were next. The blue or red light drug us in. And it would be so dark you had to stand in the corners for a while till you recognized somebody you knew. You had to make sure you could see, no matter how dark it was. To see who was with who and who was doing what, and whether any bad guys or gangs was in there. If it was a gang in there I'd hit the silk, especially when I went to parties alone. And I did a lot of that once I'd moved from the West Side back to The Hill and had a period when I didn't run regular with the Cavaliers or had yet hooked up with the Hillside Place dudes.

The quartets were what was happening at the parties. The Orioles was the stars and with them a host of other birds, Ravens, Flamingos, Swallows, Cardinals, etc. Larry Darnell and Wynonie Harris, one on the soft crooning side (another poet), the other shouting and driving us across the floor or up the street, had to be at your party.

Remember Ivory Joe Hunter? "When I Lost My Baby I Almost Lost My Mind." That was the hit that night the Dukes started some shit up in North Newark and one dude got beat with a meat cleaver. But that was so pretty. ". . . I almost . . . lost . . . my mind." We were rubbing and the odor and heat would go through us and we tried to press the sister for all we was worth and sometimes had to get off the floor quick cause our spirits had suddenly rose.

On Belmont Avenue, I lived right down the street, the next block, from two social centers, so to speak. One was the National Theater, a movie that showed reruns, that was truly the neighborhood movie. More conversation ran around between the audience than you could hear on the screen. But it was a good place to go to catch up on what you missed or to see the goodies once or twice more. I was a teenager now and my parents let me go to the National fairly late Fridays and weekends or not too late other nights.

I got some note in there one night when *The Three Musketeers* was playing, the one with Gene Kelly as D'Artagnan. They find his girlfriend's bag or brooch and it has her initials "C.B." on it, and as they handed the bag up before the camera I shouted out, "Crime Buster," which was Dick Tracy's funny-paper crime fighters. People howled and a couple of the dudes in the neighborhood liked that. I saw a lotta people going in and out of the National.

And I guess I had started running into the Hillside Place dudes around that time. I had seen some of them earlier in a renegade boy scout troop up at Camp Mohican that counselors warned us to eschew. Some of them had been hooked up some way with this Charlton Street boy scout troop but only to go to the free summer camp.

Then I discovered, when I moved back to The Hill, that a bunch of them lived right around the corner a couple blocks away, on Hillside Place. Little Jimmy Scott lived around there too, also Babs Gonzales's family. I ran with Babs's younger brother T-Bone, who was part of the Hillside Place group. Little Jimmy was always singing around in Newark somewhere and gambling in the hallways of Hillside Place. But we all dug his "The Masquerade Is Over" and imitated him everyday, including his caved-in-chest stance and sway as he whispered his tragic blues.

But it was at the Masonic Temple that I got really involved with the Hillside Placers and we became great friends. Every Sunday night at the Masonic Temple they had a "canteen." I guess they had got the name from the teenage canteens that were popular in the movies taken from the troop cool-out shelters, the Stage Door Canteens, the USO used to hook up or make believe they did during World War II.

The Masonic was right next door to the National, one flight up off the street. Proceeding up either of two grand curved staircases, you got to the main ballroom, where the canteen was held. The canteen was simply a dance, not too expensive, that was held every Sunday, with various groups. One dance got so wild, Lynn Hope and his turbaned screamers were on the set, that we all ran out into the street, Lynn Hope included, and disrupted traffic for a couple hours. (Vide: "The Screamers.")

But most Sunday nights it was just a lot of black teenagers, some a trifle elderly, grindin' and dancin' fast to the sounds of that time and place. We loved Ruth Brown, and tunes like "Teardrops from My Eyes" were not only our dance favorites but emotional anthems of our lives. Dinah

Washington and the many bird quartets also thrilled us. And Larry Darnell and Wynonie Harris and Charles Brown and a young dude who called himself Mister Blues who used to sing "I'm a real young boy just sixteen years old/I'm a real young boy just sixteen years old/I need a funky black woman to satisfy my soul!"

The Honkers really turned us on when we wasn't grinding, doing the "slow drag" off Ivory Joe or Earl Bostic's beautiful sound ("Flamingo"). We would be going crazy with Big Jay McNeely when he laid out flat on the floor blowing his soul with his legs kicking. Jay had a shirt that glowed in the dark and he played with that on sometimes. Or Illinois Jacquet (his detractors called him "lotta noise racket" but they was square). Bullmoose Jackson, Lynn Hope, Hal "Corn Bread" Singer. What about Joe Liggins and his Honey Drippers? I thought "The Honey Dripper" was a perfect piece of music. I could listen to that over and over. And you had to if you lived near Spruce Street and the shoeshine parlor with the jukebox blasting out into the open air.

Johnny Otis's "Harlem Nocturne" I loved so much. I'd whistle it Saturday afternoons in anticipation of the Sunday sets. One time I sat up in the laundromat waiting for the clothes to wash and dry and whistled the whole Masonic repertory and the little pretty girl who worked there who I saw in the canteen from time to time asked me if I was a musician. I was whistling "Harlem Nocturne," "The Honey Dripper," "It's Too Soon to Know," "Teardrops from My Eyes," etc. All those words and those sounds carried what I knew of the world, they brought me as face to face with it as I could be then.

I hear that music and not only does the image of Belmont and Spruce, the Four Corners, The Hill, come in but also names like Headlight, Bubbles, Rogie, T-Bone, Kenny, Sonny Boy, Rudy, my main men from Hillside Place. When I first went into the Canteen, it was like a minefield, you had to watch your step, like really. Somebody wanna pull a Fanon slash on you. You know, Fanon says, the oppressed, because they will not kill their oppressors, take out their suppressed violence on themselves, their brothers, every weekend we kill each other for minute affronts, while The Hill itself is a major affront.

So you had to watch out. Dudes was bashing each other for stuff like stepping on each other's shoes. "Hey, motherfucker, you stepped on my suedes, I'm a fuck you up!" Also who was going with who and who was looking at who and who danced with who or tried to rub against who. Or maybe dudes fell into disfavor with headwhippers because they was going with someone who put said headwhipper down, little dudes going with real pretty girls that headwhippers figured was too small to go with girls looking that good. There was many reasons you could get your head beat about a girl.

But once I started hanging with K. the rest was cooled out a little. We watched folks do they thing. The heavy dancers in our group would do they number and we would cheerlead or razz lead. If they got a really nice looking girl we'd line up to get a dance after them, if it wasn't one of their special numbers. But I was as interested in looking, checking everything out, as I was in dancing. Though I would get down a few times a night.

With the brothers from Hillside Place it was not a sports thing they were into, though some could really play any sport. But they were more into a social number. Going to parties and dances and a lot of times just standing around bullshitting. We went in and out of some dark dark joints, Jim, blue light red light "rub" records on the box, and nothing but big hats all around the walls. The silhouettes was frightening. But we had strength in our collective sense. K., short and bright, who hiked people almost bad as I did. He was much like me only K. was black. R. was my walking buddy it turned out. We spent a lotta time together. He looked like Malcolm a little, red top and mariney looking skin. He stuttered when he got excited. R. and K. were the most thoughtful of the bunch. And red or not, R. was definitely black. He had two brothers who also ran with us, one older and one younger. The older one was a sweet dude but crazy as daylights. He didn't like to argue, cause he couldn't talk that well. So if you pressed him it was like pressing a button. And he was a Golden Glover, could knock dudes cold with a stroke.

We had a couple flakes too with that bunch, B. the worst. He was a straight-out hood, a headwhipper from the word whip. But he ran with us and half of the time we were with B. it was keeping him from mashing somebody. Especially at the canteen. You be grooving and doing the one step you knew or rubbin' hard up against some queen of the night and look up out of the corner of your eye they'd be a disturbance and you'd see B's mouth and teeth working usually right up in some ill-fated pilgrim's face. I'd say, "Excuse me," like some nut I saw in the movies and bolt over there to play Ralph Bunche. K. would usually get in on that too but sometimes he would slap B. side the head and say, "You always messing up the goddam party goddammit stop messin' up the goddam party." But only K. could do that and even when he did it I felt like I was watching that crazy blond dude in Ringling Bros. that let the lions and shit jump on him.

Somebody had (a) stepped on B's shoes, (b) rubbed up against B's chick, (b) took B's chick, (d) wanted to take B's chick, (e) looked like he wanted to do any of the above. Or was just a Mickey Mouse-lookin' mf.

The canteen was our world. Sundays our day to show out, to come slidin' in in our cleanest shit. By this time I had a green Tyrolean with a feather band and a checkered swag. And I would slide in too, happy to be with my comrades, and eager to be in that world and suck it all in.

We went to dances and parties all over The Hill. And sometimes we even ventured into other wards. There were a couple of gangs, but we weren't really into the gang thing on the offensive. Ours was mostly defense and camaraderie. We loved to bullshit and put each other down. But we dug each other and felt for each other and even worried about each other. Yet it was funny when one or some of the Hillsides came up to Belmont and came upstairs to my house, it was always a tentative thing. Ours was a little apartment, maybe five rooms with hardwood floors and a porch overlooking Belmont Avenue. Right near the crossroads of the world. But the floors were waxed (my gig), there was wallpaper on the walls (my old man put it up), a piano and television. New linoleum on the kitchen floor, and doilies, cabinets with glasses and dishes. All the remains of the yellow dreams of a brown family. As modest as that was, and it was very modest, the Hillsides could be very quiet and respectable in there. They tried to be on their best behavior. While in others of the boys' homes they were subdued to a certain extent, but never with the almost icy deference I saw in my spot.

And dig this, I was still going cross town every morning to the Vatican and watching white boys and girls do their thing and was bitter and envious at the same time. Yet when I would see them at some after school dance (I would be peeking in on the way to the 9 Clifton) it would crack me up. The little bouncy shit they did and doctrinaire "Lindy Hop" took me out. Though there was a couple of dudes like Frank B. who did not bounce when they danced and who talked just like we did on The Hill. I understand he is still locked up!

I was going from my sophomore year to my junior year. I wanted to try out for football. I knew I could make the team cause the playground ball we played was at a high level. I knew I was fast enough, yet the whiteness of the team, of the experience itself, put me off. I was embarrassed because I was small that they might not even give me a tryout, and I didn't want to get embarrassed by those dudes. (Like the shoes on the desk bit!) I went out for track and cross country because I had more confidence and made those teams. I first got a junior varsity letter in track. It was a little white "B" with blue outline with a "2" inside it and I loved it. Especially since over on The Hill people wasn't as familiar with Barringer letters and didn't know quite the significance of it. The next year when I got a varsity letter, a big "B" in cross country, it actually got less play, even though it was much bigger, because it didn't have the little gimmick "2" on it.

We were City Champs in track my last year and that was a really big thing. I had a letter jacket and could stroll all over Newark showing it off. But I got the letter jacket when I got the JV letter and that was my special dressed up everyday look. The high school athlete tip carried more note than even the old Cavalier jacket and I alternated it, according to the crowd. I also got track medals for finishing fourth in the All City Broad Jump and fourth in the Low Hurdles and I was trying to figure out a way I could wear those, but my sister made necklaces out of them and lost them (along with my college track medals) once I left Newark for college.

But the contrast was amazing (though I guess in some senses there were many similarities between the life of a young Italian high school student and an African American high school student in Newark). At least on the surface and in my feelings, how I was regarded and how I regarded my surroundings was totally different. To me, the high school and everything in it was as serious as a letter on a page. Not much.

Not just my day-to-day life, where I lived was naturally more important than the superficial academic high school formalities, but my life on The Hill had a door which led inside (the Hill and me) to much deeper experience. The canteen was a center for a time, and the Hillside Place dudes my fellow travelers in digging all that: the life and the sounds of our time. But wedged up in there was some brown and yellow shit (I told ya) along with the white. And that is a crisscross of reference, as well as emotion.

For instance, there would be parties arranged by secret yellow sources like birthday parties for W. from Bethany, which might be held at the Jones Street Y. And I would sit and watch what passed for dancing and drink the punch and keep my eyes peeled for the harder dudes who would be passing by outside. S. and R. from the Cavaliers were in this yellow-brown combine to bring yellow life onto The Hill. And we at least had reference to something real, our wheeling and dealing—"in your face, turkey"—out in the Waverly Avenue apartments playground. A lot of the dudes at these little gatherings, like at the church and the special Y sets, were funny time. Didn't play no ball or nothing. It was some mixed up stuff.

But some of the same records would play as in the blue and red light parties. And Mr. Lamar, who ran the Jones Street Y, was a tough hip old man. He conducted big bands of ghetto youth (like they say). And heavyweights like Woody Shaw, Walter Davis, Wayne Shorter, Buddy Terry were coming through there. And some of these youth bands were so good they began playing gigs all over the town. They even started playing at the canteen.

These youth bands were playing in the canteen for a while. And they were good but they added another element that speaks to the whole nature of that time. As young people we were blues people; it is and remains African American popular music. It was the most natural element in our lives, the sound of those lives, as they were lived. In the late '40s and '50s the whole of the U.S. was going through changes and we were going through changes in it. What the blues said and says is the flow of our blood and the flow of us through this world. The old blues came into the cities before, even in the South, got hooked up to European instruments and marching bands and whorehouse employment post funeral enjoyment and became not just jass but jazz and not just that but us in a different way, somebody black with some other stuff to say. Some more stuff, what the city did, was propose itself to us as our new place (and home even away from *home*, which is still the South).

The music took on everything we ever did, which is why we loved it and made it (being us). So come into Newark, Jim, about nineteem and something, close to or into the twenties. And what you got? Some up North show time stuff. Some gay ballads, like Bert and Jim Europe and Eubie and them made. Could get raggy or barrelhouse, a strut come all the way out of the Gay Nineties.

But here come the blues. From out of the South, barrelin' in on them trains, lookin' for work. Moved into wherever, kept alive with a gut bucket. ("A bucket of guts to go, please, sir!") The blues would come into these cities and take over whole neighborhoods, not to mention horns and pianos and the rap of the drum always been there. Rap rap rap rap, drummer rappin'. Like "I rather drink muddy water an' sleep in a hollow log." "Why, you ain't even in New York, boy. This year's New Ark."

The blues would get dressed up. Put on some shiny brass and hang out in districts so out they was called red light, like our dark parties full of menace and joy. And the blues would be dressin' up and stretchin' out and soundin' like it was somebody else, but we knew it was always the blues. It would take in and take on anything it needed to survive and grow and still be us.

Blues would show changed but itself anyway. Talking about different places it had been and what it had seen. How it had been treated, using anything it could to get our attention, its only love. So here they come with horns and electric guitars. (Was named Blind Lemon, and Leroy, then come up here and plugged theyself in, *turned on* for modernism, called theyself T-Bone!) Somebody put some slick shit in they heads to match they ideas. Like Red mud for the Nuer. Grease was the newer, conk! City shit.

As for jazz, we could dig the Dukish presumption, made you see how blues could show out. Could expand and talk history like a suite of symphonies. Where we been. How we got there. How we changed. (How some got strange!)

There is a heavy thing to us, blues says. A heavy thing, which always want to get out. It's in that song and dance, that levitating stroke of walk (strut?). All the tragedies and high comedies, the constant grim ironies of tears or laughter. And beyond that. Beyond that. All the past, zoomed like a *real* silver bullet toward the future. The long glittering song of motion which is now thinking about itself.

The "romance" of jazz is that it does not let go of its crowded past, its blue shadows nor the wisdom of the lone banjo at sunset near the anonymous plantation. Yet it wants to speak of everything in this place (even the shit it ain't supposed to understand) since it is fed by everything even on the cool. Blues was naturally dismissed, some slave shit. Jazz would get smacked as payback for its presumption. No matter the rhythmic sophistication of naked savages so naive they used gold to sit their black asses on and fan themselves with peacock bennies. And then got the nerve to send messages through night black fingers smacking animal skins in Congo Square here in the New World.

Blues is our poem of New World consciousness, jazz our articulation that we is familiar with all the shims and shams of the machine (vertical American Class society, plus the international advertisements of the planet's beauty). Blues is our father and our mother, our grandparents, our history, plus our daily black soulful lives as brothers and sisters against and within the reality and the idea of this place. Blues is the basic pulse and song, the fundamental description and reaction. A slave's music, a peasant's music, a worker's music, the music of a people, a whole nation, expressing that nation's psyche, its "common psychological development." And jazz, as

Langston says, is the child, the blue/black prodigy of the earth mother/ father, that wants to take its inherited sensitivity (could etch a blue outline of hope against a grey sky made reddish by fire and blood) and presume to claim (to know and understand) all that exists in America black brown red yellow or white. Jazz, the most advanced music of the African American people, not only begins by being thrown by its parents through the shiny channels of alien sound machines, and then claiming them (like Mr. Sax of Germany might not have dug or understood John Coltrane) but then it even wants to describe the whole of this society, its multinational reality, to that society itself, and propose alternatives to the very society (from the fundamental *sound* of the culture, its publicly stated matrix of creativity and profundity). Jazz challenges Europe because Europe cannot even get in America without jazz' help. And then jazz want to take the real credit— it be legitimate American music, when Brahms and them is only visitors (get its arrogant drift?).

Jazz said, "We can deal with this hardware and them harmonies too, and we is rhythmically sophisticated, and can create what you call, uhhh, syncopation." And to the inquiring stiffnecks, the academic deadbeats who had come out from under they hoods momentarily so they could write their essays on the relative worth of these Aframerican melodies, jazz would stare politely and whilst beset with multisyllabic descriptions of the towering greatness of all that is "west" or white or European or merely dead, jazz would answer, and without malice, "It don't mean a thing if it ain't got that swing." And jazz' parents would smile, being proud of their presumptuous offspring.

Other people would say "But how can you say all this, jazz, you was not even in the classroom?" (This was before integration!) "So you did not even hear what is being taught. All you knew was the blues and that's downright paltry." (That was before the New Orleans Rhythm Kings, Bix Beiderbecke, Paul Desmond, Dave Brubeck, Stan Getz, Stan Kenton, Chuck Mangione or Elvis Presley, Bill Haley and the Comets, the Beatles, Rolling Stones, Kiss, and John Travolta. A long time before dudes started *calling themselves* PUNKS!)

And jazz would repeat its message from its Duke or stare monkishly just off to one side of the questioner's ashen face.

So we had come into the world bathed in spirituals and blues. And by time I came to consciousness up in that northern city, blues also had large scale come out the country, had come into cities and even went with a buncha people up North lookin' for work, or runnin' from the Klan or they animal counterparts, the boll weevil.

We had give up the "Spanish" (Mississippi-Louisiana-Texas) guitar for the industrial one, the urban worker's guitar that needed electricity to tell its tale. In my generation we came up with the rise of rhythm and blues, the big city blues of screaming horns and endless riffs. The big bands were actually big blues bands, and even the jazz bands were blues bands that also had another kind of story, one that included deeper histories and music so heavy it could call on an ology if it needed to explain itself.

The spirituals we carried with us even into blues. We needed quartets like the Ravens and the Orioles to translate our real funk, past the Mills Brothers and Ink Spots, who were chosen darksters white folks could believe in. Dinah and Ruth B. were gospel sounds inside the blues. And the gospel itself was an urban spiritual that wanted to bring blues right on into the church and forget the devil sposed have something to do with it.

When Big Jay, and Illinois, Jug and Gatortail, the honkers and screamers of our day, came on, it was blues church we groaned and stomped to. Those screams were like black folks in sanctification, brown folks when they quit bullshittin' and let the full spirit take 'em.

But a lot of us were leavin' the church (even while we sat in there bein' pinched by brown grandmas), leavin' it to yellow folks or black and brown fantasy folks who still wanted to sit on the porch rockin' endlessly to familiar groans strainin' and squintin' they eyes tryin' to look into the nothin' mist for a sign that Jordan was close on or that angels was actually motorin' our way in those sweet chariots we sang about.

But urban industrial United States was teaching a lot of us. The material reality of being urban workers and shaky middle-class members of an oppressed nationality. These things were teaching us in the factory classrooms and other sweatshops, on the streets, over the radios, and over television, in the movies, in school classrooms. The world was here and some people was heavy into it suckin' it dry. Our sad streets seemed to some of us to have maps and paths drawn on 'em glowing in the dark. We saw arrows away from the plantation in green-glowing neon under our eyelids just before we went to sleep. Ways out, even when we didn't know we cared. Ways away. We wanted to go where the factorie's conception arose and the intelligence of the sparkling machines came from. We wanted to go where that money went. Or we wanted to step into the books or understand more than the streets, we wanted to understand our feelings about them. We wanted to step into the radios (we sent messages and notes). We wanted to step into the movies and television screens. The grey steel streets were indeed paltry (not our feelings, and no, not the blues) but those gray streets were dead and cold, despite our warm living selves celebrating the life in us dancing across their surfaces. What was most important about the survivors was our will to be more than those streets proposed, to be happier than possible (in your philosophy, Horatio).

So the blues was myself and my life and the lives of those around me. But we were all in motion. The R&B life on the streets of the Central Ward, in the Masonic, on Hillside Place, and Spruce was natural to me. But something else was developing as well. In me, in us, in the music, in the society. It's all connected.

The horizontal quality of black life, that is, the smashed flat quality of life for the oppressed, proposes that we is all generally equally mashed. So that one whole can incorporate us in our parts, though even so there was always a slight verticality. A yellowness and brownness, from the slavery time days when the Tom Jeffersons and other great philosophers would throw black women down and fuck them up (get them pregnant) with yellow life. And many of their yellow sons and daughters was the first petty bourgeois we had, even during slavery times. Though there was a black bourgeoisie in minute quantities, a slave-owning black bourgeoisie even during slavery. That is, free slave-owning niggers!

But as the verticality extends and gets larger so the contrast within our ranks. So the wider divergence of ideologies within the nation, reflecting the sharpening of objective economic division. The blues band of the '30s becomes both the rhythm and blues band of the '40s and '50s as well as the jazz band and combo and later bebop combo of the '40s and '50s. It is simply one people showing its divergence socially though the aesthetic reflections of different sectors of themselves.

The youth bands we began hearing at the Masonic were just a few years older than I was and I was on top of middle teens then. Bands like Nat Phipps and Jackie Bland had the most note for us. And they played both the blues numbers and the incoming rhythm and blues hits and jazz and even a little new jazz. They were playing the whole of the continuum, like most of the big bands then, still able to play both big blues and jazz, they had a blues singer and a jazz singer, or one singer who could sing both. And we danced to all of it.

They would play "Harlem Nocturne" and "Flamingo," stock band arrangements of anything danceable, Ellington, Basie, "Caledonia." Jackie

Bland was probably the most advanced. He had them playing "Ooopapadow" of Diz, and Wallington's "Lemon Drop." Herman's takes of Diz were popular. They wasn't prejudiced, they even ended the sets with Kenton's "Intermission Riff." But mostly it was rhythm and rhythm and blues and blues ballads. Wayne Shorter played with Jackie and Nat, and Grachan Moncur III played with Nat as well as Knobby who's now with Herbie Mann plus some great young players like Ed Lightsey on bass, Nat's brother Billy on reeds (the whole Phipps family played—Nat a pianist). And hip musicians liked Hugh Brodie, Allen Shorter, Herbie Morgan went through the bands. Hank Mobley was blowing with Billy Ford and his thunderbirds at the Howard Bar and James Moody lived on Monmouth Street up the street from my girlfriend D.

Jackie had the most strange presence and he would conduct the band (really like Diz) with head, arms, legs, butt, even his eyes shooting in all directions. These bands played the whole spectrum of the music, our whole history, from old blues to new jazz, and we danced to all of it. "Hucklebuck," "Honey Dripper," "Four Brothers," and the band members were great heroes to us.

Nat and his brother Billy and a couple other members of that band (like Pretty Boy F., who turned out to be a four-hundred-pound cop) went to Barringer and I knew them, but they were older and in higher grades. Nat and I even ran track together one year and got to be pretty good friends.

All that music was at the Masonic. Some I was very familiar with and some new stuff I heard and began to dig. It was all part of the same cultural matrix to us—black from every which a way and brown plus even yellow and white translated by our main men stomping on the stage.

K. and R. and I also did some other steppin'. We might go to Lloyd's Manor, which had a different crowd plus some of the same folks who was at the canteen. I met Little Esther at Lloyd's one night. She had a big hit (and she was about my age, fourteen or fifteen or so) "Double Crossin' Blues" with Johnny Otis. Between sets I came up to her and she was foolin' around with the bandleader's trumpet. I wanted to say something. She had really big pretty lips, bright red, and her hair cut short and straightened. She was smiling and talking to one of the musicians. I just looked and thought, Hey, I got close to Little Esther. She and Mel Walker and Johnny Otis would sing (and I would too in those bright blue Saturdays of my teenagedom.)

L.E.: You way out in the forest
      Fightin' a big ol' grizzly bear.

M.W.: How come you ain't out in the forest?

L.E.: I'm a lady!

M.W.: They got lady bears out there!

We also went to mambo sets which were coming in about that time too. Once at Lloyd's there were so many people mamboing you couldn't move. We were stuck fixed in the crowd, breathing everybody's passion. (It was also the first time I ever remember seeing what I later found out was a Puerto Rican. Two young girls near my own age, one with a blond streak in dark reddish brown hair at the corner of Belmont and Springfield, going somewhere. I didn't even know what they were.)

This was also around the same period my cousin George lent me (forever) some of his bebop records. I had listened to a couple in his house on Wallace Street. Then he brought some over to my house on Belmont.

They were Guilds, Manors, Savoys (a Newark company), with groups like Charlie Parker's Reboppers, Max Roach and the BeBop Boys, Stan Getz, Dizzy Gillespie's "Ooopapadow," "Hot House," "Ornithology," "The Lady in Red," and waboppadapaDam! my world had changed!!

I listened to bebop after school, over and over. At first it was strange and the strangeness itself was strangely alluring. Bebop! I listened and listened. And began learning the names of musicians and times and places and events. Bird, Diz, Max, Klook, Monk, Miles, Getz, and eventually secondary jive like *Downbeat*, *Metronome*, Feather, Ulanov, began to be part of my world and words.

I want to explain how much bebop changed me. Not in the superficial movie way that said, look, yesterday the hero wore glasses and had a limp, today he's whole and looks more like Ronald Colman than he did with that funny disguise. Maybe there were some changes on the top some people could peep. But mostly it was interior. I heard this different music and different ideas, different images came to me. I thought about different things.

I was still in the Central Ward, up over the oil heater Polish couple, and could look down on Belmont Avenue weekends and see slick folks strut and drunks stagger into the Chinese restaurant for some chow mein. I was still going to the canteen on Sundays, and the National, and hanging out most times with the Hillsides, but mostly K. and R. But now some other kinds of yearnings turned me around. I wanted to go to some other kinds of places, and usually by myself. Not because I suddenly felt "estranged" from people or whatnot. But because bebop, "The Music," had got into me and was growing in me and making me hear things and see things. I began to want things. I didn't even know what.

And I wasn't even sure what the music was. Bebop. A new language a new tongue and vision for a generally more advanced group in our generation. (Though that could always be turned around by the rich and the powerful and this will be the case until the oppressed have control over their own lives!) Bebop was a staging area for a new sensibility growing to maturity. And the Beboppers themselves were blowing the sound to attract the growing, the developing, the about-to-see. Sometimes even the players was carrying out the end of another epoch as they understood it. Though they knew they was making change, opening a door, cutting underbrush and heavy vines away to make a path. And where would that path lead? That was the real question. It is the real question of each generation. Where will the path you've shown us lead? And who will take it?

The sound itself. The staccato rhythm and jagged lines. The breakneck speed and "outside" quality. Joe Carroll sang "In the Land of Oobladee." "Outside." Strange. Weird. Weird. That word I read and heard. Weird. Thelonious. That's a weird name. What did it mean? Why were they sounding like this? They even looked weird.

My first hero was Diz, Dizzy Gillespie. That's because he was the wildest. For the same reason the media picked up on Diz. I looked in *Esquire* (which my father used to subscribe to) and there was an article on Diz. "The High Priest of Bebop" (later I got to understand that that was Monk). The title of the article hit me. "To Be or Not to Bop." The Shakespearean overtones, the picture magazine hype, turned me on. Diz in windowless hornrims. Also the shades and beautiful beret. I had never really looked at a beret before. We called them "tams." And there were dudes and women who wore them. But Diz (and the magazine) provided a pique I'd never checked before. A guy down the street from me who went to Barringer named G. and I began to hang out. He was a bass player. He played with the school band and also made some of the gigs with the various teenage bands around town. He hung with with a trumpet player named Pinball who I thought was one of the hippest dudes in the world. He even had a sound like Miles.

I had gone from piano lessons to drawing lessons to drum lessons and now I was at trumpet lessons. My mother kept throwing yellow W. in my face as someone who would stick to piano lessons. (He had an uncle who played piano occasionally for the church. He, the young uncle, was yellow with a slanted high side part, the epitome of yellow mischief as far as I was concerned. Glasses. A sort of Hollywood character actor type. Had a name like Percy, dig?)

Bebop had brought a wind of other connections, interconnections in all directions. Like wires strung up and looping out of the Third Ward, yet that, for me, was its center, where you had to be to pick up all the communications coming in. I had a skate box, without skates as I remember, because I couldn't really skate. Though I went to the rink a few times. But that was a social thing. Thursdays was Colored Night in those days, even in Newark. The joint was called Dreamland and other nights you'd get turned away. Those were for white kids and the joint was really in the next town, Elizabeth, and there was always talk that if you showed up the other nights not only would you be turned away but you'd get into a rumble with the white kids.

Usually, I'd just show up down at the White Castle hamburger place on Elizabeth Avenue and check out the cars until I saw people I knew and we'd rap. I'd check the beauties and maybe see a couple of my familiar fantasies. Sometimes I'd get a ride back to Belmont, other times I had to hoof it. But it was a regular stop. The only thing I ever did pertaining to skating was paint the skate box, which was made of plain wood. I had some red sticky paint and painted Dizzy's picture, with the bebop glasses and bebop tam and around the hopeless painting I scrawled "To Be" on top of the picture and "Or Not to Bop" underneath. I don't even know if I took that skate box out of the house. I might have taken it to Dreamland a couple of times, I'm not sure, cause once I got into Dreamland, I'd just stand around and watch. Even when I put on skates. But that was it, I never even had skates. When I went down there I had to rent skates. So it woulda been stupid to carry the box. However, I mighta carried it.

But I did show the picture a couple times in some context. I began to buy records now to try to add to my core collection which was really my cousin George's. George had also given/loaned me some "Jazz at the Philharmonic" (JATP) records. The Norman Granz production of everybody in those mostly blowing sessions that traveled around the country. Bird,

Coleman Hawkins, Lester Young, Roy Eldridge, Ella Fitzgerald, Flip Phillips. He asked me if I had any records, bop records, and up until that time I would only occasionally buy an R&B or quartet record. Like Orioles, Ravens, Honey Dripper, or Hucklebuck. I showed him my parents' album (those four-record 78 collections) of Nat King Cole's trio. And they was pretty hip but that was all I had.

Everything was still 78 and very fragile. One of the first records of the new music I bought was Charlie Parker's *Repetition*. I hadn't heard it, but something I read in one of the magazines turned me on. I pored through those magazines and the mystique and the fact that they were mentioning landmark sides which I didn't know anything about and dropping names and showing flicks and I knew nothing at all about them—except the little bit of knowledge I got from George's present—made it seem that I was being let in, now, on something very heavy that had been going on all around me without me knowing anything.

I had just started trying to play the trumpet and still didn't know how to read music very well. The band I started was embarrassing in that regard, cause I had to have them play the heads over and over till I could read it, I was so slow. We wanted to play Shearing's "September in the Rain" and a tune we'd heard Sarah Vaughan sing, "Tenderly." That's when we discovered that those were really the same tune.

The alto and drums were the only really consistent members of the "band." The bass player, G., was too advanced for us. (And of that band the bass player is a street vendor, the drummer an architect, and the altoist a commercial artist, the trumpet player does write something about the music, but he sure can't play!) The band was a brown enterprise connected in its strongest tone to black and blue. But my mother let us play in her living room on her sacred hardwood floors. She "didn't mind," in fact I'm sure she was happy we was there rather than snakin' through the streets which was pure black and blues.

And then I was going through some other changes as I was about to leave high school. In school my grasp on the day-to-day academics had slipped altogether. Though I still got passing marks in most stuff, I had just waved my hands at stuff like algebra and just sat up in the class listening to the white boys crack jokes. The teacher we had, Mr. H., was no teacher at all but just the brunt of cruel high school First Ward jokes. The kids would sometimes curse him out in Italian or call him names consistently like "Baccala" (fish) which invariably cracked everybody up. I laughed because the others did. But I could ask V. sometimes what the Italian words meant and he would tell me. Where before I'd been much more serious and concerned about my grades and school behavior now I cared less and less.

In fact around my junior year I'd begun to take off (play hooky) from time to time. Mostly, when there was something happening downtown at the Adams, when they had live shows. Like the whole of the Newark school system turned out for Nat King Cole. But why would they have an 11:00 A.M. show? Once they had a guy come on stage and get a rah rah session going where he said, "Everybody from Barringer," and they'd cheer. "Everybody from Central," and they'd cheer. "Everybody from South Side," and they'd cheer. And so forth. And then they busted all those that raised their hands and any others they could see and made 'em go back to school.

The bass player and I used to cut together. We lived near each other, on the same street, way cross town. But still went to Barringer. How we got over there I'll never know. He was older than I was and was actually driving a truck. I think it was his father's fish truck, (though I could never understand how his father could use it to sell fish if G. had it daytimes cattin' around with us).

But that was superhip for its time, that fish truck. A few of the selected would meet near the school and take off. Or else we'd be in school and after letting them mark us present in their homerooms we'd break, meet outside, and take off. Just the idea of riding around in that fish truck while school was going on thrilled us. We felt real big time. Though we had deep paranoia about the truant officers and our parents. Much more probably than is possible today when the truant officers are so secondary in the present "philosophy" of education that they have been fired in Newark because of budget cuts. So your child could be absent any number of days these days and you wouldn't know it. In those days you couldn't do that. They would be onto your case in a minute.

We'd go the Adams, if there was a show. We'd go to other high schools' lunchtimes and hang out. We might go to somebody's house. For instance, G's girlfriend Mary was living with an aunt, and the aunt would be away at work. We might pick up Pinball or Calvin, a drummer, or some other developing hipsters (later the word was "hippies," before white youth took the word over in the late '50s) and just breeze around being *cool*.

Because if the blues and rhythm and blues especially had made us hot as blue flame, now we, in hooking up one way or another to bebop, wanted to be cool. As we got more conscious of bop we got more conscious of wanting to be cool. (The word as it was used before Chet Baker and Lee Konitz absorbed it.)

Cool, for us, was to be there without being into nothing dumb. Like, the whole thing. The society—right? But this was an accretion, a buildup of consciousness. Though we were talking about being cool in that fish truck or when we played hooky or as we strode out of Barringer homeroom on the way outside and down to the Adams, we were being cool. We did not want to be attached to anything stupid, though in those days we did not yet understand how widespread stupidity was nor how valuable to those who ruled us.

I got a job, my mother got me a job, really. Next door to where she was working then. The white-collar experience my mother had in the war she had used since (once the war was over and they started letting the war boom people go, especially the black [include brown] Rosie the riveters, as the slogan went). She now had a job at the community hospital as an assistant administrator (the administrator's name was Romeo Brigs) and she got me a job, working Fridays after school and Saturdays at a grocery store next door to the hospital. After I checked out OK I began working everyday after school and all day Saturdays. It was OK with me because it was a new experience and kept a few coins in my pocket. I was making about forty-five big ones a week, which allowed me to start buying my own clothes and go the various places I was coming to decide I wanted to go and to buy my own records.

I was a more solitary night traveler now. Though sometimes I would walk around with G. to someplace where music was playing or with a dude we called "Limes" because people thought he dressed and carried himself like Harry Limes (Orson Welles in the movie *The Third Man*. Limes is now a New Jersey politician and he still looks like Limes). The trombone player, Little Jay Jay, was another one of my sometimes late night walking buddies. (He was called that cause he worshiped J. J. Johnson.) Because that late night walking was more and more about music. I might meet them at one of the various places we knew where the music was being played. We were looking for bebop. The Hillside Place dudes I didn't see as much now because they were still going to the canteen. Sometimes I would go to the canteen and see them or just go around to K. or R.'s house or they come round to mine. But they did not dig bop like I did.

I was with G. or Little Jay Jay the night we went to the Silver Saddle on Clinton Avenue and checked Bird. It was a burst of magic to me. I didn't know what to make of it. It was a burst of magic. It was blue and pink and white (or were those the lights over the bar, which whirled around and shot spears off a globe of many refracting surfaces?). It was blue—but a blue that shattered into many unknown moods. Moods unknown to me. Different modes of thought. The playing in the bar shattered (was it the lights?), it showered me with blue and red dancing things held in blinding light. It was moods. Modes. Ones breaking into twos and them breaking. It was a burst of magic.

The dark crowd that night—you walk up Belmont to Avon, then turn left, go down three blocks, turn right at Hayes Circle and the Silver Saddle is right there—I couldn't even see them clearly. They might have been one large head bouncing under the music taking it in! But the music was magical and it covered me over and turned me into myself.

Afterwards, I was by myself now (for some reason), I came out and began walking down Clinton toward Hayes Circle and there was Bird sitting there smoking a joint with a white woman. I didn't know that's what they were doing because up till that time I didn't know anything about marijuana, just as some strange reference in the magazines. The idea of heroin seemed to me some crazy jail-death idea that people wanted to down you with. I didn't fully understand it or even what it was.

But it was the woman who had played piano with him in the club. (I found out later her name was Lorraine Geller.) But I passed close to them and Bird was talking and Lorraine was lighting up the joint he had just handed to her. They didn't even pause as I came close and I did not even pause though I had them fixed in my eyes and in my head as I passed, turned the corner, and went up the street. When I got a little distance up the street I turned and looked back at them and they were still smoking and talking and joking. A white woman, I thought, that's weird!

Saturdays I brought my trumpet to work with me. Steve, the owner, said I could take a long lunch cause that's when I took my trumpet lessons, not far from the store, over on Springfield Avenue. And I loved the idea of walking with my trumpet, in a brown imitation leather bag I'd got that looked like the trumpet bags Diz and Miles carried. I didn't want the hard square cases, I had what they called a "gig bag" and I tucked it under my arm and bopped those five or six blocks to Springfield and dug the idea of people looking at me thinking I was a trumpet player.

My father had asked me one day, "Why do you want to be a bopper?" Who knows what I said. I couldn't have explained it then. But bebop suggested another mode of being. Another way of living. Another way of perceiving reality—connected to the one I'd had—blue/black and brown but also pushing past that to something else. Strangeness. Weirdness. The unknown!

I guess that's what it was. The music took me places I'd never been. Literally. One night I found myself snaking through the darkness up to the Orange Armory for a dance. The dance had Larry Darnell as one part of the bill and Stan Getz as the other. I remember the fags was cuttin' the fool with Bermuda shorts in bright plaid colors. I came in and stood in front of the stage unmoving and checked two sides of that equation out. To show the mix of the times. Getz and Max Roach had played together as part of the BeBop Boys on records. I dug Getz's "The Lady in Red." That wispy romantic tone. And a lot of the bebop groups were mixed in that period. Later, I even dug Stan Kenton and went down to Symphony Hall when he had his band with Art Pepper, Maynard Ferguson, Bob Graettinger, June Christy, Frank Rosolino. I bought that album which consisted of pieces named after the players, plus something of Bob Graettinger's called "City of Glass." And that stuff was really weird. But I dug it, for that reason, and it seemed linked to the whole experience that bop had opened up for me. The fact that they were white people meant nothing to me. What they were playing was linked to something I dug.

But my deepest experience of that period was with Miles. For me Miles was what *cool* meant. (And later, over the years, his various getups on the record covers, and the music that went with them, have always remained the highest explanation of that definition.) My last year or so in high school I ran into Miles's "Venus de Milo" and "Move." In fact all the tunes in that series of recordings he made with the big band: Max, Lee Konitz, John Lewis, J.J., Gerry Mulligan, and those tunes by Mulligan, Denzil Best, George Wallington, John Lewis, Bud Powell and Miles himself, Johnny Carisi, Cleo Henry. To me that was where the definition of "high art" began. But especially "Venus de Milo," "Move," and "Darn That Dream." I liked all of the tunes and once I found out it was a whole series, I pursued all those records, which you had to get on 78s then.

The music was heavy to me almost like what they called "classical" music, which had only interested me in those terrible themes they played in the movies. I liked movie music and I dug Aaron Copland's music "Salon de Mexico" in one of those Esther Williams MGM musicals. And somewhere I heard the "Firedance" of de Falla, but it was all in tune with the movie happenings, though I did continue to think about "Salon de Mexico" for a long time. And I'd heard and liked the popular themes from Rachmaninoff, Tchaikovsky, and Chopin the movies played.

I would be carrying packages across High Street delivering them. (There were still some white families, mostly Jewish, living then on High Street, in what were then spacious luxury apartments and some one-family houses. Some black doctors had moved in there and on a couple of streets some other links in the black middle class. But only a couple blocks away, even then, was nothing but bloods, though they were a little more mixed in with Polish Jews and Catholics.) I'd be whistling "Venus de Milo," then "Move," then "Darn That Dream." I would sing "Darn That Dream" like I was Pancho Hagood, who sounded like a hipper kind of Mr. B. to me. Cause I always dug Mr. B. and even had a couple shirts with "Mr. B." collars earlier, around the time he was in the movies and sang "I Left My Hat in Haiti."

I was delivering packages and singing "Darn That Dream" or hearing those wild harmonies of "Venus de Milo." I'd hum and whistle the opening of that tune over and over. The big band weight of the music and strange harmonic voices made me think of "classical" music but it was *my* classical music, because it meant something to me. Something serious and personal and out there. It was *weird*.

The trumpet teacher I had was an Italian classicist and he had me blowing those hard round whole notes like I was playing the overture from some Italian opera or at least that's what I thought. He was really trying to teach me to play "legitimate" trumpet, if you can dig that. But I didn't want that. I wanted to play like Miles Davis, so I had to slide the horn to the side of my mouth sort of to try to get that sound. Because the way the trumpet teacher was teaching me, only those big old round notes would come out and I thought they were square. (Though I listened to Maynard Ferguson play those same kinds of notes. But he was playing so high up in the stratosphere the novelty of that hid the fact that he was playing the same kinds of notes as my trumpet teacher was trying to mash on me!)

When I was in grammar school I would take my father's clothes and wear them to the Court, the late night recreation program. He must've known it but I guess that's one of the trials of parenthood. His sweater and shirts and even a couple of ties I would wear, like it was secret, and then try to slip them back in his closet when I came home on Dey Street.

They bought clothes for me at Larkey's (where a friend worked and they could get deals) and Ripley's which leaned a little toward Hollywood. They used to have a store in Newark with palm trees sitting outside like it was Hollywood and I went in there too.

In high school my ideas must've changed somewhat. I know by the time I got a high school letter, the big one, I had on a red corduroy jacket to go with the white "B" sweater. But earlier in high school some guy had made fun of me for wearing a green sweater and blue pants. My clothes thing was fairly scrambled up.

In the canteen I'd got, I mentioned, the checkered "swag" coat we called it (a single-breasted English type overcoat with slit pockets). The green Tyrolean, I guess both of these were influences of my peers, and the peacock band I saw somewhere. I know. I was reading *Esquire* because my father subscribed to it for a long time. And I looked at the fashions and as I got older began to try to buy some of the things. I know that's where I saw Dizzy and the *Esquire* jazz polls which dropped all those names I picked up.

It's complex though. I did not just leave out of The Hill or up off it. The Masonic and the house parties and the Hillside Placers and the yellow mob plus white high School Barringer all continued to have some influence. For instance grey flannel was being talked about. That's what college dudes was beginning to wear, so spake the whatever that I picked up, maybe it was *Esquire*. So I went where those of us who was hip on The Hill had our clothes made, Wohlmuth's, and had a grey flannel suit made. The only thing was that it was a Hill suit with twenty-two-inch bottoms. (The style on The Hill was bellbottoms at the time.) I remember a girl at the Jones Street Y say it was a "black wool" suit. But she said it was a hip suit, a hip black wool suit. It was a black suit, dig it?

I went to a Howard-Lincoln basketball game for some reason at the Newark Armory and checked out those people. I was a little kid, by myself. Knowing no one, really, though there were some folks there I thought I dug. And something about that was really hip, but something else about it was disturbing. I was going to the Golden Gloves matches up there by myself and the basketball game was OK too, my parents seemed to approve.

I saw white bucks being worn. And I'd read (again, *Esquire*?) that that's what college kids were wearing. And also that they wore them dirty. Dirty? That was weird. But I bought a pair. And a couple of corny people remarked on the white shoes how dumb they were. (They bought them a year or so later and wore them until they really were dumb!) One Negro, B.P., a yellow stuck-up nee-grow from way back (he was a cheerleader for Barringer briefly till he gave that up and began driving the library truck which was some uppity shit for bloods in them days. The first nee-grow cheerleader was, yes, from yellow headquarters, and never spoke that I knew of. He ran on white approval, much like Jeckie Raw-bean-son. He was soft, like a pudgy yellow mistake. And only made sounds when cheering, "Gimme A, B," etc., clapping with pudgy little yellow paws) actually took the lead in kicking dirt on the shoes. He thought it would make me mad. What made me mad was the idea that this turkey would kick dirt on my shoes. But the result was what I really desired. At least I knew that was supposed to be hip, so I didn't really mind. In fact I treated it like they were just doing work for me, saving me the work, of having to dirty them myself. I even ran around the track with them after school at track practice to show the stupid buggers that I wanted them dirty. And what was so satisfying was that these very dudes was the kind of stiff five-and-ten-cent Ivy Leaguer types who a few years later would *have to* have them a pair of such shoes.

I began to go to a store on Raymond Boulevard. A kind of English store the likes of which are found no more in Newark, obviously, but maybe still exist in some of these wealthy Connecticut or New York towns. With saddles and riding boots and crops for decoration, cloth laid about. Very traditional and English and it impressed the hell out of me. That was a new world, too. And the clothes now I began to buy out of that mold. The English conservative clothes that the Ivy tradition is the natural extension of. I guess what was called Ivy League was the commercial surface of the older English and Eastern school tradition.

The son of the owner was there every day and I would stare in awe at his oxford flannel pants and red belts and plain-toed shoes and button-down blue shirts and paisley ties. I would stare around the store in amazement at the very hip clothes. Some I'd only heard described that now I saw.

It was part of the *coolness* the music conveyed to me. And it was a vector from black and blues with veins, tributaries going all directions. We were cool because we were not "country," not first generation. We'd been up here and dug what it was and we could sound like we had been up here and knew what was going on. The hot quality of R&B we dug, but we translated that into *frantic* I guess because that described us to ourselves and what we sounded like. *Frantic*. In sharp endless motion. But even frantic was cool in the blues sense. Because weird, frantic, hip, cool all meant to be *other* than that which was everywhere perceived deadly in its dead-end of day-to-day horrible American reality. The life of America that it talked about in the movies and on the radio was one thing, there was some imagination and vision, some honesty in that, but that was not American life. The dead end of American life meant that you could go *nowhere*. It was nowhere. It was not sharp (what the Egyptians called the "Angle of Success"), it was blunted, going nowhere, *square*. What the Egyptians called the "Angle of Failure." And we perceived most of these things only semiconsciously.

Our cool, which went hand in hand with bop (not the later commercial definition), meant other than regular America—we were not in gangs, we were not loud and unruly, we did not want to get sweaty and still be frustrated (when just a minute ago we were sweaty as we could get under Lynn Hope and Big Jay McNeely). We still might go up to parties and dance to Lloyd Price, "Lawdy Lawdy, Miss Clawdy," and that was in us, but even in those sanctums we was cool, we moved through those blue lights under those red lights trying to sidestep the ugliest parts of our American ghetto reality.

We did not want to be beat up by headwhippers or have our hats blocked by the Dukes or Geeks. We did not want to get some little girl "jail bait" pregnant and end up tied to our mutual frustration; we did not want to fail school or get thrown out or have to go get a job and just work. We did not want to be from the South or be so poor people felt sorry for us or talked bad about us. Where I was comin' from, the brown side, we just wanted to keep steppin'. The black had shaped us, the yellow had taunted us, the white had terrified and alienated us. And cool meant, to us, to be silent in the face of all that, silent yet knowing. It meant knowledge. It meant being smart, intelligent too. So we hooked up the weirdness and the intelligence. Dizzy's hornrim bebop glasses, the artist's tam, these spelled some inner deepness to us. It was a way into ourselves further, and sometimes because we went into ourselves, we seemed quiet on the street.

But throughout my life, our lives, there is music. And for me our attachment to it is one deep definition of who we are and where we think we're going. Bop was deep in its connections, its frantic side its cool side. Flame itself has different colors. The old blues, spirituals, quartets, and rhythm and blues, the jazz and bebop plus the multicolored pop, the identifiable American flying object—like Martin Block or movie and stage music (I could even speak to what we called "hillbilly" when I got in the air force and collective ignorance—my own included—was used to torture me). All this and there is a *beyond* we already know about, from here, all this has made its mark, is shaping and has shaped a world and complex interconnections within that world. They cannot be exclusive, yet we are "hung on a line" (as Chas. Olson said), somewhere or everywhere these collectively or singly or however we perceive them, are located. We know people by what moves them, what they use as background sounds for their lives, whatever they seem to be. We are talking about feeling and thought, emotion, aesthetics, and philosophy (and science). We will investigate all of them to one extent or another.

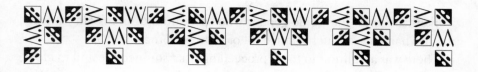

Four

Howard
(Black Brown Yellow White Continued)

I got a couple of scholarship offers through the cotillion. One was a four-year scholarship to Seton Hall, something else to Holy Cross, and a two-year scholarship to Rutgers Newark. I also got an offer, as a result of a test I took at the Y, for a two-year scholarship to Lincoln. A couple of these offers were even in the colored papers.

I decided I didn't want to go to Seton Hall (or Holy Cross) because I wasn't interested in religion. (Though, for some reason, much later I was to tell people that I once wanted to study religion!?) But I had the good sense then at least to nix the religious aggression. Some of the people I'd met at cotillion practice did accept those holy assignations. A doctor, a politician, a schoolteacher were the result and perhaps the conversion of a girl I knew's brother to become a priest, a few years later.

I suppose the cotillion was some preparation for me going to college. Those were the people that made me focus on that more than I ever had before. The cotillion hookup was brown children for the most part (with both black and yellow connections) being readied for yellow farm. The underlying animation was definitely yellow with the necessary white blessing. Not just Mrs. B., who ran the thing, she was a light-skinned social worker-teacher, a frantic do-gooder who sped around rooms almost tearing her hair she so much wanted all of us to be somebody.

There was a dullness to these proceedings that stunned me and made it obvious to me that whatever this represented I wanted no part of it. We practiced waltzing and marching. And kids from Morton Street would be looking through the windows, under the shades, and sometimes banging on the windows. And after practice we went home in groups and I ended up walking with one group all the way into Clinton Hill, where blacks were beginning to move now in large numbers.

My partner in the practice was a slightly plumpish, oddly taciturn brown girl named Betty, who apparently had made a deal with another girl, a friend of hers whose partner I was at first, to switch up. And so we became partners, walked home together with the group, once or twice a week. And later she was my partner at the cotillion. But these partnerships in the cotillion did not necessarily mean that those two were "going together."

In my mind, at that time I was going with D., the little light-skinned advertisement for sitting quietly in living rooms on one's best behavior. It was her long brown mother I watched very carefully. But I assumed that I would be taking D. to the cotillion. But, as usual, the day-to-day contact with brown Betty took its toll. I found myself, on leaving after dropping her off, up across the tracks on Jeliff Avenue, wanting to kiss her and one night I did.

From D.'s friend, who was also in the cotillion, I began to hear that D. had got a special dress for this set and was wondering why I hadn't yet asked her. Actually I was just shy, but I did think that we would be going.

From Betty's friend, who walked with us in the group to their house after practice, I also found out that Betty thought I would eventually be more than just her partner at the official part of the cotillion, and I was moving closer and closer to asking her.

I had never before had such troubles. Not from my closemouthed perspective to the various subjects of my would-be amour. When I was little I had great numbers of instant loves easily forgotten. On the real side, one little girl sent me a note to meet her at the movies. But she didn't show up. Another brown beauty with glasses she used to grin behind told me she "liked" me and I started walking her home to Baxter Terrace and we squeezed up in the hallway kissing. I thought I went with her too but then some rogue knocked her up and tearfully we took our leave. There'd been some little-boy attempts to rock and roll with a couple of brown girls and a few black ones too, but they were surprisingly minimal. I was young, I guess, even when I thought I was in full control of my senses.

But the Betty and D. thing I'd never been in before. Now, from a loose and quick-moving blue brown wraith of Belmont Avenue (and points in all directions) I found myself caught up in some stuff I didn't even properly understand. The D. thing was dry and staid, like I said. Though it maybe could have been otherwise, had I been otherwise. But I was as what went on in these pages (and a buncha other things) had made me.

Finally, I think I took D. to the cotillion. Though Betty and I were still dance partners in the grand march, so called. When I told Betty a week or so before the cotillion that I was taking D., her face got pulled tight, her eyes rolled around like fire would come out of them. And when I left I could hear her crying.

I came home after the cotillion with D. and sat in her kitchen. My black bow tie untied, I talked and pretended I was drunk (I had had something in some Coca-Cola, probably Seagram's Seven or some other abomination) and talked and talked, feeling daring in a way. But I never even made a real pass at her. A week or so later, Betty and I started sleeping with each other. It was my first time, on the real side. We made it on her couch mostly, after the family was asleep. But any and everywhere else we could. I think I might have talked to D. maybe another time or two several years later, when Betty and I had split. But for a long time, up into college, Betty and I were a well-advertised duet.

Now I was out of high school and began to go to Newark Rutgers. It was even whiter than Barringer. I was now taking another bus downtown to Rector Street and Washington Street, where the school was located in two office-type buildings. I felt even worse than at Barringer, completely isolated, though at least here no one spoke in a foreign language. But they were like foreigners to me. It was so weird they had an intramural track meet and I won the 100, 220, 440, and took second in the mile. I knew I was in some strange place then. I was pretty fast, but there was no way even in Barringer I was Jesse Owens. This joint is fulla deadbeats is the only way I could figure it.

And in school itself everything did seem a foreign language. There was a midget named Marks (really!) who taught us English literature, heavy on the Eliotic trip, and that sent me rolling into Eliot and Pound. (I asked a guy in a bookstore near Public Service did he have a book of Ezra Pound's and the guy said I was "too erudite." I didn't even know what the fuck he meant, and he probably knew it.)

I sat in a trigonometry class and learned absolutely nothing except that some process they were fooling with was called "identities." I was still wearing my Hill grey flannels. I got a light grey pair with the dark pair of the suit, both with twenty-two-inch bellbottoms. And I still walked the streets with a few friends looking for "The Music." I began to read e. e. cummings in the library quite accidentally and brought some of the poetry home one day, for some outside reason, and told my parents I had written it and must be going crazy. No telling what they said.

That summer I took a chemistry course and at the end I could not even remember the symbols for simple elements and made up some stuff on the test. (Wrong again!) But there was a guy (white) sitting next to me from Princeton who knew about as much as I did and cared about as much. Khaki pants, seersucker jacket, striped tee shirts, bucks and sneakers and Princeton cut and I checked him out. That's really what I learned that summer. My Hill suit was now an embarrassment.

The blue/black Hill was still the real world and downtown Rutgers some cardboard boredom somebody had dumped on me. I knew who it was, too. But could not have articulated it. The same isolation and alienation I'd felt at Barringer was the main decoration. Carrying books on a bus back and forth. It was the same.

I was in ROTC band that summer and we had to go up to Upsala campus in East Orange. There was an old white man who called us Sambo, me and a black kid named Conrad. He was telling us something about how to hold our horns. I was playing tuba in the band. I didn't say anything and I could see Conrad's eyes flinch and his skin turn sweaty. I walked off in a corner playing Miles licks I knew on the tuba and tried not to think about the sick gray old man even though he stood just a few feet away. Me and Conrad talked about the incident after practice, just briefly, but for me, I thought, fuck them. I'll throw that motherfucker down a staircase and be a locked-up little nigger wanted to go to college. That was it, really.

It was a time for me of mixing and swirling. Like smoke or mist or some way-out position you are in and somehow witness to but cannot even see clearly. Betty and I still went together though we didn't say a hell of a lot to each other. We were always together and she was always smiling or laughing, teasing me about something or being mock angry about something I did. She was a well-shaped little brown girl with pouting, smiling, luscious lips. And she was my companion just before manhood and I guess just before her own womanhood. There was another little girl I knew who lived closer to my house, but we were never intimate. I only saw her a couple of times when Betty and I had fought or something. Her name was Lillian and I gave her one of my track medals. She looked a lot like Betty. Plump, brown, quick-humored, and capable of a healthy heat. She got some blood disease that summer and died quickly. And I was treated like her deep boyfriend, even though I wasn't. But I carried that because it seemed her parents wanted and needed it.

My band had also come to an end, just wandered apart as a normal circumstance of our own growth and widening. Sometime that summer I told my parents I wanted to go to Howard University in Washington, D.C., a "Negro college." I didn't really know why. Maybe it was the basketball game. My mother told me years later that she had kept showing me her Fisk and Tuskegee yearbooks and making suggestions. It must've worked and whatever else went into that "decision." In the fall I was going to Howard. I was already saving money for clothes.

In some ways Howard was a continuation of the old black brown yellow white phenomenon. But now I was more conscious of what was going on. More conscious, yet not conscious enough and still with no means of full articulation. Inexplicably (and I didn't even think about it) I stopped playing the trumpet. I just did not think of it. But the whole process of what Howard was and what it meant and means begins when I started thinking about it. Because from that time I began to make changes and to change in a number of ways.

Right off the bat, by the end of the summer, the coming trip to D.C. seemed real adventure. I was off, going away, really for the first time. I had gone away to boy scout camp but that was only for two weeks at a time. Though that seemed a long time then. But now I was going to be going off on my own. And what kind of people would I meet? I thought about a Howard basketball game I'd seen while I was still at Barringer. The clutch of faces I could recall. The people there had a kind of "importance" (to themselves) that I liked but at the same time this put me off. Or made me feel maybe because they felt they were that important what would they think of me who was only a brown boy whose hair did not always seem wavy.

That ball game seemed a place of note. (And a track meet I'd gone to.) I couldn't think of much note I had—the "B" sweater and I could play football and basketball pretty well. I was fast. No note. Postman. White-collar worker. Night watchman. Ladies Aid Society. Hairdresser. Belmont Avenue. No note. Importance. (To whom? I never asked.) But that was something gnawing at me—quietly—silently, I wasn't even clear that's what it was. Note?

But there was something about those faces, the dress, the carriage, the air, that both intrigued and turned me off at the same time. What?

Now I was riding on the train headed for D.C. A trunk had been sent ahead and I sat with a couple of suitcases overhead. We were near Delaware—that godforsaken place—and I was very hungry. I had a bag of fried chicken and biscuits, a tomato, and some potato salad packed for me by my black/brown grandmother. She'd given it to me. I heard her preparing it in the kitchen and winced. Damn, she want me to have to carry some greasy bag down there. People gonna make fun of me. But I took the bag, which had a few grease spots on it, and hugged my grandmother, who I loved anyway. It was just that she was old-fashioned. Some chicken in a greasy bag, damn!

But, Jim, when I got near Delaware, after having hid the bag carefully when I got on so the important passengers wouldn't see my brown origins despite my shiny face, I broke that bag open and ate like a savage. I didn't care really, or maybe I did, but that didn't stop nothing. I ate all but one piece and I stuck the bag rolled up tight back in its hiding place and ate it that night down in D.C.

In D.C. I finally got from the train via cab to the campus. And walked wobbling with the bags up the long campus walk to Clark Hall, my residence my whole stay down there. There were dudes sitting around on the campus. It was still warm and summerlike. I expected some stuff like when I got to Barringer or on The Hill, some kind of negative welcome from somewhere or another. But no, there was dudes sitting around rapping. Some in groups collectively "capping" on the women. And the women, wow, I screwed my eyes around and around, checking, the joint was full of a whole lot of women. And from what I could see they were very very fine.

I was taken upstairs on the second floor in a corner room overlooking the stadium and gymnasium. I was disappointed at first, because I wanted a room looking out on the campus so I could look out at the "gorgeous babes" (as they were called at HU). The first day I got there there was nobody in the room, though there were clothes being unpacked. I changed from my white bucks (too cheap and too new) and put on my sneakers. I walked out across the campus trying to look like I knew where I was going, but I was just going, walking fast as usual, but trying to take it all in.

I walked off campus finally, down by Freedman's Hospital, where Howard's medical students, dentists, and nurses trained. There was a basketball court down there and a group of HU students (it seemed) playing a pickup game. I got in it and played hard, hard as I could to dispel some of my anxiety. A couple guys in the game I knew later on, but that day, after the game, I walked back to the campus, sweaty and alone, and wondered what would become of me.

I had a roommate who was not altogether suitable (I remember he was square in a number of ways). But what was interesting and important is that everyday I met someone else, many from New Jersey and Newark itself. I'd known there were some Newark folks at Howard but I didn't think it would be a bunch. But it turned out to be quite a few. And the New Jersey-Newark thing became a kind of binding point for some of us. We were "Jersey boys." In fact throughout the campus there was a joining together to a significant extent of students who came from the same state and town. The "Philly cats," the "New York cats," who we considered the most sophisticated. Cats from "Chi" were high up in that pantheon. NJ-NY-Philly-Chi hung close together plus for some strange reason some Texas cats as well. There were sprinklings in our mob from North Carolina, Florida, even East St. Louis, but the NJ-NY-Philly-Chi grouping was the core of our thing. Because not long after being there on the campus and up in falling-down Clark Hall (built in 1880-something) I was part of a little mob, "the boys," and we were something else again.

In this travailing motion from me to me (which is the underlying question in putting all this down, how did you get to be you?) different questions come up at different stages and states. We answer them in motion, casually, with our actions, no matter what comes out of our mouths. Whatever may be going through our heads. We are, meanwhile, actually doing something, actually going somewhere. There are all kinds of scenes (seens) on that road, all kinds of stops (like on an organ), what we call changes, chords, in traveling the way we do, in making the map of ourselves, though some of us may never even look at it, or even understand that it exists.

If I could have asked a question here? (And I asked many questions every day.) But the heaviest question. The question that would have summed up where I had come from and where I was and where I was going, right then, what would it have been?

Sometimes such a question can be heard inside other questions. For instance, "What do you want to be when you grow up?" (That's a question from an earlier period.) At this stage, and stop, it might be heard inside statements like my own protestation that I was "taking a pre-med course," therefore one would assume, as I did, that I wanted to be a doctor.

Obviously that did not prove to be true. Though I have been known to doctor on the truth. But why did I say it? (Which is the question on the inside, which one ought to prepare oneself to answer when one can.) So where did the "doctor" bit come from? I mentioned I had said that same thing in grammar school to a little dude who had the good sense to deny it. But where?

Perhaps it was a standard "intelligence," a reaction to what others considered important. Obviously, if I had some of the Bethany banana tone stuck to me, trips to the Y when the masses were not there, practices for cotillions behind drawn shades, the Gettysburg Address at the Old First Church, some "good hair-bad hair" training, strange picnics and pacts, and lived in a vault of hardwood floors on the other side of a secret passage which would let you out on Belmont Avenue right in the middle of a group of unsuspecting black people. All this could contribute. Though my folks, I've said, denied they had a hand in that "decision." "A doctor" is what I would say if pressed. "I'm taking pre-med." Which sounded regular at Howard. Pre-med sounded about best.

The Secret Seven, Cavaliers, Hillside Place brothers were mostly lost to me. The canteen was gone and dark night trips to Lloyd's. Though not so strangely, one dude I met, who was later a close friend of mine at HU, had been at the canteens and when he said it I remembered him in a flash. He'd been there once, I remembered. Over at the side of the stage. He and a dude named Split with a congealed wave over one eye. There were maybe four dudes and four girls with them and they did a "routine." Prepared steps in unison, throwing the girls out and spinning them, together. It was like an MGM musical—*Brownies Uptown*. The one girl, Harriet, was considered the femme fatale of them neck of the woods for a certain circle, though not in the one I ran in mostly. But we Hillsides looked over at them and smirked and B. made an ominous suggestion that would have squashed that routine all over the Masonic. It was too cute and artificial, like Mickey Rooney and Judy Garland in brownface. And they were the yellowest of the browns and/or the brownest of the yellows. Actually, what we called "sididdy," "hincty," "stuck up," "snobbery"-time motherfuckers. They gave that off the way they stood and related to each other and the rest of us. In the big black smashed-flat vat of our American concentration, we did not even hear the word "ghetto" then (unless maybe we remembered headlines from Poland in World War Two).

But now here I was with this dude Tony, and he was nice enough. With the same stuff going for him as then. The only difference was now that I was closer to him it did not irritate me in the same way. I did not feel excluded (by him), but he radiated exclusiveness like a cologne.

Yet this dude did come from somewhere in the Third Ward, in fact he lived in the apartments that my father had to bring us out of during the Depression because they cost too much. I guess they had been considered akin to some kind of semi-luxury apartments then. But this was twenty years later almost, though the apartments were still fairly nice and most of the people who moved in them never moved out. (Just maybe their sons and daughters "moving on up" to higher ground.)

These people obviously did still consider these apartments, Douglass-Harrison, some kind of luxury or aristocratic exclusive enclave of the browns and yellows. I remember always liking those apartments. Though white folks, to show them where it was really at, finally surrounded those apartments with the poorest of the black projects; in fact, dropped in the highest concentration of population per square mile in the whole country, yeh, just to show them what was happening with that cardboard exclusiveness. Exclusiveness without real money or real power!

There were quite a few folks from Douglass-Harrison at Howard. I remembered some of them. I had even heard of a couple of them. Like magic yellow celebrities "at Howard" at those yellow parties or in the *Afro* or *Herald News*. A few of them, of course, were sons and daughters of some of my father and mother's friends.

There was a bicycle raid one early evening at Central Avenue playground. Somehow, through some connection my father or mother had made, a challenge was issued to the Sutter brothers, who were sons of a guy who had worked with my father at the P.O., but had moved up to work for the IRS. One of them was a good player and it was me who arranged the game. They all swept in on bicycles (which was unnerving in the first place). We never seen that many bloods on bicycles, about ten or eleven of them. They came in complete with bats and gloves and identical caps. And they were good. We had got together a pickup team, with some of the Cavaliers (called Newark Cubs for baseball) and some other playground stalwarts. But these other guys apparently played together all the time (we only did that with basketball) and they beat us. Then climbed back on their bicycles, without having said too much to any of us, and swept back off towards Douglass-Harrison. It was like those pictures about World War Two where you see the squadrons of planes coming in to do daylight low-altitude bombing. It made us feel like we were at Bremerhaven or Cologne.

While we playing, these guys kept to themselves and they would "keep a lot of chatter going" from the infield and outfield, just like in the big leagues, but that was all they said. You got the same kind of exclusiveness. That they were some kind of mystical unenterable lodge of Negro exquisites. And wherever I saw any of that crowd, I always got the same feeling. Some of them were in a social club called the Golden Boys. A little later they had a club called Los Ruedos. I always got the same feeling from them. The standoffish self-anointed wunderkinder. And that, all that, was very very yellow to me. They even had a *whistle*! Actually, it was the old slave whistle. The whistle the slaves gave when they wanted to contact each other in the process of some clandestine operation. The whippoorwill imitation. When I first heard it, I thought it was some exclusive invention of the Golden Boys, Los Ruedos (and a later spinoff called Los Cassedores) but I found out different once I began to consciously try to become conscious.

So now these were some of the guys walking around Howard and it made me uncomfortable. These dudes had never had anything to say to me, nor I to them, really. And now here they were. Plus I was a sophomore when I got to Howard. I had already been at Newark Rutgers, so I had to come into a sophomore class that had gotten seasoned down there last year, when it was the freshman class I tended to hang out with.

One by one and in small groups I ran into the Newark contingent, not only the freshmen and the sophomores but some of the older types as well who'd been down there for a time. East Orange, Montclair, and the like were also in evidence. People I couldn't have known any other way.

There was a different thing happening with them now, it seemed, or so it seemed. I expected the straight-out straight arm of their normal elitism, but that was not there in the same way now. At least it was not turned toward me as sharply, like the "we cool—you ain't" signs they wore in their eyes when they were home. We talked as if those rare encounters in Newark, when there were those, had no bearing on anything, that there was no social (emotional/political) character to them. And I accepted that, wondering why it was that we could now be friends and what had caused the distance before.

What was different was that I was there, with them, in a higher grade than some, though we were generally the same age. I was there with them. In whatever this was. And I didn't know what it was. I was trying to find out, trying to see myself clearly, find a place for my feet to go down solid on.

As the "Jersey boys" grouping came together and its various departments from other states, Bill and I roomed together. One of the same Sutter boys who'd come swooping in in the bicycle raid to bomb us flat. Bill was a good guy, just a fraction of an inch taller than I but thick and muscular, a solid 140 pounds or so. My mother wondered did his mother feed him vitamins. That was in the days when vitamins were new and still had mystical advertising qualities. "Carrie must feed that boy vitamins the way he's growing." But she put it in a question as if it was something clandestine. And that was the only reason he was thicker and more muscular than her son. I was short and skinny and even though they came from families with taller, larger people, my mother and father were short and slight, in those days, as well. But I guess that didn't occur to her at that moment.

Bill was an athlete, even short as he was. He was a football player and baseball player. In college, most colleges, football is the most holy of all athletics and the football players are regarded with the awe once reserved for the mendicants of the sacred orders. The Dragon Slayers and Crusaders, the rescuers of fair maidens. (And the unfair too, I found out.)

It meant that the room we had together became a kind of center. Bill the athlete, and the rest of the crowd that I hung with. So we had the football and baseball players there plus the sulky little mob I belonged to. This did not happen immediately, but it represents the most typical arrangement of myself there at HU. One highlight of my integration into that society, whatever that meant.

The room got to be called "The Boys Club" and I put a sign on the door: "13 Rue Madeleine," which was the name of a Jimmy Cagney movie—Gestapo headquarters in the film. Perhaps the name meant to me some kind of subversive relationship to the whole—to the ideas I thought the school had of itself.

I was a member of the mob, of really great guys, in the sense of those times. We were great bullshitters (a trait I apparently appreciate), and we spent hours, months, years, sitting around bullshitting. And in the mob were my closest friends at the school. We thought of ourselves as city boys, somehow sophisticated, for all our youth.

The New Yorkers were the coolest and most sophisticated, we thought, I guess because they were from New York and that was the relationship Jersey had with New York and especially Newark to New York City. We thought they were among the coolest dressers. One of the coolest of the cool was a dude named "Smitty from the City," who was for us the epitome of what school cool meant. Well dressed, "dap," "clean," "hooked up," "down" were some of our words for what Smitty was. (He became an air force officer and later a dentist.) Smitty was around us, lived on the same floor, bullshitted with us, but Smitty was older and into some other things than the mob core. But he was one example we followed.

The dudes from Chicago we felt were the cleanest finally. Though they did not always, not all of them, show it. But they had, it seemed to us, the heaviest vines. The first time I ever peeped desert boots was on one of them dudes and it shot me out. What the hell are those, I thought, and immediately felt primitive because I'd never seen them before. Cashmere sweaters. This one dude Kurt had about five or six and another dude, Stone, had about ten of them! (There are probably white boys in some of these schools got thirty, but wouldn't nobody hip go to those schools in the first place!)

Dress, style, those were some of our standards. How you dressed and how you carried yourself was a big part of it. Though what you had to say, I guess, went with how you carried yourself. Were you "cool," "down," or were you corny or "flait" (a Howard word which meant worse than corny, of no value, worthless, etc.)? A couple of dudes in the mob were not especially good dressers but they were "heavy," meaning smart, and had a good rap. So they were in. Though sometimes the slicker cats would get on them about the way they looked. If they were too way out and still wanted to hang, they were the butt of unmerciful unending taunts.

We had our own language, on campus generally, but inside the group there was a sharper focus to it. Some of the stuff was even made up by us. Pretty girls were "phat," pronounced "fat," ugly ones were "bats." We would even go to elaborate metaphors to let people know what we thought about their companions if they wasn't up to snuff. We'd call somebody with an ugly girl "Bruce Wayne" (meaning Batman) or say something smart like "He the cat be with Robin all the time." Or we'd make flapping motions with our arms like a bat flying when they approached. Or go up to the cat while he was with this unlucky child and say, "How do you do, Mr. Wayne, I'm a reporter from the *Daily Planet*." The dude might just get embarrassed or get pissed off. But mob members took it as just our way of being with each other.

Really ugly girls (or objectionable people) we'd "blow up." We'd make motions like we were throwing a grenade. I developed a variation on that which was to walk up to the person and make believe I was putting a wire in their hand or on their person, then retreat a few feet and make mashing down motions like I was pushing a detonator box. This was big in our circle. We would even "throw grenades" at teachers. Or we might go up toward the front to throw a piece of paper in the wastebasket, make the "contact," then go back to our seats and blow the whole front of the classroom to kingdom come.

Something great was "way," meaning past merely "too much" (the standard applause), but "way too much," which was shortened to "way." Oh, man, it was "way"! People could be "heavy," meaning really bright or good in school or generally intelligent, or they were "light," meaning they had nothing upstairs but the wind rustling through the trees. Woolright's standard putdown of such people was that they were "lightweights." He'd say, "All you lightweight cats gonna get run outta that valley." The "valley" was just down a flight of stone stairs from the main campus where the physics and chemistry buildings were housed. One knew you had to be heavy to be in the valley. If you wasn't, you would soon "punch out," which meant flunk out of school.

Woolright was an austere, acerbic little dude who was a main part of our mob. He was not a great or flashy dresser but he was very very heavy. Plus he had a black background from Philly, a scholarship student who later had trouble passing the bar because of a slight juvenile record from gang bopping in the city of brotherly love.

Woolright was like a commentator of the mob's doings, always slightly amused but never releasing more than a mere mirthless chuckle. He was a good man, very straight and trustworthy. Our conversations were like ironic exchanges, with Woolright (who was small himself, just about the same size as I was) calling me "this little cat."

The footballers who edged into the mob on the fringes, really because of my roommate, came up with some of our language. "Over you" meant to hell with you, loosely. "Up your chest" meant you had been defeated verbally, in some activity or in some commentable way. That could be embroidered sometimes to "up your chest for ten yards" or "over you for a TD." "Over you's" and "Up your chest's" were sprinkled liberally in all our conversations.

Plus one of the mob, a guy from Upstate New York, introduced a method of speaking which also caught on. He would say, "It's me saying" or "It's him saying" or "It's me thinking" and we picked that up. He also called people suspected of or jokingly teased about fucking homosexuals "Dick Brown" for obvious reasons.

So we might sound like this: "It's me saying that my man over here, the lightweight dude with the funny sky [hat], is nothing but Bruce Wayne disguised as Bruce Wayne. Now if you wanta see some phat babes, it's you checking me out, as all the babes I have on my arm, Jim, are phat and way way too much."

It was a campus argot mixed with the language of the black streets with the spice of the jazz musician. The core of that mob was like this. Woolright, I talked about. Donny, also from Philly, another heavy dude from a browner background, but he and Woolright were old friends before school. Donny was always thought the heaviest of our crowd. He was in chemistry and went on to become a doctor. He was curly-haired and always smiling. A guy who never got angry, straight and true.

Shorty, from the city, even shorter than I was and distinctive not only because he was always "clean" and had a little dough, but because he tried never to tell the truth, about anything, no matter how small. The dough he got from his old man, who was a gangster (on the real side, though he always embroidered his activities), he spent quickly and steadily. He was like the jester of the group in one sense but everybody liked him and he was a legitimate part of the mob. The only thing is that all of us got to know him better than to believe him.

Rip Day, from Newark, I'd seen maybe at some games in Baxter Terrace. He had cousins that lived there. I think he lived up the street somewhere, but I didn't know him until I got at school. He was the "superstar" of the group, in his terms. Most of us thought he was a blowhard, full of shit, and not really a nice guy in the final go-down. A self-centered, grasping individual who was big and strong enough to threaten most of us, though we agreed he was corny. The dialogue that went on among us, between he and we, about how great he was and how corny we thought he was, was the unending background music of our collective relationship.

C.D. (the initials were his name), from North Carolina, later a little no-horse town in Virginia. He'd first shown up on the campus with highwater pants and a Mickey Rooney hat with the brim pinned up in front. I'd thrown the hat in the reservoir because it was obvious that if C.D. was going to hang with our mob he couldn't do it with that sky. He was our archetype of a country boy, but in a few months he'd gone through some kind of thorough change, for the most part, though even as clean as C.D. attempted to get over the years, we would never let him forget how country he had been. And even when he did jump into our version of Ivy League, there would always be something about C.D. that was just a little off or sticking out.

We had our first argument about who was the best tenor player in jazz, Charlie Ventura or Charlie Parker, but he painfully recanted that and later used that as an example of how far he'd come in his sophistication process. C.D. was perhaps my closest friend on that campus. Certainly he was one of the longest-lived, though I still see Shorty even today, but he is much changed as well, for the better.

But C.D. also became a writer, though at the time he was pre-law. In fact C.D. and I later were among those few students at Howard that the great Sterling Brown taught something about African American music in a series of unofficial classes in the Cook Hall dormitory. At that time, Howard still did not admit nigger music to its campus. I think the first jazz to get on in an official concert was Stan Kenton. (AAAAHHHHGGGGGGG!!!!!!) Shit, I was liking Gerry Mulligan and them and Dave Brubeck and Paul Desmond when I was at Howard. Along with Lloyd Price and Claude McPhatter. "Work With Me, Annie" and "Annie Had a Baby" etc. A dude used to walk around in the hallways of Clark Hall and make up words for Buzzy that went: "Better get yourself a white girl, a colored girl ain't no good." That kind of stuff was always being shot at us.

For this reason and others with our background, what constituted "the intellectual life" was always complex and unclear. C.D., for instance, went high up into the Howard Players, whose plays I think I went to only once the whole time I was on campus. I thought they were just in some yellow shit, some sideways upside-down shit I didn't have no use for. But then when I was in school, the idea that I might be an intellectual never oc-curred to me. Not really.

C.D. got in the goddam Howard chorus, too, the one hundred famous colored voices. The high point of their number was the choral part of Beethoven's Ninth, which they got sent up to NYC to sing. I thought all of that was boring, not to mention corny. In fact, like I said, the only thing I know I did a lot of at school was sit around and bullshit. Tell jokes, lie, insult people, and try to get out of schoolwork. I learned to drink at school, to smoke cigarettes, and something else a little deeper but then I wasn't even aware of that part of it.

I sat up in some heavy folks' classes, too. Sterling Brown. The music classes were something intimate and wonderful to me. He was opening us up to the fact that the music could be studied and, by implication, that black people had a history. He was raising the music as an art, a thing for scholarship and research as well as deep enjoyment. Brown's music classes were the high point of my "formal" Howard education. Almost everything else of value I learned outside my classes.

Nathan Scott, in a humanities class, gave me something, too. Not in the actual materials that he taught (though I did go back to some of them because of him) but in the enthusiasm of his teaching. He seemed actually to dig what he was teaching, to *love* it. Brown's taking us into another context outside any provided by the school showed his love of us and of the material. But Nathan Scott's preaching about Dante conveyed an *intellectual* love for literature that I hadn't seen. It was like some minister pushing us toward Christ, but Scott was pushing us toward Dante Alighieri. And it was directly due to this that I later went back to Dante to read what I was able.

Miss Byrd taught us social science and whapped us cross the knots with Fichte and Kant and Hegel. She was OK, some of that obviously got through, without me even knowing it. She always looked like she had just woke up and that in itself was intriguing.

There was a Mr. McSweet (not his real name) who taught biology and who the mob (or prominent members of it, me, Bill, and Tony) almost drove crazy. Sometimes I feel sorry for this man even today. He was from Mississippi and a junior teacher not at Howard too long. And he had a Mississippi accent that we would wreak havoc with, especially in the kind of intolerant hippy elitism that I was being baked in there. I would stand up and repeat his name the way he pronounced it (Mac-Swe-at) and ask him some inane question. Like he pronounced intestines "in-test-eynes." I would ask him, "Mr. Mac-Swe-at, what is an in-test-eyne??" Wide-eyed and cold as a brandished penknife. The class would crack up. He was so put upon by us that he told the three of us that we would most likely fail, that the highest mark we could get even if we got an A on the final would be a C. He was tired of being mocked. But we went into the office through an open window and stole the test, took it back to the dormitory, showed it to the mob members, then returned it. The next day in the test I finished so fast and looked up at McSweet, he knew something was up. He looked at me with real pain in his eyes. Goddam you, Jones, he was thinking. He said, "Mr. Jones, how is it you have finished so soon?"

"I studied, Mr. McSweet." I softened the mockery because we had beat his ass to ribbons now. I got an A, the two others got B's in the final, so he gave us a C and couldn't flunk us after all. That's the real shit I was learning.

In the mob was Lattimer, who walked around like a sharp maestro, always carrying his trumpet on campus. He was one of my first real friends, a music major from Virginia. Quiet and a good sport, who threw jibes, though soft ones, with the rest of us. He became a dentist, dropping music in his last year.

Lee, the artist from East Orange. A yellow boy with a yellow pretty sister we never ceased to tease him about. Though sometimes he would pick up his omnipresent umbrella and chase us down the halls. Lee was supercool, so cool it almost turned into its opposite. We were close. And it was he who called Tony "Hollywood," to capture that neon sididdy attitude Tony always had, even amongst us. I mean, Tony was a snob even when dealing with us. And there were dudes among us who came from families that had much more money than Tony's. But with Tony it was a built-in attitude he'd probably been taught since his early days. He was from Douglass-Harrison, and his family lived in a tiny apartment where they had to fold down the "front room" (colored folks' living room) bed every evening so Tony would have a place to sleep. But still he was "Hollywood." His nose in the air, loping across the campus with a bowlegged strut, a cold-blooded elitist. So much so we openly called him on it. But Tony never changed or even explained, that was the way he was and we took it or took it. We talked about him, but took it, nevertheless.

Stone from Chi, who carried scotch in his big briefcase. His family owned shrimp stores on Chicago's South Side, and he was always superclean even if he looked like he was about to come apart. Cashmere, desert boots, expensive tweed coats. But an open bad-mouthed two-fisted drinking dude. You just couldn't rely on Stone if you wanted something serious carried out. We lived together in an apartment in the city in our junior year and I had to speed home once a week after a late philosophy class to catch him before he spent up the allotment his parents sent him. He was told to buy food but he would buy alcohol. That's what he called it, "alcohol." "You boys want any alcohol?" and he'd go in his briefcase. When you got to the spot the icebox would be loaded with alcohol. But all there'd be to eat would be hot dogs and those waffles you put in the toaster. And we didn't even have a goddam toaster.

Kurt, also from Chi, short and intense, another pre-law. He and Stone always argued, because they were childhood friends. Kurt I stayed with later when I was in Ilinois in the service. When I visited Chi on the weekends, I would crib at Kurt's place. He was a good friend, reliable, hotheaded (and I liked that). He took care of his school business but it was never a problem that caused him not to be able to hang out. His father was a lawyer too.

That was most of them. Me, Bill, Tony, Shorty, and Stone roomed together one year and that was wild and focused our lives together, perhaps more tightly for a time than the others, but these guys were our dormitory crew.

Some of us were in pre-law or government. Some in pre-med, pre-dent, some were taking just general courses, trying to figure out what kind of degree. I was taking, as I said, pre-med, a chemistry major. But I didn't care nothing at all about that. So school was not the worst of my worries on the real side, although it clearly should have been.

It was a brown mob—I guess—really. That was still the stance from which I tried to understand and be in motion in America. (To the extent I understood that.) But look! C.D.-petty bourgeois/father a lawyer—yellowish. But Donny was a little smarter than that. He fell for certain doofdum but he could make fun of it, look at the whole of that, even his father's little country squire bullshit (in really nowheresville) as essentially comic.

Anyway, Donny was brown and black, from Philly's urban twist. And Woolright, black dude, scholarship-cunning to try to deal with America, USA! Bill, more yellow than brown, and Tony the same. This ain't got to deal with skin color, exclusively—Tony was darker than me, skinwise!

Lee, straight yellow (on the rambunctious side), his brown quality— and so there's a blue side to that.

Shorty, the criminal as middle class. If you mix black and yellow what do you get?

Our internal villain, Rip, was a penniless yellow. The worst kind. All grimace and illogic with the merest civil servant's economic base upon which to base his wild antisocial acts and ideas.

Kurt and Stone, the Chi connection, the middle middle and even the pitiful small capitalist himself. Hey, if we had called Stone an "upper-class Negro," he woulda grinned and said, "Look, Leee-Roy, kiss my ass!"

We were not inside the rumble of crazy Negro yellow Crazy. The stiff middle-class lie. We were touched, some bashed-smashed-ruined by it, but in the mob, our collective sense stared that shit down and laughed at it.

Johnny Jackson and Ned Smythe, two footballers who ran in on us noondays with my roommate, were brown kids from D.C. "D.C. boys" we called them, though that had real meaning only with the big hat wearer of S.W. And maybe Johnny was connected blacker too and came out on a scholarship tip. Though HU was playing "Ivy" and pretended not to give athletic scholarships. But they did, some kinda way.

(I had a track coach named Hart at Howard, reminds me now of Malcolm, those glasses and penetrating stare—ironic smile. He'd say, "Jones, I don't know if you really want to be an athlete. You don't want to work hard enough.")

We even had connections with gorillas like Tippy Whittington the all-star fullback who rumor said had been at Howard ten years. He'd come in the room from time to time with his stiff-necked growling pronouncements. The other footballers joked about him and imitated his noncommunicative speech.

But it was a brown mob. Connected to reality, to black life, and the blues. You see, Howard itself was a blinding yellow. So eye-melting some out people might say "white" and try to mash it on the Capstone. (That's what some of them dead yellow MF's had thought of to call it, "The Capstone of Negro Education." Boy, we mocked the shit out of that.) It reeked of it, that stiffness and artificiality, that petty bourgeois Negro mentality! And the top-upper Negroes is in on that, too.

We could define ourselves by where we'd come from. The teeming black cities. A whole other thing the "urban" shit defined.

So in a sense we stalked the campus as city boys connected to direct agonies of the black streets. (Though when we spun the combinations to the doors of our houses and went in off those streets, we were somewhere else.)

The geographic hookup was a social hookup. The jibes we used to throw at "South" and "country." Even on big money, big shoe, big hat Texas friends, we talked about funny for coming from outside the urban thing. Though that wasn't always altogether true.

All black schools have more peasants' and workers' children in them, though except for the very small schools, it is the yellow and brown sectors of the petty bourgeoisie that constitute their majority.

We had a sense of ourselves as being something other than the main-stream HU student, too. Even with the couple a buzzards we had in our group. The nuts were nuts because of their *pretension*. Not money. The really rich dudes did not hang with us nor we with them. Though Stone was the black bourgeoisie, in brown smoked glasses wobbling across campus with his bag of tipsy-getter. But Stone was cool. His problem (ain't it?) is that he wanted to spend all his little bitta money on the wrong shit! Shit, Stone, we need somethin' to eat! Not just no "alcohol."

We were kind of like outlaws in a way. Neither school nor mainstream
HU yellow-ass social functions were our real thing. (Though most of the
dudes hung with us did get out in the normal way without "punchin' out"
like your reporter!) Our real thing was hanging out, bullshittin'—talking
bad to each other and about everything else.

"Shit, this funny-lookin C.D. and his homeboy Wilsey." (Woolright talking typically one afternoon.) "Y'all is so funny lookin', it's a wonder they
even let you on this campus. Funny lookin' dudes."

"Woolright say your mama funny lookin' too." (Shorty agitatin'.)

"Woolright, how you gonna call somebody funny lookin'?" (C.D. coun-
tering.) He laughs loud so everyone will get his point.

Woolright goes over and pinches C.D.'s big schnozzola. "Look at this
big schnozzola. Colored people don't have big schnozzolas like that, C.D.
Who gave you this Jimmy Durante smellin' machine?" (Woolright
cappin'—we howlin'.)

Donny: Who got the wine?

Me: You can't drink no wine!

Donny: Woolright can. I'm his manager.

All: A wine drinkin' contest. Get the wine. Get the wine!

And so to work. There were bid-whist freaks (some for poker, some bridge,
but mostly freaks for real). Day and night and weekends and holidays.
Chess dudes we thought of as visitors. But we didn't play none of that shit
heavy. A poker and blackjack game occasionally. But even that shit was too
much effort. You had to pretend to be serious to play. And the dudes that
was serious about bid-whist we talked bad about. A fuckin' bid-whist freak!

We wasn't in no mock-serious, artificial, school-time shit nor the unofficial official extracurricular stiff shit of the yellow peril. At first I did go to a
few dances. You had to get "tight in the collar" for real—black tie. Some
dudes wore white tie, tails, to the shit. Various frats and sororities giving
their stiff funny shit. Naming various "queens" and super-Negroes to reign
over that banana republic.

But the glamour of that shit ran out for me pretty quick, plus the other
problems I had—like who was I gonna take, and whatnot. (A Jack Scott
phrase—the same guy who gave us "It's me saying," etc.)

All of that was part of the fraternity-sorority hype in which we were all
involved—at one degree of brainwash or another. Greeks! We wanted to
be Greeks! Alpha, Kappa, Omega-AKA-Delta, and the rest.

Our mob were not real frat types (except for Tony and Rip) but some of
us kinda drifted into one or another, we even took some sides around the

shit. But it was never a passion for any of us. Most of the frat dudes were assholes as far as we were concerned. All that rah-rah shit. The Alpha sentiment, in the main, touched our group. That's because there were bunches of Alphas from Jersey on campus. And they had a considerable influence.

I tried out for the shit the first part of my junior year and flubbed. For one thing, so-called big brothers banging on our doors or the door to 13 Rue were met with a variety of responses, mostly negative. They'd be coming in to get some note and try to order new pledges around. In Alpha, the new pledges were called Sphinxes. And me, Bill, Tony, Allan Shorter (Wayne's brother) because we were older had pledged and were officially Sphinxes. The name had to do with some of their secret ass rituals and being inducted, which was characterized as "crossing the burning sands"!

A dude named Skeffton came into Rue one night. After we open the door, about six of us inside, we see this reject-lookin' motherfucker. He was a third-string defensive lineman on the football team, even though one of his arms was withered.

Skeffton snorts, my roommate wasn't there was the first answer he got. He snorts again, looking sterile, inamicable, around at our good-for-nothing faces. Like I said, most of us didn't play on any of the teams (though I was on the track and cross-country teams), wasn't in this dude's accepted social whirl—that being the aroma of cheese back behind the mousetrap—so he feels, what with him being a "big brother," not vaguely but distinctly superior. So he says, to nobody in particular, but actually to me because I was the only Sphinx in the room, "I need something from the D.C. Donut Shoppe." D.C. Donut Shoppe was all the way downtown around them government buildings and shit. All them dudes in the room, their eyes light up like somebody flipped a switch and they all peepin' over at me.

I told him I had a sore foot or sore knee or had a stomach hurtin' or something, but I wasn't goin' to the D.C. Donut Shoppe. But these dudes in the room couldn't let well enough alone, they start agitatin'. Like, Woolright with his shit, "Hey, man," to the lame "Ain't this little cat over here supposed to be your little brother, a pledge and stuff?" Dimwitted Skeffton is getting more heated up. C.D. throws in some stuff. Donny comes in with some stuff. Skeffton still rising.

Finally he peeps, "So you ain't goin' to the D.C. Donut Shoppe?" That seemed obvious before. "Well, you know payback is hard, right, Jones? You gonna get yours." Then he turns and stalks out the room. All these dudes start howlin', but somehow it was not that funny to me. But fuck him, is all I could say. I definitely was not going to no D.C. Donut Shoppe in the middle of the night.

The frat, not just that one, but all of them, had a collection of creeps no doubt. There were some real lulus in the Alphas, but I'm knowledgeable just about them. The Omegas and Kappas had some easily identifiable nuts you could spot without even having to rub up against them too tough. But Henry Lucas, for instance, Reagan's new star knee-grow from California. He was the president of the Alphas when I was coming through. This dude wore a three-piece suit to school everyday. I never saw Henry Lucas on that campus, or anywhere else, without being totally "pressed." He had that stiff goofus quality about him, very formal and mirthless with a gigantic set of lips that must have distressed so turned-around a dude as he. When he saw me he would say "Good morning" or "Good afternoon, Jones." He always called me "Jones" like at Barringer. In all the years we knew each other on that campus we might have said a paragraph to each other. And even then when I saw him it was like seeing somebody official. Lucas was stiffer than even the professors and everybody called him by both his names, Henry Lucas, not one or the other.

That goddam Tim Bodie, who is now a three-star general in the air force, he was in there too. But he was a much nicer dude, though he was an ROTC freak even then. But Tim would laugh with you. He was an upperclassman but you see where that ROTC shit could lead.

There was a football player, a Kappa, Andy Chambers, who was a pretty popular dude on campus, he's a goddam admiral. I could rattle off a bunch more, not just frat dudes, although I bet these top-flight American warrior types were all frat dudes. But HU filled some of the needed spaces for yellow bellies. If you look and see how many of the chosen coloreds sashaying through America with "good jobs" you'll find the HU kids personable and finally in the shit after all.

Probably even psychopaths like Harry Johnston, Leon Harris, Don Bradford are hooked up somewhere. As a matter of fact I know Harris is a big-time dentist not far away in one of the suburbs, Johnston is also some kind of doctor (both these dudes were officers in the service for a while), and Bradford is some kind of bureaucrat in city hall, which was one constant hookup for folks like these. But these guys were all jangle-brained. Johnston, a light-skinned dude with a white streak down his chin like George Macready, he liked to torture people coming into the frat. He called himself a torturer. He would think of different ways to inflict pain on people.

Harris was just a violence lover. He loved to punch and beat. He always seemed slightly frantic about his kicks. Johnston was grim and chuckling— You never seen a George Macready picture?

Bradford was big, he played football until his grades got too shaky so he dropped it. He was barrel-chested and a good guy in some ways but he was so egotistical that being in the frat and an upperclassman meant that he thought he actually was a great great guy, so he could be used by real torturers like Johnston and Harris.

These, along with Skeffton, jammed me up once at one of the "sessions," actually what the white frats and shit called "hazing." We just called them "sessions." They would take us somewhere and beat us. Behind my refusing to go to the D.C. Donut Shoppe these four got me, and Johnston and Harris actually rolled up *Esquire* magazines (these have been formative in my life), wrapped them in tape, dipped them in water, and put them on the radiator to dry, so they were hard. I was running track at the time and Skeffton with his ruined self got much pleasure saying this aloud as they prepared to beat and while they beat me, on the legs and thighs until red welts and large hardening black swellings covered my legs, thighs, and butt. I could barely walk when they got through.

At the next day's track meet I couldn't run. My coach hit the ceiling. He didn't like the frats anyway though he was a goddam Alpha himself. But who really got pissed off was my roommate Bill and the mob and some of the other athletes. For them, this was beyond the call and kin of what the frats were supposed to do. Yeh, everybody knew they paddled people, but this shit was out. (The Kappas actually got suspended for a year when Lee's sister's boyfriend, PeeWee, got his arm broke by the Kappas and he was a popular kid.)

No official shit went down in my case but there was a kind of mass uprising. A few nights later at another session down on Banneker Field the pledges led by Bill and a couple other footballers erupted and turned Johnston and the others on their heads, knocked them in the mud, and generally whaled the daylights out of the big brothers under the cover of night and confusion. I ripped a few shirts and fell on a couple motherfuckers.

But that was it for me anyway. The shit seemed too unconnected to my real desires. What were they? I donno. But this shit wasn't in me. I now got much more passive about the frat. I just was not available for anything. Neither meetings nor anything else. Where before I would have great fun ducking these nuts, now I was just not around. It didn't matter too much. Both Shorter and I got blackballed (only one blackball could keep you out). Shorter used to show up for ROTC without his socks and with a "war hat" with no grommet in it so it was pulled down over his eyes like Diz might wear it. Shorter was playing tenor then. And I told you the frats were full of ROTC freaks, later generals; you know what they thought about that "weird" Shorter. In fact, I heard that's why he got blackballed, being weird. But that was not true. For me, it was said that I was a snob, that I did not mix well. But that was not true, I was still much mixed in the middle of me own mob and we would hang out with anybody (long as they wasn't square). But the real trick was that my grades had got so out that I didn't have the grade average to join the fraternity anyway. I got drunk one afternoon and fell out up against a clothes hamper lamenting my waywardness which always seemed to disqualify me for what I wanted, though who knew what I wanted. "Pre-med" would come out of my mouth, but that was so far up and away from what me wanted, when I said it it echoed like in a huge open corridor, no lights, just echoes. And sometimes it hurt my ears.

It was clear to me even then that if Howard represented something, it was something quite different from blue Newark. I said the urban troops had some special panache on the campus because we brought a kind of outside blue/black quality onto the campus. We were aware of that, too. Just as we were aware of the group of actually yellow folk who sat in the cafeteria together. And just as we were aware of the parties we weren't invited to. Like the ones given by the Turtles. They even had a password, but it got leaked due to some romance between the colors. "Are you a turtle?" was the question they threw at you on the door. "You bet your sweet ass I am" was the countersign. Except if you were not known (i.e., were a trifle brown and unruly, etc.) you couldn't make it. We mostly ignored such shit, though Tony was always sniffing around for just such as that so he could try his luck. Tony and Rip did connect and got into a lot of the high-yellow sets. Rip could have qualified anyway, though he was broke, but he had some jingling money cause he was an only child. Tony was an only child too and a cheap motherfucker, so he was always pulling hidden dough out of his safe-deposit vault somewhere inside his room. But the two of them was high up into such things as the Turtles and whatnot and other light-skinned stuff.

The med students were the pinnacle of that society. If you was light-skinned and a med student and had a car *and* an apartment, you were on a par with Zeus or one of them other gods. Dent students were next, then law students. I mean up in the med, dent, and law schools, not the "pre's." Tony and Rip's conversations always had a lot to do with what the fashionable med (and dent and law) students were doing. The sets they'd been to and how grand life at the top was. We listened but it was like movies to us, something to pass the time until somebody thought up something really out to do like that time we played hockey on the second floor with brooms and bottles till old man Butts came up on the floor and we scattered. He came to the door of Rue anyway, and busted all of us. "Mr. Jones," he'd say, "Mr. Jones. What can we do about you?" In real despair.

The doings of the real socialites at HU were relayed to us by yellowish-brown Negro radio, two of 'em, so that's really as close to that shit as we got. We did get uptight one day in the cafeteria and was close to popping some little pale Negro motherfucker in his jaw for saying something too far out while he was sitting with a dazzling collection of yellow babes all with their noses pointing at other galaxies. (Of course we were jealous, and we hated that part of it, too, since we knew they were vapid little flowers of unknowing, yet why should they be allowed to think they shit didn't stink?!)

But the divisions on the campus were *known* by all but the most unconscious. And we could get very loud talking about "sididdy yellow bitches and these jive lames" who are gonna get their asses broke in a minute. Tony and Rip, however, were tipping on all those scenes.

There was some big hullabaloo when a brown (skinned) girl, really gorgeous babe named Pat Adams, was elected Homecoming and Alpha Queen. She was a very stiff number on the real side and split for nothing but bananas, her boyfriend was Mordecai Johnson's son. When Mordecai was stalking out of his house right across from the girls' dormitory, like God walking across campus. (Mordecai used to have our ass for a whole semester sitting in chapel every Sunday, mandatory if you were a freshman or transfer student. Chicks had to be in at 7 P.M. their first semester and it would be light outside and warm and great love affairs would be getting formed. And much thrashing and moaning and loud lamentations as to the cruelty, etc., of fate and Mordecai but that made it like some Romeo and Juliet shit and that spiced it up for some.)

The frats and yellow folks ran Howard's official student life. Everything else was improvisation. We'd find ourselves trailing through black night in southwest Washington headed for parties. Dudes would say, "Some a them D.C. boys gonna split your heads open!" But we, being officially fearless, would go on and come to a joint looked just like those sets we'd left back home. Big hats and all. And the only problem we ever had was one night Tony went with us and some little black chick he wanted to impress threw an aspirin bottle at his ass, and we all thought it best to vanish.

The D.C. connection was then a connection with real black life, though Howard itself to a certain extent is black life no matter its yellow distortion and the class repression the one-sided class struggle on campus enforces. (Though probably in the '60s there could've been something else happening for the same reasons, mass uprising and a general influx of black and brown types from the cities came on campus. You'll have to ask Stokely Carmichael about that!)

The woman thing could spell it out further. All the time I was on campus I went with about four girls, and "went with" is too strong in most of those instances. On campus it was only three on the real side. Elizabeth Donald and I were tight, after a fashion. I took her to a couple of them dress-up things when I first was getting hooked up with campus life. They seemed flashy enough, but no real laughs though Liz seemed happy to be there amongst it all. She in a gown and I in a black tie. We talked to some people and posed and even danced.

But we were tighter than that. We had a couple of classes together. Zoology and physics. I was beginning to write some poetry, at first, under the Elizabethans—Sidney, Vaughan, Shakespeare, the rest. I would send her fragments of poems for her to add a stanza, then I would add another stanza, this is while the class was going on. By the end of the class we'd have a whole poem of sorts. But it was great fun and we would write poems about Peanuts (the comic strip characters) juxtaposed with our "Zo" teacher's ear or some acquaintance's droop in a chair close by on the way to a peaceful sleep.

And Liz was a really nice girl. She was always cheerful and smiling and I think she was a "Zo" major, on the heavy side. (Her sister went with one of them goddam Alphas, a big brother, now a New Jersey architect. I came to the house one time this blood gets drugged thinking I'm coming to see his squeeze, such cross-eyed explaining especially in those days I thought the Alpha gestapo would mash me up but he cooled out but was never what you'd call pleasant.) I think we went to a couple of movies, a couple of dances, I walked her home a few times, more than a few. Anyway, I began to think that Liz and I were "going together." Dudes would drop her name in a certain way so it seemed like people were picking up, had picked up that that was happening.

Then one day I said something at a mob "meeting" as to how I was gonna take my old lady out somewhere and these dudes all looked at each other and me with a smirk like I had just shit on the floor. (Or like the time Mr. Butts was banging on the door to make us shut up and I didn't think it

was him and I called out "All right Butts, grease your nose and slide under." Then we opened the door and it's him—that kind of look.) There's a
skinny four-eyed turkey whose name I can't remember (fuck you Freud-
ians) to this day. Or was it another guy? Hmmm. But anyway there's this
four-eyed dude who had been around a few times, no he was known to all
of us, Philip, I think his name was. He says, like a guy asking directions of
a traffic cop, "Your old lady?" These dudes look at me, Woolright is about
to split open with his jive ass. "Liz and I are going together."

Particularly I remember there was some kind of deadly set coming up
and Liz and I had been discussing whether we wanted to go to that (the
on-campus dress-up) or see the ballet. But obviously there wasn't much
discussion going on on the real side. I remember this Philip saying, or was
his name Al, "Liz and I are going together." Uhh, man, did that sting. And
these cats fell out. You could see some concern in some of their eyes but
they had to laugh, otherwise it would have been admitting too much and
they didn't want to have to go through that so they howled.

"God damn," was about all I could get out. "God damn." And took his
word. I saw Liz a day or two after and she was gentle and somewhat melan-
choly but she did confirm that she and Al were going to the campus set,
but it was more than that and we both knew it. (Plus half the goddam
campus!) I spoke to Liz the rest of my time on campus and we remained
good buddies in class, but not like before by no means. And she went with
this dude, a pre-med who actually did become a med, and they lived happily ever after, I guess.

Liz was a brown girl, she was, hooked up by the same yellow strings of
gold and manipulation. But she could laugh at certain of the things that
make those little phony worlds go round and this is what I liked. I couldn't
understand why she did what she did. Perhaps she was always going with
the dude and I was imposing my dull ass in the way. Maybe she should
have told me if that was the case. No, I think it was the pattern of
lackadaisicality she saw in me. Perhaps I was too casual and my jibes were
too shrill. Certainly she saw that my steps did not lead into med school and
I was almost ready to admit that too. This dude was also on his way into the
frat. He was a good solid dude. And what was I?

No sour grapes now, Jim. But that could tell somebody something, I
hope. I went with two other girls on campus, one named McKeesport.
That's not her name, it was Blanche or something, I can't even remember.
So that will tell you about that. She was inordinately skinny and quiet and

from that ugly steel town. We went out a couple of times and became friends more than anything else.

Audrey, from another wild place, a West Virginia coal mining town. These were both brown girls. Audrey was very tiny and plump with big, almond shaped eyes. Also quiet. I never found out what she liked. But we went to a few flicks. (I didn't know what I wanted to do. Some of the movies blacks couldn't even go to. We used to drive these crackers in the Peoples Drugstores crazy by ordering stuff then they'd bring it in a bag, like a Coke or something. And we'd say we wanted to drink it there. And they would say they couldn't serve us and we'd leave the shit on the counter. But you had to hat up cause they would call the law.)

The only girl I could really say I went with, in a kind of heavy way (and even that didn't get heavy as all that—not on the flesh side), was Baby. That was her name—not a nickname, her parents named her that. So she was from the country, High Point, North Carolina. She came from the same town an old crazy vet we used to holler at lived in, Terry. Terry was drunk a lot and loud but a very good dude. Kinda dude you liked to drink with. Could think up all kind of weird shit to talk about.

I mighta met Baby through Terry. She was a student at Miner Teachers College, which was right down the street, cross the street, from HU. Shootin' at Miner girls was a pastime for one sector of Howard students. But it was generally frowned upon by the mainstream. Hey, they was who? They had no note. A lot of 'em talked country (Baby shure did!). There was a few cracked yellow ones but not many. The Miner ladies was at another level ("lower" than our own coeds on The Hill. That meaning had changed for me. "Hill" now meant the yalla lights, the Capstone, not Third Ward/ Central Ward black and blue folks). That was vouchsafed.

But I ran into Baby. And she was not brown, dear readers, she was very black. Skin color and whatever otherwise. Black gleaming skin unblemished and these bright sparkling eyes, behind pinkish-brown plastic frames.

It didn't strike me as anything until I got the campus reaction. Baby was sweet and the way she sounded, that black belt peasant twang tripped me out. But she was high up into readying for the teaching thing. She was maybe a year ahead of me and was already getting ready to practice teach.

I'd go up there a couple times a week. She had a new yellow Ford. An apartment she shared with another Miner student. And she dug me, I'd say. She'd even cook most times I showed, or at least had something ready. Which was great because my old man only sent me $30 a month for odds and ends. The food money he sent directly to the cafeteria people after I'd spent it up a couple times in a week then had to go broke for the rest of the month.

But she'd have some grit because everybody knew most of the Howard students was walking around kinda hungry. Except the blindingly yellow! Mostly we'd talk and laugh a lot. She was a bright girl. She was always teasing about my (HU) origins and how HU students acted generally, which was wild to hear from that side. It even made me clearer that there were sides. But she was definitely country. Terry'd come up there sometimes and we'd get to drinking, though I still wasn't no heavy drinker.

We went to a few parties her friends gave in D.C. and to flicks and stuff in the D.C. community. I had already passed my dress-up frat period—which I guess is obvious. (And the stuff was just idle window shopping to Baby.) But I hadn't summed up as a categorical anything. I was just going along, living my life, trying to love it and let whatever happened happen.

Baby, as I said, was not particularly interested in HU society either. I think myself (and Terry) were the closest she wanted to get at that point. But we had laughing, sometimes riotous, discussions about HU and environs and the mores and customs therein.

Baby came up on campus a couple times. One Saturday afternoon she pulled her bright yellow new Ford outside Clark Hall. I was supposed to be out front waiting, but was still inside bullshitting, so she tooted the horn. The front-step jockeys got her message and my name and began screaming them out. More from a few other reasons than mere communication or aid. One was they had nothing else to do. I could hear my name ringing outside, the horn, and now in the hallways. And they all wanted to sound like Baby, Leeeeeeeee Royyyyyyyy Joooooooonessss. And I came running downstairs and when I hit the bottom step out in front, heads were thrust through windows all over the front of the building. It was somebody in our mob that started it but they were calling in unison Leeee RooooyyyyLeeeeee Rooooyyyyyy—and waving at us. You could even hear some of their comments as we got away—she had a convertible. "Broad with a car," "Goddam," "Who's that chick?" etc., etc.

For Bill and Tony and Rip and some others, however, Baby's looks (albeit her car and apartment), and the fact she went to Miner, made me Bruce Wayne. And that's what I was greeted with when I returned. "Hey, Bruce" and whatnot. And these dudes kept it up, they even had some of their hambone friends continue it and they weren't even proper in the mob. I'd cut my eyes funny at them. But mostly I just took it and continued seeing Baby, mainly cause I dug her and it was about the best place I knew to go around those parts (HU mores to the contrary). Anyway one time up in the room, I don't know quite how it got started, Rip starts this shit about Bruce Wayne and he was going with this little limp starlet, a candidate for Homecoming Queen in a couple of years from the looks of her. And I made some remarks as to what a dead-ass bitch whassername was. Goin' with her was like lookin' at pinups in *Esquire*, all it did was get his whatname hard, as he definitely wasn't gettin' any of that! And what's more, half these Negroes on this campus walking around talking about this girl like she's Lena Horne or somebody, so really, Rip, you sharin' what you ain't gettin' with all the other dumb jerkin' off lames on the campus.

Rip didn't like that and began to imitate Baby's speech. He built a great rep in his countless monologues about his prowess as a "cocksman." And to have someone imply that he masturbated, that just wouldn't do. But it got very nasty and ended with fists being rolled up though Rip was a big guy, a swimmer, and though there was a little dancin' around the room no blows were struck. What was struck was a gong inside my knot that twanged some realization. The dudes in the mob generally did not give a fuck who I went with. Though there was a streak of plain out envy. These little babes on campus had to be in the dorm at certain hours and to get out overnight they had to go through elaborate lies and for those frosh and sophomores they wasn't getting out except in extraordinary circumstances and most would not put their behind so squarely on the chopper as all that. So whatever Rip was doing, which wasn't anything anyway, it had to be done in broad daylight, off campus. You went to flicks and ate dinner in Georgia Avenue restaurants, sat up in the dorms giggling, and held hands crossing campus with the Howard ladies. But stashed back in an old northwest apartment after finishing a big dinner and then sippin' some grog squeezed up in the shadows of your own spot with a lady of your own choosing, that was what them med students and other royalty could pull off. But one of your own? "How the fuck did you luck up?" That was Woolright's comment and Donny and the straight-ahead dudes. But we had, as I said, some yeller bellies in the group. The only good thing about that is that they were like antennae then for the rest of the joint, they would be letting us know what a whole lot of the messed up and soon to be messed up would be thinking about or not thinking about.

Rip and dudes like that were into the social fabric of the Capstone mainstream and their sashayin' across the campus like the Easter Parade being looked at by others under the glass bell was all they needed. It was a form that was being followed. The little limp yellow girl (his was a blonde), being gladly and humbly craved by potential frat brothers, going back and forth to class or sitting in the cafeteria, was a distinct social form as well as a readying for service in the great lost cause of petty bourgeois hypnosis. Slave mores. Exactly what the racist gurus prescribe for keeping us under wraps. Except down in southwest D.C. or on U Street or T Street they wasn't under these kinds of wraps. They had to keep the blue/black actual strugglers under gun wraps, that's the only wraps that work on them.

I made no great rebellions, no explosions. (Cussing some future government bureaucrat out in his Ivy threads.) Just went on my way. Just moved on where I was going. Not even fully conscious, except I would do such and such and not do something else. I would like something for some reason and not like something else, and maybe not even have a reason.

I would sit up in the room sometimes with green glasses and put a yellow light bulb in the fixture. Why? Who knows? I would paint big paintings on the wall of the room — 3-D paintings of Tony's high society babes and put curtains over them so they could be drawn back dramatically to reveal the painter's madness. Or sit out on the campus eating half a watermelon and scandalize poor Butts and the patron saints of middle-class Negroes way off in Negro heb'n.

The next year is when some of us came off campus. We'd got too grown up to relate to dorm life anymore. Mr. Butts was clearly overjoyed. But that summer more wild things were happening, like being blown through a wind tunnel and the wind tunnel is inside your head. You trying to "concentrate" on something and a thousand-mile-an-hour wind is blowing behind your eyes, blowing all kinds of shit through your head blotting out your vision.

I had been blowing science courses regularly now. They didn't interest me, yet the form of what I was supposed to be doing called for science. Laboratories. I was blown out of organic like with a timebomb. I never understood qual and quant and rushed out of there in near panic. It seemed like I couldn't *understand* anything. I couldn't learn. Maybe that's why all the other shit was strange. Why I couldn't get in a frat or even get a "respectable" girlfriend. I was one center of a mob yet it seemed that that ring of friendly faces had receded to the edge of the horizon. The best of these dudes, the straightest of them, were my friends (some have remained close friends until this day and almost any of them I run into on the streets or in some airline terminal or wherever, we sit down and can get ecstatic talking about these HU days), but still, now it seemed there was more space around me than I could use. Space between me and them. Space where strange lights and shapes and voices could get in. Weird decisions and postures. The frat thing, the woman thing, seemed like they cleared space around me or something.

That summer in Newark something similar was happening but it was happening under camouflage. I was now cut off from the Hillsides and had been cut off from the Cavaliers. But there was a whole new cast of friends and people to run with by way of the HU and general college hookup. The college thing in a town like Newark did provide a special bond and the college kids even from different colleges tended to run together. There was a social club formed, really while we were in school, called the Esquires. It seemed like the requirements for membership was going to HU or some of the other schools (a couple of dudes went to local colleges like Bloomfield, Newark State, etc.), paying the dues, and wearing Bermuda shorts, which were just coming out in our generation. The Bermuda shorts with the long socks, we thought that was really hip and that was our badge that summer. I had a cord jacket, tuxedo pants, and white sneakers I also started sporting, snaking through the streets late nights by myself.

The Esquires were really Los Ruedos, Golden Boys, etc., plus a few stragglers like me now pumped in my college. We gave one big successful set which was the social hit of our circle that summer. But the one dude who didn't go to college and who'd got a rep as a kind of drugstore Lothario/ cut-rate pimp got accused of lifting some dough from the kitty and Bill and a couple of the athlete dudes jacked him up in the back. I guess it was true.

We went to parties in the Oranges and Montclair, exotic places. Me and a dude named Joe Brown would sit on the stoop outside the parties after passing through looking at the babes. We'd sit outside and talk to whoever or just with each other, or sit in the car with the door open. Joe was the key, he had the short. We'd be out there listening to Symphony Sid and talking shit, passing comments on the women that went in and out and the dudes too. Joe was very hip, a little like me I guess, but carried to the extremes. Joe would not talk to anybody he didn't know, not because he was some kind of snob but because he was shy and he didn't know how people would react to the things he wanted to talk about and be about. Joe ended up a writer as well, plays and short stories. But in those days we'd talk about the music, about the girls, about our Northeastern version of the mob. He was going to one of those local colleges as well.

The other cats would be inside cattin'. Moving around in there talkin' to babes and drinkin' punch and we'd be outside bullshittin' on the steps or in the front seat with the car doors open listening to Sid.

To me the whole party thing we did, though I really liked it, to get away from Newark and soar up through these other sparkling places, was more Howard stuff. Though I didn't think I felt anything about Howard except digging it. The funny shit was just that, funny shit, but I dug Howard, it had become my identification of myself to myself. Yet really? Beneath that? What were the other modes of response being built up? I cannot say with any more precision than this narrative.

It was tinselly, glittery in an artificial way. There were people I liked in between all that. For instance, though I looked many many of those little girls up and down with serious intent it was no realer than what I thought the rest of that tableau was. It was admiration. But I couldn't even conceive of what I would say to any of them, I didn't know what they talked about. When I took a girl out I still went out most times with Betty, and the people she hung with were still on a basically Newark scene. But the college thing always threw a damper on those kinds of romances unless one had pledged undying love, which we hadn't, even though we seemed to like each other, and still rolled around clutching each other in her house or mine on couches or on beds or cots or whatever. I wish I knew what she was thinking about all this. I do know that one evening I was talking and said "Bawston" for some reason, maybe that was the first evening I ever said it, certainly I have not said it too much before or since. And Betty said, "What? What are you saying?" And grinned.

And I repeated it, "Bawston." And that probably told her something. Also since I had gone away to school, actually just before I left, I had started spelling my name with an "i" on the end instead of as it was given, Leroy. My justification was that my father's name, seeing his birth certificate named him Coyette Leroy, was French, so why wasn't the "y" an "i"? But also I'd read that summer, just before I went away, Roi Ottley's *New World a Comin'* and I think that's what did it. At any rate, after my first year at Howard I spelled my name with a capital "R" and an "i" on the end. LeRoi.

I knew what I was doing saying "Bawston" to Betty and she knew what she heard (maybe she even knew what I was doing too) but the grin, later a laugh, "What are you doing?" was all she asked. (And then we made love in a new, more exotic way — but that was later!)

A sense of isolation had developed again. It had never left, maybe. Just quieted down by the roar of new surroundings, new faces, and a new set of customs to imbibe and assimilate. Driving around to the parties was great, sitting out front with Joe listening to Sid was great, but what? I worked in the grocery store, went to summer school trying to take scientific German. It was at Seton Hall in Newark. Across the street was a bar that looked like it had been shipped straight from Heidelberg. After the last class we all went over, mostly whites, and each bought a round—about ten of us in the class. So that was ten glasses of beer (they only cost about fifteen cents apiece) and I got really trashed for the first time in my life. Wobbly spitting-up drunk. I got home some way. We had moved when I went away to school that first year down to Hillside Avenue, across Clinton Avenue. We lived in a two-family house with the colored landlord downstairs. A little brown and yellow house with a porch on the first floor and one on the second out through our living room. I reached the downstairs porch and plopped into the rocking chair and fell out sick and twisted. My mother and father had been out that night too, so they came in and there I was blasted flat like some ominous casualty. My mother cried, she clutched my father and cried at her poor son her only son her oldest son and so forth being dead drunk right out on the street. I tried to explain the next day, it wasn't serious, but the words did not even impress me, coming as they did through the Plexiglas construct of the great primordial hangover I had. I thought I was dying.

But it was like being backed away from everything and everybody. And no whys came in. I knew what was happening to me, and even the "Bawstons" and name changes were false alarms, diversions, from what was happening to me. But what was happening to me? I felt like a lost child. When I wasn't careening around the streets with Joe and them in search of the great party, I was, for some reason, feeling almost sorry for myself. But I did not know why. The isolation, the aloneness, sometimes it was almost sweet. And I had started reading in school. Whether from the urgings of teachers or what, but suddenly I was going into Howard's library looking for Gertrude Stein. And who the hell was Gertrude Stein? I read her "Primer for Dogs Who Are Learning to Read." I showed it to Liz Donald, a girl I "went with" for a while, and we laughed and quoted from it, but why was I reading that in the first place? I had had the Pound book, a thin little collection of selected poems, but I couldn't understand much of that. What with the Greek, some of the Latin I could piece together, but I had no idea, for the most part, what he was talking about. I still read the Elizabethans. But I had got a book, a really heavy book, that I liked very much. It was Selden Rodman's *One Hundred Modern Poems* with Apollinaire's

"Zone" and work by Blok and Lorca and Rilke. I couldn't understand a lot of that either, but I liked that book and found myself looking at it from time to time trying to decode it.

The next year at Howard was my last year, though I didn't know it. I began by moving into the city with Bill, Tony, Shorty, and Stone. We painted the place a wild shade of pink. It was riotous. I was always walking in on Tony trying to seduce some suspecting charmer or we stayed up all night "studying," drinking beer and scotch and wine and bullshitting. We hung in places like the Kenyon Grill, where the elite drank martinis and I learned to drink martinis too. But not many. I got drunk and fell out at one party just as I was about to impress this sensuous beauty (we met a few months ago and she is married to a white advertising executive) who thrilled me because she was a painter.

Now that all my money was being sent directly to me again I was even broker than before. I would go to my aunt's once a week in northeast D.C. and eat like a starving soldier. My Aunt Bessie would smile and fill up a big bag for me to take back. I would try to ease it in but the niggers would spot it and gobble it down like locusts.

What Howard connect I still had weakened and drifted even further. Where before we would lay up in our corner room and watch Bill play football with our feet hung out the windows screaming, now we would only go to the stadium and get a big megaphone, put a bottle inside the megaphone, holding the bottle by the ring at its neck, and when something would happen we would "cheer" and by halftime drain a gallon of cheap red.

I would go to class, hang around on campus and up in Clark Hall, and then shoot home about four blocks over and a few blocks up. We liked living off campus because it made us feel more adult than we were. But most of the people we knew off campus were HU students and I could never get hooked to the little House of Love routine that these apartments were supposed to be according to student mythology. We had a couple of parties there, got threatened by the landlord; but personally it was just another step away.

I found myself more interested in reading and personal revelation than in the laboratories and science courses I supposedly existed for. I had a philosophy course that was interesting, teaching us bullshit like syllogisms and useless logic, but at least I could understand what they were talking about. The great silent creep of my organic chemistry class, who came in and merely wrote equations on the board that we must commit to memory and who rarely talked longer than one sentence at a time (he was so heavy, said the yellow press), bored the shit out of me. I would be sitting in class dozing, shot out, uninterested, except in the chirping of the students afterwards, what they said and made out of the shit was more interesting to me but it didn't stop me from being on Georgia Avenue alone, moving swiftly up the hill to see if Stone left any grit in the icebox.

I began to live in a halfway world, of mostly shadows and silence. With advertising of unknown whatevers slowly crawling through my head in klieg lights and marquee-type bulbs. Dazzling obscurities, questions. Embarrassing gaps in my concentration. I had not the slightest idea what I was thinking about nor much of the time what I was talking about. Unless I was bullshitting with what part of the mob remained in some focus. I thought there was a sickness around that place. It was in the stiffness and artificiality, the walking-on-water quality of references to a life that none of us would ever see. We were being readied for "good jobs," "professions," prestige and wealth. I did not have the energy to be a doctor. I was not willing to try hard enough to master the things I had to master. I was not interested in any of the shit I could understand. I didn't even feel like running too hard after the girls. I drank wine and smoked cigarettes because that was easy to do. I read books, but mostly thin ones because fat ones repelled me. I did go to movies whenever I could. I listened to music but the Howard jukebox went from Gerry Mulligan and Dave Brubeck to "Work With Me, Annie" and few of us had record players. I went to the Howard Theater. I saw Diz and Bud Powell down there and that was something I did regular. I especially liked the midnight shows. I would go downtown where the big white folks' stores were and look in the windows. I even put money down on a slick suit I saw at Lewis and Thos. Saltz and never got it, so they got my dough. I continued to go to parties out in the city. But something had drifted for good.

I think I understood that I was not getting any closer to reality. Not understanding it any better. (Though I was, just that dissociation makes you heavier, by several ounces.) Words in the wind, dull classrooms, dead folks. Corny people laughing. Rules and regulations and customs and mores. What people did. I couldn't use it.

The second semester I even moved out of our apartment, or more exactly the landlord threw us out and Bill moved in with another footballer. Tony and Shorty and Stone moved back on campus and I moved just a few short blocks into a house that was filled completely with West Indians. In our U.S. chauvinism we called the African students the "Suji boys" and the West Indian students the "Mon boys." And we mostly never mixed. They were rather separate circles. (Ain't nobody knew nothin about no Pan-Africanism!) One of the guys was in my class and he told me about the space at this house they all rented and I jumped on it. I got to know a few of the West Indians, mostly Jamaicans and Trinidadians, well. But people wanted to know why I was with these Mon boys all the time now. I didn't know. I lived with them. They had their own parties and I was in the house and started going. One night a bunch of white marines followed one dude who had brought a white girl and tried to turn the place out, so I found myself punching white dudes in the face and running in the street trying to smash some with bottles before the white police came and pacified us. But there was no more to the incident.

Actually they had a nice thing going down there. The woman who rented them the whole house said she liked to rent to West Indians because un-like these sorry U.S. bloods the West Indians had the dough and would pay. So now it was not only space but a cultural warp I had stepped through, a whole nother set of folks I found myself with. Not that I was cut off entirely from the old mob or the bloods on campus. But I could come down to the house, which was only a couple blocks from campus, and go into my room, which was clean and quiet. There might be some calypso playing somewhere, which I dug. And I'd be there mostly by myself. I could do homework (which I almost never did except the night before the test) or do what I did mostly look at stuff and think about stuff, maybe read something, or maybe go for a walk or eat or drink a beer, or just let strange stuff fill up my head in absolute silence.

By now, it was clear that I was flunking out of school. I had some good marks but in my major I was hitting on naught but the lonely heart. I went through some frantic changes, told myself and some other people some tales. But in a month or so I had "punched out" and went reluctantly on my way. (Which was where?)

Actually, I went through to the end of the semester and when I made my various goodbyes there were some deeper goodbyes being made. But still I thought maybe I would come back to school. I had nowhere else really to go, I thought.

The summer was something else, and was actually prelude or preface to another stage of my life that began much later. But I spent some time that summer going to the Village, in New York. I hadn't known anything at all about Greenwich Village, but now a guy I'd run track with and idolized in high school, Stephen Korret, was rumored to be living there and being "weird." I did not know around what this weirdness manifested but I was vaguely interested. But somehow we got invited to a party, a dude named Willie Washington and I. His sister Cynthia really interested me, but Willie was a new acquaintance. I met him, I think, through Joe Brown. Willie was very hip, always clean, was interested in and followed the music. I saw him at a few parties I went to. Another guy I knew was trying to be an architect and had an apartment on Hillside Place painted all black. He was part of it. It had to do with music and maybe painting, I didn't know. With some kind of social adventure I couldn't quite piece together. A face here and there, a name. I was at a party then and Cynthia was there. I tried to see her a couple times that summer. But at this party she was enthralled by Korret, who was now tall, slender, dark as he had been, very dark, but bearded. I remember digging the beard, what it gave to his face.

I had remembered him a slim half-miler in high school, city champ one year. Then rumor had it he had started living with a girl, her name was Cynthia too, but not Willie's sister. Then he started getting beat and seemed out of shape. This is what the scuttlebutt was around the locker room. The fact that those kinds of rumors could be spread about him, true or not, made him even more fascinating from my point of view, though he always kept me at more than arm's length. I was younger and screwy as hell I guess.

But that summer I was drifting into something else of complete unintelligibility, to me. Me and Willie hung and a couple of other guys. I tried to press his sister and she seemed willing but in a way unavailable. But it was probably me, cause I was twisted up inside in so many ways. Who knows what I sounded like or looked like or seemed to want? I might have thought I was saying one thing but something distinctly else was coming out.

I think I might have gone over to Steve Korret's house with Cynthia one day. Korret was "married" or maybe really married, I didn't know. It didn't matter. His wife was a black Canadian who'd lived in Newark for a few years and they'd come to the Village to live. Steve Korret was the talk of one aspect of one part of one circle of Newark's college-aged youth. Cynthia and I rode the subway that day and she had on some sandals with a little flower that came out between her toes where the strap was. I really dug those, and the way her feet looked in them. We'd talked when I came up to see Willie, and then I was coming up to see her and Willie, and then came up to see her alone. But Willie and I were still tight. We were cool with something else rolling in us. What? The music? He talked about painting. I knew nothing about that. He had some books I knew nothing about. Or maybe just enough to talk surface about. But now Cynthia and I sat up in Steve Korret's bright orange and white apartment on Bedford Street. And he talked, in an English accent, and she was very impressed. So was I, really. Plus his wife, Lita, was very slender and brown and lovely, with an accent that was her real Canadian one and that was fascinating. They had a wall of books in the apartment that I glanced at but that was all. Somehow we were speeding through this visit, though it obviously pleased Steve to impress us. But I had the feeling of being rushed out and suddenly we were outside starting home. I had heard some words I didn't understand, some I did, but in new contexts, from people who lived outside of Newark, I mean way outside of Newark, and maybe in what? Another world?

In the fall I returned to Howard, but I couldn't get back in school. I knew that anyway, but went down just for the trip, I guess. Just to see people coming back to school. September, the fall. I like the new tweeds and flannels dudes wear then. The raincoats and hats. The briskness of the air without its being a menace. The clarity of it, the seeming clarity of it.

I wandered around campus a day with nothing really to do once I was certain I was being put out. I could come back next semester or the next year, if I could go somewhere else and pull up my chemistry grades. But I gave not even a small shit about chemistry, except not giving a shit carried a penalty which I only began to understand. I hadn't known any other kind of life but a student life.

I bumped into friends, mob members mostly, and told them some crisscrossed stuff about why I wasn't coming back. Rip was with a group and said, "Hey, look at bohemy look at bohemy." And I realized then that my trips to the Village were known about and not only that but had been *judged*, by one group. "Hey, look at this little beard " and he plucked at a little nothing growth of peach fuzz on my chin. I had never shaved or had reason to. Maybe since seeing Steve Korret's beard the idea of it had poked out at the point of my chin. That's the only explanation I got, I certainly didn't think I had any beard.

Some more bantering, distorted discussions, lies, bullshitting, and laughter and I felt myself leaving, waving for real and now in my head waving at that place. What had I learned? A great many things, most of which I could not speak about. I had not the tools. For one thing we were being made sick. We were being gathered with the fondest motives but being made sick. (And I was not with the sickest, or only a few.) The brownness of me, in me, I certainly had been touted off of and me always yearning for an even darker explanation. At least that was what had been my measure, the blue/black streets of Newark. The gray steel of its relentless hardness. Love, for me, was music and warmth, high-pitched sounds and jagged or regular heavy grinding rhythms. It was collective and so dark you had to tighten yourself up to look it in the eyes. Stop your shakin'. Is that the way you want your hat to look? Is this the way you want to walk? How you sound? On the real sound, who did you sound like, the yellow picnic churchboy alien or the smooth blue rolling down the streets laughing at your collective hipness? (It was always dangerous, in Newark, to be alone! Or anywhere else.)

We'd been readied for the blowout, the vertical sweep up to sunkissed heaven. It was clothes and words and postures, the seeking of a secular Jordan. In coldly sociological terms, under national oppression, it was the Sisyphus myth given numbers to chart the exact degree of pain. Or ants piling up tidbits of zero to build the Empire State Building, and then not even own it. But the piling-up motion was all. We were not even being taught to pile up, like the common petty capitalist of the xenophobically abused South and East Europeans. All we were being readied for was to *get in*, to be a part of the big ugly which was that ugly because it would never admit us in the first motherfucking place! We were being taught integration and nothing of the kind existed. If so, why were we here in the second motherfucking place? We were readied for a lie as a lie. We were readied for yellow and the best of us were black and brown. We were read-ied for utopia and that is bullshit in the third motherfucking place. Only craziness could be the result. (E. Franklin Frazier was on leave when I was in school. Locke had retired. Sterling Brown taught his best classes unoffi-cially on his own time.)

We were not taught to think but readied for superdomestic service. (Su-per to who?) The school was an employment agency at best, at worst a kind of church. Hypnosis was employed. Old cult practices. Collective individualism. A church of class and caste conceit. Church of the yalla jeeeesus. And so we worshiped there and loved it.

HU was the great launching pad of the flight to this God's heaven. The launching pad of the projected verticality. The pimple of pretended progress by the "colored" few. But because within that desire is a legitimate need by the whole black of us to *rise up in reality*, the sugar and butter on white bread sandwich can get over to some extent in places you wouldn't expect.

So you say, Come on, prove the pathology, Jonesy.

My roommate became a Secret Service man. After playing a little pro-fessional baseball (double or triple A) he was magnetized to the "good job," some place he could use the muscle and continue to drink the excitement of the field. And so he's been a field man, going ahead to make certain that various cities are safe for the president. To see if all the known nuts have been sequestered or are under surveillance, like his old roommate. He has been in the protective entourage for Johnson, Nixon, Ford, Carter, Reagan. He who slept on the other side of the room.

At least five of us became generals, and many more at lower levels. An admiral or two. Reagan's top Negro. Agnew's top Negro. Negroes at all levels of state bureaucracy and madness. Negroes in the society pages. Negroes grinning just behind the robbin' hood on television strewn through the pages of our ebony sepia hue jet Afro-defender dam news. Mostly hugging a lie and laughing or hugging a laugh and lying. — He works for She works for He's the first Negro to murder white people for bigger white people You remember whassaname, well she Remember whatnot, he got they got we got Still masquerading at the top of a hill distant silhouettes removed from the blue/black streets of our collective reality. The cheap little political manipulators and bureaucrats gesturing hypnotically in black people's faces promising freedom but delivering more bondage. The yellow rat on a chain dancing for the slave masters' amusement as "the best" of "the worst."

(And do not intentionally misunderstand, the black schools have taught most of us. What we have of value and what we must despise. We did not even consider these other folks at these white schools as being in it. They've got their own sad stories to tell! You bet. Howard. The barbarians at Lincoln. Fisk. Hampton. We fought with the niggers at Morgan and broke folding chairs over their heads. In our crackpot little elitist world, if you didn't go to these schools you wasn't even in the world. No, really. You wasn't even in the world. But what did we know?)

I turned with tears in my eyes and whispered so that I couldn't even hear it in my brain, Goodbye!!

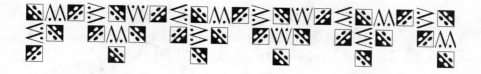

Five

Error Farce

I was completely unslung. Disconnected. I was isolated before, sometimes I seemed even to enjoy it. I never understood it. But I knew I was somehow "alone" even in the middle of a loud bunch.

Sometimes I felt nutty. Sometimes just stupid. Like how could I flunk out of school, who had never had any problems in school? I was supposed to be some kind of prodigy (I never understood why). I could read early, they said, and I had some kind of early verbal skills. I even won a spelling bee in grammar school during the summer program and that was in the paper. The news of scholarships in the colored papers. The Gettysburg Address in a boy scout suit, etc.

But now I didn't know what to think. I'd flunked out of school. All the people I knew were in school. The old Cavaliers and Hillside Placers, where were they? I didn't even know how I would relate now. I had been shot so full of yellow. Pumped so full of middle-class fakery. That was my partial perception though I certainly hadn't raised it to the theoretical level. I was going on touch and sound and smell, moving on vague feelings.

I came back home but didn't go out. I had to do something. I didn't think I could be walking Newark's streets when I was supposed to be in school, and I couldn't even explain it. What had happened or what I felt.

I talked to a few people. Maybe if I'd gone back over to New York, something else would've happened. But I didn't think that. That was all too vague for me. I didn't even have an understandable pattern.

So, for some reason, I joined the air force. I did. It sounded weirder and weirder all the time. But in those few days that all this went down, I justified it. It was something I could grasp at some level. It was escape.

The streets, the thoughts of Howard, pressed me. I didn't know what my parents thought. My grandmother. My sister. Relatives. I never thought clearly about it, I just acted. That was how I could get away, get off these streets, disappear again, and be somewhere other than being stared at by people who were putting together their own explanations of what had happened to me.

So I went down to Broad Street to the recruitment station. The common (dumb) understanding among the young college-age youth was that the army was shit but the air force was OK. Who started that lie need to be . . . but maybe it ain't a lie, or probably the thing should go, the army is shit and the air force is, too.

Going down there and waiting, then standing amid those strange unrelated kids unnerved me too. I had no idea of what that would be. I looked around the room quietly, depressed more than I had ever been because it seemed now suddenly as if I was being swept down the sewer or something. I could see no recognition in any of the other faces. They probably saw none in mine. A practiced observer would have seen pain in mine, though. I could not see pain in the other faces, just reaction to the various subdued stimuli.

We had to take an oath. We were quiet, unconnected, a few kids mumbled. We were taken to a bus; I'd brought a few clothes. When I's told my immediate family, I didn't think there was any undue concern I could see. But my grandmother told me to take care of myself. That whatever I did, do it the best way I could. My mother looked sadder than most times I've seen her. My father grabbed my arm and said write, let us know how you're doing and where you are. My sister looked tearful. And I'd gone down to where the swearing-in was.

When the bus pulled out, rolling through grey Newark, I remembered it was the day before my twentieth birthday and the city was quickly behind us.

Sampson Air Force Base was cold, grey, ugly, resembling nothing but empty hopelessness. No one sang "Off we go into the wild blue yonder." Pat O'Brien did not greet us (or maybe he did). Nor was there any other memorable background music, though later that was taken care of. I was in basic training now. We went through the usual—the haircut, the giving up of our clothes, the issue of fatigues and uniform and other equipment. For weeks we would be trained to be in the air force. I was there from October until just before Christmas.

What was most impressive about the service and especially basic training was how quickly any self-esteem was erased and with what dispatch one was transformed from Mister Whoever to nobody at all. And for me having fallen from the great yellow tower of upward to everything (admittedly a lie, but that was known only partially at that time by me) to the ground of least concern was a rude jolt to my tender sensibilities.

The class and caste shaping that the Capstone gives tells you you're somebody great even if that caste and class madness is beating your ass with its open and implied exclusion every day. I mean you can know that the little yalla boys and girls or the med and dent students are "igging" you and be igged and conscious (to the degree you *are* conscious) of it, but still because you are even permitted to let that house slave artifaction pass gas in your face (AS TRAINING, BOY, TO READY YOU FOR THE WHITE FOLKS) you feel like somebody special. Some extra-cool Nigra passing through the streets of yon ghettoes. We were permitted to float a sixteen-millionth of an inch off the ground—of course we thought it was slightly higher—as chosen Negroes of the yalla god. But bam whap mash like Jack Palance as the mad magician fell out of the tower to show he was *not* God (God was with Paul Newman and them) we were dashed to the hard ground by some social mishap like this. Was that what my grandfather and them felt like, having been thrown out of the nigger bourgeoisie all the way to the lower middle class? I see. It's rough, as Conrad Lynn would say. Rough!

Because now I found myself in crowds of people going nowhere. Or being rushed to someplace where you then had to wait for hours. For what? Nothing you would like or give a shit for. You were always standing with groups of boys your own age, black and white, not knowing what was going on. Having to do things thought of by what dumb motherfucker? (You might think that if you could raise up enough energy to put such an edge on!) Mostly you just dragged to the next place. Submitted to the next indignity, colorless and dull. You were herded and crowded and pushed and pulled and talked stupidly to and disregarded or harassed.

At first we were just run around and walked around and only a few dead-ass directions, "instructions," were given to us. It was definitely a kind of punishment. You got that early, if you were awake. It was a penalty—every-thing, walking, running, standing, waiting. The only humor provided those first days, except the jokes we began to make after we could feel at least our common lot, was the food. Eating was funny! I mean you sat and were confronted suddenly with this *stuff*. You would turn and look at some dude you didn't even know and he would be looking back at you, at first shyly, then after a few of these displays and performances, more casually, and grin. The grin got wider. In a week, there was laughter. Not gay, not grim, but a nervous release. An alternative to the banal pushing and standing and waiting and rushing to nowhere that went on otherwise.

"Like what is this shit?" we would whisper finally. "Have you tasted this shit? Wow!" I think this conversation went on initially among the most sensitive and intelligent. That's how we could tell each other. Some others would just keep their head down and ladle it in. But that was something else that was at least for me part of the penalty that the "army" is. You can find some motherfuckers in the service dumb as their surroundings, dumber than the chairs and tables. The table could get up and leave some of them there holding the food. Naturally, on the food trip, the blood relation was strongest because the food was also not only bad but the complete oppo-site of their national cuisine. Tasteless, bland, gravyless. You could pour a ton a salt on some of the shit and it would suck it in like the Blob. So they would grumble and talk shit about it first, rolling their eyes at each other.

After a couple weeks of being walked and run and dragged around we got to recognize a few faces among us (a few had come in together) and we'd venture some exploratory phrases. It is the same general process, I guess, in any structure of society at any level. How the herd gets sectioned off. How friends are made, acquaintances. Sometimes you can only get close to some people in situations like the one you meet them in. In any other situation, you might not have anything to say to that person at all. It was like that for me in Barringer, Central Ward, Howard, and now the process was unfolding again at Sampson Air Force Base, Geneva, New York.

In situations which are ostensibly mixed like the service, you can also see the national character define the various groups that form. And within those national forms, regional forms, the culture pinpointing itself. So for the most part the blacks hang out with the blacks, the whites with the whites, and northern and southern contingents of each larger group also tend to hang together.

In basic I found myself with bloods from South Jersey mostly, for some reason. Dudes from Camden and Trenton, mostly black dudes looking for a way off the streets. Trying to keep out from under the final bust. Seeing in that air force blue some trace of sky that they might get away in.

So the friend, acquaintance, "buddy" it's called in the service, thing gets hooked up like it always does. Around common experience (which might just be only the one you find yourself in then), common desires or understanding or even common misunderstanding. Certainly, most of us, after just a few weeks, knew we had made a terrible mistake to come in "this shit" and began the drawn-out mumbling and grumbling that goes on in the service as long as most of us are in.

In a couple of weeks whenever we were herded or whenever we would be run somewhere to wait ("Hurry up and wait," we called it) I would be more and more with a specific group of dudes. I guess another collective formed basically for defense and commiseration. You had to have somebody (if you were at all well) to talk bad about the shit to and to hear them talk bad about the shit. So that you knew you were still alive in the world and not in some hell of your own imagination.

We were not nationalists but we thought white dudes mostly presented a problem. They were the ones in power, in authority, or that wanted to act like they were. They were the ones who would give you the most hassle even if they were just Airman Nostripe, Airman Basic like ourselves. Though some, obviously, were better than that. For the most part the black troops, while not looking for prejudice or racism or bias or any bullshit and not carrying an excessively large chip on their shoulders, would invariably come to face all that bad shit just by being somewhere alive.

The service itself is such bullshit that the white noncoms and officers because they are the face of that authority, the "reasoning" behind that structure, are identified with it and are responsible for its stupidity and ugliness. What mitigates that somewhat is that there are white boys in there, too, catching hell and complaining just like us, and the louder they complained the closer we'd be to them. But the ones who thought the shit was good or correct or to be obeyed to the letter we thought of as simpleminded shitheads and said they better keep their ass over the fuck where they was and away from us.

Roy and Henry were two dudes that I got closest to. Two black dudes with conked heads (which the people made them cut out) straight out of the Camden ghetto. Roy never played nothing, no sports or anything, just cards. He was one of those dudes that wore a chain with his fatigues from his belt into one pocket, looped like he had on a zoot suit. He rolled his fatigue pants tight on the bottom so the knees would droop and take on a draped look. The dude always carried a knife no matter what the activity. He was a nice smiling cat could talk shit with the best, but he was not to be played with.

His man Henry (they had known each other on the streets and agreed to come in together to escape a bust for something) was a tall straight athletic dude with a short fuse. When Roy went off, death was imminent. Henry was always going off and threatening people. Plus thay had a few dudes they walked with, actually we walked with, from down around that neck of the woods. A big fat dark dude who cracked jokes all the time and was always getting into trouble with the training instructors or somebody. I think his name was Humphrey. No, that wasn't his name. We called him Humphrey cause that was a big fat dude in Joe Palooka comics. Humphrey didn't like to be called Humphrey. Sometimes we called him Humph when we were in normal relationships; sometimes we called him Humph when we wanted to bruise his gigantic ego (Humphrey thought he was strong); or when we wanted him to go crazy, on anybody but Roy and Henry who he had the good sense not to mess with, we'd call him, very sweetly, Humph rey, Oh, Humph rey! and he would chase us.

But I think I was quieter and silenter than I had been on the outside. That's my recollection. I would joke and make fun and advance the sardonic perception I'd grown up with to punctuate our collective perception of the joint, but I was quieter, more internal now. I don't think I was quite as loose-lipped as at HU, though I still had an acid tongue. Maybe because it was a different crowd, with reality mashed down on us like an elephant big as the sky. Our illusions were different—they could not be the hysterical yellow-feather brand the Capstone gave out. They were more cautious, less advertised (by us). I cannot say we were illusion-free, otherwise we would not have been there in the fourth motherfucking place.

We were orphans in the storm, come from our various other illusions to this nowheresville way up in the north woods. They called it the Finger Lakes region. The closest big city was Rochester and we couldn't go there until much later in our basic training. It was very cool when we got there and in a couple of weeks it was cold as hell. Thanksgiving Day 1954 I sat huddled in front of a fake airplane in the middle of a storm, practicing guard duty. As I sat there, completely invisible under the blinding torrents of snow, I thought I had reached the absolute bottom, the nadir, of my life. I thought I was being tortured. In this freezing dismal place I stood freezing for what reason? Why? It was a payback for my stupidity and lack of seriousness. I've never felt sorrier for myself.

We were out on bivouac during the storm, so when I was relieved of guard duty to eat I came back into the general bivouac area and hundreds of us squatted in the snowstorm and ate cold turkey under congealed gravy. Happy Thanksgiving, you dumb motherfuckers, everything seemed to be saying!

We lived in open-bay barracks and slept in double-decker bunks with our footlockers, in which we had all our earthly possessions, at either end of the bunks. Henry and I bunked together, Roy right next door and Humphrey on top of him. We had a little ghetto right in the barracks, though there were other bloods sprinkled around as well.

Those first weeks we rose at 03:27 when it was jet black outside and the wind raged. We staggered into the latrines to wash up—some dudes never changed their underwear—then made up our beds and lined up for the first quick inspection. Then marched off toward the mess hall (certainly an accurate name) to grin at the catastrophe of breakfast.

I developed a funny kind of reputation. I'm not sure what it was in toto but among the black troops I hung closest with, since I could always come up with some answer to the strangest phenomena which we encountered, they felt that was positive. I could understand certain terms and relationships, certain procedures, and would in turn translate the bureaucratese into direct black language. And the general obscurity, at a certain level, necessary to disguise the fact that the American Nightmare is what really exists, not no Dream, I could penetrate these dull surfaces because of my lightweight education and brown training up off the common streets. Roy said one day, "It's like having a goddam dictionary or encyclopedia with you." And I took that as my greatest compliment.

The other half of that was problematic. I was cordial with most of the white troops around us. Basic was fairly transient, so some of the deeper conflicts I later experienced when I got to where I finally was going did not quite surface. But there was some square-head, bland-faced, sky-blue-eyed white boy from Mississippi who was describing something and said, "Nigger." His name was Hall. But he apologized and said he was used to talking like that but was sorry. I didn't even answer and he put out his hand. I walked away. And whenever he saw me he would color, turn red, and try to grin.

One of the dudes who came up with us, a tall husky blond Polish dude, was made an assistant flight commander of our training flight and he took it just the way he was supposed to. He became part of the structure and chugged along calling cadence when the TI's let him, like he was high up in the shit. We just looked at him and then at each other and grimaced. There was some kind of disorder around something, somebody going in other people's footlockers or a stinking white boy who was thrown in the shower with all his clothes on and scrubbed with scrub brushes and Octagon soap and Henry figured in it some way. In fact, the white boy, Stenkowski, had probably never liked the way Henry and Roy and I acted in the joint, we were so openly hostile to the system itself. From almost the moment we got in it we were trying to beat it any fucking way we could. And it was very obvious now that Stenkowski liked the shit, even more so now that he had been raised up in it.

So he said something to Henry and Henry told him he would cut his fucking head off and stuff it in the motherfucking toilet! He left Henry alone. He said something to Roy and Roy did not even answer, he cocked his eye up at him and slid his hand very slowly into his pocket. So the dude acted like he hadn't said shit to Roy neither. He walked away.

But the next day at the morning inspection he comes over to me and I'm standing half asleep as usual and he says to me out in front of everybody, "Jones, why don't you stand up and be a man?" He goes in my footlocker next and uncovers from under the regulation bullshit Eliot's *Selected Poetry*, Dylan Thomas, some other stuff. He holds the stuff up, the TI and his assistant are walking with him this morning. He says, "You like this stuff?" Holding the books up like his own dirty drawers.

I said simply, "Yes." The TIs, a long thin-nosed Polish sergeant named Konuz and a short blond drunk whose name I never remembered, stepped over to look, grin, then toss the books back. Stenkowski meant to embarrass me or show the flakiness of one of the hated little trio—maybe disrupting the little defense group we'd hooked up. But those dudes knew I read "way out" shit. That's all they had to say about it when I was reading it. But it was my business, and how otherwise could you be a dictionary or encyclopedia? Henry balled up his fist and showed it to Stenkowski and Stenkowski tried to let Konuz see it but Henry wasn't no fool. Stenkowski had to move up into the special part of the barracks where the TI's had their office. But I set a new base record for KP, pulling it some twenty times before we got out of there.

It was almost twenty-four hours of stinking labor. Report at two in the morning to the mess hall. Work till almost two the next morning. Throwing slop in the trays, washing the trays, moving the garbage cans, cleaning out the grease pit (a particularly nasty task reserved for the troublemakers), mopping and sweeping the floor, stopping only to eat and drink the coffee or Kool-Aid. All the time in that mess hall the jukebox is playing. In those days the country and western tune "I'm in the Jailhouse Now" kept playing; I almost wept. Or what about Patty Paige singing "We'll Be Together Again"? It was deadly. And at the end of your day, completely covered with foul-smelling grease, dead tired, you'd wander back toward your barracks and fall out completely exhausted.

Before I got out of basic training I caught the crabs and didn't even know it until I went on the one leave I got, going alone to Rochester and staying in a hotel, and they itched me so bad I took off my clothes and looked closely and was horrified—really my blood ran cold, I'd never been exposed to shit like that. Though most of the troops took it lightly.

I had smuggled a grey flannel suit and red belt and corduroy vest up in basic training. You weren't supposed to have civilian clothes there. But somebody found my hiding place, I think it was the short, drunken assistant TI, and they got ripped off. I never went to town again because I'd have to wear the uniform. There was nothing in my life before or since like the feeling of hopelessness as I watched Staff Sergeant Konuz turn and step or teach us how to march or salute. In his nasal dead voice and water-blue sightless eyes. His starched pants and cap. His policeman's coldness and casual racism and ignorance. He was my leader. I had to do what he said, what he ordered. But the days did pass, not fast enough, but they passed, they did pass. And I found myself going back home just before Christmas, with one stripe on my arm, having successfully completed basic training.

I was sent for some reason to Chanute Air Field in Rantoul, Illinois. I was to be enrolled in weather school. Their aptitude tests said I was supposed to be a weatherman. A radiosonde operator or rawinsonde operator to be exact. Which meant I was trained to send helium-filled balloons aloft and, looking through an instrument like the surveyor's transit, chart the airspeed and direction, air temperature and pressure. I was supposed to work at a weather station or at an airport, going out to check the little white weather shack with its latticed sides and slanted roof. (You can see these little white shacks at airports out near the runway.) I didn't mind this idea really. Weathermen in the air force had weird kinds of hours. You usually worked three days on, two days off, or something like that, so it was not the normal nine-to-five day. The three days you worked you stayed out at the airport or at the weather station and didn't go home and sometimes you would be at out of the way places, Greenland or the Azores or somewhere wild. It seemed OK to me. Even the isolation, though I did not want to go to Greenland. Thule, Greenland! But then, that was so legendary that I wouldn't even have minded that. But that did not happen.

There were only whites in my training squadron now. And some of the others, maybe all of them, had some college. I guess that's why they'd chosen us for weather school. And I guess that's why there were no other blacks in that squadron. And in some ways it felt like Barringer again. And, Jim, that part of Illinois is a crime in itself. Flat and hostile, like the real South crept up on you. Southern Illinois: towns like Kankakee, Champaign-Urbana, Decatur. Stuck halfway between Chicago and St. Louis. (When I could I started to go to Chicago every weekend and stay at Kurt's house and roam around the South Side near the University of Chicago.)

But that was a strange place altogether, and for me especially. The dead of winter, in little wooden barracks heated by coal furnaces. (It turned out later, in a heavy scandal, that the brother of the commanding general owned the coal company, which is why the base heating system had never been converted. Meanwhile they had one of us per barracks each week keeping the coal furnaces stoked, and if we let them go out we'd get court martialed.)

The same disconnection and isolation characterized my stay at Chanute. And the first days were even worse, certainly now that I was just among white dudes again. As isolated and lonely as I might feel among bloods, to be the lone spot in the buttermilk is totally a drag. You have to assume a whole other character, just to communicate! You must speak a different language, adjust culturally, stay at a point of tension in which there can be no real relaxation.

Before our first test I went into the latrine and studied the materials. The next day I got a perfect paper, 100. It was pronounced with such weightiness the entire class looked around at me; I was surprised, but better, it made me feel somewhat restored after my heavy defeat in school. Maybe I was not totally stupid.

After that there were a few white guys who'd come around the bunk to check up on why I'd gotten that perfect paper. A blond jock with a perfect German crew cut, a good-natured All American named Van Allison. Two ex-college dudes, one the hypertypical Ivy specimen, University of Maine, named Kreeger, and a short swarthy guy from the University of Maryland named Voster. (Hey, were all these guys German or something?) Kreeger, Voster, and I did some running close by the base. A few bars. We kept up a more or less steady conversation, though as I said, my conversational form had retreated somewhat. Kreeger had the classic "Princeton cut" and wore plain toes, grey flannel slacks, and blue button-down oxford shirts with the sleeves rolled up. He had a real Maine accent and was really a nice guy. He'd gotten tossed out for something and his obsession seemed to be to get back into the Ivy. Voster was a self-proclaimed intellectual, wanted to be a science major of some kind. I don't know how he ever got into the air force. (But then I don't know how I got in either, now!) It was a funny trio when engaged. Kreeger, off-the-top Ivyisms; Voster, deep mock-probing philosophical; and whatever the fuck I was then. That was a college-type intellectual hookup, but bright enough and interesting in that context.

Later, I ran into a guy named Strassbaugh (another German?) who was in another squadron. He was the first hip white boy I met. Strass liked jazz and talked like a blood. He wanted to play saxophone and always talked about it. He was always looking for someplace to practice. And the "squares" and "farmers" that made up a large part of our companions in arms constantly drove Strass to distraction. He was always cussing out some "farmer" or "square" and I was one of the only dudes I ever saw him with. Strass couldn't stand Voster. "Little square cat!" But Kreeger was all right though Strass was always raising one eyebrow at some of Kreeg's Ivyisms. Strass and I went into Champaign-Urbana looking for music one night, like trying to ice skate in Death Valley.

There were two bloods I knew fairly well. One, a guy from one of the maintenance squadrons, was in the mold of my running buddies in basic and Hillside Place. But he got further advanced in training and was gone in a minute. The other guy was really out. I met him one time at the University of Illinois library, where I started going from time to time. I even started taking a couple of courses, General Psychology 1 and 2, and got good grades. We walked back to the base talking. He was carrying a thick Dostoyevsky under his arm, *The Brothers Karamazov*. I never saw him without that.

John Karamazov (I'm lying about his last name) saw me coming toward the library a few days later and the maintenance brother was with me, Jerry, in his civvies, which were bright as tomorrow. Karamazov and I, of course, were dressed in less color—in honor of our training. We were headed for the university's weekly movie showing which some of the base intellectuals would make and John leans over and whispers in my ear, "Who is that person?" referring to Jerry. He was lucky I didn't tell Jerry or he would've found out. But that's the kind of guy John was. He was slender and stiff, he wore sweaters then but later he was always in a suit.

John became very wealthy later in New York, after an early fling at a respectable bohemianism. I think he married four different white women and was last heard of (by me) living in a penthouse on Park Avenue (he'd made money in advertising, one of the first black advertising agencies), but rumor had it at last hearing that he'd lost his bux. But then he was roaming around in southern Illinois in the error farce too. I never found out why.

The weather squadron I was in had a strange collection of types. But, thinking about it, I'm wondering why so many Germans? Aside from the friendly dudes I mentioned, there was also a straight-out Nazi. Not just philosophically, this guy had been a glider operator in the goddam German army, the goddam Luftwaffe. Now he was becoming an American citizen. I guess, if you can't beat 'em, etc. His name was Helmut Meisler and he sat on his bed, mostly, shining his boots and writing letters. He came on like he was intelligent, but with no real evidence except what came out of his mouth as assertion. And that was just irritating. Stiff and blond, be looked and sounded like a fucking Nazi, though he never said any out of the way shit, to me.

But he did get people up in arms about some anti-Jewish shit he'd said, in his usual "I can smile it's so obvious" manner, to this guy named Lewis Felzer, a thin spider-skinny blond Jewish boy. Meisler had said that yes, Jews were inferior, he believed it, and Germans superior. I didn't hear this directly, but they were all ranged around the barrack when Strassbaugh and John and I come in from somewhere. Meisler had just said this and he's continuing to polish his fucking boots. People are standing around him, not quite menacing but very very interested in the statement. A Dutch guy, an ex-pilot in the Netherlands air force, is sitting watching, his pipe in his mouth. He wore Dutch pilot's wings. Meisler wore glider operator's wings. A wild set. Kreeger and Voster were also there standing. Voster, it turns out, was indeed Jewish, a German Jew. And he's working himself up, like wringing his hands. And Felzer is wide-legged, agitated around the mouth, his eyes like spinning around in his skull. But Meisler's talking normally, matter-of-factly. "I told you what I think is the truth. There's no reason for anyone to have to believe it."

Voster was trying to agitate, but he really didn't know how. Kreeger tells me what's happening. John makes a noise, blowing air out his mouth with his tittering little laughter. (John didn't really like white people, or I should say white men, though he emulated the shit out of them. But to him it *was* funny!)

But I sure as hell knew how to agitate, that was my trade, it turns out. "Well, how come if you superior, everybody kicked y'all's ass?" says I from the back of the almost crowd. The light laughter broke the spell. Meisler turns and looks at me, smiling.

"That's a good question," he says. "But how do you know you have?"

"You in the goddam American army. You surrendered and then joined the conquerors." Felzer hadn't said anything. He just stared at Meisler like he couldn't understand what was being said.

"But I was not making a speech." Meisler still did not look irritated. He was smooth. In wartime I would have killed him immediately. "And certainly I was not talking to you." That was as aggressive as he wanted to make it. But it was OK with me if he took it even further out, but I knew he wouldn't.

At this point Strassbaugh says in the loose singsong of the white bebopper, "Say, man, why don't you carry that square-ass shit back to the Third Reich or whatever that shit was called. We got enough problems over here as it is without no goddam Nazis. Shit!" Strass had said it like he was talking to an annoying security guard who was stopping him from getting into Bop City or something. Squares and farmers were always doing something to Strass.

The crowd had indeed formed, thickened would be the word. Our words had drawn the others together and they stood glaring a little at Meisler, who now returned to polishing his shoes. After a while he said, "I'm not going to say anything else."

Later we tried to get Felzer to bounce one of those metal bunk legs off Meisler's head but Louie was still quiet and just generally drugged that the shit had even come up. Voster told us the guy was sick. Kreeger agreed but also agreed Felzer should bounce something off his head. It was discussed briefly that maybe somebody else should. Strass said he'd be glad to but we thought it wasn't a cool idea. Meisler never said anything else I heard, not even good morning, the whole time we were there.

I would go up to Chicago as often as I could on the weekends. A bus from Rantoul up to Chicago, or the train. The train was better. I might walk up under the El and check out the loud blues life. I went to see T-Bone Walker one night at the Crown Propeller. Kurt a couple times had some people over and he introduced me to some. We talked, the two of us, about Howard. The semester before was his last one and he was trying to figure out what law school to go to. But I also ran a lot by myself as I was wont to. I snaked through the South Side and up to near North.

One time I was drifting around the South Side, near the University of Chicago, feeling alone, as usual, isolated, as usual, my usual emotional stock in trade, and I bumped into this bookstore called the Green Door. It had a green door, and kind of orange plastic in the window so the sun wouldn't ruin the books. I came to rest staring into the window. There were books there I didn't recognize, a few I did. Like we'd had *Portrait of the Artist* my first year at Rutgers and I'd looked at it, but it was a *school* book and for that reason I didn't take it seriously. Though parts of it vaguely fascinated me even then. A copy of this was in the window, and next to it *Ulysses*, the book opened to the first page so you could see the words "Stately plump Buck Mulligan " I stared at the words and tried to read them. I saw other books, Pound, Eliot, Thomas, philosophy books, art books, statistics, and poetry. Something dawned on me, like a big lightbulb over my noggin. The comic strip *Idea* lit up my mind at that moment as I stared at the books. I suddenly understood that I didn't know a hell of a lot about anything. What it was that seemed to move me then was that learning was *important.* I'd never thought that before. The employment agency I'd last gone to college at, the employment agency approach of most schools I guess, does not emphasize the *beauties* the absolute *joy* of learning. That is what came to me. Cut off as I was from the artificial concept of education, I suddenly appreciated what real education might be. I vowed, right then, to learn something new everyday. It was a deep revelation, something I felt throughout my whole self. I was going to learn something everyday. That's what I would do. Not just as a pastime, something to do in the service, but as a life commitment.

I went in and bought some books. *Portrait of the Artist* and Thomas's *Portrait of the Artist as a Young Dog.* In a couple of weeks I bought *Ulysses.* But I went home this first time in a daze, having leaped past myself, to myself. All kinds of new connections yammered in my head. My heart beat faster; my skin tingled. I could understand now a little better what was happening. I needed to learn. I wanted to study. But I wanted to learn and study stuff I wanted to learn and study. Serious, uncommon, weird stuff! At that moment my life was changed.

Another month or so and I was leaving Chanute. I was glad, even though I'd met some people, but I did not see myself remaining too long in the flatlands of Middle America. Sometimes I felt like there were witches and devils out there. Plus every morning at about 4:30 the guy in charge of putting on the lights would throw them on and the switch was connected up with his own radio, which brought the "shitkickers," as Strass called them, at us full burst. At that time of the morning most of the city boys were not interested in country and western.

But I had been elected class leader in weather training school because of the high marks I received consistently and one time Airman of the Month, for the academics, not the soldiering. I even began to look forward to tech school ending and being sent somewhere as a weatherman, with lots of time to myself to pursue my newfound cause of learning, something every day! However, they pulled a trick on me of sorts. As the highest-finishing airman in the class I was given first choice, along with a few others, of where I would be shipped, out of a group of bases that needed weathermen. The choices were right outside D.C., which I seriously considered. If I had done that, no doubt I would've gone back to Howard. Bermuda was also mentioned, plus Germany, Okinawa, and Greenland. But the one I wanted was Puerto Rico. Actually it was a tight choice between the D.C. base (Andrews AFB), Bermuda, and Puerto Rico. The enlisted man scam had it that "Puerto Rico was a country club—light duty and good weather, cheap prices and fine women." Hey, dudes was saying, you need to take Puerto Rico. And that was that, my choice was Puerto Rico. "A country club." But little did I know.

In choosing Puerto Rico I had then to sign up to go to gunnery school down there and become not just the normal weatherman but a *weather gunner*. That is, I had volunteered to fly in B-36 bombers as a rawinsonde operator as well as a "right rear gunner." I hadn't wanted to fly when I came in, my early romance of flying had slipped by. At a certain point most boys want to soar through the sky, at least in my generation. So even after they dropped this "volunteering" on me (to pay you back for thinking you could actually *choose*) I was not drugged because I thought, Hey, I'll be flying after all. Even the gun shit was part of an old romantic image of tail gunners in the Second World War, chewing gum, cracking jokes, and firing at the enemy. But reality, my friends, is always something else again.

Plus, the "country club" that I'd signed for apparently *was* a country club. Or at least *had been* a country club until we got there. The gargoyles at Strategic Air Command had also heard the airman scuttlebutt about Ramey AFB and they were determined to do something about it. So they chose to start doing something about it the same time I got sent down there. Talk about some bad luck! (I wrote something about this in a play,

A *Recent Killing*.) The same time I arrived and a few other guys from Chanute, perhaps even the same day, the SAC commander sent his son-in-law (rumor had it) Bertram Harrison, a thirty-eight-year-old "insane" brigadier general, to clean the joint up. It seems that Ramey had the highest venereal disease rate in SAC, the lowest efficiency rating on the mock bombing raids that SAC stages pretending to bomb large cities in the U.S. and other places. So Harrison was sent down to "gung-ho" the base back in line and make us the efficient trained killers we were supposed to be.

Interestingly, since there was no world war when I was in the service, the general aura I encountered might be something found only in "peace" time, but I think not. At least it seems that way to me from other stories I've heard about the so-called esprit de corps in wartime. If anything, it's probably worse during wartime, when dudes think they might be getting killed for some bullshit they didn't have anything to do with.

I could see, once I got down there, how Ramey could and probably was being run on the casual side. The standard work uniform was white tee shirt and blue jeans and either the regular fatigue hat or, if you were in one of the flying squadrons, a baseball cap in your squadron's color. I was assigned to the 73rd Strategic Reconnaissance Squadron, which was later changed to the 73rd Bombardment Squadron. We wore blue baseball caps, though I never had one. I always wore my fatigue hat. (Except, strangely, there is a photo of me with the rest of my crew—the first crew I was on, N-45—standing with the rest of the troops with a baseball cap. But I don't remember owning one. I always wore my fatigue cap. Maybe it was borrowed for the flick. Or maybe it's not even really a baseball cap?)

Puerto Rico was the first permanent base I was assigned to. My first permanent assignment (it turned out to be my last). Before I went down I was given a short leave and I went home. I remember going to Steve Korret's house in the Village. He had a new wife now, Charlene, a beautiful dancer—she's now a slightly older but still beautiful novelist. We talked and he introduced me to various people, white and black, streaming through his house. (Or maybe this was after I had already gone to Puerto Rico for a time and then come back on leave. I'm not quite clear.) But I remember talking to a white painter named Norman who painted strange unconnected quasi figures that had mystical significance. A tall black woman painter, Virginia. A short dark man, a poet whose name was Karl. At any rate the visit I remember, Steve and his wife had to leave and left me there. I was reading something. I was leaving from his house directly for the airport and thence to Puerto Rico. I was sitting alone reading and musing, then I looked at the time and I had to go, if I was going to catch my plane. I put the book down. My duffelbag, packed full, was standing in the corner. I made ready to leave. I grabbed the bag and went to heave it up onto my shoulder as I had done many times before. But this time I couldn't move it! The duffelbag would not budge! You'll say, it was psychological. You didn't want to leave. Your mind was playing tricks on you. Be that as it may, I couldn't move the bag. I strained to get it up onto my shoulder and it would not move.

I panicked for a minute, then sat down. My hands were shaking! I said, out loud, I've got to pick up this bag. I've got to get back to the base or I'll be AWOL. I went on cajoling myself, pleading with myself, and finally I tried again and the bag came up easily. I hefted it up to my shoulder and went out the door, down the stairs, and got a cab to Idlewild Airport.

Because Ramey was a permanent base and a big SAC base, I met a buncha people. And they were from the various classes and sectors of the base. One thing, if you are at all serious about understanding this country, arrogantly called "this society," you'll see after any close investigation how absolutely structured according to class and caste it is in all areas. Nothing, no piece, of U.S. life escapes! It is a class society in every nook and cranny of its total existence. Its material base and its ideas. Its economic foundation and its institutional and ideological superstructure. And this was clearer to me in practice than it ever was in theory until very recently. I always dealt with it as it came up, as I had to or was able to deal with it (just like you!) but I didn't always call it anything. But as I got older I recognized it more and more clearly for what it was, class and caste divisions. The rich the middle the poor. The white the light the brown the black. Everywhere in you, America!

At Ramey, since I was in a flying squadron, I was again with mostly whites. The flying squadrons were the "high-class" groups on the base. Certainly the service makes all these things more obvious than ever before. There were officers and noncoms then enlisted men. That was the basic class structure, the fundamental hierarchy of the joint. And these were in all the squadrons, but the flying squadrons were tops, the upper class. Then came the maintenance squadrons and within that division there were divisions. Then underneath the maintenance squadrons the air police, then motor pool, then cooks or food service. Most of the blacks and other nonwhites were in food service, the motor pool, or maintenance. Only a few were in the flying squadrons. And this made some of the ones who were in them mad as all outdoors. Like the yellow madness of my childhood grew up and gone to college—now gone and joined the air force! I remember one Negro who never spoke to or was ever seen with any blood the whole time I was on that base. All he did was ride his motorcycle and sometimes ride his motorcycle with some white boys who rode motorcycles. I met the dude and he wasn't a bad dude, he was just crazy. He even talked like a white boy. But not the pursed lip stiff jaw of the academic white imitator. This guy "towked" like a working-class white boy from the Northeast. It amazed me. And even when the other bloods on the base would say funny things about this dude I would tell them (though I hadn't penetrated it down to theory level) that the dude was a nice cat, he was just out of his mind! I guess he talked to me because I was in a flying squadron too.

So again the relationships I developed were somewhat complex. I had friends, a lot of them white, in the flying squadron I was in as well as in the 60th Bomb and 301st Bomb. The 73rd, as I said, had blue baseball caps, the 60th red baseball caps, and the 301st yellow baseball caps. Dudes in other bomb squadrons I knew because we would go to gunnery school together or target study (studying Russian cities from aerial photos so you would get familiar with the cities you were going to bomb from high up in the air). We sometimes went to embarrassing harassings like so-called Character Guidance. Where they would march us down to the theater and teach us how to be good airmen and stop getting venereal disease, etc.

So I got to know guys from the different flying squadrons, but especially gunners and other weather gunners. There was a little group of white weather gunners I hung with, and other crew members. They were mostly good guys, young like I was, some younger, naive about life and brash enough not to give a shit too much about our racial and national distinctions. They were the kinda guys who talked about "roaring into town." They'd go steaming off the base and get staggering, falling-down, singing drunk and not even know where they'd been the next day. That was one group and sometimes I'd be with them puttin' away watered-down beer like there was no tomorrow and cracking stupid jokes. These were the kinda guys they mighta shown in the war movies but not corny like that. Burke, a French Canadian from up in New England. Reilly, a big red-faced Irish lad from Boston. Goodsen, a freckled-faced all-American Jew. Burset, a short, funny-grinning, perpetually joking and staggering Welsh American who aspired, he said, to the heaven of perpetual drunkenness. We greeted each other with shouts and there was always pushing and patting and horsing around. These guys were all good soldiers, good airmen, but they liked to have a good time and many times that's not possible playing war.

Another group was formed really around the painter, William White, a black dude from North Carolina. He was a weather gunner in the 301st and always wore the yellow baseball cap. Tall, introspective, and serious, White had a barracks room full of paintings when I first met him. He later went to New York to continue painting after first going to Howard, even though I warned him continually not to go to that sorry joint. Except my protestations must have seemed to him like a simple case of unrequited love. White became one of my best and closest friends in life. He died, still trying to paint, in New York, mixing methadone and whiskey.

But somehow one time I got to White's room. Oh, yeh, I'd met him in gunnery class not long after I came to Ramey. He'd come a little earlier. And the incident that brought us together was when some dude, a fat young white farm boy from Colorado I had known at Chanute (in fact it was he, Bodey, Clifton Bodey, who was in charge of snapping on the lights and hence the shitkicking sounds there in Illinois), pulled my chair out from under me one day in tech school, apparently thinking to make an imprac-tical joke. I wheeled on his ass and fired right into his face (not a gun but my bony brown fist). He staggered backward, a big question mark on his face. I said, "You didn't think I could hit that hard, did you?" Really, at a loss for words myself and half expecting him to make a sudden counterat-tack. For sure he hadn't gone down and one of the old bits of folk wisdom I remember has always said, if you throw your best and they don't go down it's time to get in the wind. But Bodey only pulled himself up straight, other dudes in the class laughed, and White was among them laughing his ass off into his hands.

I guess Bodey was too surprised to do anything. He said some things designed to give battle but since he just didn't charge and start throwing me on my ass (he must've outweighed me by about a hundred pounds) nothing happened and as it turned out Bodey and I never really became enemies, in fact he was closer to me than a lot of people. Because in a few months he had married a Puerto Rican prostitute about ten years older than he was (he was eighteen) and a lot of the dudes made fun of him for it, especially the white Southerners.

After that I would go to White's room a lot, since I had weird room-mates. We bunked three in a room, if you were lucky two, and all of that was considered luxury. The luxury of the flying squadrons since all the other squadrons still lived in open bay barracks. I think my first roommates were Bodey and a white guy looked like Steve McQueen, named Cooper, from somewhere in Tennessee. Cooper was a buck sergeant (three stripes), Bodey and I two stripes (airman second class). Cooper was the classic taciturn Southerner, probably filled with all the prejudice of that particular specimen but with the quiet dignity that made acting nasty about it impossible. Bodey was loud and wrong, naive and corny as the little Colorado farm he'd come from. He was every stereotype you could think up and more. He collected gun magazines and motorcycle magazines and girlie magazines (Cooper read these last ones too on occasion) but had nothing to do with guns, motorcycles, or women. He claimed to know all about cars and eventually he did get one, he got a motorcycle too (so did Cooper), and when Cooper finally shipped out going to another base I left Bodey there with a wife who spoke very little American and no English at all and two kids, one on the runway and one in the hangar (in airman talk), a stranger in a strange land, completely ignorant of reality.

So I had to go to White's room to hang out when I wasn't on the drinking bouts with Reilly and Burke and the others. White had collected a weird little group around him. They were mostly black though there was one white dude who hung around us, Vincent, a pudgy almost feminine Italian dude from the Bronx, with skin so white he looked like he never got in the sun even though we were in Puerto Rico. There was also an almost blond-haired Chicano dude named Lopa who looked like a white boy even to the close observer. It was only when he talked that you could hear the lilting syllabics of his accent and it still always amazed me when I thought that Lopa was a Mexican. This got Lopa in trouble before he got off that base too. Once in a bar some "farmers" were talking bad about "spics" and "greasers" in the charming official speech of the white American, and Lopa was leaning against the jukebox staring right into their mouths. I think there were three of these farmers. It was in Aguadilla, the closest town to Ramey, but in a bar frequented by a lot of airmen. Lopa let them know he was Chicano and that he didn't like what they said and that they were generally and unreconcilably full of shit. One guy went to throw on Lopa and Lopa cut him, across his face, sliced the shit out of him, leaving a scar, hideous and flaming, going from this farmer's ear down to the point of his chin. Lopa did almost a year in the stockade for this shit and when he got out he still had to do that year again in the regular service since that was looked at as "bad time"! But it was great when we walked across the base together and we would see this little knot of Southerners approach us and we'd see the one Lopa had cut, marked this motherfucker up somethin' terrible. Lopa would cut his eyes at the dude and smirk with utter contempt and the agitators in our group would cut the fool.

The most way-out dude in this group was Yodo. His real name was something else. And people were always startling us by calling him that name, especially if they said Airman Lambert, because Yodo hadn't had any stripes (I think he might even have had three one time) in a very long time. Yodo's full name was Yodofus T. Syllieabla—"the high priest of Swahili, the czar of yap," he'd add, "and Phersona Figues is my pal." Phersona Figues was another one of the group whom Yodo had named. He named every one of us, some odd name or another. Some of us he simply turned our names around. Like he would call me Yorel Senoj. White was Mailliw Etihw. Though he always called Vincent, Vincent, and Lopa, Lopa.

Yodo was absolutely committed to jazz, African American improvised music. His whole imaginative and creative life revolved around the music. You never saw Yodo without albums in his hands. Even during work hours. (He worked in the base dispensary.) White uniform and blue "cunt" cap, long striding somewhere. Yodo usually carried a cane, or some stick he'd fastened a plastic top to with a red ball or some such inside the top. He called the stick his "all-purpose" stick and named it too. The stick's name was Anacronobienoid. He was great for holding dialogues with the stick whenever it suited him. Like he might say, after holding a conversation with one of us about something, "Well, Anacronobienoid, what do you think of that?" Or he might say, if he disagreed with something we'd said, "Anacronobienoid disagrees." Or something. Once, a white noncom was giving Yodo a hard time about something and Yodo, without blinking, said, "Look, Anacronobienoid is laughing at you! Anacronobienoid thinks you're a joke." And he would stretch his eyes and make weird gestures with the stick. The poor noncom, rather than go on with it, just got in the wind.

Yodo was one of the funniest dudes I'd ever met. By the time I met him he'd been in the service about nine years. And during that time he'd floated around going from one base to another and reenlisting simply because he didn't know what he'd be doing once he got out. Also, I think at one point he might have thought he could make some kind of career as a medical technician which he didn't think was possible in New Orleans where he'd come from, and so he thought the service would give him a career then he could retire relatively young and just cool it. But he'd run afoul of the service, gotten into some trouble and had his stripes removed, and this had crushed him, though he never admitted it.

Yodo's dialogue or sometimes monologue about the music was almost nonstop. He'd talk about Bud and Bird and Brownie and Monk. When he showed up at the door he'd swoop in with albums under his arm. On payday he'd buy whatever was in the BX, which wasn't much, and immediately come over to White's after work to play the side. He'd also write away for sides where possible. We'd play the sides and drink whatever was available to drink. Usually rum, since that was the cheapest in Puerto Rico.

Payday was only once a month, so that took on the character of a monthly bash, a big payday party. And much liquor and whatever else got bought. There was much going into town, usually Aguadilla, which was right down the road. Some would go further away to Ponce, Mayagüez, Arecibo, and the most ambitious would go all the way to the other end of the island to San Juan, usually by guagua (bus) unless you were a noncom or officer and had a car.

The music had always been a heavy part of my life, but Yodo raised it up in another way. Cut off as we were, and as he had been for so long, the music was a connection with black life. It was also a refuge, a way out of the agonizingly boring dreary white cracker-oriented service life, especially in Puerto Rico, where one felt even more cut off from the normal channels of American and African American life. One could not shoot up to Chicago on the weekends or Rochester. Airmen piled into the Puerto Rican cities whenever they could and there were places in Puerto Rico full of adventure, beauty, all kinds of pleasure, but despite all this you knew you were away from home, on the real side. And what's more, stuck in some intolerable madness you now had almost no understanding of how you'd got sucked into.

We talked about that all the time. How silly we were, how dumb, etc., we had been to get hooked up in this bullshit. For one reason or another. Some without other opportunity. Some looking for a way out of a dead end situation. A way into a career. Adventure and excitement. The claim of manhood. There were many reasons, but at this point, none of them were satisfactory.

There were some guys in the air force who did dig it. I have to believe they were a minority. Though there were a good number who'd signed up to do long stretches, some even to do a whole twenty, to retire. But these people were strange to us. They were among the "lames" we identified casually, squares and cornballs, gung-ho freaks and warcats who made us squirm for their simple-minded pleasure. We would always get on Yodo about the fact that he'd re-upped and had been in so long. We called him the oldest airman basic in the service.

So White's room became a kind of haven. And once Yodo and some of the others started showing occasionally at my room, which would send Bodey and Cooper out right smart, then sometimes we'd all gather in there for our record and booze and nonstop rap sessions. That was our basic life in the air force. We'd drink rum and play music and talk—project our desires or reminisce about what we'd lost or wanted people to think we'd had. And we became a kind of defensive unit for ourselves, a kind of salon.

White, of course, was the most serious painter. And when I first met him he was painting in mainly realistic style but occasionally veering off into surrealism. Later, in New York, under the influence of the abstract expressionists he developed a kind of surreal-abstractionist style that was very much his own. It was, of course, his nationality that slowed him down in his ascent in the world of fine art.

Yodo drew too, and painted some outright surrealistic pieces that revolved around the music. Bird with a duckbill Yodo named "Klacktovedisteen." Yodo said the duckbill made a sound "klack klack klack," which is why Bird called his tune "Klacktovedisteen." He had a painting called *In Walked Bud*, after Monk's tune. Yodo would enter the room sometimes, saying, "In Walked Bud," and then dance in like Thelonious Monk danced next to his piano when the rest of the band was playing.

We met a couple of other guys in the air force who began to hang with us or hang with me. One was Jim Mitchum, from New York City, who walked around even then taking photographs. He was never anyplace without at least one camera. Jim Mitchum was kind of a snob and he talked in an exaggeratedly near "proper" style, which was funny if you thought about it. He'd been in the service a while and his speech was meant to impress you that he was not just your regular airman deuce (two stripes), that he was some kind of intellectual.

Phil Peakes was another photographer with the bunch. He was white, Jewish. Apparently from some pretty heavily endowed suburb of Boston. Phil also was kind of snobbish, though he was still young enough for that not to have completely got the best of him. He was the kind of guy who needed to be an intellectual to pull it off and at the time hadn't got it all sufficiently together, so he was a mixture of nose up (he had a large one too) and nose regular. Phil and Jim and I would have the most openly arty conversations (according to our standards at the time), though on the real side Yodo and them were actually talking about some deeper questions, even casually.

Jim and Phil always felt slightly perturbed when Yodo was on the scene. And Yodo, sensing this, would pick at them in his not-so-subtle way. Having Anacronobienoid speak haughtily to them or chide them for their lack of knowledge about African American improvised music. Phil could cop by waving his latest acquisition, Glenn Gould playing the Brandenburg Concerto or the Goldberg Variations or some such. But Phil didn't have such a heavy knowledge about that stuff either, not really. Jim would haltingly try to scoff at what Yodo might be asking, like for instance did he, Jim, like "Glass Enclosure" or "Un Poco Loco" best? Or who was playing drums on "Ornithology"? Or was he a Blakey fan (Yodo called him by his Muslim name, Buhaina) or did he dig Max?

Still, we were an enlarged salon and the contradictions inside that entity brought out all kinds of conversations and conflicts that were usually at least funny. We thought of ourselves as the base cognoscenti, the real hipsters or the base intellectuals, depending on what part of the group would be together. We all were unified by our hatred of the air force. Phil and Jim acted as if they had been kidnapped from their intellectual pursuits and now had been forcibly surrounded by unwashed idiots. Yodo, like Strassbaugh, thought there were too many squares, lames he called them, around the joint. And though he had re-upped before crossing our paths (and him losing his stripes) he confirmed that he would be leaving for good as soon as he could.

We had nothing but contempt for the "old soldiers," especially those who remained in the service for security, what they called "three hots and a flop." The sergeants who would counsel us that there was nothing outside for us, no jobs, no future, that we had better stay inside where we knew we had something going.

Something going? What? The fool, Harrison, was fanatical about trying to get all of us soldiering, like his brother-in-law wanted. He'd roam the base and show up without warning. He even came into my room one morning when I should have already been down at the flight line and scared the holy shit outta me. I thought it was my man JWT and I looked up at the one star on this guy's cap like the one-eyed Cyclops and babbled some shit trying to get outta there.

To check the VD Harrison even started passing out negative awards. To the squadron with the highest venereal disease rate on the base, he would announce this honor at the Saturday parade. (We started having weekly parades, Saturday morning, in full class A uniform!) This squadron then had the honor of marching to work every morning at 07:00, complete with the base band marching in front of them. The band members despised Harrison because before the VD marches, they had it mostly made. An occasional parade or officers' affair. But now they had to march every morning and play a full parade on Saturdays. We hung around with some of the band members, naturally. And they were death on Harrison.

The 73rd got the VD award one month and I think it really did cause some of the borderline VD cases at least to question the cleanliness of the *choche* before plunging in. I don't think it mattered too much to the wilder ones. When they got the little scratch each month they'd go charging off the base and lay down with the first *puta* they saw. "Hey, GI! Two dollars short time four dollars long time!"

But, God, could that shit make you feel sorry for yourself! Not even light out, line up, atten-hup!, then some jive march music and go poking through the darkness down to the flight line. If you wanted to eat those mornings (that month you had the marches) you had to rise up still earlier. Though the food was so bad I changed my eating habits. A couple Sundays they had chicken in the mess hall and the shit was bleeding. Rare chicken! Sunday evenings they had some thick wet baloney. I gave it up. Found out I could get people's salads and desserts in exchange for that bleeding chicken. So I became a vegetarian. I was always walking around the base with nuts and raisins in my pockets. The wildest thing about the mess hall was when the maintenance dudes would come in. Some of 'em didn't want to wash up. You could see it especially on the white dudes (at least that's what we said) and the sight of somebody eating a slice of white bread with the black greasy fingerprints all over the bread could take your appetite. It helped reinforce the elitist tendency our salon took on.

There were a couple other members of the Ramey Air Force Base Intellectuals Salon. Sid, a guy from Syracuse, who had gone to the University of Rochester, pre-med. He later got out and became a doctor. I guess he was drawn to some of us because we came on like intellectuals and I had gone to college. Jim to CCNY. Phil to Brandeis. Though we'd all dropped out for one reason or another. Sid was the kind of dude who smoked a pipe. He had a job in base supply or some such paper-pushing gig. Jim was in a maintenance squadron, open bay barracks, with the plebeians, and this bugged the hell out of him. "They're ignorant of everything important," he'd say. As stiff as an unused hardcover.

Another dude I got close to was a very short shriveled-up Jewish dude named Laffowiss. We called him Laffy, though he had usually a sad and forlorn expression on his face but it didn't stop him from constantly making jokes. His favorite entrance was bent over pretending to have a cigar in his mouth or fingers like Groucho Marx. Sometimes Laffy would stand like that or slightly modified even in the presence of a noncom or officer. He was from the Lower East Side, old style. The Lower East Side that Mike Gold talked about in *Jews without Money*. He was the true mensch, son of the Jewish working class. Cynical, full of a crystal-clear sardonic humor that cut through the crass bullshit of the air force with ease. But like the rest of us he was always running into trouble because of it.

Laffy was always complaining about the air force cuisine. He missed the East European specialties that characterized the Lower East Side. He was always loudly wishing for smoked herring, or pickles, or pickled tomatoes, or whitefish. He was a nonstop questioner of everything. Slumped over, either pretending to be Groucho Marx or actually being Louie Laffowiss. He hung with us easily, laughing at us and with us and at himself. And the most common quality he had was an absolute and uncompromising hatred of the service, and the people who thought they were important because they had some kind of rank or status in it. Yodo and Laffy together would make a classic TV sitcom if TV was in the real people's hands instead of the few gimlet nitwits that run it now.

I guess the salon—I'm calling it the salon now, but actually it was a defensive unit, a sanity-maintaining collective of aspiring intellectuals—taught us all something. We had the jazz foundation mixed with concern for the graphic arts—painting and photography—a couple of academics ensconced among us for laughs, and a few of us interested in literature. Laffy was a nonstop reader, as I had developed into being. The rest of the guys liked to talk about books; Phil and Sid were always talking about what they read. Jim always carried a book along with his camera. White read what he thought was serious and Yodo read *Downbeat*, *Metronome*, and any book on the music.

The high point of our salon structure came when I took a part-time job evenings in the library. The money was negligible, but I spent quite a bit of time in there. And when this big WAF, a sister from Texas, who was the day clerk, let me know there was a part-time job at night, I leaped at it. Joyce was about six foot two and I guess had some kind of undefined crush on me, but she was a good friend and earnest sister who'd gotten in the WAF to try to see the world. And she'd been to Europe and was now in Puerto Rico suffering under the shit like the rest of us.

The librarian was a little plump middle-aged career service librarian who saw that I not only knew how to run the library in the evening quickly enough but enjoyed being around the books, so she gave me the run of the place. In a month or so she actually let me order the books and see to the stocking of the entire library. We had a hurricane in '55 and it blew every wooden structure on Ramey down and destroyed the town of Aguadilla. The rebuilt library was modern and even had a brand-new hi-fi set in it. The music library was mostly European concert music, but we were into that too. And for me it was really a learning period about this music and I was buying Bach, Mozart, Beethoven, Stravinsky, trying to fill in my knowledge, so that between our own collections and the library collection we were giving ourselves a collective education.

So that was smooth. In the evenings, a group of us from the salon would go into the library. This was after hours and we had the whole building to ourselves. And we would read and bullshit and drink and listen to music turned all the way up. It was the closest thing to paradise we ever encountered down there. Years later I met a guy who had also gone through Ramey and he said he'd seen my name in a bunch of the books there, A/2C E. L. Jones.

But in every way, like it or not, pleasant or not, the service was my graduate school or maybe it was undergraduate school. For one thing, I began to keep a journal, a diary, of what was going on. I can't find the thing now, though I guess it's still around somewhere. But it was the pain and frustration of this enforced isolation that began to make me scrawl my suffering, to seek some audience for my effusive self-pity. As the journal went on it became more and more a listing of the various books I was reading. Because now, so completely cut off, I read constantly, almost every waking hour I wasn't actively soldiering or bullshitting with the fellas. I began reading the *New York Times*—you could only get it Sundays—and at the time 75 cents was an exorbitant fee, but I paid it. And that in itself was an adventure because I had never had much knowledge of the *Times* and its presumptions.

The best-seller list became a kind of bible for me. I tried to read everything on it. I ordered through either the library or a book club, one of the "serious" ones, the Readers' Subscription, which offered Joyce and Melville and James, etc. But I was in a very conscious and very agitated search for information, and it was focused more and more directly on literature. Later,

I could see even how my handwriting changed in the journal. How it took on new shape and spoke of further comprehension and consideration of questions which before I could not have formed. I wanted to become an intellectual. It seemed, for some reason, that for me it was the only thing left.

The world of Howard University and its brown and yellow fantasy promise had faded, leaving a terrible frustration and sense of deprivation. That I had, through my own irresponsible acts, deprived myself of something valuable. I thought the sharp and relentless striving to become intellectual was the answer to this void. At some point I wanted to be back at Howard, at another point, and more and more consistently now, I was almost contemptuous of it and the people there, children. Though the constant self-pity I felt being there "among heathens" was an endless rebuke.

And then, on top of all this, I would actually, every once in a while, see some Howard people. Officers now. We were completely removed and separated from each other now. And the class realization I got from that, the class consciousness, was stunning to me. I could see that we were in different spheres. Of course I could not verbalize it as class, etc., but my perception of it as class, as a separation upheld by the society itself, was keen and staggering. Most of those Howard dudes who were officers in the air force simply avoided me. One I did meet at a base in the South and we talked in his room, and it was cold and frustrating. Our speech had been separated by reality. We no longer linked up. Our interests were different. I could hear the simplistic careerism. The prepared sheepdom of the read-ied-for-the-slaughter Negro pursuing his "good job" into hell itself. And "Who was I?" was going though my head. Who was I? Where did I fit in? Standing now on the side of the road as the select browns and yellows marched by heroically, triumphantly, toward that shaft of gold leaned out the sky to call them home to yalla jesus. Some calendar shit! I mean it reminded me of the somber glories of the calendars one got in funeral parlors right across the street from the yalla folks' church.

There were a few black officers at Ramey. One was even on the same crew with me. N-45 "Not ready" was what the N meant. It meant we were a bunch of trainees, or ne'er-do-wells, or misfits. Gadsen, the Negro officer on that crew, was classic, I guess, though I never knew many of them well. He was dark brown but absolutely yellow in his aspirations and kind of brownish despite it all. He was a link with the past, in some sense, for me. I think he'd gone to Lincoln. He had a big blue car with a plaid top, a convertible, and was considered, by whomever, the most eligible black bachelor on the base. He was young, not much older than me, a second lieutenant, so he fit into the power structure in a commendable way, plus he was single and independent and could fly back and forth up the island pursuing what limited pleasures the island might offer to someone in the service. Though, for sure, we all surmised that those pleasures were much more than we would ever be exposed to. It was rumored that Gadsen always had one woman leaving the room as one was entering. And he enjoyed a kind of prestige among some of the base's blacks, a mixed love-and-hate thing emotionally. But the white boys, ever cognizant of the caste-class structure of the real America, constantly made Gadsen the butt of their jokes, so he could not be too uppity, at least in their heads.

That was probably a weird position to be in, like the yellow/brown situation generally in the context of working for white America and somehow relating in some way to the rest of it, including black America. One fat first lieutenant, a yellow Negro straight out, got caught up in some weird stuff that socked it home to me, the sheepish quality expected of the careerist Negro. A fat white master sergeant got into a "game" being played by some of the younger officers near the flight line. They were tossing each other's hats around, which was questionable in the first place, what with the Articles of War, the so-called RHIP (Rank Has Its Privileges, the motto in the service that spells out the class structure of that society and U.S. society in general clearer than I've ever seen it elsewhere). But they're tossing hats and fat Sergeant Mullarcy gets in it. Catches this black lieutenant's hat and tosses it, but too far for one of the other officers to catch. The black officer tells him to pick up the hat and the fat sergeant refuses!

A guy stood me up in front of the barracks one day, a white first looie, and made me salute over and over because he didn't dig the black salute (though Laffy saluted the same way). Black troops had a tendency to bend their heads sideways down to their hand when saluting rather than bringing the hand all the way up military style. This guy made me salute maybe twenty-five times until he was satisfied. I was determined in my sly way not to understand what he was talking about and went on saluting in the hot goddam sun and he stood there over me, the gung-ho sonafabitch! And it went on and on.

I knew what would have happened if I had just nutted out and refused to go through the saluting game. And at the end, I don't think I'd really changed my salute, but he was satisfied that he got me some extra duty or extra harassment for taking such liberties. But the fat sergeant refused to pick up the hat. I was squatting in the corner with some other airmen watching. And there finally was some compromise, like somebody else picked up the hat. But why? Why hadn't the officer just given the fat master an Article 15 or got one of his stripes? The fat sergeant was an old soldier, the yellow lieutenant, a short-timer, and probably in transition to his dentist's office in a few years. But still, to me and the others that watched and heard of this, this was a clear display of the dickless stance such yellow status predicted.

But I never felt really part of all that. In it, I was, for sure, and it pained me like the great tragedies of my reading. And I began to scrawl my agonies into my journal regularly. My findings. The ideas that came out of the books. Proust and *Auntie Mame*. Hemingway and *The Man in the Gray Flannel Suit*. And Joyce, Faulkner, Melville, Dostoyevsky, Hesse, Flaubert, Cummings, Lawrence, Pound, Patchen, Hardy, James, Balzac, Stendhal. I would read *Bonjour Tristesse* and Robert Graves in the same day. A book on Buddhism and *The Communist Manifesto* in the same afternoon. I enjoyed plunging into long books that I'd read were difficult to get through. The Proust and Dostoyevsky were glad tasks for me. I'd find an author and read everything of his or hers I'd find. Puerto Rico made that difficult, but being the night librarian aided this quest. And when I was given guard duty, which was always, I would squat out in the hot sun twelve hours trying to read clandestinely, because reading was not permitted during guard duty. Plus Harrison said we were to have nothing on display on our dressers or windowsills, so that after a while the books I began to amass had to be put inside my closet or otherwise stashed, though at times I got sloppy and put them on the dresser with a bookend like normal people.

I also began writing poetry more regularly. I'd written some light verse and some Elizabethan doggerel during my HU days, mostly hooked up with the doctor's lady, Liz. But now I was more serious (though still not altogether) with what I was doing. I was at least trying to put down what I knew or everything I thought I felt. Straining for big words and deep emotional registration, as abstract as my understanding of my life.

At the Green Door, I'd also stumbled into the literary magazine. *Accent*, a small magazine from somewhere in Illinois, impressed me most. With the strange abstruseness of doctrinaire modernism heretofore unknown to me. "Pity Poor Axel the Spinhead" was the name of one story, author now unknown. I tried to penetrate its murky symbolism. The poetry also swept past me. I had since been getting the *Partisan, Hudson, Kenyon Reviews*, even *Sewanee* from time to time. I was getting beat over the head with the New Criticism and didn't know it. I strained to understand, to find something for myself in those words. I read Empson's *Seven Types of Ambiguity* and plowed into all the fashionable literary McCarthyism coming out then, as my entrance and baptism into the world of serious letters. All the time a radio would be screaming in hillbilly at the top of its voice and drunken airmen would be clattering through the hall goosing each other in memory of the most recent *puta* they'd banged.

I'd say the irony of all this is what someone far removed might think of as "delicious." The reality of my day-to-day air force life fairly terrified me—despite the collective resistance of our salon elitism. The daily grind of guard duty, or fortnightly "alerts," fake missions announced by the screaming of hellish sirens which sent us scrambling down to the flight line and up into the very wild black yonder, were driving me up the wall, or at least to drink. Yet the reality from which I wanted to escape was replaced by my reading, which often was the most backward forces in American literature, teaching me the world upside down and backwards. But despite the New Criticism and the word freaks and the Southern Agrarians and Fugitive propaganda that I imbibed as often as I could as a supposed antidote to the air force, it gave me enough solid reflection on real life so that it had to change me. That and the service.

I began to send poetry out to these magazines. And unerringly in a few days, rejection slips would come in. I wish I had saved these. For a time I did, but they disappeared somehow. I got rejection slips from all the quality magazines and *Accent* and some others I dug up. *The Saturday Review,* *The New Yorker, Harper's,* and *The Atlantic Monthly.* They all showed the good taste and consistency to turn me down flat and very quickly. And these rejections only served to fuel the deep sense of despair, so ultimate and irreversible with a twenty-two-year-old. None had any use for my deathless immortal words but I kept trying.

One afternoon I had gone to San Juan by myself. I had found some places in Old San Juan I could walk around. They had a tourist section, fairly arty. There was a painter there named Juan Botello (a funny name) and I would go in his shop and walk around that area trying to get close to some professional art. I had the *New York Times* under my arm. I was in civilian clothes and I remember I was reading *The New Yorker.* I'd stopped at a bench and sat down near a square. It was quiet and I could see a long way off toward the newer, more Americanized part of the city, the Condado Beach section, where I could only go if in uniform, so they would know I was an Americano and not a native. I had been reading one of the carefully put together exercises *The New Yorker* publishes constantly as high poetic art, and gradually I could feel my eyes fill up with tears, and my cheeks were wet and I was crying, quietly, softly but like it was the end of the world. I had been moved by the writer's words, but in another, very personal way. A way that should have taught me even more than it did. Perhaps it would have saved me many more painful scenes and conflicts. But I was crying because I realized that I could never write like that writer. Not that I had any real desire to, but I knew even if I had had the desire I could not do it. I realized that there was something in me so out, so unconnected with what this writer was and what that magazine was that what was in me that wanted to come out as poetry would never come out like that and be *my* poetry.

The verse spoke of lawns and trees and dew and birds and some subtlety of feeling amidst the jingling rhymes that spoke of a world almost completely alien to me. Except in magazines or walking across some campus or in some house and neighborhood I hadn't been in. What was so terrifying to me was that when I looked through the magazine, I liked the clothes, the objects, the general ambience of the place—of the life being lived by the supposed readers and creators of the *New Yorker* world. But that verse threw me off, it had no feeling I could really use. I might carry the magazine as a tool of my own desired upward social mobility, such as I understood it. I might like some of the jokes, and absolutely dig the soft-curving button-down collars and well-tailored suits I saw. The restaurants and theater advertisements. The rich elegance and savoir faire of all I could see and touch. But the poem, the *inside,* of that life chilled me, repelled me, was impenetrable. And I hated myself because of it, yet at the same time knew somehow that it was correct that I be myself, whatever that meant. And myself could not deal with the real meanings of the life spelled out by those tidy words.

I made no dazzling proclamations as a result of this crying into the *New Yorker* experience. I still felt sad as I took a *publico* back. I still wrote the same kinds of deadly abstractions about love, death, tragic isolation. I still went on reading whatever I could get or find out about. Sartre, Camus, de Beauvoir, anthologies of poetry. I learned about Apollinaire and Rimbaud. I read every novel of Evelyn Waugh's I could find and wondered often how to pronounce his name. I thought Sebastian Flyte in *Brideshead Revisited* was marvelous! I still got the reviews and stiff magazines. I even subscribed to *Partisan Review.* And I went on scribbling nightly or whenever, but regularly, in my journal. Writing haughty reviews and deep analyses of what I read. I was aware of an intellectual world—it had existed all this time—

people were walking around knowing about it, knowing these various ideas, books, phrases, histories, relationships, and I didn't. Why hadn't I caught on in school? That there was an intellectual *life* that could be pursued. A life of ideas and, above all, Art.

I brought no great selectivity to my reading, though I began to understand after a while that some literature was more serious, more probing and thought-provoking than other, lighter stuff I might mash on myself as a result of reading *The New York Times Book Review*. But I found signposts and guides, references and printed directions. I might see a certain reference in a book or magazine—for instance, I saw the word "Kafka" in *Esquire*. What was a Kafka? I looked in dictionaries, no Kafka. Finally I stumbled on an article in some literary review about his work. The stiff abstruse language of the article only bade me rush harder after its sense. And all the sub- and counterreferences, the foreign words and jargon of the New Critics, I tracked down like Basil Rathbone, but it was not elementary.

During this period I also went home over another Christmas break. Again, I went to the Village and visited Steve Korret and his beautiful golden brown dancer wife. Their apartment on Bedford Street was stark white, except for the kitchen, which was orange. The books that ranged up and down one wall now pulled me to them and held me there. Steve laughed at me standing by his bookcase hungrily gobbling up titles. A lot of them Eastern and Buddhist. Steve had become a Zen Buddhist. I did not know how fashionable this was becoming in the Village and its counterparts elsewhere. It was still the middle '50s ('56) and the tremendous popularity of the East in bohemian circles had not yet reached its full peak. Steve was an early acolyte. He even worked in an Eastern bookshop called Orientalia, around 12th Street. I came to the bookstore before I went back to Puerto Rico and I was transported by the hundreds of scholarly books on various schools of Buddhism and Eastern thought in general. I bought two of R. H. Blythe's books on Zen, analyzing Western art for parallels with Zen consciousness. I was swept up.

Dylan Thomas was also very heavy in those days downtown. People passing through Korret's house talked of "Dylan." One black poet there lilted some of Thomas' verses and then some of his own which were amazingly similar.

Korret was a writer! The idea of this made me drunk with wonder. A writer! What a thing to be—so weird—so outside of the ordinary parade of grey hellos and goodbyes I could begin to measure my life with. A writer. In the mysterious jumble of Greenwich Village.

Steve and his friends treated me like a little boy, which I guess I was. A little boy off in the goofy hopeless world of the army? No, the air force. How comic. How tragic. How odd. How romantic. How petty. I thought the last myself. These painters, dancers, writers, thinkers, witty makers of brilliant statements, and here I am on the fringe again. Unconnected and without note once again, just like at Howard.

I think it was now that the duffelbag incident occurred. Yes, it was now, at the end of this leave.

But I did get back to Ramey on time. Even sadder and more hopeless. I still had almost two years to go on my four-year enlistment. And my new intellectual life made soldiering harder and harder.

I had been moved to another crew, R-32, a "Ready" crew, which meant we were among the actual strike force of any bombing mission. It meant I had to go regularly to gunnery schools on base and in Tampa, Florida; Mobile, Alabama; Shreveport, Louisiana. In Tampa I met the Howard officer. In Mobile I shot down the drone aircraft during the gunnery sessions, because an old gunner told me in Puerto Rico that the shit was fixed and that the sight was rigged so you couldn't hit the drone cause the drones cost $10,000 apiece. So you had to use "Kentucky windage"—just shoot a little ahead of the thing, like deer hunting. And I brought it down, which meant I was supposed to go to a "Select" crew or at least a "Lead," but I didn't.

In Shreveport, Reilly, Burke, and I tried to go off the base together, but the locals discouraged it. I ended up two days AWOL. I had gotten lost and laid up with a sister down in the Bottom (one black community of Shreveport—see *The System of Dante's Hell*) and finally came back rumpled and hung over and absolutely broke.

Once we got downtown, Reilly got on the same bus. At first neither of us recognized the other. I couldn't recognize him because his face had been beaten till it was puffy and distorted. He couldn't recognize me because his eyes were all but closed. He'd run into some little guy with a cowboy hat and they'd had some words about the jukebox. Cowboy hat, it turned out, was a professional boxer.

The new crew I was put on had an AC (aircraft commander) named Major Smart—no shit. He was from Mississippi and had gone to the eighth grade. He'd been a master sergeant when the war started (World War Two), got made a temporary captain and most recently a temporary major. He had a broad supernasal accent and looked at me with wicked twinkling eyes. I guess I was his cross—integration and all that shit.

He used to get to me by telling racist jokes over the intercom once we were upstairs. When he found out I would shut off the intercom, he'd put it on "command" so as to override all cutoffs and be heard simultaneously throughout the whole ship.

He would ask me how far in school I'd gone—it peeved him—and he would mock me, again on "command." Jones is ed-ucated. He told a joke about a white man got on an airplane with a colored woman and the hostess brings them black coffee. The man says, "I didn't want my coffee like this."

The hostess says, "I thought you liked your coffee like you like your women, strong and dark!" I cursed in the isolation of my lower right rear gunner's position but that was all. When the flight was over, Smart, with his narrow hooked nose and grey shit colored hair would stride past me, eyes twinkling.

At least once a month we'd have an "alert." The sirens would rage and we'd have to get up in the middle of the night and dress and fly off to "bomb" some city, usually American, and then return. It was a recurring nightmare to me. The siren, after midnight, was like hell's actual voice. You'd throw on your flight suit, the grey slick coveralls, check out a parachute, get your weapon, load your cannon, wait for orders, and take off. Sometimes we took off and came right back. Sometimes we'd go and land somewhere else and stay a few days. Sometimes we'd go right back to the barracks. And I was the only guy on my crew with the big awkward .45 automatic and a shoulder holster. Putting a parachute on over that getup was painful and dangerous. The rest of the crew had .38s, small and compact and buckled on at the waist. I was the only one that looked like Smilin' Jack. And try as I might to get a .38, I never did.

When we weren't flying we had to guard the plane. I was low man (stripewise and castewise), so I spent the most time. Like twelve hours a day. Everyday, except when we were flying. The sun breaking your head, white and scorching. Trying to read and having to keep something covering the book for fear of detection. And unerringly, whenever I flew, I'd catch cold! Those planes (B-36s) were not comfortable like commercial airliners. They were cold and drafty. Colder than air conditioning! An hour or so out, my nose would start running. I'd have on my flight jacket, but the whole flight I'd be freezing to death. My feet felt like ice cubes.

The K-rations we'd have to eat were always cold though there was some johnson in the plane that was supposed to heat up the food like a hot plate. But it wasn't near my station so I forgot it. We'd have, like, cold canned spaghetti that would slide out of the can in a single solid blob. Or canned pound cake, or how about the hard tack, the round cement crackers, also canned, which were your bread? I couldn't use any of it.

When we came back from flying, I'd feel like I'd been tortured. But, even then, I'd try to get on with my reading—being bothered by the AC's instructions, the crackling radio, the racist jokes, the freezing airplane. But the next day we'd have off and I'd lay in bed and read or wander down to the BX and buy something if I had the dough or go to the library.

I'd have to wait most times till after duty hours to hook up with the salon, except those who were off or "sick." But you had to notify the first sergeant the day before you went on "sick call," i.e., the day before you got sick. So that put a crimp in that malingerer's device. Sometimes when we got together to bullshit we'd have to have "music wars" to quiet out the hillbillies across the hall. They'd be playing something like "I'm in the Jailhouse Now," which was standard, but if they got aggressive and turned it up to drown us out, we'd counter, turn up Diz or Bird or else we'd blow 'em off the map with Beethoven's Seventh or Ninth!

One time a guy named Muck—no shit, a big thick terrible white mechanic from Chicago who was always covered with grease—came roaring down the hall cursing. He shouted he was gonna kill these nigger bastards and came rushing down toward my room. The room had one louvered wall, so you could hear clearly. I got my .45 and climbed up into the top bunk. Muck slammed open the door, slamming it against the bed, and rushed in. I was crouched on the top bunk and shoved the big gun down in his face as he turned. His eyes rolled up under the grease. He was drunk and sure enough he had a .38 like the crewmen had, snapped on his belt. But I had the .45 in his face and started cussing him, "You fat ugly stupid motherfucker, I'll blow your fuckin' brains out!"

He gasped. He stood still, his head wobbling from side to side in a circle of dead drunkenness. He took a step back, turned, and split.

Muck was sufficiently pacified, but a couple days later a friend of his, a guy from upper New York State, exhilarated by the open displays of racism he must have seen on the base, wakes me up and he's standing over me, a fist cocked, daring me to rise up. I said nothing. There was nothing to say. He spat out his threats, though none were specifically racial. He hated me, he said, for playing that fuckin' classical music when I had CQ (change of quarters, like a nighttime security guard) in the hallway and we had clashed on this before. I looked warily up at his face as he kept talking and daring me to get up. I relaxed a little hoping some of my friends would come in. I wondered did this slob have a piece. But it was only his nasty fist. After a while he got tired and turned and left. I jumped up and got my .45 and stood by the door listening. Then I went out in the hall. No one there. Then I heard the motorcycle racing out by my window. Muck and this guy Martin were standing near it laughing. I rolled the louvered window open and stuck the big gun through the slats. "Hey Martin, Martin," I called. "Come here, you bastard!" He laughed and threw me a finger. He got on the back of Muck's cycle and they jetted. I never got revenge!

Going into town meant you were going to drink or go whoring. Laffy and I once bought two *putas* and screwed them in the same bed. Him pumping away at one end and me on the other. Afterwards, his woman tried to raise her price and we fled off into Mundango, the red light district, with these unfortunate creatures screaming at our heels.

But mostly, I didn't go off the base too much. I read. I read. I read. I sulked. I bullshitted with the salon members. I played music. I read.

Dudes would tease me about not going off the base. They said I was going to whack my doodle off. I don't think I was ever in danger of that, but what did I know? What changed my life and brought my air force days to a close was an anonymous letter. A letter was sent to my commanding officer saying I was a Communist. No shit! Why I, who at this time thought I was an aspiring Buddhist—I guess—was singled out as a Communist, I'll never be completely sure. Except years later, Sid the Doctor met Amina and me at some party and he said he's always remembered how rebellious (and, he said, "courageous") I was in the face of various officers and non-coms. I'd never thought that. I always thought of myself as very quiet, retiring, reserved, painfully shy. But his description of me to me surprised me. "Whatta you mean?" I said.

"Well, you were always challenging those guys, disputing them. Putting them on. Dropping not-too-veiled insults on them. Defying them. Your hat pulled down over your eyes like a bandit. The dark glasses [I'd forgotten], the little illegal wispy hairs on the chin, the constant book under the arm or in the pocket. It was inspiring to me. The way you attacked those guys and never compromised!"

Shit. I had no idea at all who he was talking about. My whole life was worse than a compromise, to me. I remembered maybe a few exchanges and encounters. Like Lt. Col. Jones (he had become our squadron

commander) and I bumping heads in the laundry. I was shoving my nasty
fatigues in the washer and in comes a little beady-eyed baldheaded guy
with powder blue pistol pocket pants. The pistol pockets were in dark blue.
He also had on one of those manic Hawaiian shirts. I glanced up to see
who it was and then continued my washing. He cleared his throat. "Airman, don't you salute an officer?"

"I didn't know sir you didn't look like uhh I mean I didn't recognize "
and saluted. He scowled and turned and walked out. I stood there holding
the dirty fatigues and grimacing until one of the dudes walked in and asked
me if I'd seen Colonel Jones.

I wonder if Sid was talking about shit like that? Accidental, inadvertent
shit. The warnings for books and albums on the dresser. The Article 15s
for cutting out on parades. Being late to work. Reading on the flight line.
Needing a shave. Outta uniform. Playing music late. Back to the base after
hours. Having to paint the whole barracks for fighting on CQ (Martin).
Being weird in the plane (being out of position when given the order to
"fire"). Reading. Being an elitist, a member of a khaki and fatigue salon of
crying young boys.

But I was trying to become an intellectual. I was becoming haughtier
and more silent. More critical in a more general way. More specialized in
my concerns. More abstract and distant. I was being drawn, had been drawn,
into a world that Howard prepared me for on one level—blunt elitism.
Though the deeper resolves of intellectualism I knew mostly nothing about,
even though I'd been prodded to hook up self-consciously with the
profoundest art of the African American, black music, by one man, titil-
lated by another, I knew nothing consciously when I got out and went into
the death organization—error farce.

Yet my reading was, in the main, white people. Europeans, Anglo Americans. So that my ascent toward some ideal intellectual pose was at the
same time a trip toward a white-out I couldn't even understand. I was
learning and, at the same time, unlearning. The fasteners to black life
unloosed. I was taking words, cramming my face with them. White people's
words. Profound, beautiful, some even correct and important. But that is a
tangle of nonself in that for all that. A nonself creation where you become
other than you as you. Where the harnesses of black life are loosened and
you free-float, you think, in the great sunkissed intellectual waygonesphere.
Imbibing, gobbling, stuffing yourself with reflections of the *other*.

Finally, I am an internationalist and it is clear to me now that all people
have contributed to the wealth of common world culture—and I thought

that then, if only on the surface! But I had given myself, in my quest for intellectualism, a steady diet of European thought, though altered somewhat by the Eastern Buddhist reading. That was what intellectualism meant! To me. It was certainly not conscious. But I had never been warned. (An old man in the South one time had said to me, "Some folks speaks too clear," talking about my clipped northern speech. But, hey, that never registered.) Be careful in giving up the "provincial" that you do not include the fundamental and the profound.

I was being drafted into the world of quattrocento, vers libre, avant-garde, surrealism and dada, New Criticism, cubism, art nouveau, objectivism, "Prufrock," ambiguity, art music, rococo, shoe and non-shoe, highbrow vs. middlebrow (I'd read the article), and I didn't realize the deeper significance of it. I reacted to some of it, emotionally, like the *New Yorker* crying incident, but even that, the realization it brought, didn't reach deep enough.

I was going down a road. Positive in the overall, but just now I was taking a twist and I'd answer for it, you bet.

The letter said I was a Communist. One day I got a message to report to the first sergeant and the adjutant and they said I had been removed from my crew, taken off "flying status," and my "secret" clearance rescinded. I knew what was happening, I'd known from the giddy-up. In a week or so I had to go back again and they told me I was being transferred out of the 73rd Bomb to Air Base Group.

In group I was put on a gardening detail with other troops, who had mostly been busted down for various infractions. We were supposed to be planting flowers to beautify the base. One ex-tech sergeant I met, his arms bare except for the traces of his removed five stripes, was planting collards next to the flowers. So all over the base he had collards growing he'd pick and cook or sell. He'd gotten busted for sleeping with some warrant officer's wife. When they were walked in on, she screamed "Rape." Now the sergeant was on his way to Leavenworth to do nine to twelve.

I was a gardener for a month or so and the salon regulars thought it amusing, but I didn't, in the hot sun digging holes for flowers. At least on flying status I got to sit in the hot sun guarding and reading.

I was then moved to another job, in the registration office at the visiting officers' quarters. I also had been moved to an open bay in the Air Base Group barracks, which was like the torture of Chanute and Sampson. But with the move to the visiting officers' quarters, I was moved into a room there, in the back of the joint. This was really the best job I had except for the library. I slept in a small room and came out to the front office to work my eight hours. Giving out blankets and pillows, making up beds, then going back in my room to read and drink.

The guy in charge of us (three of us) was an Italian dude, short, plump, perpetually smiling, named Cosi. That wasn't his real name, but it's OK. Cosi is an Italian word which means "like," used like the blood use of "like," like, you understand? Like this and like that. Cosi had an accent and had been born in Italy. He'd come over and after a few years of seeking opportunity had finally settled for the air force.

He was a sweet guy, a nonstop talker, always laughing and making jokes and saying "cosi." We sat up talking on his shift or mine. He went out occasionally, but almost as seldom as I. He marveled constantly at my reading. He'd come in and whistle, "Hey, reading again? Maron' a mia!" And start kidding me. Once he came in and I was reading *For Whom the Bell Tolls*. I was at the part where the hero, Roberto, is killed by the fascists and I was weeping like a baby. Cosi said, "A goddam book can make you cry? Maron' a mia!"

I was in limbo for months and heard nothing from anyone about my case. Then suddenly, one day, I was brought in and questioned. I was shown a sheet which listed organizations and they asked me had I ever belonged to any. I put down the Civil Rights Congress because I had once gone to a meeting where a guy had talked about this organization. I wrote about this meeting in the space provided on the form. I was shown a copy of the accusatory letter, which had been sent anonymously. I got a chance to glance at a sheet which said that among the artifacts the air force was amassing as to my offense were copies of the *Partisan Review*!

I was asked if I belonged to an organization called the Congress of Cultural Freedom. (According to Lillian Hellman, a liberal defense mechanism to outdenounce the McCarthyites, thereby clearing themselves!) I said, "No," and was shown the magazine which they'd gotten from my room. I hadn't known the publishers. I had letters in my drawers with rejection notes and that address. It was lucky my ass wasn't on the line. Shit, I *wanted* to get kicked out of the service.

The thing dragged on and I began writing letters home about headaches I was having. (The biggest one was the fuckin' air force!) I had received a couple letters from Steve Korret, one in particular made reference to Zen and quoted Thomas. Korret said in answer to one letter I'd written him that I "was always crying. Cry, Poet!" And that was the first time I'd ever been called that. Poet. It dug into me. I had a photo he'd given me on my last leave. Taken at a party, with various of Steve's friends, in particular a slim-faced white girl with a long ponytail and heavy eye pencil sending her eyes around the corners of her head. This flick fascinated me! Not just the wild-looking woman in black stockings, but the whole scene. A Village party with all the hair let down, all the cultivated wildness on display. This was the Village. Weird! Something else was happening other than what I knew about. Wild stuff. Free open shit. Look at that weird looking woman. I bet she'd fuck. I bet she knows about all kinds of heavy shit. And I bet she'd fuck. Not like them stuck-up bitches at the Capstone. Wow!

The shit dragged on for months with me still in limbo, still making beds at the visiting officers' quarters, and at last I got orders to leave. We were sitting where we could see the flight line, drinking vodka ($1 a fifth) and cackling about the commander of all Strategic Air Command (Curtis LeMay) driving face down on a go-cart back and forth, back and forth, on the flight line like a juvenile delinquent!

We kept saying, screaming really, "This is the motherfucker in charge of us?" It made us hysterical!

Cosi brought me the orders. In the multicopied ditto those things come in. He was breathing hard and grinning, like he knew it was important. It was just that Special Orders were an event for any airman. You didn't know what the hell was happening.

I had been discharged. *Undesirably*! What? UNDESIRABLY! I was to be discharged in thirty days. Being shipped to South Carolina in about two weeks, then undergoing two weeks' processing.

The guys there whooped and hollered. What the fuck, Undesirable or up your ass and gone, getting out was what was happening. That news shot around to the salon members and other folks. The hip folks were happy for me. I was getting the fuck out. The squares were sorry I'd gotten a funny discharge. UNDESIRABLE!

Hey, I wanted to get out. It didn't matter, long as I was sane and healthy. I wanted out. Out! Undesirable or not, here I come.

And in a few weeks I was on my way to South Carolina. While I was being processed I got a chance to go up to Columbia to see my relatives. My aunts and uncles and grandmother. I spent most of the time talking to my tall, thin, dark, fast-talking aunt.

I was happy to see everybody else, including my tall, light brown, light eyed, slender aunt everybody agreed was beautiful. But to the tall dark aunt I poured out my heart, such as I could muster. I had been kicked out. My parents wouldn't like it. Would they understand? I wanted help and she gave me that by listening, commenting on the obvious, and reserving comment on the abstruse. I stayed there talking a week or so and then got discharged formally and got a bus to ride twenty some hours back to Newark.

My air force career was over.

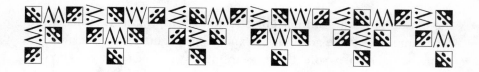

The Village

In the South I was again formally disconnected. Although I was happy, very happy, to be out from under the torture of the air force, still it had been a form, it had given my life a shape, as hateful as it was.

I wandered around, just outside everyone's reach. And then going north, back home on a bus, a seemingly endless ride. And finally to be back on the street, in the house, undesirably discharged from the air force, even talking to my parents and sister, my grandmother, wasn't sufficient to snap me out of it. It was like being in a city of ghosts, even in my parents' house. That recognition that it was *their* house was one aspect of that. I was no longer connected with that from the inside. I was a long-removed visitor returned to look through my old things for what few things I might need before I went off again, somewhere.

The strings from my old life, the HU college crowd, the older darker Hillside Placers, the brown Cavaliers, high school, even the yellow agents of Bethany Church picnics, had been cut. Not just by attrition but a willful kind of de-identification process that had gone on in various stages and identified as various things since high school.

As far as I was concerned the air force had formally ended the great shot-from-cannons stunt of brown folk myth where they are blasted through the plastic tarpaulin of their obvious limitations out at the yalla sun of Jesus' smile. He smile good jobs, "haimes," prestigous "slaves," maybe you could be a general or something, wear suits to work, be connected up with well known white folks? Maybe you could be T. Rockland Johnson, M.D. or H. Bernard West, D.D.S. "You remember Jinxy Red? He's got a very good practice! You remember Wilson McCall, he's a captain in the air force, flies a jet. When he gets out he's going to start a practice. "

It seemed all I could see was brown bodies shot flailing into the air, flapping their arms like weird birds. It made me see the masques I'd danced and worn. The skins I'd already shed. And in my parents' house I felt like I was wandering through a carnival of ghosts.

One evening at dinner, after I'd been "home" maybe a month, seemed a kind of farewell. I argued with my mother with all of the family members at the table. There was probably no reason except there had been some mention about what I was going to do. Was I going to get a job in Newark? I told my mother she just wanted me to get some factory job in Newark. (She probably wanted that even less than I did.) My confusion was showing and being sounded.

But what did I *want* to do? Why not work in a factory (the post office was probably more like it)? No, I wanted something else. For one thing I wanted to be gone from here. From Hillside Avenue and even, yes, from Newark.

I'd gone into New York a couple of times. And one day I started looking at the *Times'* want ads. I had got close to two dudes I'd known before the service, who had not gone away to school. One was Tim Wilson, Cynthia's brother, he was still talking about painting. The other was Brad Davis, the thin, thin haired acerbic vibraphonist with Jackie Bland's band. He had also been aloof from the HU scene. It came out he also was thinking about moving to New York. Because that's what had grown more clear in my mind. New York. The Village. An apartment of my own. Or at least with one or two roommates to keep the cost down. Brad worked in NY and had gone to a business school there. He worked down around Wall Street for an importing firm. He was always lithe and hip looking in his blue suits and shirts, the one lock of his straight hair hanging over his forehead like Horace Silver's. Brad was the coolest talking and coolest walking dude any of us knew.

So we made a loose pact. We three would go to the Village. We would take our fantasies all the way into reality. We would be hip and cool and in touch, a peer of the mysterious and romantic names like Steve Korret and some others who apparently lived exciting meaningful lives there.

But in the end that was not the way it happened. I saw an ad in the *Times* to work in a bookstore on 47th Street. The Gotham Book Mart. I went over that morning on a bus and walked in and met the old grey civet of a woman and was told I could start the next day.

So I started everyday going to New York on the bus, getting off at 42nd Street and scrambling up to 47th between 5th and 6th to the Gotham Book Mart to work. I told my parents I'd gotten a job in a bookstore. I don't know if it made sense. This announcement was not met with wild applause. Though my father did note it, putting a half question, half revelation on the end of the word "New York."

Mrs. Steloff, the owner, was an impossible person to work for. I was a stock clerk and occasionally delivered books to nearby apartments and hotels. I once delivered a book to Thornton Wilder at a hotel and thought I would see him, but the doorman took the book away and I was left walking away drugged that I didn't get a chance to see somebody famous.

Mrs. Steloff shouted at everybody, customers, the help. She seemed to get easily aggravated and impatient with any number of things. She screamed at me for not knowing where the stock was, not moving fast enough, the usual. Mrs. Steloff asked, after I'd been there a few weeks, if I was cripple — she was referring to the slightly dragged leg of the cool hipster hop I carried with me from Newark, a legacy of black. It was ironic to me, Shit, this bitch think I'm cripple and I'm hip.

Now I began to read the real estate section. Apartments to Let. It gave me something to do on the bus in the mornings or during the forty-five-minute lunches Mrs. Steloff gave us. Talking to Tim and Brad was occasionally encouraging. They wanted to move too. They were ready. But then one morning I saw an ad in the paper for an apartment on East 3rd Street. An ex-UN worker was leaving, he had sublet the apartment, down just off First Avenue, and now he was splitting to go somewhere! Lunchtime I found my way down there. I'd wanted the Village proper, but this was close and it cost only $28 a month for three rooms, a cold-water walk-up. But to me it was right. When I walked in the apartment a couple of people were there talking to an Indian-looking guy about this and that and various qualifications. I walked in saying, "I'll take it! I'll take it." It didn't matter to me. I'd take it! And in a few minutes the business was all but concluded.

An apartment in New York? What? How can you handle that? These kinds of questions bounced subtly off the walls of my parents' house. (I didn't have much to take. Most of my civilian clothes had thinned out being in the air force. I had no great library to transport. It wouldn't be that bad.)

"But how can you deal with the rent? That job?" Fifty dollars a week was what Mrs. Steloff was paying me. I'd have money to spare. I had no other responsibilities and besides I'd have roommates. But Wilson and Davis squared up on me. They never left Jersey at all.

At the Gotham, I was constantly picking up on whatever in all directions. Authors' names I'd never heard of before, books I knew nothing about. Gotham has always been the home of "We Moderns," as it was listed in the catalogue: the post-WWI explosion of Western art and literature that brought these expressions into the 20th century, redefining the form and content of Euro-American life, still explosive as the French Revolution and Commune of 1871, but distorted by the cynicism and disillusion created by World War I and the abject crumbling of the Brotherhood of (white) Man on the battlefields of Belgium, France, and Germany. The maturation of Imperialism!

The New Directions books, the sacred texts of '20s modernity: Sartre, Cocteau, Djuna Barnes, Fitzgerald, D. H. Lawrence, Stein, and the contemporary bridge into our own day, existentialism. *The Little Review*, *Blast*, stream of consciousness, the mythology of Eliot, Pound, Joyce, Shakespeare & Co., Hemingway, the *Cantos*, all these things I was picking up on much deeper than before, buying books and carrying them back on the bus readying for my move.

Then one day I went over with my few things and few books. It was after work one evening I went over. There was a little furniture, a bed, a couple chairs. My father drove me, my mother went with us, searching East 3rd Street and First Avenue for some sign she could understand or feel comfortable with. The joint looked even grimmer inside, going up the narrow dark halls, opening the door and into the tiny cold-water flat. I could see my mother's eyes misting over. She looked hurt. My father went on talking about how I had better get some furniture. (They'd given me some sheets and towels, a blanket.) He was trying to make a joke of it all. I guess he knew, at least, that I was determined to do it, that I was off on my own, like it or not! And that, in itself, was encouraging. But my mother could barely see or speak. She mostly grunted at the place and whatever she thought the future held. And suddenly I was alone!

There were no lights burning. Con Ed hadn't yet turned on the power. There was no gas. I couldn't even cook—not that I knew how. I was using candles and they shed their eerie light, stuttering and crooked. I was where

I wanted to be, I thought. Living by myself. (I'd wanted that, hadn't I?) Throughout the service I'd groaned under the weight of different room-mates from the unobtrusive to the repulsive.

But now I was alone. Yet I sat up in the candle glare and was almost feeling regret. I knew no one for miles. I was a stranger in New York. The few friends I still knew in Jersey had vanished. Wilson and Davis had copped out. I had no phone, I couldn't even call anybody. That's a lonely feeling. But I had an apartment and a job. I was in New York on my own, by my lonesome, and that was good enough for me!

I started walking around now after work, mostly on the West Side, Green-wich Village. Looking. Watching people. I walked around Midtown where I worked. I had very little money. I'd gotten the gas and electric turned on. I made contact with Steve Korret and would go there once in a while. He seemed amused that I'd moved over. "So many had said they were coming (like Tim and Brad) and they were never strong enough to do it," he said. Like some ominous editorial. But I didn't want to hang around him too much. The stuff he was doing was on another level. Though I longed to be really included in his circle of friends. I'd seen a few people on the streets and spoken. "Yes, I've moved to New York. I'm on East 3rd Street." Not the Village, but close, they seemed to say. (This was before the Lower East Side became fashionable. It was then just *outside* of the Village, the ro-mantic center.)

I began to stop by the few places I knew or heard Steve went to. Rienzi's, a coffeehouse on MacDougal Street. The San Remo, a bar at the end of the block. I found out about Romero's, on Minetta Lane, run by a flashy mulatto, Johnny Romero (who later left for Puerto Rico, it was rumored, because of some run-in with the Mafia). It seemed to be the maximum hangout spot for many blacks in the Village then.

There was also a coffeehouse on West 4th near Sheridan Square called Pandora's Box, where Steve McQueen used to sit on the steps and watch the passing parade until he went off to Hollywood and became one of its drum majors. Coffeehouses, at that time, were very popular. The post-WWII decade of American visitors to Europe had brought back the coffee-house as one evidence of a new reacquaintanceship with continental cool. Certainly, for me, the coffeehouse was something totally new. Downtown New York coffee smells I associate with this period of my first permanent residence in the city. When you came up out of the subway or the PATH, the smell of coffee seemed to dominate everything.

I made the rounds of the coffeehouses, checking them and the people in them out. I'd heard certain names around Steve Korret. In fact one afternoon we'd gone over to Rienzi's and had espresso, caf, au lait, hot cider, or cappuccino, which I really liked. That might even have been before I got out of the service. But coming in the old Rienzi, with its gestures in the direction of continental sophistication, had turned me on. I thought everyone in those places was a writer or painter or something heavy.

Even when I got out of the service and was floating in and out of these places, I still thought for a while that all the customers were heavyweight intellectuals. Intellectual paperbacks were just coming out about that period as well. And people could be seen with the intriguingly packaged soft pocket books, folding and unfolding them out of bags and pockets. Sipping coffee and poking deeply, it seemed, into *Moses and Monotheism* or *Seven Types of Ambiguity* or Aristophanes' comedies, mostly reissues with the slick arty covers that made merchandising moguls attribute "genius" to the young men who conceived and orchestrated this paperback explosion.

But I was struck by the ambience of the place. People in strange clothes. (One dude I saw on the streets then dressed up like a specter from the Middle Ages, like some *jongleur* wandering through the streets, complete with bells and all. I wondered then, what wild shit lurks behind this creature's eyes?) The supposed freedom well advertised as the animating dream of that mixed-matched Village flock I believed as well. It was what I needed, just come out of the extreme opposite. Suddenly, I *was* free, I felt. I could do anything I could conceive of. Some days walking down the streets, with the roasted coffee bean aroma in my nose, I almost couldn't believe I had gotten out of the service and could walk down the street. And though I still had to get up work-early, to get uptown to the Gotham Book Mart and Mrs. Steloff's madness, I felt liberated on the real side.

My reading had prepared me for this trip as well as my friendship with Steve Korret and what I had perceived to be the life of "the Village" through his spiritual stewardship. My last few months in the air force I'd even started getting *The Village Voice* and began to read more specifically about contemporary Village types. I even wrote a note, a letter to the editor, that was printed, regarding a controversy about the "meaning" of Beckett's *Waiting for Godot*. My first signed article, "E. L. Jones, Ramey AFB, Puerto Rico." "Godot means God and/or Death. The ending of the word is simply death in German turned around." Such intellectual pomposity leaning up out of the 73rd Bomb Squad.

I first met Ted Joans, then a surrealist painter, in those pages. With his beret and symbolic rhinoceros. He had a small gallery somewhere on the East Side and featured in one show the works of Reggin Nam. Gross, but at that point fascinating. Though I wondered why. But I had then, even from across the sea, some forming image of what was going on downtown.

The idea that the Village was where Art was being created, where there was a high level of intellectual seriousness, was what I thought. And the strange dress and mores that I perceived even from the distant jailhouse of air force blue I thought part of the equipment necessary to have such heavy things go on. The trips home, on leave, and before that, from school life, helped cement these notions in my mind. So that I did think that coffee-house after coffeehouse and the other establishments down around West 4th and MacDougal, Bleecker or 8th Street, were filled with World Class intellectuals. And I felt a little uneasy just appearing on those streets or inside those places with no real qualifications save desire.

The streets themselves held a magic for my young self as well. Names like Minetta Lane and Jane Street and Waverly Place or Charles or Perry or Sheridan Square or Cornelia all carried with them, for me, notions of the strange, the exotic, and I dug it all, believed in it all.

I was meeting people or seeing them in one way or another through Korret. He was my center, and his circle the pinnacle of my social and intellectual aspirations. He had an integrated kind of court. His second wife was a dancer and she had danced with Merce Cunningham. Those groups of young white intellectuals were hooked up with Cunningham and John Cage and David Tudor; Korret and his wife, Charlene, knew and had some degree of social relationship. Though at the time these names were just part of the rash of information I had to file and build my own understanding with.

Steve worked in a bookstore, Orientalia, along with Cunningham and Cage's and the Living Theater's lighting designer, Nicky Czernovitch, whom I had now got to know going in and out of Orientalia, staring in awe at the thousands of titles relating to Eastern thought. Zen had come in even then with some groups of Village intellectuals. It was the so-called Beat Generation people who later popularized this attention to Eastern philosophy, especially Zen. But Korret, Czernovitch, Cage, Cunningham, Renny Charlip, and their circles were intimately involved with the philosophy even then. And because of Steve Korret, so was I.

The most obvious facet of the Zen trend in the Village in those days was the Zen "jokes." People in that circle would make ironic statements, funny or with pretensions of being funny, that were supposed to reveal some basic Zen truth or insight. I guess this came because in the various books about Zen, especially Blythe and Alan Watt and Suzuki, humor was supposed to be an intrinsic part of the doctrine. And many times individuals were supposed to have gained "enlightenment" through laughter. In fact, the Zen masters and monks and other initiates were always supposed to be "roaring with laughter" in revelation of one Zen truth or another.

One of Korret's friends was a painter named Norman, a Jewish dude who had strange, almost slanted eyes. I was sure this was because he was deep off into Zen. And Norman played the part. When I first met him, he gave me one of his strange-ass paintings. It was a seated woman, painted very flat against a very flat background, with no eyes. I sat and looked at that painting for a long time trying to figure it out. I never did.

Norman, in his sandals and long reddish-brown beard, was for me, in those days, the prototype of the Village intellectual. A painter, involved with Zen and its high antic truths, who walked around in sandals (though with socks) even in the winter and a big turtleneck sweater, cracking ironic anomalies about a world I was still trying to understand.

Because of William White and his paintings and my own attempt at doing some painting under his influence while I was in the service, it crossed my mind a couple of times that maybe I wanted to be a painter. I remember standing in the cold-water flat on East 3rd Street batting painter or writer back and forth in my head for a minute. But then I settled quickly on being a writer since as broke as I was I could not buy the materials to paint with. Hence my decision.

Still, I was fascinated with painting. And Korret's circle contained, I found out after a while, quite a few painters. The black painters, Harvey Cropper, Arthur Hardie, Walter Williams, Sam Middleton, Virginia Cox, and the great Vincent Smith, were all part of Korret's circle, inner or outer. Later, many of these people went to Europe, convinced, probably, that the U.S. is really home only for barbarians.

Certainly, Europe was the intellectual center for many in Korret's circle. I guess for one part of a whole generation, they were more connected to the vision the emigré Richard Wright or the '20s "modernists" had about America, with Europe as some sort of haven. There was a whole section of that generation that came just after Wright, Jimmy Baldwin's generation, perhaps, who took up residence in Europe, or who came back and forth. Some finally deciding it was better to be formally foreign in a foreign land. There was still the mythology of black people being able to make it better in Europe, especially Paris, away from the diabolic torture of American racism. There was no doubt that for many black intellectuals, like their white counterparts, white intellectual Europe was the source and site of the really serious intellectual pursuits. But for black people this assumption has very serious implications. (It has, finally, for all Americans.) The intellectual worship of Europe is in one sense only the remnants of colonialism, still pushed by the rulers through their "English Departments" and concert halls!

It was Harvey and Arthur I had seen in a photo Korret sent me in Puerto Rico. Bird had some indirect hookup with this circle, I'd heard. Harvey Cropper had tried to teach Bird to paint in exchange for Bird teaching Harvey to play the saxophone. But Bird was dead by the time I got to the Village (contrary to what Ted Joans wrote in 1981 in *Coda* magazine saying that when I was around in the early days of beatnikdom I didn't "consistently fly on bird wings"). Bird died when I was in the error farce. I remember Yodo and I talking about it. I didn't reach the Village (except on leave from HU or the error farce) until March 1957!

There were writers too in that circle. One I remember, Clyde Hamlet, who imitated Dylan Thomas. But many people did then. Korret's work at this time was connected very consistently with Thomas, who was roaring around the Village, especially the White Horse Tavern. Hamlet was a very short, very dark brother with owlish eyes who ran with jazz musicians as well. He was reputed to have lived with Buhaina, Art Blakey, up in a loft on 29th Street. Hamlet was suave and sophisticated, I thought, he was hip to me. That's why I couldn't understand his poetry sounding so exactly like Dylan Thomas's (nor Steve's) when it seemed to me, once I'd read Thomas, that anyone reading him would realize immediately that their poems (especially Clyde's) were simply Thomas imitations and little else.

What I'd said before about how my reading was taking me into something and away from something at the same time is relevant here. Because this circle of Korret's and indeed his influence, to a certain extent, was merely a continuation of the other "whitening" influences I had been submitting to enthusiastically under the guise of information, education. That was true. But, again, there was something else being taken in. I guess not for the first time, but adding weight to whatever other similar tendencies come with anything you take in in this white supremacy society.

So that Europe as intellectual center was yet another stone to the weight of "alienation" from black (if that is not too strong a word) that was building up in me. Exiting from one world and entering another. That's the way this learning I'd committed myself to had taken shape. As fragmented and personal as that learning was, the sources I went to most consistently had more the weight of the white than the brown or black (though the yellow trailed its source, as it does, like a shadow).

And I learned quickly that the Cages and Cunninghams were very highly esteemed in that circle. Almost mythological beings, and ditto "Dylan," as Korret called him, like they were cutbuddies. So I was heavy into Dylan and Yeats too because Steve Korret quoted Yeats so often. He'd even quoted "Lapis Lazuli" in a letter to me in Puerto Rico, and I treasured those few lines and eagerly sought to know their source. "Gaiety transfiguring all that dread./All men have aimed at, found and lost;/Black out; Heaven blazing into the head. "

There were deep assumptions these people lived by and I did too, but who knew what they were? I didn't, and I am clear that unconsciousness is a ubiquitous condition. The rule of confusion is terrifying. But I followed now, eagerly, happily, assured in myself that this, finally, was what I had been looking for. Not only as the place where my intellectual pursuit would take place, but the life there, as I knew it, as it seemed to me then—this was the life I wanted.

When Charlene, Steve's wife, served cheese omelet and black bread along with ale, for me it was the sheerest revelation. Korret's white apartment to me was the essence of hip bohemianism. I knew nothing (consciously) about omelets (nor black bread, nor ale). It was "Village food" and I adored it. I had known nothing about white apartments. Even the word "bohemian" I thought of as intriguing, positive, something to be found out about and emulated. The conversations, both their form and content, heard around Steve or in those coffeehouses, or around Washington Square and MacDougal or Bleecker. The long-haired mysterious women with their eyes painted, "free-looking" in sandals. Dudes with berets or bookish pipe-smoking people. I was drawn to all of them and all of it. Who knew that all of this sat in a particular way in the world of meaning? Who knew the significance of all of it measured against a real world? The world Norman called (since he worked at not having to work) "The World of Effort." Echoing the superhip metaphyiscs of Bodhidharma or the second Patriarch.

But it is significant that most of those blacks I met through Steve Korret, who were artists, left this country, finally, never to return. Virginia Cox lived for years on Bedford Street, very near where Steve Korret lived before he went to Scandinavia in 1960. Vincent Smith, who was perhaps the most legitimately bohemian (in the sense that he had no money and was not just some middle-class juvenile having his way paid through bohemia, as I later was to find out some of the white folks I met were, but coming out of a Brooklyn ghetto had to struggle against society and even against what it tried to make him into, in order to paint). And then finally, when he began to paint consistently, Vincent developed a style that was thoroughly black; completely connected to the history and tradition of Afro-American painting, but at the same time, original and fresh. Vincent still lives in the U.S., and though he still, even at his high level of artistic accomplishment, has difficulty getting major shows, this is also part of the black tradition in this country, and will be until we get our own cultural institutions. But his work is still strong and still triumphantly beautifully black, and all those streets and voices and music course through his images with a daring and sense of color that is his alone yet collective as the African American experience itself.

At the time Vince was joked about, not harshly but lovingly, in Korret's circle, because he was such a hard liver. (Though, thank goodness, this changed many years ago.) He was a wine bandit, for a minute, the talk had it. And he lived in a loft that had neither heat nor light. It was the bohemianism of necessity, in one sense, rather than the fake poverty of the well-to-do little boys and girls. But Vincent's vision was black, and the soul that pulsed through his work was dark as our history and he has survived!

This was 1957. Eisenhower was president and jokes were made about his backwardness, much like the gibes that were tossed at genius Gerry Ford. The Montgomery bus boycott had just scored a success, desegregating Montgomery's buses. Martin Luther King, the leader of this black victory, was just coming into the public's eye when he had cooled out large numbers of armed black people who were spoiling for a fight as a reaction to racists' bombing of King's home. This had taken place on national television. A few months later SCLC—the Southern Christian Leadership Conference—was born. This was the year that Jimmy Brown, the great fullback, also shot into national prominence. Later that year, Orval Faubus and Little Rock would also come to widespread public notice.

So this was a time of transition. From the cooled-out reactionary '50s, the '50s of the cold war and McCarthyism and HUAC, to the late '50s of the surging civil rights movement. And I myself was a transitional figure, coming out of the brown world and its black sources but already yellowed out a bit by the Capstone employment agency on The Hill. And then to add insult to injury, or maybe attempted homicide to assault, I had offered myself to the totalitarian "whiteness" of the military. Running away from it, I dived into the books, only to get involved in a deeper, more "profound," more rational version of the same thing. And then suddenly the unaware chump, seeking escape, runs into, strangely, a slender white woman with painted eyes, ponytail, and sandals with a copy of Strindberg under one arm.

The Village, of course, is where I first met with white in any social situation portending equality (though that is a story still to be told). The underlying tone of that social circle was that black men and white women could make it, if they wanted to. Steve was not hooked up with a white woman nor had he been that I know of. In fact, later, when I began to go out with one white woman I met (whom I later married), Steve spoke somewhat disapprovingly of this, in his way. And I believed, for some reason at that time, that he did not even like white people, though I had never thought of it before. But when he said what he said to me about the white woman I was seeing he tried to embarrass both of us saying that she had caught me "with coon fruit" (watermelon). And seeking to legitimatize his seeming objection to this woman or at least understand it, I said Steve hated white people. Though it never occurred to me that he did, or for that matter that *anybody* did or would bother.

Strange then, that after Korret left for Scandinavia he would marry a white woman and be content to live over there with her and the family they created. Though I guess it is not strange, since if you are going to stay in a place where there are mostly white people, there is certainly a greater chance of becoming hooked up with one. And then, like we used to say, So what?

That circle, however, did seem to have the white woman/black man connection as one of its underlying themes. Certainly, Clyde Hamlet was always hooked up with one white lady or another. And so were many of the now emigré painters of that group. But I thought nothing of it except that it was hip. The idea that you could go with a white woman seemed like one of the "down" aspects of the whole bohemian scene. Before coming to the Village I had never really thought about white women. In Barringer High, I certainly looked at the various sweaters and skirts and insinuating walks and lyrical smiles of the mostly Italian female student body. But that was nothing and barely registered. (At least I didn't think it did at the time.)

I think that was the tone of perhaps a whole generation or two of black intellectuals, who, seeing segregation and discrimination as the worst enemy, sought a more open contact with the world. And certainly, those who were taught that Europe (the Holy Grail of "whiteness") was the source of intellectual life and measure could have that understanding shaped in some specific social context into a liaison or affair or long-term relationship with whites, a romantic connection. This was one of the advertised characteristics of the bohemia I came into. Though a black and white couple could still cause a few heads to turn, even in the Village. But by the late '50s such connections and relationships were on the obvious increase.

Bird was probably the patron saint of the generation preceding mine, as he was an arch-bohemian in the downtown Village sense, including his famous trysts and marriages with several white women. Wild flights of art, heroin blind, and "pulling grey bitches" were Bird's trademarks. Or so at least it was told. Jimmy Baldwin's *Notes of a Native Son* had come out about that time and I stared at it in the old Eighth Street Bookstore, admiring the cool black face that stared back at me. And to me, Jimmy was the last great black arts figure who related to Europe as center. But even Jimmy is transitional in this sense, since he began to travel back and forth and was no longer the classic black exile in Europe.

I was like blotting paper for any sensation. All perception, watching and looking, listening, trying to emulate and understand. A young boy just back from the outlands, still outlandish himself, but wanting to learn whatever anybody claimed was valuable to be learned.

And now I wonder what I looked like then. Wandering the streets trying to check something out, not only thinking that almost everyone I saw or met hungered and thirsted after knowledge the way I did, but figuring that they had been around the Village, that they had been on the scene for a while. I doubted anybody I saw in the San Remo or Pandora's Box or Rienzi's had been stuffed away in the brown-and-yellowness of HU or imprisoned in Aguadilla in an air force suit. Who could be that stupid and gullible? Only your reporter.

Meanwhile, I no longer had a job. One afternoon I went to lunch and never returned. I really went out to lunch. Suddenly, leaving the Gotham Book Mart with Mrs. Steloff's freshest hoydenisms ringing in my ears convinced me that on my newfound freedom trek I did not need any new top sergeant. So I simply split, no explanation, nothing, just gone gone gone.

This made for problems though, like cash. I was not sure what I would do. Didn't think about it and in the suddenness of my "decision" didn't even care. I just walked, and was glad to. It crossed my mind a couple days later that maybe I could get on unemployment. I hadn't worked long enough, but I remembered someone had told me that veterans had some weeks of unemployment compensation coming. But then the contradiction to that, I thought, was that I had been Undesirably Discharged. Maybe that would cancel out that unemployment. I had to find out.

The little apartment on East 3rd Street was stark and cold. When they said cold water they were not shitting. I turned on the slender gas range, opening the oven door and lighting up all the "eyes" on top. Sometimes I'd sit reading with my feet thrust into the oven, the chair tilted back, with a heavy sweater on. I had also begun to write a little, a few scratchings, but not much. Everything was still too new, too strange to do any real writing. I didn't even know what I wanted to write about. Except the kind of poems I'd written in Puerto Rico, abstract and big-worded, talking about stuff of which I had only the remotest idea.

For eating, I'd usually buy a few canned foods. I shouldn't say "foods" because the shit I ended up getting was only marginally edible. I couldn't (and still can't) cook, so mostly what I did was heat up canned garbage. I'd always be eating something like Spam (ugg!) or canned Chef Boyardee spaghetti (double-ugg!), really loathsome stuff like that. Sometimes I'd heat that shit up, then didn't want to eat it. And it would sit there getting cold in an already cold apartment and I'd stare at the concoction I was supposed to dump down in my stomach. Usually, I would get hungry enough to gobble it down very quick and still be hungry.

The hungriest I've ever been was at HU, where, spending the money my parents sent me right away, I had no money left for the cafeteria (before my mother and father got wise and started sending the money directly to the cafeteria food plan). Broke, I'd live off Nabs (those little Ritz cracker and peanut butter sandwiches) and orange soda.

But even in that hunger there was a kind of collective kid glee, probably at the prospect of actually being hungry, a virtually unknown phenomenon, so I guess that was kind of exotic. East 3rd Street hunger maybe had a little of that element in it. Alone, in my cold-water flat, knowing almost no one in the whole of that huge city, and now without a job and very little money, the exoticism was not the factor that I thought about. Such a hunger as can come to exist in such circumstances has a much more dire impact, because of the aloneness, the kind of solitary nature of your situation.

I could have called my parents, but I absolutely did not intend to do that. That would have been an admission that I had failed, that I was still a little boy. I was twenty-three, an adult, I could take care of myself. Actually, the college and air force stints had made me more self-reliant and even though I was getting ready to get in a bad fix, I knew I could handle it.

So I sat with my feet in the oven and read or tried to scribble on a yellow legal pad. Or I would walk around peeping in windows, looking at books and people, finding out things I thought I needed to know. And had no money. But I started to react in more aggressive ways to my new state. I began going into various delicatessens, usually on the far West Side, Greenwich Village proper, and trying to boost certain things I needed to survive. My best shot was those nice barbecuing chickens they sit on the counter after taking them off the spit. Occasionally, I'd catch the store clerks in the right position, off one of the chickens, and hat. I also began to discover various ways of advancing my economic position (at least easing my hunger) just like the big corporations, and in the true spirit of American free enterprise I began to rip off what I could, modest enough, but effective. I discovered that the bread trucks and milk trucks left their wares in the doorways of the stores before those stores were open. I'd shoot out early in the morning and cop a couple quarts of milk and a half dozen rolls. So I had breakfast. Somehow I'd cop some hated Spam or some cheese and I had lunch. Dinner I'd deal with the flying chicken routine, when I could.

Sometimes Steve Korret invited me to dinner and that was, to me, unbelievably great. Sitting in that neat white apartment with all those books and talking and eating, staring respectfully in awe at Steve's gorgeous wife, Charlene. I'd also begun to meet some other young people on my own, usually around the coffeehouses I'd stop in from time to time. There was Ernie, a young brother from the West Indies, who was also trying to write poetry. And we hung together, after a fashion. Sometimes he'd even come over to my scrambled-up little joint and we'd sit around talking about poetry, looking at each other's work, and figuring out how to survive with no money. (Some years later I think Ernie did go back to the West Indies and away from the hated cold weather.)

There was Ed, who was still in school up at CCNY, majoring in philosophy. Ed was a robust, actually a big fat dude, always smiling or about to smile. He was a poet as well, but deep off into Eastern philosophy. Both Ed and Ernie knew Korret, but they were too young to be in that circle. The three of us would sit in Rienzi's over cider or cappuccino (I never liked espresso) and talk about what we knew and what we didn't. We liked the idea of sitting around being young poets, young black dudes trying to find a way in the world. Sometimes that world seemed wayless, sealed up, surrounding us with high walls of anonymity, racism, penfrom, the norms of U.S. life for young black men (or old black men, or young black women or old black women, or middle-aged, etc., etc.). But we all gave off optimism like life rays, and actually encouraged each other by our willingness to be out there in that world saying, "Hey, we gonna be writers, dig it?" And not caring what anybody thought about that.

I still was in general awe of being "free," brown, and twenty-three, post-HU, post-error farce, and swarming all over the Village in search of myself, but now I was becoming somewhat more acclimated. I was meeting people my own age and saw that many of their problems and designs were like my own. Our conversations helped bring the Village and slowly the entire world of the intellectuals and artists more clearly into focus. I could begin the process of measuring what actually existed and how I stood in relationship to the real, not the youthfully subjective. I could begin to see what had really been accomplished and by whom. My perception was slowly deepening.

Also, a little later, Jim Mitchum showed up downtown. He'd gotten out of the service later than I had gotten thrown out. And now he'd finally wound his way around to where I was, still carrying the camera over his shoulder and still speaking in that stilted roundabout way of his. He was still living up in the Bronx but I'd see him too from time to time and he'd hang out with us, or just the two of us. Ed, Ernie, Jim, and Roi sitting in some coffee shop, late winter/early spring 1957 and for a couple years after that, plotting our rise to the tops of the buildings. Laughing at each other's jokes and each other's conceits, taking serious interest in each other's work; I guess trying to understand the world.

There was also a wilder guy I met about the same time, Tim Poston. Tim was also a poet, but older than the rest of us. He lived in a furnished room over near Cooper Union. In fact, you could look out of Tim's window and right across the street from Cooper Union was a big billboard with a picture of Trujillo on it, then dictator of the Dominican Republic. U.S. support for Trujillo was so great in those days (like its support for the Peruvian fascists today) that they allowed him to have this really huge billboard bringing greetings to gullible U.S. citizens. Some days we'd sit there drinking wine with Tim (Tim only drank wine) and staring out at Trujillo.

Tim had been around the Village for quite a while when I ran into him. Both Ernie and Ed spoke of him as a talented poet. Ernie and Ed, though young, had also been around the Village for a while. Ed making his forays from the Bronx, but based at CCNY. And Ernie not long over, but longer than I, from the islands. When I finally did get to see some of Tim's poetry,

I was also impressed. He'd been influenced by surrealists of one kind or another, and he was kind of wiggy anyway. Tim's problem was that he drank too much and when he drank too much he acted even wiggier than usual. He would scream and laugh too uproariously and even occasionally get into bad scenes with folks who did not appreciate his essentially fun-loving innocent nature. Tim drank so much he developed certain mental problems or perhaps the alcohol just emphasized certain problems he already had. But he was a hard case when he was in his grapes and he was in his grapes much of the time.

Tim and I got pretty tight. At one point, he was one of my closest friends. But he was a definite pain in the ass, a problem to know. If you knew Tim, then you not only had to put up with him but had to try to help him out of the various scrapes he'd get into. Or he'd come over to your crib and nut out, just collapse and lie across your bed with his mouth open, snoring like the Charge of the Light Brigade. But he was a good poet. At the time I knew him, he had already (unlike most of us) developed a distinctive style — surreal, cynical, and funny, just like him. He had scraps of poetry all over his nasty little furnished room. Tim's room looked even wilder than my apartment, I guess because he'd been there longer, in a smaller space, and had more time to accumulate mountains of debris. All kinds of bottles he hadn't thrown out, books thrown everywhere, in a room not much bigger than a cell.

I liked Tim, I guess, because he was a *real* poet. He had a sureness to his hand (not as sure as it would have been if he'd managed to stay sober over longer periods) that came with practice and knowing what it was he wanted to say. The rest of us, Ed, Ernie, and I, didn't know what the hell we wanted to say. Ernie was under the Dylan Thomas tarp which those years threw upon so many. Ed was trying to write haikus or tankas and deal with Eastern philosophy in the traditional forms of the East and Middle East, and I don't know what I was doing, just abstractions and big words about whatever — who knows?

Plus Tim gave me a look at the Village, at the life downtown, that I couldn't get from Steve Korret. Steve had a circle that functioned at the fringe of another, more fashionable circle (I see now). Steve was who I wanted to emulate. Straight, erudite, slightly mysterious, knowledgeable, ensconced in a beautiful little white apartment with a gorgeous brown wife. But Tim was out, he was on the fringe of everything. He looked at the whole scene with another eye, a jaundiced, drunken, very cynical eye. The way he lived was bottom-of-the-barrel bohemian, no frills or pretension. He was almost a bum. He had a harder life, hence a harder view, than Korret's, and somehow this fascinated me. Also, he was older and I felt this gave me some kind of security or something, some kind of basic connection with the whole life and style of the place and its varied denizens.

I think that another important quality I got from Tim was that he helped me, with his cold cynicism, to see through the make-believe fairyland subjectivism I had about the Village. He allowed me to peep the widespread stupidity and even racism of the place. (Hey, I even came to the Village thinking the people there, those vaunted intellectuals and artists, "World Class Thinkers," could not possibly be "prejudiced" because that was dumb shit. That's how naive I was, how deeply subjective and desirous of a new world!)

Tim would tell me some outrageous story, laced with his steely cynicism, then fall out, as much at the story as at my reaction, my widening disbelieving eyes and childish grimace. That would knock him out and he'd hand me the bottle of cheapest wine to turn up just like him.

Like it was Tim who hipped me to the dangerous state of race relations in the Village. And other of my friends did, too. I found out myself from a few bad incidents. But Tim would fall back in his chair chortling and spilling the wine on his pants or shirt. "And watch out for the Italians, Leee-Roy, they'll bop you in the head. They don't like us black boys. They'll beat you up. Especially if you with a white woman. I always carry a blackjack with me or a knife." And he'd show you this limp-ass blackjack didn't look like it could do anything. "Watch out for the Italians, Leee-Roy." It'd crack Tim up.

He was right, to a certain extent. The "local people," as folks were wont to call the largely Italian population that was intermingled with the more exotic Villagey part, apparently did not care for the wild antics and bohemian carryings-on of the permanent visitors to their neighborhood. It was like the "townies" and the campus types. Like the "D.C. boys" and those of us up on The Hill down at the Capstone. Except with the blacks it was, as usual, even worse. The general resentment the locals felt toward the white bohemians was quadrupled at the sight of the black species. And there were plenty people with grim stories to verify Tim's charges. Like a guy I came to know named Will Ribbon, who went with this one white woman for years and lived down below Houston Street, where it was really reputed to be dangerous for white-black liaisons. He got jumped on by a gang of the young locals and they pummeled him and called his woman names.

Will goes home and gets his pistol, it was a Beretta, and he walks up and down Thompson Street and Sullivan Street down by Broome and Prince and Spring, looking for these guys. He even goes into some of those private clubs (reputed Mafia relaxation stations) hunting for these guys. When I started working down around that area I used to carry a lead pipe in a manila envelope, the envelope under my arm like a good messenger, not intimidated but nevertheless ready.

All this brought back harsh memories of Barringer where I had been part of a harassed minority under the Italian majority. I thought, Jeez, bastards followed me all the way over here. But it was Tim who prepared me for all of this.

I had another close friend, and he was from Newark as well. Tom Perry, older but runty like myself, maybe even shorter, much darker, and a dandy to the bone. Tom came out of a group of Newark black Hill intellectuals. Dudes I had glimpsed when I was coming up and just getting aware of my clothes, stalking Newark's Hill in search of the music. He was an old friend of Steve Korret's on the New York side. But in Newark, Tom was more closely linked with dudes like the super-hip "Stein" (called so because people thought he was heavy as Einstein), always "dap" and clean, Melvin Kemp, Ralph Brown, and Grachan Moncur, the trombonist. These dudes were so bad they used to *talk* about their clothes. They had definite tastes, were heavy into the English thing when most of us thought it was "Ivy." In fact Stein and Kemp were so far out they wouldn't hang with certain people if they had on the wrong shit.

Tom Perry was hip like that. Dark and quietly humorous with the kind of biting irony to his observations that I felt close to. You'd see Tom and he had some kind of job in a store, and he'd be coming down the street with some impeccable Harris tweed jacket, charcoal-grey pants with just a hint of a flare at the cuff (in honor of Newark), maybe a cold-blue shirt and a beautiful paisley or Indian madras tie and a handkerchief stuffed in his breast pocket that set it all off almost rakishly. Coming out of some bullshit job somewhere where he had to listen to some dull-assed white dude load him up with sorry shit, and Tom cleaner than sunlight!

Tom moved into the apartment under mine on East 3rd Street. When I first got to town he lived way over on Hudson Street with his wife, also from Newark, Maureen, who was even younger than I was. Maureen and I had gone to the same church and her mother was one of the movers and shakers in the Bethany class wars, a friend of my mother's but older and somewhat more flashy than my mother. She had an older son, who knew

Tom and Stein and the others, a very hip and intelligent dude. He got out of high school and went to work in one of the auto plants and he's been there ever since—almost thirty years. Still, when you see him on the street or with his binoculars going to the track meets or other sporting events—that's his thing, sports—he looks like some really taste-setting executive on his way to a late conference. (But his sister was something else again.)

The first time I went over to Hudson Street to see Tom he introduced me to the "speedball." I didn't know anything about drugs, not even marijuana. And my first years in the Village didn't change much. I had neither the money nor the inclination to get into drugs. They just didn't interest me. It was no moral thing, I just didn't know anything much about them. But Tom mixed this heroin and cocaine, which people on the street call a speedball, and offered me a couple snorts. I didn't know what the shit was too tough, just the names of the stuff. But Tom was into "chippying"—using scag now and again—and his boy, Ralph, who came over every once in a while from Newark, would bring some stuff over. Tom would give me a little snort and it would take me up, but this speedball business was something else. I'd never really been that high before. The heavy drugs almost dropped me to my knees, but somehow I made it out and down the stairs. Tom was saying, "Hey, man, you gonna be all right?" And I staggered all the way crosstown to East 3rd Street, throwing up any number of times as the world whizzed in circles around me.

After that, Tom and I, on some weekends, would score and I'd get fairly mashed up. Not so much at this point, but some time later, Tom and I would always be copping and getting zonked and wasted. But around this time, Tom and Maureen moved into the same building. They had to move out of Hudson Street, and I saw one of the apartments vacant in the building and told them and they moved in. Maureen had just given birth to a little girl and Tom had gotten another of the store-type jobs he'd get to make ends meet. But that entire apartment building was kind of funky. On one floor there was a family of Gypsies, and during this cold winter the door of their apartment couldn't quite shut, so that the blasts of icy air would shoot straight in on them. I don't know whether they had any heat at all. Tom had a couple of kerosene-type heaters and I had my stove with all the eyes on and the oven door open.

I'd begun to write now. Slowly, pitifully (to me), I began to eke out a few words. A couple of poems I wanted to keep, though I don't think I kept any. I'd even written a few pages of a play, a musical, because the girl I'd been almost going with when I got home from the service had a musical troupe and said she wanted a play. I'd begun to write it not knowing what the hell I was doing. I titled the play *A Good Girl Is Hard to Find*, probably in reflection of my generally womanless state. I'd mentioned I was going to write a musical at Steve Korret's one night, if not full out before the attendants of Korret's court, at least to one of his friends who was known in the circle as "a composer." In my naive pretension and presumption I asked if Silva, the composer (who was named this because he looked like a villainous actor, Henry Silva), would do the music. He nodded yes. Other people in the circle assured me that Silva was a composer, and I assumed he was serious. But I never finished the play. And Silva never produced any music that I know of. I think he was one of those people I began to find out about who never *did* anything but hang around the Village claiming they were this or that but who were just that—hang-arounders. Some of them only hung around for women, some just to hang, but I was surprised as I discovered more and more people like this.

Really I was fearful that maybe I was one of these people too. Because as it dawned on me that these hang-arounders abounded down in the old Village, then I began to be more and more skeptical, in some moments, about myself. After all, what was I doing? Hanging around. Walking the streets. Sitting in coffeehouses talking. Reading a bit, quite a bit actually. Trying to find out anything about everything. But what, really, was I doing? Nothing took me down as much as that pessimistic perception.

What it meant really was that I was developing some critical faculty, I suppose. Beginning to peep through this "paradise" of my own making, created by my own needs, and see its reality. There were many people who were earnestly trying to create Art (which more and more I focused on as my "purpose"), but there were a whole lot of people—and Korret knew quite a few of them—who were all pretense and prevarication. Sham artists whose claim to being artists was a justification for their bohemian lifestyles.

This became even clearer once I began to get into the habit of writing. Once I started actually writing more regularly, it caused all kinds of other things to happen. For one thing, people began to look at me, regard me would be more like it, a little differently. I think some people down there actually thought that the act of my writing harmed them in some way. Maybe because they were just profiling and here was some naive young dude trying to write for real. They mighta been around for years tap-tapping every once in a while, now some know-nothing colored kid is gonna come on the scene—what? writing? Bullshit!

I wrote a story, a rather longish story, at that time my maximum creation. It was called "The Marathon Runner" (hopefully, it is lost), influenced, I would imagine, by Franz Kafka, who I had gotten into deep. The short stories really turned me on, even though I didn't fully understand them. "The Hunger Artist," "In the Penal Colony," "The Metamorphosis," plus *The Trial* and *The Castle*. I liked that eerie otherworldly style of Kafka's, the heavy symbolism. Yet I was too young and inexperienced to understand the heavy social commentary of that symbolism. I got mostly its air, Kafka's style, feeling that that style carried something of deadly seriousness about it. I did not really understand that Kafka, indeed, was talking about the rise of fascism.

But I worked away at "The Marathon Runner," writing in my yellow legal pad, for weeks. I even had drawings of the course the marathon runner of the title ran. It was a somewhat metaphysical rumination about the runner running, I guess inwardly and outwardly aspiring to some unknown absolute as I was, the narrative full of philosophical abstraction and labored symbolism. But it was mine. And after this story, I no longer had as much difficulty getting some of my feelings down on the page.

I brought the story to Steve Korret to read. He would be the person I brought this sign of genuine promise to (so I thought, shyly enough). I was no mere hang-arounder, I was for real. I was going to write. This was no bullshit. Korret seemed startled when I handed him the story. He had seemed somewhat startled, or maybe it was just sardonically amused, when I told him I had written a long story I wanted him to read. But now that I'd handed him "The Marathon Runner," he almost colored (except he was too dark complexioned for red to register). He grinned in a fixed way like I had done something to him that was not really all that pleasant, and he was surprised I would do that to him, my old friend and maximum mentor.

When I saw him a couple of times before he finished reading the story he would comment aloud to Charlene or to whoever was around, that I had written a story and had given it to him to read and that he was reading it. He made it seem more portentous than I thought it was—the giving of the story to him to read—it was almost as if it was some kind of challenge that I had issued to him. And I could pick that up.

It was at this point that I reflected that I had never seen any of Steve Korret's writing. Except the letters he had written to me when I was in

Puerto Rico. Two letters. I remembered also that he had once spoken of his "work" and showed me vaguely some pile of papers and note cards. He said he jotted things down on note cards. And now I think he showed me some more of his work, typed irregularly on yellow Swedish bond, interspersed with hosts of note cards. This was after he had announced that the story I'd given him was "ambitious, very ambitious," but he said no more, grinning broadly when he pronounced my ambition. What he showed me was rambling, yet trying to find focus for focus. It was abstract and philosophical; it was speculative philosophy of a metaphysical bent, deeply influenced by Eastern religion. Yet I had not the vaguest idea of what it was trying to say. I blinked and kept scanning until he took it from me. Steve laughed deeply, he had given me back "The Marathon Runner" as he pronounced my ambition.

I didn't know what to make of that, though I could sense a kind of tightness—the accepting of a challenge that I hadn't meant to issue. I was just trying to be true to myself, to my own dreams and fantasies. I hadn't realized I'd encroached on someone else's and I still didn't know how.

It was Percy Knight, an old friend of Steve's and a very fine person, who shed some light on the situation. Percy was part of Steve's circle, but Percy had no pretensions that called for membership in bohemia. Percy lived in Brooklyn and worked for the Transit Authority. He was an intellectual and, I always thought, a philosopher. It was Percy who always pronounced the most ironic and thoroughly comic of the Zen "jokes" and tales. I looked to Percy as an older brother, a *real* person from whom you could receive some actual information about the world. Always smiling and cool, Percy said to me simply, "About that story you've written, Steve tells me it's very good." He paused. "I knew it would be." And smiling coolly, as was his wont, he talked about other things.

The story came at a time when I was beginning to roam a little more on my own. It was probably the confirmation of this development. Before, I had been under Steve Korret's tutelage, armed and guided by his stance and opinions, but now I moved a little away from this conscious and unconscious center. The story had a lot to do with it. Perhaps it was the pronouncement of an independence I didn't even realize I needed to pronounce. I was living from hand to mouth, very tenuously. The rent, increased to $32 a month, seemed an enormous amount. Finally, Mitchum moved in with me to share the rent, but still I had no consistent source of money. Jim had some sort of job and this kept me from getting tossed out of that joint on my head. Tom lent me a few dollars, and there were some other scams. But I had to get a job. I looked in various newspapers, followed certain clues, but still nothing. I was getting desperate.

A couple times people from Newark came over to see me, but they generally did not dig the horrible little cold-ass apartment with no furniture. I'd "built" a desk from a tabletop hooked by belts to one wall so it could be let down to sit on some milk crates that I had books put into. The bed was never made, the sheets a stomach-turning grey, and shit thrown around everywhere. When Mitchum came in he also brought his darkroom equipment and turned one of the rooms into a darkroom and another room into his bedroom, which left me a bedroom and the kitchen. When Mitchum had women over, the shit really got complicated. But it beat being out in the street and at this point Jim was paying the rent until I got straight.

Two of my old flames came over. Betty, who I'd gone with in high school, was so horrified by the apartment she vowed never to come again. In fact she thought the place was so bad that she wouldn't let me sleep with her, saying the sheets made her sick. And given Betty and my previous hookup with nonstop teenage copulation all over the place, this was a rude awakening, not to mention a deadly drag!

Later Joanie Johnson, the singer I'd been going with most recently just before I'd left home, also came over. We had never made it and I thought that now that I had an "apartment" she would let me make love to her. But when she got over there, she froze and pushed my panting face away and unpeeled my hot fingers, shaking her head. I thought, "this prudish bitch" and said to her only "Why? Come on." But she shook her head and looked away. I was crushed.

But one thing positive happened. Looking in *The Village Voice*, I spied an ad that said "Clerk wanted, jazz magazine, inquire *The Record Trader*, 271 Sullivan St." I shot over there bright and early. The guy I talked to was the proprietor, Dick Hallock, a youngish, though five or six years older than I, blond guy with one lock of hair falling constantly over his eye. He wore glasses and kept a gentle warming smile that really made you know the guy was all right, whatever else he might be.

The Record Trader was in a narrow grey storefront. All over the front of the store and in the back were records, mostly 78 rpm's, stacked every which way. I came in bullshitting, but not really. I told Dick I knew about the music but not much before Louis Armstrong. Dick told me not many people knew about the music before Louie Armstrong. But aside from my own tastes and what I'd learned formally from Sterling Brown and casually from dudes like Yodo, I didn't know much about the formal history of the music.

We talked, Dick relaxed, a small dog jumping up into his lap which he petted for a while, then the dog jumped down to wander around between the myriad boxes stacked all over. Dick sat wheeled sideways from an old rolltop desk. A tweed cap sat, bill straight up, barely on the back of his head. The desk was the resting place of papers, record albums, opened and unopened letters, and a whole lot of other stuff that would otherwise have been lost from the world. Dick was a collector, it turned out, not only of old records but of old (and new) everything else. A few old cylinders from antique cylinder machines were on the desk, Rolls-Royce fixtures, a clarinet case with the clarinet lying across it, the dog's (Noel's) leash, and thousands of other objects all lay relating to each other on top of, around, or near to that sprawling desk. And the desk itself was very large, the room very small. The records, boxes, walls of shelves with more records, an oil heater, Dick and I and Noel, all made the small storefront even smaller.

The Record Trader was a magazine for "moldy figs," i.e., those diggers of the old jazz. Actually "figs" were mostly white worshipers of pre-swing, pre-big band jazz. The diggers of the "original," "New Orleans" stuff, the music before it got newfangled and weird. What delicious irony that young whites would be the upholders of the old jazz when most times they would have little use for contemporary, deeming it an expression of the savage woogies. But once the expression was not contemporary, once the bloods had moved to a newer expression, then the old jazz could be appreciated. Because, as one critic turkey said, "It brings back the old days, when things and people were simpler." Then the new jazz, the contemporary expression, could be put down (as the old once had) as "noise" and "savage ruckus." Ah, well.

Dick and company had a little of that to 'em, I discovered, and I got to meet many of the Ivy-trained slick young white critics who were just coming into the open (some of the older ones as well) and got a chance to peep close-up on the development of the species. Though, to be wholesided, I must say I learned a great deal not only from Dick but from the many types who wandered through the *Trader*, as we called it.

The magazine's function was to provide commentary and analysis of the music (as I said, in the main, the older, more traditional styles) and at the same time to hold auctions of various people's collections so that people could get hold of some of the old records they wanted for their own collections. A typical issue of the *Trader* would have a couple of feature articles, maybe on Bunk Johnson or Jack Teagarden or Kid Ory or the white hopes, Bix Beiderbecke, the New Orleans Rhythm Kings, etc., plus several auction listings. In those listings you'd see some things like "Armstrong, Louis OK 8447 N[ew] $12.50" or "Keppard, Freddie Para 12399 N $11.00." There'd be records that featured a brief Beiderbecke solo amidst Whiteman's or Goldkette's cacophony, or even early Bing Crosby singing with Whiteman would fetch a pretty penny. The collectors, mostly middle-class white people—"figs."

My gig at the *Trader* was to consist of being the shipping clerk. I would get the letters after they'd been opened and the money taken out, find the records among the stacks, then package them and mail them out. I needed a job, any job, but the *Trader* job seemed to me something heavier, something maybe I could dig, who knew?

After talking to Dick a few minutes and getting some indication of what the job entailed, and with some measuring going on by Dick and myself of what the prospects looked like, I was told I could have the job if I wanted it. It was paying $40 for a part-time slave, which wasn't bad, 12 noon till 4. Hey, in those relaxed (albeit chaotic) circumstances, and with only Dick and Noel to bug me, it looked great to me. I was going to start the next day.

Before I got out of the narrow storefront, a stocky little white woman with big owlish glasses came in grinning, huffing and puffing from hurrying back (I couldn't understand why) from her lunch. I was introduced to Nellie Kohn, the *Trader's* secretary, who laughingly made a funny little curtsy and slid between the record shelf in the middle of the floor and the wall where there was a typing table and a pile of letters. In a couple of minutes, Dick and I still exchanging parting small talk, a tall slender light-brown-haired woman came rushing in, also out of breath, but from shopping. Her hands were filled with bags. This was Barbara Weiss, Dick's roomie and fiancée. Dick and Barbara had been going together about five years, living together about three, and shortly before I was gone from the *Trader* or it was gone from me, they were married.

Barbara's father was a famous anthropologist who had done important studies of South America, particularly Brazil. He taught at NYU and Barbara's family lived in a sprawling eight- or nine-room apartment overlooking Washington Square. One of the old-time luxury apartments. It was Barbara's father who first translated the Brazilian genius Machado de Assis.

The funniest thing in the world was witnessing Barbara and Dick have a conversation. It consisted of Barbara talking nonstop about any number of things, sometimes at the same time, and Dick nodding, saying a few words, petting the dog, or noodling on his clarinet, while Barbara went on jetting out language faster than sound. But she was a nice, well-meaning woman and shared all of Dick's interests, but in a lighter, more airy, more casual way. Dick dug traditional jazz, playing the clarinet (which he did with several Dixieland groups, including one called the Red Onion Jazz Band), Noel, antique cars (he had a 1922 Rolls-Royce), writing, and, as he put it, "facing" around the Village. Barbara was stashed in that hierarchy, fairly high up.

In a few minutes, a black dude named Will Ribbon (he of the searching Beretta) came in. Will was one of the only young black men I knew to play traditional jazz. He was a trumpet player and sounded then like a slightly younger version of Bunk Johnson. Only slightly younger. Will came in talking and laughing as he crossed the threshold. He and Dick were old friends. He pecked Barbara on the cheek and called over to Nellie, "How's your crotch?" Not knowing the exact meaning of that greeting, I blanked on it, though I could hear Nellie's distinct embarrassment in their exchange.

Finally, I got out of there, but the next day, getting acquainted with my tasks, maybe ten or twelve people came through the *Trader* offices. Most of them old friends, school friends, Village friends, musician friends of Dick's. I was introduced to all of them. There was Martin Williams and Larry Gushee, who were writers. Martin and I became pretty good friends, though we had our differences about the music. But Martin was not a fig, he did have a scholar's regard for the traditional but at the same time he was very much into the contemporary music. He dug Monk, which brought us closer, since Monk was my main man. Martin was also one of the first persons I knew who dug and hipped me to Ornette Coleman when he blew into town a little while later. And one of the best magazines about the music, the short-lived *Jazz Review*, which was edited by Martin, remains one of the hippest magazines ever to appear. It was in the *Jazz Review* as well that I published my first full-length article, a piece on saxophonist Buddy Tate.

I also got to meet guys like Dan Morgenstern, who thought the music ended with the big bands, though later he was willing to admit certain latecomers into the pantheon. Williams, now is the jazz person at the Smithsonian; Morgenstern, the chief scholar, etc., at Newark's Institute of Jazz Studies. At the time, Morgenstern was a *Downbeat* regular. Bob Parent, the jazz photographer, was a *Trader* regular. Bob lived in a loft right around the corner, when SoHo was just a bunch of industrial buildings and factories. He came into the *Trader* every other day to shoot the shit, walking his own dog. Sometimes he and Dick would go down the street, each strangling a little dog as they half flew up the block, talking about who was playing where.

What made an impression on me was that there was a whole group of young university-trained, fairly well-to-do white dudes who had come up with the music in their youth, listening and playing or hanging out in the clubs. And, generally, these were the critics, and the ones I met, the most *advanced* critics of the music. Nat Hentoff used to come around from time to time and he and I got to know each other fairly well. I always respected Nat because he was and remains serious about his concerns. In fact, Williams, Hentoff, Gushee, and Ross Russell remain some of the most astute critics of Afro-American music, though they are all white. But it began to dawn on me that there were not many black voices focusing (or at least being published) on black music. I'd written Leonard Feather (or was it Norman Grantz?) a letter when I was in the service, attacking him for patronizing Charlie Parker by saying on the liner notes of *Bird and Strings* that "Charlie Parker had to be on his best musical behavior" because he was playing with the likes of Mitch Miller and the strings. I knew that shit was racism, young and twisted up as I was, and shot Grantz-Feather a note telling him that "one day I will be a jazz critic" and that I would waste his ass for such bullshit ignorance and racism. That was an assertion that came from somewhere deep inside me. As I wrote it, I wondered at its reality, but whatever emotion prompted it was real enough for me to send it.

Being around these people now made my desire to know and write more about the music bloom. Every day I came to the *Trader* I had to go through stacks of records looking for the ones ordered in the auction. I studied bands and players from different periods, labels, and trends. I got to know the key personalities in the different periods of jazz and began to understand when and how the music changed. Later I would do my own deeper research to find out *why* it changed, which remains to me the most important question. (Later, I got a job with a guy called not-so-lovingly "Jake the Snake," a big record trader. Jake had literally thousands of records in his cellar which he sold to collectors by mail order all over the world. It was my job to put those records in alphabetical order. These jobs were like graduate school, though for the Snake I was in semidarkness in a dank cellar, thumbing for hours through the records. From both jobs I gained not only a great deal of knowledge but also a respectable collection of traditional jazz and swing and blues. My job with the Snake ended when someone rushed by him as he was about to enter his car one evening, closing the door on his hand and cutting off his thumb. A lot of the people around the *Trader* suggested that this happened to the Snake because he was so evil.)

I would see Nellie Kohn at work each day and we would trade a few light sentences but that was all. She had been in the Village a year or so after graduating from Mary Washington College of the University of Virginia. UVA was the Yale or Harvard of the Confederacy and Mary Washington its Radcliffe. Nellie was a Jewish girl from Long Island trying to make it in the Village. She was interested in the theater and literature (her major), but being in the Village, it seemed at this point, was her major focus. She was going with a guy who came by the *Trader* on a motor scooter and took her motor-facing around the Village.

My own life had gotten a little more stable and a little more directed with the acquisition of the job at the *Trader*, but there was a problem, and it surfaced not long after I had gotten there. The problem was money—there wasn't much. Hallock ran the *Trader* on pennies, some of it his own. Dick was one of those staunchly "anticommercial" idealists who litter places like the Village. Middle-class people who think they can somehow preserve "standards" in the holocaust of monopoly capitalism. They yearn for the epoch of the handmade, of the old craftsmanship, of a sentimental "integrity" that permeates all they hold in reverence. It was a major breakthrough when Dick decided to take advertising other than for the record auctions. And after a couple issues, around the time I came on board, the magazine got more irregular and so did my salary. I got paid when Dick had money, in bits and pieces. But I didn't mind as long as I had a little pocket money. I liked the *Trader* because it brought me close to things I cared about. I thought of it as something like a school for me. Plus I liked Dick and his soon-to-be wife and Nellie and the assorted stream of characters that came in and out.

Steve Korret and company now did not occupy a central place in my life. And in the tiny crib, Jim always had one woman or another, till finally he installed one semipermanent lady, the plump Bernice, and they laughed and cried among the negatives while I was coming in and out. When I wasn't at the *Trader*, I might be at some club with Martin or Will Ribbon or Dick or hanging with Ernie or Tim. I'd started to go also to clubs which featured poetry readings.

One night I went to a party that a painter friend of Korret's gave at a loft in the '20s, probably Walter Williams. I met a white woman there, Dolly Weinberg. I don't know how we met, I wasn't doing much dancing, probably just circling around the walls, a little shyer than is healthy. The party was one of those hollering and running and pushing and drinking bashes where a hundred or so people are mashed into a big old loft. I was looking at people, maybe I talked to some. A few I knew from Steve, but when I left I was with Dolly Weinberg and we walked slowly down Seventh or Eighth Avenue to her house, which was way down below Houston on Thompson Street, near the *Trader*, down there where Tim had warned me against going, especially with white women.

Dolly was much older than I was. She was in her middle or late thirties then and I was twenty-three. She had grey hair with a little black tied into a bun, and she dressed like a classic bohemian, peasant skirt and blouse, sandals, etc. We talked and walked and talked and talked. She was curious. I was so young, she said. One time she took my face in her hands while we were waiting for a light. I was so young, she said.

When we got down to her place, a five-flight walk-up on Thompson Street long before SoHo fashion arrived in those parts, we stood out in front of the building still talking. I had never talked to any white woman before at such length or with such intentions. Because as we wound down toward her place I could see sleeping with her. It seemed to me part of the adventure of my new life in the Village. The black man with the white woman, I thought some kind of classic bohemian accoutrement and so this meeting and walking and talking fascinated me.

But Dolly was not altogether all together. This began to register, some of her conversation was strange to me. She talked about things I didn't completely get because they were out of different epochs and I had been scarcely educated formally. For instance, she talked about the radical '30s. In fact, later I discovered she had been a Communist. She was still, she thought, some kind of fellow traveler. But her relationship, even ideologically, had grown vague and unfocused. She knew about the "fascists" and the "bosses" and she made reference to them in her conversation. But Dolly was no middle-class Jewish girl from an Ivy League school. She worked in some sweatshop. She had come from that kind of Jewish family, her people from the Lower East Side when it was full of Mike Gold's people. The life she talked about seemed mean and cold, the product of a dying economic system. But it had done something to her psychologically—she spent half her weekly salary on a psychiatrist and had spent some time in at least one mental hospital.

As the sun began to come up on Thompson Street she took me upstairs into her apartment, where I stayed until the middle of the afternoon. When I woke up Dolly had split for work. There was a note and stuff laid out to make coffee. But I didn't like coffee. The apartment was small, maybe three rooms, and though it was cluttered, there was a sense of someone living there, not the chaotic storage space I lived in. She had a few books and records, though it was not the same kind of stuff one saw the youngish fashionable paperback readers carrying around. She was more into secondhand bookstores. The style was old-line radical bohemian, like the faded '30s memories she reflected but really had no direct part in. I sat around, clearing my head. I'd had quite a bit to drink. I sat quietly, browsing through her meager library. There were also a few drawings of Dolly around, in different-colored charcoal, and little Villagey things here and there around the rooms. But there was a meanness, a poverty to the place, that brought something else in with it along with the easy label of bohemian. It was bohemian but it was bohemian poverty. A starkness and bareness that was in no way fashionable. I sat there idle and reflecting. I had slept with a white woman and I wondered what it meant. The act itself had been like any other, but there was a mental "excitement" that this hookup brought that was "other." No matter that Dolly, as I said, was really an older woman and no goddam beauty queen. A mental excitement. I pondered it as I rose and went down those stairs, ducking my head as I met a few of the other residents of the building, who were mostly the local Italians. It seemed they were all scowling at me and so were the ones in the street, including the clutches of men standing and sitting in front of the private clubs and coffeehouses as I walked up the street a couple short blocks to the *Trader* offices.

For a couple of days things went on as before. I was coming to the *Trader*, packing boxes, and going my way. I was still trying to write, scratching away when I could on my legal pads. I still had no typewriter. But then one afternoon Dolly came into the storefront. I had told her where I worked, and though I hadn't tried to get in touch with her, had only barely thought about her, now she had come into the *Trader* and leaned up against the boxes grinning at me. In the light of day, even the half-light of the *Trader*, she looked even older. We talked a little about the party, about what I had done when I woke up. What she had done at work that day, how she felt.

I was alone for an hour or so, but now Nellie and Dick came in one after the other. Dolly made a bad joke when she found out that Dick was my "boss."

"This guy don't look like such a big-time capitalist," she laughed. And Dick, of course, didn't. I could see him peeping over and through his glasses as he prepared to take out his clarinet and practice. Nellie was making faces over at her tiny typing table. I guess they were signals, but I couldn't pick them all up.

Dolly spoke exactly like the stereotypical Lower East Side worker Mike Gold might write about, even though she had wandered around the Village for almost twenty years. That middle-class panache that is supposed to come with the bohemian life she had not picked up at all. She spoke almost exactly like a stage working-class white person and it embarrassed me a little (sad to say), that tough New York accent that bought trouble as easily as it described it.

We left the *Trader* together, going into a coffeehouse and talking some more, and finally we went back to her house. I must've stayed there two or three weeks, maybe more, going back and forth to the *Trader*, and only occasionally back over to East 3rd Street, when I needed more clothes or to get something or other. Jim took it in stride. I was still giving him a little dough for the rent, and by now he was deeply involved with Bernice. He had heard that I was keeping company with Dolly from someone else, who it turned out even knew Dolly, so they said, so he just mentioned it to me to confirm it. He nodded and chuckled at the thought.

Living there with Dolly was a little out, because Dolly was not a little out. The longer I knew Dolly, the more I could see that she was very deeply disturbed. To her the world was a horrible, frustrating place (as it is under the rule of the ancient minority). In this sense she was like Tim and his wined-up, cynical self. But Dolly not only had the radical background, she had gone for the Freudian psychological trip as well. So she actually, literally, spent $20 a week out of a $75 salary on the headshrinker. And she had been doing that over *ten* years! She told me this as matter-of-fact exposition, though she seemed, upon my naive open-eyed questioning, to be a little embarrassed because the shit had not worked. The pain she felt, she still felt, and all those $20s going to this slick psychiatrist had not changed any of that.

She had another male friend she talked about incessantly. An older dude who, as the ironies of class society would have it, was the brother of a friend of my sister's. The woman, Shelley Ransome, went to Teachers

College with my sister, and Shelley's brother, Luther Ransome, had come to New York seeking to be a sculptor. They were his drawings strewn around the house. But "Mensch," as she called him, seemed only to hook up with Dolly when he was broke. And while they had lived together in a loft on Great Jones Street, Dolly said she couldn't take his beatings, his arguments, his blaming of the world's ills on her, his taking her money and her love and leaving her nothing but the imprint of his flailing hand on her face.

The whole story chilled me. In fact, Dolly's life, the apartment, the weekly psychiatrist, all chilled me. A little boy from a little brown house and family. All these things, including her speech, seemed out to lunch to me, too extreme and pathological. And Dolly peeped as much, telling me what a child I was, what a little boy. She even told me one blue night high up over the street that I didn't know anything about sex. What with the straight-ahead stuff I knew, the same thing going in the same place, that was truly humbling and humiliating, though thinking about it, how much could I know? Though I had sneaked and read Krafft-Ebing when I was in high school and *The Kinsey Report*, but I had scant experience except with Betty from Newark and I never saw her anymore. She had never complained except that she thought that doing it during my lunchtime on the family couch was a little abbreviated.

But I was still mostly there at Dolly's but drawn away in a funny way, tilted away from her. I had never been there all the way I guess.

One night after work Nellie's boy on the motor scooter didn't show and I walked her home. She lived just a few blocks from the *Trader*, in the opposite direction, on Morton Street. In the central, more fashionable Village where the middle-class, hardly bohemian residents cribbed. We had talked in pieces every day I went to work, but it was distanced and polite. She was always friendly and helpful. I always wanted to ask her why Will Ribbon greeted her the way he did. But Nellie was funny. I'd seen her one night dressed in black, leotards and top, from head to foot. She was so little she reminded me of a mouse. But she had been jumping up and down talking to someone, the scooter guy (his name was Guy, as well), and it knocked me out. She seemed so antic and clownish.

Nellie said she had wanted to be a clown. She liked circuses and show biz. She liked making people laugh, with her little hopping walk and neat Mary Washington clothes, combined with instant bohemian getups. I was walking her home, I had no other intentions, maybe because we worked together everyday, and that was as far as I saw it. But when we reached

Morton Street, she quickly invited me up for coffee. I didn't drink coffee, so she offered me a piece of watermelon she had in the refrigerator. (The source of Korret's gibe a few months later.)

We talked about literature, she could see I was serious and that made her want to know how come and what it meant or maybe she just wanted to get laid, I donno. Anyway, by the early morning hours I was still there and still talking. We were talking about Shakespeare, Hamlet or Lear or Macbeth when I made my move.

Nellie lived in a one-room efficiency-type apartment, painted white with bullfight posters and Mexican hats on the walls. She had a narrow wall of books, many of them from school, a white rag rug, a tiny kitchen section with a table and refrigerator and stove and not much else. But it was in a really fashionable West Village area and one paid for that.

By now Nellie was looking for work in the mornings because it was clear that the *Trader* was not long for this world. She was gone when I woke up and I rummaged around and went over to the storefront. When she did come in we looked at each other from time to time and smiled, and after work, as Barbara and Dick looked on, we went off together towards her place. I didn't have much at Dolly's, maybe nothing at all. But whatever it was I got it out, though there was one scene where just before I left we were together one last night and then the next evening Dolly sees Nellie and me coming out of a coffeehouse. She called me at the *Trader* the next day and says, "You're with me one night, the next night I see you with the little whosis. Do you think that's right?" I said I didn't, but that was the last time we spoke as people relating to each other intimately. I had "moved in" with Nellie and went on sleeping there and going back and forth to the *Trader*, while Nellie looked for another job.

Though the relationship with Nellie had its tentative aspects as well, still there was much more a sense of us actually "going together," to the extent that such a definition could apply to us. I was open, naive, in the sense that I did not know what such a relationship involved—i.e., the black-white thing. I don't think Nellie knew much either, on the real side, about such a hookup. But she was much less naive than I thought about the general man-woman connect.

We were working at the *Trader* and generally going home together after work. We'd go to a few places, very few, because neither of us had much money. We might go out in the company of Dick and Barbara and some of the other *Trader* regulars. It was light stuff. People around us, I think, took our hookup as light stuff—casual. Ribbon winked and chuckled when he found out. But it was all still vague and offhand, even to us.

Occasionally I would go back to East 3rd Street and holler at Jim and whoever. Sit down and talk with Tom Perry. I might bump into Tim, but I didn't see Korret that much anymore. I was taking on a new group of friends, or at least drifting away from one circle.

Nellie and I did talk, about a lot of things. Our plans, I suppose. What we saw or wanted to see for ourselves. Who we thought we wanted to become. For one thing, Nellie had something of an inferiority complex. First, she'd been out in Long Island under the heavy sun of gentile suburbia, trying to grow and having to relate to whatever the dominant image and peer pressure was for the Jewish middle-class yearning for American middle-classdom but finding only Jewish middle-classdom. Plus she was very tiny but almost chubby, "zoftig" I heard a store owner friend of ours describe her, with a very Semitic-looking face (if such a concept is scientific). But the prescribed stereotype, East European, prominent nose of aquiline proportion, etc.

Going to Mary Washington had done nothing to eradicate her feeling of inferiority. The black middle class suffers from the same kind of malady, a lack of self-esteem caused by the great nation chauvinism that is so much a part of American life. White supremacy, anti-Semitism, they not only work on the victims to deprive them of material and spiritual ease but they can, with some of the victims, actually convince them that they are hated for correct reasons, and the victims take up this same view, only, of course, it is now self-hate.

With Nellie, this lack of self-esteem took on a personal cast. It was not so much expressed as being anti-Jewish as by feeling that since she was small and plain looking, she could not be a glamorous figure in the theater or the world of lights and action. She was also attacked psychologically by the effects of struggling to overcome the anti-Semitic stereotypes syndrome. The attack that national minorities feel or the immigrants before they got integrated into the great white (racist) American Dream. I read in a diary of hers one night: "I think I'm losing my Jewishness. . . . Grrr, what is that?" That is, a debate about whether there was such a thing as "Jewishness" and, if so, was it a quality worth maintaining? The cultural aggression that is the norm of U.S. life creates such paradoxical questions in the minds of its victims. And so the swarm of self-doubts that confused the young Nellie Kohn.

I read in that same diary a list of men's names. It was shocking for some reason. (Where had I obtained such fake morality?) Nellie actually listed the names of the men she had slept with—at least that's what I took it to be. I wanted to remember the names, most of them I didn't know. But since I saw my name, "Roi," at the bottom of the list, I assumed that's what it was. Plus, my man Guy's name was there just before mine. I wondered why a person would have such a list, what it portended. It was no short list either, and I wondered if perhaps it went back into high school or something. Another thing she had in that diary was a running day to day or every few days entry about what was going on in her life. I had stumbled on the diary rummaging around in things, as I usually did when I awoke and Nellie was already out looking for a new job. I'd go through things, and look at things, read different books—at least a few pages of ones I was only a trifle interested in. Being in the calm white apartment, in an orderly clean setting, was new to me since the beginning of my Village days, so I was fascinated. Being in the apartment gave me a sense of well-being, plus I was very nosy.

I stumbled upon a recent entry that seemed the dreamy reflections of a young woman—"What is ahead for me? What am I going to do with my life?" And then she added: "I'll be all right if Roi doesn't continue to live here." Well, that hurt. Nellie and I seemed to get on smoothly enough, though there was no great passion. There was sex, fueled up a little higher maybe by the mutual curiosity each of us felt about the other. We mentioned sometimes different stereotypes we'd heard about black-white romantic relationships and we'd laugh, above and beyond such stupidity. But mentally we'd check to see if such was true about us.

I never mentioned to Nellie that I had read her diary. But in a couple days, over some pretense, I cut out for East 3rd Street. A few days later, while I was scratching away in the dank little pad, there was a knock at the door and Nellie stood outside asking could she come in. And I was back on Morton Street. A week or so later, I was supposed to meet her at the Randall's Island Jazz Festival. I couldn't go but wanted to hang around outside after it was over since I was always interested in jazz musicians and the people who dug them. I spotted Nellie standing talking to Dick and Barbara, and when I come up she colors—turns an unfashionable pink. I look from one to the other while we're exchanging small talk and by the by young Guy comes up wheeling his motor scooter. There are a few words, some embarrassed bullshit, then she climbs on the back of the scooter and goes off with Guy. So I was gone again. But in a few days the same thing

happens. She's tapping at the door and I come to the door and she's standing there with tears in her eyes. (It was my sister, Kimako, who said once,
"You don't understand women." The male chauvinism that would let me
accept such a copout must be obvious.)

After that, though, there were other stages, other openings and closings
in our relationship. For one thing, now it was certain that there was a
relationship, whatever it was. It existed. Not only did we know each other,
but we related to each other. We liked talking to each other, apparently.
Maybe we liked sleeping with each other, but there was never any passion.
But maybe that's idealism. Maybe I didn't know what passion was in the
first place, since there's no truth in advertising. We always related to each
other calmly and rationally.

We were living together now too. It was her apartment on Morton Street,
but we went about what we went about like that was where we both lived.
Nellie had gotten a job with a publisher. It wasn't quite what she wanted
but it was more money and it was consistent. The *Trader* had just about
gone down the tubes. I was still there. But Martin William had hooked me
up with a job proctoring for examinations at New York Law School. I stood
in the room so students couldn't cheat. It paid a few dollars and was a
welcome addition to my lack of money.

For the first time, I was "going with" someone in New York. Some kind
of stability had been reached in the relationship. We'd go to a few places.
Movies, sometimes a club. That's when we ran into Steve Korret up near
the old Loews Sheridan. He said, "You're the one who's been keeping him
away from us," glowering at Nellie in a mixture of mock outrage and his
normal arrogance. When the story of the watermelon got told, he responded,
"Coon fruit you got him with coon fruit!" A few more words and he was
gone and I tried to explain what I didn't understand.

I did begin to understand what the interracial relationship was in this
society. The stares from people on the street, the tension that rose in my
own self in certain situations, though for the most part I didn't give much
of a shit what anybody, not no white people anyway, thought about our
hookup. But there is a mutual mythology that gets built in those relationships and built by the people in them. Information about the other's world
becomes one main topic of discussion. Though, I think, black people by
and large know more about the "white world" than whites know about the
life and times of even the middle-class blood in America. But the differences in the cultures between the American culture and its various ethnic
variations and the African American are points of departure for discussion.

The conflicting opinions that come with those lives are discussable as well and the dynamic that makes the meeting interesting. But white supremacy creates an inequality in those relationships that probably most of the people in them cannot identify by name but certainly they can by what emotions and ideas it produces. For me, suddenly, there were no more black women in my life and it had happened quietly, "normally," without fanfare or recognition. Betty and Joanie I had struck out with in the nasty little East 3rd Street pad. Neither of them were bohemian. Betty had said openly the joint sickened her, Joanie hadn't said anything but she'd turned down my romantic blandishments flat. During one of Nellie and my split-ups I'd tried to get Betty to go to the apartment again. But she refused. And she'd heard that I was going with "some white girl" and that chilled her even more. What did I want with her? she said. "I heard you going with some white girl." I took it only as jealousy, but it was really a farewell speech from the distaff side of the nationality. I didn't know.

One night Nellie and I got into a discussion about children. We'd been living together for a few months now. I was beginning to meet some of her friends. A couple of girls from school, a cousin, some old boyfriends. And we're talking about children, the subject having come up in some strange fashion. "I wouldn't want children," Nellie was saying. "I wouldn't want them to grow up in this kind of world. Children in a mixed marriage would suffer." (We'd never talked about marriage or anything that square before.)

I disagreed with her. I thought I heard something else in that, that one shouldn't have children as the result of any mixed situation. I protested and acted, was, hurt. Not that I intended to marry her, but her saying that the issue of an interracial union was negative slightly inflamed me. The more I thought about it, the more inflamed I became. We had yet another split-up and I went to East 3rd Street. I called Betty but she wouldn't come. I could sniff her disapproval over the phone. "No, I'm not coming over there. For what?"

When we got back together, Nellie told me she was pregnant. That flattened me. Pregnant? Great balls of shit what was going to happen now? But I just smiled at her and touched her arm. "What are we going to do?" she was saying. "It's already a couple of months." There was a fitful harassed look on her face.

I asked her what she wanted to do and she told me about some doctor in Pennsylvania who did abortions. In a week she had gone, stayed the weekend, and returned unloaded. But she looked drugged with the whole situation. I offered to leave for good. In a few more months she told me she was pregnant again. "We'll get married," I said. It came out of me without my having inspected it. Clear and audible: "married."

When she repeated the word, I could hear it more clearly. But I have the kind of personality that will take on any kind of commitment if I can feel any real connection with it, and not blanch or shake (at least not outwardly) at whatever consequences. "Yeah," I assured her. "We can get married."

What I said had opened a trap door into our deeper feelings. Married? To whom? For what? Forever? I felt a little pushed, more than a little uncertain, but I couldn't think of anything else to say. What? Go get another abortion for crissakes!!? What was terrifying deep down was that I felt nothing really. There was no passion. It was quiet and rational. Our words back and forth. There were smiles. Nellie looked at me smiling, half smiling, uncertain. She didn't know what to do either. What kind of life would this be? How long would this last? Who was this, anyway?

The fact that this was a white woman that I stood close to in a small New York apartment talking about marrying was not significant at first, but it grew in significance the more I thought about what I'd said. Those same words, that same information, had to be relayed to various out- and inposts, this marrying, especially this marrying across the normal borders of cool. The running bohemians of the black-white hookups I knew didn't (I didn't think) get married. (But I didn't think about that anyway.) Hey, but here I was going off into some normal U.S. social shit, it was out. Some of that slopped around in my head, but at the same time I got the feeling that, after all, marriage was some normal U.S. shit, there was a fixture to it, a stasis I perceived (my youth in rebellion?) that I didn't know whether I dug or not. Hey, it was a kind of middle-class thing to do. I didn't come over to the Village for no regular middle-class shit, yet here I was in it. And what was so crushing, yet pulsing on the subtlest of emotional wires, was that I had a *responsibility*, I was expected to do something. I couldn't just walk away. And no, there was still no real passion.

We decided that we would get married in a Buddhist temple on the Upper West Side. It meant to me that I could avoid the normal straight up and down middle-class thing. Korret's prior coaching paid off in this expression. We contacted the Buddhist temple and arranged to be married there. Nellie's parents nutted out, and while her mother would at least talk about it, the father declared Nellie *dead*! (A male relative was sent to talk to us, but he was too young and the only thing we succeeded in doing was getting drunk together and I put him on the train wondering was he going to make it.)

My parents took it in stride. There was not even any eye rolling or excessive questioning. (Such is the disposition and tenor of the oppressed, they are so in love with democracy.) They just asked me was I sure about what I was doing. "As long as you're sure," my father said, looking at me not quite directly. They came to the wedding, and so did the Hallocks and Will Ribbon. That was it.

A few weeks before I got married, I met Tim Poston in the street and he was drunk as usual. He beat me on the back, whooping and hollering a mixture of greetings and biting commentary on why he hadn't seen me. "That's your girlfriend?" he was screaming. "That's your girlfriend? How're you, girlfriend?" he shouted, shoving his thick paw at Nellie. Then he grabs me around the shoulder and pulls me over to the side and in a mock whisper begins to harass me. "Whatta you, eatin' pussy now, Lee-Roy? Ha-ha-ha! Whatta you, eatin' pussy?" I pushed him away, telling him something he already knew, that he was drunk.

A couple days later, Tim found out where I was living, on Morton Street. He camps outside under the window screaming up at me. "Whatta you, eatin' pussy now, Lee-Roy? Huh, whatta you doing?" I had to come downstairs and wave my lead pipe, pulled out from inside the manila envelope, at him. To drive his drunken howling ass away from there.

Korret, Tom, and the rest of my friends had nothing to say about the marriage because I was not seeing them regular now. Jim knew something was going down (or coming up) since I'd gotten almost all my things and told him I would be moving.

I had managed to get on unemployment as a result of having been in the service, though I had to do some writing back and forth and get interviewed because I had a funny discharge. But in the end I got it, $38 a week. It beat a blank. Also I was still working from time to time proctoring. Nellie was taking in manuscripts to proofread and edit and doing typing to supplement the other editorial job. The Morton Street rent was pretty substantial and now the space began really to be too small. Two young people hugged up and in and out don't think about the space. But now, with more stability to the relationship, and the promise of another boarder, we began to think about moving as soon as we could.

In the meantime, I'd published a poem in a magazine put out by a guy named Judson Crews from Taos, New Mexico. The publication was called

The Naked Ear, the poem "Preface to a Twenty Volume Suicide Note," addressed to a daughter I did not even have. But the publication was encouraging, even though who the hell read *The Naked Ear* which was only half the size of a regular paperback but you could see it in some of the bookstores. I became a familiar figure in the Village bookstores, especially the Eighth Street and the Phoenix (run by a guy who was later a very close friend of mine, Larry Wallrich).

I was also going to the different poetry readings at clubs and bars in the Village. In the late '50s the poetry reading circuit came into its own. I began to meet other poets, Jack Micheline (the great populist) I heard read for the first time down at a club on Sixth Avenue, where Mingus was playing. On Mondays they had open poetry readings, and one night they had a contest and Jack won and I cheered him on. Howard Hart was another of those poets. Both Micheline and Hart wanted to read with jazz, which I thought was a hip idea. Steve Tropp was another reader and his wife Gloria. He was a white jazz drummer, his wife black, both of her arms crippled, but she was made up like in Hollywood science fiction movies about what blacks will look like in the future. (Later they had a child, a boy they called Tree Tree Tropp.) I even caught Langston Hughes reading with Mingus at a new club called the Five Spot. I spoke to him that night, very shyly, when he finished. Later, when I began to publish poems, Langston wrote me a note telling me he liked them. And he began to keep up with my publishing and from time to time wrote me and told me what he thought. Langston was always very sweet and extremely helpful and encouraging to young writers. When his *Selected Poems* came out he sent me an autographed copy, "To LeRoi, From Langston, Harlem, U.S.A.," and later he sent an autographed poem, "Backlash Blues," which I have on my wall framed today.

About this time I heard talk of Allen Ginsberg and his poem "Howl." I was moved by this poem so much because it talked about a world I could identify with and relate to. His language and his rhythms and the poem's contents were real to me. Unlike the cold edges and exclusiveness of the *New Yorker* poem that had made me cry, Ginsberg talked of a different world, one much closer to my own.

I thought "Howl" was something special. It was a breakthrough for me. I now knew poetry could be about some things that I was familiar with, that it did not have to be about suburban birdbaths and Greek mythology. I kept watch for more of Ginsberg's poems. And somehow I found out that he was living then in Paris, on a street called Git Le Couer. Wanting to be as weird to him as I thought he was to me, I wrote him a letter on toilet paper asking him was he for real. He sent me back a letter, also written on toilet paper, but the coarser European grade that makes better writing paper. He told me he was sincere but that he was tired of being Allen Ginsberg. (The notoriety was just starting.) He signed the letter and had a drawing under his signature of a lineup, a parade, of different beasts and animals, all with halos over their heads in some weird but jolly procession.

It was around this time I decided to publish a magazine. Poets. Writers. I knew that not only me but young dudes like Ernie and Ed and even Steve Korret and Tim Poston didn't publish for one reason or another. With Ernie, Ed, and me, I knew it was turndowns.

A guy named Brayton (Brady) Harris had a printing shop on Cornelia Street, just around the corner from where we lived. When I'd go into the Phoenix Book Store to poke around, I'd pass the shop. Eventually I went in there and asked about starting a magazine. We could be co-publishers, I improvised on the spot. I know all the young poets and writers. Do the printing at cost, you distribute some, I'll distribute the rest. Micheline was getting ready to publish his first book, *River of Red Wine*, and Maurice Kenny was publishing a book there, so one day when Micheline went over to see about his book, I raised the question about the magazine and Brady went for it. In fact he said he'd start a series of books and magazines. Jack's would be the first and our magazine could come out about the same time.

Nellie went for the idea. She was working in publishing. She had majored in literature. She thought it was a good thing to do. She'd type the manuscripts on our electric typewriter we rented when she took in typing. The name of the magazine would be *Zazen*. It was a Zen word, a special quality of being, a texture of perception reflected by the term "mystery." It had to do with attaining a high state of grace and relationship to divinity in whatever you did, especially in the arts. I had read the Japanese philosopher Seami, *On Attaining the Stage of Zazen*, and to me this was the quality the magazine must have, must attempt to put out. The attaining of a mysterious grace linked to spiritual revelation! And so the magazine would be called *Zazen*.

I wrote to Allen G. for manuscripts. I talked to Ernie and Ed and even Steve Korret and Tim Poston. I talked to some of the poets I'd met at the readings, they gave me other names. Work came in. Ginsberg sent four small poems for that first issue and told me about people like Philip Whalen, Gary Snyder, Gregory Corso, William Burroughs, Jack Kerouac, and others. Whalen sent some poetry immediately and Allen passed the word around. He was the poetry advertiser of that age, the role that Ezra Pound played during the '20s, hipping people to each other, trying to get various people published. He was one communications element, a very important one, in the mobilization of all those young poetic forces so that they could find some concrete expression.

I also had met some painters. A guy named Peter Schwarzberg was actually the son of one of Nellie's relative's friends. Peter was really out, out, out. He was in graduate school at the New School, in philosophy. He said he was a "phenomenologist" and his endless discourse about "the self and the *other*," existentialism and phenomenology, made me begin to study these philosophies myself. I began to read Heidegger and Wittgenstein and Husserl. Wittgenstein's *Tractatus* became an emotional reference for me. And Peter's paintings, heavily influenced by the German Expressionists, made me check their works out and study them. I came to dig Kirchner, Schmidt-Rottloff, Beckmann, Nolde, and the others, relating to that wild sense of color and exaggeration. But also to their deep sense of distress and social calamity.

Peter did our first cover and a few others, plus many illustrations in the magazine. There was also Tomi Ungerer, whom I met through the bookstore. Tomi was a painter, illustrator, writer, and mordant self-proclaimed existentialist wit. He did covers and some illustrations for us as well. Tomi went on to become very wealthy and famous for his children's books and other kinds of works plus his shows of paintings. The first issue of *Zazen* said: "A New Consciousness in Arts & Letters." We thought that. We used collages, illustrations, and drawings because we wanted to. We had no heavy weight of bullshit literary tradition staring us down.

When the first issue came out with its brownish-yellow cover with a face receding into a background of apparently shifting forms, I walked them all over the Village getting them in bookstores. I think we did five hundred and in a short time they were gone. There was no money in it, of course, but we wanted to get the work out. I was open to most directions of work (though my main thrust was unacademic, later anti-academic). I was looking for a "new consciousness." I didn't have any analytical treatise prepared on why my own consciousness was new, but that's the way I felt. And there were the vibes I picked up from the young people around me who were trying to live in a contemporary world. The people who had not been mugged so severely by various "English Departments" that they were still battily swamped in iambic pentameter, not to mention starchy-ass ways of living.

We saw "the man in the grey flannel suit" as an enemy, an agent of Dwight Eisenhower whose baby-food mentality we made fun of. We could feel, perhaps, the changes that were in motion throughout the whole society. We reflected some of that change. Though in those days I was not political in any conscious way, or formally political at any rate. But my first published poem in *Zazen* is about an angel who thinks that the segregated bathrooms of South Carolina marked "others" must be for him. "I wonder, could they have known?" So there is a political consciousness lurking, albeit somewhat submerged, under the focus and banner of my attention then to "Art." (A year or so later I could even be heard arguing with Kenneth Tynan that I was not political, as he struggled with me at some Beat poetry reading, ridiculing the nonsense I was spouting.)

It was 1958 and the first issue included Philip Whalen, Ed James, Judson Crews, Tom Postell, Allen Polite, Stephen Tropp, Bobb Hamilton, LeRoi Jones, Diane DiPrima, Ernest Kean, Jack Micheline, and Allen Ginsberg. Works by Tim Poston and Steve Korret were also included. The second issue, also 1958, had Gregory Corso, Tuli Kupferberg, Thomas Postell, LeRoi Jones, Barbara Ellen Moraff, Ron Loewinsohn, Diane DiPrima, Oliver Pitcher, James Boyer May, Harold Briggs, Bobb Hamilton, Gary Snyder, Ben (A. B.) Spellman, George Stade, and a poem of Poston's.

The magazine opened up a whole world of back-and-forth correspondence among other young writers. It also created some beginning recognition of my own name and work. I began to get word of other publications and sometimes exchanged issues. There was also news of new publications and various readings near and far. With *Zazen*, I had plugged into a developing literary world and I was beginning to see its outline. But new or not, there was still definite connection with the old world. For instance, one of the young editors of a magazine dedicated to the new writing had written me a letter saying that while he liked some of the work, some of it reminded him of "the old nigger writing of the '30s." I held the note, staring at it awhile. First of all I didn't know what he meant, except that there was some "nigger writing" he didn't like. (Do you think he was talking about the writers of the Harlem Renaissance?) This young editor was hooked up a little with Pound's work and ideas, but strangely enough, later, this same editor became a friend of mine and I never asked him about the remark.

So I could see the "newness" and the openness of ideas and forms that now began to come in to me as an editor. I was given a broader overview about what was going on that young people wanted to call literature that could be sent to a youthful Buddhist-tinged, "new" asserting publication that any close observer could see was hooked up in some way with somebody black. The first issue was evenly divided between black and white writers. By the third issue there was not one black writer at all (though I was still an editor)! At the same time the normal trepidation I felt when confronted with anything in the U.S. which I knew historically must be in some way linked to white supremacy made me wary as I entered into these new relationships. I did think that white people would be opposed to a black dude even being a writer, even saying it. I thought maybe it was like coming into some place where they wouldn't want you. That maybe there were *passwords* or dress codes or certain signals you had to learn. By this time I had met enough outright boobs and dumbasses to know better than my initial misunderstanding that the Village was the home of all World Class intellectuals, but I thought maybe there would be, for instance, purposeful confusion between the Silvas' and Clyde Hamlet's hanging out or just looking for white women and my own seriousness. I could assert anything, of course, but also I knew that there was a legitimacy and depth to my concerns. I did not as yet have a whole lot of confidence. But that came later on as well.

Nellie got a new job around this time that made some other changes in our lives. She got a job as a secretary at *Sectarian Review*. (Ironically, the same magazine mentioned in my USAF bust!) This brought in more money. The *Sectarian Review* was an established literary magazine, probably the best known of its kind. Even more ironic was the fact that the very things that *Zazen* wanted to oppose and transcend were the essence of the *Sectarian*. Nellie liked the job because it was the kind of thing her education had prepared her for. She not only got to meet, every couple days, the well-known editors of the magazine, but now and again, famous writers would blow in and she'd meet them or talk to them over the phone.

Our first child was still a couple months away, so the job raised our spirits. *Zazen* was at the same time creating a new set of friends for us. The magazine was becoming widely known, within a small circle of young writers and people who read them. One couple, George and Dolly Stade, we had gotten to be friends with. George had sent in some poems that we printed and they'd come over to talk. He was going to grad school at Columbia. (He became head of the English Department at Columbia College and a reviewer for the *New York Times Book Review* and a successful novelist.) We were even supposed to be moving into the same apartment, we decided, since we both needed more room, up on West 20th Street between Ninth and Tenth Avenues. But George said Dolly's parents hit the roof when they found out that the other couple was mixed and the colored guy might rape Dolly.

But finally we moved anyway, up to West 20th Street. The rent for us alone, without the Stades, was much too high. The unemployment checks were running out and in a couple months a baby would be here, so I had to go out and look for a job. I got a job as a technical editor, up on 49th Street. This meant I had to read the deathless prose of some semiliterate engineering majors and try to put it in readable scribble-scrabble. It couldn't be done. But that was a sobering experience, working 9 to 5 among some granite heads. I got the job because I could pass a typing test. The place was filled with real characters, mostly suburbanite, lower-middle-class whites whose vision of what the world is is so narrow the very look of them can suffocate you. There was Miriam the secretary and assistant office manager who was always getting into as many people's business as she could. When she left the office every night she'd gurgle, "Nightol," like the product, making a weary joke. There was Kent Manner, a big husky vice president, who really ran the company. Every day coming out of the subway I'd see him as he whizzed past me to work without speaking. I was glad, who the fuck wanted to speak to him? At one point he called me into the office saying, "Jones, what is it Lumumba wants?" My answer was a cheap copout, I said, "Whatever everybody else wants, I guess." And by that time I'd gotten much more political. There was Arnold, another technical editor who worked at the next desk. Arnold was funny because he was so mock serious about everything. He was like the underside of New York, the grey tedious side that is lost in the banter about the Great White Way. Arnold lived in a furnished apartment not far from the office. He lived there because it was close to the office. A two-button, patch-pocket jacket with no pretensions of anything but covering his narrow butt was enough to make Arnold sashay around telling me how well dressed he was when he looked like the j.v. floorwalker at Sterns. Arnold was the kind of guy who still went on "dates" in his late twenties. There was McMillian, the good-natured drunk who walked around telling jokes, always running scared of his job. And Monica, the older woman who was chief editor, she was quiet and scary mornings, her age probably telling her she was losing her capacity to turn it out like the biggies wanted. But afternoons, buddy, after she got a couple of them martinis under her belt she was a terror. In fact, McMillian and Monica were alike in that respect. After lunch, Jim, they were dynamite, full of confidence and raring to go, unless of course they had that fourth martini and then they had to be carried home.

Just as I was getting into the literary life, I had to drag off to labor and I resented it. Perhaps that is why I resented the people working there so much. I would rush down into the subway and rush out, always just making it or late. But it was a must. The *Sectarian Review* had just published an article putting down the Beats. I didn't even think I was Beat or even know what that meant, except as a media term, but I resented the writer's basic bias and stupidity. It was Norman Podhoretz who wrote an article called "The Know Nothing Bohemians" (from the same guy who later came out beating his tits with an article called "My Negro Problem and Ours" in which he revealed his essential racism. And then this same boob became Reagan's far-right hand "intellectual" man. Oh well, just to think I watched him as he grew!)

In a few months I had had much correspondence from Ginsberg and some of the people he turned me on to. *Zazen* 3 had Gary Snyder, William Burroughs, Ginsberg, Peter Orlovsky, Philip Whalen as well as Robin Blaser, Gilbert Sorrentino, Diane DiPrima, and a young guy who was still in prison, Ray Bremser. (I was Ray's guardian when he got out of the slam.) I was not only in touch with the Beats, but I now had found out about the Black Mountain poets, also through Ginsberg. Ginsberg had also hipped me to the San Francisco School (old and new, some of whom were known as the Beats), the New York School (Frank O'Hara, Kenneth Koch, John Ashbery, Jimmy Schuyler), and a host of other young people. Older poets like Charles Olson and Robert Duncan. Trendsetters like Robert Creeley and all kinds of others. Kerouac and Burroughs, of course. John Wieners, Ron Loewinsohn, Paul Blackburn, Denise Levertov, Ferlinghetti, Jack Spicer (his notes were like quick courses in contemporary American poetry). I think by that time I had even met Allen G. and his running buddy, Peter Orlovsky, just back from Paris. We'd even hung out one night at a place on Seventh Avenue South where Kerouac was reading with Philip Lamantia and Howard Hart. There was a sense of community growing among some of the young writers, and I was one of them as well as the editor of one of their magazines. I told Nellie I wanted to answer the Podhoretz letter, was it possible? And sure enough the famous noble editors allowed it. In answering the letter, not only was I beginning some public stance as an anti-academic polemicist, but it helped to consolidate some ideas in my own head about what we all were about and why Podhoretz was full of shit. In fact, why he represented a full of shit point of view.

Zazen 3 was the first from West 20th Street. It was a nice neighborhood, very surprising. Stade had gone to put down on the apartment, that was our agreed-upon tactic for stopping the usual New York racism. There were really fabulous-looking brick houses and brownstones on that block. Across the street from us was a seminary and huge church. It was a strange neighborhood. Expensive-looking and clean, I'd known nothing about it before. Going east there were still brownstones and single-family houses pitted against the larger apartments and tenements. There was a heavy Irish population strewn around from old Chelsea, and stashed between them the middle class of many nationalities (few blacks). Bill Manville, the novelist, who was writing a column then for *The Village Voice*, "Saloon Society," lived on the top floor of our building. There were only three floors. I don't think I ever found out who lived on the second floor.

Our apartment was long, railroad style; from the living room to the study where I wrote was like half a block. But the ceilings were high, the rooms fairly large, and if we had had any money we would have been thought to be living in luxury. West 20th Street was tree-lined, the quiet elegant brownstones were on our side of the street, a large garden belonging to the seminary was on the other side. It was a lovely neighborhood.

We never had any direct harassment there for being interracial, or, more precisely, because I was black. Manville never invited us up to his sets — but then we never invited him to ours. But just looking at him you could tell he was a cold-blooded snob — his column confirmed it — so I stayed out of his way.

From literary connections, social hookups resulted. West 20th Street saw many of those we published in *Zazen* and all kinds of other folks coming in and out. The magazine was identified with the Beats, but the people tied to that name by specific identification were every which place — in San Francisco, Paris, Tangier, Mexico, London, New Mexico, and points north, west, east, and central. The groupies produced by the media, the would-be Beats, were usually a little gritty and willfully bohemian for our tastes — though there was always some media product or other showing up at our door. To rub up against what they perceived as necessary to the carrying out of their roles.

A circle of sorts developed at West 20th Street. Poet Gil Sorrentino and his first wife, Elsene; Hubert Selby, the novelist; Joel Oppenheimer, the Black Mountain poet, and his wife, Rena; poet Max Finstein — a hip redhaired double of the younger Shylock; novelist and painter Fielding Dawson (the unofficial then, later semiofficial historian for Black Mountain College); A. B. Spellman, the poet and jazz critic (an old friend from HU); poet Joe Early, an old friend of Sorrentino's from Brooklyn, and his wife, Ann, a department store buyer; painter Basil King and his wife, writer Martha King (both Black Mountain alumni); poet Paul Celento and his wife, Ceeny, also from Brooklyn; another HU updated memory, C. D. Transan; Mark Fine, the poet; Joe Heisler, another poet, who wrote like Joel Oppenheimer, and his wife, Rene; poet Sam Abrams and his wife, Barbara; painter-writer Philo (Fy) Duncan; Larry Hellenberg, a steelworker; and a few other folks could be considered the core. But there were always people in and out, staying a few days, longer than that, or whatever. We had no guest rooms, so most of the time the couch in the "front room" was where visitors stayed.

The pattern got to be that on Fridays, after leaving my slave job, I would stop at a liquor store and get a bottle, usually Old Grand-Dad bourbon, and head home. As it got later, others would start to drift in. (From the Bronx, from Brooklyn, Lower East Side, etc.) For one stretch Fee Dawson stayed for several months on that couch. Max Finstein also cribbed with us the same way. And A. B. Spellman.

By late Friday there were usually five or six or more people in the front room. And we had what amounted to a party, all weekend. By Sunday night most of us would be wasted, from Friday night, all day Saturday and Sunday impromptu sets. So that Monday morning was a hellish arrival.

The whole weekend we whooped it up. Nonstop rap sessions, putdowns, literary councils, adulterous initiatives, boozing it up and using whatever drugs existed on the scene. It was fun but a lot of it was, at least, irresponsible.

Poetry, literature, was our undying passion. Most of us would agree. That was the reason we all came together. But under that rubric (and defense) how many other less-than-kosher practices and relationships got put together?

For instance within that crowd, C.D. was sleeping with Paul's wife, Ceeny. Fy Duncan had to leave the Celentos' house where he'd been staying before he came to West 20th Street, because he'd also been sleeping with Ceeny. Mark was sleeping with Joel's wife, Rena. And, yes, later these marriages did break all the way up because of these ongoing breaches.

A typical weekend spontaneous bash at West 20th Street might see two or three affairs swirling around in plain view, with almost everybody in the crowd knowing what was going down, even the offended against.

All of us hung at the old Cedar Tavern, down on University Place. It was the hangout of a bunch of abstract expressionist painters. Jackson Pollock died just as I got there, but he had been one centerpiece. Franz Kline, Bill de Kooning, Philip Guston, Ray Parker, Norman Bluhm, Mike Goldberg, Al Leslie, John Chamberlain, David Smith, Dan Rice, and even Larry Rivers were regulars. They were the big names, people we respected. Franz Kline's style, not only painting-wise, but his personal idiosyncrasies, was one genre of lifestyle some of us imitated. Kline seemed always a little smashed, drink in hand, cigarette dangling, talking in drunken parody as abstractly as he painted. Basil King, Dan Rice, Joel Oppenheimer, and Fee Dawson used to do takes on this style, personalized but legitimately drunk. To talk in a fragmented, drunken but hopefully profound ellipsis was the goal. The torture of genius, genius unappreciated, genius assaulted by philistines, this is what was implied. Genius was not easy to understand or put up with. Basil was always getting ready to get into fights because he wanted to be too energetic with his parody of Franz. Dan and Joel almost became alcoholics, but then had the strength to go past that. I don't know about Fee.

It was from this circle that I got to know the Black Mountain school of poets and learn the fabled history of the place itself. Black Mountain was an experimental school, loosely based on somebody's idea of the Bauhaus (Josef Albers) and advanced "education" in the arts. Charles Olson, the poet, was the last rector and he was always spoken of in that circle with awe. Fee and Joel and Basil and Martha had been Charles' students. Gil and Max and Joe admired the myth and reality of the place and the literature and aesthetic that seemed to issue from it.

The house was always full of Black Mountain stories. Fee was the great storyteller (in more ways than one). And he was in the house day in day out. He might take off Monday to go stay with one of his various women. But unerringly on Friday he'd return. It was a long time before I even found out why Fy had had to leave Paul's house. I knew he had stayed there and then he'd gone. Week after week the Celentos would be there too. Paul and I got to be good friends, but the kind of wild morals of that crowd permitted them all to be mashed up together without open incident. (In a blood community or even in a working-class community of any nationality, death would've been the price of those liaisons, at least serious violence and disruption. But we were more "advanced.")

I learned about Charles Olson's work and began to read it. Also Robert Creeley and Robert Duncan. I got hold of copies of *The Black Mountain*

Review and witnessed real excellence not only of content but design. One, a thick white-covered book, had a Dan Rice pre-minimalist abstraction that I thought was the hippest thing I'd ever seen. I learned about *Origin*, the forerunner of *BMR*. Not only those writers, but younger writers like Ed Dorn, John Wieners, Michael Rumaker, Ed Marshall, had studied there, and painters like Kline, de Kooning, Guston, Motherwell, had shown or taught there along with Albers and Reinhardt and musicians John Cage, Morton Feldman plus Merce Cunningham. All these people had come out of Black Mountain or been there at various times and we upheld its memory and its aesthetic.

I came to understand the differences in the "schools." The Beats, the San Francisco school, the older San Francisco Renaissance group, the New York school, the Black Mountain School. Some of us were hooked up to one or the other or all at the same time. These schools were mentioned sometimes, in literary contexts, as schools, trends, realities, circles of history, experience, friendship. They did have specific styles, obvious aesthetic correlations, models historical and contemporary, teachers and even some organizations or publications to further their interests.

I had come into poetry from a wide-open perspective—anti-academic because of my experience, my social history and predilections. Obviously, as an African American I had a cultural history that should give me certain aesthetic proclivities. In the U.S. and the "western world" generally, white supremacy can warp and muffle the full recognition by a black person of this history, especially an "intellectual" trained by a system of white supremacy. A cultural history is at once the result of a particular psychological outlook which has been shaped by the sociopolitical and economic context of its development, as well as the raw material for a particular aesthetic. It determines what you think is beautiful or even intellectually significant.

The dead bourgeois artifact I'd cringed before in *The New Yorker* was a material and spiritual product of a whole way of life and perception of reality that was hostile to me. I dug that even as young boy weeping in San Juan. Coming out of Howard and getting trapped in the air force had pulled me away from the "good job" path which is also called the Yellow Brick Road. The Yalla heaven of the undead!

I'd come into the Village *looking*, trying to "check," being open to all flags. Allen Ginsberg's "Howl" was the first thing to open my nose, as opposed to, say, instructions I was given, directions, guidance. I dug "Howl" myself, in fact many of the people I'd known at the time warned me off it and thought the whole Beat phenomenon a passing fad of little relevance. I'd investigated further because I was looking for something. I was precisely open to its force as the statement of a new generation. As a line of demarcation from "the silent generation" and the man with the (yellow) grey flannel skin, half brother of the one with the grey flannel suit. I took up with the Beats because that's what I saw taking off and flying that somewhat resembled myself. The open and implied rebellion—of form and content. Aesthetic as well as social and political. But I saw most of it as Art, and the social statement as merely our lives as dropouts from the mainstream. I could see the young white boys and girls in their pronouncement of disillusion with and "removal" from society as being related to the black experience. That made us colleagues of the spirit. Yet I was no stompdown bohemian. I had enough of the mainstream in me, of lower-middle-class craving after order and "respectability," not to get pulled all the way over to Wahooism. Yet as wild as some of my colleagues were and as cool as I usually was, the connection could be made because I was black and that made me, as Wright's novel asserted, *an outsider*. (To some extent, even inside those "outsider" circles.)

The understanding that there were several different "schools" of new writers excited me. As an editor I thought that all the different relevant new schools should get published. Yet in this admirable "catholicism" a bug was sewn up in my rug that had to eat its way clear before too long was over. *Zazen* 4 saw the picking up on the Black Mountain people, also my new social relationships. The issue had a black cover with white abstraction by Fee Dawson. It was striking and the whole issue much more professionally done—Varityped instead of the old IBM, not as many of the weird little paste-ins and collages. The lineup was Olson, Orlovsky, O'Hara, Finstein, Dawson, A.B., Bremser, Marshall, Oppenheimer, Crews, Snyder, Kerouac, Wieners, Creeley, Corso, Jones, Sorrentino, Mason Jordan Mason. Mason was supposedly black but actually it turned out he was really Judson Crews. Crews had several noms de plume and several personalities. Mason Jordan Mason was his "black" personality. But interestingly enough the M.J.M. poems were better than the Judson Crews ones, because in "being" black Crews assumed a simplicity and directness that made the work more forceful. The Crews poems were too full of literary allusion and stuffy syntax.

The black cover on one hand does represent to me the coming into full force, or full consciousness, of one circle, at a relatively high literary level. But there is only one black writer, LeRoi Jones. (At the time I might have thought it was two!) Ernie, Ed, Steve, Tim, Bobb Hamilton, Allen Polite, Tom Postell are not there. But I was not with them socially either. (Though around that time I had had to get Tim out of Bellevue, where one of his drinking bouts had taken him right into the nut ward. I had to testify to his sanity and become his guardian.) I was "open" to all schools within the circle of white poets of all faiths and flags. But what had happened to the blacks? What had happened to me? How is it that there's only the one colored guy?

But I answered that the same way the National Book Award committee answered inquiries to it in the '80s about why there were no minorities or women among their nominees. "We were looking for quality literature and that is what we got." Amen.

So obviously my social focus had gotten much whiter. White wife, co-editor. The weekend hollering and drinking trysts were hooked to the same social focus; they were it, actually. Our first child, a daughter, Kellie, was born. I had come back from reading poetry somewhere, with a couple other poets, and we came back to the hospital and squatted outside, until I got to go in. That was the high point of my life, another mystery uncovered. I was a father at twenty-four and a half years old.

Nellie and I never hassled each other, in the main. Though she had a bright pixie quality, like a child insisting it be allowed to celebrate. She had had to come to terms with the marriage in her own way. I can only guess what whites who think they belong in the mainstream of U.S.— American Dream—society think when they find out for some reason (in this case an exploding black penis) that they will not be allowed in that stream. She had that quality that marks survivors, a dogged will that haunted her twinkling eyes. A strength to her laughter that made it richer. Yet for these reasons a kind of lonely atmosphere accompanied her no matter how she tried to mount it or quiet it.

She liked the weekend bashes we had because it cast her in another light. We were, in some repects, at the center of a particular grouping of folks. The magazine both created that circle and connected people to us that we didn't even know. Nellie had not been such a popular kid, she'd told me many times. She was unpretty, she'd said, in a pretty world. Unglamorous in a world ruled by glamour. So she loved the attention that even such a modest circle as our drunken, adulterous poets provided. The fortuitous link with *Sectarian* gave her a look at two worlds.

The world we were in was off to the side of the one she'd prepared for. Nellie was always laughing, scolding our house guests, or rollicking with the bashes, and she must have been drawn, as was I, into its values and mores.

When we heard first about why Fy had to leave Brooklyn (and then he was with us), he and Paul were rubbing shoulders. Then we learned (she first from Rene) that Rene Meisler and Mark Fine were a number. Mark lived with them in the Bronx and when John went off to his printing gig, they had at it. When Paul went off to his gig, Fy and Ceeny did it. CD stood at the side of people swirling in a larger party and wept (months later) in confession to Paul that he'd been jamming his lady. Why he picked a party to put on such a drama I will not speculate upon. During this period I myself had an affair of sorts with one of the campfollowers Gil brought over from Brooklyn. That was the first in a long series of affairs and liaisons, mostly with white women.

The various "schools" of poetry we related to were themselves all linked together by the ingenuous. They were a point of departure from the academic, from the Eliotic model of rhetoric, formalism, and dull iambics. Bullshit school poetry.

Under the broad banner of our objective and subjective "united front" of poetry, I characterized the various schools: the Jewish Apocalyptic, biblical, long crashing rhythms of spiritual song. "Howl" and "Kaddish" are the best examples. Kerouac's "Spontaneous Bop Prosody" is an attempt to buy into the "heaven in the head" of religious apocalypse, which Ginsberg inherited from his rabbinical sources (and his historic models, Christopher Smart, Blake, Whitman). It is a hyped-up version of Joyce with a nod in blacks' direction because of the heroic improvised character of African American music, especially the improvising soloist.

The wildest of the literary-social schools was the full-out bohemians of "turn on, drop out" fame. People in "pads" smoking pot, listening to "wild sounds." But these were the most politically open of all the schools, the most radical and furthest removed from the university. These were the forerunners of the hippies and flower children. The "punks" of today.

The Black Mountain people linked me to a kind of Anglo-Germanic school, more accessible than the academics, but still favoring hard-edged, structured forms. Olson and Creeley were its twin prophets, but Olson had the broader sword, the most "prophetic" stance. His concerns went further and touched me deeper. Creeley was closer to the William Carlos Williams style—sparse and near-conversational, though much more stylized than Williams and influenced by someone like Mallarm, in the tendency toward using the language so precisely and literally it became at times "abstract."

Olson shared Williams' word usage but also was a Poundian (though opposing it seemed to me, Pound's social pathology and worship of the European Renaissance as the beginning and end of all culture). Olson's *Maximus Poems*, his major work, is a direct descendant of both the *Cantos* and *Paterson*.

If in one space of New York City you'd have neo-Ginsbergian poems all over the place, wander into the West 20th Street circle you'd have beaucoups Creeley poems and neo-Creeley poems every which where.

I met Frank O'Hara through Allen Ginsberg, like so many writers I met. Frank was assistant curator for the Museum of Modern Art. He was a close friend of the whole community of New York painters, abstract expression- ist as well as the loony pre-pop figures like Larry Rivers, Alex Katz, and Bob Rauschenberg. Frank was one of the most incisive and knowledge- able critics of painting in New York at the time. The New York school was chiefly, to me, O'Hara. And if you were anywhere around Frank, as he launched into this subject or that, always on top, laughing, gesturing, ex- claiming, being as broad as any topic, and the easy sense of sophistication which gave him an obvious "leadership," you'd understand. (He'd turn red at such a suggestion. "Listen, my dear, you can take that leadership business and shove it!")

Kenneth Koch, whose poetry I dug because it was almost always hilari- ous, especially the great "Fresh Air," which single-handedly demolished the academic poets (even if they couldn't dig it), and the later Pulitzer- National Book Award winner John Ashbery were the other chief practitio- ners of the New York school, so called because its writers not only lived there but—at least with Frank—expressed a sense of the high sophistica- tion and motley ambience of the city. This was (in O'Hara's hands) a French(-Russian) surreal-tinged poetry. A poetry of expansiveness and high emotion. Sometimes a poetry of dazzling abstraction and shifting colorful surfaces. It was out of the Apollinaire of *Zone* but also close to Whitman and Mayakovsky.

Williams was a common denominator because he wanted American speech, a mixed foot, a variable measure. He knew American life had out- distanced the English rhythms and their formal meters. The language of this multinational land, of mixed ancestry, where war dance and salsa com- bine with country and western, all framed by African rhythm-and-blues confessional.

Whitman and Williams and Pound and Apollinaire and the Surrealists were our prophets. Whitman, who broke away from England with his free verse. Williams, who carried that fight into our own century, seeing the universal in the agonizingly local. Pound, the scientist of poetry, the translator, the mover and shaker (and fascist)! Apollinaire, a whole tradition of French antixbourgeois openness and aesthetic grace. And the Surrealists, because they at least figured the shit had to be turned upside down! (This plus the improvised zeitgeist of black music!)

All these I responded to and saw as part of a whole anti-academic voice. So that the magazine and Nellie and I were at the vortex of this swirling explosion of new poetry. And I moved from one circle to the other, effortlessly, because I sincerely had no ax to grind but the whole of new poetry.

The Cedar Tavern would be bursting with the Black Mountaineers on one hand, maybe just come down the hill from West 20th Street. And the New York school people, Frank, Kenneth, would be holding court along with any number of painters (Larry Rivers, Mike Goldberg, and Norman Bluhm were special friends of Frank's). A.G. and company were not too heavy on that scene. The Beats were more "pad" people or "On the Road" and more into bush smoking than boozing. Also they lived mostly on the Lower East Side and tended to hang there more regularly. The cold-water flats of East 2nd, 3rd, 4th, 5th, 6th, 7th, 9th, etc. The tenements of Eldridge Street, Clinton Street, Allen Street, East Broadway. The Lower East Side was still sparsely populated by arty or bohemian types in those days. It was poor—on the real side.

I started meeting Frank for lunch some afternoons at joints near our workplaces—Frank's, the MOMA at 53rd Street, mine at 49th Street, Technoscopic Productions. We'd meet at some of those bar-restaurants on the Upper East Side and drink and bullshit, exchange rumors and gossip, and make plans and hear the latest about the greatest. Frank and I were friends. I admired his genuine sophistication, his complete knowledge of the New York creative scene. A mutual friend, editor Donald Allen, brought us together. Don was an early admirer and champion of Frank's poetry. Don was an editor for the Grove Press at the time and the man who made *Evergreen Review* the standard of excellence it was at that time. He looked like the quintessential Roman aesthete, a haughtier John Gielgud, with the same impeccable diction. Don had been putting together an anthology of new poetry and new poets. He worked meticulously, and he went to great pains to investigate the poetic scene, inquiring after new poets, buying all the magazines, going to all the poetry readings and events manqué.

(He had found me through *Zazen.*) *Evergreen Review* charts the late '50s-early '60s U.S. poetry explosion. The results of his work, the standard-setting *The New American Poetry: 1945–60,* is clearly one of the greatest anthologies of poetry in the American language.

Frank O'Hara was also part of the high-powered New York City homosexual scene in the arts and, as far as art was related to money, certain aspects of flashy jet-set society. It was Frank whom I first heard pronounce the word "camp." "Oh, that campy bastard!" or "My dear, the production was entirely too campy." Or he might just run someone down while tossing down a drink: "It was a trifle tacky, don't you think?"

I found myself going to the ballet, to cocktail parties, "coming over for drinks," to multiple gallery openings with Frank O'Hara and his shy but likable "roommate," Joe LeSeur, who looked like a blond movie star of the ingenue type. With Frank O'Hara, one spun and darted through the New York art scene, meeting Balanchine or Merce Cunningham or John Cage or de Kooning or Larry Rivers. Frank, A.G., and I even had a few notable readings together at the old Living Theater, when it was on 14th Street and Sixth Avenue. Another at Princeton with Diane DiPrima. I had taken the day off to do the Princeton set, calling in sick. But when I came in the next day my picture, plus A.G.'s, Frank's, and Diane's was in the *Daily News* or *Mirror,* so that vice president peeped it and let me know it. Just before lunchtime he comes through and drops the paper on my desk. "Sick, huh?" was all he said and turned on his heel. But I didn't get fired. That job did get a trifle complicated because the president's daughter, a young woman my own age, was trying to become a dancer and working part time at the family business and living down on Thompson Street, near where Dolly lived. We hit it off and started lunching together occasionally and standing around being in the office. There was no romance (not that I would have minded) but our friendly comrades-in-the-arts manner ticked off a few of the science majors and the vice president's eyes began burning holes in my back.

My standard hangout was the Cedar Tavern. Jazz at the Wagon, a joint down on Sullivan and Bleecker, had opened with the music, and cokes, but that was doomed. But I met Leroy McLucas, the photographer, who was manager of the joint while it lasted. The Five Spot was on the rise and in the third issue of *Zazen* we had a Five Spot ad: "Home of Thelonious Monk—Home of Jazz-Poetry—Home of America's Leading Painters, Sculptors, Composers, Actors, Poets, PEOPLE." They had jazz and poetry every Monday night at 9:30. The Terminis who ran the joint, Iggy, the quiet one, and Joe, the big extrovert, were two of the nicest guys in the business. It was a real drag when they got out.

I had gotten a small offset press and was now trying to do the magazine on it but failing, though a little guy named Chuck Irving ran some of the magazine for me and some other things. I managed to do a couple of small-run pamphlets. We decided to put out books, to start a small publishing operation, which I called, for some reason (maybe I was reading Jung at the time), Totem Press. I met Lucia DiBella through Ginsberg. She lived over on East Houston Street, pregnant with her first child. The guy who fathered the baby she would constantly make reference to as a square. I'd gone to see her to get work for *Zazen* and she gave us a couple short stories and some poetry.

Lucia was an ultra-Poundian when I first met her, with as much communications-for-poetry energy as A.G., but being a woman, and a pregnant one at that, she was more restricted. Lucia was toying at the time with the gay scene, and the black poet Audre Lorde was an old friend. But even as she talked theoretically about the gay life, she was always relating to one man (even some gay ones) or the other in some aggressive redhaired way. Later, we became lovers and still later coeditors of another publication, *The Fleeting Bear*.

Lucia was publishing her first book, *This Kind of Bird Flies Backward*. She sent it to Ferlinghetti and he sent a weak little "caveat emptor" as an introduction. We included this in our Totem series. Ron Loewinsohn's *Watermelons*, with introductions by William Carlos Williams and A.G., was the second of our publications. This was 1959, the civil rights movement was rising with every headline, and for the last few months I had been fascinated by the headlines from Cuba. I had been raised on Errol Flynn's *Robin Hood* and the endless hero-actors fighting against injustice and leading the people to victory over tyrants. The Cuban thing seemed a case of classic Hollywood proportions.

So I proposed that we come out with a little pamphlet in honor of Fidel Castro, when the *barbudos* finally burst into Havana and sent Batista flying. Fee Dawson suggested we call the quick little pamphlets "blue plates," as in the great American blue-plate special. Fee was a great one for Americana. He was the All American Boy gone haywire and turned to adultery, sly panhandling, and drink.

The reactions to my proposal were interesting. Sorrentino, always the classic debunker of the political in favor of the high aesthetic, said, "I hate guys in uniforms." Alas, he should have told it to Ezra Pound. But he gave us a poem. I remember there was a rather sharp discussion during our weekend bashes of my poem in that "blue plate" where it ends up saying, "Sunday mornings, after we have won." The general line being that poets and politics ain't cohabiting. That was my line, had been the words coming out of my mouth. Yet perhaps the intensification of the civil rights movement, the daily atrocities which fat sheriffs in Dumbbell, Georgia, could run on blacks, began to piss me off much more deeply than I thought. I rejected Martin Luther King's philosophy. I was not nonviolent. I had written a poem about this time that ended:

> We have awaited the coming of a natural
> phenomenon. Mystics and romantics, knowledgeable
> workers
> of the land.
> But none has come.
> (Repeat)
> But none has come.
> Will the machinegunners please step forward?

I was not entirely sure what it meant myself. But I knew I rejected King's tactics. I would not get beat in my head. I would fight, but what was I doing? The poem had asked earlier:

> What
> industry do I practice? A slick
> colored boy, 12 miles from his
> home. I practice no industry.
> I am no longer a credit
> to my race. I read a little,
> scratch against silence slow spring
> afternoons.

The title of the poem was "A Poem Some People Will Have to Understand."

The static over the poem and the whole "blue plate" did crystallize some things. It made me see certain real differences among those of us in our little circle on West 20th Street. Differences which often registered anonymously in my head, registered near where the brown consciousness still existed, tied to a black soul base. I had wandered away only so far, though. I came to a Halloween party we gave at West 20th Street as a "shade," with an old window shade around my neck and hanging down my back like a cape. A.B. and I were the only bloods. I still pronounced the brownness but saw how caught it was in the ironies of that context, a comic manqué of Halloween identity.

The morality of the place, of that crowd and personal stance. There was not much black I related to except deep within myself, however that was stirred. It was not, ever, that I consciously desired not to be black or the brown consciousness tied irrevocably to the black mass soul—I had just wandered off, had gotten isolated to the extent that almost all of my closest friends, the people I saw everyday, were white!

But none of that really registered as such. In the wildness of our groping lives there was a deadly hedonism that answered all questions. That offered all explanations. The pleasure principle, that finally was the absolute, what gave pleasure, and that alone. Our lives were designed (to the extent they could arrange themselves according to our love of spontaneity) around pleasure. "Anything goes" was the word. Like Raskolnikov's line, "All is permitted." The same stance.

Flashes of what that was, a rush of sparks, kicks, comings, lies, sadistic exchanges, masochism, a swarm of individuals sucking on life for instant gratification. It didn't matter how. With the cover story of Art to provide an arrogance and sense of superiority for some finally low shit.

As part of the social circle at West 20th Street people blew into town announced or unannounced. Poet John Wieners, just out of some institution, came and stayed with us a few weeks. He was wearing a long ponytail before they were even in with the outs. I walked him around the Village, going to the Eighth Street Bookstore, with people's heads turning, staring at John, who said maybe two words the whole time he stayed with us. John, like the rest of the younger poets, had picked a piece from this school and that. He liked Charles Olson's work. John, from Boston, called him Chawles. He had a crazy half-black (maybe Cape Verdian) friend, poet Steve Jonas, who plagued him. Jonas rambled nonstop about Pound. Blacks and Jews and Poundians all, scrambled by talk of Art. We'd look at all the "kikes" and "niggers" in his work, gloss it, look over it, justify it, and right on, Pound, right on!

Ray Bremser was another dude that showed, but this after much back-and-forth correspondence between us. Bremser's weird rhythm and gnarled efflorescent style turned us on, plus his jailhouse humor. He and a young black poet, Harold "Wine" Carrington, wrote us from the joint. Bremser made it out, Carrington didn't. Ray showed finally on West 20th Street and for a while I was his legal guardian. (In one publication on the Beats there are about ten poets whose address is c/o L. Jones, West 20th Street.)

Ray seemed determined to live out his own criminal projections as well as the myth of the Beats. Tall, hawk-billed, with the long slicked-down mop of the juvenile hoodlum, he was from Jersey City (no wonder!), but I liked the guy. He was wild but good-hearted and no punk (old usage).

One night Joel Oppenheimer comes into West 20th, blood everywhere. Some guy at the Cedar had bashed him. I pick up my iron pipe and say, "Let's go!" That surely was the black connection; the response to that kind of personal aggression is "Fight!" But Joel didn't want to go near a couple of those assembled, i.e., for help, not that we needed them. There were always some shoot-outs at the old Cedar. One night Sorrentino and I are standing in there swapping literary unniceties and in come these guys in grey flannel suits, sleek with ties, and for the hell of it they start some asinine conversations as to who we are, are we artists or what do we do, are we bohemians? In fact, whatever we're talking about this one slob wants to connect on. The conversation went from bad to worse. With these guys finally waving the flag or something and I raised Little Rock and one guy says, "You're just saying that because you're colored." Which was true or could have been—but then, no, there's whites who would've objected to Orval Faubus. Gil would've, as unpolitical as he was. So I spit in this guy's face. But I got to hand it to the guy, he was all class. I say, "So what do you think of that?" The spit is literally hanging off his starched and stiff puss. I say, "Spit is dripping down your face."

He says, "No, it's not." Goddam. Now tell me that's not the height of absolute subjectivism. That's how these people can torture, kill, and oppress people. "No, it's not," he says, with my nasty saliva rolling down his cheek.

Big John, the bartender, who was always grumpy in his good-natured way, comes over and looks at these two solid citizens and says, "What are you guys, starting trouble?"

I was beginning to see Lucia DiBella every so often. She'd resisted that liaison, protesting about Nellie. But finally it went down. Lucia was an arch-bohemian, the writer (person) on the fringe of society, par excellence. She liked that projection and held up the continental models of Cocteau and that crowd as historic disrupters of manners. And she was first and most deeply a literary person, a creature after and of the Arts. Always in jeans, her long red hair twisted almost any kind of way, so little she thought of that kind of style. Nellie was a much more "middle-class" person. She could be the homemaker, the wife, though she was a great help with the magazine. Lucia and Nellie were clearly in contrast. But in that life of hedonism, all that finally matters is the pleasure one gets from something or someone, little else, everything else recedes into the background.

But one night I'm in Lucia's house and I pop awake and it's maybe two in the morning. I sit up and say, "Wow, I've got to get out of here, get home."

Lucia, I guess not wanting me to leave then but at the same time letting me in on something that she thought would transform our relationship, looks at me and says in a soft but signifying voice, "Suppose I told you you didn't have to go back now, that Nellie is not there?"

"What?" I sat straight up. "What?" Ah, the injuries of spirit the male chauvinist must endure, doing his thing, but certainly in no way ready for the woman to do hers. I threw on my clothes. Lucia is protesting, "Why are you goin' now? She's not even there."

But I was on the street in a few minutes, sprinting almost all the way from Avenue C and Houston to West 20th Street and 9th Avenue. When I got in the house, it was true, Nellie was not there. A.B. is on the couch sleeping. I prod him awake. "Where's Nellie?" I shouted. He shook his head, shaking off sleep. "Where's Nellie?" I shouted again, right close to his face. And then it hit me. Every week Nellie had gone out with Celento's wife, they were going to "dance class" and then they'd go have a drink at the Cedar, the girls hanging out. The notorious Ceeny was seeing CD and one night I'd walked in and Nelly's sitting with her talking to a painter, Luke Sashimi, a Japanese. It didn't make any difference at the time, but now it did. I said to A.B., "Sashimi? Is she at Sashimi's?" He nodded yes.

I knew where Luke Sashimi lived because it had been pointed out to me before. He was a friend of Frank O'Hara's, an abstract expressionist of the Kline school. I ran over to his loft, which was only a few blocks away, shot up the stairs, and began hammering on the door. Sashimi opened the door and Nellie was sitting inside, on the side of the bed, as if she was waiting for me. All I said was, "Let's go. Come on." She began to cry. Sashimi walked toward me and I stood with my fists balled up. But this bastard had offered once to teach me judo.

He said, "We civilized people. We civilized people." I got Nellie's arm and pushed her out the door.

At home we screamed and I slapped her around. But she kept saying, "You were seeing Lucia. You were seeing Lucia." I kept screaming at her, telling her that she was stupid and that Sashimi was stupid. Then I left her standing in the middle of the floor and rushed out, going back to Sashimi's. I got to his door, then looked for something to bash his head in. I found a metal post from an old bed that was lying in the street and charged up the stairs. I hammered on the door with my fists and then beat the door with the post but Sashimi, no fool, had either gone or wouldn't answer it.

I walked all the way back to Avenue C, not to see Lucia, but to find a friend of mine, Bob Thompson, a black painter I had gotten friendly with. Bob lived in a huge loft on Clinton Street. He was there with a couple of bohemians, getting high, shooting heroin. I didn't know he used it, but he was sending one of the bohemians out to cop. I dropped some money in the mitt and meanwhile used some of Bob's "smack" and we took off together, down, down, and right here! Bob and I were a number after that.

That's what that life had become. Joe Heisler was moving out of the Bronx too. He and Rene (he reluctantly) were splitting, and Rene and Mark were supposedly moving to New Mexico. Paul and Ceeny had also agreed to split. The thing with C.D. had been the last straw. But one Saturday I get a phone call, some of us were sitting around drinking. It's a guy I don't know named Richard Gibson and he asks me if I want to go to Cuba, as part of a delegation of black artists and scholars whom the Cuban government wanted to get a look and spread the word. Relations with New Cuba and the U.S. had not gotten outright funky but they were getting that way. The U.S. could dig a Batista, their boy, but Fidel Castro was making noises like a democrat and you know they can't abide that shit. The agrarian reform had already sent these white racist monopoly capitalists up the wall. I agreed to go, turning from the phone and telling people, "I'm going to Cuba!"

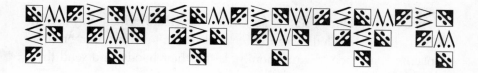

Seven

The Black Arts
Politics, Search for a New Life

The Cuban trip was a turning point in my life. Langston, Jimmy Baldwin, and John Killens were supposed to go, but didn't. I was in a group that included Sarah Wright, the novelist, and her husband. Ed Clark, the painter, whom I knew. Harold Cruse, the writer, whom I also knew. (I'd met Harold in my MacDougal Street days, often in the Caf, Figaro at Bleecker and McDougal. He lived then in a furnished room on West 23rd or West 14th and was always complaining about how Broadway producers were turning down musicals he was writing.) Julian Mayfield and his wife, Ana Codero, a doctor, born in Puerto Rico. Also with our party was a man I didn't know until then, Robert Williams. It was Williams who had organized the most militant NAACP chapter in the States, a chapter composed of black workers and returning veterans, in Monroe, North Carolina. They'd had "wade-ins" to integrate the pool in Monroe, and Rob had summoned black militant attorney Conrad Lynn down to North Carolina to defend a ten-year-old boy who had been *locked up* for kissing an eight-year-old white girl. Rob had also organized a self-defense group in Monroe and when he made the statement in 1959, after a white rapist of a black woman had been freed by an all-white jury, that blacks should "meet

243

violence with violence," he was summarily ditched by Uncle Roy and the NAACP. Later, Rob led a group of armed blacks to surround a group of menacing Klansmen, disarm them, take off their hoods, and send them scurrying back into their rat holes.

He was wearing a big straw hat like a *campesino* (Cuban farmer) when I met him, with a wispy tip of beard. He was a big man, maybe six feet three inches and about 240 pounds, imposing, strong-looking. One never doubted that, aroused, Rob could be a mean mf.

Traveling with us, as well, were John Henrik Clarke, the historian, plus some other people—a black model, two strange-looking sisters who were members, along with Gibson, of the Fair Play for Cuba Committee, and a journalist from a Philadelphia newspaper. (For a detailed account of this trip, see "Cuba Libre," an essay in *Home: Social Essays*.)

But we went to Cuba (this was 1959), after a false start courtesy of the U.S. government, and we stayed a couple days in Havana talking to various people, meeting various Cuban and Latin intellectuals and officials. I met the great Afro-Cuban poet Nicolás Guillén, who asked me straight out where was Langston and did I think that Langston had gotten more conservative. I smiled, but I did not know then that Langston had testified, under duress, before HUAC, denouncing some of his own earlier work, to keep great patriots like the filthy cracker bastard James Eastland off his ass.

I met Pablo Armando Fernández, the poet, and people at La Casa de Cuba, an arts center. We also visited various ministries and got lectured to about what Cuba was trying to do. I talked to a young minister in the National Agrarian Reform Institute, António Nuñez Jiménez, and was very much impressed. And then we traveled, with thousands of other people, on a slow train to Oriente Province, on the eastern tip of the island, where the revolution was born. I met intellectuals from all over Latin America, including a young woman, Rubi Betancourt, from Yucatán and Jaime Shelly, a poet from Mexico. These young people assaulted my pronouncements about not being political. It was the first time I'd been taken on so thoroughly and forcefully and by people my own age, my contemporaries. I was not Eisenhower or Nixon or Faubus, I protested, I was a poet. And so you want to write your poetry and that alone, while most of the world is suffering, your own people included. It is bourgeois individualism, they screamed. That is all it is, bourgeois individualism. For twelve or fourteen hours on the train I was assailed for my bourgeois individualism. And I could see, had seen, people my own age involved in actual *change*, revolution. In my sinister American cynicism, my inherited world-weary arrogance of theoretical know-it-all-ism, I was little better than my friend who'd said, "I hate guys in uniforms." In fact, I was the same.

I could fight back with what I knew of my own seeming disagreement with my U.S. peers, how I did have sensitivity to what was going on. But that seemed puny in the face of what I'd already seen in Cuba and in the faces of these young Latino activists and intellectuals, already politicized, for whom Cuba was the first payoff of a world they had already envisioned and were already working for. I was the oddball, the weary traveler/tourist from the U.S. of A. As much hot hatred as I could summon for the U.S., its white supremacy, its exploitation, its psychological torture of schizophrenic slaves like myself, I now had to bear the final indignity—which made my teeth grate violently, even in reflection—the indignity and humiliation of defending its ideology, which I was doing in the name of Art. Jesus Christ!

In Oriente, we went up into the Sierra Maestra for the celebration of the July 26 invasion of Moncada by Fidel Castro and his forces, who called themselves the July 26th Movement. There were hundreds of thousands of people up there. It could have been easily a million people. We trucked and walked and wound up and up. I rode partway with Françoise Sagan, the French novelist, who had attendants everywhere, befitting her great celebrity. I had known her from the covers of her books I read down in Puerto Rico in the error farce. All of us were thirsty, the hot sun whipped our ass, plus the long walk. But we made it up to where the celebration was held. And I heard Fidel Castro speak for perhaps two hours nonstop, relating the entire history of the revolution to the *campesinos*, soldiers, intellectuals, and foreign visitors. I even got to meet him and say a few words. It was a rare moment in one's life and if the harangues of Rubi and Jaime and the others weren't enough, this final stroke was, my head spinning with recognition, revelation, and the hot-ass sun.

We had a few more days in Havana. I hung out with Rob Williams one day, and everywhere he went people in the street cheered him. The Cubans had made his confrontations with the Klan and *yanqui racismo* known to people throughout the island, even though in the U.S. they tried to play it down.

Even when he was in Havana, Rob got word from the Cubans that the Klan was stirring again, trying to intimidate his family. Rob, with me trailing along with him, went to see the U.S. ambassador. Rob was wearing a shoulder holster and his language was so hot you could hear him through the door. "If the U.S. government don't protect them, then I got people there who will." (And he did!)

A year or so later the government framed Rob in the famous Monroe kidnap case, when Rob saved two whites who'd wandered into the black community, during a shootout with the racist state police, from being jacked up by a crowd of blacks incensed by the state police's racist terror tactics. He went to Cuba, Algeria, and finally China, where he never ceased to be a thorn in the U.S. racists' side with his militant publication *The Crusader*. When we got back to the U.S., the newspapers even pretended that the Cuban celebration had been rained out.

But I carried so much back with me that I was never the same again. The dynamic of the revolution had touched me. Talking to Fidel or Juan Almeida, the black commander of the revolutionary army, or to the young minister of agrarian reform, Nuñez Jiménez, or Jaime or Rubi or Pablo Fernández. Seeing youth not just turning on and dropping out, not just hiply cynical or cynically hip, but using their strength and energy to *change* the real world—that was too much. The growing kernel of social consciousness I had was mightily fertilized by the visit.

When I returned, I was shaken more deeply than even I realized. The arguments with my old poet comrades increased and intensified. It was not enough just to write, to feel, to think, one must act! One *could* act.

First, I wrote an essay about my Cuban experience, "Cuba Libre." I remembered that the Cubans had changed the name of the Hilton Hotel in Havana to Havana Libre, and a U.S. telephone operator, in making the hookup of a call there, insisted the hotel was still the Havana Hilton. But the Cuban operator would have none of it. "Havana Libre!" she shouted. "Get used to it!" That was the spirit I wanted to invest in the essay. It won an award after being published in the *Evergreen Review*. The award was $300 and was the most money I'd ever gotten for something I'd written.

At the same time I had begun a long prose work. It was as if I wanted to shake off the stylistic shackles of the gang I'd hung with and styled myself after. I consciously wrote as deeply into my psyche as I could go. I didn't even want the words to "make sense." I had the theme in my mind. My early life, in Newark, at Howard, in the air force, but the theme was just something against which I wanted to play endless variations. Each section had its own dynamic and pain. Going so deep into myself was like descending into hell. I called it *The System of Dante's Hell*.

I would focus on my theme and then write whatever came into my mind as a result of that focus. I called them (later) "association complexes." I was tearing away from the "ready-mades" that imitating Creeley or Olson provided. I'd found that when you imitate people's form you take on their content as well. So I scrambled and roamed, sometimes blindly in my consciousness, to come up with something more essential, more rooted in my deepest experience. I thought of music, I thought of myself as an improvising soloist. I would go into almost a trancelike state, hacking deeper and deeper, my interior rhythms dancing me on. Only in the last section is there what I called "fast narrative," something approaching a conventional narrative. It was almost like what Césaire had said about how he wrote *Return to My Native Land*. That he was trying to break away from the heavy influence that French Symbolist poetry had on him. So he decided to write prose to stop writing poetry. And what he came up with was a really profound new poetry, showing how even the French language could be transformed by the Afro-Caribbean rhythms and perception. (Though I did not find this out about Césaire until almost twenty years later!)

I wrote in jagged staccato fragments until at the end of the piece I had come to, found, my own voice, or something beginning to approximate it. We were also going through the process of moving. Another little girl child had been born, Lisa, so we had two little girl babies. We were moving to East 14th Street, between First and Second Avenues, into a terrible though huge barnlike apartment over a Gypsy storefront. It was not the sleek, quiet West Side apartment in Chelsea. We moved into the grimy East Side just before the still vague East Village changed abruptly into Chelsea East. Our lease had run out on West 20th Street. The rent had been high for us in the first place, but now I had also gotten fired from my job for having gone off to Cuba. I had to get back on unemployment, so there was no way we could support West 20th Street.

It was a weird time for me altogether, what with the political impulses the Cuba trip had set in motion. There was an unused metal sign over the Gypsies' place on which in some critical moment in U.S.-Cuban relations I'd painted "Cuba Si-Yanqui No!"

When I finished *Dante's Hell*, it was Lucia to whom I thought I should show it, and she thought it should be published immediately. I also showed it to a friend, John Fles, who was publishing a one-shot anthology of new work, along with Artaud, whom Fles dug. It was called *The Trembling Lamb*. I felt, then, that I was in motion, that my writing, which I'd been deadly serious about, was now not just a set of "licks" already laid down by Creeley, Olson, etc., but was moving to become genuinely mine. I felt that I could begin to stretch out, to innovate in ways I hadn't thought of before. And in all my poetry which comes out of this period there is the ongoing and underlying contention and struggle between myself and "them" that poetry and politics, art and politics, were not mutually exclusive.

Lana wanted to be a "mistress." She took that as a real identity, Brook Farm, I'd thought before, when I discovered the Nellie-Luke Sashimi hookup.

When I discovered that Luke and Nellie were still seeing each other, I just left, moved out, and Lana, a young dancer I'd met, wanted me to move in with her. Lucia didn't know what the hell I was doing, but she was half hip to the Lana scam, so we were not as close as before. I'd picked up the phone one day and it was Luke, maybe drunk, trying to disguise his Asian accent, like an alligator "disguised" in a tuxedo.

Nellie had started work again at the *Sectarian Review* and we'd hired a West Indian woman to watch the kids all day, while Nellie worked and I wrote. But now I just split. I said a few words to Nellie, gathered my shit, and was gone. Luckily I had found a place to sublet that was just three blocks up the street on East 17th Street, in an elevator building, one of the old luxury-type apartments. A young white piano player who was working with Jackie McLean was splitting and he wanted to get rid of the place, so I leaped on it. It was a nice little three-room spot, between Second and Third Avenues, the only run-down-looking building in a block of extremely high-priced luxury apartments.

Lana started coming around to that apartment, spending the night (when she wasn't hooked up to Butler). She was hinting that she wanted to move in with me, but I wasn't hearing those hints. The solitude, being a young man with some knowledge of the town now, not thrown back and forth at the whim of whoever as guides, was sweet.

During this period, I'd tried to start a group known as the Organization of Young Men (OYM). It was one fledgling effort at building some political consciousness downtown. And not so strangely, it was all black. Not that I'd planned it that way, but that is who was in it. And not so strangely, almost all of those in it had white wives or lovers. Archie Shepp, Steve Cannon, Leroy McLucas, Walter Bowe, Harold Cruse, Calvin Hicks, A. B. Spellman, Bobb Hamilton, and a few other folks. We weren't certain just what we wanted to do. It was more like a confirmation of rising consciousness. We issued at least one statement, but the sense of it was that we knew it was time to go on the offensive in the civil rights movement. We did not feel part of that movement. Most of us were isolated now from the mainstream of the black community and we did not reflect, in an undistorted way, that consciousness. Our consciousness, in the main, was that of young black intellectuals "integrated" to within a hair's breadth of our life.

We talked vaguely about going "uptown" to work. But what work we did not really understand. We had a few meetings, but then Calvin Hicks had already organized a stronger, somewhat more experienced group, the name of which came to be On Guard. It was the same kind of group, mainly black intellectuals living downtown, many of whom were married to or "going with" white women. And in that organization, it was an unwritten rule that our wives, lovers, etc., weren't to go uptown with us. The exception to this was Hicks' wife, who was explained as "an Egyptian," though to the untrained or spontaneous eye, she looked extremely white.

Finally, after a few clandestine visits back to East 14th Street, I abruptly decided to go back. Why? I can't really say. Perhaps a sense of family, a feeling of being somehow insecure living "by myself," or whatever. But I came back, to much hand wringing and moaning from Lana and the old goodbye to some others.

The West Indian woman was still "minding" the children while I tried to write. One time she took them to the park that is part of the Stuyvesant Town apartments, and while sitting on a bench next to many black "governesses" with their lily-white charges, she was asked did those children live in the complex. These security guards knew they didn't, because at the time Stuyvesant Town was lily white. So they asked Miss Brown to leave!

I had also become a part of the Fair Play for Cuba Committee under Richard Gibson's urging. And this brought me further into the world of political commitment. It was as if I had two distinct lives, one a politically oriented life, with a distinct set of people I knew and talked to, the other the artsy bohemian life of the Village.

Zazen had come, finally, to an end. So Lucia and I began to put out a small newsletter, which would come out monthly or thereabouts, called *The Fleeting Bear*. It published poetry, reviews, snippets of essays, fiction, and was distributed to whoever wanted it for a contribution of one kind or another.

Working with the On Guard people, I would go uptown. We had opened a small office on 125th Street and got involved in a few struggles. The most important battle we took up was when the government tried to frame Rob Williams. We set up a committee, the Monroe Defense Committee, to raise money and put out propaganda about the case. We ran into trouble with the Socialist Workers Party, which wanted to have some grip on the group. I was very naive about sectarian left politics and didn't really understand what was going on. All I knew is that the SWP wanted to put a woman named Berta Greene on the MDC and Richard Gibson was always complaining about the SWP and, particularly, Berta Greene as interfering obstructionists to the work he was trying to do with Fair Play. We met one day at my house on 14th Street. Calvin, Virginia Hamilton, Archie, and some others and SWP people gave us a check for a couple hundred dollars and wanted to talk about Berta's being an officer on the committee. We went into secret caucus and subsequently told them we didn't want Berta on the committee. So SWP took their check back. What was so wild was that some of us were talking about how we didn't want white people on the committee but we were all hooked up to white women and the downtown Village society. Such were the contradictions of that period of political organization.

But Rob's frame-up brought us into that struggle in a big way. We put out a little publication called *In/Formation*, which talked about the case and which we began to distribute mostly downtown. We had the uptown office, but most of us (all of us) still lived downtown.

The SWP started a rival defense committee, as they usually do when they cannot steer things their way. So the two defense committees struggled with each other and at the same time we were trying to get out information about Rob's case. I became a member of the Fair Play for Cuba Committee and eventually chairman of the New York chapter. I started also to speak at different places around the city about Cuba and also the Williams case. Both these issues had caught the imagination of a certain sector of young people of my generation—harbingers of things to come. I began meeting a lot of different kinds of people than the sequestered artistic types I'd been running with, but I was still very much a part of a downtown art scene, though the positions and opinions I was beginning to take were always opposed by most of my artsy world. "Cuba Libre" was reprinted by the Fair Play Committee right after it appeared in *Evergreen Review* late in 1960.

In some ways the East 14th Street apartment was the scene of even larger bashes than those on West 20th Street. The West 20th Street sets were, in the main, in-house kinds of things—close cutthroat friends. On East 14th Street we had one New Year's Eve party that looked like it had half the Village there. And there was not only anything people wanted to drink or smoke (and whatever they wanted to snort somewhere in one of the rooms) but we had taken to buying these amyl nitrate capsules, which were normally used to revive heart attack victims. Cracking the glass tube inside a bright yellow net and whiffing that boy gave one of the oddest kinds of instant high. It made things hilarious (do people with heart attacks feel instantly sad?), but its effects were very short lived—perhaps a minute. For this reason people were always whipping out the yellow-clothed capsule, popping it, and falling all over cracking up. People who didn't know what was happening thought we were nuts.

The Fleeting Bear was coming out regularly and became the talk of our various interconnected literary circles. It was meant to be "quick, fast, and in a hurry." Something that could carry the zigs and zags of the literary scene as well as some word of the general New York creative ambience. Lucia and I were very serious about it, sending it to anyone who wanted it or who we thought should get it and asking for any contribution they wanted to give. Usually that meant people might drop a dollar on you when you couldn't possibly have "charged" a dollar for that skimpy little thing. But the publication had real impact and influence and was greatly talked about. And though it had a regular circulation of about 300, those 300 were sufficiently wired for sound to project the *Bear's* presence and "message" (of a new literature and a new criticism) in all directions.

Fleeting Bear 9, however, got another response. We were sending it to a couple of people in the slam and the authorities intercepted that issue, which contained Burroughs' take-off on Roosevelt, called "Routine: Roosevelt after the Inauguration" (an excerpt from *Naked Lunch*), plus a dramatic section of my own *Dante* called "The Eighth Ditch," about a homosexual rape in the army. In the middle of the night (about 3 A.M.) treasury agents, FBI, and police showed at East 14th Street. I was awakened with these nabs standing over my head. Nellie told them not to wake the children and they threatened to arrest her. One of them asked me, "Is that your wife?" Just to show that they did not like the interracial business.

I was being charged with sending obscene materials through the mail. So you can see that certainly was another day, just a little over thirty years ago. The words used in those two pieces can probably be found in most films released now. I was locked up but got a lawyer, and when Lucia turned herself in later, we were both released on our own recognizance.

I defended myself before the grand jury, however. I read all the good parts of Joyce's *Ulysses* and Catullus aloud to the jury and then read Judge Woolsey's decision on *Ulysses*, which described obscene literature as being arousing "to the normal person." I went on, saying, "But I know none of you [grand jury] were aroused by any of these things." They dismissed the case.

During those East 14th Street days, Timothy Leary showed up. He was teaching up at Harvard and doing research on hallucinogens; he and another guy (Alpert) who became a guru and changed his name to Baba Ram Dass. Leary was floating around the downtown artistic community handing out the drug psilocybin, also called "the magic mushroom," to get the reaction of writers and painters and dancers and musicians to hallucinogenic drugs. LSD was a later development of this same stuff.

I had my reservations about taking that bullshit. My rationale was that while traditional drugs (bush, scag, cocaine) were OK with me, I didn't know anything about this kind of shit Leary was pushing. But I went for it anyway and took some of it. I was high about eight hours! And then when I thought I was down I had a relapse. The shit made stuff seem like it was jumping around on my desk and in the house. Papers, pictures, furniture all would suddenly leap to another spot or jump up and down. After a while I began begging to come down (in my head). And then aloud: "I wish this shit would go away!" Finally, it was late at night and I thought I had shook the shit off. So I went for a walk up First Avenue, which was just a block away. When I got up in the 20s, suddenly I started hearing these wild screams and moans. "Goddammit, that shit is back again. Goddammit!" I was whining out loud, but then I looked up and I was walking right near Bellevue and it was the noise the nuts were making. I never used it again, Leary or not!

I had gotten together enough poems for a first book and was thinking of publishing it through Totem. But I hit on an idea of getting Ted Wilentz and his brother, Eli, who ran the Eighth Street Bookstore, to co-publish with us. They had started a publishing company, Corinth Books, to publish a book that Eli had done on New York City history. Ted was a good friend of Allen Ginsberg and generally a warm and fairly knowledgeable person about the new literary scene, since people were always coming into his place mashing new stuff on him to sell out of his store. We'd always got a good response with *Zazen* and the Totem books and he carried much of the new literature from all over the country. So in 1961 my first book of poetry, *Preface to a Twenty Volume Suicide Note*, was published.

The Totem-Corinth collaboration published a number of significant books. *Empty Mirror*, early poems by A.G.; *Myths and Texts*, Gary Snyder; *Like I Say*, Philip Whalen; *Second Ave.*, Frank O'Hara; *Hands Up*, Ed Dorn; *Scripture of the Golden Eternity*, Kerouac; Gilbert Sorrentino's *Black and White.* Plus Totem, by itself, published Max Finstein's *Savonarola's Tune* and Charles Olson's seminal work, *Projective Verse*, which was for many of us the manifesto of a new poetry.

But soon we had to move again. This time the landlords wanted to tear down the old building to make way for a new apartment complex. So the apartment-hunting routine had to begin again. I was still not doing anything but writing. Nellie still worked for the *Sectarian Review*, so that was the steady money; other than that, there was, for a time, my unemployment check. Then only some other very little bits and pieces. I was doing articles on music for *Metronome* in its new reemergence and that provided a few pennies here and there. I had even had a cover article, "Blues, Black and White America," which tried to look at the music from a historical perspective. The editors wanted to come on more radical than the dreary *Downbeat.* One of the editors was a friend of Lenny Bruce's. The cover of the issue in which I had the big article showed a white referee on a football field kicking a black baby over the goalposts!

But I was writing reviews consistently for *Metronome*, and another publication was initiated, first by Marc Schleifer and later by Lita Hornick, called *Kulchur.* The title was taken from Pound's title *A Guide to Kulchur.* Schleifer was a young Jew who had come out of the University of Pennsylvania as an arch-conservative, then was transformed by the various Village forces and became more radical than most of my other colleagues. He was later to interview Rob Williams in Monroe and publish the introduction to the first edition of Rob's important work *Negroes with Guns*, which was one of the first contemporary statements in support of black self-defense. Schleifer also went to Cuba later and, finally, during the intense period of estrangement between certain blacks who had been living downtown and their erstwhile white friends, Schleifer went to Algeria, then Egypt, changed his name to Abdullah, and became a Muslim!

Lita Hornick was the wife of Morton ("Mortie") Hornick, who was, when I met him, the president of the Young Presidents Club, whose members had to be presidents of large corporations before they got to be thirty. He died a few years ago. They lived up on Park Avenue, but Lita had a literary interest (which she still maintains), and becoming familiar with the Beat scene and with people like Frank O'Hara and myself, she decided she wanted to buy Marc's magazine. For a time, Schleifer continued as editor, then Mrs. Hornick took over. Sorrentino was poetry editor; O'Hara was arts editor; I was music editor. The magazine was more focused on commentary than poetry or fiction, though it did have a drama issue, which I edited. And while there was no money being made, it offered still another vehicle for expression of our broad common aesthetic. It allowed us to resume our attack on the academy, for instance, at an even higher level than *Zazen* provided. Plus, our editorial meetings at the Hornicks' were always a treat for us downtown frayed-at-the-edges semi-bohemians passing into the Park Avenue pad to view some sho nuff wealth. Mortie Hornick and I always had a running banter going, he needling me because he knew I always talked against the rich, and me accepting the needling good-naturedly, but still adding a little doo doo in the contest.

I had hit upon another idea in our search for some dust, however. I made a copy of Nellie's key to the *Sectarian Review*, and unbeknownst even to her, I began to make clandestine visits to the offices. My object was to cop the review copies of books they always had there, or I figured they'd have, and resell them to various bookstores. I figured they'd take the books they were going to review and send them out. But the other books, the big art books and coffee-table books, plus the various kinds of fiction and non-fiction in which I knew the Sectarians had no interest, I'd drop into my army gas mask bag and slide on out before the whole building closed. I used to make this move about once a week, more if there was a big crop. I never took too many, since I didn't want to get anyone suspicious or Nellie fired. But I'd wait till I knew she was gone, and she was the last one in the office. The two famous editors rarely came in. Then I'd take the books to Strand or Phoenix or Briggs' Books and Things and get something like 25 cents on the dollar. If a book sold for $20 or $25, I'd really be in clover.

I used to get review records normally as a reviewer for *Metronome*, Martin Williams' *Jazz* magazine, and even *Downbeat* occasionally. I'd sell these as well, if I didn't want them, and get the same price, 25 cents on the dollar.

A small crisis arose when the deadline to move out of the East 14th Street barn came up and we still didn't have a place. Finally, we had to move one way or another. Fee Dawson, by now, had moved into a loft, down at the other end of West 20th Street, right near Fifth Avenue. He was leaving to visit, but the loft had nothing in it really. I'd found a small group of rooms, the strangest-looking little apartment I'd ever seen, down on Cooper Square, a few steps from the Five Spot. Though the Five Spot was moving now too, up a couple blocks away to the corner of Cooper Square and St. Marks Place. The apartment had concrete walls and little winding halls, and a room that would be the kitchen with windows that opened out onto a roof.

It was a wild place, but it needed work badly. It could not be lived in by small children. It needed doors and pipes for bathroom and kitchen, for tubs, commode, and stoves. It also was filled with debris. I found a guy who would do the work of fixing up the joint if I agreed to help him so he didn't have to pay a helper. Nellie would go to Newark to stay with my family, with the two babies. I would stay at Fee's place while this was going on.

At this same time, an old girlfriend of Jack Kerouac's, Joyce Glassman, now Joyce Johnson, had become an editor at William Morrow. She told me if I submitted an outline for a book, something like the article I had published in *Metronome*, "Blues, Black and White America," she could get it published, since some folks up at Morrow liked the article. I did an outline, Morrow liked it, I got a small advance—enough to pay Jeff, the carpenter, give Nellie some money, and at the same time have a little to sustain me at Fee's loft. And so I began work, at the same time as we were fixing up the loft-like apartment on Cooper Square, on the book *Blues People*.

The feeling that went with moving plaster and garbage all day and helping with the plumbing and carpentry and in the evenings working feverishly on *Blues People* was elating. After a week or so I didn't have to do so much to help the carpenter, so I could spend the whole day doing the research, reading, and writing. I'd go by Cooper Square every day to check on the progress and call Nellie about what was happening. She'd come over a day or so every week.

In a month plus a few days, the apartment, such as it was, was finished. Coooper Square is really a continuation of the Bowery and the section between the Bowery and Third Ave., they are the same street. I had made great gains on the book, gotten my basic premise together, and was clear about how I wanted to flesh out the *Metronome* article. In the next few months I was to finish it. The Cooper Square apartment had an ambience, a sense of place, as Charles Olson would have called it, that was unlike either West 20th Street or East 14th Street. Perhaps, for one thing, it was my own deepening sense of myself that was at large within those rooms: what the Cuban trip had begun to urge onto the surface, something that had existed in me as seed, as idea, as perception still to be rationalized. The political work that I was doing more of meant also that I had to offer another face to the world; maybe I was becoming someone else. Fair Play, On Guard, Organization of Young Men. I began to feel, even though I was definitely still a member of the downtown set, somewhat alienated from my old buddies. Perhaps alienated is too strong a word, but I peeped some distance had sprung up between us. I was writing the poems that would come out in a couple years as the book *The Dead Lecturer*, and again and again they speak of this separation, this sense of being in contradiction with my friends and peers.

For another thing, my writing on black music had increased in very large measure and, for certain, that was an answered promise that went back to my youth as a set of fresh ears trailing across Belmont Avenue listening to black blues and knowing that was the real language of the place! I even got something like a gig about this time. Esmond Edwards, the A&R man for Prestige records, gave me a gig writing liner notes. I got a disc about two or three times a month, and for each set of notes I wrote I got $50! I wrote liners for Gene Ammons, Shirley Scott, Arnett Cobb, Willis "Gatortail" Jackson, and many many others. *The Blues People* research also meant that I had to study not only the history of African American music but also the history of the people. It was like my loose-floating feelings, the subordinated brown that was hooked to the black and the blues, were now being reconstructed in the most basic of ways.

I was still drifting around the Village hooked up to any number of completely transitory, mainly white, female liaisons. But even that was somewhat altered. For one thing, I got involved with this beautiful black woman who was the mistress (on the real side) of this rich Village publisher. She was so out she'd go by there and get money from this dude and then we'd take off and go somewhere. In one sense, I guess I identified with her, because she seemed completely sealed off in an all-white world. He, the publisher, handled her like expensive merchandise. And one night, we look up, and we're the only black people at this book party, and our eyes collided so heavily I swore someone could hear it. But she was even more confused than I. One day she comes to my house on East 14th Street, with some friend of hers, under this completely phony guise, and she says something to Nellie and wants me to leave the house and go with her at that moment. That was a little out even for me. She was still chippying around as an omnisexual or whatever, so our thing was short-lived. The wild thing is that one night, maybe six or seven years later, I see her at some function and she's become a Muslim, a member of the Nation of Islam. We said nothing to each other, we even pretended not to recognize each other. But that really twisted me up.

Another kind of salon or circle began to form at Cooper Square. The tenor saxophonist Archie Shepp moved downstairs sometime after we did.

At that time he was completely unknown, his first glimmer of recognition was playing in the jazz group that was part of the play by Jack Gelber, *The Connection*, which opened at the Living Theater, Julian Beck and Judith Malina's avant-garde theater.

The altoist Marion Brown was also part of that circle. He had come up from Atlanta University to the big city and was still not certain he even wanted to play music. He was into writing, acting, whatever. William White lived right around the corner just off Cooper Square, in a basement apartment on East 4th Street, with his wife, Dorothy. He'd just come up from Howard University, where he went despite my telling him all those months in Puerto Rico not to. He was trying to make it painting in the big city. White had several friends whose main focus was scag, and that's what they contributed to the circle.

The black painter Bob Thompson and I had gotten tight a year or so before. I'd seen him in the Cedar and at some parties. A big, husky, homely dude with hair standing up all over his head. I was always in and out of his loft. (The poet Quincy Troupe reminds me of Bob sometimes.)

A. B. Spellman was still around, now married to a French woman and living not far away down near Houston Street. C.D. was also around. And the painter Joe Overstreet, with his loud-ass self, was there.

Some of the people from the West 20th Street group were still coming by. Joel Oppenheimer and Gil Sorrentino perhaps more than anyone else, and "Cubby" Selby (he'd be looking for shit as well). But there was a distinct change in this circle, one I understood much later. Marion might come around in the morning and we'd bullshit and get high on whatever. We'd go around to bug White or maybe Marion'd come with White and we'd get high and listen to music and bullshit. Archie or Joe might be on the scene. Sonny Murray, the great drummer, lived not too far from us and he'd like as not come in with Marion or, later, by himself. He had just begun to work with the jazz innovator Cecil Taylor. Cecil wanted to rehearse in his loft most of the days. But that was part of it—the time necessary to be put in, to reach the level we all wanted, those of us who were really serious! You got to put in that time, as Max Roach would say.

Sonny was always looking for smoke or whatever and some conversation. He was always full of his chuckling humor and talking about the music. We would sit around and get blind or blind-blind, talking about whatever came into our heads. Whenever someone would show, we had no bell, they had to stand downstairs and holler up; it would be the end of my work day and bullshitting and getting high was the order of the day!

But these were mostly black men that I began to see in the daytime hanging out, where before at West 20th Street, any daytime hanging out was with the Black Mountain crowd and mostly on the weekends because I had the technical editor gig. I was not doing any day gig now, I was writing, actually pretty prolifically. But my daytime hang buddies were black.

White, Bob Thompson, and I (mainly at Bob's urging) were always putting in "bag time" walking around looking for dope. We might go wandering up Eighth Avenue in Harlem, in and out of some greasy joints, chasing the bag. We were all "chippying," using scag from time to time, but mainly anytime we could get it. I mostly snorted it, but I was shooting it, too. Bob and White were shooting much more than I was. But all of us up in that group snorted scag like we'd drunk booze at West 20th Street. Plus my old friend Tom Perry would come by and we'd really get it on. (Steve Korret had left the States in 1960, as a new decade came in, connected up perhaps to a previous generation that saw Europe as center. At one point, he'd stopped Joel Oppenheimer and me in the Five Spot and jokingly made reference to a Blues poem of Joel's in the magazine. Korret was very ironic and curt with Joel but in his humorous albeit quasi-nasty way. He said something to the effect that he wanted to check Joel's blues, which was also the name of the poem, to see if it was *authentic*. I'm going to study this aesthetic you've roped this boy in with, is what he was implying. Later, on West 20th Street, we'd had an argument. He'd said, "Why are you talking to me in this way?" He was telling me about something he'd been doing at the UN. He'd left the bookstore and gone to the UN to work, divorced Charlene, and he was living with another woman who worked at the UN. In a month he was gone, to Scandinavia, where he lived until 1992, when he died.)

I still went to the Cedar and bellied up to the bar with Basil King or Joel or Gil or A.B. or even Bob and White would come along, but now I was much more into the jazz clubs that were opening and some coffeehouses and lofts that were playing the "new thing" rather than the old stiff formal expensive nightclubs. The Five Spot was the center for us. When Thelonious Monk came in for his historic eighteen-week stay, with John Coltrane, I was there almost every night. I was there from the beginning listening to Trane try to get around on Monk's weird charts, and gradually Trane got hold to those "heads" and began to get inside Monk's music. Trane had just come from playing with the classic Miles Davis group that featured Cannonball, Philly Joe Jones, Paul Chambers, and Red Garland. The Club Bohemia was where I'd heard them "max out" and make their greatest music. And that was a slick nightclub, albeit in the Village. But the Five Spot was on the East Side, on the Bowery. C.T., Cecil Taylor, had really inaugurated the playing of the Music in the place. Before that it had been one of those typical grim Bowery bars, but some of the painters who had lofts on the Bowery and in the area began to come in and drink and they used to ask Joe and Iggy to bring in some music. So the completely unorthodox Cecil was one of the first to come in. By the time Monk and Trane got there, the Five Spot was the center of the jazz world!

In one sense our showing up on Cooper Square was right in tune with the whole movement of people east, away from the West Village with its high rents and older bohemians. Cooper Square was sort of the border-line; when you crossed it, you were really on the Lower East Side, no shit. The Music itself, rapid motion during this period. Trane's leaving Miles and his graduate classes with T. Sphere Monk put him into a music so expressive and thrilling people all over tuned in to him. Miles' group was classic because it summed up what went before it as well as indicated what was to come. Miles' "perfection" was the interrelationship between the hard bop and the cool and in Miles, sassy and sly. So that on the one side the quiet little gurgles that we get as *fusion* also come out of Miles (all the leading fusionaires from "Cannonball" on are Miles' alumni) as well as the new blast of life that Coltrane carried, thus giving us the Pharaoh Sanderses and Albert Aylers and the reaching searching cry for freedom and life that not only took the music in a certain direction, but that direction was a reflection of where people themselves, particularly the African American people, were going. It is no coincidence that people always assciate John Coltrane and Malcolm X, they are harbingers and reflectors of the same life development.

And so I, we, followed Trane. We watched him even as he stood staring from the Club Bohemia listening to Miles and going through some personal hells. We heard him blow then, long and strong, trying to find something, as Miles stood at the back of the stage and tugged at his ear, trying to figure out what the fuck Trane was doing. We could feel what he was doing. Amus Mor, the poet, in his long poem on Trane says Miles was cool, in the slick cocktail party of life, but Trane would come in "wrong," snatchin' the sammiches off the plate.

The Five Spot gig with Monk was Trane coming into his own. After Monk, he'd play sometimes chorus after chorus, taking the music apart before our ears, splintering the chords and sounding each note, resounding it, playing it backwards and upside down, trying to get to something else. And we heard our own search and travails, our own reaching for new definition. Trane was our flag.

Trane was leaping away from "the given," and the troops of the mainstream were both shocked and sometimes scandalized, but Trane, because he had come up through the ranks, had paid all the dues, from slicksteppin' on the bars of South Philly, honking rhythm and blues, through big Maybelle and Diz on up to Miles and then Monk, could not be waved aside by anybody. Though some tried and for this they were confirming their ignorance.

But there were some other, younger, forces coming in at the time and this added still other elements to the music and spoke of still other elements that existed among the African American people. Ornette Coleman had come in, countrified, yet newer than new. He showed at the Five Spot, first, with a yellow plastic alto saxophone, with his band dressed in red Eisenhower jackets, talking about "Free." It was "a beboppier bebop," an atomic age bebop, but cut loose from the prison house of regular chord changes. Rhythmically fresh, going past the church revivals and heavy African rhythm restoration that Sonny Rollins, Max Roach and the Messengers, Horace Silver had come out with attempting to get us past the deadly cool of '50s "West Coast" jazz. Ornette went back to bop for his roots, his hip jagged rhythms, and said, "Hey, forget the popular song, let's go for ourselves." And you talking about being scandalized, some folks got downright violent. Cecil Taylor was on the scene first and his aerodynamic, million-fingered pianistics, which seemed connected to the European concert hall, made people gloss over the heavy line of blue syncopation that Cecil came with, and the percussiveness of his piano was as traditional for black "ticklers" as you could get. But that was new too and sassy, even arrogant (like Cecil himself), as if he had gone to the academy (he had) copped what they had, and still brought it back *home*.

Plus, all of Ornette's band could play, they'd start and stop like it was *in medias res*, it seemed there was no beginning or formal ending, yet they were always "together" — Don Cherry, like a brass pointillist, with his funny little pocket trumpets; Charlie Haden, the white bass player who got down on his instrument, strumming and picking it like a guitar, showing that he had heard Monk's great bassist, Wilbur Ware, and knew which way that ax was going, but at the same time original and singing. And Billy Higgins, of the perpetual smile, cooking like you spose to, carrying the finally funky business forward. They all could play, and the cry of "Freedom" was not only musical but reflected what was going on in the marches and confrontations, on the streets and in the restaurants and department stores of the South.

The '60s had opened with the black movement stepping past the earlier civil rights phase in many ways. One key addition and change was that now the black students had come into the movement wholesale. So that from 1954 (when *Brown v. Board of Ed.* showed that the people had forced an "all deliberate speed" out of the rulers instead of the traditional "separate but equal"), through 1960, Martin Luther King and SCLC, mostly black, southern, big-city ministers, leading that struggle for democracy, were at center stage. But in 1960, the student sit-ins began, and, on February 1, black students at Greensboro began a movement that brought literally hundreds of thousands of black students, and soon students of all nationalities, into the struggle for democracy as well. So that soon we would hear the term SNCC, who, at first, were still hooked up with the middle-class ministers and their line of nonviolence, but that would change. But now, the cries of "Freedom" had been augmented with "Freedom Now!"

So it was in the air, it was in the minds of the people, masses of people going up against the apartheid South. It was also coming out of people's horns, laid out in their music. People like Max Roach spoke eloquently for an older, hip generation. He said "Freedom Now," and Sonny Rollins had his "Freedom Suite." And nutty Charlie Mingus was hollering his hilarious "Fables of Faubus." I even got into a hassle with a bald-headed German clerk in a record store on 8th Street. I'd come in and asked for Jackie McLean's terrible side "Let Freedom Ring," and the clerk wanted to give me a lecture about how "you people shouldn't confuse your sociology with music." (It was mostly a European concert music-selling store). I told him to kiss my ass, right now. Yeh, kiss my ass . . . that was also getting into it.

So there was a newness and a defiance, a demand for freedom, politically and creatively, it was all connected. I wrote an article that year, "The Jazz Avant-Garde," mentioning people like Cecil, Ornette, and the others, plus Trane and the young wizard Eric Dolphy, the brilliant arranger and reed player, Oliver Nelson, Earl Griffith, onetime Cecil Taylor vibist, and my neighbor Archie Shepp, who had come on the scene, also shaking it up.

I also wrote a piece for *Kulchur* called "Milneburg Joys, or Against Hipness as Such," taking on members of our various circles, the hippies (old usage) of the period who thought merely by initialing ideas which had currency in the circles, talking the prevailing talk, or walking the prevailing walk, that that was all there was to it. I was also reaching and searching, life had to be more than a mere camaraderie of smugness and elitist hedonism.

Ornette Coleman's "Free Jazz," the completely "free" improvisational record, with the cream of the new players, had set the tone. It was as if the music was leading us. And older players like Trane and Rollins took up that challenge. Trane played chordal music, but he got frantically chordal. The critics called it "sheets of sound," many at a loss for words, like they'd been when Bird had first appeared. *Downbeat* and *Metronome* had to re-review all those old records, because they had put them all down as fakery and they were classics of African American music, so they tried to clean up.

What was being generated by the new blacker circle I mostly hung with was quite different in effect than the earlier circles. Our overall large circle was, of course, well integrated. But now, I'd be sitting and talking to Marion or White or both, or three, add Bob Thompson. Or we'd be at Bob's loft, checking his wild paintings, all kinds of different-colored women with scenes taken from the Italian renaissance classic painters and reinterpreted through Bob's way-out mind. White was painting wry symbolic abstractions, where instead of the pure motion-paint of the "action paintings," White relied on more or less "organic"-looking shapes swirling and dancing on his canvases. I still wonder what White's work would have been like today had he lived. Or Bob's, had he lived. Overstreet, at the time, was doing brilliant but highly sexy drawings. And usually we'd be getting high, about to get high, or talking about getting high.

We had some bigger, wilder parties at Cooper Square, in Archie's loft, with some of the hippest music of the time. And Archie and I used to do some mean tipping around those streets, or when he played we'd go cheer him on. Sometimes with Bob and White and Marion and me, Tom might be walking with us, or hanging with us, and sometimes Elvin Jones or Hank Mobley. Dudes be sitting around heads about to wear they chest out and Elvin would look like he wasn't even high, smiling his lit-up smile like a neon sign. But Hank eventually got into bad times.

One time I was sitting with Marion and White and somebody else up in my study at Cooper Square and we were shooting cocaine. Somebody also had given us a vial of liquid procaine, which was like fake cocaine. I get the bright idea to melt the real cocaine in the liquid procaine and shoot it up. I had got the needle out of my arm and I feel the rise coming but this time it's sweeping up through my body to my head like it won't stop. I was sitting in the big overstuffed desk chair for my rolltop and this hot surge seems to sweep up past my eyes shooting out the top of my skull. I rose up, almost paralleling, I guess, the rise of the drug. I said, "Whooo-ooo," and then wheeled around in the middle of the room and fell over backwards like I'd been shot. And then, on the floor, semiconscious, it seems to me like some big blue thing is trying to hit me between the eyes. They say I was thrashing around on the floor, turning my head frantically from one side to the other. I thought I was trying to keep the blue thing from hitting me between the eyes. I didn't know nobody could OD off "coke," but that felt mighty close to something bad, and it scared the shit out of me. But it didn't stop me or our drug activities.

We were in the old Half Note on Hudson Street watching Trane slay all pests. Between sets, Bob (who was a great friend of Elvin's), White and I go up the street, fetch a bag of whatnot, then Bob wants us to stop by this painter's house he knew, a pretty hip white dude who lived down there. We all high, but Bob wants to go up and talk to the dude. His wife comes to the door in her gown and lets us in. It was a very sheer gown and you could just about see through it. there's some music playing so after Elvin is introduced, he starts dancing with this dude's wife, grinding like he's trying to start a fire. I'd always thought the shit made you unsexual, but it didn't affect Elvin that way at all. We'd be nodding and he'd go back and play the drums like mad.

There were now a few lofts scattered around where you could hear the music as well as European avant-garde music. I especially liked Morton Feldman's music, Cage's audacity and some of the other things. But we were mostly into the new black music. Coffee shops like Take 2, the White Whale, also had the young musicians in when they couldn't work in the larger clubs. In one of those coffee shops one night a really wild episode went down. It told me something about downtown and myself and some of my friends. Archie Shepp had been playing in this place on 10th Street, the White Whale, the decor even had a big anchor on the wall with huge chains hanging down. It was early and people were sitting around talking and, at a couple of tables, playing chess. There's one guy sitting there, they called him Big Brown. He was big, about six feet three inches, and much darker than brown. He was slender like he was in shape. Plus, he had this slow, bent-knee hop he walked with that was more peculiar than hip. Brown made his mark downtown by first standing around various places like Washington Square Village profiling. He had muscles, so he liked to preen and twist, stand like a body builder in a show. He was a proto Arnold Schwarzenegger.

Brown's whole demeanor used to turn me off. But even worse was the fact that not only would he always be in his exaggerated strut, but during the summer months he'd walk the streets in a loincloth, like an Indian fakir or something. And sometimes he'd come into the Cedar when we'd be sitting there and he would come walking down the aisle rubbing his crotch, like he was showing off his wares to the various females. One night he even came up to a booth where one couple was sitting and stood rubbing his crotch just a few inches from this woman's face! Her companion said something and Brown talked in rhymes putting the dude down. Brown loved to recite singsong versions of Shakespeare or the *Rubaiyat* or his own rhyming doggerel. A couple of times, I saw him get in some woman's face who was sitting with some man and I vowed inside my head that that motherfucker better not ever do that to any woman I was with. In fact, when he'd walk down the aisle I'd loudly ridicule him, and one time he cut his eyes over my way, scowled, made some remark, and kept swaggering on up.

But as he was playing chess, the dude he was playing checkmated him, calling "Check!" I laughed, as it happened just as I was passing close to the table where he was sitting.

I said, "Wrong again!" and broke up. Some of my friends, notably A.B., Marion, and Joe, were in there and this cracked them up and some others nearby. Brown always pulled his shit off in the spirit and demeanor of "Bogarting" people. He would run his silent or rhymed gorilla act on people and they were supposed to be intimidated. But I didn't dig him.

So Brown says something, maybe "Fuck you" or "What you got to do with it?" or something, but the catalyst was me saying, "Big Brown, the African Queen!" So he leaps to his feet and goes into his menace/gorilla stance. But I kept talking, kept putting him down. Not only "African Queen" but all kinds of other things my instinctive sense of danger now has blanked out. Not only that, I start taunting him: "You supposed to be bad. You ain't bad, dressed up like some fuckin' genie or something. You just silly. A silly-ass nigger! Shit, I bet you can't even fight." Yeh, it really got out. And I can see with some kind of split vision my various buddies flung about the room, frozen stiff as respective Statues of Liberty or Colossi of Rhodes or whatever. (A.B. told me later he kept thinking, "Shut up, little nigger, shut up.")

I can't even say what made me go so far. Except I felt Brown's whole thing was an act, some second-rate vaudeville. Actually, he looked like the dude who used to run with Mandrake, because he wore a turban sometimes. But in some fit of absolute frustration, most likely, Brown reaches and grabs the chains from the wall decor and holds them like he's going to bash my head in. So I started laughing and taunting him even more. "Yow, a six-foot-three two-hundred-pound bad dude got to get a chain to bash me!" I cracked up. "Hey, man, you must be pretty bad, you gotta get a chain. God damn!" And that broke it open. It was absurd. And in the end, the room was bathed in laughter and Brown stood there with the chain in his hand, then slowly let it fall to the floor. He turned and grimly stalked into the night. My nerves shot more laughter up and out after him, then we got some wine, threw it down telling various bullshit versions of the same event, and trailed out of the joint, with people still pointing and cackling. We looked both ways when we got outside though we still were animated by a frivolity that both masked and carried our deep sighs of relief.

Hey, it wasn't even the real world. I guess that was my reasoning. In the real world, of Newark's steel-gray streets, all that mouth would've got me killed or at least forced me to set a new indoor and outdoor Olympic hat-up record. But down there, wow, even the bad dudes was cardboard Lothars afraid of their own shadow.

The work with On Guard on Rob Williams' defense and the Fair Play Committee had given me another and, I think, deeper perspective. I could reflect on revolution and struggle as concrete phenomena. It made the posturing and fakery of much of the downtown residents even more absurd. Though I was still involved in quite a bit of it myself. Lucia DiBella had gotten pregnant. I tried to tell myself it wasn't mine. And Lucia had one dancer friend of ours living with her from time to time. I thought maybe it was his. But he was a homosexual, a beautiful but tragic dancer who was always slightly fantasizing about himself as a young Nijinsky. One night at a cocktail party, probably high on acid, he stepped through the open window, claiming he could fly, and killed himself. Plus one of the dancer's men friends, piqued by something he, Neddie, had done, or both of them mutually pissed off at each other, had ended their relationship and the friend, a tall blonde fashion model, Chris Bartlett, and Lucia were rapidly becoming fast friends. However, such "might be's" and "maybe's" didn't change the reality. No matter how many of the endless one-night stands I might get involved with, I'd always show up at Lucia's.

Actually, the magazine I ran with Nellie, *Zazen*, had continued to issue No. 8, coming out the same time as *The Fleeting Bear*, the sheet that Lucia and I put out. Lucia's pregnancy alerted Nellie, however, and she asked me what I knew about it. I didn't know anything about that, just because I went over there to put out the *Bear* didn't mean anything. But it did. I had asked the poet Harry Schulman, who was a friend of Lucia's, over the phone, "What does the baby look like?" And he said, "White." I felt relieved. But in a few days, Nellie came home with our babies from hanging out in Tompkins Square Park near Avenue A where the Lower East Side mothers congregated, as the West Side mothers did in Washington Square Park. She said to me only that she had seen Lucia's baby and it was "one of those black-and-white kind." Then she cried some, asking me from time to time, "How could you?" And that was a very good question. I wondered myself.

To make bad things worse, in a few months the house next to ours was vacant and Lucia moved there, baby, model friend, and all. I had said before, it was like Brook Farm. Eventually, the model assumed fathership of the baby, and Lucia and he even had a baby of their own. Lucia called the child she'd had by me Dominique, in honor of the Frenchified LeRoi.

I was now taking published potshots at the nonviolence movement. "Tokenism: 300 Years for Five Cents" was one article, "What Does Nonviolence Mean?" another. *Kulchur* had published the first, and the conservative Jewish publication *Midstream* the other. I was becoming much more openly involved with movement questions. The mood downtown was changing, there were many more signs of some people getting involved with various struggles, especiallly the Cuban struggle and the student struggle. Plus, there were now a great many more blacks downtown than when I had first arrived half a decade before. I had been on the scene now from the period when there were relatively few blacks and when the sets had gotten fiercely integrated, but now there seemed to be further change. More and more I found myself sitting and talking or walking and making parties with black dudes. We began to feel a certain kind of community, perhaps a kind of solidarity as blacks that was unspoken in the old MacDougal Street days, but was now an openly acknowledged emotional binder. And the various sets we'd go to would always take on a distinctly different tone once we'd enter. Especially with Bob Thompson laughing at the top of his voice and "snatching bitches," as the saying goes. And White and Marion and I would be blind as the night.

But we knew what was in our hearts, something open and bright. We wanted what was new and hip, though we were connected in a lot of ways with some stuff that was old and square. We knew the music was hip and new and out beyond anything anyone downtown was doing, in music, painting, poetry, dance, or whatever the fuck. And we felt, I know I did, that we were linked to that music that Trane and Ornette and C.T., Shepp and Dolphy and the others, were making, so the old white arrogance and elitism of Europe as Center Art was stupid on its face. We could saunter into a joint and be openly critical of whatever kind of show or program or party, because we knew, number one, it wasn't as hip as the music, and, number two, it wasn't as out as we were out, because now we began to realize or rationalize that we were on the fringe of the fringe. If the down-town Village/East Village society was a fringe of big-time America, then we were a fringe of that fringe, which put us way out indeed.

Patrice Lumumba was assassinated by the CIA in 1961 to stop the newly freed Congolese people from nationalizing Union Minière and other Rockefeller properties. I found myself marching outside the UN in demonstrations, while others, mostly blacks, took off their shoes and threw them down in the gallery as the gallery guards were called in to toss the demonstrating blacks out. Sisters were bashing the guards in the head with their shoes and throwing the shoes down out the gallery. Ralph Bunche said he was ashamed and scandalized by such niggerism, while we were scandalized and ashamed of his negro-ass tom antics.

Outside, in front of the U.S. mission to the UN, the police also attacked us. One sister, Mae Mallory, Calvin Hicks, and I were marching and we looked up at the top of the stairs just in time to see James Lawson, the so-called nationalist, pointing us out to the police, and then they attacked us, clubs flying. Mae put up a terrific battle and the police were sorry they ever put their hands on her. It took several of them to subdue her. She was one of the people in On Guard and she remained very active in the Black Liberation Movement.

As the police put us into the paddy wagon, a couple of them would catch us by the elbows and hoist us through the back door, banging the top of our heads on the metal doorframe at the same time. You felt like you'd been whacked yet another time with a nightstick. Dazed in the back of the paddy wagon, I reached into my pockets and found some Benzedrine or Dexedrine pills that I took every once in a while to stay awake if I was writing all night. I threw them all in my mouth, figuring the nabs would charge me with possession of drugs. But I had taken so many I was jittery as a flea. The police must've thought it was nerves.

I began to meet some young black intellectuals connected with the Black Liberation Movement and strike up friendships. One I met in this way was Askia Touré (then Rolland Snellings), the poet. We were on those picket lines and I didn't even know he was a writer. We became friends as part of the movement.

Sometime later I began to get some word of *Umbra*, a magazine that began to come out from the Lower East Side that featured black writers. Lorenzo Thomas, who published as a very young person in some of the places that the New York school writers published, I think I was aware of first. His work appeared about the same time that Ted Berrigan and Ron Padgett and Joe Brainard, the Oklahoma free association semi-surrealists began to appear. I was especially impressed by Thomas and Berrigan, and very curious about Thomas because he was black.

One later afternoon, as was my wont, I wandered into the Five Spot, the one on the corner of St. Marks and Third Avenue. I'm sitting there sipping and probably glancing at a paper or something when two bloods come up to me. *Blues People* had come out recently and I was elated and surprised in a way because it was my first book from a mainstream publishing house and I was impressed because of the hardcover. The publisher had even had a party for me at the New School, where I was teaching a course in poetry. Ornette Coleman came, and there is a photograph with the two of us grinning. My mother and father came as well, but one of the biggest disappointments was that my grandmother had died before I had a chance to show that book to her. She probably would've cried and told me, "Practice makes perfect."

But one guy says to me, "You LeRoi Jones?" I probably just nodded or grunted. One of these dudes is sort of big-headed and bulky, the other taller, with midnight-dark glasses and a rough complexion of skin stretched tight in what I'd have to call an ambiguous smile. The big-headed one says, "I like your prose. I don't like your poetry." The other guy just continues smiling like he knows a secret.

"Oh?" I left it pointed up like someone had let a pigeon shit on my shoe, but said no more. But the big-headed one wanted to go on and he did, saying some other things. But then he introduced himself and his companion.

"My name is Ishmael Reed. This is Calvin Hernton." And so I'd met Ishmael Reed and Calvin Hernton, but I didn't know them from Adam's house cat. Though it did seem that Hernton's name rang some kind of bell, someone had mentioned it or I had seen it. But the introduction seemed to me like some challenge, I didn't know, casual or not. But I took it as such, the way you had to deal with these various ersatz artsy gunfighters roaming around the Village who thought that confrontation in the name of art was the highest form of hanging out.

But I didn't take the bait. After that intro, I kept sipping my drink. And in a few minutes, Sonny Murray or Marion or White or somebody came in and we got into our serious drinking in peace, probably conjuring up our next bag chase. Reed and Hernton sat awhile and then eased into the early evening. I remember questioning my buddies about them and was told something about *Umbra*, the folks in it and what it was about. It sounded interesting but I still didn't know why Reed had wanted to come on like Skippy Homeier looking for Gregory Peck.

We used to hang in the Five Spot in the late afternoon/early evening too, drinking and bullshitting. There'd be a mixture of the artists in the area—musicians, writers, painters. It was a good easterly drinking spot in the daytime. One time Sonny Murray came in and told me he had got into a hassle with Charlie Mingus and had to break a chair over Mingus' back. Charlie was always in the habit of cursing musicians who were his side men right up on the stage, in front of the public. It was really humiliating. I heard him one night cuss out Lonnie Hillyer, Charlie McPherson, and Jaki Byard, using all kinds of wild language. I wondered how they had gone for that.

A few evenings later, after Sonny related his confrontation with Mingus, allegedly about Mingus calling Sonny "jive" for his free style of drumming, I meet Mingus outside of The Five Spot. I say something to Mingus, like "What's happening?" or whatever, just a typical greeting. Mingus starts talking some off-the-wall stuff, most of which I didn't even get with. But then he pushes me, and I'm laughing like it was a joke, which I figured it ought to be. But then he advances, as rapidly as he can with all that weight— Charlie was about a hundred pounds overweight—and he slapped me! It was light, partially because he was off balance and partially because as I saw it coming I tried to pull my head back.

I said, "Hey, man, what's going on? What's happening?"

And Mingus starts this spew of profanity, saying something like "You goddam punk," and I could hear that it had something to do with something I'd written, that I was sympathetic with the avant-garde musicians, or something like that. But this time when he came forward, I went into my Newark Sugar Ray stick and run, jab and duck, and started popping him side his fat head. After a round-and-round of a few minutes Mingus stops and people all around us are telling us we oughta stop and stop acting crazy. I didn't think I was acting crazy, I was defending myself as best I could against some two- or three-hundred-pound nut.

Mingus stops, then he puts out his hand to shake. He says, "I'm sorry. I made a mistake. I was wrong." I guess he meant because he thought he could just slap me and walk away, having chastised some jive intellectual. But I'd ducked and dodged around some much-meaner-with-they-hands mf's than Charlie Mingus. Like I said, in many ways, the downtown scene was completely cardboard.

People like Pharaoh Sanders also began to show up on the scene. When he first arrived, everybody called him "Little Rock" cause that's where he was from. Pharaoh had the wildest walk, like he was stepping over them rows in the fields. It actually made you break up to watch him bobbing up and down as he walked toward you, horn in hand. But from the first time I heard him play, it was obvious that he was something very much else.

The power and beauty of that music was something again. And now there was so much of it coming out and everybody was talking about Freedom.

I had also got an offer from the Communist Party to edit their literary magazine. I had got some modest name, I guess, as a black intellectual, with an obvious left bent. One day I get a message from a photographer I knew who tells me that someone will be calling me from the magazine. I go over to the building the CP had the magazine's offices in. The building is dusty, the office is dusty. The whole impact on me was of dust and oldness. I thought maybe these people had been sitting there with cobwebs twisted around their heads since the '30s. But what was wild is that this guy makes me an offer to become editor of their literary magazine. I wasn't in the CP, I knew very little about them, except the clichés that we tossed around about the "failure of the '30s," not even really knowing what that meant. Though the CP, since its 1957 Congress, had become even formally revisionist, saying that socialism could be brought in the U.S. through elections. I guess they were offering me this job to bring in some new blood, but the whole operation looked too dead to me. I was really flattered, but refused. Later, they started a "black magazine" called *Dialog* and made the photographer the editor.

I'd also started contributing articles, mostly on music, to a magazine called *African Revolution*, coming out of Algeria. The progressive Ben Bella government was putting the magazine out and it featured writings from people all over the world. Richard Gibson later became associated with that magazine when he had to leave the U.S. when the government tried to frame him by implicating Fair Play for Cuba in the Kennedy assassination. But before that, Fair Play had been having harder and harder times, based on the fact that as U.S. policy toward Cuba stiffened, many of the liberal types that had supported Fair Play cut out. Also, there was a great deal of internal struggle caused by the SWP and the CPUSA slugging it out in their sectarian battles within the organization and creating chaos and havoc.

But a year or so after Gibson got over to Algeria, the Boumedienne coup came and the left-leaning Ben Bella was overthrown and Gibson and his staff had to run for their lives, barely getting out of Algeria with their skins.

It was a bizarre time, in so many ways. Attempts at new ways of life were clashing with the old. India and China had gotten their formal independence before the coming of the '50s, and by the time the '50s had ended, there were many independent African nations (though with varying degrees of neocolonialism). Ghana's Kwame Nkrumah had hoisted the black star over the statehouse in Accra, and Nkrumah's pronouncements and word of his deeds were glowing encouragement to colored people all over the world. When the Chinese exploded their first A-bomb I wrote a poem saying, in effect, that time for the colored peoples had rebegun. Frantz Fanon's books were popular, Grove Press had brought out *The Wretched of the Earth*. My own reading was broad and wilder than I knew. I was reading people like the right-wing Sorel's *Reflections on Violence* as well as the Italian Marxist Gramsci. But it was all mixed up and unsorted. However, I was plodding "forward" at the quickstep.

New ideas were clashing with old ones too. For one thing, with all of our attempted forward thrust, we were still chippying, and for some it was even more serious. White was now bordering on being strung out. He seemed at times to come back, but then for long stretches every time you saw him he'd be nodding. One night a group of sick white boys bashed me in the head on St. Marks Place and left me on my back wondering what hit me. I'd run up and down the streets trying to locate them and when I saw them eating in a Second Avenue Romanian restaurant, I'd gone into a phone booth across the street and called White trying to get some help. There were four or five of them. When I got him on the phone he sounded wasted. A few minutes later he responded and came walking around the corner. I could see him from where I was, hanging, high as planets. I told him to go home, shit, it was better just to be out there by myself. White would get killed trying to pug blind as he was.

The white boys spotted me. When I wheeled around from dealing with White they were not in the restaurant, but as I was walking toward the corner they suddenly leaped out from behind a car on a side street just off Second Avenue. I whipped out me trusty blade as the four of them spread out, one of them with an old burned Christmas tree. But the myth(?) of the crazed Nigra with a knife worked. I screamed that one of them would have to die and they couldn't decide which, so they threw the tree, which cut my hand pretty badly somehow, but split, up the street and back to their caves.

Bob Thompson had also gotten much the worse for wear, from his constant use of scag. Whereas some of us were merely chippying, Bob and White had been serious. Perhaps because the frustration in the painting world was more intense. Though Bob was beginning to get some recognition and shows. He had even finally gotten hooked up with the Martha Jackson Gallery, which was one of the more prestigious of the galleries dealing with the downtown folk.

Bob had married one of the white bohemian women and her sister was also hooked up with a black dude I knew. Bob's sister-in-law went with a dude from the South who had been one of White's best friends, and both this dude, Earl, and Bob were hooked on shit! Earl's nodding was notorious around us; a once handsome dude, he'd gotten progressively more like Dr. Hyde with each bag he shot up. It got so bad with Bob that he could no longer shoot shit into the veins of his arms, but now stuck needles in his legs and hands, even the tips of his fingers, looking for uncollapsed veins. He started wearing woolen gloves, even in the summer, to hide his ubiquitously punctured hands. One of the musicians we hung around with had developed a huge black knot of a vein on one of his arms, where he shot up all the time, and it seemed all he had to do was jam the spike anywhere in that huge black knot and blood would creep up in the dropper indicating he'd hit. This brother was and is a famous musician, but the last time I saw him, he was so blasted and pitiful he couldn't even recognize me.

A major point of change for us came with John Kennedy's assassination. Kennedy, for many of us, even unconsciously, represented something positive. The Kennedys *were* liberals. (The liberal wing of the bourgeoisie, at least.) JFK's pronouncements were meant to be progressive-sounding. And his and Jackie's style, their youth—"They bought paintings from " was one repeated line you could hear at the Cedar. But many of us did have some emotional investment in the so-called Camelot and the New Frontier.

The day Kennedy was assassinated, Bob Thompson and I were walking down Cooper Square and radios and televisions everywhere carried the grim scenes. Bob walked out in the gutter, near my house, and wept openly. That shook me up, because though I was disturbed, curious, about the assassination, I hadn't realized it until I saw Bob sitting now on the curb, weeping uncontrollably about Kennedy's death. I wrote a poem which had to be tipped into the winter issue of *Kulchur* called "Exnaugural Poem," with a subtitle, "for Jackie Kennedy who has had to eat too much shit." I was trying to move to a revolutionary position, but I was still ready to weep for Jacqueline Bouvier Kennedy!

Malcolm X had begun to reach us. I'd heard of the Nation of Islam and had even heard Malcolm speak on television and he charged me in a way no one else had ever done. He *reached* me. His media appearances made my head tingle with anticipation and new ideas. He made me feel even more articulate and forceful, myself, just having seen him. But I was not clear about the Nation of Islam and not being in a black community am sure I did not receive the full impact of Elijah Muhammad's teaching and image, but Malcolm had begun to get some media coverage.

When Malcolm was silenced by the Nation for commenting on Kennedy's death—that it was "chickens coming home to roost"—I was very deeply puzzled and disturbed because I didn't understand why Elijah Muhammad would do that. Malcolm was his sword, his chief, the most articulate man in the world, as far as I was concerned. Why had this happened? When he had said that the March on Washington was a black bourgeois status symbol, I'd roared.

Also, I'd read about how Malcolm had led a small army of Black Muslims to a Harlem police station to stand in silent protest against police brutality and how the precinct finally had yielded to Malcolm's cold dignity. They knew they were not playing with some schizophrenic Negro but a strong black man, a black leader.

To me, the March on Washington, which happened the same year that JFK was assassinated, marks the end of the second phase of the civil rights movement, in which SNCC and the students had come to center stage, even though King was still seen as the maximum leader. Malcolm's cold class analysis at Selma, talking about the House Slaves and the Field Slaves and how the House Slave identified with his white Master so completely that when the Master got sick, the House Nigger did too, and when the Master's house caught on fire the House Nigger would scream, "Boss, *our* house on fire!" But the Field Slave would *fan the flames*. That bit of class analysis dug into me, cutting both ways.

And then, the little girls in the Birmingham church were murdered by a bomb planted by a white racist and King wanted to kneel in the streets and pray, but Malcolm talked bad about nonviolence, saying that those people who had done such a thing and indeed all the white racist crackers in the world could only be reached if one spoke the same language that they spoke. That language was not peace and love, said Malcolm.

One night I saw Malcolm lay waste completely to Kenneth Clark, Constance Baker Motley, and some other assorted house Negroes, just as he had wasted David Susskind and Mike Wallace. (The Wallace program, "The Hate That Hate Produced," had shot Malcolm X and the Nation into the public eye.) This kind of thing would thrill me so completely because what Malcolm said were things that had gone through my mind but he was giving voice to. Or he'd say things and instantly it'd make sense or confirm something I'd not even thought but felt.

At one point, Kenneth Clark was saying, "Come, come, Mr. X, I don't believe Negroes will act the way you say." Malcolm had told him that blacks would not continue to turn the other cheek, that the young people would not stand still for the kind of white supremacy bullshit, of water hoses, police dogs, homegrown Nazis like George Wallace and Bull Connors. No, black people would not stand for it, especially not the young ones. But Kenneth Clark wanted to go on talking his house-slaveryism. This was early in 1964.

I felt that way. Malcolm X spoke for me and my friends; Kenneth Clark did not. C.D. used to walk around during this period and ask us, "Suppose all the Negroes did leave America to be in their own nation, would you go or stay?" C.D. also had married a white woman, with a charming French accent and a bit of continental spice. That's the way some of us saw the contradiction. Would you go or stay?

For me, Malcolm's words had me turning tricks whether I knew it or not. What it meant to my life immediately was words in my head coming out of my mouth. (I thought about Tim Poston, wandering down Third Avenue, completely off his rocker. He was mumbling, "The Jews are talking through my mouth. The Jews are talking through my mouth." And he tried to clasp his hand across his mouth, spitting these words out as if in terror. The society and the wine had done him in.)

How did we act in the face of the world now, with all its steady wave of new meanings coming in? What did we do? How did we *act*?

For one thing, unconsciously at first, but then very openly, dramatic dialogue began to appear in my poetry. Suddenly there were people, characters, talking in them. The tiny play *The Eighth Ditch*, which I put into the *Dante* book and had gotten me busted, some of the people connected with Lucia asked to produce—probably because they were gay and the play was about a homosexual rape. It opened on St. Marks Place in a place called the Poet's Theater, but the police closed it after a few performances.

I began to be interested more directly in drama. I'd written a play called *The Baptism* and one called *The Toilet*. *The Toilet* was published in the drama issue of *Kulchur*. (As editor, one of the plays I had turned down was Douglas Turner Ward's take-off of Ray Bradbury's "Way in the Middle of the Air," in *The Martian Chronicles*; Ward called it "Day of Absence.")

I can see now that the dramatic form began to interest me because I wanted to go "beyond" poetry. I wanted some kind of action literature, and the most pretentious of all literary forms is drama, because there one has to imitate life, to put characters upon a stage and pretend to actual life. I read a few years ago in some analysis of poetry that drama is a form that proliferates during periods of social upsurge, for those very same reasons. It is an action form, plus it is a much more popular form than poetry. It reaches more people and its most mass form today is of course television and, secondarily, film.

I got involved with a drama/playwright's workshop initiated by Edward Albee and his producers at the Cherry Lane Theater, Richard Barr and Clinton Wilder. The workshops were held down at the Vandam Theater, a tiny but attractive theater on Vandam Street, a few blocks below Houston Street. One night I sat up all night and wrote a play I called *Dutchman*. I had gotten the title from *The Flying Dutchman*, but abstracted it, because *Flying Dutchman* had been used and it didn't quite serve my purposes, whatever they were. It took place in a subway and was essentially a confrontation between a slightly nutty (and wholly dangerous) white female bohemian and a young naive black intellectual. The director, Ed Parone, read it and liked it and so there was talk about doing a workshop performance.

We did the workshop performance and it was very successful. I even got Marion Brown a job as an extra and quite a few people I respected dug the play. So it was decided to do a commercial production. In February 1964, James Baldwin's *Blues for Mister Charlie* opened on Broadway, directed by Burgess Meredith, and, while it had mixed reviews, it was one of the great theater experiences of my life. A deeply touching "dangerous" play for Jimmy, it not only questioned nonviolence but had a gutsy (but doomed) black hero and his father go at each other's values, echoing the class struggle that raged between Dr. King and Malcolm X. Al Freeman played Richard, the Malcolm type, though Jimmy couched his rebellion in sexual symbolism (including, as far as I'm concerned, the character's name). Diana Sands, as Juanita, gave a marvelous performance, showering us with Jimmy's questioning even of "God in his heaven" for his part in the conspiracy that leaves us powerless and our young men killed. It was an extremely powerful work, so powerful I believe that the bourgeois (mainly white) critics at that point read Jimmy out of the big-time U.S. literary scene. He had gone too far. And as critical as I had been before of Jimmy and what I perceived as his stance of avoiding reality and confrontation, now I was elated and almost raised up off the ground by this powerful play.

Dutchman opened the next month, downtown, at the Cherry Lane, with Robert Hooks and Jennifer West in the leads. I went out late that night after the opening, up to the corner of St. Marks and Second Avenue, and read the reviews. They were mixed too, but there seemed to me a kind of overwhelming sense from them that something explosive had gone down. I had a strange sensation, standing there like that. I could tell from the reviews that now my life would change again. I wasn't sure how, but I could perceive that and it sent a chill through me. I walked back home slowly, looking at my name in the newspapers, and I felt very weird indeed.

When the magazines and electronic media coverage of the play and local word got out, I could see that not only was the play an artistic success, despite my being called "foul-mouthed," "full of hatred," "furious, angry," I could tell that the play had made its mark, that it would not quietly fade away.

Suddenly I got offers to write for the *Herald Tribune* and the *New York Times*. One magazine wanted me to go down South and be a civil rights reporter. I got offers to rewrite Broadway plays in tryout, including *Golden Boy*, with the producer flying me down from Buffalo, where I'd gone as visiting lecturer in American poetry, to eat breakfast in his well-appointed brownstone on the Upper East Side. There was all kinds of interest and requests and offers and propositions. It was as if the door to the American Dream had just swung open, and despite accounts that I was wild and crazy, I could look directly inside and there were money bags stacked up high as the eye could fly!

It was clear, I could get it. An article came out in the *Herald Tribune*'s Sunday magazine, "King of the Lower East Side." The phone leaped with people calling for interviews, my name began to pop up all over the place, coming out of the mouths of people I didn't even know. It was a swirl of attention, pregnant promise was being popped for my pleasure. Oh? I could feel myself being raised, lifted by some strictly finite presence, but it was like some wind, full of names, some historic presence that I could casually identify as anything. Anything I understood. But that was the ripper, señor, the contradictory motions of my life must make it obvious, how confused I was. I had to read the play *Dutchman* again, just to understand it. And those words led in all directions, away from the page and into my life and memory. And what was it really saying, after all? I was asked that again and again. A confrontation between two people, between two symbols? I improvised from my deepest feelings. "It is about how difficult it is to become a man in the U.S." That, I knew, was true and honest. But a naive black youth, a *soi-disant* intellectual murdered by a mad white woman he had hoped to seduce? Shit, and it was only that crazy Dolly I'd dressed up and set in motion and some symbols from out of my own life.

I was at Barbara Teer's house when she was married to Godfrey Cambridge. It was Barbara Ann's party, they were mostly her friends. Godfrey sat in the kitchen fiddling with a camera. Barbara Ann and Bobby Hooks were close. Later, they even started an actors' group that evolved into the Negro Ensemble Company, somehow without Barbara Ann. There was an actor-model who also wrote plays, and he was alarmed that my play had gotten some attention. All of us know that there is no black person but ourselves that deserves to be that noble savage in the buttermilk, but ourself, dammit, ourself, goddammit, and double, ourself!! So he says to someone else, really as a gibe flying in my direction, "That's why the guy gets killed, hahahahaha."

My normal reaction would be to say something really low as to this dude's gender or sexual orientation or maybe just about the sexual orientation of his father or mother or both. But I just looked in his direction and smiled really as pleasantly as sulphuric acid could. And that was because I could tell, even though I hadn't heard the entire remark, that there was some element to it that was, indeed, legitimate.

But in the barrage of attention and unbalanced huzzas, I went inside. When I got an assignment to write an article in the *Tribune*'s magazine section, I took it as the main question being asked and I wanted my main answer. I can see now, it was just my confusion that allowed so much of the

Great White Way to flow in my direction. It was the contradictions in my life and thinking, the unresolved zigzags of my being that permitted them to hoist me up the flagpole to wave, for them.

So as I wrote that article, "LeRoi Jones Speaking," there came over me this most terrific sense of purpose and focus. It rose up within me like my grandfather's ghost. Yeh, I was some colored bohemian liberal living on the Lower East Side in hedonism heaven, yet I could not sound like that. What "fame" *Dutchman* brought me and raised up in me was this absolutely authentic and heartfelt desire to speak what should be spoken for all of us. I knew the bullshit of my own life, its twists and flip-outs, yet I felt, now, some heavy *responsibility*. If these bastards were going to raise me up, for any reason, then they would pay for it! I would pay these motherfuckers back in kind, because even if I wasn't strong enough to *act*, I would become strong enough to SPEAK what had to be said, for all of us, for black people, yes, particularly for black people, because they were the root and origin of my conviction, but for anyone anywhere who wanted Justice!

The article was really, then, a commitment to struggle. I said, "Let them know this is a fight without quarter, and I am very fast." Brash, arrogant, sophomoric, but it was smoke from a moving vehicle! There now began in my downtown environs and elsewhere a dervish of forums, speakouts, intellectual shootouts, not just in reflection of my own mind's motion but as reflection of what the whole society had become and was still to become.

One forum at Carnegie Hall with Lorraine Hansberry, I remember as the kind of document of this event, which was packed to the rafters, me jumping up and furiously putting down liberals and liberalism with such vehemence that it made not a few people's teeth rattle. *The Village Voice* and several of the other liberal journals carried sympathetic disclaimers of the event for the liberals.

There was also another kind of motion downtown. Added to the initial coming together of blacks in the Village there was now a distinctly militant kind of black emerging as well. I began to come in contact more and more with them.

One night at a party at Marzette Watts' loft, who lived on the first floor of the Cooper Square place, there was some kind of battle, a fight it turned out and finally Sonny Murray had it out with this bone-slim wiry dude with a permanent bitter smirking smile on his face. What wigged me is that this dude, Tong he was called because of his Asian-looking eyes, had popped Sonny in the nose and broke it. I couldn't conceive of anyone beating Sonny. But then, as it turned out, I didn't even know this dude.

And he is posturing over in the corner talking to a friend of his and his brother and when I come up he says, "Yeh, I did just what I thought I could do, broke this motherfucker's nose."

The blood rushed into my head and I got into the dude's face, "So what you spose to be, bad? You can get killed, too, my man. You know, you can get laid out right here in the street." It was not even with a desire to fight, or maybe it was, but it was anger and shock at seeing Sonny disabled. Tong said nothing to me, he just put on his coat and hat with the jerky, manic motion I was to become familiar with and with his running buddy, Jimmy Lesser, split. His brother, Shammy (real name Chase Hackensack), didn't go with his brother Tony (real name Bobby Hackensack). I guess to show there was some distance between him and his brother, he laid. But though I'd seen him before, I didn't really know him. But now I would.

There was another forum down at the Village Vanguard, probably on a Monday night. It was Archie Shepp, Larry Rivers, somebody else, and myself. We were discussing racial problems in the U.S., and Larry, I guess, because we had been friends and had had a lot of laughs together, did not feel particularly threatened by me or Archie, both of whom he had sopped up much alcohol with. Larry was even an old scag man from way back when he was an uptight young Jew looking to play the alto like Charlie Parker.

But Archie made some distance, and when the question of struggle and change and, yes, revolution came up, Larry backed off. But I cut into him perhaps too cruelly, for that context. I said, "Hey, you're all over in these galleries, turning out work for these rich faggots, you part of the dying shit just like them!" That shocked a lot of our friends who were there, not so much what was said, I suppose, but the viciousness of it, the absolute distance raised, not only between Larry and ourselves but whole bunches of folks tied to him, who likewise had thought there was some intellectual and emotional connection between us. But now it seemed there was fire in me that could rush up and out even directly into the faces of some of my old friends.

For Nellie, this period was also a contradictory thing. Obviously, the attention and celebrity of *Dutchman* pleased her. I guess it was, in one very nasty sense, some justification, even legitimization, of our marriage to all her old familial connections. The inner-circle hauteur that only the cognoscenti who read *Zazen* or *Evergreen Review* could appreciate had now been replaced by a wider spread of public talk. It was not just some colored guy, she was married to somebody. (Apologies to Jesse Jackson.)

The rounds of cocktail parties and receptions we got invited to, the "sudden" literary presence that even her old employers at *Sectarian Review* must have appreciated, obviously warmed her. In the same year the book *Dutchman* was published (although with another play she distinctly did not like, *The Slave*). *Dutchman* won the Obie Award as Best American Play, and since I was out of town during the awards dinner, she had to accept the award on my behalf. I know these are the kinds of things she had unconsciously prepared for, though in another context, a great part of her life.

The trouble was that now there was some kind of slow drift by me away from her. For the past period the liaisons I had with other women had grown less frequent, but now, from no open or conscious plan I put forward, the women I began to see were black. Though they were hooked up or on the fringes of the same shit. Plump brown Rose and I staggered out of the Five Spot together late one night, down to her place in Brooklyn, which looked like a hurricane had hit it. Or yellow Joanie, trying to make it in advertising, from one of those schools, saying goodbye in the subway station and roaring off rather than be used by some white woman's man after business hours.

I was invited to a writer's conference at Asilomar, Monterey, "The Negro in American Literature." My recent celebrity made me the bull's-eye of the joint. Not only to be shot at but hit on. I found myself inundated with lovely black women. I mean, just to sit and talk and remember what they were like. What it meant when I put my hand out and they put their hands out to shake, innocently enough, to see how our hands matched so and to hear their voices lilting, full of questions about my work, or Baldwin's or Wright's, was kind of thrilling. Not to mention the heavier stuff that went on later in the evening, in this small cabana-like apartment with a glass door opening down to the beach.

The last sister I was with and I roared up the coast in her MG after the conference was over and we stayed at her place in Oakland for a couple of days, walking around Berkeley, going into San Francisco. I even got into a fight with this white writer, later a famous novelist, who was then a lousy poet (I've never read his novels). It was really, I think, about the same kind of thing as the Village Vanguard shootout. He wouldn't fight but the woman he was with, a poet of deservedly small reputation, tried to jump me for roaring at her man. I mean, she wanted to scratch me or jump on me with her hands and I swatted her while the young sister, Gwendolyn Buck, full of southern petty bourgeois gentility, watched in a state of half alarm, half amusement. And we discussed the episode over drinks into the wee hours.

While I was in Oakland, a local dude and his friends heard I was there from this sister, Gwen's running buddy, who'd been at the conference, and he came over to get his copy of *Blues People* autographed. He was working as a standup comedian in a local nightclub, his name was Bobby Seale. A couple of years later, he and Huey Newton were to put together the Black Panther Party for Self-Defense!

When I talked to Nellie on the phone, she could only say, "Why are you still there? Come back. You should come back, now." It was like she could sense something was very much awry. There was a note of desperation in her voice.

At home, a collecting up of this heavier black circle went on, still casually, but fueled by reality. I could sense some distance now between Nellie and me that had never existed before: a darkness into which words disappeared. I saw Shammy again, he began hanging around this little gym where we played basketball, where my kids were in nursery school. He'd be on the sidelines cheering, though I could sense he could play, too. But he could see that I was no stranger to the court, and if I made some hook or jump shot it seemed to connect him to me more closely. I guess he could see I was a real person.

Since our struggle with the SWP in On Guard, a couple of the black SWP cadres had come around and I'd talked to them. The one I got closest to was Cornelius Suares, called Corny. He was a black worker, working almost all his adult life (except for the time he was in jail) in the garment district, pushing, as he called them, "them Jewish airplanes." He pushed the garment racks up and down the streets. Corny was the loudest person on record, check the *Guinness Book of Records*. He had a hard and willfully rough exterior but he was a very sweet and gentle dude in many ways. If he felt really put upon or pissed off, he'd break down and cry.

His running buddy, whom I also got to like a lot, was Clarence Franklin, another worker, doing New York City messenger work. He was once SWP's candidate for mayor and is a sensitive poet, though Clarence talks only as a last resort. Plus, Clarence's brothers Doll and Robert, who are the talkingest dudes, next to Cornelius, you're ever likely to meet. All of these brought another air into my life, a wind of further reality, of actual concrete life.

I went to Buffalo for a month that summer, with my family, as a lecturer in poetry, in some program put together to get Charles Olson, Creeley, and some of the other new poets up there lecturing. I still had a great admiration for Olson. I had gone up to his house a couple of times, up in Gloucester. Once in the late fifties with McClure and Wieners, later with Don Allen and Irving Rosenthal who had just quit as editor of the *Chicago Review*, to write a novel, *Sheeper*. Olson had taken us one night to this castle in Gloucester that this rich dude had imported stone for stone from Europe. And now it sat in Gloucester, overlooking the bay. The guy's father had invented the electronically controlled boat. And he used to steer these boats by remote control up and down in that harbor.

We had some interesting evening. Olson, center stage as usual, was telling these stories and the son or grandson of the inventor, who was now master of the house, had a few friends over, all, I think, gay. I think the only non-gay persons in the crib were Olson and I. The castle was full of statues and hanging tapestries. At one point, the owner excused himself and then we heard organ music. We figured it was him, but then he returned and the organ was playing, we were told, by remote control. He then started to make weird effects — slurs, eerie moans, and ghostly sounds — on the thing. Olson and I were catching each other's eye, but Olson kept talking.

When we go to bed that night, I got a room that's right off this patio in the middle of the castle. After midnight sometime, I hear this noise like splashing and men's voices high and tittering. I go to the door and prop it open and this guy's friends are diving from a second-story balcony down into this pool in the middle of the patio. They're butt naked. It was like being woven into a tapestry of exotic otherness, but the next day when we get back to Olson's place he is roaring with laughter at the whole business.

What fascinated me about Olson was his sense of having dropped out of the U.S., the "pejoracracy." He said in his poems we should "Go Against" it. That we should oppose "those who would advertise you out." It was a similar spirit that informed the most meaningful of the Beats, and Olson was a heavy scholar. His "Projective Verse" had been a bible for me because it seemed to give voice to feelings I had about poetry and about society. When Charles came down to Cooper Square, there was another sense that what we were doing he could use, that it was something he thought useful and correct, the *Zazens* and Totem Press and the rest of it. I had even seen remarks he made at Berkeley letting me know that he thought *Dutchman* was an estimable work. It was Olson, because of his intellectual example, and Ginsberg, because of his artistic model and graciousness as a teacher, whom I thought most about in terms of the road I was moving along. Where would they be in all this? Also, my friend Ed Dorn, the poet, who was living out in Pocatello, Idaho, in a place so American it didn't understand itself. How would he relate? We wrote many letters back and forth. And the book *The Dead Lecturer*, which came out that year (1964), is dedicated to Ed. It included the comic-book hero Green Lantern's code: "In Blackest Day/In Blackest Night/No Evil Shall Escape My Sight/Let Those Who Worship Evil's Might/Beware My Power/Green Lantern's Light!"

Ed and his family and Nellie and I and our children lived together briefly up in Buffalo that summer. It was like the last touching of the old places, though I didn't know it. I liked Ed so much because he had (and has) an intellectual toughness that perceives the worst in the U.S., but he has the energy needed to survive that worst. His Idaho and New Mexico sojourns, I think, were meant to keep him from the sickness of big-time America. Yet the leaks of that sickness are themselves communities, even on the geographic outskirts of the various big apples and pears and plums of gimme-gotcha melican society.

These white men saw that I was moving away from them in so many ways and there was some concern, because it wasn't that I didn't like them any longer, it was just a feeling that where I was going they couldn't come. Where that was, I couldn't even articulate. Those who were physically close to me, the old New York crowd, I was less concerned about, because we had our day-to-day confrontations. There was no room for decent concern or sentimental concern either, we were too concretely close and for that reason getting away from them was a physical and intellectual syllogism.

While I was in Buffalo, the Harlem Rebellion broke out. There had been a couple rebellions in other cities just before Harlem went up, in Jacksonville and then in a suburb of Chicago. But Harlem had the media coverage. It was like the proof that the ticking inside our heads had a real source and was not subjective. It bore out what Malcolm had said at the beginning of the year. It made *Blues for Mr. Charlie* and *Dutchman* seem dangerously prophetic.

I left Buffalo, to get closer to what was happening. The events rang in me like the first shots of a war, which I not only knew would break out but one that I had to get into because I felt I had helped start it. I remember getting a .45 automatic from where I had stashed it. Lana Solon looked surprised, I hadn't seen her in months. But I had left a piece there back behind some suitcases. She said, "I knew you'd come. I felt it." I got the piece from where I'd hidden it, put it in my gas mask bag, and split. I never saw her again.

After the Harlem Rebellion it was a rush of events, confrontations, tempers, even histories that I witnessed and was part of. For one thing, the sense of being more and more estranged from Nellie was reaching an openly rising quantitative peak. We were seldom together now, the way we had been. I was hanging out and meeting with mostly young black dudes, both my brothers from the earlier Cooper Square circle and the later crowd of people. Shammy, his brother Tong, who I still did not feel comfortable around; he gave me a cold and clammy feeling. Jimmy Lesser came by now, usually with Shammy. He dressed like a classic Black Muslim and I accepted him as that. One of White's old junkie friends also began to dress up like a Muslim and he seemed to have cleaned up as well. But that didn't bother White, Jim; he was still getting higher and higher. Corny, usually with Clarence, would show. Plus, Overstreet might breeze by and we'd drink a bottle of vodka. One time White, Overstreet, and I go to a party around the corner and Overstreet and I get into a fight, or I should say a "fight." I don't know what happened and he claim he don't know either, but when we woke up the bottle of vodka was empty, most of my clothes were ripped off, and Overstreet was laid out drunk. We didn't know where White had gone.

Marion and Archie were around and Bob when he wasn't drilled flat by the scag. A young dude named Dave, light-skinned, heavy glasses, interested like all of us in the music and also poetry. Both of the Hackensack Brothers were part of *Umbra* and I began to get more word on what that was or had been. I found out later that they had had some intense struggle over a poem that was to be published that was critical of JFK. One group wanted to can the poem because Kennedy had got iced, the other, more militant group thought the poem still needed to be printed. And there were all kinds of recriminations. I still saw C.D., but not in the same way as before. He was very much married and the French lady had, it seemed, a rather abbreviated tether.

I'd see Tom Perry, and if Tom and White and I got together with maybe Marion or even Bob when he could see, we still got wasted. And walked around, in and out of parties, being even more removed by the shit, and our sense of removal from that whole scene. But even that enlarged circle had its sectors, and it would, at a later time, split in half as well.

The public verbal shootout that remains most clearly etched in my memory is one that was held at the Village Gate. In this there were questions from the audience and I had now grown into a stance of actually putting down white people. I had long done this in my writing, from a concrete point of origin. These torturous years the African and African American have spent as slaves and chumps for this white supremacist society obviously provided enough factual resources to support a tirade against whites. The Muslim example, particularly and most inspirationally the role of Malcolm X, supported my attack. But still I was married to a white woman; I still had many white friends. I still thought very highly of innumerable white intellectuals and artists. But I felt justified in talking about the horrible bullshit that white people had put on the world, bullshit they are still putting on the world (though now my view is tempered by the science of class analysis — but then so many whites go for the ghost of white racism, and whether they actually benefit from it or not, still *do* go for it and actively support it — and the poison of white chauvinism warps some of the otherwise hippest white minds in extant).

A woman asked me in all earnestness, couldn't any whites help? I said, "You can help by dying. You are a cancer. You can help the world's people with your death." She seemed flabbergasted. Another mentioned Goodman and Schwerner, they had been slaughtered along with black James Chaney in Philadelphia, Mississippi, by Klansmen in police uniforms. And certainly their sacrifice is to be upheld and the willingness of young whites to put their lives on the line for the struggle for democracy *is* a noble thing, an important thing, and any people sincerely interested in making revolution must have allies. Only people not really serious about making revolution can dismiss sincere allies. But in my fury, which had no scientific framework, I could only thrash out at any white person. The fact that Chaney was never mentioned, and Goodman and Schwerner were, pissed the hell out of me. I told the woman, "I have my own history of death and submission. We have our own dead to mourn. Those white boys were only seeking to assuage their own leaking consciences."

And in this last outrageous diatribe I was confusing Schwerner and Goodman with the young white poseur-liberals who sashayed safely through the streets of Greenwich Village, the behind-the-lines bleeding hearts. When, on the real side, if I could have stood some hard truth, Schwerner and Goodman were out there on the front lines doing more than I was! But Chaney had been beaten beyond recognition; he had so received the fury of those maniacs but all these people wanted to talk about was the white youths' deaths.

I guess, during this period, I got the reputation of being a snarling, white-hating madman. There was some truth to it, because I was struggling to be born, to break out from the shell I could instinctively sense surrounded my own dash for freedom. I guess I was in a frenzy, trying to get my feet solidly on the ground of reality. And during this period, whether publicly or not, there was a lot of snarling, and cussing out of white folks, and punchin' people in the mouths to justify our growing sense of ourselves.

Albert Ayler had come on the scene around this point. He appeared at my house one afternoon with a dude named Black Norman. I had heard of Albert and think I'd even heard him on some record where he was still playing with a group that was sounding the standard bebop changes, *My Name Is Albert Ayler*. But Albert had already moved beyond that. Albert had this white shock of beard that shot out of his chin, though he was a little short stocky dude, that made him look extra weird. Plus the intensity in his eyes and voice. Norman was his sidekick mystic, chuckling always about something the rest of us was just a little too square to dig.

Albert had asked me about the music and about my writing on the music. I think he wanted to challenge me because I didn't really know who he was. He asked me did I think it was about me? He said, "You think it's about you?" I did and didn't know what he meant. In some ways, I guess, I did think it was about me. Albert meant it was really about *Spirit* and Energy. This is what it, life, everything, was really about. Not personalities and their yes-and-nos. Albert was always jumping on folks by saying of corny people, "He thinks it's about *him*," with the "him" said so disdainfully, as only Albert could say it, so you really could dig that was some stupid shit. "It ain't about *you*!" Albert would say. "He thinks its about Him! And it ain't about Him." And he'd stretch his eyes wide and maybe spit out a jagged hunk of laugh.

Plus, Albert, we found out quickly, could play his ass off. He had a sound, alone, unlike anyone else's. It tore through you, broad, jagged like something out of nature. Some critics said his sound was "primitive." Shit, it was before that! It was a big massive sound and wail. The crying, shouting moan of black spirituals and God music. Pharaoh was so beautiful and he had a wildness to him too, a heavy force like the world could be reopened, but Albert was *mad*. His playing was like some primordial frenzy that the world secretly used for energy. Yeh, the music. Feeling all that, it touching us and us touching it, gave us that strength, that kind of irrevocability we felt. Like the thunder or the lightning or the ocean storming and mounting, crushing whatever was in its path.

At Lincoln Center one night, Trane's group with Eric Dolphy and Pha-
raoh too, plus Cecil Taylor, was on the same bill and Art Blakey and the
Messengers. It was a beautiful night of music, but the high point was when
Albert, whom I had come up to the hall with, came out on the stage, at
Trane's invitation. He came out in the middle of one tune, horn held high
up in the air, blowing like the world was on fire. His monster sound cut
through all the music, he was blowing so loud, the timbre was so big.
People in the audience and the musicians on the stage were electrified.
After the performance, backstage, Trane asked Albert, "Hey, man, what
kind of reed you using?" I could dig that!

Marion and some other people were playing in D.C. Marion and I were
very close in those days, he'd come by and tell me all his plans and projections and co-sign some of mine. Marion sometimes seemed very bohemian and disconnected. He was heavily introspective, I guess like many of
us. But he also had a practical, opportunity-seeking side of him. He wanted
to meet people and when he finally did decide he wanted to go back to the
Music, being in and around Cooper Square got him quickly connected up
with Archie Shepp. And just as Shepp's first major side was "4 for Trane,"
so Marion's first side was "3 for Shepp." So Marion was quietly but effi-
ciently building his own career while watching close up on mine.

So I wanted to go down to D.C. to hear him play in what amounted to
his first big gig with his own group. A group of us were going down, but as
we were getting ready a feeling of dread descended on me. Like nothing
that I had ever felt before. I found myself dreading taking Nellie down to
D.C. with me. I was perspiring and agitated as the time approached. I was
pacing around in the house, trying to get high and drunk at the same time,
but doing neither. I was cold sober. It was the feeling that Nellie was *outside* of my concerns, that we did not connect up. I think now I resented
her. It was the black-white thing, the agitation, the frenzy, always so deeply
felt and outer directed. It had settled in me directed at my wife. I had
begun to see her as *white*! Before, even when I thought she was white, I
had never felt anything negative. Even to the point of our beginning de-
bates in the Village and the rising political consciousness I was developing. I had never felt anything abstractly negative about Nellie.

There had even been a magazine satire about me as the great white-
hating militant finishing one of my diatribes and then going back to the
dutiful white wife. But that had not bothered me, it had not affected my
sense of myself or my regard, in whatever way that was carried, for Nellie.
But now it was different. There was within that shadow I described before

not only a deep vacuum where words could disappear, there was now a coldness, a sharp disaffection that existed.

"Nellie, we can't go down to D.C. together. I don't want to go with you."

She looked puzzled and tensed, somehow expectant. "What do you mean?"

"I'm black, Nellie. I'm black and you're " I trailed off. "White. I can't do this, Nellie. I'm black."

That look in her eye then was of such deep hurt and confused amazement that I almost covered my face so I did not have to look at her face. "Oh, Roi," she said. "That's silly. You're Roi and I'm Nellie. What are you talking about?"

What was the correlative or parallel scene being played all over the world which meant the same thing in all the different sectors and levels of human experience? That open call for that splitting up. As if the tragic world around our "free zone" had finally swept in and frozen us to the spot.

The play *The Slave*, which shows a black would-be revolutionary who splits from his white wife on the eve of a race war, was what Nellie called "Roi's nightmare." It was so close to our real lives, so full of that living image.

We talked awhile, saying really little else. Actually, we repeated the things we had already said, in other ways. But finally, I was gone, down to D.C., where Marion was playing. But when I got down there I had a kind of relapse. I thought I had done wrong to leave Nellie that way, though I was coming back. The serious business of what was to happen to us and with our marriage was still to be done. The set was in a hotel and I paced back and forth and called home, but no one answered. Nellie was wherever she had to go to deal with such conflict. I called again and again, pacing, now feeling somehow I was trapped in this high building, unable to get back and cut off from this woman I had lived with for almost seven years. I was nervous and confused and though there was a party after Marion's set, I went to my room and laid up brooding about what the fuck I'd said and done. I called again; no answer.

Finally the drink I was nursing ran out, so I went down the hall to where the party was. When I stuck my head in looking around for the alcohol, there was a very slender red-brown black girl with the kind of "Mariney" red-brown haircut, very short and worn natural. She looked at me and smiled and not only did she not avert her eyes in some false modesty, she winked at me mischievously. I stood my ground, still looking for the big drink. But smiling, trying to be cheerful. So she comes over, drink in hand. She says, "You look hip, what's your name?" Her name was Vashti.

We breezed out of that joint in a few, and wound up in my room, talking eight thousand miles an hour about everything we could think of. She was a young woman, still college age, but she had dropped out, she said, cause she wanted to be a painter. Vashti was skinny and had a tendency to be knock-kneed, but I thought she was one of the most gorgeous women I'd ever seen. It was like her quirky red looks turned me on, and the little knock-kneed walk and slightly protruding teeth. Plus, Vashti was dressed up, she was styled like she thought she was in some play where the woman painter goes to a cocktail party and meets the famous writer. Slouch hat pulled down over one eye, drink in one hand, cigarette in the other. Full of wisecracks and laughing at her own ironic humor or mine. We wound up in bed much much later in the morning with Vashti saying, "You better not give me a baby. I'm not playing."

I told her she reminded me of Alice in Wonderland. She said, "Yeh, and you're the Mad Hatter." And so I referred to her as Alice for a while. I was going back to New York and she was staying in D.C. But I knew even then that I would see her again. I knew that she would come to New York.

The crowd of dudes I was hanging with had swollen, it seemed that that place on Cooper Square became a meeting place for a certain kind of black intellectual during this period. But it was not just a casual circle anymore, there was clearly something forming, something about to come into being. We sat around trying to talk it and coax it into being. I met Max Stanford, from Philly, who'd recently moved to New York. I didn't know it at first, but Max was with the Revolutionary Action Movement (RAM), which had just formed. Larry Neal became a part of that group. Larry, clean as blue wind, would sit in and contribute to those discussions of what was going on in the world, who were we in it, what was the role of the black artist? What should our art be? Larry was a poet, and he too had come up out of Philly and was also, unbeknownst to me, with RAM.

One night, after talking to Max, who had communications with the exiled Rob Williams, and who was actually distributing his newsletter, *The Crusader*, I felt particularly whipped and beaten. Why? Because, to me, the young tireless revolutionary I saw in Max was what I felt I could never be. I had said outright that the black and white thing was over, but I did not think I could act. For one thing, the little girls, now, were walking around and there was certainly both a deep love and a sense of pressing responsibility there. It seemed to me I was caught, frozen between two worlds. I told this to Nellie, almost weeping, but dragged off to get high and tried to push it out of my mind.

One evening when a large group of us were together in my study talking earnestly about black revolution and what should be done, I got the idea that we should form an organization. On Guard had been long gone, because of its obvious contradictions. We needed a group of black revolutionaries who were artists to raise up the level of struggle from the arts sector. There was Dave Knight, White, Marion, C.D., Leroy McLucas, the Hackensack brothers (Shammy and Tong), Jimmy Lesser, Larry, Max, plus Corny and Clarence. We would form a secret organization. Tong asked me what would it be called, it came into my head in a flash, the Black Arts.

But all those people who'd hung around were not the serious core I felt would cohere with such an idea. I also thought it should be a paramilitary organization. At the next meeting I announced this, and if there were any doubts that some folks would stay and others breeze, that put an end to it. Max and Larry hung back because they were in another organization. Askia, too, who was around there, was not in that core because he too was with RAM and apparently they had been "assigned" to work with us.

White, though he worked with us contributing his art, could never make that core, which was probably a little too fanatical anyway, because of his scag habit. There were other people who came in once we got uptown and who worked with us as strongly and as closely as possible. But while we were downtown the core became McLucas, the Hackensacks, Jimmy Lesser, Dave, Corny, and Clarence. We gave ourselves military ranks, at which Larry smiled, it seemed knowledgeably, saying only, "You'all think you're ready for that?"

Marion spaced on that, being a little too sophisticated for such playacting, I guess. Bob Thompson was off battling the white powder. Overstreet came up to work at the arts but avoided some of the nuts in that core. So it got down to McLucas, Dave, the Hackensacks, Lesser, Corny, Clarence, and I, with C.D. straddling the fence.

We talked black black, being downtown, amidst the white world, even more frustrated and bitter in contrast to our surroundings, and less realistic than we needed to be. We formed a cadre, but looking at it now, my oldest black friends downtown did not go for the science fiction blackness our downtown core presented. All those people, with the exception of C.D. and McLucas, I had met only relatively recently.

What we did, concretely, was polarize the people downtown. We talked a black militance and took the stance that most of the shit happening downtown was white bullshit and most of the people were too. The fact that we, ourselves, were down there was a contradiction we were not quite ready to act upon, though we discussed it endlessly. With all militant black groups that form downtown, the point of demarcation is always: they are downtown and the masses of black people are elsewhere. For us it was Harlem, that was the proper capital of our world and we were not there.

So we settled for jumping on people, mostly verbally, and preaching the need to be black and ultimately to get out of this downtown white hell.

Because of this "blacker than thou" stance, several relationships were disrupted. We were sincere, most of us. But we carried the fanaticism of the petty bourgeoisie. White through, yesterday; Black as heaven, today!

For one thing, we kept talking and talking about "going uptown." The On Guards and OYMs came up, partially dissected. *Umbra*'s struggles were partially discussed. I learned that Ishmael Reed, Hernton, Lorenzo Thomas, Askia, Tom Dent, David Henderson, Steve Cannon, the Hackensacks were grouped among its ranks. Theirs was a positive self-conscious black effort that had existed for some time down on the Lower East Side. But with the twists and turns of U.S. reality and new contradictions, one was splitting into two, they were about to come apart.

Rival sectors of different arts groups, particularly poets and writers, were polarized. The Black Arts group still moved downtown, still my house the unofficial HQ. Some of us had guns and we talked endlessly about black liberation. So that we might go to a poetry reading of Ish's and Calvin's and be there both to dig them and also to measure how black they were.

Our deepest feelings were correct, but we had no knowledge of the realities of revolution, not even the realities of the Black Liberation Movement. But still, helter-skelter, twisting and turning, we were putting out the seeds for a Black Arts Movement and the bit of that which we perceived astonished us.

Vashti came up to New York to live. She had a girlfriend she stayed with up on the West Side (who became part of a group of middle-class black women who came to the aid of Betty Shabazz, Malcolm's widow). But soon we had arranged something. I'd meet her different places, occasionally she even stayed at the Old Albert Hotel on University Place. She began to meet the various people in the Black Arts and go in and out of the watering holes of our downtown world. Sometimes we would go to a friend's loft and she would talk bad about me getting high, but mostly we talked and laughed and made love. Vashti became part of our crowd, speeding with me through those nights of uncertainty. I came to feel more and more for her. It was like we were at the outset of a great adventure, the deepest part of which we picked up just by watching each other laugh. There was so much love in our eyes. Plus, we felt we were snatching that love from out of some dying white shit. Vashti never talked bad about Nellie, but she would look at me, sometimes, with her hands on her hips, not quite smirking, when the subject came up. There was nothing left for me at Cooper Square now but memories and the little girls. But I felt backed up against the wall.

When the "going uptown" talk started to surface and be talked about, with whatever bias, naturally still more relationships got disrupted. Some of the white women who were with black men (and I guess those white men with black women—though I knew far fewer) got visibly uptight. C.D.'s wife, Françoise, stopped talking to me, and when I started to cross St. Marks Place to talk to him one afternoon, he crossed quickly to say a few words and she stayed on the other side of the street glaring.

I didn't know most of those who formed this downtown Black Arts "core" very well. But I'm sure some stuff passed publicly that took everything that might be said around me even further out. After all, I had obvious limitations, as leader, hooked up with the white woman. There was some antagonism now between some old friends.

Both of the Hackensacks always made me nervous because I couldn't understand them. I hadn't known them long enough or seen them in action and, apparently, they and Askia formed part of the militant wing of *Umbra*. I found out later, someone had threatened someone else's life.

But Shammy showed at my house and seemed to want to be my friend-student. Tong was distant and had a bitter cast about him, dipped in a kind of acid silence, that made him seem edgy and challenging. Both were writers, Tong a poet, Shammy a playwright. At a number of places, Shammy, Vashti, and I became a trio.

I got appointed as guest lecturer in drama at Columbia, for one semester, as a result of *Dutchman*. There was an article I'd written in the *Voice*, probably it was an interview. Vashti, Shammy, and I were sitting in the West End Bar and Grill after class. I went to the bar to get a beer and these two white guys approached. One a smallish eyeglass-wearing person, the other, a half step behind him, large and bulky. The little one said, "You're LeRoi Jones?"

"Yes."

"I saw that statement you made in the *Voice* about whites. You're sick."

I stood, flat-footed, a mug of beer in my hand, and eyed them carefully.

"Why don't you stop spouting sick things about whites in the paper? It's blacks that cause the problems."

"Yeh," I said. The big guy was grinning.

"I wanted to talk to you." It was the little guy. "I brought my football-playing friend so you'd agree."

My forehead heated up quickly at the idea of a henchman intimidator. "You gonna talk to us?"

"Fuck you." I was turning to go to my table. The big dude moved forward hesitatingly. I hit him full in the forehead with the beer mug and, with no break in the motion, bopped the other one headside as well. They screamed, the small one fell, others stood and shouted. Vashti and Shammy were at my side. We backed out of the West End like gunfighters.

"Very good, Mr. Jones," was Shammy's comment. Vashti laughed and pulled on my arm.

One other event to show how far the thing had gone. I was sitting with Shammy, who had begun to accompany me different places, in line with our paramilitary pretensions. We were in the restaurant of the Fifth Avenue Hotel, where I'd met with my editor about some book. As we ate, unknown to us, C.D. entered the sleek restaurant. He came up to our table and said to me and Shammy, "Leave me alone. Leave my family alone. I'm not going uptown." He touched his belt. "I have a gun here. If anyone bothers me or my family, I'll shoot them!" He turned and left.

Shammy and I laughed, but for me, it was a deadly portent somehow. C.D. had been one of my oldest friends in New York. But the two of us at the table made light of it. He was hooked on white women, etc. I could talk.

February 21, 1965, a Sunday. Nellie and I and the two girls were at the Eighth Street Bookstore, at a book party. I had a cap, hunting jacket, and round dark glasses, the dress of our little core. I was being personable and knowledgeable. Both Vashti and Shammy and some others were in the bookstore, discreetly separate from my party.

Suddenly, Leroy McLucas came in. He was weeping. "Malcolm is dead! Malcolm is dead! Malcolm's been killed!" He wept, repeating it over and over. I was stunned, shot myself. I felt stupid, ugly, useless. Downtown in my mix-matched family and my maximum leader/teacher shot dead while we bullshitted and pretended.

The black core of us huddled there, my wife and family outside that circle. We were feverish and stupefied. McLucas wept uncontrollably. I called a couple fellows in the corner over, but they were dazed and couldn't hear immediately. Joel Oppenheimer said, "That's the trouble with the black revolution. Roi's giving directions and nobody listens!"

But who and what was I to give anything, or he to make such a statement? "It's all bullshit!" went through me. "All!"

In a few days I had gotten my stuff out and gone uptown. We had seen a brownstone on West 130th Street and this was to be the home of the Black Arts Repertory Theater/School.

My little girl, the older one, Kellie, picked up instinctively a sense of my departure. She said to me, "You can't go anywhere. You're one of the funny things."

But in a minute or so, I was gone. A bunch of us, really, had gone, up to Harlem. Seeking revolution!

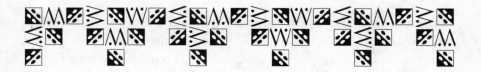

Eight

Harlem

The arrival uptown, Harlem, can only be summed up by the feelings jumping out of Césaire's *Return to My Native Land* or Fanon's *The Wretched of the Earth* or Cabral's *Return to the Source*. The middle-class native intellectual, having outintegrated the most integrated, now plunges headlong back into what he perceives as blackest, native-est. Having dug, finally, how white he has become, now, classically, comes back to his countrymen charged up with the desire to be black, uphold black, etc. . . .a fanatical patriot!

When we came up out of the subway, March 1965, cold and clear, Harlem all around us staring us down, we felt like pioneers of the new order. Back in the homeland to help raise the race. Youth in their fervor know no limitations, except they are celebrations of them. Narrow, because they lack experience, yet fervent, super-energetic, super-optimistic. If we had known what faced us, some would've copped out, some would've probably got down, to study, as we should've, instead of the nowhere shit so many of us were involved with.

The building on 130th Street was an old brownstone, like you can find in Harlem. Right off by Lenox with its crab sellers, the permanently out of work taking a stroll or in knots, summing up USA, its working people going and coming. Grey with black is the dominant color. Brown gives it flair, the yellow an edge to its conceits. The occupation army of white police beady-eyed and ubiquitous, stupid as the one-day-to-be-slaughtered-without-knowledge-of-why-they-died.

We set up shop and cleaned and swept and painted. We got a flag, White designed, the "Greek" theater masks of comedy and tragedy, rendered Afro style, like a shield, with spear behind, all in black and gold. The Black Arts Repertory Theater/School.

Malcolm's death had thrown people up in the air like coins in a huge hairy hand. Even before I'd left Cooper Square people had showed up. Carrying various perceptions. Some crazed or halfway there. John Farris, the poet, showed for the first time, like he was Malcolm's bodyguard, and told stories about imminent revenge. The mosque on 116th Street burned up and took the edge off, but people were vowing to go to Chicago and kill Elijah.

Whatever Malcolm had laid out was now just in the wind to be grabbed on the fly. The Organization of Afro-American Unity (OAAU), the united front structure Malcolm wanted to build, styled after the Organization of African Unity (OAU), was not completely put together. There was no doubt it would soon be gone. The fact of Malcolm's death meant, for us, that the Nation, of Islam, had also died. Though there were arguments about who was right: Malcolm or Elijah? But up close to us, Malcolm, Malcolm, semper.

The mood? I came downtown one time during these early days and was sitting in the Orchidia Restaurant, down on Second Avenue. We had just come from the St. Marks Theater, Vashti and I, where I'd been talking about plans to stage my plays The Toilet and The Slave. Lonnie Elder and Douglas Turner Ward were sitting there, loud in conversation. Elder said something about Malcolm. "Why did Ossie [Davis] call him a prince? He wasn't no prince."

I came out of my chair like the black plague. "Don't ever say anything about Malcolm. Nothing. Don't let nothing come out of your mouth ever about Malcolm." Whatever the rage did to my face made them quiet. They only stared. I got Vashti and we went back uptown.

What was really interesting during this period is who came up and who didn't. Some, of course, the smaller core, augmented by a few uptown heads, were at the Arts every day and night trying to do whatever they thought they were doing. Others constantly came by and helped, many artists from various disciplines who contributed what they could. Doing programs, being in forums, helping us with our major arts project in the streets that coming summer. Still others we saw from time to time wanted to help in deeper ways, talking to us, trying to counsel and help us. There were others whom we very seldom saw and then mainly downtown. There were others we never saw who nevertheless, in being true to the vanity of illusion and dubious social distinction, were also there, invisible except for their inadequately disguised disdain.

A basic core was the Hackensacks (Shammy definite, Tong most of the time), Jimmy Lesser, Dave, McLucas, a friend of Tong's who came along, Tub, a largish, sourly succinct dude; and after work, Corny and Clarence, and, a little later, Clarence Reed, the poet, who was hanging around on Lenox Avenue at the Progressive Labor Party offices, due in large part to his friendship with their black organizer, Bill Epton.

Larry Neal was one of those who was always in and out, helping with programs and giving us some rational counsel. Askia was there a lot in that same role and from time to time Max Stanford. Vashti was there all the time, trying to deal with some of the people who started acting like "crazy niggas," as she called them, often at the top of her voice. Tong was married, but I don't think his wife ever came around. She was always at home or at work. But I think Tong never encouraged her to come by the Arts or else it was her own idea. All the rest of those brothers had various, often frequently changing, lady friends, but I was the only one of the core who had a regular, fairly stable relationship.

I developed a great deal of affection and respect for Larry Neal, but I think Larry knew a little more about the nature of some of the more nutty dudes the Arts was to attract, so he was in and out, but constantly on the scene. We picked up a lot of people in those few months. It was a socially and intellectually seismically significant development, the leaving of some of us (and more we didn't even know) from downtown and the implied and actual cutting of certain ties, and the attempt to build a black arts institution, and that in the heart of the past capital of African American people in the U.S., Harlem. The reality set many fresh and needed ideas in motion. The idea set even more ideas in motion and more concrete realities. In many ways it was something like the period of the Harlem Renaissance. Black intellectuals drawn to a common spot out of the larger commonality of their national experience. A rise in black national consciousness among the people themselves is what set both periods in motion, and whenever there is a high level of black national consciousness, a militant affirmation of the African American national identity, then the whole country is in the midst of wrenching social movement, eventually revolution.

But even more than the Harlem geography, the Black Arts movement reflected that black people themselves had first moved to a political unity, despite their differences, that they were questioning the United States and its white racist monopoly capitalism. And they were doing it with *mass action*! Just as the Garvey movement, the African Blood Brotherhood, the thousands of socially conscious actions in the '20s agitated an "African" consciousness and a spirit of African American self-determination in the black artists identified with the '20s renaissance, both within Harlem and all over Afro-America, so in the '60s the struggle of Dr. King and Rob Williams and the Nation of Islam and SNCC and Malcolm X had agitated a young black intelligentsia who could not find self-respect except in opposition to black oppression. The people themselves were in motion, the artists just reflected it!

The emergence of the independent African states and the appearance of African freedom fighters, fighting guerrilla wars with white colonialism, had to produce young intellectuals (and older ones, too) who reveled in that spirit and sought to use that spirit to create art. An art that would reach the people, that would take them higher, ready them for war and victory, as popular as the Impressions or the Miracles or Marvin Gaye. That was our vision and its image kept us stepping, heads high and backs straight, no matter some of the wacky bullshit we got into on occasion.

Sun Ra and Albert Ayler were always on the scene. For some, Sun Ra became our resident philosopher, having regular midweek performances in which he introduced the light-show concept that white rock groups later found out about and got rich from. When Ra would play his "Sun-Organ," when he played low notes, deep blues and dark colors would light up on it. When he played high notes, oranges and yellows would light up, and we sat, sometimes maybe with fifteen or twenty people in the audience, and thought we were being exposed to the profundity of blackness. Jim Campbell directed the bigger plays at the Arts and that's where I first met Yusef Iman. When we got our regular programs going, concerts, readings, plays, in the downstairs auditorium we made by tearing down a couple of walls, black artists flowed through those doors. Some for single performances, some for longer relationships, some to absorb what it all was. We were all trying to grow together.

Milford Graves was another regular, and Hugh Glover, who was just starting. Andrew Hill, soft-spoken, blinking, sometimes in disbelief, behind his cool glasses, was our music director for the summer program. Overstreet became our director of graphics along with Betty Blayton.

One of our first official actions was a parade across 125th Street. With Sun Ra and his Myth-Science Arkestra leading it, Albert and his brother Don blowing and Milford wailing his drums, the core of us, as it had grown, some other black artists from downtown and those in Harlem who'd now begun to come in, plus Baba Oserjeman and his Yoruba Temple. We marched down the street holding William White's newly designed Black Arts flag. I've seen one photo that survives of this (in a magazine put out by Asian activist, Yuri Kuchiyama, *North Star*). A small group of sometimes comically arrogant black people daring to raise the question of art and politics and revolution, black revolution!

We had little money. But the mortgage on the brownstone was only about $100 a month and it was in generally good condition. I was the main source of funds. I had a couple of plays running downtown at St. Marks Theater, and we had put on a benefit just before we left, doing *The Toilet*; Charles Patterson's *Black Ice*; another play of mine, which I directed, *Experimental Death Unit #1*; and a play by a guy named Nat White called *The Black Tramp*. We charged $20 a ticket, the audience was mostly white, and we used the money to pay down on the brownstone and help put the building in some shape.

Tong was supposed to direct my play *Experimental Death Unit #1*, but after a few days he had slapped the star, Barbara Ann Teer, so I took over and directed it. The slapping situation unnerved me, but I got it done. But slapping? Barbara wasn't going for it, whatever the cause, and I could dig that. Yet Tong said it was Barbara's fault, she had done something, it was implied that she wouldn't let herself be directed. The problem was that Barbara knew theater, she was a professional, and Tong could probably never be. I sensed that at once. The problem was to get the play directed, not to make Barbara Ann Teer "submit" in some kind of way. But that was the kind of shit that Tong got into, with all kinds of people, many people I felt kindly toward or who were my friends. He even got into a hassle with my sister during our Operation Bootstrap summer program because my sister was given an office which Tong thought was too large for a woman, plus my sister smoked. She was another registered theater professional, probably thinking also that her brother would certainly make things easier for her, whatever the uncertainty. That was a major battle.

What began to be obvious to me before too long was that Shammy was volatile and unpredictable, but he had a basic respect for me as a writer, certainly for the downtown huzzas. But he was unpredictable. His brother had a deep malady, probably some kind of advanced paranoia. What was predictable about him was the negativity he carried with him, no, *wore*, like a wet suit.

Dave was younger than the other two, and influenced by both, but he was closer to Shammy. Dave and I were alike in a number of ways. Dave wrote poetry and music criticism. He was steady and assumed a lot of the daily arts programming and scheduling. He handled the artists and was a serious student of Sun Ra.

The first forum we had at the building was about which way the arts were going and the responsibility of the black artist. Tong, incensed by some point Sun Ra was making, leaped up and tried to walk toward him before being forcibly restrained, calling Sun Ra "an old woman." I was literally shocked. I was deeply embarrassed. Certainly Dave didn't like it either, but he could never be openly critical of Tong. In some ways Tong resented anyone who had some leadership role or qualities. For one thing, any intellectual who might shine in his younger brother Shammy's eyes, Tong was *jealous* of. He was against Sun Ra because Sun Ra, in Tong's mind, was alienating Dave. That's the kind of wild paranoid Tong was.

The only person to try to give Tong what he needed as far as African American street therapy, a good ass-kicking, was his brother Shammy, and once, during the middle of an exhibit of painting, suddenly Shammy and Tong rolled into view, fighting each other, rolling on the floor, till the rest of us separated them. The two of them became the new talk of the Harlem nationalist and Black Arts community. I was told later, I think by Larry Neal, that these two dudes are always getting into that. Shit, now he tells me!

Shammy had a love-hate relationship going with me. He envied me, I think, the celebrity of the well-known writer, and liked, I think, being associated with me. But at the same time he did not like to be in my shadow and secretly he thought he could write as well as I. His brother Tong hated me, because Shammy emulated me in many ways, even down to mannerisms and the way we dressed. So not only would they fight, but I had to struggle with Tong because of his craziness, often directed at me. I also had to stop the wild-acting Shammy from getting jumped on by any number of Black Arts regulars and Harlem citizens who wanted to kick his ass. Finally, there were more people wanting to kick the two Hackensack brothers' asses than you could kill with a submachine gun without a lot of extra clips. They were a major problem at the Arts.

After we had first moved in, one morning I see this tallish, long-striding figure coming down the street with a suitcase and a red tarboosh on his bald shaven head. It was the bony-faced, acid-looking Tong. He had not come up with us; in fact, he was, in our deliberations, against the move. We even thought he might just drop out and not hang with us. (I was hoping.) But then there he was, asking could he have an office and work with us. He touched the red tarboosh, which at the time I was unclear about, and said only, "Yeh, this is me." Then he went inside and Dave found him an office. The fighting and other backwardness started not long after that.

Cornelius, as the various struggles between the Hackensacks or between them and any number of other people would go on, used to ask why I put up with it. He would say, "Goddam, LeRoi, these mf's must have something on you." Later, it got so bad that Corny and the others would come in with plans for the two brothers' destruction, which I would naysay. They even came in with a smiling bespectacled murderer friend of theirs (who was a very sweet dude) who would have left either or both of the brothers in an alley perforated in some deadly manner.

Dave was all but frozen stiff trying to function rationally and get the real work we wanted to do in motion. He was always caught between the two brothers, ideologically and factionally. And there were different factions throughout the Arts. For one thing, Shammy would work. And he would do most of what we agreed on, though he might come up with some improvisation or alternative reading of it that would be puzzling. He wrote plays of some real value and was ready to direct them and find actors and do the work necessary for us to get an audience. Tong did nothing. He would sit in his office with a small court that quickly developed. Jimmy Lesser, who looked like a Muslim and talked Elijah Muhammad's program up a storm. He was sort of Tong's left-hand man, because Lesser had a relationship with Shammy, but Lesser would always hook up with where he thought the momentum was careening, which he assumed to be Tong. Tong's right-hand man was Tub, about six feet three, two hundred pounds of muscle. Tub was actually a good man, dependable, but he had been swept up all the way by the red tarboosh rhetoric of Tong Hackensack and he functioned mostly as Tong's yea-sayer and enforcer. When I last saw Tub, he had become a Hanafi Musulman, a small sect of Islam associated by some with religious fanaticism.

At the time I knew little of Islam, either the orthodox, Sunni kind or any other kind. What I knew of the Nation of Islam, the so-called Black Muslims, I had picked up, like most people, through Malcolm X. The religious practice interested me less than the black nationalism. It was only after I left Harlem that I became more interested in the religion of Islam. But, apparently, in Tong's office the study of orthodox Islam became the central focus and people were warned that they could not smoke in Tong's office. What went on in that office mostly was discussion, we used to call it bullshitting, but I don't know if the aspirers to Sunni truths bullshit or not. Maybe it is called something else.

With the smallish Majid, a pleasant, smiling little brown intellectual with horn-rim glasses, the basic Tong faction was formed. What they did was mostly criticize and undermine whatever went down in the Arts. They opposed most programs if only by doing nothing. Yet they were even more arrogant than the most arrogant of the rest of us. But they never proselytized for their faith in front of me, for some reason. So I knew even less of the formal mechanisms of their "worship" than I needed to. They were content, in the main, to talk bad about and undermine the rest of us, any way they could.

Perhaps what Tong had in mind was to become the de facto "leader" of the BARTS. I sensed that often enough. He thought he was a superior person. He had not been downtown wasting his life as a traitor to black people. He lived downtown, yes, but he was married to a black woman. A light-skinned proper-acting lady from Philly. I think she was a Philadelphia social worker. But all during the time I knew Tong I saw him with his wife socially perhaps only once.

Tong had not been downtown married to a white woman. He had not just hung around with white dudes trying to screw every white woman who had been turned away from the Miss America pageant. I know that the light of Islam helped that rhetoric, scowling at the swine-eating, wine-drinking dudes the rest of us were. But I have never met a person as violently male chauvinist as Tong. He would make women (at least black women) walk several feet behind him, and he was consequently always getting into struggles with most of the women around the Arts who didn't even know what the fuck he was talking about (i.e., the religious "justifications" for his bullshit); they just wasn't buying it.

Vashti was slick enough to stay away from Tong. Though she would light up most of the Arts dudes when they were bullshitting, which was often. But with Tong, Vashti just smiled her slightly lopsided smile and would say to me, nodding her bead, "Tong is crazy, Roi, really pretty crazy." And I'd look at her and roll my eyes.

The first large rally we held, out on Seventh Avenue in front of the House of Proper Propaganda, created the first major open conflict between Tong and me. The older black nationalists always talked on their ladders across the street in front of the Hotel Theresa. Larger forums were held in front of Mr. Michaux's bookstore, called, affectionately, the House of Proper Propaganda. Malcolm had spoken in front of the store often and there was a sign in front of the store ringed by Pan-African leaders from everywhere in the black world. There was a major reason for our rally, probably mobilizing people against police brutality. We got out the literature, even got a car to use a sound system. But just as things were ready and we were about to proceed down the one long block to Seventh and then down to 125th, Tong declared to a small group of us left at the building that he opposed the rally.

The people were already assembled, new music was playing out of the speakers, which was the trademark of our rallies, the use of the most avant-garde black music, and our people were there waiting. I was momentarily speechless. I didn't believe he had said that, and certainly I had no understanding of why he had said it. "What?" I said, staring as if at a monster. "Why are you saying that?"

"Suppose it's a setup? Suppose the cops just let us put this together so they can attack?"

I must have been sputtering "What?" I wanted to keep saying it, but it would've betrayed my absolute lack of understanding of what was going on. Finally, I got myself to say, "That's a pretty wild idea."

Tong said, "You just want to get black people killed!" And his face twisted into the acid scowl it always threatened to be.

"I just don't believe that it's any setup," I went on. "I think we should have the rally. We planned it and did the work to get the people out. We've got to get over there and do it."

Tong stepped close to me. We were in the hallway, readying to go out onto the street. "You're a wise guy," he said, the terminology temporarily nonplussing me.

"I *am* wise," I said. He had his face just an inch or so from mine, though he was taller and seemingly tougher. But I stuck my face close to his like in a cartoon.

"You know what I mean," Tong went on. But after the freeze-frame face-to-face I walked around him, and the few of us went on to the rally.

I heard Vashti's words echoing and this confirmed it for me on one level, though now I knew I would have to deal with this Tong openly and quietly as well. He was mad as the maddest goddam nut I'd ever met. Or was he just that intent on undermining my "leadership" and "taking over" the Arts? Tong's faction held him as the real moral and spiritual leadership of the Arts, but even they had to retreat partially in the face of the reality of trying to set up a functioning black arts institution. His faction did very little of anything but sit around. Plus the artists, mostly, did not relate to them, plus the staff of folks that we took on when we did our summer program not only thought Tong and friends the lunatic fringe of the Black Arts, but despised them because they didn't even think they were serious artists. Tub and Lesser made no pretensions of being artists, but neither did Cornelius. But Cornelius was our greatest propagandist. He probably talked to thousands of people a day and handed out literature. People running into Tub or Lesser or Tong would be put off from even wanting to be around us. Shammy had that charming way about him as well, but he was not in the Tong faction because of their conflicts.

Tong was so mad that he would try to disrupt the rally probably to become the real decider of direction in the Arts. As it was, he was constantly initiating little bullshit Islamic-related "rules" for his office. As hat-wearing a bunch of bloods as we were, Tub would announce when you came in Tong's office, "Take off your hat. No cigarettes." While the rest of us, informality's children, would be wandering around trying to get stuff printed, or see that there was enough space for a rehearsal or a class, or talk to some artist about doing something with us or for us. While Tong and company scowled either behind the closed door or with the door left open, sitting back in tilted chairs, a red tarboosh on the desk, upon which not one speck of any productive labor crossed. So that when people would come up to the Arts you could figure out after a time where they were coming from by who they hung with. The Arts types would be swinging with Dave. Sometimes he and Sun Ra would stay holed up for hours. The arts/politics dudes and the political dudes would crowd into my narrow office, like Larry Neal or Askia or Ted Wilson or Overstreet and the others. The weirdo-mystical irritators would gravitate to Tong. It got so when I saw Tong and company coming I would get depressed, expecting open tension to reflect the constant tension that developed in the place.

What Tong wanted, I don't really know. Leadership of the Arts, perhaps. Though once, when he was borrowing some money, because he had no job and his rent was not paid, he told me that I was the quarterback and I ought to keep my fullback (him) in good shape. He was a strange, often deadly quiet man who probably fancied himself many things, but the only thing I knew he was good at consistently was making trouble.

The Supremes' "Where Did Our Love Go?" and Mary Welles' "My Guy" reached me in 1964. And Dionne Warwick's "Walk on By." These tunes seemed to carry word from the black for me. Monterey, the downtown streets of the forming Black Arts core, the dazzle that black women pre-sented to me now. Marvin Gaye's "Stubborn Kind of Fellow" was playing when we got uptown. "Keep on Pushing," which poet David Henderson made into a great poem, was one of our themes, and all of us would try for Curtis Mayfield's keening falsetto with the Impressions. Plus their "We're a Winner" also moved us and spoke, it seemed, directly to our national desire.

It was as if I had a new ear for black music at that point in the middle '60s. I was a jazz freak, though we rhythm-and-blued to Ray Charles' "I Got a Woman" and "Drown in My Own Tears" at our downtown loft sets. But now the rhythm and blues took on special significance and meaning. Those artists, too, were reflecting the rising tide of the people's struggles. Martha and the Vandellas' "Dancing in the Streets" was like our national anthem. Their "Heat Wave" had signaled earlier, downtown, that the shit was on the rise. But "Dancing in the Streets," which spoke to us of Harlem and the other places, then Watts and later Newark and Detroit, seemed to say it all out. "Summer's here and time is near/for dancing in the streets!"

We did the Philly Dog and the Boston Monkey, whirling and being as revolutionary in our dancing as we were in our own thoughts. Somebody told me that Tong had said that I "danced like a white boy." I guess that was part of the reason he thought he should run the Arts. I used to dance pretty well back home, but when I heard that, I figured maybe my living down-town had cooled my cool. Ruined my rhythms. That was part of the whole sense of myself that I carried at the Arts as well. I *was* guilty for having lived downtown for so long with a white wife. I think that was the kind of trump card that Tong and them thought they held. And it did make me reluctant at times to come down hard on people who obviously needed exactly that, because I was still insecure and tender-headed about my recent life. So certain people could play off that, and probably did. Certainly, Tong and company did.

I even stopped going downtown, and I'm sure certain aspects of the stances I took were based on my feeling of revulsion when my Greenwich

Village days were focused on. Others in that Harlem community mouthed similar kinds of charges. Though most of what they said, on the legitimate side, was that most of us were from downtown and knew next to nothing about Harlem, which was very much correct.

An opportunity presented itself that we were lucky enough and hip enough to seize upon. We had no money for any really well advertised programs at the Arts, but we did the best we could. We turned out flyers and little booklets which Dave had designed and circulated them, building up our audience. We did *Dutchman* again and a new play of mine, *Jello*. I also wrote the play *A Black Mass* in my office at the Arts. It is a work that dramatizes the Nation of Islam's mythology about the origins of the white man, having been created by the mad scientist Yacoub. Patterson's *Black Ice* was another of our staples. In trying to get money to put on programs, we searched for various sources. One very successful set was a benefit concert which was recorded by ABC Impulse. I knew the producer of Impulse, Bob Thiele, fairly well, having done liner notes for him, one the enormously important *Live at Birdland* album, for which I interviewed Trane in the little telephone-booth dressing room in the back. So Thiele liked the idea of doing an album dedicated to the avant-garde in black music, which he could then market as an anthology and as a sampler of albums he would bring out later. He called the album *The New Wave in Jazz* and it featured Trane, playing the beautiful and frightening "Nature Boy," and groups led by Albert Ayler, Archie Shepp, Grachan Moncur, Bobby Hutcherson, and Charles Tolliver. The only person left off the tape, which infuriated me, was Sun Ra. Dave did one section of the liner notes and I did the other. So we got some money for our programs and also got a very hip record out.

Then we heard about the HARYOU Act programs around the corner functioning out of the Hotel Theresa. HARYOU was the first antipoverty program set up by Lyndon Johnson in his continuing assault on the Great Society. They were trying to set up a stop-riot program for the summer of '65, the summer after the "long hot summer" of '64. There was to be an Operation Bootstrap functioning that summer in Harlem out of HARYOU. What it would be was anybody's guess and we found out when we started coming around there that most of those folks at HARYOU didn't know either.

Livingston Wingate, now a judge, was the director of HARYOU. He was Adam Clayton Powell's man, I was told, and a very popular dude uptown. However, the guy running the summer program was an egg-shaped, light-skinned man named Frank Stanley, who tried to be likable but seemed just a trifle on the slick side. Some said, more greasy than slick. My job was constantly to rush back and forth between Stanley and Wingate and a few other folks trying to get some money. Finally, we hit on the idea that we could do a summer arts and culture program. I wrote up the proposal with help from my old HU buddy Shorty, who was now an accountant with some firm. Shorty was also married to a white woman in the Bronx, but that spring of '65 when we met I was talking so much shit that Shorty soon moved out of his situation and was at the Arts as our accountant. Shorty knew a couple of Bronx operators on the semilegal side, Ricky and Tony, so they became the triumvirate of our financial dealing and accountability, which, with all the headaches, crazy niggers, crazy government, crazy whiteys, they did remarkably well.

There were always many versions of how much money we got out of HARYOU that summer for our Arts & Culture sector of Operation Bootstrap. But we must have got away with a couple hundred grand and even more in services when it was all over. It was really a great program, running that entire summer. We brought paintings into the street with outdoor art exhibitions. Overstreet designed the easels we used to show the paintings and he brought artists with him to oversee and contribute to the shows. Each night the show would move to a new location in Harlem.

We brought new music out in the streets, on play streets, vacant lots, playgrounds, parks. I think perhaps the Jazzmobile came from our first idea. We had trucks with stages we designed from banquet tables, held together by clamps (another Overstreet design). And Pharaoh, Albert, Archie, Sun Ra, Trane, Cecil Taylor, and many other of the newest of the new came up and blew. The only bad incident was when a white-media-famous tenor man came up with an integrated group and someone threw an egg at him. We told the musicians we wanted black groups and boycotted them if they refused to make their groups all black. But there was music at these different sites every night moving all over Harlem.

We brought drama out in the street as well. We set up our improvised stages and with a little fanfare we quickly got a crowd. One evening we sent Shammy with a pistol chasing one of the characters in *Black Ice*. The bloods seeing a brother with a gun chasing somebody who looked like a white man made a crowd instantly, and the show began! Or just the sight of us unpacking and setting up would be enough. We performed in projects, parks, the streets, alleys, playgrounds. Each night a different location, five nights, sometimes six, a week.

We brought street-corner poetry readings, moving the poets by truck from site to site. So that each night throughout that summer we flooded Harlem streets with new music, new poetry, new dance, new paintings, and the sweep of the Black Arts movement had recycled itself back to the people. We had huge audiences, really mass audiences, and though what we brought was supposed to be avant and super-new, most of it the people dug. That's why we knew the music critics that put down the new music as inaccessible were full of shit. People danced in the street to Sun Ra and cheered Ayler and Shepp and Cecil and Jackie McLean and the others. It was a great summer!

We set up crews for each of the arts, each with its own truck, sound equipment, stages, or whatever else was needed. Harlem residents were our technical staff and quite a few of the more sympathetic folks from downtown who came up, like Overstreet and White. All those beautiful people who did come together that summer whose names I cannot recall have that sweet memory as their final unspendable paycheck.

Getting paid at HARYOU was always a drag. There was always something happening which slowed the checks down. What we would do is simply unleash our staff and crew on the HARYOU bureaucrats and they'd sail over there and talk so bad and threatening that our checks, though late, would get there before the other projects.

Hanging out in front of the Theresa was hip anyway, because people always gathered there, plus the old Garveyites would be there on their ladders with the red, black, and green flags beating the white man to death every evening.

It was a great place to argue and I had some furious mouth shoot-outs at that site quite a few times. One of the most memorable was arguing with Robert McBeth, who later became head of the New Lafayette Theater, about black art. McBeth told me that there was no such thing as a boogie man. That art was simply art, that it could not be black. I said there's Russian art, French art, Spanish and Chinese and English art, etc., but not black art? My problem was that "black" is not a nationality and I wasn't clear on that. But African American art is the creation of African American people.

Barbara Ann Teer and I got into a similar argument, I think out in front of the Black Arts, slinging the pros and cons of black art. Though I think Barbara Ann was convinced, as her National Black Theater now attests.

Being able to hire people that summer gave a big plus mark to our cry of Black Arts! It was a powerfully constructive program and word of it spread not only through the city, up and down town, but across the country. Not so weirdly, when I had done *Dutchman* downtown I had got an Obie Award, but uptown it was called by some newspapers "racist drama." From the "fair-haired black boy" of Off-Broadway, as Langston Hughes called me with his tongue stuck way up in his cheek, I got to be a full-up racist. So strange that the victims, once they began to scream and shout at their oppressors, can now be termed the oppressors. We accuse whites of racism, so—Presto! Change-o!—"black racism" is the real problem. "Hate-whitey dramas" were what I and my colleagues on West 130th Street were writing. And, the white god help us, when we were trying to find out how we would carry out our all-black aesthetic when most of our plays had at least one white in them, it was Shammy who came up with the idea that we should do them in whiteface. We loved the idea and it became a tack one associated with the Black Arts. Blacks in whiteface! What racism! My God!

We also gave classes in playwriting, poetry, history, music, painting, and martial arts. A young black poet named Ojijiko was our resident martial artist. Harold Cruse was our history teacher and at one time he had two FBI agents in his classes. One, Donald Duncan, was later implicated in framing Max Stanford and Herman Ferguson for some bullshit FBI-fabricated attempt to assassinate Roy Wilkins and Whitney Young. Another one of the agents had also penetrated Malcolm's OAAU. One guy was tall and light-skinned with red freckles. I'd see him going back and forth to Harold's class. Later we put out flyers and circulated them to many cities with these dudes' pictures and one of their lady friends, alerting people to these agents' presence.

Bringing art to the people, black art to black people, and getting paid for doing it was sweet. Both the artists and the people were raised by that experience. But we were just going on instinct and our own skills at what we did best, arts. We knew next to nothing about bureaucratic games or the subtlety needed to preserve so fragile a program as we had erected, so fragile because it was so important and we had no funds of our own and no correct understanding of the economic self-reliance needed to push a program calling for black self-determination, even in the arts.

We met a lot of people, many who had our best interests at heart, but we did not take some of the best advice. We did not benefit from the wisdom of our elders. We met Bumpy Johnson, the grand old man of organized Harlem crime. Bumpy was one of the first to insist that black dudes run their own rackets and stop paying off the white boys. He was a respected

elder, straight as a board, with an office in a warehouse that sold extermi-
nator supplies (so help me!), a legit front for his widely known and widely
respected operations. For an hour or so Bumpy talked to me like my father, telling me I had to meet different people and get hooked up really to
the community and not get too far out so that negative folks could shoot
me down. I listened and was proud to be there with the bald-headed, dignified Mr. Bumpy Johnson, but I couldn't really hear what he was saying.
I didn't really understand. But Bumpy could see we were heading for trouble
if we didn't get fully conscious in a hurry, but I was too naive to dig. I
thought that if I roared and roared and took it all straight ahead, as hard as
I could, relentless in attack, we would get over, we would win. The question was, would we survive?

Sargent Shriver, Kennedy's brother-in-law, was head of the antipoverty
program. He came to New York to tour HARYOU's various programs. When
he came with his entourage to the Black Arts building, we wouldn't let
him in. Bad us! Dave came up to my office and told me Shriver was outside waiting to get in. I could peek out my front window and see the crowd
of white D.C.-type bureaucrats along with some of the Negroes from around
the corner. I told Dave, "Later for them motherfuckers."

"It's Shriver," Dave told me.

"Fuck Shriver." And Dave carried the message back. And looking out of
the window you could see the white faces turning red and the Negro faces
turning Negroier.

So it was about this time that word of the "racist" Black Arts program
began to surface in the media — "teaching racism with government funds"!
In retrospect, that obviously wasn't cool. With a good grasp of skating on
the thin ice of government grants and with a smart grantsman around, we
could have not only bit deeper into the federal pie, we could have gotten
some of the foundation money. But we were too honest and too naive for
our own good. We talked revolution because we meant it; we hooked up
programs of revolutionary and progressive black art because we knew our
people needed them, but we had not scienced out how these activities
were to be sustained on an economic side. Later, after the word "black"
had cooled out some and the idea of even "black art" had sunk roots deep
enough in the black masses, where it could not simply be denied out of
existence, the powers-that-be brought in some Negro art, some skin theater, eliminating the most progressive and revolutionary expressions for a
fundable colored theater that merely traded on "the black experience,"
rather than carrying on the black struggle for democracy and self-determi-

nation. Then the Fords and Rockefellers "fount" them some colored folks they could trust and dropped some dough on them for colored theater. Douglas Turner Ward's Negro Ensemble is perhaps the most famous case in point. During a period when the average young blood would go to your head for calling him or her a knee-grow, the Fords and Rockefellers could raise themselves up a whole-ass knee-grow ensemble. But that's part of the formula: Deny reality as long as you have to and then, when backed up against the wall, substitute an ersatz model filled with the standard white racist lies which include some dressed as Negro art. Instead of black art, bring in Negro art, house nigger art, and celebrate slavery, right on!

But we made it easier for them to take us off—we acted so wild and woolly (get it?). From the point of our publicly nutting out on Shriver, news of our "black racism" steadily accelerated. And the funding of the most obviously successful arts and culture program any poverty program ever had was made "highly controversial." But we thought we could simply trample the racist rulers with the sincerity of our feelings. We hated white people so publicly, for one reason, because we had been so publicly tied up with them before.

There was, however, a positive overall effect of the Black Arts concept that still remains. We showed that we had heard and understood Malcolm and that we were trying to create an art that would be a weapon in the Black Liberation Movement. In August of that year, while we were still conducting our nightly black art in the streets, our Operation Bootstrap program, Watts went up in flame and blood, and a war raged in Watts for five days. That's what we thought, that it was out-and-out war. When Malcolm was murdered we felt that was the final open declaration of war on black people and we resolved to fight. The Harlem move was our open commitment to this idea. In our naive and subjective way we fully expected the revolution to jump off any minute, Watts or Harlem style. There had been rebellions in many cities since the year before, when Jacksonville and Harlem went up. For us, it meant black people had taken the offensive and we despised those who did not equally commit themselves to the struggle. Young writers and other artists were drawn to this stance and its furious patriotism and outright despising of whites. Poets Sonia Sanchez, Clarence Reed, Clarence Franklin, playwright Ronald Drayton were among those that flowered out of the Black Arts. Sonia, then a wide-eyed young woman, quiet and self-deprecating, was herself coming out of a bad marriage and she came to our programs announcing very quietly and timidly that she was a poet. The two Clarences had walked the streets of Harlem all their lives, but the Black Arts saw them flower as poets. Sam Anderson and Ed Spriggs developed out of that Black Arts movement, participating in the readings we gave, at places like the Club Baron and the Celebrity Club or in the small Black Arts auditorium. We had one hugely successful reading at the Baron, Milford Graves on drums, plus the African dance company from Oserjeman's Yoruba Temple.

Some of us were very much influenced by the Yorubas. When we first arrived in Harlem, Oserjeman's group was very political. They dressed as traditional West Africans from Nigeria but upheld the right of black self-determination, declaring that Africans in Harlem must control it. We gave many rallies at which Oserjeman or some other speaker from the Yoruba Temple spoke. I had known Baba Oserjeman through a host of image changes. He was Francis King from Detroit, a friend of Steve Korret's, where I first met him. He was always spoken of then, by his friends, as a kind of con man/hustler. He wore English riding outfits and jodhpurs and affected a bit of an English accent. He then became Francisco Rey, Spanish for a minute. Then he became Serj Khingh, a little Indian, and he opened one of the first black-owned coffee shops (of that era) on the Lower East Side, called Bhowani's Table, where some of us used to go. The next I heard of Oserjeman, he had become Nana Oserjeman of the Damballah Qwedo, "practicing the religion of our fathers." And finally (?), Baba Oserjeman, chief priest of the Yoruba Temple.

I had no formal definition of cultural nationalism. I didn't even correctly know what it was. But certainly it was all around us then, the Nation of Islam the most known. But Malcolm's death ended any would-be hookup with the Nation for me and most of my friends. Lesser stoutly maintained he was a follower of the honorable Elijah Muhammad, but he belonged to no mosque and his commitment to the Nation seemed to be the carrying of a Qur'an and the wearing of the funny little suits and bow ties popularized by the Nation, plus carrying a briefcase and standing sluefooted ("45 degrees") the way he thought a good Muslim should.

All of our politics were confused. Tong and his boys thought they were focused on a kind of Islam, but the only results I saw were negative. Some of us were influenced by the Yorubas because we could understand a connection we had with Africa and wanted to celebrate it. We liked the African garb that Serj and his people wore. The lovely long dresses, the bubbas and lappas and geles of the women. After so much exposure to white women, the graceful dress of the sisters in their African look, with their hair natural, turned us on. Plus, Oserjeman and the rest talked about and practiced polygamy, and certainly for some of us who were used to ripping and roaring out of one bed and into another, this "ancient custom of our people" provided a perfect outlet for male chauvinism, now disguised. But that was a basic cultural nationalist influence.

All of the various influences focused on white people as enemies, devils, beasts, etc., and our thinking fell in perfectly with this. One question white reporters never seemed tired of asking me was if I hated all white people, were all white people the enemy? When the last question was asked I would say, well, I haven't met all white people. It was our intention to be hard and unyielding in our hatred because we felt that's what was needed, to hate these devils with all our hearts, that that would help in their defeat and our own liberation.

So if "Hate Whitey" was our war cry, it was also reason for me to be attacked. That was Tong's main method of undermining and attacking — to point out how a few months ago I lived downtown with white folks, now here I was directing black people. Plus, the press and the white power structure had definitely set us up, exploiting my recent fame to turn it to infamy, before people's eyes. Larry Neal and Eddie Ellis had articles on this phenomenon in the *Liberator* magazine, but I still slept what they were saying, that I was being propped up so I could become an all-purpose whipping boy to show the absurdity of our cries of Black Art.

We faced both internal and external conflict. Every day brought a revelation of one aspect or the other. One day Shammy got into a struggle with a dude from the Yoruba Temple over a woman that Shammy wanted and the Yoruba dude did too, plus Shammy had talked wise to one of Oserjeman's wives. When I looked up, the entire Yoruba Temple, which numbered a couple hundred in those days, came over to the Arts. They had come, they said, "for satisfaction." One of their priests' wives had been insulted and it must be rectified.

At first our people wouldn't let the Yorubas in, but I came downstairs and let them all file in. They stood silently around the wall, some with walking sticks, a couple, I suppose, with heat. Shammy wanted to act mock-heroic and defiant, but finally I got him to beg the priest's pardon and so his face was saved and likewise Shammy's ass. But Oserjeman lectured us on our bad manners and our lack of African perspective. We could not come up to Harlem and act like Europeans. I was boiling mad and embarrassed again by one of the Hackensack brothers.

The program that summer built a great rapport in all sectors of the community, especially since we were able to give out some jobs. We worked constantly to agitate the community and to further inflame it against the white racist system. But it seemed that fools like the Hackensacks did everything they could to break down that rapport and isolate us. When the program was over, we faced the bleak prospect of trying to raise money to continue our programs at the level to which we'd grown accustomed. I went downtown one night, backstage, to see Sammy Davis in *Golden Boy*. He made me a gift that night of $500 in brand-new $100 bills right out of his pocket. We also got Sammy to come uptown and do a benefit for us. It was at a HARYOU facility on 125th Street. Sammy appeared with his entire entourage and made those surroundings seem even more spartan than they were. It was wild how white Sammy's act seemed in Harlem. But he did all right by us, whatever his motives.

There was one school of thought, not wholly shared by me, that we could simply gorilla the bux out of anyone, that we needed not only black celebrities but the government as well. That proved wrong on both counts. We pulled some thoroughly juvenile delinquent shit on Harry Belafonte after demanding some money which he wouldn't give up, writing his name on some paper and then tearing the paper up as if that signified his imminent disposal. But it didn't work, Belafonte wasn't cowed by such shallow theatrics. Or at least I didn't think so.

Our trips down to the various regional offices of the Office of Economic Opportunity, which was the funding agent for HARYOU, were legion. We still have photos of Dr. Proctor (later pastor of Adam's Abyssinia) sitting with his head in his hands listening to our frantic spontaneous treatises on why we had to have some money, or some more money, etc. We felt that we had a right to demand money for our operations—some of us, I guess, felt we had a right to demand money for our personal lives, but I never had that problem.

So this gorilla attitude did permeate one aspect of our public image. While I did not think such an image was an absolutely correct one, there were only a few things I could do about it. I mean, I thought it was all right to present that image to the state, i.e., to the white racist government and those linked up with it ideologically or through employment. But I did not think that that should be our image as far as black people were concerned. With the Hackensacks and Tong's clique on the scene, that problem was also a constant. They were always having some confrontation or another with someone and then justifying it in the name of blackness. So I spent a lot of my time cooling out that image, trying to rectify it, or in hassles with our own perpetrators.

What our image was at large, outside of Harlem, I can only guess. Though the large motion in black communities to set up Black Arts equivalent institutions meant to me that the image was, in the main, positive.

Downtown some people still smarted over the disrupted social organization that the "mass" move uptown had caused them. (Fifteen years later a white woman came up to me in a bar and talked to me in a bitter accusing tone about how I had personally estranged her black husband away from her. With my wife, Amina, sitting there listening to her. It *was* sad.) The downtowners who came up to work and contribute to the Arts, I guess, had some contradictory words to put out against the straight-out maniac line that was being run by some. We heard fragments of the tales and emotional dislocation coming from downtown, from both black and white, and it was curious to me, like listening to one's obituary. Perhaps like Cross Damon in Wright's *The Outsider*.

One night a group of the black downtown residents came up for a reading at the Arts. Ishmael Reed and Calvin Hernton among them. Vashti got into an argument with one poet, Luther Rupcity, about the nature of the Arts, what we were trying to do. What we were trying to *be* would have been Rupcity's phrasing. He and Hernton were very close and Vashti had little use for either one. Calvin had a problem with black women downtown and up that year because he had come out with his book *Sex and Racism in the USA*, which roots the problems of black national oppression in sexual conflicts and psychological antagonism stemming from those conflicts. Interesting that both Cleaver and Jimmy Baldwin, to varying degrees, also made this analysis. Calvin's statement that lit many sisters up was that many sisters are lesbians because black men do not relate to them sexually.

Rupcity was spouting some aspect of Hernton's theories and Vashti lit into him and Hernton with such ferocity that everyone else in the small gathering suddenly stopped to check out what was happening. Vashti was gesturing and backing Luther up, when Luther stopped talking to her and turned to me with his hands palms up and said, "Will you get this lesbian off me?"

There were at least a dozen persons in that room who would have gladly and without remuneration beaten Calvin, Ishmael, Rupcity, and entourage into fragments and slivers of confusion and foolishness. But obviously I had been called. As I stepped toward Luther, he began crying, like real tears formed and rolled. My jaw was tight and my fists obviously shaking with anticipation. Rupcity says to me, "Don't hit me. What do you want to do, hit me? I know you've got those big hands. You want to hit me?" And he was quite right, that idea did cross my mind. But his display was further out than I expected and it unnerved me. I felt sorry for them. I jawed at him, talked bad to him, and then they all dragged out of there.

Vashti and I were living on Seventh Avenue right up near 145th Street. After struggling with the Arts all day I would walk up Seventh Avenue to our little three-room flat which overlooked a courtyard full of new, middle-aged, and ancient garbage. It was a fifth-floor walk-up, over a West Indian bakery. So I was always eating them hip meat pies smoking hot, but I could never deal with the ginger beer. We went to the Zambesi bar across the street, and around the corner was the Lagos, African named even before our new African consciousness. We hung out up and down Seventh Avenue. Count Basie's and Wells', home of the famous chicken and waffles, were our special hangouts. We'd fall by the Red Rooster, the stakeout joint of the black middle class. For special meeting meals with whites or certain kinds of Negroes we'd go to Frank's on West 125th Street, which had, at the time, white waiters who circulated playing Gypsy violins! Occasionally we might go by Shalimar, across the street from Sugar Ray's, or Small's (which Wilt Chamberlain had bought). I saw Redd Foxx in there one night and he made a joke about black militants and I said something to him from my table. It was a brief exchange but I could see his embarrassment come out from under those red freckles. They made a Sammy Davis film, A Man Called Adam, about a weird Louis Armstrong-Miles Davis combination, at Small's, and we got some of our actors on as extras. I even met Cicely Tyson and exchanged pleasantries while Vashti smirked just off camera.

Not just Vashti and I, but some of the dudes from the Arts and myself would hang out. We were always in the Apollo. I even went backstage and talked to Dionne Warwick, whom I fancied I had a crush on, trying to get her to do a benefit for the Arts. Some brothers opened a coffeehouse right around the corner from the Arts called The Truth. It was meant to cater to the Black Arts and those with similar tastes. There had been a rush of folks from downtown up to Harlem, but also from outside New York. People had come into New York as usual, but now there was a very definite magnetism to go up to Harlem.

Harlem had its share of nuts and bolts. Not all of them came with us, but we did bring more than our share. There were resident paranoids and schizophrenics we ran into as well as sane people reacting normally to our abnormality. Most people were not running away from white people and a "shadowy" life as "King(s) of the Lower East Side." So sometimes we probably confused some people's normal reaction to our nuttiness as nutty reactions to normality! But, all things considered, like they say, there were some bona fide nuts we ran into and some of the best people we have ever met in life.

Around us, at this point, there were people from RAM and also from the *Liberator* magazine, run by Dan Watts. There were the Garvey people, young and old. The neo-Garveyite followers of Carlos Cooks, like the AJASS society (African Jazz Arts Society) led by Elombe Brath, who first featured the "Naturally" programs that made natural hairstyles popular among some advanced groups of black people. They also modeled African clothing styles with their "Grandassa" models. And they definitely had some grand assas. Some fine ones too.

There were all kinds of other nationalists. The street-corner variety, which included not only the Garveyites but folks like Eddie "Porkchop" Davis, who was on the ladder daily giving white people hell. There were the cultural nationalists like the Nation of Islam, the Yoruba Temple, and even smaller cults and the orthodox or Sunni Muslims, who also had many variations, and the black Jews or Hebrews, the Egyptian Coptics, and various other "consciousness-raising" religious cults and sects. There were black militants of all persuasions and those on the left like Bill Epton around the corner at the Progressive Labor Party. Epton got arrested during the '64 rebellion and charged with "criminal anarchy." Bill was a soft-spoken likable dude whose relationship with the black community, from a little ramshackle office over top of a restaurant on Lenox Avenue, gave PLP a little credibility before it came out with its bullshit position that "all nationalism is nationalism," negating the revolutionary aspect of liberation struggles against imperialism which are not direct struggles for socialism. The white chauvinism and petty bourgeois subjectivism of would-be white leftists like PLP have always left them isolated from not only the black community but also the other oppressed nationalities, and their connection with white workers is even more dubious.

Bill and I appeared on programs together and got along all right, but I was a nationalist and he a Marxist. We argued about whether PLP would come to his defense adequately. I told him I thought they would leave his ass to rot, while letting him take the weight. PLP did get him out, though I think he later resigned from the organization and joined a mainly black organization based in Harlem. PLP did, however, leave another of its black cadres in prison to rot and take the weight and expelled this brother as a "nationalist." I never found out what Epton thought of this.

There were also the basic working people, moving out of Harlem most times to work and struggle and then returning at night to the indignities of ghetto life. There were Harlem office workers and bureaucrats and politicians. There were other cults like Democratic and Republican blacks. We disrupted several of their rallies, at one of which Mayor Lindsay was to speak. There were right-wing nationalists like James Lawson who acted as bodyguards for the white and black politicos, and we had constant run-ins with them. There were people like Charles Kenyatta who got great notoriety as "Malcolm's former security." Kenyatta spoke on the ladder every day as well. But our comment was terse: "Motherfuckers who say they was Malcolm's bodyguards need to be killed. They shoulda died along with Malcolm." And HARYOU, because it had got some dough, drew all kinds of hustlers and con men, religious and secular. There were people like baldhead Omar, who wanted to talk his way up on some money and power, or Donald Hassan, who got a reputation for being as crazy as Shammy, trying to gorilla his way up on same. There were the good-timers who wanted to hang out all day and night. Corny would lead us around to the various after-hours joints, where he would hold forth and introduce me to everybody and we would argue about Shammy and Tong and whether there was a black middle class or not. Corny said there wasn't. (Years later Cornelius was shot to death in just such an after-hours joint by some gunmen who, when robbing the place, turned for no reason and suddenly filled Corny full of lead!)

There were the gangsters and hoodlums and people in "the life" and all kinds of people who had been overlooked or peeped and popped. There was, as in any large urban black community, all kinds of promise and all kinds of frustration and bitterness. The sickness, the pathology that Fanon talks about that exists in the communities of the oppressed, it was all full out and openly roaring around and over and through and within us. The Black Arts itself was a pastiche of so many things, so many styles and ideologies. We had no stated ideology except "black," and that meant many things to many people, much of it useful, much of it not. But we shot from the hip, came always off the top or near the top of our heads. Our sincerity was our real ideology, a gestalt of our experience, an eclectic mixture of what we thought we knew and understood. What we wanted. Who we thought we were. It was very messy.

Vashti and I were a pair for those times. She young and aggressive, so full of her own sense of what everything was (even as she was in the act of finding out) that she was intimidated by nothing. Probably some white women hated Vashti (some black ones, too) because she was not just a symbol of something new, she was the whole drum set. People must have thought, this young girl, how'd she get into so much? But the brash young lady from D.C. was just what the doctor ordered and she knew it. Whoever it was — nuts, nationalists, Muslims, Yorubas, artsy types, politicians — Vashti handled them. "Hey, you betta get outta my face!" was one of her favorite statements. And our struggles were many and varied, for whatever reason. But we took all that in stride because we knew we had something deeper, we knew we actually dug each other, that we were *friends* as well as lovers.

Even my waywardness and roving eye she tried to deal with straight up and straight ahead. She'd say, "Roi, you gonna make me kill this bitch," of any object of my dalliance she would perchance to spy. And there were those. At Dolores Soul, the actress, Vashti merely laughed. "That old bitch!" And at Maria Cuevas, the writer, she just put her hands on her hips and when either of them was around the Arts she'd stand and watch them so intensely they felt a laser on their intentions that cooled them into distance.

One time we fought about my intentions. Vashti wanted to know when I was going to get a divorce. She said, "You think I'm just living with you for my health?" And we went off. I stalked out the door, headed for somewhere. The next day I went to the bank, and goddam Vashti had withdrawn all the money and split for somewhere. Then she called me up at the Arts, laughing. "Fooled your ass, didn't I?" I was rising in smoke like the Phoenix. I got home and she'd bought a goddam antique rocking chair.

We had a real falling out another time about something very similar. She says she's tired of my bullshit, she's going home to D.C. When I get up to 145th Street that evening she has taken most of her shit and gone. I was depressed not only with this personal wipe-out; the day-to-day shit at the Arts could be extremely depressing with that cast of nuts to deal with. I was trying to figure out how we were going to sustain the program now that the federal moneys had been stopped. The phone rings and it's Brandy, a friend of Vashti's she'd met through Shammy. (Shammy's female thing was astonishing. He ran through so many women so quickly it was impossible to keep track. They'd appear, be on the set a few minutes, and then disappear as if Porto Rico, the dude with the hook at the Apollo amateur night, had pulled them off accompanied by crazy music.)

Brandy was a Shammy ex and she'd got real tight with Vashti. But now she's on the phone and I tell her that Vashti is not in. She says, "I know. Do you want me to come over?" In truth, the only reason I said I was busy, some dudes were coming over, was because suddenly I got the image of Shammy and that crazy-ass Vashti converging on me with waving swords and I couldn't handle it.

A few minutes later, Vashti calls from Washington. She asks me what I'm doing. She says, "I bet you got some woman over there, don't you?" It was funny now, so I told her about her friend Brandy and Vashti goes up in smoke right on the phone. "That bitch. I was the one who told her I was going to D.C. and to watch out for my interests. That bitch. Wait till I get my hands around her throat!"

But when she didn't come back I got into all kinds of dubious shit. For one thing, during the summer cultural program, the Yorubas had sent people over for some of the jobs. One of them, a young little girl named Olabumi, caught my eye. She was tiny but built like a dancer, with, as the nationalists say, an impressive history (a shapely behind). I started watching her go up and down the stairs at the Arts wondering what was under the long African lappa she wore.

At a program we had at the Baron, the Yoruba dancers are wailing and then Olabumi, or Bumi as we called her, falls out. One of the Yorubas then spreads the story that I was staring at her so intensely it made her faint. At any rate, I found myself going by her place, but then I found out she lived with two other women and one of the Yoruba, a dude who sold incense. I didn't know what it meant, but I didn't care. Maybe I was interfering with some of their polygamy. Anyway, we found ourselves in one of the worst flophouse hotels in Harlem, but once getting in there she said she had no intention of doing anything. She said that Olatuni, whom she lived with, was her guardian, nothing more. But she would not give it up. So this became one focus for my after-Arts hours, trying to catch up with this little teasing Bumi.

I met another woman at the same time, a little light-skinned woman with glasses who walked like she thought she was a musician or at least a street hipster. This Lucille had been downtown and had moved up, but she was living in Harlem and hanging downtown and had come uptown before most of us. When I ran into her she was staying with some girlfriend and implying she might be going to lead a life of Lesbos. Goddam, I thought, why I always have to run into these.

The influence of the cultural nationalism on all of us at the Black Arts was real. For instance, when I finally succeeded in getting Bumi to come up to 145th Street and spend the night, I immediately got the idea that both Bumi and Lucille could move in, that I should begin to live as the Yorubas at Serj's temple. As an obvious justification for male chauvinist bed rambling there is little to discuss, but the extent to which these ideas had penetrated my thinking on the real side is what is interesting. But not only my thinking. I did convince the two of them to move into 145th Street. Bumi, a teenager, an African dancer, child of the new age, seeking some new revelation of changed black reality. Lucille, an office worker who loved the music, whose quest for blackness was made all the more ironic (but necessary) by her very light skin.

Lucille, the office worker, liked the idea (but maybe she just wanted to get next to little Bumi), but Olabumi, who was associated in the temple with polygamous marriages, seemed less impressed with the idea. The three of us sat and discussed it, with Lucille marveling at Bumi's sewing machine, a portable she was carrying with her to make bubbas and lappas for wearing and for the temple's performances. But why had I found it necessary now to offer such a relationship to these sisters? I had never asked any of the white women I had been with to enter into some polygamous relationship. Though that is just a formalism, since the many affairs and one-night stands that went on amounted to something like polygamy. Engels says adultery is the partner of monogamy. None of that went through my mind; the idea of polygamy was "new" and "black," so we went for it.

After a day or two, this relationship, such as it was, got reported back to me by Lesser, who said, "I understand that you're living according to one of the most illustrious traditions of our ancestors." But by the time he said that shit, it was already just about over. Vashti had decided she was coming back, so these other sisters had to cut out.

Things at the Arts were getting dire. When the summer program was going and money was flowing in, things were great, there were conflicts but they could be handled. The noise Tong and company sold, the antipathy the community people, professional artists, and the like felt for them, I could cool out somewhat, at least keep the shooting war off. But without the cash flow, raising money here and there with handouts and our programs, people started to get more sullen. People kept coming to me with plans to dump Tong or Tong and Shammy in the river or off the roof. One old friend of Tong's from childhood sat in on one of these frenetic discussions and he agreed that the dude was dangerous and needed to be took off. Then he slips a note to Tong telling him to watch out.

Tong bursts into my office and says he understands that somebody is planning to do something to him. That he is ready and that no one would survive. I had a huge blue-steel cowboy-style .357 Magnum I used to carry in my briefcase. And while he is woofing I run my eye over the briefcase and his eyes drift in its direction as well. He knows full well what is in there. But I keep scribbling notes for a play I'm trying to write and look up at him only barely. "I don't know what you're talking about." And he goes back into his office. But the tension between us and his mob after that was unbearable. It was like you couldn't do anything for fucking around and being fucked with by these unproductive nuts. One little dude took Tong out in Mount Morris Park and kicked his ass one afternoon after Tong kept woofing at him, and that made me feel much better. Tong thought he was bad bad, but the little dude was a boxer and jabbed and hooked him dizzy. We stopped it, why I don't know.

Our politics, first and ultimately, was the reason the program and its development were in such disorder. Our politics which flowed from our mix-matched and eclectic ideology. We had straight-out white supremacy bourgeois opinions mixed with mass-felt revolutionary ones. We wanted to destroy a system and didn't realize that we still carried a great deal of that system around with us behind our eyes.

In one of our confrontations, for instance, Jimmy Lesser, one of Tong's black blacks, confessed that he could not get as deep into the militant thing as we could. (I didn't quite understand the difference then between bourgeois nationalism that just wanted to get in on the exploitation and a revolutionary democratic view that wanted to destroy it, so-called revolutionary nationalism. I thought they were all the same. This is the reason so many of us slept on what it meant that Malcolm and Elijah had split. That split between the politics of an oppressed bourgeoisie and the politics of the exploited and oppressed revolutionary black masses.) Lesser then says, "Look, man, I have to admit I'm a traditionalist. I need a snowy blond white woman at my side, whatever I'm going to do."

I was so horrified because I realized I had been, was being, vilified by motherfuckers that wasn't even as straight as I was, who had problems even much deeper than my own. The fact that I couldn't believe there could be suckers much sicker than me was what had left me open to these clucks. And I resented it, deeply. It made me even more sardonic and terse in dealing with these dudes.

The reason this conversation had come up was that all the lights had blown out in New York City, I guess for the first time. In Harlem this Great Blackout had a special effect. Suddenly, at the corner of Lenox and 125th, a group of white people were being taunted and robbed. The police swung into action—saving white people is their second most important function after their most important function, saving white people's property. They had to do some property saving too. Windows were getting smashed and commodities were disappearing at an alarming rate, well below their established exchange value.

We got the idea that we should agitate for more of what was going on, as if people needed us to tell them what to do. By the time we got our sound truck in action, one piece of 125th had been stripped as clean as most bloods' pockets. But we started speaking over the loudspeaker, riding up and down Lenox and Seventh. "Now's the time," we shouted. "They can't see you. Rip these stores off. Take everything. Come on out and get it!"

We had just come back up the hill near 130th Street when police cars hemmed us in. White cops leaped out, guns drawn. They dragged us out of the seat, sticking a gun to my head. We were running off at the mouth, driving their temperature up even higher. They were dragging us to their car. I think it was me and Dave in the car. But just as they are getting us into the car a crowd forms. They came together instantly, those bars and corners emptied, and suddenly, yeh, the surrounders were themselves surrounded. And, Jim, if they thought my mouth was bad, they hadn't heard nothing. Bloods lit them up on all sides. One old sister, her hands on her hips, stood between us and their car calling them "White motherfuckers! You white motherfuckers need to be killed! Leave them young boys alone, goddammit!"

And the others joined in. There were maybe a half dozen police and now, very quickly, about fifty or sixty people. The police had to decide what to do. They were caught between training their guns on us or the crowd, which was getting louder and louder and prettier and prettier (the cops would say "uglier"). Plus, the people were closing off the space, drawing the circle in tighter. But one cop gets on the radio and starts calling. The goddam precinct house was right around the corner at 135th and Seventh and they push us toward the car, pushing the confrontation toward its explosion point. But then some colored cops arrive. That's why they were calling. The Buffalo Soldiers were needed once more and they arrived riding their trusty backwardness. We get smashed into a police car and talked bad to with a gun at our heads by the white cops. They are threatening to kill us. "Like Gilligan did? Huh?" we screamed. (Gilligan was the cop who had shot the young black boy in an incident that helped set off the Harlem Rebellion and wanted posters appeared the next day with the caption "Wanted for Murder: Gilligan the Cop!" The PLP was reputed to have done it and that's why the police wanted to bust Epton.) The cop tried to strangle us.

When we got to the precinct they were pushing us into the back room, where they said they were going to finish us off, but as we entered I spied the newly appointed black commander of the precinct, Eldridge Waithe, a West Indian dude with a fairly good reputation, for a black cop. He came over, and we started screaming that these freaks were gonna kill us. So Waithe intervenes, questions the cops, questions us, and after an hour or so in which many of the Black Arts people had come over to the precinct or were calling the precinct over the phone, Waithe cut us loose.

That's what Lesser meant. He wasn't as militant as us. He thought the revolution had to do with wearing bow ties and standing sluefooted. But at least that involved some activity. Some did even less.

I was growing sick of most of these people, because even some of the more productive brothers and sisters would only come around at times when they thought they didn't have to put up with the Hackensacks and the rest of that crew. Corny sat and broke down in tears one night because Shammy had said something to him and Corny wanted to kill him and, because he couldn't, the frustration ate him up, and he wept, trying to threaten Shammy still, but at the same time wailing like a child.

Askia, Dave, and I sat up all night after we got released from the joint, talking of revolution. The blackout itself was an agitating element of romance in our concept of revolution. We were still so unclear. We still did not even understand in anything approaching a scientific way what were the purposes or the methods for making real revolution. We were angry and we had heart. We thought those were most of the prerequisites. But the Hackensacks turned people like Larry Neal and Askia off. Larry thought they were seriously ill—"counterproductive," he called them. But Larry was going through some personal problems himself. One of his close political comrades had run off with his wife. He'd told me in that same narrow little office. That seemed shitty and ugly, like it was happening in another world. The wild ins and outs of our various relationships I could take as they came, but something like that seemed, somehow, foreign. Like a bourgeois movie.

After that, Larry had gotten involved with a sister that Tong had some design on, and that put even more distance between them, as if there needed to be any more. Plus, Larry had been openly critical of the way the Hackensacks, in general, liked to fuck things up. So there was bad blood between them.

The screwy Tong, in what he conceived as some secret strategy, tried to get his young disciple, Majid, to follow me around. He was supposed to report on my activities, where I went and whatnot. I guess because he thought that allowed him to undermine even more, interfering with stuff he didn't like. But then, also, I guess I was his meal ticket. There was no money changing hands anymore. The little money I got, from royalties and readings, I needed to support myself. But I did give up some few dollars to keep the Arts functioning. We did programs that brought in a little money and contributions, but we were just barely paying the bills. Tong and his nuts might have resented the fact that I did have some money, and they chose not to work, at anything, and that was yet another edge between us. I let Majid walk around with me sometimes, but when I wanted to I'd lose him easily, if I wasn't in the Arts. I wasn't doing anything, I just didn't want him with me.

But now the bullshit was rising so high that I was getting more and more distracted. When Vashti found out about my nutty liaison with the two sisters she went up in smoke, started throwing plates and pots, a steam iron, her fists, then she repacked her bags and split. She moved downtown with a girlfriend, or at least down to the East 90s. I guess I was wasted. When she'd been in D.C., that was one thing. I figured she'd be back and the separation didn't seem permanent or the final solution. But this walk-out had bodings of finality, termination. Plus, now, I felt naked. It was the kind of loneliness that can descend on you at the end of some personal relationship or phase of your life. Vashti had been for me, no matter my craziness, a real companion, an extension of myself, as I was, I guess, an extension of her. We'd always felt like two hip young things against a crazy world, and we were time enough for it. There was a groping tenderness to our relationship that came from experiencing sweetness in the midst of the unknown and clinging to that sweetness as life itself.

So the days passed now with an edge of gloom to them, and the weight of the growing madness at the Arts weighed even heavier on me. For now, I literally could not stand the asshole Tong or his unpredictable brother.

I hung with Corny and Clarence in and out of the Harlem bars or holed up in my office drinking cheap orange wine. The goings and comings of Tong and his litter of nuts did not interest me. The programs we put on, Dave and I took care of. The artists that came through, the two of us talked to. We regarded Tong and company as bad weather and dealt with them as little as possible.

We had a public image. We still spoke at rallies and programs, firing away intensely as we could against the white beasts who oppressed black people. Earlier in the year 1 had finally published the book *The System of Dante's Hell*. The moiling, twisted experience of my youth still moiled and twisted as an aesthetic form of rhythmic images, searching for a voice that finally begins to emerge at the end of the book and its "fast narrative" of a perpetually gloomy reality. But I had already gone past that stage in my life. (I hoped!) When I had, at the end of *Dante*, "woke up with white men, screaming for God to help me." I had served that apprenticeship to my own real spirit. I had left the Village and that education I had given myself, reading and feeling myself through great parts of the Western world. I had dashed out at full speed hurling denunciations at the place of my intellectual birth, ashamed of its European cast. Arriving full up in the place of blackness, to save myself and to save the black world. Ah, the world-filling egos of youth.

But now I felt more alone than ever, bereft of Vashti's kindred spirit and love. Facing dumb dissembling motherfuckers who wasted time conspiring against advance and productivity. My head was a swirl of images, disconnection and new connection, its focus vague, dulled by my own subjectivism. Most of our intentions were good. We wanted to help free black people. We, ourselves, had got back a self-consciousness of our nationality, but we were bogged deep in nationalism, a growing, ever deepening cultural nationalism, it was to turn out. Malcolm's death, certainly, had left many people scrambling and unprepared. There was no revolutionary party we understood. No science we could relate to. Those people calling themselves Communists we despised. They were stupid-ass white people—shit, they were part of the enemy. Hadn't they even come around saying that "the nationalism of Malcolm X was just like the nationalism of the KKK" and that "Malcolm was a police agent"? Shit, they needed to be fired on.

But we were a clutch of kids, some of us never even got past that and remain kids even to this very day. We needed to be directed, we needed guidance. We needed simple education. There were next to no black institutions where we could learn, that's why we had tried to put one together. We could understand what it was to be uneducated in a world of airplanes and skyscrapers. I, certainly, knew what it was to be suddenly conscious and then be made ashamed of your own unconsciousness which had ended only a few seconds before.

When I finished whatever tasks I had given myself at the Arts I would take off, unless I was talking to some of the artists or Corny or Clarence or a few of the other people or Dave. But now there was little to say to the others, who had their own powwows, which produced nothing I could see but metaphysical double-talk and empty leers pretending toward consciousness.

I discovered where Vashti was holed up and started calling her. I could tell that she hadn't frozen up on me completely but she did think that I was too much trouble. There was too much wear and tear on the neurons. And was it worth it? But a couple of phone calls and we were at least sitting in some bar sipping drinks and staring out at the world trying to put something back together.

The first night I slept over where Vashti was staying proved to be the beginning of the end of the beginning. We ate breakfast and talked. I was restless and she wondered why. I was supposed to show up at the Arts around ten o'clock, but I didn't feel like it. It was nothing formal, just a bedraggled, out-of-it feeling.

We went out to a bar, then we decided to go downtown to see a flick. They were doing Evelyn Waugh's *The Loved One* and we sat through that. When we came out I told Vashti to call the Arts and see what was happening. She said they were wondering where I was. Tong had asked Dave and Dave passed it on. At that point I felt, "Oh, bullshit; fuck them." I had Vashti by the hand and told her simply, "Hey, it's finished. Fuck those people. I'm not going back there."

I went to the old apartment and packed a few clothes. I called Shorty and told him to watch my shit—I was cutting out for a while. Then we went to Vashti's place and got her clothes and took off. At first I didn't know where we were going, I just didn't feel like seeing those gloomy nuts on West 130th Street. Finally, after several bars and another flick, I decided we should go home, to Newark, to my parents' house. I called up, made arrangements, and then cut out. A couple of young people who had started coming up to the Arts were from Newark. We contacted them through Shorty and got them to help us move out our clothes and most of our belongings. Except I left a huge record collection, with Shorty supposedly minding it, that I never got back. Shorty let Corny and Clarence and some others know where we were, but that's all. We didn't even tell young reliable Dave, because Dave was always the object of manipulation by the Tongs and Shammys.

When Tong and Shammy found out I had split, moved out with Vashti, they got nuts, I guess. They went running up to the apartment and threw whatever was left around. Then they stormed around Harlem, claiming they were looking for me. For a couple of months, whenever I came to New York, I carried a sawed-off shotgun inside my hunting jacket in such a way that I could put my hand on it, open the coat, and fire almost simultaneously. But happily I had no confrontations.

In the first heat of that split, there was a casualty. Apparently Larry Neal, Askia, and some others went to inquire of Dave about my whereabouts and were met with even more hostility from the now thoroughly lost and desperate survivors at the building. Now there was no money, the programs had stopped. Of those still around, only Dave would do anything consistently to put together the programs, and now there were no resources. Shammy was frustrated and angry because I had split. Tong was now free to run amuck and that amuckness ended up with Larry being shot as he emerged from a subway by Shammy. It was a small-caliber weapon and Larry was hit in the leg. But now it seemed a war threatened to jump off, of forces colliding in the vacuum of my sudden removal. But I didn't care, except for some twinges of feeling about my failed responsibility. When I saw Larry he questioned me and said that some other folks wanted to know why I had brought those nuts into the community and then left them up there.

But now I had other things to think about. Like, what was I doing back in Newark? I had just completed a book of essays called *Home*, which meant coming back to one's self, one's consciousness, coming back to blackness. I ended the introduction to the book: "By the time you read this, I will be even blacker." That was true, albeit the grand stance. But I could also have said: "and confused like a motherfucker." But, at least, I was, literally, Home.

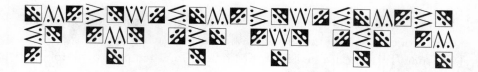

Nine

Home

It was just after Christmas, the last few days of 1965, when Vashti and I arrived at my parents' home on Eckert Avenue in Newark. Now a state of shock started to develop in my mind, faced with being back in Newark, an unknown quality, except in my brown memory. I had left New York. In a week or so it was behind me. But what was ahead?

We sat and absorbed the atmosphere and brooded a lot. But in that frenetic high-strung way those suffering from anxiety do. There was now, also, a continuing relationship with the two young brothers, Donny and Barney, who'd helped to cart our stuff over. They brought us news about the nursery of maniacs left at the Arts, their foolishness and increasingly manic actions. The shooting of Larry Neal shocked me. That was the reason for carrying the sawed-off shotgun. In March the news came out that the police had raided the Black Arts. Headlines: "Arms Cache and Six Seized in Harlem"! Tong, Tub, Lesser, Majid had coalesced into some weirder stripe of destroyer. Now to some extent hooked up by metaphysical ideology—some loose, some actually calling themselves Hanafi Musulman.

The police said they had found guns and a basement shooting range. (That was Shammy.) My name came up in the papers: "Police Raid LeRoi

329

Jones Theater: Find Guns, Bomb." Implicated by association, but I had been gone for several months when the bust came.

Later, Tub was arrested, with two others, for attempted bank robbery and the name Hanafi Musulman came up again. Tub, a believer, got fairly heavy time.

Majid got involved with a Washington, D.C., orthodox Muslim group that the Black Muslims (Nation of Islam) were accused of assassinating. The assassins killed wives and babies, plus a couple of the men, in what was a horrible crime. The leader of the assaulted group went on television accusing Elijah Muhammad and swearing revenge. Still later, this same group occupied the offices of B'nai B'rith in a protest against vulgarization of the Prophet Muhammad's life in a film. Majid was the negotiator with the police, in that incident, for his father-in-law, the head of the group.

In a year or so I saw Tong again, now haggard and gaunt, wandering through New York City streets claiming to be Pharaoh and talking unintelligibly. Shammy I saw many years later in Washington, D.C. He had just come back from West Africa, where for several years he made a living selling drugs on the continent. Dressed like a real operator in a white double-breasted suit, he was with a tall blond woman he introduced as his wife. She looked like the high-powered wife of a high-powered drug dealer. We talked quietly and listened to music.

In Newark, I was somewhat at loose ends. First of all, being back in my parents' house had so many overtones and shadows obscuring some aspects of reality, but at the same time overemphasizing certain other aspects. Vashti and I weren't married, yet I'd brought her home as if she were my wife. We were staying in the guest room in the little two-family house I'd lived in during my final days at Howard. At first I had not even thought about this point—what my parents, certainly my mother, would think. But in a week or so it occurred to me that maybe they might not like it. Vashti and I acted the way we acted. We had good times together, but at the same time we fussed and fought in a very open way, and I know my parents didn't dig that. But I was trying to figure out what to do.

I was writing poetry, naturally enough. Nothing could affect that. A poet writes because he *has* to. It is like breathing—you can stop only at grave peril. But what should I *do* now? Vashti began taking classes at the College Division of Arts High. I was writing various articles and working on some plays as well. I even did a script for a film I figured might not ever be shot: *The Death of Malcolm X.* But what this did was get me interested in making films. I bought a camera, a 16mm Bolex, some editing equipment, including a Moviola for viewing what I shot. I began to do pieces of film, a couple reels, mostly mood studies of Vashti and environs. I even wrote a couple of mini-scripts. (Ten or eleven years later, when I got copies of the COINTELPRO papers the Freedom of Information Act entitled citizens to, there was mention of one film I was making out in my parents' backyard that involved a noose and an American flag!) I enlisted a few other people's services in making the film. Donny was a filmmaker himself. And I began to meet some of the arts-oriented people in and around Newark. Only Shorty from the Arts came over a few times to visit and fill me in on what was going down in New York. Ben Caldwell, the playwright and painter, lived in Newark then. He was painting and managing a rundown old transient hotel on Broad Street. He came over one day, invited by Barney, to participate in the filmmaking. He brought a young woman with him who was interested in acting. Her name was Sylvia Wilson. By 1967 she was my second wife!

I was doing various things but I didn't know overall what I was doing. Or why I was doing. However, I was meeting people and getting reoriented to Newark. I felt that I had failed in New York. The last days at the Black Arts had thoroughly disgusted me. Rather than continuing to struggle with Tong and the others, I had opted to cut out. There was no particular event or incident. I had just gotten filled up with all that. I had wanted to create a revolutionary art and a revolutionary institution to bring that art to the black masses. And while we had made some real contributions we (I) had also gotten bogged down with nonproductive nuts. Why? was what plagued me. Why had all that happened? Probably it was something about me. The guilt I carried about my life in the Village always undermined the decisive actions I had to take to preserve any dynamic and productive development in the Black Arts. Plus, obviously, I didn't know enough. I knew that, but what I thought I needed to know about was not what I really did need to know about. I needed to know the art and science of politics and how to run an institution. It was a long time before I learned either.

But something had happened that was good. The idea of the Black Arts, the concept of the black revolutionary artist organizing arts institutions, particularly theaters, in the black community, caught on. By the summer there was word that people in Detroit had pulled together the same concept. They even had a Black Arts Convention there. There was also talk of a Black Arts West opening in San Francisco, and word came from several other places of similar activity. In fact, by the middle of the year it became evident that there was a Black Arts movement spreading throughout the

United States. Traveling around to these cities and speaking and reading poetry was another one of my activities and a source of income. Word of the concept of the Black Arts far exceeded what we had actually done, but the concept itself was important.

In Newark, Vashti and I had a few friends. Donny, Barney, Ben, a friend of his, Russell Lyle, an alto saxophonist, and his older brother Henry. My mother and Vashti became famous friends. They'd even go down to the Owl Club and sit and drink cocktails and rap to each other. But by now it was evident that we had to move out of there. I had been asked to direct a local staging of *Dutchman* at Arts High, produced by a black Newark production company, the Calabar Society, which was run by some childhood friends of mine, Wilbur McNeil and Gene Campbell. Rehearsals would soon get started and I had some of the feeling of getting back into the theater.

After a month or so of being in Newark, Olabumi called me and told me she was pregnant! That wiped me out altogether. Pregnant? Shit, how? Hey, goddammit, I felt, we only made it a couple of times. But apparently, according to some scientists, one shot can do it. I arranged to meet her in New York to discuss it. I was pissed off. "How'd you get pregnant?" was behind any words I spoke to her. We stood near a statue of George M. Cohan on Broadway and I was not warm and friendly. "So what's going to happen?" was what I was saying.

"What's going to happen?" Bumi got furious—she was young and now she was hurt. I was throwing her favors back in her face. Now what's going to happen? So she spun away from me, running into the Broadway crowd crying, "I hope the baby dies. I hope the goddam baby dies!" I was left alone in the swirling crowd, and wound my way forlornly to the Newark bus.

In a few days Bumi called me again and we talked. I felt there was nothing I could or wanted to do. "Get an abortion" was my counsel. I thought I ought to convince her. So I told her to come over to Newark. I would meet her down at Ben's hotel to discuss it further. When she got down there I couldn't convince her to get an abortion. Not only that, she stayed the night down there and I stayed with her.

Vashti was smoking the next day when I saw her, making up some lie or other. What was really outside was the fact that Bumi didn't want to leave the hotel. It was the world's worst place (or at least no better than the world's worst). It was a flophouse, full of prostitutes, hustlers, petty thieves, and some recent Southern immigrants. Ben ran it like a big commune and several of the guests were weeks behind in their rent. And Ben seldom pressed them. When I went down there to hang out with Ben, we'd sit and bullshit, drinking bottles of very cheap wine in his cramped little room, which he also used as a painting studio and storage space, or we might sit out in the "lobby" of that stinking joint and have a quick forum about anything. All the other guests who wandered in would join the discussion. What was so interesting about Ben and the joint is that I had forgotten that there were people outside of New York who painted, wrote, danced, etc.

So Bumi began staying at the hotel. I didn't want her there, but now here was some other guilt, her pregnancy, to whip my head. I thought maybe Ben and she had got tight and that's why she wanted to stay, but that seemed so convenient an out for me I rejected it. I'd been going down to that hotel from time to time to bullshit with Ben anyway, but now I'd go down more often. Vashti became more and more aggravated and stayed on my case about my late-night returns and absences. Some of those nights, however, I was just sliding through black Newark streets, going in some Central Ward bar I'd stumbled on, just to sit and rub my head wondering what the fuck I was doing with my life.

Rehearsals started for *Dutchman*. It starred Iris Spielberg and Marvin Camillo (who later moved to New York and formed the theater group The Family, which produced Miguel Pinero's *Shorteyes*). I thought the production was pretty good, even though Iris and I had a fight, in which I told her I didn't like white people—she had complained that I hadn't related to her enough as a director. She said I didn't like white people because I was immature. There was probably some truth in that, though there are probably some other reasons white people could be disliked by any colored person.

The night of the opening, Bumi came up to see the production and Vashti spotted her. Vashti had gotten friendly with Sylvia and some other folks in Newark, and she had been complaining to them bitterly about my male chauvinism, my hanging out all night, and about Bumi, whom she had got word about. After the performance that night all of us went to the Owl Club down on Clinton Avenue. The place was founded by a friend of my grandfather's, another black Republican and a prominent Elk. My grandfather was a Mason. So there was a mix most times of young middle-class types and the older bloods who'd been going down there for decades.

Vashti and I had a fight about Bumi, not only verbal, but she slapped me and I pushed her, right in the Owl Club. My mother was there and she was so embarrassed she came up to me with tears in her eyes, her voice and person shaking violently. "I have to live here. This is where I live!" So much for the brown promise of yellow spotlight. Tussling in a bar in front of the colored citizens. Wow.

For Vashti and me that was it. That was the finish. She went back to my parents' house, got her stuff, and blew. She went back to New York to stay with a friend. I could not reach her. It was a very low point in my life. The Smokey Robinson hit "The Tracks of My Tears" was popular at the time, and for me that summed up what was going on in my own life. "Take a good look at my face/if the smile seems out of place/look a little closer it's easy to trace/the tracks of my tears!" Fuckin' Smokey, the poet of the age.

I got out of my parents' house as well and went down to the flophouse to stay. As depressed as I was, that raunchy joint took me even further down and out. Bumi was a kid, almost completely unshaped. She was no Vashti, who was also youthful but sophisticated to within an inch of her life. Me and Vashti were like partners, like Nick and Nora Charles, brown style. Bumi knew next to nothing about music, art, poetry, politics — none of the stuff that animated my life. Yet for some absolutely stupid pathological reasons I found myself with her in some flophouse on Broad Street in Newark! The irony, the psychological cruelty of that punished me unmercifully. The same grey streets. The hopelessness and despair that walks through that city like its real owners. I was back here with it, without, even, the promise of youth.

First of all I had to get out of that hotel. I pored over the newspapers looking for some way out. The depression was unbearable. The wine drinking increased. Days filled with a listless frustration, a self-condemning tone to my thoughts mocked me without end. I spotted a house for rent on Stirling Street. Just as you left the downtown area of Newark you'd pass through the Stirling Street area, just above the courthouse and Hall of Records on High Street. It was a short street, bounded on one side by High, on the other by Howard. It was only a couple blocks away from my old church and right around the corner from the church my father told my mother he was a member of so he wouldn't have to go to Bethany regular.

Also, there was a building just a couple blocks away from Stirling Street on Shipman Street where they had music and poetry readings down in the basement and an arts group upstairs. That building contained just about all of arty Newark. Plus, you could shoot right down the street and be at Penn Station or the bus station if you were removing. It was close to downtown, convenient, yet it was edged up into the community. It was about

$200 a month to rent the whole wooden house, three floors. I went up and looked at it. I could get the $200 plus another $200 security, if I strained. And I had to strain, I had to get out of that hotel.

Something happened to flush me out even more quickly than I'd intended. The owner of the hotel sent a man down to check on why he wasn't getting his rent money on time or no time. The reason was that Ben wouldn't bug anybody for the man's money. If you had it, cool; if you didn't, that was cool too. Ben would say, "Hey, man," to the nonpayers, "the white man gonna throw your ass out in the street," and everybody would laugh. But the white man did come down, or at least sent someone down to harass the tenants.

Some people had come over from New York to see me, Shorty and some others. The money collector sees us coming through the lobby and he wants to know who we are and whatnot. One thing led to another and I'm saying, "Fuck you, kiss my ass," which seems normal in these kinds of situations. The guy picks up a stick and charges me. I guess he was some kind of small-time enforcer. But luckily I kicked him with a fake karate kick right in his real testicles, and he keeled over, folded up like a newspaper. You mean you gonna kick some white man in the balls on Broad Street? Some landlord's flunky? You can't make that, my man. Something like that could have gone through my head as if it was Clarence Franklin talking slow and drunkenly inside my knot. For a second I froze. The guy was still laying in the floor like he was knocked cold. I backed off him, scrambled up the stairs to get what I could out of the room. Most of my stuff was still at my parents' house. Then I split, jumped on a bus, and went just where any detective would look, my parents' house. I didn't think anybody at the hotel would say anything. I lay low a couple days, and when I got my money together, I headed for Stirling Street.

So I found myself cleaning and painting yet another group of rooms, yet another place. I was moving to the third floor. Bumi would come, too. Barney wanted to move into one of the rooms with a little girl he'd hooked up with, the daughter of a famous black novelist. Ben figured he wanted to move out of the hotel, after that last incident. So he was going to move in, too. In a minute, Shorty would move over, too.

I wanted the downstairs floor to be a theater, something like the Black Arts. So we tore the walls down again. Joe Overstreet came over to help and at one point the whole ceiling nearly collapsed on our heads. Joe thought it was funny. There was a bunch of young boys in the neighborhood I soon got to know and they helped us. While we were clearing the theater part I even put together a quirky little film in which the kids starred. Putting that building together gave me more of a sense of purpose than I'd had in a long time. It was possible to do work in Newark. I was not an exile from New York. I could do work in the city of my birth. And that positive idea began to grow.

One of the first things I did was organize the Afro-American Festival of the Arts. The World Festival of Negro Arts was being put together in Dakar under Monsieur Senghor's direction. The idea of a world festival of *Negro* arts was a drag, many of us agreed about that. But the overall idea was a great one. But there was no mistake, Léopold Senghor *was* a prominent Negro!

The Newark festival took place mainly outside in the park of the Douglass-Harrison apartments. Those were the most successful sessions. The speeches and music and dance got over biggest. We were supposed to have a few forums and roundtables inside but they were not well attended. But the outside programs were very successful.

Ben Caldwell designed the brochure, which showed some folks sitting on the steps of 33 Stirling Street. The festival brought Stokely Carmichael, Harold Cruse, Baba Oserjeman, and the Yoruba Temple Dancers and Drummers into Newark. While some of the things didn't work, some worked very well. Carmichael, for instance, had just projected the concept of "Black Power" in the press. When I read it, in the *Times*, quoting Stokely down in Georgia or Alabama calling for Black Power, it lit me up. I had heard some things about Stokely when I was in New York and he still at Howard. I followed the SNCC struggles, of course, and the change that had occurred in SNCC, from a replica of the black preachers' SCLC until now, when under Malcolm X's influence, a nationalist perspective was growing in SNCC. Many of the whites had left. And now Carmichael was talking about Black Power. Next to the article I penned: "God bless you, Stokely Carmichael!"

The festival was my first really organized attempt to bring political ideas and revolutionary culture to the black masses of Newark. Though, in retrospect, a lot of what was said could hardly be looked at now as revolutionary. Though it all *was* resistance to imperialism in one aspect or another. The festival also connected me to many of the young people in Newark who were trying to do something in the arts and alerted some of the political types in that city that something "new" was happening.

We published a magazine called *Afro-American Festival of the Arts*, which featured works by Larry Neal, Sonia Sanchez, Ed Spriggs, Yusef Iman, Ben Caldwell, Clarence Reed, S. E. Anderson, and myself. Later it was called *An Anthology of Our Black Selves*. I met a young writer who worked for Johnson Publications, David Llorens, and he followed us around from place to place taking notes which in a year or so blossomed into a feature article in *Ebony* on our work in Newark.

Art Williams was running the Cellar just down the street from where I lived. He brought New York musicians in on the weekends. There were some very good sets. He also had poetry readings and I even read there myself one evening with a poet, Ronald Stone, who later changed his name to Yusef Rahman. Yusef's poetry was a revelation to me. He was like Bird in his approach to the poetry, seeming to scat and spit rapid-fire lines of eighth notes at top speed. It was definitely speech musicked. This was my first exposure to his work and I was mightily impressed. It confirmed some of the things I had learned in the first surge of the Black Arts movement, how different the black poetry was that emerged in that rush of new blackness that came upon us then. Poets like Larry Neal and Askia Tour, were, in my mind, masters of the new black poetry. Larry coming out of straight-out bebop rhythms, but actually a little newer than bop, a faster-moving syncopation. Askia had the songlike cast to his words, as if the poetry actually was meant to be sung. I heard him once up at the Baby Grand when we first got into Harlem and that singing sound influenced what I was to do with poetry from then on. To me, Larry and Askia were the state of the art, where it was at that moment. Yusef was good, in some ways on a par with Larry and Askia, but Larry's syncopation was a little more elegant. Yusef was dead-on a Charlie Parker bebop, straight ahead, blue wings flapping up a hurricane of funk. But Yusef was a definite new measure in the poetry, an innovative style that had to be absorbed by any who wanted to reflect where the word was circa 1966.

The fact of music was the black poet's basis for creation. And those of us in the Black Arts movement were drenched in black music and wanted our poetry to *be* black music. Not only that, we wanted that poetry to be armed with the spirit of black revolution. An art that could not commit itself to black revolution was not relevant to us. And if the poet that created such art was colored we mocked him and his inspiration as brainwashed artifacts to please our beast oppressors!

Another poet I heard during this period had a great influence on me, Amus Mor (once David Moore) from Chicago. I heard him read in Chi his masterwork, "We Are the Hip Men." The way Amus put the music directly into the poem, scatting and being a hip dude walking down the street letting the sounds flow out of his mouth—putting all that into the poetry—really turned me on. We wanted to bring black life into the poem directly. Its rhythms, its language, its history and struggle. It was meant to be a poetry we copped from the people and gave them right back, open and direct and moving. Reading in the vacant lots and on the sidewalks and playgrounds of Harlem that summer of '65 had opened many of us all the way up. We had been able to reach deeper into ourselves than ever before. We had been able to touch sometimes that dark brown feeling that is always connected with black and blues.

Reading with Yusef was a good heavy experience, like playing opposite another horn (his an alto, maybe, mine a tenor) and wailing blue/black magic for the soul's use. I began to come down to the Cellar often. It was only a block and a bit from my house. I became a regular, showing for most of the programs, sipping the beer and wine and mingling with the folks, digging the sounds. Maybe Barney and Donny and Ben and I would show. I was writing a column called "Apple Cores," meant originally for Ed Dorn's magazine *Wild Dog*. I had published a couple of columns in *Downbeat*. I began to fill them with what was going on at the Cellar.

Actually, Art Williams, who ran the Cellar, I knew before I left home. His younger brother and I had been fairly close even though we went to different high schools. Art was a bass player, much maligned by some musicians, who called him "the silent bass player," because Art's sound was so small. But Art was a good dude at heart, one of those classic free spirits that float through the black community trying to raise up beauty in the midst of ugliness. He'd been part of the Jazz Arts Society, which ran the third floor of the building the Cellar was housed in. But they'd split up because there was a growing Muslim influence on the Jazz Arts, resulting in them not wanting to deal with whites either as performers or as audience. Art had no such restraints on what he wanted to do. He wanted to bring in the music, whoever was playing it and whoever wanted to listen to it, and groove.

I was hooking up a production of A *Black Mass* and *Jello*, two plays written at the Black Arts. Calabar was putting up the bread and we were using the Proctors, an old movie theater that no longer functioned as that. Marvin Camillo, Barry Wynn, and Yusef Iman had the leads. Olabumi was in *Mass*, and Sylvia Wilson. Yusef and Charles Barney, a Newark actor, had leads in *Jello*, and Bobbie Riley, the mother of the major-league catcher Earl Williams, played Mary Livingstone. I thought it was a good evening, a professional production and aimed at the many.

It was during the rehearsals of these two plays that I came to know Sylvia Wilson better. She played the role of Tiila in *A Black Mass*, the young woman whom the beast (Bob Davis) touches and changes into a raving creature. Sylvia always drew applause the way she acted out the transformation.

Bumi and I were living together, but that was a thing of circumstance and inconvenience. I felt like her father more than her lover. She wore her Yoruba gele up and down those Newark streets and made friends with the young kids in the neighborhood. But we were in two different worlds. I could, however, and did feel responsibility for her quickly rising stomach and no matter what I felt, I was determined at least to serve that responsibility as best I could.

I found myself staring at Sylvia Wilson, who was married and had two children. One night at the Cellar she asked me was I really staring at her. Yes, I mumbled, maybe I shook my head, uh-huh, I had been. You know, some people get off just by staring. Sylvia was in the midst of separating from her husband. It was over already, the moving out was all that was left. In a few nights we found ourselves hugged together up in the loft, thinking it was just a brief coming together caused by our propinquity at the rehearsals.

But that was not the case. We saw each other again. We held hands and walked around Lincoln Center. Sylvia was tall and very slender, a brown woman with long, straightish-looking hair. I had seen her in the loft world a few times, before the tryouts that got her the part in *A Black Mass*. One night she was dancing in a company doing African dances and her halter slipped down, but she was so intense about the dance she didn't even bother to pull it up. I wondered about that, was that just for effect or was she intense enough to let the damn halter stay down. Bumi had snickered when we saw that, saying she thought Sylvia was "phony," but by the time the production at the Proctors was over, we had gotten tight indeed.

Sylvia also performed with Yusef Rahman, dancing while he read his swooping jazzical lines. It was my idea that Yusef liked Sylvia as well, even though he had a wife, Aishah, who had moved away from him for a time. Sylvia was one of the initiators of the Jazz Arts Society, which tried to bring some new art into the city, but the split meant she and the folks upstairs at the Jazz Art Society went one way and Art Williams another. But nobody could deny that what Art was doing downstairs was successful.

So her own cultural work was in and around Newark, against much heavier odds. But it was hooked up objectively to the same kind of thing we were doing at the Black Arts. In those cities like Newark, grim industrial towns in the real world, these kinds of projects are necessarily smaller but at the same time tougher and blacker because they are rooted in the absolute necessities of people's desired sensibility. People must fight to bring art to a place like Newark; it is not the tourist stop or great advertised mecca of commercial intellectualism as New York has been styled.

And so she had a whole life as cultural worker in Newark that paralleled what we were trying to do at the Black Arts in many ways. Therefore, a sensibility that was like mine in some ways, but without the tiresome "spaciness" of the middle-class intellectual, subjective and selfish as I and much of the New York crowd tended to be. There was much less room or tolerance for the "fake art" syndrome that is so ubiquitous in Manhattan, therefore much less fertile soil for the maddening and finally vapid "artsy-craftsy" personality type. Art was literally lifeblood in a place like Newark and its tenders and developers were, given the limitations of resources etc., dedicated valuable people, with usually a great deal more of a sense of responsibility than their average New York counterparts.

The unwavering focus of responsibility, especially as it relates to the African American people, was what the whole of the Black Arts movement was about. People like Sylvia, in the Newarks all over North America, had had that sense of focus and responsibility because, finally, there was much more of a black working-class underpinning for what they were doing. Such an intellectual and philosophical basis for their efforts was a given. For me, on the other hand, it was something I was still trying to *win*, even when I met her.

Our new relationship moved swiftly toward some resolution. Sylvia fascinated me. Before I'd gotten to know her I was still trying to hook up again with Vashti, but now that was surely over forever. We'd met once more in a bar, after an African wedding Bumi and I had gone to. Vashti stood there holding my arm, telling me it was all over. That we had had some fun but it was over. "We had some fun, didn't we?" She was crying, at first softly and then racked by more tears. "Didn't we?" Bumi had walked out so that we could talk. "Why can't I be the one in the beautiful African clothes?" she said, weeping, referring to Bumi's Yoruba dress. "Why can't I be the one that is beautiful in the African clothes?" And then we parted.

I heard that after our final split Vashti took up with a cameraman. A year or so later, I heard that she and the photographer had gone to Mexico for a vacation. It was in Mexico that Vashti went swimming one day and drowned.

What to do now? Bumi was a girl, yet she was about to become a mother. Sylvia was from Newark, too, though she'd been born in North Carolina, but she'd lived mainly in Newark, mostly the Central Ward, what used to be called the Third Ward. And she'd lived for a long time as a child, with her grandmother and father, on the Ward's most famous street, Howard Street. What seemed so strange to me now was that I had made something of a full circle. To have gone away so far, so many places, yet to be back with a black woman from the Central Ward. The irony was somehow mocking. I told her how many steps we'd wasted only to come back to our source, love in black life.

So I told Bumi about Sylvia. I told her I had been seeing her. Our relationship had just started. There was a fine intensity to it, a dazzling sensitivity to it, of us together, sensuous and alive. Sylvia was very slender, one could say skinny, but she carried with her (as so many dudes would remark to me while they were still in the running) an outright black sensuousness that was thrilling.

I felt my life had been blown around. I had been thrown by my own appetites across a whole cosmos of feelings and relationships. But the idea of Home was heavy on me, that I could come back. That I could somehow reclaim whatever I'd given up in going away. But there was Bumi and a baby coming. I thought she was too young and naive to handle it alone, which I guess was naivete of another sort, perhaps male chauvinism of one variety or another. So I proposed to Bumi that we practice polygamy, that we go to Sylvia and explain it and get her response.

The whole Yoruba cultural nationalism was influencing me. Bumi was still tight with Serj and the Temple folks. Olatuni even came to visit us with incense from time to time. We had a small altar in the house, as part of the religion. I did have a sincere belief in the need to go back to my roots. As Amilcar Cabral said of the black petty bourgeois intellectuals who have been so thoroughly wiped out by white society, they then all too many times freak out by diving headlong into a super-Africanism. (This was still to come!)

What we must have seemed like, the two of us, coming into Sylvia's house with such a proposition, I cannot guess. Sylvia lived in one of the middle-income town-house complexes that the administration put up to try to make a gesture toward the black middle class. The only thing was, these town houses were only a few steps away from the lower-income straight-out projects, though they did look different. It was a well-kept apartment, with the dramatic gesture of art readily apparent. (Though we were critical because there were white people's images in some of the paintings. I who just a couple years before not only had lived in a house full of paintings with white images, but had lain beside another white image, a flesh-and-blood one, as my wife. The pretension of these stances was fantastic, yet they came as a reflection of some legitimate desire to change.)

Sylvia did not like the proposition at all, except she did have some real feelings for me and that made her hesitate. She was also in the act of leaving this home, separating from her husband. The two daughters by that marriage she had already taken to her mother's to stay until she got herself situated. That marriage had already shattered. Her being with me had made it absolutely impossible for her to try to repair what was smashed and finished.

What our proposition did do was give Sylvia a place to move until she could see what she had to do. So she moved into Stirling Street with us. I had named the building the Spirit House, trying to raise up to another level the idea of what soul was to black people. The Spirit House was a place to raise the soul, to raise the consciousness. It was to be another edition of the Black Arts.

But no such thing as polygamy could work for us. Bumi was pushed because, even though she had been exposed to this madness, as an honorable black social form, she had her own instinctive feelings bred of being raised as a lower-middle-class girl in America. Sylvia did not want it either; her experience was completely the opposite. She was a light and a live wire in black Newark even with male chauvinism and a backward society. She had hung with musicians and artists, whom she made view her as equal and not as a piece of sexual baggage. But she would not say all this because of me. And I, so long whited out, now frantically claiming a "blackness" that in many ways was bogus, a kind of *black bohemianism* that put the middle class again in the position of carping at the black masses to follow the *black* middle class because this black middle class knew how to be black when the black workers did not. Hey, all that shit was yellow, very very yellow. Another kind of clique and elite. How to move from, say, Francis King to Baba Oserjeman and not miss a stroke.

Sylvia was in the house a few days when she decided she was moving out. The polygamous setup could not be consummated. The many head-to-head conversations we were having led Bumi to protest that she had been left out of this new family. But it had never been a family, only a bad idea sponsored by a middle-class black intellectual deeply confused and legitimizing male chauvinism. There was a party up on Clinton Avenue at someone's house. I knew Sylvia was going to be there. I had been in New York dealing with my agent and trying to cash some checks. I got back and went up to the party. Sylvia and I talked. She could not go on with this sad charade that I had tried to put together. Maybe, sometime later, things would be different. I stared out into inner space, wondering what was going to happen now. Someone was calling me. There was a phone call. It was one of the older women on Stirling Street. Bumi had gotten sick, it was late in her pregnancy, but she had gotten suddenly sick. An ambulance had been called and they had taken her to the hospital. When I got there she was in a coma. She never regained consciousness.

For Sylvia and me, Bumi's death was a torturous calamity. Not that we did not understand that now the way had been cleared for our relationship, which only a few minutes before had been doomed. But it was the very *guilt* that came with Bumi's death that was so unbearable. The guilt we carried was enormous. She was a young girl, almost a little baby, and we didn't need her in our lives. Now this frightening stroke of coincidence had removed her from our lives. We knew we should be relieved and that was the terrible guilt that plagued us for years afterwards.

What was even wilder was that one of the poets whom I most admired intimated to some people that he wanted to *investigate* Bumi's death because he suspected foul play! On top of that, Bumi's parents acted pretty wild as well. They asked for the baby clothes back, as if somehow I was going to steal them and do what with them!? They too seemed to hold me responsible for her death. This on top of everything else. (The book *Tales*, which was published the next year, has stories in it relating to this period.)

But despite the enormous guilt Bumi's death caused for us, it did not split Sylvia and me. Both of us felt that the cycle of completion represented by our coming together could not be thwarted. We tried to go on with our lives. Sylvia did move now completely into the Spirit House and we began to live together on the third floor. We began now to try to love each other as best we could in a crazy primitive world.

What combustions and reorganization our new lives together caused, I won't speculate upon, only to say that it was obvious they did, maybe they still do. Sylvia was from a black working-class family, one sister and four brothers, of which she is the oldest. She is eight years younger than I, and though we were raised not too far from each other, the difference in our generations and the difference in our class backgrounds meant that chances of our meeting before this last part of the '60s were not good.

Not because she lacked any sophistication; if anything, what I was coming to emotionally and intellectually, the sophistication to understand who you are and to be ultimately responsible for your development, she had never really gone away from. But I doubt that she would have threaded through the deathly white cells of downtown New York not-yourself-ville searching for death, as I and so many other blacks had and are. She is too completely connected to life as vitality and development, too certain of herself as herself (black, female, intellectual).

The '60s represented a great coming together of the brothers and sisters. The parts of the whole assembling to see further and do more. This is what national consciousness proposes. It is, in the deepest sense, a reunion with our selves, even the farthest-flung.

And so the journey that I made, which can be characterized as "the Prodigal's trip," only to be summoned (not only by myself but by all the others of us who were conscious that we were not together). Summoned where? Why, home, emotionally, intellectually, and in some cases physically and geographically. And who do you meet? Your brothers and sisters, the other parts of yourself. The people who be home!

Sylvia was raised by her grandmother and grandfather. He a construction worker and she, when she worked, a laundry worker in a Chinese laundry and a hairdresser. Sylvia had gone to Arts High School and wanted since her childhood to become an actress, then a painter, and then a dancer, or all three at the same time. It was this vector that had put her in motion in a direction that caused our paths to cross. An early bohemian, thought of by her mother and teachers as "weird," she was once sent home from high school because the teacher accused her of looking like "she belonged on a reservation." But hers, for the most part, was a black bohemianism. A white guy had come to her parents' house to try to see her when she was younger and her grandmother had driven him away, saying, "None of that!"

She had known my name first, she said, from a set of liner notes I had done for a record called *Billie Holiday in Germany* and then she had read the splintered "association complexes" of *The System of Dante's Hell*. She had been active in the Newark arts scene and even knew some of the New York people through the Jazz Arts Society. She'd heard of the madness of the Black Arts through some folks who'd come over to see us in the throes of youthful bombast and struggle. "They said you dudes were *out*—crazy as hell," was the way she described it.

But different people made different evaluations, naturally, of what our coming together meant. They still do. Some folks were disturbed (some still are); some were elated. I think the latter is the norm, but there were significant deviations from this reaction. For one thing, there was a group of people in Newark who'd either been after Sylvia or at least thought she was not to be gotten. She was not only married but principled. There were some other folks who thought that Vashti was a momentary phenomenon and Bumi was even more transient. (Many people who thought this way were not white, either.) They thought I was going eventually to get in motion in their ocean, not go home to a warm southern sea.

I am not even sure that Sylvia and I understood what our coming together meant, except we were in love, we had just come through fire, so we thought we deserved each other and none of the bullshit we were getting. We plunged into life as we felt it, determined to do things our way, no matter who thought what. We were strong on feeling but light on analysis. And sooner or later this one-sidedness must return to haunt you.

We began building a block association on Stirling Street. I had gotten a mimeo machine down in the basement and an electric stencil maker. When I taught all the kids who came around how to work these, we started a little community newsletter, *Stirling St. Newspaper*. We conducted interviews with the residents, editorialized about the city to the extent that we could, and drew people in the area together with this project.

The youth that worked with us in those days—Bobbie, Herbie, Larry, Junior, Stanley, Moosie, J.B., and the others—we grew very close to. Some of them are still our close friends, though they have grown up and are struggling right now to raise their own families. But in those days they were early teenagers full of all that energy and promise. They found they could come into the Spirit House and learn something. We gave them a newspaper to run, to write and print and distribute. We taught them to use business machines. We put them in plays. We got them politically in motion.

When we discovered that the children around Stirling Street had trouble reading the scripts I was writing, some of them especially written for youth, we went into the local school, Robert Treat, later changed to Marcus Garvey, and began to raise hell. The deeper we got into the community, the more openly political were our actions.

The concept of Black Power had reached me and I would walk around stenciling a black fist with the words "Black Power" over it. We had not completely focused on the meaning of the term, but we knew it was correct and ours! That year there were rebellions in Atlanta and Chicago, but the most shaking blast came out of the Hough section of Cleveland, where they called in two thousand National Guardsmen. Roy Wilkins denounced Black Power, and I wrote a poem saying, "I'monna stick half my sandal up his ass."

I was also finding out what was going on in the community at large and began easing into certain meetings. Hugh Addonizio was mayor of Newark, he and the Mafia, and he had a crew of niggers and Negroes crawling around on all fours working for him that would make any honest person's hair stand on end. My old college-years buddy Calvin West was jam up in that as a legacy from his sister, who'd always been "the man" of that family. Even her name, Larrie Stalks, suggested that. There were others, petty gunmen and pimps, muscle boys and dirty white-collar workers, who all slithered around using up our fresh air and replacing it with farts.

I was investigating, looking and listening, thinking about Black Power. I discovered, for one thing, that Newark was over 50 percent, maybe close to 60 percent, black. The idea of this set wheels turning inside my noggin. I didn't even peep myself. It was truly *Home*, like a replica of down home. Once in an antipoverty meeting supposedly open to the public, at the point where the community was supposed to vote on an issue, one of Addonizio's thugs, Jack Nicks, stood over some people and openly threatened them if they voted "incorrectly." It seemed like some straight-out fascism. A guy named Ken Gibson, a black guy, was running for mayor. I didn't follow it down to the detail, but I could check it from the corner of my eye. Somebody put caricatures of Gibson as a rat all over the city. Once, I saw black dudes pasting them up. I was still stenciling "Black Power" on abandoned buildings and sidewalks.

We were starting to have regular productions at the Spirit House and trying to raise an audience. Our theater could seat maybe fifty people if we squeezed. Stokely Carmichael had gotten arrested in Atlanta. The book *Home* was published. Also, I started Jihad Publications. *Jihad* means Holy War. Our first publication was a slim pamphlet of poetry, *Black Art*, with a cover photo showing young Larry Johnson (later Tarik) being trained in karate in the Spirit House by Clarence Reed's son, Clarence. People were coming to the plays and music and poetry, not only from the Stirling Street area but from all over Newark, and even from out of town. We had a small intense audience, an audience that influences others.

We were getting to be known not only by our community but by other forces. One night when we were rehearsing up in the loft, the Newark police crashed through the door and barked at us. They snatched the script out of my hands and took it, I guess, as evidence. But most likely they took it just to bust our balls.

One Sunday we had scheduled a poetry reading down at the loft and the police sent word that if we tried to hold the reading we would be arrested. I walked down the street to the loft and there were plainclothesmen all over the joint. They were going to stop any Black Power poetry before it started.

Barney got arrested in an old car I bought going for a juice one night late after rehearsal. He was arrested as being "suspicious" and we had to go down and bail him out. Everywhere we'd leave our mark. When I asked who was in charge in the precinct, the captain started screaming that I was gonna get arrested for being so presumptuous as to ask a question of these cavemen. Another of our friends was arrested over at a precinct on Runyon Street and we walked in to bail him out and told the desk sergeant that we could kick his ass and in fact would do it very soon. Anger and youth!

Added to this was the bad publicity that the media would hype us with. But some of it was our own doing. I had published a play, *Experimental Death Unit #1*, in the *Eastside Review*, which was edited by a guy named Shep Sherbell, who at the time was tight with Diane Wakoski, the poet. Sherbell promised me $100 for the play but I never got it. One night I saw him at a concert at a theater on Second Avenue. During the intermission I ask him for the money and he says he never promised me any money. The anti-white thing is working very strong. Barney and Donny were with Sylvia and me. Barney, Ben, and I always had a habit of getting into arguments with white folks. Whenever they said something we thought was off the wall, we'd jump on them. So that Sherbell's rap and his attempt to brush the matter off as some nigger lie I'd made up to hustle off him made smoke blow out my nose. In the flash of an eye we were rolling on the floor. *The New York Post* said, "LeRoi Jones Accused of Beating Publisher." That dragged on for a little while but was finally thrown out when Sherbell didn't show. Why only I had gotten charged when we'd had a fight in which we both participated I leave for you, gentle reader, to figure out. Diane Wakoski tearfully begged Sherbell to drop the charges but he wouldn't.

There was a deep anti-white feeling I carried with me that had grown deeper and deeper since I left the Village. I felt it was a maturing, but in some aspects it was that I was going off the deep end. To the extent that what I felt opposed white supremacy and imperialism, it was certainly correct. But to the extent that I merely turned white supremacy upside down and created an exclusivist black supremacist doctrine, that was bullshit. Bullshit that could only isolate me from reality.

But who was clear? Sylvia and I were trying to live and find out about each other. I was resolved that I would clean up and straighten up, that I would stop trying to make it with every attractive woman I came in contact with. Before, it was white ones, and then it changed to black ones, but it was much the same business, sad to report.

I also had to straighten out other parts of my life. I had been seeing my two daughters on the weekends when I was able to. They were getting older, growing up in the Village world. Nellie had never ceased to relate to my mother and father, especially my mother. The children had been her links and she was building strong (though, I think, devious) ties. Perhaps my mother thought (as Nellie might have too) that these black women I was with were just passing fancies and that one day I would get my good sense back and return to good-hearted Nellie. The idea that someone could think that makes my teeth grind. At any rate, the longer Sylvia and I lived together, the more complex the relationship between my mother and us and Nellie and the children became.

Sylvia and I had growing pains too. She got suddenly angry because I had not voluntarily thrown out the bed Bumi and I had cohabited in. Sylvia's anger distressed me. I had not known it was so sudden and direct nor as hot. Many people in Newark could have told me this about her had I been close to them. But I had to learn the hard way. We would also struggle about my disappearing late nights into the ghetto to go in and out of the taverns and hangouts, sopping up the atmosphere the way I liked to do. I might go out at midnight and hang in the Howard Bar or some real dive and sit there till the joint closed, sipping and listening and looking. My accountability in a living-together situation was not too strong. Downtown New York it was light at best, and even though it strengthened with Vashti, I was still unpredictable and spoiled and a stomp-down male chauvinist. And these struggles were to come up again and again.

The Newark community was restive, going through surface changes but also changes in psychology, like myself. The Addonizio thing was so low that only the basest mongrels could defend it. Even mediocre civil servants shuffling papers in the dark castle of City Hall, like Gibson, could see something was happening and something further still needed to happen. The undercurrents were no longer completely under; there were bubbles in the water that suggested deep turbulence. Calvin West won a City Council seat, so now there were two Negroes seated on the nine-member council. One an old-line blood who had had some note—even honor—as the first Negro councilman, Irvine Turner, an old friend of my family's. I had looked up to him as a child. But since then he had turned into his opposite. He was looked at now as an old Tom, mouth puckered from kissing Addonizio's ass for so long. Plus, he had grown senile in office and stared into space like a dead thing. He was now an object of ridicule.

Calvin was raised by his sister to be Addonizio's junior crony. And he had become that, exactly. We used to tease Calvin, when we were all college age, by rubbing the fingers of one hand together to suggest how dearly Cal loved dee dollar. With his little, naturally hoarse, high-pitched voice and comic-opera sense of style, hey, like a black homburg and big cigar— Mr. Big Time Negro heself!

This is what we had, like, to represent us. Even in our kid-operated *Stirling St. Newspaper* we began to raise the fact that Newark was over 60 percent black. We asked, "What do you think of having a black mayor?" And sent the kids up and down the block and around the corner to ask the questions like the inquiring reporter. We began to harass the school administration at Robert Treat to find out why the children couldn't read. "Wouldn't it be better to have a black principal at an all-black school?" we asked, not innocent at all.

I wrote leaflets, and circulated them, about the local situation and the national and international situation. We distributed them at the plays and dropped them off at meetings and put them in people's mailboxes. The FBI even suggested that I had circulated a leaflet on how to put together a Molotov cocktail. I found this out from a nigger I later discovered worked for the sheriff's office. One thing about the FBI, they're always trying to make you famous.

We began to take people down to the Board of Education, particularly to deal with the Robert Treat situation. Sylvia had gotten friendly with many of the women on the street, personally and through the block association. We were building ties and mutual support. We were friendly and intimate and Stirling Street resembled a country street down in the black belt most times. But Newark itself reminds one not a little of the black belt South, northern industrial city though it be.

Another issue that began to surface that year was the proposed building of a medical school in Newark's Central Ward. The authorities proposed that the medical school be built on 155 acres of land in the central city! This was supposed to mean that 23,000 black people would have to be moved out of the Central Ward. As this situation gradually surfaced, it became clearer and clearer that what was happening was an attempt by the white power structure to undermine completely any motion by the black majority population toward democracy and political power. It also came out that there was no medical school on the planet that took up 155 acres of land. One of the most prestigious medical schools in the United States, Johns Hopkins, took up only an acre and one half of land. This kind of information was distributed in the black community on a mass basis. As the hearings for the school began, at first the administration wanted to keep them closed—they didn't even want to have them. But the black community pushed, black agitators appeared, even those middle-classed blacks who simply wanted to run for office but who dug that without a constituency, running was futile. Hearings were called for. They were resisted, then they began to be held. And with each resistance, all that happened was a further building of momentum. Whitewash crews were put into the streets now to try to white out the Black Power signs we'd made ubiquitous. Different black groups began to emerge, as well as some white groups, like the visiting SDS spinoffs that people like Tom Hayden were associated with. The question of Black Power had set things in motion. The civil rights movement of the late '50s and early '60s was in the act of being transformed. A few years earlier, questions like whether to fight back, whether to turn the other cheek, how to resist, how much to struggle, had been dominant in the movement, put forward by the middle-classed black ideologues associated with people like Dr. King and the SCLC. But the civil rights movement was giving way to a Black Liberation movement. Jacksonville, Harlem, Watts had announced this. Hough had confirmed it.

One early evening, a short, stocky, bald man dressed in a green olive-drab dashiki, accompanied by two brothers dressed very similarly, came up to the top floor of the Spirit House to see me. The short, stocky man introduced himself as Ron Karenga, from Los Angeles. I didn't know the name. The two brothers with him also had African, Swahili, names. Both of them were also bald and wore the same kind of wooden pieces of African sculpture around their necks—talisimus.

We talked generally about the movement. But Karenga began by telling me he knew my work. He said he liked *Blues People*, but that he thought the blues were reactionary. That blues were talking about slavery and submission. I blinked and politely disagreed. But Karenga is nothing if not aggressive. He went on, elaborating his theories on culture and nationalism, talking at high speed nonstop, laughing at his own witticisms and having two members of a chorus, yea-saying, calling, "Teach!" when Karenga made some point he considered salient.

Surveying this dynamic fat little man, who spoke his mind with such authority, I could see things from the point of view of my highly styled conscious aesthetic that I questioned. The little cheap nondescript shoes, highly polished. The bargain basement overcoat and sale socks. But what that meant, I told myself later, was that I was some kind of elitist; trained that way by my long-term residence in and worship of the white elitist culture and aesthetic. This brother was more likely to be rooted with the people. (Now if you can dig the real elitism of that supposedly anti-elitist construct, then we in business. You mean they with the people cause they corny?! Gad!)

At any rate, I was obviously impressed by this visit. Karenga was in town, he told me, helping to plan the Second Black Power Conference. Adam Powell had called for the First, which was held in Washington, D.C, in 1966, with his declaration that black people must seek "audacious power."

Strangely, in a couple of months Sylvia and I were in San Francisco. Not to stay, but I had gone as a visiting professor at San Francisco State College, invited by its Black Student Union. The president of the BSU, Jimmy Garrett, had come to Newark, visited me, and asked me to come out to San Francisco to organize some cultural presence among the students. By now, Sylvia was pregnant and it was just beginning to show. We went West as "Mr. and Mrs. LeRoi Jones," and this rankled her in a way I didn't appreciate until later when she came out with it.

Garrett had impressed me as a deeply serious and willingly militant young man. Though I guess I also thought he was a trifle arrogant from the way he told me that "we [young people] don't say Negro anymore," when I had used "Negro" in some context. But it was good to see this kind of spirit.

The BSU at the time was pretty tightly organized with a strong sense of centralized leadership (Garrett's). They had an office on campus that I was to work out of. Later I got my own, still not far from the BSU's. I wanted to put together a "Communications Project," really a means of bringing black consciousness to the students and the community. I wanted to organize a company of students and community people to put together a repertory of plays and travel throughout the area and all this, the preparations, the plays, community response, travel, would also be filmed. This was my proposal. Garrett liked it, and we also got good support from artists in the area, principally Ed Bullins and Marvin X Jackmon. There were also people like Duncan Barber, Hilary Broadous, Carl Boissiere, who helped form the core of that company, even though they were not students. Plus, the students themselves participated, both as actors and as technical staff and publicists in a very enthusiastic, positive way. Emory Douglas, who became the Black Panther Party's "Revolutionary Artist," was my set designer and graphics specialist. George Murray, who became the BPP's Minister of Education, was the star of Ben Caldwell's *First Militant Minister*, which I directed for our tour.

San Francisco is a very special and lovely town, shrouded, it seems to me, in a kind of provincial charm, very colorful and exciting and even a trifle mysterious. It has a kind of bohemian character to it, not just from the herds of real and legendary bohemians who do animate the Fillmores and Haight-Ashburys and North Beaches; the landscape itself, those sharp rolling hills that the city is built upon, seems out of the ordinary—as if the landscape itself was some kind of bohemian. The weather, as well, is romantic, raincoats everyday, without a sharp winter or summer, just raincoats and then the bay and those two magnificent bridges, one going to Oakland and Berkeley, the other to hip Sausalito, where once I lived for a minute or so on a houseboat owned by Godfrey Cambridge, Shammy and I organizing tours of young black women to go back East.

Bullins and Marvin X were extremely supportive. They had put together Black Arts West, along with Duncan, Hilary, and Carl, down on Fillmore Street. Marvin X and the rest were into Islam (though I think only Duncan actually joined a mosque, in New York, and remained with the Nation fourteen years). Bullins was, in some senses, closer to my own type. He had been hooked up more directly with white bohemia and had stepped past it.

Working together, with us pushing the program from one direction and the students pushing from the other, we got a whole lot done and created a dynamic movement and program that reflected the tide of the times. Duncan, Hilary, and Carl were actors. Bullins and Marvin X were not only writers, they would help direct and connect the program with different aspects of the black community.

The repertory we put together to tour with ended up as Ed Bullins's *How Do You Do*, directed by Duncan and Ed, with Carl and Hilary in leads. *Taking Care of Business* by Marvin X. *We Own the Night* (with the title taken from a poem of mine) by Jimmy Garrett, which I directed. I also directed Ben Caldwell's *Militant Preacher* and my own *Mad Heart*.

In the programs we would also include poetry readings by Marvin X and myself as well as Sonia Sanchez, who had come out to live in San Francisco. There was a brother named Willie X, who wrote a song, which he sang much like Joe Lee Wilson, called "Babylon." These programs were heavily political and black-nationalist-oriented, with a strong overlay of Islam and other cultural nationalist tendencies. We traveled to schools all over the Bay Area as well as local halls in San Francisco. We even went down to Los Angeles and did the CORE convention, which is when I got a chance to see Karenga again.

The Communications Project had a great attraction for the young, politically turned-on blacks of the Bay Area. Here too, there were bubbles that suggested deep turbulence. It was early '67 and Watts was not even two years in the past. The Black Panther Party for Self-Defense had just formed, based across the bridge in Oakland. The audiences at Merritt College and Laney College, which were two heavy Panther enclaves, were some of our best. We also did performances outside in an Oakland park, Marvin X lighting people up with his poem "Burn, Baby, Burn!" which immortalized the mass cry that had come out of Watts as the bourgeoisie's property went up in smoke.

The Panther message was also being pushed afternoons out at San Francisco State, with literature and speakers. We began to do regular programs of poetry and music out there and so it all intensified. Our base in the community was at the Black House, which actually closely resembled the Black Arts in many ways. We rehearsed there and did regular programs of poetry and song. The Panthers pulled security for those programs, with armed brothers flanking the stage in a symbolic gesture showing the links between black revolutionary art and political struggle.

The day Bobby Seale and the Panthers went up to Sacramento with their guns, the state campus sparkled with anticipation. The word spread like only good news can. Black students were beaming from one end of the campus to the other. The real shit was not too far away, was what was in some of our minds. The real revolution is just around the corner, we felt. The photos of Bobby and Bobby Hutton on the front page with their heat strapped on or in hand did something wonderful to us. It pumped us up bigger than life. Black men demanding democracy and justice and ready to fight about it! Those were heady times.

On the campus, as we built our program and put the parts together, we began to get some opposition. A reactionary group of white students who had control over the student activities monies resisted giving the black students the funds necessary for our program. In the true spirit of white-racist-controlled anti-poverty programs, they wanted to give up mainly the monies to bring me out there and a little chump change for the actual program. They didn't want to give up any money for the film at all. And we had already got most of the program in motion, now we were being stopped.

But to show just how much of the spirit of those times animated different sectors of the black community, a meeting was called with the white student body that controlled the funds. This was to be a showdown. We had already talked back and forth in memos and letters, over the phone and in small conferences. But now this was to be the push. The people at Black Arts West and the Black House got the black community elements interested in this struggle, the most politically tuned-in elements, to come out to the mass meeting. The BSU mobilized the main body of black students.

When we got to the meeting place we were greeted not just by the white student government body which was refusing to give up the money, but these jokers had gone out and rounded up a group of white S.F. State athletes to be their security! White football players and wrestlers stood around the perimeter of the room, seeking to surround the group of us when we sat in the seats in the middle of the room. And it got even funnier. The speeches back and forth naturally got hotter and hotter. The place was bulging with people. I made a speech near the end characterizing the white students as student racists trying to get degrees in white supremacy so they could carry on the traditional U.S. program of black national oppression, but that we were going to stop their shit before it even got going good.

Finally, people were talked out. We had shown that, according to the percentage of blacks on campus and the amount they paid in student fees that were supposedly designed to create programs such as ours, the black students were not getting "too much money" but were being robbed, as usual. Now there were calls back and forth and that rising turbulence in a crowd that means very soon the shit will be on. One blood said, "We oughta just kick your ass," to the white students and their security and their white faculty advisers. There were some brothers and sisters from Fillmore, a mainly black community, and from Oakland, and they thought the only alternative was to "knock these motherfuckers out," as several put it very directly.

Hearing this, one of the white wrestlers stood up, big and burly, and shouted, "You wanna fight? You wanna fight? Hell, we'll fight you, if you fight fair."

At this point a short little black dude who obviously was not a student stood up and, almost like he was telling everybody the time of day, called, looking directly at the wrestler, "Fair? Shit, I'll break my motherfucking knife off in yo' head!" The meeting, for all intents and purposes, was over. We got the money.

Nathan Hare was also at San Francisco State during that period and he and Jimmy Garrett helped put together the first Black Studies program in the country. Humanitarian California? No, some niggers with guns had just walked into the California legislature. It was during this same period that black people got their first U.S. senator since Reconstruction (Edward Brooke of Massachusetts). For the same reasons. It ain't everybody that can go one hundred years between senators, not and be some thirty million folk!

I saw Eldridge Cleaver one afternoon at State. He had just got back from Alabama, where he'd interviewed Stokely Carmichael for *Ramparts* magazine. There were many tales about Cleaver at the Black House. He was going with a young sister, who was pregnant at the time, who rehearsed with us at the House. One sister, who was going with Marvin X at the time, told Sylvia that Cleaver was tipping around still seeing his lawyer and old love, Beverly Axelrod, who was white. The sisters around the Black House were highly critical of him for this. Plus, this same sister took Sylvia upstairs to peep in Eldridge's room. It was different from the rest of the house, which tended toward a minimalist militance as far as its furnishings went. Cleaver's digs were somebody's idea of plush, with wall-to-wall carpet and color television.

At State, Cleaver sat and listened to the poetry, the song. When we were finally introduced, he grimaced as if I had done something wrong to him. I had heard of Cleaver while he was still in San Quentin. Somebody had called him "the new Malcolm X." But he was curt and uncommunicative and I couldn't figure out why.

The CORE convention was being held a short time later and our entire Black Communications Project went down to perform. I was invited as well to read poetry at the headquarters of Ron Karenga's organization, US. Some people claim that US meant "United Slaves," but Karenga told me it meant just what it said, "US" as opposed to "THEM." I also attended what Karenga called the first Afro-American wedding in the United States. This was said because Karenga had put together a wedding ceremony, an Arusi, that drew on certain generalized African customs, "updated" and supposedly made relevant for black people in the United States.

Karenga did a great deal of work with culture. It was he who, with his organization, US, pushed a program that called for first having a "cultural revolution, to win the minds of our people," and then the political revolution would be a matter of course. So he put together a group of rituals, holidays, and programs that were aimed at politicizing black people with *blackness*. Karenga's line was that he was combining "tradition and reason"—i.e., what was traditional African with what had to be utilized from the American experience—to create a revolutionary Afro-American culture.

So the Arusi was one of these revolutionary rituals; the holiday, Kwanzaa, which is still very popular, as an alternative to Christmas, beginning December 26 and extending seven days until January 1, was another. The seven days of Kwanzaa corresponded with the Seven Principles or Nguzo Saba, upon which the US organization and Karenga's doctrine of Kawaida (African traditionalism) rested.

Swahili was used by Karenga, as he explained in his doctrine, ostensibly because it was a nontribal language, a kind of lingua franca for all the continent. So that the Seven Principles were to be memorized in Swahili as well as English. They were Umoja (Unity), Kujichagulia (Self-Determination), Ujima (Collective Work and Responsibility), Ujamaa (Collective Economics), Nia (Purpose), Kuumba (Creativity), Imani (Faith). The practice of these principles by black people would give them a new value system, theorized Karenga, a value system which would make them revolutionary.

There was also a pamphlet, *The Quotable Karenga*, which some of "the advocates," as members of the US organization were called, had put together, which consisted of quotes from Karenga. Karenga also had a formal *Doctrine*, some of it published in bits and pieces in the *Quotable*, some other parts in the *Kitabu*, the book of the Kawaida doctrine.

The advocates I saw looked well disciplined and dedicated. All had Swahili names. Karenga's practice was to give out a Swahili name as a last name, the way it existed in many East African countries, such as Tanzania, Kenya, Uganda. So that a person could be James Tayari or Ken Msemaji. Karenga gave out the names, naming each advocate according to his attributes. So Tayari meant "ready," implying that that advocate was *ready* to make revolution. Or because Msemaji meant "orator," it was given because Ken Msemaji could heavy rap! Just as I was impressed by Karenga's first appearance in my house, I was even more impressed by the images presented by this well-disciplined organization. By the seeming depth and profundity of his Kawaida doctrine. I felt undisciplined and relatively backward. Here was organization. The worst thing a person could be, as far as Karenga was concerned, was Ovyo, a Swahili word meaning "random," a person acting at random, disorganized and unpredictable. This was the problem with the "basic blood," as Karenga called blacks. No values or the values of their oppressors; no organization except the church.

Karenga's doctrine, as I found out after following it politically and socially for eight years, was very eclectic. He had borrowed and copped from some-a everybody. Not only Elijah Muhammad (Karenga had once been in the Nation), but Nkrumah, Fanon, Touré, Nyerere, Garvey, Malcolm, all ran through his doctrine, plus Mao and even Lenin and Stalin and Marx. Karenga hid the bits and pieces he had taken from the white revolutionaries. Even today I think that there is much in Karenga's doctrines that is valid. Certainly the idea that oppressed people practicing and believing in the values of their oppressors cannot free themselves is true and unchallengeable. But what are those values that will oppose black oppression and where do we find them? The idea that somehow we had to go back to pre-capitalist Africa and extract some "unchanging" black values from historical feudalist Africa and impose them on a 20th-century black proletariat in the most advanced industrial country in the world was simple idealism and subjectivism. Cultural nationalism uses an ahistorical, unchanging never-never-land Africa to root its hypotheses. The doctrine itself is like a bible of petty bourgeois glosses on reality and artification of certain aspects of history to make a recipe for "blackness" that again gives this petty bourgeoisie the hole card on manners to lord it over the black masses, only this time "revolutionary" manners. Cabral and Fanon also expose this to the core, but Karenga only quotes bits and pieces. The fact that he could quote only bits and pieces of Mao shows how this quoting out of context to make a point works. So that Karenga could "borrow" from anyone, even those whom he disagreed with or who were saying some things absolutely opposite to what he was. It was the fact of Karenga's education (a Ph.D. student in African history and languages) and his nervy aggressiveness that gave him a leadership quality. He had the ability to take from anything and synthesize something that one could identify as "his." What he had created was a cultural nationalist organization that had aspects of, and indeed became, a *cult*. Karenga was *Maulana*, self-named, as he named all the advocates, "the master teacher." Karenga means "nationalist." So he was the Master Teacher of Nationalists.

Because I was so self-critical, especially from a black nationalist perspective, the fact of the US organization—i.e., that it was an organization and not just a bunch of undisciplined people taking up time mostly arguing with each other about what to do, or what method to use, even about things that most agreed should be done—that I was drawn to the US and Karenga. He was quick-witted, sharp-tongued, with a kind of amusing irony to his putdowns of white people, America, black people, or whatever, that I admired. Plus, there was no doubt, when you were around Karenga, as to who was *the* leader, even if you weren't in his organization. And if you were, *all* things revolved around Maulana. He named the advocates, married them, named their children, even suggested where they should work and live. When I first came out to L.A., many of the advocates lived very close together, several in the same housing development. In fact, I thought maybe Karenga owned this one development, because not only did he live there but his principal security lived on either side, plus some of the other important people in the organization lived both downstairs on the first floor as well as on the floor above.

It seemed to me the kind of next-higher stage of commitment and organization as compared to the Black Arts or what was going on in the Spirit House in Newark. There was a military aspect to it, a uniformity that I regarded then as indispensable to any talk of black revolution. Also, Karenga's doctrine, some of which had been printed, summarized and ordered an approach to the revolution we sought. He had various lists, like the Nguzo Saba, but in almost any category you could think of. There were the Three Criteria of a Culture, Three Aspects of a Culture, Two Kinds of Revolution, Seven Aspects of Malcolm X, all of which were for memorization purposes. Advocates were questioned about these parts of the doctrine and were supposed to respond with the answers by rote.

There was a heavy emphasis on karate, named Yangumi by Karenga to give it an African cast. His security was always armed. All the advocates had shaven heads, "in mourning for African people," and the high-collared olive-drab bubbas with the US emblem and the talisimus added a kind of neo-African military quality to the organization that impressed me and I suppose a bunch of other people. It seemed that Karenga was serious. In my right-around-the-corner version of the revolution, I thought that Karenga represented some people who were truly getting ready for the revolution.

Even the day-to-day greeting Karenga had stylized and "Africanized": "Habari Gani" ("What's happening?") was the greeting and the response was "Njema" ("Fine") or "Njema, Sante Sante" ("Fine, thank you"). The men shook hands with one hand on their arm and then pounded their right fist on their chest, something like the Roman legionnaires. Greeting women, one crossed one's arms and embraced each cheek. When Karenga passed, advocates would pop their fist to their chest, the women "submit" — i.e., cross their arms on their breasts and bow slightly in an Afro-American adaptation of West African feudalism.

Because, also, Karenga's whole premise was of cultural revolution, I was pulled closer. Being a cultural worker, an artist, the emphasis on culture played to my own biases. And no doubt in a society where the "advanced forces" too often put no stress on culture and the arts at all, I thought his philosophy eminently correct. Culture and the arts can be used to help bring the people to revolutionary positions, but the culture of the black masses in the U.S. is an African American working-class culture. The "revolutionary culture" we must bring to the masses is not the precapitalist customs and social practices of Africa, but heightened expression of the lives and history, art and sociopolitical patterns of the masses of the African American people stripped of their dependence on the white racist monopoly-capitalist oppressor nation and focused on revolution. All nationalism leads to exclusivism and chauvinism, and the imposition of old social forms from earlier, less advanced periods can only lead to reaction and backwardness. But because African Americans have suffered from cultural aggression, having their culture and history attacked, their art denied or defined as "primitive," they are naturally attracted to things African. The attraction is correct, but all cultures, as Lenin says, reflect both the ruled and the rulers of any nation. And what is the irony of black people celebrating some of the very African kings and queens who sold them into slavery in the first place?

It is Cabral who said that the African petty bourgeoisie, because they were too often exposed only to the master's culture and history, when they become radicalized want to identify with things African as much as possible. This was obviously my problem, and Karenga's US was a perfect vehicle for working out the guilt of the overintegrated.

After my trip to L.A. I remained in close contact with Karenga and very quickly I assimilated the Kawaida doctrine and began pushing it wherever I went.

When I got back to San Francisco, a strange thing had happened. Cleaver had gotten the Panthers, ostensibly through Huey Newton, to throw the artists, many of whom were cultural nationalists of one kind or another, out of the Black House, saying that all the artists were "reactionary." I had heard before I had gone to L.A. that Cleaver was going to Socialist Worker Party meetings and I thought this strange. We had just gone through a "get away from whitey" push in the East. That, I thought, was the root action of revolutionary motion, getting away from white people. What was with Cleaver? I didn't understand. The idea of his being Marxist-influenced I wasn't clear on. Some weeks later the Black Panther paper came out with an editorial warning black nationalists not to attack the Panthers' revolutionary allies. Did they mean hippies, the flower children, or white women lawyers? There was never any clear ideological breakdown of what was going on, no clear polemics with the nationalists. There was just the summary breaking up of the Black House and the creation of an even deeper split in the movement which was to go down a few years later. But from the time of the Black House split, I always thought Cleaver was aptly named, because he was one of the important catalysts in the deadly split that soon went down in the Black Liberation movement.

It had never occurred to me that a variation of what had gone down inside the Black Arts could happen again on a larger scale. But it did, and even worse. But at this point there was still some effort by various developing factions to work together. Sometime after the Black House ouster, the artists who had been around the Black House and the Black Communications Project agreed to do a benefit for the Panthers. That was during the period just before the Panthers tried to "draft" Stokely Carmichael and Rap Brown. Stokely and Rap appeared at this benefit, along with Huey, Bobby Seale, and Eldridge. I directed BSU head Jimmy Garrett's play *We Own the Night*, with Willie X as the black youth revolutionary and poet/radio host, Judy Simmons as his domineering mother, whom the youth shoots when she tries to warn the police of the black revolutionaries' plans. This last act got a roaring standing ovation from the capacity audience.

We continued to travel all over the Bay Area with the Communications Project repertory, and some of the actors and technicians who were being drawn into the Panthers still contributed to the project. But there was talk and rumors about the widening currents of the split in the movement. We got the film equipment and were moving ahead putting the film together. When it was finished it was called *Black Spring*. One of its main sequences was the Panther benefit.

All during this period in San Francisco, I had left Sylvia at home more and more. I thought it was because she didn't want to run back and forth to the Black House after I came back from the campus, but what it was, was that I would simply go from the campus to the Black House or, after the ouster, from the campus to wherever we would be rehearsing (for a minute it was over Richardson's Garvey bookstore). She resented this, though she would go out occasionally with Sonia Sanchez and the brother Sonia lived with at the time, Chuck, the father of her twins. Sylvia was, by this time, very pregnant. The program was drawing to a close and she was anxious to get back to Newark, afraid the baby would be born in San Francisco. We still had not finished the film and I didn't want to leave until we did. So that was one basic bone of contention, though the selfishness of putting the film before the woman or the child-to-be should be obvious. Male chauvinism disguised as dedication to Art.

We struggled about what would go down and in the end I put her on a plane, weeping under my chauvinism. When I got back to Newark a few weeks later, my first son, Obalaji Malik Ali, was a week old. He had been born while I was in San Francisco. I had let Sylvia have the baby alone.

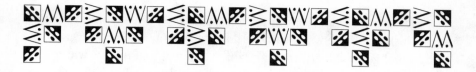

Ten

A Continuing Journey

The same motion that had been rising when we left Newark was at a higher point when I got back. The hot bubbling surface speaking of depths of frustration and unrest. The medical school issue had gotten even sharper. There were several different groups contending with the powers about this obvious ripoff, and a main coalition pulling people together to fight was agitating throughout the city. I got active in this and drew the forces around the Spirit House very active in this as well. Groups of us would go to the meetings and attack the various administration spokesmen, city or state. I also began to identify various groups and trends in the city and enter into general discussions about Newark politics. It had become obvious to me that, since Newark was at least 60 percent black, Black Power here meant that we had to control the politics of the city. I printed leaflets and stated this thesis in the issues of the *Stirling St. Newspaper*. When I made public appearances I would dwell on this issue, intent on raising the national consciousness of the black masses in Newark.

Another equally incendiary issue was the question of the appointment of a secretary to the Board of Education. Wilbur Parker, a black CPA, had gotten to be the favorite of the black community for the job. He had a master's degree and was certainly academically and technically qualified.

But Addonizio resisted. He wanted to appoint one of his cronies, as usual. In this instance there was a catch. Addonizio's man, Callahan, was only a high school graduate. His major qualification was that he was white. Like the medical school conflict, this issue was one that could tighten the jaws of all classes of blacks, whether black workers or black professionals. Both issues were attacks on the whole of the black community.

Another factor in the general increase of tension was the constant incidents of police brutality. The Newark police whipped heads with impunity under the neo-fascist police director Dominick Spina, a "kindly" gray-haired administrator who reminded me of one of Mussolini's murderers. I had had already, since returning home, several direct conflicts with Spina, and not just the general ones. In any public gathering where he was, I never resisted the opportunity to talk bad to and about him. I was told later, by one of Spina's paid informers, that Spina was a member of the Klan. It seemed that the Klan in New Jersey had become progressive enough to recruit Catholics.

We were still putting on plays and using the Spirit House for community meetings, broadening the block association and focusing much heat up at the Robert Treat school. Newark was a city of widespread and clearly understood corruption. Everybody in public office was known to be on the take, and not just from hearsay—most people had had some direct experience of it. Calvin West was one of Addonizio's "classiest" niggers and Cal had the kind of personality that might make one spray a room with Lysol after he'd passed through it with one of his outsized cigars.

All these things were in the bubbling. Black Power pressed these issues at a higher level. It pointed out the straight-out apartheid in the South and the neo-apartheid in the North. It raised the issue of black political self-determination and the need for self-sufficiency. The Nation of Islam preached about "doing for self" and how black people were indeed oppressed by the filthy white devil. Black nationalists talked about "the beast" getting big on black people's flesh, and Addonizio and company were living proof of all these nationalist examples. And I'm sure the "left," wherever it was, was also pushing in whatever ways it could. Tom Hayden and his classmates were around being "troublemakers," which could only add yeast to the whole mixture.

Adam Powell had gotten removed from Congress over some obvious bullshit, though white liberals would've told you, "We've formed the Urban Coalition and just appointed Thurgood Marshall as the first Negro on the Supreme Court." But as it got warmer that summer, all talk of white liberals just added some numbers to the thermometer. All over the country black people were marching or rising up. You heard often not only of Dr. King and the Nation of Islam but of Stokely and Rap and Huey Newton and the Panthers, of CORE and SNCC and Black Power. The newspapers and television, the radio and people's mouths, carried the word. Even the *New York Times* that year reported that the civil rights movement was over. I don't remember if they remarked on the rising motion of the Black Liberation movement. There was an antiwar movement against the U.S. involvement in Vietnam that was also in motion. Even Dr. King had announced his intention to come out against the war. A current of dissent was everywhere, open rebellion was not only justified and justifiable, but examples of it were growing ubiquitous: demonstrations, marches, sit-ins, arrests, civil disobedience, clashes with the police, cities going up in smoke. There was, in Newark, an atmosphere of oppressive tension. As spring moved into summer, each day and evening held a quiet, heavy aura. It was clear the medical school was going ahead, the largest on the planet. It was clear that Callahan would get the job and not Parker. Spina's blueshirts had run into a Muslim home near East Orange because it was reported that there were men in the building "armed." No arms were ever produced, though the place did serve as a kind of "dojo" for martial arts training, which apparently pissed Spina off. His boys shot the place up and brutalized some people. That word was passed around swiftly and bitterly.

We had been building a following at the Spirit House. We were rehearsing plays. Giving poetry readings. We even made a record, "Black and Beautiful," with rhythm and blues and chants and poetry of black struggle and nationalism.

Sylvia and I had also been struggling, in a different way. The child had come, Obalaji, and I viewed this with the mystical focus I had then. It was very significant to me that the white woman, Nellie, had not produced a boy child, only girls. It was clear I had gone in the right direction (more chauvinism). The boy was named after a young boy I'd known in Harlem with Oserjeman's temple, a little fresh dude full of life. Obalaji (God or the King's Warrior), Malik for Malcolm, and Ali after Muhammad Ali. But for all that, I was not ready to get married. I had not thought of it. It seemed unnecessary. Yet my son was on the scene. Sylvia and I had traveled around together, I had taken her with me on many of the poetry readings and speaking trips I went on. I had been drawn to her deep, lovely sensuality. The San Francisco business had created a tension between us I would forget more quickly than she. How selfish and subjective men can be when it comes to women. I knew I wanted Sylvia. I knew I wanted us to live together. I was full of joy that we had had a son. Yet I did not think we had to get married. It was half bohemianism, some plain-out insensitivity, but may it not have been also a kind of unconscious disregard for black women? I had offered to marry Nellie in a similar situation. Yet, with Sylvia, there I was haggling and contentious about the same kind of act. The irony is that I felt closer to Sylvia, we were more "together," there was much more heat to our relationship, much more passion. I had even been moved to the point of telling her how much I loved her, which I could not do before with women I'd been with, even Vashti, even though I'd taken the sparkling relationship we'd had as a love relationship.

Our explosions inside the Spirit House were in tune with the whole siege of tension that stalked the day-to-day streets of the slowly simmering town. There might have been rumors about us up and down those streets just as there were broader rumors twisting through the streets of the whole city as it heated up and hidden tension became open tension, and open tension became confrontation.

One afternoon I heard something about a demonstration over at the precinct across from the Hayes Homes. It was about a cabdriver who'd gotten beaten by the police the night before. When we got there, there were maybe fifty to one hundred people. It was still afternoon and most people were still working, so this was a good crowd on the line. It was thick over there. There were younger people standing across the street, watching, occasionally calling out or laughing. The picket line was being led, ostensibly, by CORE and its chairman in Newark, Bob Curvin. We talked briefly, and the couple of us who'd come over from the Spirit House got in the line. There were young people and middle-aged on the line. They chanted and walked and as we joined them it was obvious to me that it was not like a picket line at a strike or the lighter kinds of demonstrations. People talked, but there was a presence on the line and in the scattered crowd that gathered on the other side of the narrow street. It was the same precinct where we had demonstrated for a black police captain to replace one of Spina's cronies. It was like the air itself was a container for something that was pushing against it trying to break out. People turned and looked at each other, sensing this presence. They grinned nervously or squinted up at the precinct at the mostly white police who stood outside frozen or the ones who would occasionally scowl through the windows of the precinct or move quickly by, snarling, as they got out of their police cars and went into the building.

After an hour or so, the couple of us from the Spirit House got off the line, which was still moving, more people having come, others splitting. We had to go home to get ready for rehearsal and another community meeting. So we started to go home, rolling slowly across Belmont Avenue, past the abandoned Krueger brewery and over to Springfield Avenue. It seemed there were knots of people, ever moving, people in small groups, looking, peering, as if they too sensed what was ready to loose itself.

It was later in the afternoon when we got to the Spirit House. I had to eat. Sylvia and the boy were there, also Barney's girlfriend, Beverly, and Shorty's friend, Helen, who was an old friend of Sylvia's. We ate and talked and began to get ready for the evening when some of the young boys who came in and out of the Spirit House rushed in. "They're breaking windows on Springfield Avenue" was the word. Moving outside, it looked, for some reason, like the sky had a long, wide reddish streak to it. It was low and wanted to burn. It sizzled and carried images and words, buzz turning to roar. Its smell got in your nose and made you blink. You could see people in motion, like a slow-motion flick speeded up. Moving in all directions.

We stood for a second, all of us from in the house. Then Shorty, Barney, and I jumped in the bus; it was a new Volkswagen I'd bought recently, but I still didn't know how to drive. "Where're you going?" Sylvia called, and I said something, but we were around the corner and onto Springfield Avenue. When we got there the shit was already on! Farther up the street we could see figures moving fast. The sun was falling to hide them quick. Suddenly, sirens. We could see some smoke, hey, then glass started to break close to where we were.

The spirit and feeling of the moment a rebellion breaks out is almost indescribable. Everything seems to be in zoooom motion, crashing toward some explosive manifestation. As Lenin said, time is speeded up, what takes years is done in days, in real revolution. In rebellions life goes to 156 rpm and the song is a police siren accompanying people's breathless shouts and laughter. (See "Newark: Before Black Men Conquered.")

All that was pent up and tied is wild and loose, seen in sudden flames and red smoke, and always people running, running, away and toward. We wheeled the wagon around and began to head up toward what looked like the eye of what was growing mad and gigantic and hot. We went straight up Springfield, not fast, not slow, but at a pace that would allow a serious observer to dig what was happening. It had got dark fast, like the dashing bloods had reached up and pulled night down by its silver string and slam! it was down and they got on with they shit.

Boxes of stuff were speeding by, cases of stuff, liquor, wine, beer, the best brands. Shoes, appliances, clothes, jewelry, food. Foodtown had turned into Open City, some dudes jumped the half story out the window to the ground. There were shifts of folks at work. The window breakers would come first. Whash! Glass all over everywhere. Then the getters would get through and get to gettin'. Some serious people would park near the corner and load up their trunks, make as many trips as the traffic would bear. Some people would run through the streets with shit, what they could carry or roll or drag or pull. Families worked together, carrying sofas and TVs collectively down the street. All the shit they saw on television that they had been hypnotized into wanting they finally had a chance to cop. The word was Cop & Blow! And don't be slow.

Then the fire setters, Vulcan's peepas, would get on it. Crazy sheets of flame would rise behind they thing. Burn it up! Burn it up! Like Marvin had said: Burn, baby, burn! They were the most rhythmic, the fire people, they dug the fire cause it danced so tough, and these priests wished they could get as high and hot as their master the Flame.

Now we circled and dashed, zigzagged, tried to follow the hot music's beat. We were digging, checking, observing, participating, it was a canvas, a palette no painter could imagine. A scale no musician could plumb. (Why do you think Trane and Albert sounded like that? They wanted the essence of what flailed alive on all sides of us now.)

The police were simply Devils to us, Beasts. We did not understand then the scientific exegesis on the state—though we needed to. Devils! Beasts! Crisscrossing in their deadly stupor of evil. The people were like dancers whirling around and through the flames. A motorcycle leaped through Sears's window! with a blood, head down, stuck to it, booting and smoking up Elizabeth Avenue. Rifles strapped to his back. The last firearms sold legally in Newark disappeared in all directions out of Gene's and the same Sears. Devil-cars spinning meanwhile as they shot at everything that moved, everything with any grace.

We moved through looking until the rage and madness's dazzle had reached its peak. I thought it must be like what a war is, to be in the middle of it. Then we saw people getting hit. The Devils were spraying the dancers; they were enraged by their own poison. We saw a man fall near Springfield and Belmont and the police quickly swallowed him up. We had to move quickly and keep some distance and the correct angle between ourselves and them. At Belmont and Spruce we saw another brother hit, he fell into a sitting position, shot through the leg. Blood streamed down his pants and the case of shit he was carrying was smashed to the ground. His legs stuck out into the street, a car twisting suddenly around the corner would have mashed both of them off. We pulled up and dragged him into the van, then we sped off toward the city hospital.

Inside the hospital it was really a war zone. People were staggering in, people bandaged everywhere. Police brought some in. We brought the brother, Rabbit, carrying him like he was in a chair. Blood on the floors and walls, smeared on aprons, falling out of people in gasps. We got a doctor to look at him. Talked to Rabbit, who was trying to smile, he had been talking a mile a minute in the car. He seemed OK, and there were too many police in the joint so the three of us got back in the wind.

It was late at night now as we spun round and round in the streets. It looked like the crowds were somewhat thinner. We had picked up Tom Perry a little earlier and he was with us too, ducking and dodging through the streets that night. Another hour or so, another couple people picked up, and we went down to the Key Club for a drink. As wild as it seemed, there were people in there, a few, sipping and talking low about what was loose in the streets. We met Grachan Moncur, another hip Newark boy, we went past his crib and passed the peace pipe around, talked some more about what the future held for ourselves and our people.

It was very late now. Leaving Grachan's we headed up the hill to where Tom was staying. He came over now regularly because his daughter Tania was staying with his mother. His wife, Maureen, had run off with one of Monk's less exciting bass players. That had been the corniest thing that had happened to Tom since he had got old enough to bring some control into his life. And it finished him. He went from merely chippying as a working man who liked to get high regularly but not dependent to somebody chasin' the bag for a dying. One of my dearest friends, Tom later moved to Harlem, where he died violently in some drug-related situation. One of the hippest and kindest and sweetest people I had the pleasure to know well and swing with. I loved to see Tom coming, his whole life was style. And in the end it was an uncool world that killed him. (I said to him once—we were talking about his slow plunge into the abyss—simply, "Why?" And his answer: "I know what you're talking about. With what I know, you want to know why I don't live according to religion." Tom meant Zen and the Mahayana doctrine of the Wisdom Religion. That was our last conversation.)

But now, we were shaking hands. "It was a great night," he was saying. "A really great night." He stood on his mother's stoop watching us pull off.

The streets were quiet, eerie quiet, and it was pitch black and maybe one in the morning. We were moving slowly down South 7th Street—we had crossed Springfield and were approaching South Orange Avenue—when we saw the lights. Red lights like vicious eyes blinking. A riot of red lights blinking. Like Devils or pieces of hell. We were slowing down, and the lights seemed to get frantic, batting and winking, little silent splinters of scream. Then we could see under the streetlights piles of police cars, maybe five or six. For one instant we started to stop and back up or try to U-turn or even speed up on the sidewalk and go past. But the fantasy had stopped. All of us could sense that if we did anything we would die. We could see the shotguns and helmets. They had the street blocked and as we slowed pulling up to them we looked at each other and got ourselves ready.

A mob of police surrounded the van, two of them pulling open the front and back doors. They had their shotguns and handguns trained on us as they dragged us out the doors. Shorty, Barney, and I. I heard one guy say, "These are the bastards who've been shooting at us!"

Another shouted, "Where are the guns?"

Then another cop stepped forward, I think he was saying the same thing. What was really out is that this cop I recognized, we had gone to high school together! His name was Salvatore Mellillo. The classic Italian American face. "Hey, I know you," I said, just as the barrel of his .38 smashed into my forehead, dropping me into half-consciousness and covering every part of me with blood. Now blows rained down on my head. One dude was beating me with the long nightstick. I was held and staggering. The blood felt hot in my face. I couldn't see, I could only feel the wet hot blood covering my entire head and face and hands and clothes. They were beating me to death. I could feel the blows and the crazy pain but I was already removed from conscious life. I was being murdered and I knew it. I screamed, "Allahu Akbar. Al Homdulliah!" Spitting the rage and pain back out at them.

But then I could hear people shouting at them. Voices calling, "You bastards, stop it. Stop it. You're killing them. Motherfucking bastards, stop it." From the windows black people were shouting at the police. From a tall apartment building overlooking the scene. People screamed at them. They started throwing things.

I could hear the policemen shouting at each other. "Put 'em in the car. Put 'em in the car!" But once in the car, the torrent of blood was falling out of my head so fast that one of them started cursing. "Get him out of the fucking car. He's bleeding all over the fucking car!" I never lost consciousness, but I lapsed into an even lower state of semiconsciousness. I felt myself being lifted into the paddy wagon.

The next thing I knew I was being dragged out of the wagon and up the back stairs of the police station. Just before we went through the door of the station, one of the police dragging me wheeled me around and tried to drive his knee into my nuts, but I slipped it or he just missed. "You faggot," I was screaming. Shit, I knew I would make it now!

Inside the police station I was thrown on the floor in front of a high desk and then dragged to my feet. I could see in front of me the police director, Dominick Spina. He was smiling, his neck and head like one grizzly object of yellowish skin with grey crew-cut hair.

"Mr. Spina," I called. "Hello, Mr. Spina." I wanted to say more but my energy was failing me rapidly.

He turned and looked at me. "They got you," he said with the forthrightness of a well-advertised poison. He continued to smile.

"I'm alive," I said. "You didn't kill me."

He nodded and the police roughed me away.

So I was locked up the first night of the Newark rebellion. In its entirety the rebellion went on for six days or so. Thousands of blacks were arrested and thousands more were injured. The official score was 21 blacks killed and 2 whites, a policeman and a fireman. But there were many more blacks killed, their bodies on roofs and in back alleys, spirited away and stuck in secret holes. It was no riot, it was a rebellion. The $10 million damage, mostly in the black community, was mainly to white businesses. Whole blocks of small white businesses disappeared, never to reappear again. The Kerner Commission stated that the only way to change the cities was to "enhance the ghetto," which ain't happening, or convince the blacks to leave. So the Newarks of the U.S. still exist like they did in 1967, trying to drive the blacks out to the hopeless exurbs, so that the whites can urban renew, having found out the ancient teaching of Ibn Arabi is true, that the cities are the chief repositories of culture and the highest thrust of human life. Plus, they are the banking, communications, and transportation centers. Or having read Mao they know that the socialist revolutions in the Western industrial countries *will begin in the cities* and then move out to the countryside.

And these rebellions, check with Kerner, were not the work of the lumpen, i.e., those crushed already by capitalism, the pimps and prostitutes, dope addicts, that "dangerous class." The rebellions were the handiwork, in the main, of the disenfranchised young black workers, enraged at racism and exploitation.

I was taken to the Newark Street jail (Essex County Prison), a joint I used to see all the time in my youth. Either walking with my grandmother over to the election-machine warehouse on Wilsey Street where my grandfather was night watchman or playing baseball in the huge vacant lot across from the jail. I had always wondered what went on behind those walls and now I would find out.

I was put in solitary confinement by a Negro who had been an old friend of my father, "Jazz" Jones, who later testified in court that I had not been in solitary confinement. What was so strange about being in jail then is that we still knew that there was a rebellion going on outside. We could look out the windows even during the daytime and see its effects. One day, in the middle of the afternoon, we spotted a car coming around the corner and up New Street. The National Guard had been brought into the city and they were staked out in the vacant lot across from the jail. We could see them clearly from inside the prison. As the car came up the street the Guardsmen started firing at it. They didn't know who was in the car or where it was going. I guess they could see it was black people inside. The firing brought the car to a halt and it was quickly surrounded. One door opened and a black man and woman stumbled out. The woman was wounded and was staggering and bleeding. A couple of the Guardsmen seized her and dashed her against a factory wall. The woman was slumping, obviously wounded from the gunfire. The man backed against the wall with his hands up.

All the inmates started screaming out the jail. There was no way the Guardsmen could hear us, but the cops inside the prison could and they walked around calling for order. I was screaming, "We need to do the same thing to some white bitch." The cops ran up and down telling the inmates to shut up, but they kept screaming.

That night someone started shooting at the prison. They shot the lights out around the walls. The firing was coming from one of the factory roofs that extended down the block across the street from the jail. You could hear the pop, pop, pop of what sounded like a .22. Then the National Guardsmen opened up, blasting in the direction of the one .22 for about ten minutes. Then all was silence, except in the prison the guards turned up the canned music until it was almost screaming. It was Patti Page singing "We'll Be Together Again."

The Guardsmen were so frightened they had a tendency just to shoot and shoot without even bothering to aim or look squarely in the direction of what they were firing at. (Probably it was something in their own heads. The state policemen, on the other hand, were straight-out murderers. The job they did on a young boy they caught trying to liberate some liquor from Jo-Rae's tavern on Bergen Street was one grim example. The boy was shot over thirty-five times. He had six or seven slugs through the top of his head. I got hold of the photo of his autopsy after I got out, printed it up, and circulated it. The police and sheriff's department tried to catch us and lock us up for circulating the photo. The bloody killers were heroes!)

The same night of the shooting into the jail there was an escape plan that was supposed to be carried out. Word of this got to me and I agreed to go along with it, but I did not think we would make it. I wrote a piece in my notebook (published in *Raise Race Rage Raze*) which was meant to be a parting statement. It is full of Islamic and other metaphysical symbolism. It also speaks of my "wife," Sylvia, who was not then my wife, and what she had taught me, even by then, of my own elitism and selfishness. It is a demand that black people evolve to a higher stage of life, an evolution that can be brought about only by *fire*!

When I was released on $25,000 bail, which was got by putting up some of my mother's friends' houses for collateral, I discovered that the case was a cause célèbre. First of all, $25,000 bail in those days was higher than most bails—it was a blatant ransom. The racist Judge Del Mauro, who was later removed from office for improprieties, gloated like a hate junkie full of his favorite drug when he called out the bail. As the Black Liberation movement went on, the bails got higher and higher, but the $25,000 was a landmark for that time, 1967.

Returning to the community it felt like a war had been waged and was still going on. The rebellions brought clarity to many blacks about who they were and where they were and who the U.S. government was. Tanks had rolled up and down these streets. Blacks had been stopped and searched like in Nazi movies. To get up on Stirling Street, where the Spirit House was, one had to show ID. And all the time I was in the slam the police and National Guard harassed my family, Sylvia and my baby son, Obalaji. One night they shot into the windows and Sylvia and the child had to get into a closet. Then the next night they broke into the theater and tossed things around and broke things up. They went down into the basement, where I had printing machines, and destroyed what they could, papers and materials. They started up the stairs, wandered around on the second floor, and started up to the third floor, where Sylvia and Obalaji lay crouched in the same closet. She was trying to keep the little baby quiet and he was quiet, remarkable for such a tiny baby. She had prepared some Afro-American napalm, lye and hot water, to throw on them if they came through the door, but fortunately they did not. Satisfied with the destruction they were able to commit, they left.

One evening the noted religionist, activist, and educator Nathan Wright picked up Sylvia and the baby so that he could find out what he could do to help and get information for one of his articles. When they came back from his spacious home in South Orange, they were stopped on High Street. The National Guard would not let Wright drive up into Stirling Street, so he let Sylvia and the baby go up the hill to the Spirit House by themselves.

But the most indelible evening of the rebellion for me was the night I had got beaten. After the police station they had taken me up to City Hospital. The "doctor," a white man with glasses, peered at me and asked was I the poet? I told him. He said, "Well, you'll never write any more poetry!" Then he gave me fifteen stitches on my forehead and another five in the hairline, with no anesthetic, like some primitive Gestapo butcher.

I was left in the hallway, handcuffed to a wheelchair, completely covered with the drying blood, my head on fire. Then I heard Sylvia screaming in the hallway. She had run, barefoot, from Stirling Street to the hospital, at least ten or twelve blocks, after a brother named Otis had called his mother on Stirling Street, letting her know that he had seen me getting beaten. His mother told Tarik's mother and she came across the street and told Sylvia, who gave the baby to the women at the house to mind and took off, frantically running to the hospital.

She was screaming at the policemen, hammering at them. There were two of them standing near the wheelchair, as if I would break the handcuffs and do something wild. "Are you going to kill me now?" she was screaming. "Are you going to make me look like this?" A black cop intervened and pulled her away. The white cops were cursing her and I was weakly straining to come up out of the chair. But I could barely raise my head. This was it, the real America, the America of slavery and lynching. I could feel an absolute kinship with the suffering roots of African American life.

Ironically, the Second Black Power Conference opened in Newark just as the rebellion was subsiding. Karenga, Rap Brown, Phil Hutchinson of SNCC, Gaidi of the Republic of New Africa (RNA), all came up to the

Spirit House for a press conference which I had called, demanding intervention by the UN, showing the photos of the brutal murder of the young boy at Jo-Rae's. We raised Malcolm's correct dictum that the black struggle in the U.S. was the struggle of a non-self-governing people against genocidal oppressors.

Carmichael had gotten arrested in Atlanta, and a rebellion had jumped off down there. Rebellions popped like deadly firecrackers in city after city that summer. But the week after the Newark rebellion, Detroit went up in even more flames. Forty-three dead, over 7000 people arrested, $44 million damage. They brought in 14,000 paratroopers and National Guard. Yeh, even the airborne, with machine guns, because bloods in Detroit had come up with automatic weapons, not just the pop-pop of .22s.

For me, the feeling I had downtown New York was being borne out fully; it was a war. The Black Liberation movement was raising up full out. It was a war, for us, a war of liberation. One had to organize, one had to arm, one had to mobilize and educate the people. For me, the rebellion was a cleansing fire. I must come all the way, I had come all the way, I would go all the way. What I had screamed while they were trying to kill me. "Al Homdulliah!" All Praise the Power of Allah, the Power of Blackness. I felt transformed, literally shot into the eye of the black hurricane of coming revolution. I had been through the fire and had not been consumed. Instead, I reasoned, what must be consumed is all of my contradictions to revolution. My individualism and randomness, my Western, white addictions, my Negro intellectualism.

I stopped drinking and smoking (I had smoked a pack of Gauloises a day). I remember going someplace to speak, shortly after being released, wearing a bright-colored dashiki and fila (hat). I had a bandage down my forehead and the rage that came out was boiling deep and utterly genuine. If I had been able to agitate and propagandize before, now it was raised up another notch in intensity. I felt the clubs, the guns; they had even bashed one of my teeth out and loosened some more with fists and clubs. I would be scarred for life. The hottest rage had become a constant of my waking personality.

Not long after the rebellion two men came to see me; they described themselves as Sunni Muslims. Malcolm had become a Sunni just before he was killed, moving out of the social orbit of the Nation of Islam. This had left a deep impression on many of us. Kamiel Wadud was one man's name; he was tall and well built, bearded, handsome, with a mocking smile that made one think he had different ploys and approaches to anything one cared to mention.

He said he wanted me to meet Hajj Heesham Jaaber, who was the Islamic priest who had buried Malcolm X. Kamiel was light-skinned with straight hair, because, he said, he was mixed with the Italians. Kamiel was a kind of gangster at one time (anytime), but he had received the religion of Al Islam and it had transformed him into the righteous messenger whom I now beheld.

The gist of what they said was that leadership had been thrust on me, and if I really wanted to be a leader I had to have "leading information." Kamiel talked in a personal and Islamicized symbolism, mixed with the street lingo of the "wise guys" who ran the Italian sector of organized crime.

They had been sent to convert me to Islam, orthodox Islam. Malcolm's break with Elijah had raised this as a possibility for many of the black militants. The mixture of weird symbolic "logic" and conversion-oriented preaching that came out of this general historical phenomenon has to be heard to be understood. (Except today, after years of prison, Rap Brown is a Sunni Muslim and the non-Black Muslim sects of Islam are enjoying more popularity in the black community than ever before, all from the same fundamental historical source.)

I met the tall, slender, beautifully dark-skinned Heesham, Hajj Heesham, signifying that he had made the Hajj, the journey to Mecca required of all Muslims. Although Malcolm X was supposedly the first of the Black Muslim group to make the Hajj, a move that further distinguished him from the homemade Islam of Elijah Muhammad. It was Heesham who gave me the name Ameer Barakat (the Blessed Prince). Sylvia was named Amina (faithful) after one of Muhammad's wives. Later, under Karenga's influence, I changed my name to Amiri, Bantuizing or Swahilizing the first name and the pronunciation of the last name as well. Barakat in Arabic is pronounced "Body-cot"; the Swahili drops the "t" and accents the next-to-last syllable, hence Baraka. Amiri with the rolled "r" is pronounced "Amidi."

The name change seemed fitting to me. Not just the flattery of being approached by these people, especially Heesham, and not just the meaning of the name Blessed Prince, but the idea that I was now literally being changed into a blacker being. I was discarding my "slave name" and embracing blackness. It is Chancellor Williams, the historian, who points out, however, that the many new Yusefs and Omars should remember that those Arabic names for black people are as much slave names as Joseph and Homer. One from American slavery, the other from Arab slavery.

Kamiel and other Sunnis and Heesham would come around to the Spirit House. They would drop in at odd times. They would talk to me, really recruiting. We had long discussions about the meaning of Islam. They wanted me finally to become a Muslim, to take Shehada with them. They began teaching me the five pillars of the Islamic faith and taught me how to make Salat (prayer). Kamiel and his wife tended toward the mystical. He showed me how he could put his finger in a glass of water and make it sweet. He smoked chain fashion, but he said he knew the correct prayer to say after smoking to cool it out. He interspersed Masonic lore with Islam and never ceased telling me that Masons aspired to be Muslims, that that was the Europeans' way into Al Islam. And that at the 33rd degree of the Masons, the secret or code word was Allahu Akbar (Allah is the greatest!).

At one point, the Spirit House even became, unofficially, a Jamat, or gathering place for the faithful. There were classes in Arabic offered and religious instruction, though the plays and community meetings still went on. I was also beginning to meet other people in Newark, more specifically political people. They came in and out of the Spirit House, for the plays, the classes, or to talk politics. I organized weekly Sunday meetings for the political group. Harold Wilson, a childhood friend from Central Avenue; his brother Jackie (Jim Nance); John Bugg, who sold furniture and clothes and worked with Harold; Russell Bingham, an older man, even my father's senior, a retired numbers man and elegant old-time Newark swifty. He had been with the team that put Irvine Turner into office years earlier. I'd known him when I was a child being squired to the Newark Eagles games and the Grand Hotel by my father.

As we began to meet regularly, our small circle grew. Harry Wheeler, from an "old" Newark family, exactly as his name suggested, except add "Dealer." Harry was a schoolteacher who'd been niggling around politics most of his life. Earl Harris, an old half-slick Republican, who'd been a freeholder, started coming later. Teddy Pinckney, an old school friend from HU; Jim Walker, a civil servant with political aspirations; David Barrett, a Rutgers-trained mathematician; Donald Tucker, a community activist from the East Ward, along with his pal Al Oliver. Ken Gibson, a civil engineer in City Hall who had run for mayor in 1966. What we were getting was the more politically oriented middle class, those whose imaginations had also been turned on by the fact of Newark's black majority.

So that the political meetings, the weekly "circles" we came to call them, went on during the same period as the heavy Sunni Islam influence on me and the Spirit House. Sundays, we sat and discussed politics, what was going on in Newark, who was doing what. We began to arrange to be at certain meetings to make the points that we thought needed to be made. The issues of the medical school and the Callahan-Parker conflict were high on our priority list, plus Spina's police brutality and Addonizio's general corruption. As our meetings got larger and, we thought, more important, we began to discuss security. Just as the police had run into our rehearsals and seized scripts, we felt they might try to do the same thing with our meetings—especially as we began to focus on electoral politics. We wanted to run a candidate for City Council in 1968. So the Sunni Muslims began to pull security for us. (Although my personal security was Walter "Sonni" Koontz, a childhood friend who began pulling security as the Spirit House expanded. He continued until the Congress of Afrikan Peoples came into existence.) Kamiel and his constant associate at the time, a warm, amusing brother named Bassit, a park policeman, were inside and outside the meetings as security, also some of the other brothers from the group of Sunnis who lived around Newark and environs.

But the thing that most changed my life at the time was marriage. It was Sylvia who showed me the craziness of my ways and struggled with me as hard as she could to get me to change. I didn't like it. For one thing, the very hotness of her temper drugged me. I thought I was supposed to be the only one with that kind of heat stored up. Our struggles around the Spirit House got familiar to the actors who were around. The fire the police had lit my head up with changed me as well. I had the feeling that I wanted to get rid of my bohemian ways, plus the little Oba was already three months old. There was no doubt that I regarded Sylvia as a very singular woman, both sensual and intelligent, but I had thought that I would never get married again. I wanted to avoid those kinds of forever ties. But I loved the woman, so why all the bullshit? Sylvia Wilson and Everett L. Jones were married the first weekend in August 1967 by the Yoruba priest Nana Oserjeman in a Yoruba ceremony.

I was to be tried for possession of two weapons. The police, to justify their almost killing me and their beating of Barney and Shorty, said that we had two .32 revolvers in the van. Not only did they beat us almost to death, they destroyed the van so that I could never use it again. When the trial came up, I got Irving Booker, an acquaintance from childhood and one of the persons who'd sit in our Sunday circles, to defend me. Three-hundred-pound John Love was Barney's attorney, and Booker got a Jersey City attorney, Louis Sanders, to represent Shorty.

The trial was like a comic opera. Booker thought that the best thing to do with the case was to change the venue. I was so preoccupied at the time I didn't object, but later I began to wonder why in the world he wanted to take the case out of Newark. I thought we might get more black jurors in Newark. But Booker got the case moved out to Morristown, a lily-white town in a lily-white county just west of Newark, up beyond the South Orange mountains.

When they were picking the jury, at one point I asked the judge (Kapp) could I make a statement. I wanted to raise the issue of how they thought they were going to try us with an all-white jury. Only Booker was there with us that morning, the other two attorneys were late. Kapp said I could speak only through my attorney. This infuriated me so much I told them that I was leaving. I said, "These people [the potential all-white jury] are not my peers, they are my oppressors."

I turned to go, getting my briefcase. "I'll not be judged by any hundred white people!" As I turned, a big dark detective who acted as Kapp's body-guard hit me from behind. He was about 260 pounds, six foot six, and I felt like a mashed-up scatback blindsided by Rosey Grier. But as this silly nigglow lay on top of me he breathed into my ear, "Hey, man, I'm in your corner." Shit, if dropping his big-ass 260 pounds on top of my back meant he was "in my corner," what the fuck would happen if I got on his shit list?

Kapp locked me up for contempt of court. I was stuck into the Morristown jail. The sentence was thirty days, Kapp said, but it was to be executed at the end of the other proceedings. My father came up to see me. I had been whipped half to death before, and now locked up for protesting an all-white jury. The sight of me behind bars and that beating radicalized my father. A year before, when I had first come back to Newark, the FBI had come snooping around. I had just moved into the Spirit House and my father told the FBI where I was, not knowing he didn't have to say shit to them. This burned me up and I wrote the play *Great Goodness of Life*, satirizing my father's attitudes, so hooked up with an America that has historically tried to castrate him. But the trial and lockup fired him up in a way I had never seen him before. I guess he knew that if they could do this to his son, whom he *knew* was not a criminal or bad person, then they deserved his contempt, perhaps his hatred. I heard him use profanity for the first time in my life.

What really was funny about that trial was our attorneys. "Buddy" (I'd called him that since high school) meant well but many times he was just plain terrorized and terrified by the judge, who made it plain from the very beginning that he thought I should be wiped out and that he was going to see that that happened. Big John Love seemed like he wanted to be as low-profile as possible, not make any waves, for those same reasons, reasons that had Buddy pacing up and down in the courthouse hallway.

But the most hilarious of the trio was Sanders, the Jersey City dude. He had been married to one of Joe Louis's ex-wives, Rose Morgan, of the beauty-salon fame. A stout jowly man with glasses that slipped down on his nose and that he was constantly pushing up on his forehead, Sanders had a stomach that hung pendulously over his belt like a bag of suet. But he had no belt, he wore suspenders, and his characteristic stance during the trial was to lean back against a railing where the spectators sat and pull on his suspenders with his thumbs while he sagged in sleep. If he hadn't made me so mad it would have been truly hilarious. The jurors got a chance to stare up into his open mouth and I was constantly whispering or gesturing to Booker to poke Sanders and wake his sorry ass up.

However, Sanders outdid even his self. At the end of a hearing at which we were trying to suppress the two guns as evidence, Sanders said, "Not only are they not our guns, your honor but we want them back!"

My mouth flew open and must have hit my chest with the impact of a .22. In my paranoid state, I swore the police got him to do that.

The trial ended with me getting convicted of possessing two guns. In fact, Barney, Shorty, and I were all convicted. However, I was sentenced to three years with no parole, while they got a year or so. Kapp amazed me by prefacing my sentencing by reading a poem of mine, "Black People," with the lines that became ubiquitous: "Up against the wall, motherfucker, this is a stickup!" He read this to show that I was guilty. But whatever he said, I would counter it.

When he read the poem, he left out the profanity, and as he read I supplied it. He said, "You've been convicted of possession of two guns," and I added, "and a poem!" Kapp got redder and redder as I kept jumping in during his tyrannical little rant.

When we first got to the court all the attorneys weren't there, but Kapp was going to go on with the proceedings without them. I protested and urged Barney and Shorty to protest. "Tell him it's illegal. Tell him you want your attorneys," I called out to them. But both of them ignored me and stood quiet and docile before the judge like doomed chattel. (Not so strangely, immediately after this gun business was cleared up after our appeal and during the second trial, Barney and Shorty moved back to New York. Even while the rebellion was going on Helen and Beverly had cut out. Suddenly they both had things to do, and they had cut out until time for the trial.)

Finally, Kapp laid his sentence down on us, me with the three years without parole for possession of guns. And I told him again as they led me out of the court, "Black people will judge me, Brother Kapp don't worry about that. Black people will judge me!" They led me away, placed me in the back of a screened police vehicle, and drove from Newark to Trenton State Penitentiary, about fifty miles, with the sirens blasting all the way down!

I spent maybe a week in Trenton. Before that I had spent a few days at Caldwell, up near Morristown, in another joint, in an open-bay jail with a couple hundred prisoners. Caldwell had been like going back to grammar school, I saw so many old familiar faces. Trenton was like going back in time as well. All the missing dudes I'd wondered what had happened to were down there in that old 19th-century jail that stayed about 50 degrees all the time. I got a cell where I had to step down about half a foot. It was so narrow that only the single bunk really fit into it and it was very dark. I made a prayer rug out of newspaper and made regular Salat while I was there and it gave me great comfort. It is easy to see why someone in prison could cling to Islam. The sense of being supported by a higher power than the one that is downing you. It is the appeal of all religions—one is "protected" by a higher power. But not quite enough.

I met the writer Nathan "Bubbie" Heard in Trenton. He was in there doing a stretch for armed robbery. I guess he was working on his famous novel *Howard Street*. He knew me and befriended me immediately. Between Bubbie and Billy Allen, the black-sheep brother of my old track buddy Arthur Allen (New Jersey All State high jump and high hurdles during my high school days), I got a heavy reception from the prisoners. They brought boxes of cookies, tea, instant coffee, canned meats and sardines, and candy to me in the cell. Another brother came up to me in the mess hall and told me he had read the newspapers about my trial. He praised the statements I'd made. A couple others threw their fists up in the Black Power salute.

Bubbie hipped me to a plan the guards had, probably passed on to them by the FBI. They were going to come to me, demand that I shave off my beard, and if I didn't do it, they would drop me into solitary. So when they came, sure enough, about four of them, telling me I had to be shaved and have my hair cut, I said, simply, "OK," and they looked at each other, obviously nonplussed, shaved my face, cut down my mop, and split without another word.

The always low temperature and dim cells were that way, I guess, to keep you demoralized. And they succeeded. But those prisons house some real warriors and even a few scholars. The fact that big-city prisons are 75 percent black and Latino makes you know that their real function is as institutions of oppression for the poor and minorities.

I was out after about a week, on appeal. I had reached Ray Brown, the white-looking black criminal lawyer from Jersey City. He filed the appeal and took up the case. Before that I had received an offer from Bill Kunstler, through someone, that he would take the case, but being a nationalist, I refused. A well-known black star had agreed to let my wife and father come to his penthouse hotel suite and tell him about the case. While they talked to the diminutive musical star, an Italian-looking dude sat in the suite listening. Finally, he asked my wife and father, "You want me to call some of the wise guys over there to take care of it?" But they, very wisely, refused. What would I owe for such a favor? I can imagine to whom it would be owed. Apparently, the diminutive black musical star owed them several favors.

The appeal was won on the basis of Judge Kapp's demented reading of my poem in court as part of his justification for the stiff sentence. He had also charged the jury by telling them that "the boys in blue," the police, who were the state's principal witnesses against us, "would never lie." So we got a new trial. But this time, the sleeping ugly from Jersey City was not with the team. Ray Brown came on as my attorney; Booker and Love were retained to try the case again, as part of the new team.

If he were really white, Ray Brown would be one of the most famous attorneys in the U.S. He is obviously one of the best. A learned and curious man, Brown had such mastery of the courtroom proceedings that I was relaxed enough to write a play while the trial went on (*The Sidney Poet Heroical*). He kept the prosecutor, a grim crew-cut carabiniere named Zazzali, so off stride and frustrated that at one point Zazzali was chastised by the judge for flying off the handle. "If you do that again, Mr. Zazzali, I'll report you to your superior."

Plus, every time Zazzali passed the table where I sat I would boo him under my breath, but loud enough for him to hear. His face stayed hot-poker red throughout the proceedings.

Ray Brown's summation to the jury was incredible. He took Mark Antony's speech to the crowd in *Julius Caesar* ("Friends, Romans, countrymen") and using the refrain Antony laid on Brutus to discredit him ("And Brutus is an honorable man "), laid waste to the state's arguments. Brown would say, "And we are supposed to believe the police, because they are honorable men . . ." taking them all the way out to lunch and back. At the end of the summation you could see some of the jury wanted to applaud.

This was the denouement, and the verdict of acquittal seemed to me a matter of course. But the high point of the case was when Rabbit, the brother we had picked up off the street and taken to the hospital, was found by means of leaflets we circulated through the community. He breezed into the courtroom, talking shit, the same way he had that night, raised up his pant leg and pointed to the bullet hole. We were not shooting at people, we were taking people to the hospital. Brown won it going away!

The group that met on Sundays decided to call itself The United Brothers. It was still expanding and the meetings were regular and we all looked forward to the incisive informal discussions and the growing amount of planning that went on. There were also some brothers and sisters from East Orange and Montclair who knew something of Karenga's organization, US. They had formed a group and styled themselves after the US people and regarded Karenga as their leader. They were called the Black Community Defense and Development (BCD). Two men headed up the group, a dark-skinned, big-eyed brother named Balozi Zayd Muhammad, and a karate expert, Mfundishi Maasi. They also began to attend the meetings of the circle.

Karenga's influence was increasing on me personally. He came East a couple times, planning the 1968 Black Power Conference, which was to be held in Philadelphia. I was coordinator of the Arts Workshop at that conference. I began to move more and more under the sway of cultural nationalism, Karenga's brand. The two influences, orthodox Islam and the African-derived cultural nationalism, had to clash, and they did. The Sunnis were not very advanced politically. They said that blacks were really "Arabs," that the true Arab was black. "Arab" means black, but they were very derogatory about Africa and things African. Also, they were constantly counseling me against my "militance," saying that my speeches needed to be toned down. Kamiel's advice to me when I was on trial was that I should stand with my feet placed at a 45-degree angle and then put my hands on top of my head, since that was "a Masonic distress signal." He said the judge would then recognize that I was a Mason in distress and cut me loose.

What really put distance between us was that I found out that Kamiel was in regular contact with Spina as well as the sheriff's office. He would file regular reports, and parts of his regular reports were on the "fantastic" doings at the Spirit House. And what he had in his reports was fantastic on the real side. But it made good reading. How did I find out? Kamiel cheerfully volunteered this information. It paid good money!

When Dr. King was murdered in '68, rebellions broke out in the major cities. Newark, too. Again, we walked all night, but this time the people did not want to tear up inside their own community; groups of people marched down Clinton Avenue toward the downtown area to light it up. The police massed at the bottom of the hill, shotguns raised. We told people to cool it. Kamiel introduced me to a balding black dude with a walkie-talkie strapped to his belt who was carrying a shoulder holster. We wanted some assurances that the police would not shoot into the crowds. Kamiel implied that the balding man with the walkie-talkie was attached to the sheriff's office but was really a fed. Kamiel and I went with this man to an apartment building directly across from City Hall. There was a white man in a room on one of the floors wearing a shoulder holster. I was told this was some kind of nerve center for the feds to monitor the crowd's actions. At one point, the balding man said to me, "Well, you have to admit one thing about America. It's been a fascinating experiment!" My blood ran cold, this Negro was an actual creation. Someone or something had created him and what I was hearing was obviously tapes running through his brain track.

Later, this same balding man with the shoulder holster was present at the first meeting called by the Black Panthers to start a Newark chapter. But this time he was one of the recruiters. He was supposed to be a Panther!

It was during this period that Kamiel introduced me to Anthony Imperiale, the Newark racist from the Italian North Ward. Imperiale had made headlines talking about the tank and the guns he had. He'd said, "If the Black Panther comes, the white hunter will be waiting!" He'd also called Dr. King "Martin Luther Coon." Imperiale had risen to infamy as the white counter for black rebellion. If I had gotten some notoriety from the rebellions, so had Imperiale.

It was Kamiel who organized the appearance of the two of us on a television program. The angle of the show was to denounce the left in Newark. I saw it as an opportunity to denounce the young whites who were playing revolution in Newark. I was a black nationalist and saw nothing wrong with denouncing Tom Hayden and the others. It was rumored in the black community that these dudes were setting the rash of fires that broke out during that period. Old buildings in the black community. These actions were supposed to trigger more rebellions. We wanted Hayden and his classmates out of the community. We thought they were "white boys pimping off black struggle," so we put them down on the TV program while Imperiale and some police official from D.C. went out on the left in general. I thought white Marxists were just some more white people using black people to do their struggling for them. But in retrospect, to be on such a television program was asinine.

Kamiel, as our security chief, even thought up the gimmick of a "hot line" between Imperiale and me, supposedly to keep community tensions down. The phone was installed. I guess, on reflection, it probably was nothing but a listening device right in the center of the house. I never used it.

It was Karenga who, on one of his visits, suggested that we formally bring together the United Brothers, BCD, and the Spirit House forces. (The acting group was named by me the Spirit House Movers. I got the Movers' name from a bar down on Shipman Street, Daniel's, where we always went when we were down in Arthur's Cellar or after rehearsals. There was a moving company down the street, and the workers drank in Daniel's all the time too.) Karenga suggested the name Committee for a Unified Newark. We shortened it somewhat to Committee for Unified Newark (CFUN). So this larger united-front organization brought together middle-class blacks interested in electoral politics (United Brothers); younger blacks influenced by Ron Karenga's Kawaida doctrine (BCD as well as us in the Spirit House); and mostly young black artists who were part of the Black Arts movement (Spirit House).

CFUN's first project was to hold a Black Convention in '68 and then run candidates out of that convention for City Council. (The last day of that unsuccessful "Peace & Power" campaign is recorded in a film made by Jim Hinton called *The New Ark*.) Karenga came to town especially to help with the campaign. It was he who named the campaign "Peace & Power," hoping to capitalize on the peace movement that was one aspect of the anti-Vietnam War protests, as well as the Black Power movement. The visual symbols were a red ankh (peace) and a black fist (power).

Our first candidates lost and the loss brought us all down, but it was good experience. We learned a lot in that campaign and got ready soon after to go again. Nineteen seventy was the mayoral election and all the councilmen's terms would be up. Our weekly circle meetings took on even more intensity, since now we had gotten our feet wet and knew what to expect.

Karenga's influence came to dominate the entire CFUN, which alienated a few of the older political brothers in the United Brothers, all of whom would certainly not become Karenga cultural nationalists.

During this period I got deeply involved with Kawaida. Although, as Karenga was to complain in a note to himself, the things we did were never absolute copies of his Los Angeles operation. He wrote that I was a "revisionist." But many of us now, and certainly all of the younger people in CFUN, began to wear African clothes. Dashikis for the men, bubbas and lappas and geles for the women. The united front, which still remains the fundamental weapon of struggle for the oppressed black nation, was eroded in one sense by the gradual domination by cultural nationalism in CFUN, though for a while our numbers steadily increased.

I learned the voluminous pages of Karenga's Kawaida doctrine, the Nguzo Saba, the five of this and seven of that and three of the other we had to memorize. We learned the basic Swahili vocabulary that identified the organization. But I had no intention of shaving my head. The L.A. people wore the olive-drab dashiki; in the East we wore the normal multicolored West African dashiki.

The doctrine was organized so it dealt, presumably, with every part of life. And even though I was heavily influenced by Karenga and Kawaida, there were certain parts of his doctrine which made no sense to me, so I did not impose them on the Newark people. This was especially true of the parts of the doctrine dealing with women. The heavy male chauvinism that I already suffered from was now formally added to. Karenga's doctrine gave male chauvinism a revolutionary legitimacy. The doctrine said there was no such thing as equality between men and women, "they were complementary." This was a typical Karenga manipulation of words. When brothers went by, the women were supposed to "salimu" or "submit," crossing their arms on their breasts and bowing slightly. We changed this so that they did this only for the organization's officers.

Karenga also had wild stuff in his doctrine about how women ought to dress and how their clothing should always be "suggestive." He said they should show flesh to intrigue men and not be covered up so much. I could never adjust to Karenga's thing with women either on paper or in the flesh. He was always making "sexy" remarks to women, calling them "freaks" and commenting loudly on their physical attributes. In L.A., Karenga even sanctioned "polygamy" and was rumored, himself, to have pulled many of the women in the L.A. organization.

What stopped us from getting too far out in Kawaida was my wife, Amina, who not only waged a constant struggle against my personal and organizational male chauvinism, but secretly in her way was constantly undermining Karenga's influence, figuring, I guess, that I would not come up with as much nuttiness disguised as revolution as he, though I did my share. (This is the reason that the work of uninformed "observers" like Michelle Wallace, who was by her own admission in private school or away in Paris during this period of the Black Liberation movement, shows up so shabbily. To suggest, as Wallace does in her *Black Macho and the Myth of the Superwoman*, that the black women inside the various organizations of the Black Liberation movement did nothing but acquiesce to our male chauvinism during the '60s is simply white feminist chauvinism. The sisters in the organizations I was in fought us tooth and nail about our chauvinism in much more forcible and effective ways than the middle-class sistren at *Ms.* magazine could ever begin to imagine.)

All the black women in those militant black organizations deserve the highest praise. Not only did they stand with us shoulder to shoulder against black people's enemies, they also had to go toe to toe with us, battling day after day against our insufferable male chauvinism. And then later, when there was a lull in the movement, those women who were away in some school getting Ph.D.s or off in Europe soaking up "culture" or in some bohemian place learning how to make narcissistic art can return and get to be big deals running on about what the movement really was about. What bullshit! But predictable bullshit.

The US organization started out as community activists but gradually they became more and more just cultural nationalists putting out an abstract doctrine of "blackness." I myself became one of the chief proselytizers of Kawaida. Actually, if it were not for CFUN and the later Congress of Afrikan Peoples (CAP), the Kawaida doctrine, the Seven Principles, and the holiday Kwanzaa would never have been as widely known as they are. Certainly it was not through any kind of community organizing on Karenga's part, though he did have a dramatic, humorous, very charismatic way of speaking and carrying himself. And his doctrine did carry orderly methods of approaching community organizing and they sometimes worked. I wrote a couple of pamphlets explaining Karenga's doctrine which were well circulated. And because he did push tight organization and military-like rank and discipline, the US cadre did seem much more "together" than most of the other militants, especially around things like the Black Power Conferences. During those years Kawaida was very influential, and it became even more influential through CFUN and CAP.

The people functioning in CFUN as cultural nationalists began to think of themselves as US organization members on the East Coast. Balozi and Mfundishi pushed a general US line as well, though Balozi had a great store of "homespunism" that he pushed equally hard. Mfundishi was really the strong silent type and was content to walk around and be worshiped in silence. Mfundishi had about him that arrogance that only men skilled in the martial arts, especially those of other nationalities pretending to be Orientals, could have. But he was especially skilled in martial arts, a sensei, or teacher.

One event will show how skilled and dangerous Mfundishi was. He was walking with me one afternoon on the way from the CFUN building. (We had moved into an abandoned Red Feather building just down the block from the Spirit House. All we had to do was pay maintenance costs and fuel, since the city had taken it over. We painted the interior red, black, and green, put large posters and photographs of Afro-American and African leaders on the walls. It was three stories—downstairs for our weekly programs, called Soul Sessions, like Karenga's on the Coast, the second floor for our administrative offices and my own office, and the third floor for other officers in the organization's offices and the training area.) We had to go to the Hall of Records for something. We had crossed the street and were walking up the diagonal path which leads past the courthouse and on up across High Street to the building.

As we started up the path, we spied the fat, bulky Imperiale coming down the courthouse stairs and headed toward us. Part of Imperiale's rep rested on the tale that he was a black belt karate man and was deadly with his hands. He might have had something going for him Korean karate style with his huge meaty hams at the end of his arms, but Mfundishi was an artist. We walked directly toward each other, Imperiale from one direction, Mfundishi and I from the other. When Imperiale got perhaps a couple feet from us, Mfundishi stepped with one stride between Imperiale and me and, turning his body at the same time to face Imperiale, was no longer at my side but jam up in Imperiale's chest, face to face. Imperiale's face clouded like someone had shit in it. Mfundishi was just a little lower than Imperiale, he had come up and with his one sleek stride was poised just a little under Ant-knee's chest, crouched and at the ready. It was impressive; certainly Imperiale was impressed.

Mfundishi's thing, it seemed to me, was that the martial arts was the deciding factor in the black struggle, as if guns had never been invented. All the brothers in the organization took Yangumi ("the way of the thinking fist"), and Mfundishi imposed a harsh discipline and a hard training regimen. The BCD brothers were really being trained for martial arts tournaments rather than political organization.

Balozi, on the other hand, sought to be the Karenga-like figure, with a constant stream of jokes, mainly about "the nigger," such as "Nigger need to be locked up for his own good." So, for a time, there were three leaders of the CFUN: Balozi, who was supposed to be the political leader; Mfundishi, head of the troops (Karenga called them Simba, the young lions); and I, termed "the Spiritual Leader."

We functioned together for a while but before 1968 was over we had split. What jumped it off was one evening brothers were scheduled for doctrine class and Mfundishi told them they had martial arts training class. Mfundishi did not think the political training was as important as the martial arts. He was always taking the younger brothers, mostly BCD, but some of the younger brothers we had brought with us from Stirling Street, off to the dojo. They pulled personal security as well as security for the building. We always had someone downstairs on the door and sleeping overnight in the building to stop the police and the junkies from ripping us off.

On this particular evening, I raised hell about people being pulled out of doctrine class for Yangumi. There was a confrontation (one that got pretty wild, with Mfundishi ordering a couple of the troops to shoot upstairs and get their heat. Why this was necessary, I don't know. I can't believe he thought I would be scared. The shit was too theatrical). At the end of it I called Karenga and told him what was happening and he got Balozi and Mfundishi on the phone and told them to back off. But Mfundishi pulled all the BCD people out of the CFUN at that moment. They took their gear, which included Mfundishi's record "Music for Zen Meditation" by Fred Katz, and they split. Later Karenga sent a couple of his top people to the East to hang around and make sure that all was well. But I never believed any real violence would jump off.

What it was, I think, was that a rivalry was growing up between the BCD leadership and myself. I was pushing CFUN politically and Mfundishi and Balozi were not ever really deeply involved with actual politics. Except the kind found in *The Quotable Karenga*. Balozi's quips and

Mfundishi's martial arts exhibitions and mystical muscled demeanor were all they thought was needed, plus the charismatic African clothes. We had thought it was a perfect combination, the older electorally oriented political types, the young martial arts cultural nationalists, and the artists, the communicators (who were also deep into cultural nationalism). But the contradictions inside that mix had split it in half.

Karenga, that year, muscled his way into the top leadership of the Black Power Conference. He had always been on the Continuations and Planning Committee. But at the Philadelphia conference, there was a confrontation between the US forces and Max Stanford's RAM and their Black Guards (a takeoff on the Chinese Red Guards). The confrontation seemed to cool out when Stanford showed up with a black eye, never explained to me, and for the rest of the conference at least, a Mexican standoff was what was happening. But the RAM forces and Karenga were always in sharp contradiction after that. (Across from where we had the Arts Workshops that year, at least ten white house painters painted a small woodframe house in the middle of that ghetto all day! Yipes, J. Edgar, was that you?)

The split with the BCD actually left us better off, though at first we felt weakened severely because our "military" arm had been cut away. But the United Brothers aspect of the organization had grown. The younger brothers interested in political work were called Saidis, the ones interested in the military were the Simba Wachanga, in Karenga's terminology. We were better off because now we could pursue our political direction without obstruction, confident in the Kawaida ideology and at the same time continuing to work with the united front concept as much as we could understand it.

Late in 1968 something happened which changed our whole relationship to Karenga and Kawaida. Karenga had come East again for a fundraiser we were giving in Harlem at the Renaissance Ballroom. The place was packed, perhaps a thousand people. We had music and dancers, skits and political speakers. At the height of the program Karenga received a long-distance phone call backstage. I had organized the program and was walking back and forth keeping everything rolling. But I was backstage with him when he got the call. It was something very heavy that went down. Karenga questioned the caller, talking furiously and almost hysterically. There had been a shootout at UCLA, coming out of the sharply intense contradictions between US and the Black Panther Party. Two of the US brothers had shot and killed two of the Panthers, Bunchy Carter and John Huggins.

I had known Bunchy from L.A. Karenga had organized the Black Congress, an "operational unity" united-front structure that tried to bring the major black organizations in L.A. together to meet once a month to discuss important issues affecting black people. The Spirit House Movers had performed at the Congress building and Bunchy had interviewed me for the Panther newspaper. I walked into his office and it was thick with grass fumes, a no-no for a cultural nationalist, so we felt very superior. Bunchy asked me during the interview did I think the Panthers were "kamikaze niggers," as Karenga was fond of calling them. There had been bad feeling between Panthers and US in L.A. for months. James Forman had even come out to L.A. once as a peacemaker, sitting between Cleaver and Karenga. When Huey got jailed in '67, Cleaver had taken over as Minister of Information and the Panthers had gotten less black nationalist and more bohemian anarchist ever since.

I had tried to organize a national united front structure with US, RAM, SNCC, RNA, and the Panthers, but Eldridge talked bad about the idea over the phone. More and more the Panthers began to denounce the "pork chop nationalists"—obvious Cleaver terminology—and more and more Karenga's people called the Panthers "kamikaze niggers." It is proven now from Freedom of Information Act files that the FBI orchestrated much of this discord between the two organizations. But certainly Cleaver's arrogance and shallow bohemian anarchism, which he passed off as Marxism, plus Karenga's Maulana complex, helped speed up the tragic collision that finally saw Bunchy and Huggins dead.

Karenga was frozen by what he had heard on the phone. He was scheduled to speak very shortly and it was obvious he could not. His eyes seemed to dart around in his head, glassy with fear. He said he wouldn't speak, but I began to try to convince him that he must speak, that all the people sitting out front were waiting for him. But he was extremely paranoid, thinking that perhaps the word had already reached East about what had happened. He thought maybe Panther sharpshooters were sitting in the audience. Finally, he did go out to speak, surrounded on all sides by the security, the L.A. brothers, and our own people.

From that point on, the FBI escalated their "intervention" into the conflict. They'd shoot at one organization, knowing that the other would get blamed and that the organization shot at would retaliate in kind. That is just what happened. For months, tales flew back and forth between

Newark and the Coast about new shootouts. One brother we knew barely escaped, going over a fence and catching slugs in his leg and shoulder. Cars were shot up, windows shot out, and homes shot into; a full-fledged war was going on in Los Angeles, between US and the Panthers, courtesy of the FBI; we even got letters from the FBI in Newark. As the conflict broadened and cultural nationalists and Panthers across the country drew their lines and screamed and shouted at each other, we received a letter, ostensibly from the Jersey City Panthers, telling us we were "pork chop nationalists" and threatening to wipe us out. We were supposed to run out and blow them away first. But reading the letter, it was obvious that the writer did not have a firm grasp on the African American dialect. I thought it was just some white racist sending crank mail, so we dropped it into the wastebasket. The FOIA files show that the FBI sent this letter to us, hoping to widen the fratricidal clash that disfigured the Black Liberation movement!

What happened now was that Karenga and the L.A. US organization developed what we called "a foxhole mentality." Because of the constant shootouts and military encounters with the Panthers and the police, who tried to capitalize on the struggle by busting both sides, US was not able to do much in the way of community organizing. The whole function of the organization now was security and defense, all development was on hold.

At one point Karenga had a machine gun sitting in his living room facing the front door, on a tripod. He even gradually developed a dependence on pills of one kind or another. A kind of "diet pill" that kept him in a perpetual stupor. So that now instead of the swift sparkling intellect, he slurred his words and staggered around the room at times. The advocates were made sometimes to sit in his living room for hours waiting for him while he drowsed and nodded. The old Maulana complex which had shown itself by his gathering advocates around him in his living room to spill out his pearls of master teaching had been stretched out to full caricature—a static cult with a drugged prophet.

While Karenga and US were bogged down in super-security, paranoia, and pills, CFUN still functioned in the day-to-day struggles that concerned black people in Newark. Having had our public baptism in electoral politics, we were fortified for further struggle within that framework. Black Newark spelled a definite motion of Black Power. We would try to apply Karenga's doctrine in practical ways, not just as cultural pundits inveighing from on high. So that from Karenga's Four Aspects of Political Power, which called for community organization, alliances and coalitions, electoral politics, and disruption, we developed the practical capacity to utilize all or any of the four.

Our day-to-day practical movement pulled us increasingly further and further away from Karenga. One evening I received a call from some of the L.A. advocates, who, alarmed at what was happening inside the L.A. organization, bade me come West to talk to them. I got on a plane and met with about seven or eight of the brothers, most of whom I regarded as strong revolutionaries. They lamented and complained that the organization was slipping down the tubes. Some of them had already been put out; Karenga, they said, was acting weird and arbitrary. They wanted to know what I thought. Those who had been put out could come East if they wanted to, I would try to do what I could. I returned the same evening to the East.

We were getting more deeply involved with the sweep of black Newark politics. We were planning another convention for 1969, but this time we had learned about alliances and coalitions as a means of extending power. We had always been close to the Young Lords. Felipe Luciano, the first national chairman, was an old friend of mine. We had that special connection that cultural workers have. Felipe was a member of the original Last Poets. He and Gylan Kain and David Nelson had extended the form of the ensemble poetry performance that we had worked with in the Spirit House. Despite the fact that the Lords were heavily influenced by the Panthers, Felipe and I remained friends and our ties with the Newark Lords remained strong despite the anticultural nationalist bias that must have informed the national organization. The Newark captain, Ramon Rivera, and I got very tight (we remain so today) and so the planning for the Black and Puerto Rican Convention went forward.

We were extending our black united front that was initiated with CFUN. The Sunday United Brothers meetings got increasingly more animated and serious. The question of mayor was foremost in all of our minds. Who were we going to run? The question ran around and around, with too many people supplying personal self-serving answers. Inside our forum the number got reduced to two persons: Ken Gibson, the City Hall civil engineer, and Harry Wheeler, the politicking schoolteacher. Why we chose Gibson still eludes me. I guess Gibson had run before, he had his name out. We felt maybe Harry was a little too slick for our own good. People kept whispering about a "milk scandal" Harry was implicated in as a public school teacher. At any rate, at the critical moment, our steering committee hands shot up for Gibson. He would be our candidate at the convention and of course we would make sure he won.

Harry was frustrated. He plain out didn't like it. For one thing, Harry knew he was smarter, more sophisticated, than Gibson. I knew this too. And with the withering intelligence of hindsight, I can say that Harry would probably have made a better mayor than Gibson. Gibson was a civil servant, a grey yellow man from the lower middle class with not the slightest understanding or vision of what the world would be like without the present social and economic system that rules us. Ken's highest dream is that of being a GS-1000 in the great civil service in the sky!

But at that point, Ken Gibson had the weight of our steering committee behind him. He had the commitment, at that point, of the most politicized segment of Newark's black petty bourgeoisie, its left and its center (and even some of its right wing).

The mobilization for the convention was really the mobilization for that campaign. This was late in '69. The Black Power Conference that year had been obstructed by the ineptitude within our own ranks and the American imperialist state. It was held in Bermuda, with a host committee headed by Roosevelt Brown of the Continuations Committee and a member of the Bermuda Parliament. I was convinced that Brown was a thoroughly opportunistic and unserious person, and the Bermuda government kept most of the well-known activists out of Bermuda as personae non gratae, including myself, Sonny Carson, Karenga, and some others. It seemed to be a thoroughly wasted affair.

I had by now gotten onto that Continuations Committee of the Black Power Conference, so that meant I was able to put out some lines on a national basis more easily. I talked about the Black and Puerto Rican Convention and the coming election in Newark as examples of the practical pursuit of Black Power. Newark became a point of some national focus within the national black nationalist community.

We worked now to build a team of candidates who could come out of the convention. The convention was created as a mass vehicle, an instrument of black and Puerto Rican people's power. The point was to limit the wild, unfocused profusion of personally sanctioned candidates and give the people a chance to support a slate which, because it had wide backing, would have a good chance to sweep into power. And this is what we did. Gibson and eventual City Council president Earl Harris were members of our steering committee. Young minister Dennis Westbrook came to our attention as a Central Ward activist, and he was drawn onto the commit-

tee. Ted Pinckney and Donald Tucker met with us regularly and they became candidates. Sharpe James, a physical education instructor, we convinced to run from the South Ward, because in our meetings his name
came up as a good solid progressive candidate. Al Oliver, Tucker touted
from the East Ward. Ramon Rivera had some doubts about the Puerto
Rican candidate, Ramon Aneses. He didn't think he was assertive enough.
But Ramon could not come up with another candidate at the time and he
did not want to run himself.

The convention was billed as the instrument to choose "the Community's
Choice," and that was the name of the team that came out of it. The convention was widely talked about and extremely popular. Broad masses of
black people and the Puerto Rican community could see that what was
being constructed was something which could seriously contend with
Addonizio and company. And as the convention mobilization moved forward, the younger and more serious black youth joined CFUN. We also
sent out word to the various colleges in the area that we would need help,
that they should come to Newark and help us build Black Power.

Two mayoral candidates refused to come to the convention, Harry
Wheeler and the labor bureaucrats' "progressive," George Richardson.
Together they got fewer than five hundred votes in the election itself. The
convention nominated not only Ken Gibson but the whole Community's
Choice team of Harris, Tucker, Pinckney, James, Oliver, Westbrook, and
Aneses.

(The election campaign is covered in depth in an unpublished book
still in the possession of Howard University Press, called *The Creation of
the New Ark*. But that book was written from the deep backwardness of
cultural nationalism, and when I wanted to revise it in galleys, HUP refused. I told them all I would do is simply to asterisk certain ideas and then
argue with myself in the footnotes so that people could see what my nationalist ideas were, how I changed them, and the justification I had for
doing so. At this writing HU still refuses on the grounds that they don't
have the money.)

In truth, many elements converged at this time that aided us, despite
our own relative naivete. Newark was a city on somebody's list, as a result
of the '67 rebellion. Obviously some sectors of the ruling class in the U.S.
realized that the old, completely segregated, apartheid type of U.S. social
structure could no longer hold. The Kerner Commission had spoken of
"aggrandizing the ghetto" as one method to bring social peace to the large,
increasingly black urban centers. Addonizio and company had been

indirectly denounced, even in that official government report, for the "sense of pervading corruption" which existed in Newark. Every day now there were rumors of Addonizio's indictment. Plus, he was a Democrat and the national power was Republican. Our motion was coming in the midst of all this.

Addonizio and company were not prepared either, as they should have been. Perhaps their Negroes were telling them that all was well, it would all pass. But neither the racists and gangsters that ran the city nor their colored gun bearers realized how isolated they all had become. Nor did they realize how deep the ties we had run into the community had been sunk. There were those among them who realized that I was not an "outside agitator," but the self-styled prodigal returned. They didn't realize that the self-styling was a mass line, that that very prodigality held interest because I had come back with some information, some national ties, and the brutality of my reception had ignited an unquenchable fury of black patriotism, however warped by cultural nationalism. I was only one part of an entire mass movement for political democracy, Black Power. But I became one focus of Addonizio and company's attacks, because they thought my checkered past and "criminality"—i.e., being arrested in the rebellions—would turn the masses off. It acted exactly the opposite. Every knock was a boost. They were simply letting the people know what I and the rest of us stood for. Addonizio and company and the bourgeois press were our best press agents and advertising aides.

Tying Gibson and the rest of the Community's Choice team to images of my personal militance and rebelliousness helped the campaign immeasurably. It was not just a personal electoral campaign, it was a *movement*, the advanced and the middle forces, the progressive and the average, all mobilized to oppose black people's enemies and their reactionary colored house servants.

CFUN organized the New Ark Fund, which was a fundraising organization, also an excitement-raising mechanism. We brought in the biggest names in the country in support of the campaign. Isaac Hayes with his chains and shades, James Brown, Leontyne Price, Bill Cosby, Dustin Hoffman, Beau Bridges, the Staple Singers, Stevie Wonder came in and rode around on the back of a truck all day, singing and pushing the program. Manhattan borough president, Percy Sutton, walked through the streets passing out leaflets. Even Adam Clayton Powell came in and mesmerized a packed house at Bethany Baptist Church. Chuck Jackson, the Supremes. There was an endless line of speakers, entertainers, performers, politicians, militants that we brought in. We also did team advertising: posters, leaflets, billboards, and our regular newspaper, all dedicated to the Community's Choice.

Bill Cherry, who later became Richard Pryor's and Richard Roundtree's manager for a time, came in, working then for a black ad agency, Uniworld. It was he who made the New Ark Fund tick as far as bringing in the celebrities and the slick, eye-catching graphics. I thought an appropriate logo for the campaign would be a rainbow, so we designed buttons and posters with the bright rainbow band, with the names of each of the candidates in the different colors of the spectrum.

From the beginning, Kenneth Gibson was a rather peculiar candidate. He was shockingly unsophisticated, a little fat man with a close haircut and cuffs on his pants. When I took him out to Chicago to appear with Jesse Jackson at his Saturday morning Operation Breadbasket session, Jesse cracked on him, privately and publicly, about his close-cut hair, in an era of prominent Afros, and his high-water pants.

You got the feeling talking to him that you might not be making sense, that he might be misunderstanding. You could not feel much of that warmth that comes from the mutual appreciation of patriotism and struggle. He was bland and his ideas were deadly conventional. But I thought somehow we could change him, that the movement which he was riding would penetrate and transform him. I thought he had some loyalty and feeling for black people. He was so dull I could not see that beneath that bland exterior there was a truly dull mind, a mind so dull that it had not yet even aspired to embrace the collective energy of black struggle except in the most opportunistic and low-level careerist way.

But the campaign itself was a juggernaut that plowed into the masses' feelings and used those feelings as fuel. As far as we were concerned, Addonizio was just a minor obstruction, though the focus of our blasts. The specter of Black Power was haunting the proceedings and that specter grew larger and more real, it grew before our eyes, towering over everyone in the town.

Addonizio was indicted just before the election, along with some of his pratboys. That sealed his fate as far as I was concerned. Our campaign was popular and it had taken on national scope. Every weekend busloads of students came in and walked the streets. The Old Ward heelers and party hacks could not match these resources with their nickel-and-dime bought-and-paid-for loyalties. Earl Harris came up with a slogan we put out on mimeograph sheets a few days before the election. Earl came from that part of the Newark black political spectrum who were in such a position and would recognize that kind of nationalism: "Take the Man's Money, But Vote for a Brother!" was his slogan.

The backward political intelligence had said, sure, there's more Nigras in the town but you'll never get them registered. Many of our celebrities came in pushing voter registration. We made voter registration hip and exciting. We used fat-bellied Imperiale fondling his gun-penis on a poster with a slogan: "Register and Vote or This Will Be Your Mayor!"

We used the *Life* magazine photo of the killer cop (name: Capone) standing over the dead black child in the street during the rebellion, murderous weapon still smoking in his hand. "Register & Vote! Never Let This Happen Again!" It was a moral and survival issue we raised. Either you would register and vote or you were some kind of traitorous maniac.

Not only did students and others come in every week to register people, put up literature, canvass, and talk to the people. CFUN grew, even its inner, highly organized cultural nationalist cadre, by leaps and bounds. There were students and middle-class youth in the city, plus working-class youth from the inner city and even other towns.

Newark was a focus for all of Afro-America, certainly the more politically conscious aspect of the black nation. There was no way that such a juggernaut could be stopped. Yet right up until election day there were still public doubters and very public Toms. There was a group of black preachers who backed Addonizio. One of them, B. F. Johnson, whose grandson later became a city councilman, came out with a statement, as part of the "Ministers for Addonizio," that made it seem that God and Jesus wanted black people to vote for Hughie the crook. We put out leaflets—"What Does Jesus Have to Do with Addonizio?"—and picketed the man's church, passing the leaflets out to his faithful. Many of the people smiled their blessings at us, nodding knowledgeably. Even one of the old deacons expressed his support for the campaign, until old B.F. sent a loyalist deacon out to run us away. But the damage was done. That word spread everywhere, that we would go up against the biggest churches and the biggest preachers and cut their shit to the wind.

Other churches and ministers were with us. We spoke or Gibson and the other candidates spoke from their pulpits and the old ladies waved their fans hard enough to raise airplanes off the church floor.

On election day everything was at the ready. We had brought in some electoral specialists like Tony Harrison from Alabama, who functioned out of the League of Cities, until he finally went back home and won a few elections himself. Larry Coggins, an old Progressive Labor fellow traveler Gibson brought in. Coggins was very sharp, albeit oiled to the gills most times. He knew electoral politics cold; unfortunately any real connection with a genuine left perspective was long gone except as a possible justification for interracial banging.

Because of the team, we could have people at all the polling sites, both challengers and literature passers. We had radio cars, walkie-talkies, huge maps in every headquarters, groups of young pullers to go into the flagging areas and get the people out. We had security forces riding radio cars in each ward, checking on the polling places. We had a steady flow of information, from hour to hour, about what polls were doing what. We knew where our strong points were. We had to get the South and Central Wards out in majority numbers. We had to take the West, and do well in the North and East, even if they went to Addonizio (which they would).

Naturally enough, Addonizio tried the usual gangster racist tricks. Polling places in black areas got "strangely" jammed up. But we had prepared beforehand. We had notified the state and federal attorneys general that this is what would happen and requested observers and federal marshals on the scene.

Addonizio even got some renegade Muslims to ride around in blue suits with Italian flags in their lapels and try to intimidate people at the polls. But we had some absolutely hard niggers on hand that would have chewed they heads off. The black police had been contacted long ago, through our ties inside the Bronze Shields, a black police organization. They served as Gibson's personal security. Death threats had been made on him, ostensibly by the renegade Muslims out of Newark's Temple No. 25, the same mosque which produced Malcolm's assassins.

But it looked good, close, but good from the beginning, and as the day wore on it looked like we were not only holding our own, getting the votes we absolutely had to get, but as if we were edging away. As it grew later and later in the day, word was received that Imperiale and his goons had gone wild in the North Ward. They had thrown all caution to the winds and come out in knots to harass the late black voters now that twilight was moving down.

I called our security forces together, plus a whole roomful of volunteers who had come back from their puller work for the last-hour drive which means so much in an election. I talked to the group of them, about 150 people or so. I poured out our fears of what Imperiale and company were up to. They were trying, as they had all day in a number of illegal ways, to steal the election. Now they were trying straight-out force, open and un-compromising. When I finished, the people flew out of the Hekalu (Temple), as 502 High Street, CFUN headquarters, was called. Trucks and radio cars (some cabs appropriated for the election day work) flew up toward the North Ward. The young people and our own security met Imperiale and his goons out in the streets that last hour. They rode around confronting the knots and groups of goons and forced them to back off. Many of the young brothers had waited all day for something like this to happen, so they could get their thing off, let out all the pent-up frustration. They raged through the streets looking for racists. But it was too late any-way for Imperiale to do anything, the polls were closing. We were getting the first count, and it looked good. The next hour, as people began to come back, a little subdued from the tension and the expectation, but still talking and confident, more numbers began to come in. In another hour it got clearer. We saw the different candidates. The radio and television were on in the Hekalu, groups of us sat around and talked and waited, ooohed and aaahed, fretted and laughed. There were television sets everywhere, on each floor, one in my office.

The commentators talked shit, saying you couldn't tell yet, but as it got later, you could tell. And suddenly, even they couldn't bullshit about what had happened any longer. Gibson had won! And Harris and James and Westbrook. Tucker and Pinckney had not. Nor Aneses and Oliver. But we didn't believe it; how could that be true? They were all the Community's Choice. We knew that the ballot stuffers and machine jammers had got over in those four cases. We had felt "sweep" all the time. The sweep had been frustrated, but the biggest part, the mayor's spot, had changed hands.

Jesse Jackson had come to town the day before, with his Operation Bread-basket band. They had helped hype people up and pull people out. Now Jesse was in the Hekalu, "502" our enemies called it. The building where all the wild shit emanated. There was much screaming and jumping up and down. People kept flowing into the Hekalu. Not only the workers and visiting students and our own people, but well-wishers and friends. Even some people who had heard the news and simply wanted to "get near the magic" (as Gylan Kain might say).

Jesse and company wanted it quiet so they could hear the TV, but we knew already who had won. People all over the building were whooping and hollering. But finally we got people quiet so Jesse could speak (and some people were drugged by this). Jesse came on like it was His Work (and I don't mean De Lawd), that he had known it all the time and had sent instructions regularly to keep us in it. And there was more to come.

Gibson was having a celebration downtown at the Mosque, a big dance hall on Broad Street. As the Hekalu Umoja (Unity) got overflowing and the final show of victory was coming in, we decided to go downtown too. But before we emptied out the Hekalu, there was a sight on the television that made people jump up and down with pure, unrefined nigger glee. Imperiale and some of his people were shown fighting with the cameramen. They had taken exception to some things CBS had said, so now we watched as Imperiale and company, in complete disarray, started punching and cursing out the cameramen and reporters. They had "sold out white people." The rage, the running-around frustration and confusion was a heartwarming sight, especially to people who themselves were usually in that situation.

As we rolled down the streets, people were everywhere. People literally danced and whirled around, screaming and hugging each other. It was pure joy, running unabated. We had won! We had won! We had beat their ass in their own court. We had whipped their motherfucking ass! It was sweet sweet, sweeter than words can carry.

People walked and ran right down the middle of Broad Street. There was a bus parked in the middle of the street, right in front of the Mosque. The bus driver was out with the rest of the people dancing and hugging. Some people got up on top of the bus and danced back and forth. There was a dynamism loose and roaring in the street. That is the way it must be with revolutionary victories. Our joy literally knew no bounds. And those of us in CFUN swelled up big as houses, we were so proud and filled with a righteous sense of our own strength and power. Hey, we had won! We had kicked those crackers' ass!

Inside the Mosque, there were mountains of people, hugging and screaming. The victorious candidates were there as well as the losers. The losers were grim, but at the same time all of us believed that the whites had stolen the victories from them. We talked about taking up that fight, at the top of our voices. A thousand conversations going on at the scream level.

Finally, Gibson and the other candidates were ready. Jesse and I were also up front. And Jesse gave the same speech he had given up at the Hekalu. He had let Gibson speak at Breadbasket at my urging, and he had come in with his troops during the last days, and all that was good and real. But Jesse went off into this paean to himself that defied belief. We looked at each other and coughed and laughed. Jesse was being Jesse, and although he always styled himself "the Country Preacher," don't believe that for a second. Jesse Jackson is a City Preacher, very City, if you read me. As slick as the big, unpaid-for Cadillacs you see sprinkling the ghetto.

That aura of glorious victory and an unlimited future stayed with us. The next days were filled with our self-appreciating. People called from all over the country and there were interviews every couple minutes. Gibson had won, but now, it appeared, there was to be a runoff in a month, and for the other candidates too. The media held out that Addonizio would take the runoffs, but we knew that was stupid. We had tasted the victory already, the rest of it was formality.

But during this period there was a developing dimension to what had gone down that began to present itself. Gibson was so busy now that he couldn't get to the Sunday meetings, or he couldn't get to all of them. He made most of them right after the first election. But occasionally a representative of his, usually Elton Hill, would come. And this seemed cool to us, we could understand.

The runoff came and Gibson and our candidates who had won the first election skunked Addonizio. (That made it certain that Hughie would soon be in the slam. A year or so later he was sentenced to ten years for corruption.)

But now Gibson found it impossible to make the Sunday meetings. He was mayor now. He had to set up his cabinet. We had discussed this with him, but now he met with us less. Once he got into the mayor's office these meetings were switched to his office, once a week. Baba suggested that something was funny with Ken, that he was acting weird.

Prudential Insurance at first had opposed us, of course. They had put up the fire chief, Caulfield, as opposition. They had first gone with a refined Italian senator, as well, hedging their bets. But the senator struck out quickly. After the runoff, they had a change of mind. Even before this, they had given up some money for voter registration. We had got Howard Samuels, the rich Jewish New York gubernatorial candidate, to come over and support voter registration and used his image to get close enough to Pru for some voter registration moneys and even some money for the convention. Hey, wasn't that the Spirit of Good America, voter registration and public participation in the electoral process? They gave us no chance. But Baba said he had heard that they began rubbing up against Gibson after the first election, giving him a little taste. Now, after the wipe-out, they had crept even closer and Gibson was easing away from us. But I hoped not.

Actually, this would have been the time to take Gibson for a long ride and threaten to blow his head off if he pulled any funny Negro shit. But we didn't, and I have to take the weight for this. Certainly I was counseled to do this by my elders, who really knew how the shit worked.

Still, for the time being, everything was on an upbeat. We were getting ready to run the city. A black-run city—what we had said, what we had thought was the practical approach to Black Power. We had done it; now the heavy work had begun.

My view was that Newark should be a model for the country, for the black movement, of how to gain practical Black Power. In the Continuations Committee meetings of the Black Power Conference, I had advanced this. I wrote a paper called "The Beginnings of National Movement" and another called "The Strategy and Tactics of a Pan-African Nationalist Party," in which these ideas were advanced.

It was also my idea and some other people's that the Black Power Conference, with its informal structure, had to give way to an organization, a national, even Pan-African organization, whose function would be to struggle for Black Power wherever black people were in the world. This was finally accepted in the BPC Continuations meetings. The 1970 Black Power Conference would be held in Atlanta, on the campus of Atlanta University, and its main focus would be the formation of the Congress of Afrikan Peoples. CAP was conceived as a party as well as a united front, which reflected the fuzziness of some of our thinking, although the essence of what we came up with was sound. The African American Nation still needs a national black united front, a liberation front, like the struggling nations and peoples of the Third World have raised to fight colonialism and imperialism in general.

The meeting was in September, Labor Day. That same weekend, the Black Panther Party held its Constitutional Convention in Washington, D.C. The Panthers drew about 10,000 people, we drew about 4,000, so that there were maybe 14,000 people meeting that weekend trying to transform an oppressive U.S. society.

But now we ran into open conflict with Karenga. Because of the siege situation in L.A., Karenga made none of the Continuations Committee meetings leading up to the CAP conference in Atlanta. I had sent him information, and occasionally he would send a rep, but as things got worse in L.A., he could not even send anyone. Actually we were supposed to be his representatives.

However, since Karenga had not been at the meetings and had not been able to impose his personal stamp on what had developed, he now suddenly opposed having the conference. First he had someone call me and tell me this, that all those plans for having a conference in Atlanta had to be scrapped. I couldn't or didn't want to understand this. I told his caller that I needed some clarification. What did this mean? Couldn't I talk to Maulana myself? A few days later one of the advocates called me from L.A. and then someone got on the phone. He sounded drowsy, as if he were drifting through deep space and conversation was a tremendous effort he could not consistently sustain. "Baaaaa-raaaaa-kaaaaa"—his saying of my name took seconds. He began trying to tell me something about "not disobeying him." He seemed to be repeating this over and over again, from somewhere high up over the rainbow. It was Karenga. He sounded drunk or high. It was astonishing.

I kept saying that the 1970 meeting was very important. That we had already mobilized people. People were ready all over the country. I didn't see how we could just drop the idea. Why? What was the reason? What he was saying seemed arbitrary and certainly disjointed. There was no sense to it. He was saying something about how we didn't need to hold the conference. He mentioned the Panthers. But we were pulling out the whole spectrum of the black community, from one ocean to the other. We were pulling together a true united-front meeting. The Panthers couldn't stop us. They were having their own meeting anyway, there was no reason for them to hassle us, nor we to hassle them.

What I didn't count on was the extent of Karenga's bizarrerie. He had mumbled in a later conversation that he was going to "send some people" to the conference. After the first conversation, I had felt totally disconnected from him. Now I knew that was real, we had no more connection of any positive nature. He was threatening us. If we went on with the CAP conference he would send people to disrupt it.

As the time for the conference got closer, I called our people together and announced that the alliance between CFUN and US was no longer. Ex-advocates from L.A. had been coming back East for a while now with various horror stories about the organization's degeneration. So the straight-out directive that we were no longer allies was not as shocking as it would have been a year or so before.

I had met with Balozi and Mfundishi to discuss the Atlanta conference, since CAP was going to be a national front, with entire organizations as members on one level. Even though we couldn't be in the same organization, certainly we could be in the same united front. We contacted various organizations across the country, mobilizing people for the conference. We had been developing closer ties with organizations with a similar Pan-African nationalist ideology. There were some folks in the Bronx who had a community organization that Shorty had joined; also, Les Campbell, later Jitu Weusi, a friend of Sonny Carson's, had organized a cultural center in Brooklyn called The East. We had begun to communicate on a limited basis, particularly through Carson in the Continuations Committee meetings.

The security for the Atlanta meeting would be the CFUN Simba and Saidi, the BCD brothers who had gone off with Balozi and Mfundishi, and some of the ex-US advocates who'd split from L.A. and come out to the East Coast. Balozi and Mfundishi perhaps had never forgiven Maulana for taking sides with me. Balozi had come to some of the Continuations Committee meetings as well, so he felt the Atlanta conference should go on too.

The conference itself was a historic meeting very much like the conventions held during the early part of the 19th century, the black convention movement, which provided a lot of the fuel for the abolitionist movement, black and white. All of the Black Power Conferences must be compared to those early-19th-century conventions. They had the same objective: Black Liberation!

Ken Gibson, Jesse Jackson, Roy Innis of CORE, Richard Hatcher (himself newly elected as mayor of Gary, Indiana), Whitney Young of the Urban League, Minister Farrakhan of the Nation of Islam, Julian Bond (head of the Atlanta host committee), the ambassadors from Guinea and Tanzania, representatives from many of the African liberation movements, Imari Obadele from the Republic of New Africa, Howard Fuller (later Owusu Sadaukai) of Malcolm X University in Greensboro (who read a message from Stokely Carmichael), Max Stanford (now Muhammad Ahmed) of RAM, an NAACP national officer all appeared, made major speeches, and participated in the conference. But almost from the outset, Karenga's people did appear. There were six or seven of them, all dressed identically, all carrying the characteristic attaché cases in which we used to carry our heat around before the airlines put up the metal detectors. When we saw them we knew what those cases meant. Word was got to me immediately about the six, mostly new, people who had appeared and who were now marching ominously around the campus which was the conference site trying silently to intimidate people.

Their leader had asked to see me and some of the brothers didn't want to allow it. But it seemed to me that the best thing to do was to take them all the way out, as far as they wanted to go, peaceably, and to make plans for dealing with them in other ways if they wanted to take it there. The US brother told me that Maulana wanted to speak to me. He would call and then I could speak to him. All right, call him.

Karenga got on the phone and said some of the same things. They really seemed out now, because the conference was going on. There was no turning back. Karenga's shrill little voice raced up and down in his wearying attempt to make what he was saying sound rational. After we talked, the tactical leader stood looking at me. I said, "OK, we've talked. Is there anything else?" He turned and went out.

The security heads came together to discuss this problem. What were these Karenga dudes really going to do? Threats aside, what would they really attempt? George Armstrong, who had once been head of Karenga's security forces, as Weusi, said he thought we should take the attache cases away from the L.A. brothers. Mfundishi seemed to be going along with this, but I squashed this as hard as I could. Trying to take those cases away from them would mean instant confrontation, possibly shooting, maybe an end to the conference in wild chaos. Wasn't that what Karenga wanted? No, we would cool it. We would tail them, but let them go anywhere they wanted to go in the conference the public was. They could participate like anybody else. Let 'em in any of the workshops they wanted to go in. They were our guests. They were emissaries from Maulana Karenga, certainly they were welcome. But we would tail them.

A couple more times the brother who seemed to be in charge of the "killer squad" said Maulana had requested that I talk to him on the phone. We talked again, but the third time I was unavailable. Karenga was just saving face over the phone now. There were no incidents except one young brother roused the troops in the middle of the night by shooting himself in the foot while on security. This was the joke of the conference and lightened the mood as our combined units of Simba and Saidi, their blood tingling because of the possibility of confrontation, marched back and forth to their posts or drilled so that all could see we had a strong and disciplined security force. I had learned that from Karenga—a show of force often precludes having to use it. Karenga had learned it from Sun Tzu, the great Chinese military master.

I was directing the Political Action Workshop of the conference, and the most important thing to come out of that workshop was the call for a Liberation Front of black people that should include even the Panthers and the League of Revolutionary Black Workers, two left organizations that the nationalists usually would not work with. We were also supposed to go on organizing a "cadre organization" of Pan-African nationalists to continue to build the united front structure formalized in this meeting.

One of the most important points to come out of this workshop was that we should call, by 1972, a National Black Political Convention, not only to flesh out the united front structure but also to choose candidates to run in the major elections and to give black people a unified voice in dealing with the presidential election.

There was one famous photo in *Jet* of the conference in which Hayward Henry, who was elected chairman of CAP, is shown holding up Minister Farrakhan's hand along with Whitney Young's hand to symbolize the unity found at the conference. Farrakhan had delivered a crowd-pleasing address, in a style that made some people think perhaps he should pay royalties to Malcolm's family. As it was, Betty Shabazz, who also spoke at the conference, left in stony silence when Farrakhan and his party appeared. Many people were surprised that Whitney Young (called "Whitey" Young by many of the nationalists) even showed, especially since there were a couple people on the program who had been locked up just a few years before, having been framed by the FBI for planning to assassinate Young. Roy Wilkins, who was also one of the targets for this bullshit FBI assassination plot, did not show.

Hayward Henry was a young Unitarian minister who headed up the Black Affairs Council of the Unitarian Church. The white churches had begun to set up such groups in their midst as blacks in white churches demanded that these churches share some of their vast resources with the black community. Henry, along with Richard Traylor and Law Gothard, had come in with some money to help with voter registration in Newark, and we had gotten rather close. Later Henry set up a chapter of CAP in Boston and Traylor set one up in Philadelphia.

Not only was the conference a success, but what had happened also was the meeting and identification of kindred forces in the Black Liberation movement. We had brought hundreds of black organizations together and some who seriously thought along the same lines that we did. We were trying to evolve an ideology that could deal with black nationalism as well as African liberation. It was Pan-Afrikan Nationalism. (A "k" in "Afrika" because one of our theorists, Brother Ruwa Chiri, who belonged to an organization called UFOMI—United Africans for One Motherland

Indivisible—put out a newsletter explaining that "c" did not exist in African languages.) But we were also heavily indebted to Karenga's Kawaida, which remained an underlying structure we related to. We could not work with him, but we were still committed to Kawaida and its multiple lists and the Nguzo Saba and Kwanzaa.

Back in Newark, our thrust now was toward the creation of a national organization. We were CFUN, one chapter of the Congress of Afrikan Peoples. We had also met brothers and sisters who had organizations in Pittsburgh, Gary, South Bend, Indianapolis, St. Louis, Detroit, Camden, and Cleveland who wanted to hook up with the cadre structure of CAP.

Gibson had spoken in Atlanta, and his appearance, even though he wasn't much of a speaker, had been electric. The national black community of political activists honored him, honored CFUN and me for the job we had done in the election victory. It was this victory that raised CFUN's stature among the organizations. We had done some practical work and won it.

At home, Gibson's drifting continued. Our meetings were now at his office. Gradually, they became less and less regular. A couple times we had to speak to him and get reassurances from him that he wasn't trying anything. But the whole thing seemed more and more like it was getting fucked up. We were supposed to plan this shit together, the people who had put out the muscle and vision to get his ass in. But he was pulling a disappearing act right before our eyes.

One thing went down before the first year was out to make me clear on what was happening. I had put together a comprehensive cultural program for the city. What it called for, generally, was a consolidation of the cultural resources of the city, to expand the city's education capacity and transform the city into a cultural center. We did not have a lot of money but we could transform the city, I reasoned, by intensive cultural activity, even bring in some revenue and give the grim-visaged town a new image.

Gibson appeared to like the program. He formed a cultural committee to deal with the plan's implementation. The committee was designed to bring the different interests together in the city who were interested in culture and the arts or education. Prudential had a representative at that first meeting, Al DeRogatis, the old New York Giants football player, now community affairs specialist for the Prudential Life Insurance Company, the largest life insurance company in the world, whose main headquarters was in Newark. Prudential, hooked up with the Rockefeller interests through the Prudential-Manufacturers Hanover Trust group, of course, owns New

Jersey, legislature and all. DeRogatis, who was one of the Giants' game announcers at one point, was the kind of community affairs specialist who sat with the president of Prudential in his top-floor offices near the huge boardroom with raisable stained-glass windows and a view of their own communities way up in the mountains overlooking our grimy black town. On the outside of the boardroom were large paintings of the board members. It seemed as if there had been some major breakthroughs, as there were at least one Italian and one Jew on the wall among the smiling Anglos. DeRogatis was security as well as community affairs.

Before our first meeting of the cultural committee was over, DeRogatis had said to all in the room that he could not be in a meeting in which I was a participant. This was Prudential's position. But it was not even a real confrontation. It was a fait accompli. Gibson and the Prus had obviously talked about this before. But I thought it was a simple confrontation — that it was even good that it had come out so soon and could be gotten out of the way. Prudential was obviously one of our enemies and we would have to fight them. But that was the last cultural committee meeting Gibson was to call. Because of Prudential's displeasure with me, Gibson scrapped the committee. At first, when such things happened, I thought Gibson was simply ball-less, but as it went on, the pattern was clear he had been "purchased," as Baba had suggested.

Each week, after a while, there was some new affront, some new confrontation between the old team and Gibson. The city tax on out-of-city workers, who had most of the jobs in the city, since Newark is an insurance and commercial and banking center and most blacks are not brought into these businesses in any number approaching their actual existence in the society, Gibson gave some lip service to, but quickly got silent when Prudential let it be known that they were opposed to the tax. All the promises and issues to come out of the Black and Puerto Rican Convention Gibson slid away from. And before the second year of his term was up he had attacked us openly, though in a slightly indirect way.

CFUN had managed to get some influence over the local antipoverty agency, the United Community Corporation. Even before the election, we were swarming all over their public meetings, attacking UCC's administration along with Addonizio. After the election we moved quickly to grab some real control over key sectors of the agency. This allowed us to put people in positions of power in the agency, including the president, David Barrett (Mtetezi), the trustees, and, finally, even the assistant director of the agency.

An open confrontation came when Gibson secretly backed a coalition of our enemies, who had been his enemies, too, before the election. His henchman, Clarence Coggins, put the attack together, trying to mobilize people to join the UCC so they could vote for Coalition Six to replace our people on the board of trustees, thereby limiting or totally eliminating our influence. But we outmobilized, outorganized, and beat them cold. George Richardson again figured in this traitorous business, and again he got his ass beat!

Now word was running around the city that Gibson was trying to cut himself loose from our baleful influence completely. Gibson thought, and he said this again and again, through the years, that he was the mayor. To him, this meant that he had to do everything himself, answerable only to his own mind and conscience (and the Prugeoisie). What limitations to impose upon a person. Even if Ken Gibson were intelligent, he could not do this. Not being intelligent made it difficult for him even to conceive of certain possibilities. For instance, not long after he got elected, Gibson painted the gold dome on the City Hall yellow. I guess he couldn't wallpaper it; for one sector of the lower middle class, cheap gloss paint is the answer to all problems.

It was his civil servant's mentality, that heaven is a place where GS-1000s go, that ultimately restricted him to mediocrity. He could not really conceive of black people having to make their own way, of self-determination and self-sufficiency. A government check is the only way we'll make it. So he gradually moved from being some kind of spokesperson for an independent black community to being a messenger to black people for the federal government's shenanigans.

We clashed now repeatedly and more and more openly. Our Sunday meetings became a thing of the past. But meanwhile we tried to work with him. We knew we could still benefit in some ways by the association, so we still tried to relate to him as we could.

CAP grew steadily, with new cities coming in nationally, where we had developed cadres—Chicago (through Don Lee, the poet, who was now Haki Madhubuti), Delaware, Philadelphia, Boston, Albany. Even the San Diego chapter of US had broken away from Karenga and become a chapter of the Congress of Afrikan Peoples.

Our main work nationally, aside from building the cadre organizations of Pan-Afrikan Nationals heavily influenced by Kawaida, was to put together the convention called for by the Atlanta mandate. I traveled around the country meeting with different organizations. There was much political activity, and not just in the Black Liberation movement; now, as the 1972 presidential elections drew closer, a wide spectrum of people were busy getting ready to take part in those elections.

We had now gained a good entree with black electoral figures, because of the Gibson election. Electoral politics had become an obvious arena for the struggle for Black Power. We met with the black congressmen and congresswomen, who had now put together the concept of the Congressional Black Caucus. One meeting we had in D.C. with representatives of the caucus—Owusu Sadaukai, a national NAACP rep, a rep from the Urban League and the Urban Coalition, plus some of the old Black Power Conference Continuations Committee people—put the conceptualization of the National Black Political Convention squarely on the agenda. The caucus itself had a gathering a few months later, at which Shirley Chisholm declared her "presidential aspirations." She attacked the male caucus members for not supporting her. I raised the Black Convention as the only viable way to proceed. If the black masses at a national convention wanted her, then let the convention declare that and then let black people come out and not only vote for Shirley Chisholm for president of the U.S. but convince others to do so as well! I later discovered that Ms. Chisholm's candidacy was just an attempt to get a front position at Mr. McGovern's pay window, that it was not serious at all. (In fact, the whole motion of black politicians toward the 1972 elections and the relationship of their real aspirations to the needs of the black masses I put in an article first published by *Black World*, the old *Negro Digest*, called "Miami Before and After." Hoyt Fuller, the editor, changed the title to "Toward the Creation of Institutions for All African People." See *Jesse Jackson and Black People* [Chicago: Third World Press, 1995].)

In the end there was no clear place the politicians could turn but the Black Convention and seem as relevant to the movement as they wanted to seem in 1971. The endorsement by the Congressional Black Caucus of the National Black Political Convention brought it together as the most forceful demonstration of mass motion toward the realization of Black Power of that period. Gary, Indiana, was selected because it had a black mayor (one who was more progressive than our own K.G.) and because Gary was in the middle of the country, just outside Chicago.

Some nine thousand people came to Gary, and since it was all black, the convention represented a far larger concentration of the black masses than even the Panther Constitutional Conference, which also gathered many whites and other oppressed nationalities besides African Americans.

In this period CAP had become a relatively powerful, well-disciplined national organization, with chapters in some eighteen cities. I was its political empowerment chairman as well as program chairman. The strong, well-organized base in Newark gave me a great deal to say in CAP affairs, and the Newark cadre was generally considered the most advanced group of cadres in the national organization.

A triumvirate was elected to pull the convention together. We wanted to draw all sectors of the black nation together. So that Mayor Hatcher, Congressman Charles Diggs of Detroit, and I were chosen as the three coconvenors. The sight of some nine-thousand-plus black people together in and outside the huge arena in Gary was deeply stirring. We had put up signs alphabetically throughout the hall so that the different state delegates would be seated just as in the Democratic and Republican conventions. We had also worked out a formula for how many delegates could be represented from each state according to the number of blacks in that state. Gibson thought that he should be chairman of the Jersey delegation, but the delegates elected me, which burned him up. But more and more people were beginning to find out just how jive Newark's first black mayor was becoming.

A very fine film was made of the entire convention by black filmmaker William Greaves. It is narrated by Sidney Poitier and shows Harry Belafonte, Isaac Hayes, Bobby Seale, who spoke one evening, Jesse Jackson, hosts of black politicians, Richard Roundtree of *Shaft* fame, and the thousands of black people intensely participating in a sincere effort to transform their lives and the society.

The NAACP issued a statement, from the national office, telling white folks it wanted no part of this all-black proceeding, even before the convention started. But the masses were there, bodily and in spirit. When it was over, we put together a fairly progressive document known as the Black Agenda. This was composed of resolutions voted by the convention, and this document was supposed to be used on a national or local level to present to candidates so that they would know black people's concerns. I was even appointed to go down to Miami to the Democratic convention to make sure that any of the politicians who wanted the black vote had to agree to the issues presented in the National Black Agenda. But once in Miami, the majority of the black politicians who were talking much militant shit in Gary reverted to character and were simply scrambling to get on some candidate's payroll. Jesse Jackson, Shirley Chisholm, Ken Gibson, most of the Congressional Black Caucus were whoring like nobody's business. I wrote about this in the *Black World* article, which in turn made many of those folks very angry. Charles Evers was such a bold-faced "ho" it was embarrassing, switching from candidate to candidate, with his hand out and his butt cocked for ready access. In a few minutes he switched from Humphrey to Chisholm to McGovern. Whenever I raised the question of the Black Agenda, such an idea was openly scoffed at. Hey, that was just for show. Shirley Chisholm refused to come to the Black Convention, where she could easily have won the black nomination and mobilized the black masses, if that's what she had really wanted to do. And then there was the charade about which black was closer to the biggest white. Ken Gibson came out into a conference of well-known black political types telling us that McGovern's choice of a running mate was the mayor of Boston, only to have McGovern, almost immediately after Gibson's statement, on a television playing in the same room announce that it was Congressman Eagleton. Ken did get the privilege of nominating Eagleton, which was considered hot stuff by the Washington black politicos, but lo and behold it's shown that Eagleton is a mental case so Gibson's great nomination came to naught.

But the Black Convention was a high moment in my life. Several times I had to chair the huge meeting, keeping a balance and the procedure flowing at the same time. It was the kind of challenge that made the adrenaline rush through your head and your whole body tingle. There was even a bomb scare while I was presiding (probably by the FBI) and I had to evacuate the huge building without causing too much alarm.

Coleman Young, later the mayor of Detroit, got some kind of note at the National Black Convention when he led a walkout of Michigan delegates. I was dumbfounded and demanded to know what was going on. It turned out that one group of blacks was going to push a resolution calling for separate black trade unions. Young was a UAW political cadre, so he was trying to avoid blowing his own gig.

There was much infighting and confrontations between different groups. Just like in the Congress of the U.S. In truth, that was our model for the National Black Political Assembly, the mechanism we created to elect delegates to the convention. We wanted to create a focused national group dealing with black concerns, the members of which would be elected every two years. We wanted a Congress for the black nation to act on our concerns as if we were a nation with political power.

Owusu Sadaukai stopped me in the hallway and said he had been told that CAP was going to attack him if he or his people did not vote as we wanted. This was science fiction, I told him, but I wondered who would put that out. Probably, again, Hoover's Heathens. If anything, we wanted to get closer to Sadaukai and the Malcolm X Liberation University he headed because we respected what they were doing, despite our differences of interpretation about Pan-Africanism.

Roy Innis and his CORE people provided the most tension and nutty confrontations. Innis thought what he had to do was come out to the convention and straight-out "bogart" everybody with some big fat gun-toting gorillas. But as bad as he must've thought he was, I wasn't too worried because we had people with the same equipment, more of it and better training.

Innis wanted to push an "antibusing" plank through the convention, but finally there was a compromise of language on the resolution that actually passed. Most of the black masses are not interested in busing, they want to know why they can't get quality education right in their neighborhoods.

That busing resolution and the last one that hit the floor the final night of the convention, which called for "the dismantling of the state of Israel," caused the most controversy. The last resolution was widely blamed on me by the press, but in truth I had known nothing at all about it or its origins. It had come from Reverend Douglas of the Black United Front of D.C.

The shock waves caused by the Black Convention swept all across the country. We had raised up another level, we were not just militant, we were organizing. At the end of the convention, Mayor Hatcher was elected chairman of the National Black Political Assembly, which became a forum for continuing the work of the convention, and Congressman Diggs, president of the national convention itself. I was named secretary-general. The task with the most work but, at the same time, the job that would give us the most hand in organizing the Assembly and bringing in new forces. We wanted to make sure that the Assembly went on and reached out even further.

During this same period another very important formation in the Black Liberation movement was organized. Owusu Sadaukai had gone to Mozambique and had talked with many of the liberation fighters. They had told him that the best thing African Americans could do to help their struggle would be to send dollar and materiel support but, most important, to wage struggle over here in the U.S. against the U.S. imperialist superpower.

When Owusu returned he began to contact people about forming an organization in the U.S. which would focus on supporting the African liberation movements and mobilizing people to struggle over here. And so work began on organizing what was known first as the African Liberation Day Support Committee, later as the African Liberation Support Committee.

From the beginning CAP was in the forefront of efforts to build the ALSC. The first focus was to mobilize people to march in D.C. in May 1972 on what had been designated African Liberation Day by the Organization of African Unity. There was some negativity between the organizers of ALSC and people in Guyana and even Stokely Carmichael because some people had a very partisan understanding of struggle and thought that if such and such wasn't being organized under their direction and according to the ideological designs of their group then it shouldn't be supported. But we went past that. CAP sent a person down to D.C. to help with the organizing and national mobilization. Just as we had done with the Black Convention, bringing together a broad united front.

That first ALSC demo saw more than fifty thousand people march in D.C. and another ten thousand march in San Francisco. Black nationalists and Pan-Africanists, workers, students, elected officials, all participated in the mobilization and program. We marched and also stopped in front of the Portuguese, Rhodesian, and South African embassies to denounce them. We grouped at the foot of the Washington Monument, with miles and miles of black folks stretched out in all directions away from the monument. The Panthers' Elaine Brown spoke, surrounded by a crew of big-hatted security brothers. Congressman Diggs, dressed in a dashiki, denounced South Africa (and it was probably as a result of these appearances by Diggs that the racists in Congress and the FBI decided that he must be busted so that his seniority and chairmanship of the Africa committee would not stall their defense of white colonialism and racism in Africa). Haki Madhubuti read, a group sang, a preacher prayed. I spoke too. But Owusu raised everybody up as he ended with the final address to the audience, quoting Frederick Douglass.

Both the National Black Assembly and the ALSC formed in 1972, perhaps a high point of black organization at the time. But by 1975, both organizations had peaked as the result of too many internal contradictions and errors and the interference of the state. CAP also had its high point of organization and influence in '72. That fall, at our CAP convention held in San Diego, I was elected national chairman, replacing Hayward Henry.

This meant that the Kawaida influence in CAP had consolidated at the highest level, but there were also intense and still developing contradictions.

For one thing Karenga sent a few carloads of intimidators down from L.A. to pull the same shit at the CAP conference as he had pulled in Atlanta two years before. Perhaps he was still smarting from the effrontery we had had to go ahead with a project of such magnitude without his being in the driver's seat. But he had not been in any condition to drive anything. A short time later, his whole playhouse came tumbling down when he got arrested and jailed for "torturing" two female members of the organization. This and his wife testified against him as well as George Armstrong-Weusi. He was incarcerated in St. Louis Obipso in California.

In the '72 confrontation, two groups of armed brothers, dressed in dashikis, some old comrades, stood facing each other, ready to fight. For what? Some vague egotistical king-of-the-hill bullshit. But the conference went on. Owusu spoke and C. L. R. James, the Trinidadian writer. Unfortunately, for all of C.L.R.'s great work, he is still very much influenced by his Trotskyist youth and often counsels people incorrectly, telling them that spontaneous organization by the masses is a substitute for the Leninist vanguard party. It was just such counsel that delayed the Grenadian revolution when the revolutionaries tried to overthrow Eric Gairy without a revolutionary vanguard, heavily influenced by C.L.R.'s antiparty line. But he is still a great historical writer and his books of Marxist and cultural historical theory and his book on Haiti, Black Jacobins, are landmark works.

If my election as chairman of CAP meant a consolidation of the Kawaida tendencies, it also meant that CAP would be moving even more sharply to the left. Our contact with Owusu Sadaukai and the Malcolm X Liberation University had made us place more emphasis on Pan-Africanism, though we never believed as Stokely and Owusu did that our only struggle was in Africa. When Owusu ceased to believe this, he and Stokely split up.

In the CAP newspaper, we now pushed nationalism-Pan Afrikanism-Ujamaa. Our reasoning was that we had to fight the black liberation struggle here in the U.S., support the liberation of Africa, and at the same time push cooperative economics (as Ujamaa was defined in the Nguzo Saba). We didn't know it clearly at the time, but there were Communists inside the ALSC, black Communists. We had only very little to do with them consciously, but obviously we were being influenced. The Black Workers Congress, the black Marxist group that had formed after the demise of the League of Black Revolutionary Workers in Detroit, was in ALSC. The

Congress never came out directly and tried to organize as it should have; it worked on the inside insinuating and implying but never came straight out. If they had done so, I believe they could have set a clearer direction for people inside ALSC, especially those more advanced forces who were actively seeking to understand how to make revolution.

If the CAP newspaper is analyzed, the organization's move toward the left will be obvious. We went from nationalism-Pan Afrikanism-Ujamaa to nationalism-Pan Afrikanism-African Scientific Socialism. Then A.S.S. became socialism, to which we appended Kwame Nkrumah's definition. We even issued buttons for the CAP cadres which said nationalism-Pan Afrikanism-socialism.

The contradictions in our leftward move were that we were deeply rooted in cultural nationalism of the Karenga-Kawaida variety. The ex-L.A. cadres who came East brought even a heavier dose of this with them. Everyone of them who came East lasted in CFUN only a few months. One ex-L.A. advocate, from East Orange, had been one of Karenga's personal enforcers. In the end, Karenga had turned on him and got somebody to split his head open. We had to put him out of CAP because he had brought the L.A. polygamy trip with him and was running it to the brothers in the organization, implying that I was repressing them by not letting them practice polygamy.

A few months after we kicked this fellow out of CAP he shows up at the Central Committee of a Communist organization preaching against cultural nationalism. It was he who even helped put Karenga's wife out of the house one night in a fit of drowsy pique. She called Amina and sobbed this over the phone.

Mtume, the rock star, was in the US organization. He came East with the ex's but he brought so much of the same L.A. baggage that we could not work with him. The organization was a Kawaida organization, but it was not nor had never been as deeply into all the rites and rituals that Maulanism carries.

We were going to the left, and I was reading Nkrumah and Cabral and Mao. We had started to think about an Africa that was still alive and in chains, actively struggling for liberation. One heavy part of the Kawaida doctrine was based on a never-never-land Africa, the African paradise of the first chapter of *Roots*. We were finding out about an Africa of imperialist domination and class struggle. For Nkrumah and Cabral, the enemy of Africa was imperialism, not just white people. Though we had been influenced by the Black Muslim cosmology, Malcolm's assassination had served to estrange many of us from the Black Muslims. The "white devil" philosophy was shown to be too narrow and limiting. We could see its reactionary underpinnings. Though the everyday torture white people took us through made our coming out of narrow nationalism problematic.

But CAP was a Kawaida organization. On the positive side, our attention to things African came as the supposed antidote to our deep suspension inside the self-hatred of white chauvinism presented as "learning" or "culture" or simply as "facts." For the middle-class intellectuals of an oppressed people such suspension has always been quite deep, so the desire to get away from this condition tends to be extreme.

Negatively, merely returning to various forms of African dress and learning a few Swahili words cannot effect black liberation. There is (right now even this very moment) a need for a cultural revolution, but the culture must be that of the black masses, given revolutionary focus and, as a whole, part of the actual political thrust itself.

We were doing political work, much of it successful and necessary. We were setting an example of work and struggle for an entire community of black nationalists and even many others. But the reactionary nature of much of the Kawaida doctrine could not help but affect us negatively. For one thing, it encouraged a feudalistic, even dictatorial style of leadership. It was never my nature to be as absolute in my pronouncements as was called for by Maulanaism; we always had various councils and committees and various checks and balances, but that one-person "godlike" rule was evident and we were criticized for it, mostly behind our backs. Some of the criticism was accurate. We needed even more.

Another deeply negative aspect of Kawaida was its position and social practice relating to women. Some of the doctrine was so far out I never attempted to bring it to Newark. Karenga's peculiar focus on women, *all* women, led me to believe semisubconsciously that many of his statements and prescriptions about women were best left alone.

A third backwardness of Kawaida, even as it was manifest within CFUN and CAP, was the openly metaphysical character of the ideology. Kawaida was and is, if it still exists, a *religion*. On one level this had its tactical uses; for example, it enabled us to go into many of the prisons as *priests* and teach black nationalism. It allowed us tax exemption for various operations. But it was a cultural religion tracing its spiritual origins back to "the first ancestor." The "priest" appellation for the officers of "the Temple of Kawaida" was real and it was taken by the advocates as such. That is why the one-man leadership (at whatever level) could get over so easily. That is the priest's relationship to his flock—godlike.

So the big three cornerstones of our backwardness: feudalistic, one-man domination; male chauvinism given legitimacy as "revolutionary"; metaphysics. These three deeply rooted errors led to many others for which these were the base.

As we moved to the left all three of these things were challenged more and more. My wife, Amina, had always resisted the male chauvinism, not only from me but at all levels of the organization. But the feudalistic structure of the organization meant that I was away and aloof from much of what was going on, which is not to say I was above it, but simply unable to recognize certain problems and correct them, even if I'd wanted to.

To a great degree the women in the organization had developed into a separate organization under Amina's direction. This in itself set many of the male officers against her, as they tried to bring the women under their more direct authority. Her struggle against male chauvanism encouraged the women in the organization to struggle against it as well and this struggle went on behind closed doors or sometimes much more publicly.

Amina had a great innovative and creative influence on the organization as well. She could introduce new ideas, particularly variations on the Pan-Afrikan or neotraditional social organization that we practiced. It was she who actually designed in the most practical way such an impractical idea as communal living under capitalism. She named her collectives Umuzi, after the collective houses of the Zulu. Here the advocates lived together collectively or semicollectively. The Temple would buy the house and the various families would pay rent, stripped down to just the basic mortgage, to the Temple. The advocates would handle the mortgage and the upkeep. The Temple just had title.

But the morality and consciousness of people under capitalism tends to be individualistic. Some of the should-be collectivist families felt that collectivity and communalism meant that they had a free ride while others had to slave to make it. Plus, many of the people were young and they had never had a job or had to be out on their own. The organization was father and mother and all the family they had. The organization provided them with a job and a house and so some of them lost contact with the real world.

As head of social organization for CFUN and CAP, Amina presided over and planned the various weddings (arusi), feasts (karamu), baby showers (akika) that went on in Newark and created ways these should be done throughout the country. As far as I was concerned, the most important of these was the Afrikan Free School. Named after the first free public school in the United States, the AFS was started in the late '60s out of the Spirit House. It was first called the Community Free School. Initially Amina and the other sisters living at the Spirit House gathered the children around the neighborhood and began to teach them. This was after we discovered that many of the children we wanted to get to act in our plays could not read.

But after the '70 election we expanded our operations. First AFS moved down to High Street, then we got a building just for the school. It was on Clinton Avenue and Amina designed and picked out all its furnishings, the desks and cabinets, the books and maps and globes. The Afrikan Free School was a high level of accomplishment. During that period we also had a public school version of AFS in the Marcus Garvey School (which used to be Robert Treat). After the election we had renamed many of the city's schools. South Side High became Malcolm X Shabazz High; there was a Harriet Tubman School, a Martin Luther King School, a Rosa Parks School, etc. Newark Rutgers was forced to name their student center Paul Robeson Center and even give Robeson a doctorate. By the time we tried to change the name of Belmont Avenue to Malcolm X Boulevard, Gibson had squared up completely along with City Council President Earl Harris whom I had loaned some of my personal money to run, and they, along with other reactionaries, blocked this. Belmont Avenue is now named Irvine Turner Boulevard after the first black councilman, but as these politicians got more and more backward, you could tell from the names that got put on things—now there is a Floyd Patterson School! Jesu Christo, Floyd Patterson? In 1980 somebody wanted to name a street after B. F. Johnson, the man who organized the Preachers for Addonizio—to show you how far the shit had turned around.

The Afrikan Free School was a very influential institution not only in Newark, which we now called New Ark, but throughout the country. Under Amina's direction it became a model for independent black schools everywhere. The basic elements of the curriculum were African and African American history; also African and African American culture, what the universities would call humanities of course. But African and African American humanities. AFS taught world history as well and American history; we did not want the children one-sided. Plus mathematics, reading, health, science, physical education. We were accredited by the New

Jersey Educational Association as an elementary school. We even had graduates go on to high school, out of the Garvey class.

Amina organized the parents of the AFS children very well. They were expected to help the school survive, since we charged no tuition. AFS taught not just the children of the CFUN advocates, but got a following of parents from the whole Newark community. Later, when we decided that the AFS still constituted "private education" and that we had to go back to dealing with public education and resume our struggles in the public schools, these parents resisted and opposed our move with all their might.

Amina also came up with the idea that the best way to free up the women and even the men for more political work was to start a twenty-four-hour day-care center at the school where the advocates could leave their children. The women in the organization were organized into shifts so that children could be left there at any time and picked up at any time. So we had twenty-four-hour security at all our buildings (there were now three of them) and twenty-four-hour day care. Amina was concerned that in the Kawaida organization there was a tendency to deal the women out of the politics of the organization. They had their "role," which Karenga defined as "social organization, teaching the children, and inspiring the men," in the reverse order. As stated it was about as limiting as "Kinder, Kirche, and Küche." So the appointment of women to the various other departments, such as Siasa (politics), Uchumi (economics), Kuumba (arts), was important to her, and she reasoned that if the usual institutionalized societal limitations could be somewhat modified, women could participate more in other aspects of the organization and develop more.

The women had ranks within their own group as well. They were either Malaika, the good spirits, or, on a higher level, Muminina, the Believers. Amina really studied African culture, so the women and the men in CFUN and in most parts of CAP reflected that serious study. It was always a drag to encounter a group of cultural nationalists who thought that the ideology deserved no serious study and that the depth and richness of it could be expressed sartorially.

The CFUN/CAP uniform for the men was the dashiki for everyday wear and a version of the Tanzanian national dress suit for special occasions. The women wore the beautiful colorful bubbas and lappas and geles which Amina taught all of them to wear and sew. Later she developed a woman's version of the national dress suit. We established a bookstore which also sold the clothes and suits, with our own label and a department making the clothes to be sold in the store (Duka Ujamaa).

At one point we had the bookstore, Afrikan Printing Cooperative, where we also printed our own books and propaganda. Our newspaper, a monthly, we changed to *Unity & Struggle* to demonstrate our growing familiarity with dialectics. Our publishing company, first called Jihad (Holy War), as we moved to the left was called People's War, showing we had read Mao. The Spirit House Movers still traveled around performing mostly my plays and reading poetry; their name was later changed to Afrikan Revolutionary Movers (ARM).

Amina opened a dining room in our Hekalu Mwalimu (named after Julius Nyerere, president of Tanzania) where the advocates could eat hearty food for next to nothing. We did not eat meat, only fish, and otherwise were vegetarians. The dining room also had a fair-sized clientele of people in the neighborhood who liked to come in and talk and eat Amina's special menu. Many hot political discussions went down in that dining room.

Hekalu Mwalimu was a large, beautiful building. It also had a giant auditorium where we held our weekly Soul Sessions, Karamus, weddings, and other public events. This is also where we performed plays while in Newark.

The auditorium was decorated with huge photographs of Pan-Afrikan leaders, but as we moved to the left we also put up Third World leaders. In the basement, where a bowling alley had been, we built a TV studio. We got CBS and NBC to give us some of their older broadcast equipment and we put together a studio with some money we got through UCC. We set up a communications training program, taught young people television programming, and made over a hundred of taped programs ourselves. Our people in the arts were taught to use the cameras and other equipment first. A brother named David Shakes (Mchochezi) ran all this and he did it well.

The reason we built the studio is that we were determined to get a cable franchise when cable was first being talked about not only as an alternate means of reaching people but as a potential moneymaker. But again Kenneth Gibson in all his new mediocre backwardness opposed this, telling us that cable should be public. He allowed the state government to put a moratorium on all cable franchises just to stop a black organization from getting control of a couple of channels.

We had convinced the chairman of TelePrompTer, the oldest of the cable operations, to institute a training program in Newark for minorities so that they could hire them as they wired the city up. We also made a deal which would give us two channels (one for educational uses, the other to do regular black programming and sell advertising) plus equity in the parent Newark company. Gibson was so dull that he obstructed the deal and it was killed. We brought in advisers from all over the country to talk to him, including Phil Watson, who put together Howard University's School of Communications; Ted Ledbetter, who later owned a television station in the Virgin Islands and was then a candidate for head of the FCC; and Tony Brown, a television personality who became president of Howard's School of Communications and then became one of Reagan's Cheetahs. Gibson sat us down with a couple of white dudes working for the Rockefeller Foundation at Rutgers and tried to explain why black economic development was unnecessary.

What was really mysterious and unmysterious about the opposition was that shortly after this, Kahn of TelePrompTer was busted. Governor Schapp of Philadelphia was brought in to run TelePrompTer while Kahn was locked up. The moratorium on New York cable franchises lasted right up into the '80s!

We were active in politics and struggled with economic development. We wrote out proposals for all kinds of grants and got money from them but at the same time we set up businesses and profit-making operations. As we expanded, we became more and more of a community unto ourselves. We were ever active in the broader community, in New Ark and throughout other cadres in the other cities, but we provided such an inclusive range of services and goods for the advocates that they had little real interplay with people outside the organization except around political matters. Amina called this to my attention from time to time. But we were deeply and totally involved.

Our day would begin very early; by 9 A.M. we had been out in the street driving around and coming back to one of the Hekalus for administrative work. Amina would be off to the AFS. We might see each other from time to time during the day, but that would be in passing. I might call her from the Hekalu over at the AFS building, but she was involved with running the women's part of the organization and the Afrikan Free School and the day-care center. I would have meeting after meeting. A staff meeting, a meeting with Siasa or Uchumi, in the evening a rehearsal. I might have to speak in town or someplace else. I would have meetings with community groups. We sent our people to all important public meetings. They always went to City Council meetings and Board of Education meetings to raise or oppose issues we felt critical.

Every Saturday morning I went to the park with all the male advocates and we ran around the lake some two and a half miles and then played football or basketball or even ring-a-leerio (I let them play this by themselves). The advocates not only had their individual assignments in the various departments, but they were in charge of security, driving people home at night (kuchukua), they had to go to various meetings, train in yangumi a few times a week (the women too). One white man seeing a group of us training one Saturday remarked, "You all are like marines." (A noted black writer came into town one Saturday and the brothers assumed that he wanted to run around with them. They took him around the lake and he fell out on his face. This amazed them since this brother was much younger than I was. But then he wasn't doing this shit everyday!)

Wednesday mornings all the males had to fall in at six o'clock and we drilled and began to study Lenin's works about the "woman question." On some evenings the males studied Sun Tzu's military works collectively. Amina had the women studying various works as we moved toward the left. In many ways, CFUN was like some militant university committed to black liberation.

But our contradictions were deep and frequently abrasive. The men and women, married couples, frequently didn't see much of each other. They had their assignments, their jobs, their meetings. Often this was an excuse for an even deeper male chauvinism than exists on the outside. When Amina and I saw each other it was late at night and sometimes not every night. The tender sensuality of our early days was often replaced by a weary perfunctoriness which made our lovemaking resemble the way the organization was set up.

This is the fanatical aspect of the petty bourgeoisie. In one sense the organization became a fanatical driving thing that tended to remove us from our community and even from each other. Revolutionary struggle must be integrated within a more or less "normal" life of the people. Certainly, to wage that struggle, we must spend a good deal of our time and energy doing that, but we cannot so distort and limit people's lives that they lose their excitement and even their will to struggle!

As I said before, the women in those '60s and early '70s black nationalist organizations (and even, I'm told, those further to the left) had to put up with a great deal of unadulterated bullshit in the name of revolution. My own wife, who met me in what appeared to be the dying days of my bohemianism, really had got to me when that bohemianism had changed its color. It is my contention that much of the cultural nationalism young people fervently believe is critically important to the struggle is just a form of black bohemianism. Take away the attention to Africa, and the "weird" clothes and the communalism could be found in any number of white hippie communities. Some of the cultural nationalists we began to recognize when we started to read the history of the Communist Party (Bolshevik). These old Russian hippies and cultural nationalists were called Narodniks. When we read that, we recognized ourselves so clearly. Even the bit about how socialism must model itself on the form of the peasant communes in Russia. Black modern day narodnika say black people have always been communal. All we have to do is style our economic system after the traditional African communalism.

When I wanted to go into Sunni Islam, it was Amina who refused, who would not humble herself to a new metaphysics. She would not make the Salats (prayers). And though I was upset at first, I was not so upset that I insisted. It was Amina who was most suspicious of and distant from Kamiel as well as Karenga. And once I had begun to grasp and understand that cultural nationalism was a dead end and seriously to study Marxism, it was Amina who encouraged this study and pressed for its public dissemination to the organization as a whole.

She has frequently had to struggle with me to take positions that people then applaud only me for. She has also had to take assaults from people who want to attack me and see her as the most accessible point to launch that attack. Too often I have been so self-absorbed I have not helped her when I should. Obstructed by others, I might get sullen with her. Lionized by many, I would not always be as attentive and loving as I could. Traveling all the time, I would forget that she might be lonely. Involved in constant struggle, I might occasionally forget to be tender. To add to this, the white press and art world seemed only to want to talk about my first wife. The fact that I had been divorced and remarried and that Amina and I had had five children was lost effortlessly in their reams of distortion. According to many biographies and accounts of my life, it ended, both the living of it and the writing in reflection of it, when I left the "white world." They would not honor my life or my work. To raise a black woman is to raise the mothers of the black nation, the wives of that nation, its beautiful struggling daughters, and hence that nation itself!

But a man is only as strong as the woman he's with, and it is difficult for a woman to develop past the life situation sanctioned by the man she is with — it is the nature of the society itself. The man, usually with the purse strings, becomes the boss, the woman the exploited worker. The marraige is like a reflection of society, the economic system itself; it enforces the same kind of relationship. I have learned these things only after a long struggle and much study. And still I am not always able to act wisely on them.

For Amina and me, our relationship has been one that began in passion and then that passion took a backseat to nationalism and organization. It is one that has even been diverted by male chauvinism. But it is a relationship whose essence has always deepened and gotten stronger through the very adversity which has constantly threatened it. It is a relationship whose deepest foundation is an ever-ripening love, an ever-developing respect.

Our first son, Obalaji Malik Ali, born just before the rebellion, in May 1967. Our second son, Ras Jua Al Azia, born in 1969. I stayed up all night reading and studying to find a name for Ras. The ancient black name of wisdom, Ras means "the wise" or "wisdom," and, more contemporarily, "president" or "leader." Ras, people say, is the most Imamu-looking of all the children. The third child was a girl, Shani Isis Makeda. Shani means "something wondrous"; Isis, the ancient Egyptian goddess, wife of Osiris, the father of judgment; and Makeda, the Queen of Sheba, the Ethiopian beauty. Shani was born in 1971.

The fourth child was another boy, Amiri Seku Musa, named after me and born the day before my birthday, October 6, 1972. Shani and Amiri are Libras, and the fifth child as well. Ahi Mwenge ("brother of the masses," "a torch"), born October 10, 1973. So after the first two were two years apart, the next three came one year after another. This was a reflection of our cultural nationalist line against birth control, which we deemed genocide. But obviously "too many children" can be used to cover the real causes of pauperizing people, so birth control is just another modern method of environmental control. We should not confuse birth control, which is voluntary, with enforced sterilization, which the imperialists practice on oppressed people.

All the time Amina had to struggle in the organization and work and study with us she was also having child after child. Plus, she had two older girls by her previous marraige, Vera and Wanda, whom she had to look after and raise. So much pressure and never enough help. A husband whose life is used up publicly in art and traveling and speeches and common struggles and sometimes in abject stupidity and conceit. And all of it is still in motion, this very minute I write.

From 1972 on, ours was a steady march in quick time to the left. If I had been allowed to publish as widely from that point on as I had been before, all this motion would have been well documented. As it was, Jihad and later People's War put out an endless stream of inexpensive pamphlets. Many of my speeches and writings of the period were sold in many printings. We also published a book of poems of mine, *Spirit Reach*, and books by Sekou Touré, Julius Nyerere, Amilcar Cabral, and later even reprints of Lenin.

From the big publishers I published regularly until about 1970. Jihad brought out *Black Art* (poetry, '66) and *Slave Ship* ('67). Grove published *The Baptism and The Toilet* in 1967 and *Tales*, a book of short stories, around the same time. *Black Music* came out in '69 and *Four Black Revolutionary Plays* the same year from the same publisher, Bobbs Merrill. This is probably when they thought it was still good business. The last book was *In Our Terribleness*, also published by Bobbs Merrill, in '70, a collaboration between Fundi (Billy Abernathy), a great photographer who was in the organization at the time, his wife, Laini (Sylvia), a fine graphic artist who did the layout and design, and my words.

After that, until 1976, everything I published was published by Jihad, such as *Black Art*or the poem *Afrikan Revolution* or the books on nationalism such as *A Black Value System*. Haki Madhabuti's Third World Press out of Chicago took up some of the slack, *Its Nation Time* (poetry) and *J-E-L-L-O*, a play.

The words of an incendiary poet are finally less frightening than a political organizer. The one can be used merely to titillate, the other assumes a functional presence in the world that can intimidate.

Inside the ALSC we were exposed, I believe, to black Communist organizers and that had a real influence. Our exposure to a real Africa, a contemporary Africa, also helped change our worldview. But we were also exposed everyday to class struggle. We saw everyday how Ken Gibson vacillated, lied, sold himself, and showed his ass to the black community. (If somebody wants to object I'll say, OK it wasn't his ass, it was his face, but most of us couldn't tell the difference!)

We saw how a small group of blacks, a little petty bourgeois bureaucrat class, got over at the expense of the rest of us. We saw how the little "verticality" created by the election had got one group of blacks over, a tiny group, while for the rest of us the struggle had to go on, with not much change. We were seeing class struggle in reality. Reading Marxist literature only confirmed what we had already seen and gave us a scientific terminology and proven references so that we might better understand already existing phenomena.

At each ALSC meeting we got into struggles with brothers and sisters on the left, either announced or otherwise, and learned something. In a minute, I found myself moved to the "middle," where I was trying to understand what those further left were saying and trying to make a bridge for my nationalist comrades.

In the National Black Assembly, we encountered growing hostility from the elected officials and other middle-class academic and political types. On one hand they didn't mind if we did the agonizing work that went with trying to maintain and expand a national organization, they probably thought this is what CAB is for. But on the other they deeply resented the fact that as secretary general I had a great deal of influence in the organization. Plus, I did not always handle these contradictions as they should have been handled to keep them nonantagonistic. As Mao says, contradictions among the people can remain. I was quick not only to criticize but to take the criticism out as far as I could and to make it public. This created widening rifts between CAP and certain elements in the NBA. After a time, they both began to mobilize to get rid of me.

The redder I got, the more this mobilization intensified. Ron Daniels and Hayward Henry, two ex-CAP members who got off the train at social democracy, the former as "economic democracy," the latter as "black humanism," were the final executors of this mobilization.

But it was as if reality was forcing us even further to the left and this motion caused further contradictions to emerge, new tensions and explosions inside our various organizations. If we had handled this motion leftward more scientifically, perhaps there would have been less destruction with the explosions. But we were only where we were, and only knew what we knew.

In Newark, there were many things, a series of things, in our struggle with what could be characterized as the "neocolonial" reality that Kenneth Gibson represented, even though I don't think black people in the U.S. are a colony, but an oppressed nation. But the oppression we suffer is no less than what our brothers and sisters under colonial oppression suffer and have suffered.

We were trying to build housing in the Central Ward on a plot designated R-32. I got a friend of mine, an old friend of White's, Earl Coombs (Majenzi), a Howard-trained architect, to design the whole area. He worked up a fantastic neo-African design for buildings, businesses, parks, and schools in that depressed Central Ward area, but Gibson would give us no help. He wouldn't even tell General Electric they had to remove some old unused railroad tracks that were dangerous and a terrible eyesore, serving no function but the collection of garbage.

At the Housing Authority, the son-in-law of a Mafioso was the director. He took me into the conference room one afternoon and told me frankly, you take this architect, this consultant, and this construction firm and you go forward tomorrow, otherwise nothing. I told him all that was cool but how could I tell black people that I've been struggling for black development and then tell them these are the people who're going to make a profit off this development? Gibson would do nothing but burp when he was told of these things.

We joined with attorney Ray Brown in planning and getting designed another project in Newark. This in the North Ward, to be called Kawaida Towers, a low- and moderate-income housing development that we would build with New Jersey state funds since we were a nonprofit organization. We broke ground and put in a million-dollar foundation, but when we had our formal public ground breaking we ran into trouble. I had arranged to talk to Imperiale beforehand about the project, through Kamiel, so there wouldn't be any trouble. Imperiale asked for jobs, but since the main contractor was Italian I thought there would be no trouble. A meeting was arranged between Imperiale and the contractor. We had set up a "mix and match" situation: in any area or business necessary to the building, there would be whites where blacks could not be found, but there would be black subcontractors working with them learning that skill or developing a track record so that they could get the bonding the next time on their own.

But when we went public, a so-called liberal Italian, a Democratic Party, new-style ward heeler, Steve Adubato, raised a stink, because "he had not been told." Imperiale, then, not to be outdone, came out denouncing the housing project as "racist." The African name Kawaida was "threatening." It was to be "a racist housing project."

What went down next and afterwards is public record. Imperiale mobilized the racist elements of the Italian community against the housing, even though the particular area it was to be built in was a mixed area, heavily black and Puerto Rican as well as Italian. It was raised that there should be no high-rises in the area, and the New York Times came out with this story while photographing the site from an existing luxury high-rise in the area where mainly whites lived, so that it looked as if there were no high-rises!

The racist trade union bureaucrat leadership backed Imperiale and would not order their workers, mostly skilled trades, into the site to do the work.

Only the black laborers' union crossed Imperiale's picket line and some of them got jumped by Imperiale's goons. When we came down to the site to defend the workers, Gibson's police director, Redden, first allowed his cops to jump on us rather than Imperiale's goons, even though we were trying to keep the site open and they were chaining themselves to the gate to stop the building. Then, rather than have to arrest white people, Redden resigned. We had been on Ken Gibson's case constantly to get him to replace Redden with a black police director, but he refused. He had even made a public statement saying Redden was the greatest police director in the country. Great, as long as all he had to arrest were blacks and Puerto Ricans.

Gibson, with any show of integrity, could have gotten Kawaida Towers built at once, but he betrayed us again and let the state and county officials get in it and declare an emergency and close the project down, which is exactly what Imperiale and company wanted all the time. So that even in a black majority city with a black mayor no housing could be built for the poor and moderate-income people because of Gibson's backwardness and vacillation.

During the period when the project was closed down we had to go through endless legal battles and we won every one of them, but by the end of it, inflation had sent prices up some fifteen percent and we needed that fifteen percent in addition to the $6 million we had got from the state. They said we should build only efficiency apartments, since part of the cry of the racists was that all those black and Puerto Rican children would be brought into the racist project. So the state went along stride for stride and word for word with the most racist group in the city and then justified it with double-talking bullshit.

Gibson meanwhile appointed a Negro named Eddie Kerr as police director; Kerr was simply the standard colored Stepin Fetchit model to sit around, scratch his head, and take orders from whites. During this period a carload of white cops broke into my house claiming they had received a report that a patrolman was being tortured on the second floor. I was not home when they came in, but they went directly to my study, threw shit around, then left.

Twice our windows on High Street were fired into, and once they even shot into the Afrikan Free School. Imperiale and company even staged a disorder in the North Ward, and when a white man was killed in the confrontations, a month or so later a young black activist was murdered while he jogged through the city streets early one morning.

But even Kerr's appointment came only after Earl Harris, Dennis Westbrook, and I took Gibson in the back of Earl's record store and jaw-boned with him for hours. But Cur was not who we meant, Gibson was not brave enough to appoint the young Harvard graduate Hubert Williams, who was the only person with even reasonable accomplishment in Gibson's cabinet, until several years later and after several more tragic "accidents."

One of the most tragic was the Puerto Rican rebellion in 1974. It jumped off after a festival in Branch Brook Park. Two white police brutalized some of the brothers and they responded. In a flash the whole of the widely scattered Puerto Rican community had been mobilized and descended into the center of town demanding justice and the firing of the police.

We got in it immediately and groups of CAP people went downtown too and milled out in front of City Hall with the Puerto Ricans, demanding justice. Brothers and sisters from the Puerto Rican Socialist Party were out there too, but they did not take control like the old Young Lords would have. They were shaky and didn't know how to deal with the crowd.

You want to feel some deep shame, Blood, let there be some kind of half-ass nigger government in power and they be brutalizing people of other nationalities. The sense of class distinction and class struggle is keen and obvious at such times.

I was chosen as part of the group to go upstairs and meet with asshole Gibson. When we get up there he's already got a group of Puerto Rican compradors and so he feels he's got everything cooled out and doesn't even have to talk to this group of militants (CAP, ex-Young Lord Ramon Rivera, PRSP, and other activists), but as he's bullshitting, one of the brothers says, "Hey, the people only gave us ten minutes for this whole rap." Gibson starts to say something off the wall, burping and staring vacantly at some horrible abstraction given to him by "Arty Ruler," when a stone comes flying through his picture window and almost bangs him in the knot. The expression on his face at that moment was really high art!

We got back downstairs and the people are chanting for Gibson to come down. Then more stones got thrown and suddenly from around the corner, police on horses and in patrol cars. The whole of the front of City Hall got shattered and the crowd went surging up the street. The police then did what the police of any white racist monopoly capitalist government would do, they tried to kill people. They roared down the street, one car slamming on its brakes just a few yards from a crowd of us, then turning sideways so it could slam broadside into us. A young Panther running beside us was slammed high into the air but did not get hurt. Later two young Puerto Rican brothers were killed. But the Ricans did tear out the downtown windows. The earlier rebellion only fucked with windows in our own community.

One of the brothers was shot, the other had his head smashed, probably by a policeman's horse. Gibson came out after the initial violence and said that gatherings of over two or three people were banned. He was playing "white boy" to the Puerto Ricans like Addonizio to the Bloods. I hated the feeling this gave me, I could understand somewhat what radical whites must feel when white racists and white supremacy freaks are running their usual hate everybody oppress everybody bullshit.

We were working with groups in the Puerto Rican community around the clock. We had been planning a demonstration against Gibson's terrorism of the Puerto Rican community anyway, but when Gibson came out with his Hitler-like declaration that there would be no demonstrations, we really got down to organizing. Fuck him! Let him do whatever he thought he had to, we were going to organize, and march. Some two thousand to three thousand people, mostly Puerto Ricans, marched from the North Ward right down the middle of Broad Street to City Hall. The demonstration was well planned and well executed, so there were no casualties, but we could see now we were facing a little fat colored dictator.

There were so many things happening during this period. Ourselves scrambling to the left were right in the middle of all of it. Gibson was making his quick march even further to the right, taking a tiny little pimple of middle-class colored bureaucrats with him. Interestingly, many of the people who had come from L.A. fleeing Karenga jumped on that bandwagon. Every other day smoke would be coming out of my nose or my face was turned to fire by the blatant disregard for the people of Newark by our fat stupid Negro mayor. The class contradictions were what I was learning. How the different classes fared, even as black. Not to mention the wider class disparities that cut across the boundaries of nationality or were exacerbated by nationality. No, we were seeing how a little petty bourgeois coterie could scoop up and run with a whole city, yeh, carry it right back to where we had supposedly got it.

As we moved to the left, as we began to focus more on class, we became more and more intolerant of the black middle class. As we got louder and louder about Gibson, we were also getting louder and louder about the vacillating character and quick sellout capabilities of an entire sector of black middle-class so-called leadership. The foibles of Gibson, his failures, went hand in hand, absolutely in tune, with the dumb chump character of the national leadership of the NAACP, Urban League, national black church organizations, black elected officials, blacks in the academic world, black government appointees, media spokespersons, etc. They were all full of shit and our views grew more and more loud and caustic.

We were doing good work nationally on issues like "Stop Killer Cops," leading mass demonstrations against white police murdering black youth and black people in general. We headed up a huge demonstration aimed at indicting the police murderers of thirteen-year-old Claude Reese in Brooklyn. We were working for police review boards, people's trials for killer cops, publishing information and distributing it nationally. We were mobilizing thousands of black people around the country.

At the same time, I personally began to read more and more left material. I read more and more Mao Tse-tung, and where before I had simply excised his repeated references to his communism in the works, borrowing from him Ron Karenga style, now I would acknowledge his communism and try to understand it. I was trying to make Nkrumah and Cabral our bridges toward learning socialist theory, but I was not convinced that I needed to be a Marxist.

Socialism obviously was necessary, I had come to that, but how to bring it? What constituted the science of bringing socialism? The phrase "scientific socialism" fascinated me. I heard it more and more around ALSC meetings. The ALSC was really an activist gathering, more so than the NBA. Many of the NBA members were more rooted in reform and electoral politics. The ALSC people were more directly products of the militant '60s. They were closer to Malcolm X than King and more familiar with an Africa of struggle.

At some of the ALSC meetings I began to find myself almost like a mediator. I was the head of a cultural nationalist organization, one of the largest in the country, yet I was having some misgivings about my own ideology.

In South Carolina, at Frogmore, we had a meeting to discuss the ALSC's Statement of Principles. On one side the nationalists were resisting what they called the "Marxist language" or "left-wing language" of the document. Actually after some discussion in which I wanted to insert how imperialism also committed "cultural aggression," the language did not bother me so much. I recognized it as "leftist" just as the other nationalists, but I thought the essence, the content, the anti-imperialist essense, of what was being said was correct and I could uphold it. So I took the position of getting the nationalists to agree with the SOP with the few changes we had suggested.

Two of the CAP leaders, Jitu Weusi from Brooklyn and Haki Madhubuti, the poet from Chicago, agreed in a meeting that they would compromise on the language, but when we got in the general meeting they still resisted, openly contrary to our own discussion. Finally, the discussions reached such intensity that it was agreed that a few months later at another meeting, in Greensboro, North Carolina, we should all submit our overviews of the black struggle in the U.S.

The more I thought about this later, the more it resembled a setup. The left forces wanted a confrontation and while such struggle must go on in any visible united front, these new left forces took very sectarian positions rather than the necessary stance of unity and struggle.

At Greensboro, Nelson Johnson, ostensibly with YOBU and closely aligned with Owusu Sadaukai, ALSC's chairman, and Abdul Alkalimat (Gerald McWorthers before the bourgeois Negores down at Atlanta University got rid of him for steering the youth toward militance) came out with a statement which in essence was a full-blown, though ultimately incorrect, position on the Afro-American national question. The document was clearly the work of much research and study, but unfortunately it was influenced by a so-called Communist organization, the mostly white Revolutionary Union and possibly the Communist Party USA. The document dismissed the idea of a black nation, even belittling black culture as "mostly soul radio." But what was impressive was the pages of statistics and research. The pamphlet was thick and well presented and made up to look like an official ALSC document.

It was an ambush on the nationalists, myself among them. The "ALSC cover" I thought reprehensible; it was probably the work of Nelson Johnson who always gives you the feeling of sneaking around, even if he's standing in your face grinning. I didn't agree with the liquidation of the black nation or the dismissal of black people's right to self-determination, but I understood that until we had our own research and serious study done, this pamphlet would have an enormous effect.

Of course there was struggle in the meeting. Most of the nationalists looked to me to counter the attack, but I was too confused myself to offer much help. I half-believed much of the paper. But the nationalists felt used. The paper, indeed the entire confrontation, had been organized in such a sectarian manner. It dismissed with a wave of the hand most of the people in the ALSC. There was no understanding of the united front character of the ALSC, there were just some young people bellowing that they were right and that everyone else in the ALSC was a fool.

Quite a few of the nationalists reacted intensely. Even some of those who could have been won over to the positions in the SCP now wanted to resign and many did. The two line struggle that had crept out into the open at Frogmore the year before had now come full out in a steering committee meeting, and it was going to come out even further.

Since 1972, when I had become chairman of CAP, I had begun to formulate a "Revolutionary Kawaida." I was trying to emphasize the more revolutionary aspects of Kawaida and introduce more of an emphasis on Pan-Afrikanism and socialism. By March of 1974 I was now openly including elements of Marxism in this "Revolutionary Kawaida," but I was still unwilling or unable to cut Karenga's doctrine, at least the main thrust of it, loose.

The Greensboro meeting showed me, above all, that the old cultural nationalist positions which we upheld were insufficient. And instead of being a leading force in the struggle against the left, I was being won over myself. So that at the same time the right wing was fleeing ALSC and some other forces were driven out by the sectarianism and neophyte "leftism" of some of the new Marxists, we were having a struggle inside CAP.

CAP was a loosely organized assemblage of Kawaida cadres which formed a national organization. We had worked at building a national unity between the various organizations and some of the more advanced of the city groups did take on a kind of organized national quality. At any rate, we were the best organized of all the cultural nationalist organizations, and we had proven in many different ways that we could do the work. We put out a button, "Kazi is the blackest of all," referring to the constant struggle of the nationalists as to who was "the blackest," i.e., the most correct. Kazi, the Swahili word for "work," we put out was really the most correct, and those of us in the BLM should be about that work. What was that work? Building the nation!

The various CAP cadres came from different bases. Some were former community organizations, some black arts groups, others part of national civil rights organizations which had gotten disgusted with the reformism of the parent body, still others were groups formed specifically after Atlanta, of young people trying to relate to Kawaida.

As the two-line struggle that was boiling in the whole movement came up inside CAP, the organization went through rapid changes. At a meeting in Chicago, a midwestern regional meeting of CAP, I read a speech,

"National Liberation and Politics," which ended by calling for the inclusion of Marx's theories and the teachings of Lenin and Mao as part of Revolutionary Kawaida. The speech was more of a bombshell than I anticipated. At the end of the meeting, both Jitu Weusi of The East and Haki Madhubuti of Institute for Positive Education resigned. What incensed me particularly about these resignations (and the resignations of those entire cadre organizations from CAP) was the fact that neither man had the honesty to tell me while we were at the regional meeting. I got a letter from Jitu a couple days later, even though we had flown back to New York together. Haki's letter took a day or so more. I'm sure they had communicated with each other even in Chicago. I answered their letters in public in the newspaper *Unity & Struggle*, printing my reply in section after section in the newspaper for a year. While much of my criticism of them was accurate, the tone and approach were like beating somebody in the head for disagreeing, the same thing I had accused the Johnson-Alkalimat faction of doing in Greensboro.

But the struggle between the CAP faction that I represented and Jitu and Haki had been going on sub rosa for most of the period I had been chairman. As long as Hayward Henry and the black nationalists, black humanists, were in the organization, the Kawaida-Pan-Afrikanist faction could unite to criticize Henry and company who we felt were just three strides past being "straight-out Negroes." But once there was a higher level of national organization unity, namely, Kawaida-Pan-Afrikanism, then the contradictions within that grouping became clearer and clearer.

Haki, for instance, would take the no-meat vegetarian line all the way out. In the Chicago cadre organization such concerns took on the importance of our principal work. As if we had all joined forces to root out and oppose meat eating. Perhaps the closeness to Chicago's Black Muslims had some influence, but it became for me more and more an example of black bohemianism, like hippies in blackface. Haki was superior to us only because we stooped to eat fish.

But the most hilarious confrontation came at one of our steering committee meetings when Haki and company produced a "Survival Kit," a list based on the writings that Amina had done right after the Newark rebellion describing the things people must have in such an emergency. But now Haki and company took Amina's ideas further and created a Survival Kit. This survival kit included a *bath tub*.

Haki and the Chicago cache were so far into the straight-up black bohemian aspects of cultural nationalism that they spent most of their time thinking about what they could and could not eat. Much of their Survival Kit was a list of herbs one must get and store. What was lost on them is that most of the medicines in the corner drugstore come from these herbs they mentioned and the refined form could be got and stored just the same. Plus, at one point when I was saying in a meeting that we could read Marx, Lenin, Stalin, Mao, that we should read anyone and anything that could hallmark revolution, Haki had objected, but then went on to say that in studying herbs and his Survival Kit he had consulted the works of Jethro Kloss's *Back to Utopia* and various white bohemians on weeds and herbs and exotic teas and broths. He'd even gone to some right-wing madman who counseled whites to leave the cities when the final race war breaks out and go into the countryside armed to the teeth and buy land for that purpose and store various items there as preparation for the forthcoming race war.

I asked why was it that we could read right-wing and bohemian whites, but that white and other nationality revolutionaries were taboo? The speech at the regional meeting had taken it all the way out. But at the same time too much of the move left was occurring in my own head and with only the effects being passed down to the advocates. I was grappling with ideas, desperately searching for some ideological revelation that would square socialism with nationalism. I knew, after a time, that socialism, scientific socialism, had to be the answer economically. We had grasped what we called "cooperative economics" from the beginning of Kawaida, and I had been skirting socialist theory even while I was downtown in the Village. But this was different. I had a great deal of responsibility and I was trying to deal with it, but I was still acting as if I were the only person who had to be convinced or who had to understand. Rather than holding discussions with our leadership and they in turn holding discussions with the rank and file, tried to deal, largely by myself, with my own desire for ideological clarity. I figured that all I had to do was say the word and the whole organization would not only move left but would understand why as well.

By the spring of 1974, CAP had split open just as the ALSC had. At the National Black Political Convention in April that year, held in Little Rock, I made an address to that convention which openly called for socialist revolution. It stunned quite a few people in the National Political Assembly and at that point I'm certain the more conservative factions in the organization vowed to get me out of the secretary-general's post.

That was a wild convention anyway. Saladin, my forward man into Little Rock, was "kidnapped" at gunpoint by some crazy fat nigger named Shelton (who later I heard became a Black Muslim). Shelton saw the convention as a huge pork barrel and he wanted to make sure he and his fellow Little Rock thugs could make all the money with gambling casinos, after-hours spots, and hotels in which they had pre-rented all the rooms which they were going to charge us double for. He thought that we "northern boys" were going to chisel our way into his operations and get all the money.

To get Sala back we had to assure Shelton that he could make all the money on his various illegal and semilegal deals. But only two thousand people came to the Little Rock convention. This was not a presidential election year, and a lot of the elected officials and people turned on by electoral politics stayed home. So Shelton lost his ass anyway. The last time I saw him he was sweeping down the huge stairs of the convention hall, thousands of dollars in debt, crazy mad and trailed by two or three bodyguards with their pistols hanging out.

At one point in the convention, when we were debating the postion on Israel, about eight or nine New York delegates came into my office—headed by the professional militants Lloyd Douglas and Omar Ahmed, and several New York antipoverty militants and small-time politicians. I had told the security people to go outside. I knew all these people.

L.D. began by saying, "Percy [Sutton] told us that if we could get you national guys to cut out the anti-Israel resolution we can get some money for the New York Assembly and even get set up in some offices. We know you guys are getting Arab money for doing this, some Libyan money, we hear."

It was funny to me. First, because if Percy had said that, I knew exactly where that was coming from, Abe Beame (mayor of New York) and company. But what also made it slightly more than hilarious was that here were these stomp-down militants wanting to bail Israel out. I told them I knew of no Libyan or other Arab money and that if there was some of it available, they could count me in. I also told him I was voting to uphold the anti-Israel resolution. They stood there in the office, militant by virtue of being a crowd, but it was so funny there was no menace to it at all.

"We know you gettin' some Libyan money," Douglas repeated. "You need to get us some of that Libyan money!" Some of the shit you couldn't believe.

I'm certain, however, that word of the Chicago confrontation and subsequent split in CAP as well as the Little Rock speech shot around movement circles. Baraka had moved to the left. CAP had an internal struggle raised to full public pitch; split in CAP; split in ALSC. In May of that year at Howard University, ALSC held its landmark conference, "Which Way the Black Liberation Movement?" It was a forum to debate frankly and openly the two lines within the Black Liberation movement. Owusu had suggested such a conference and it was meant to benefit the left.

Stokely Carmichael, Owusu, Muhammad Ahmed of RAM (then African People's Party), Kwadlo Akpan from PAC of Detroit (a Pan-Afrikanist cultural nationalist organization), Abdul Alkalimat from People's College, and myself, representing CAP, all made presentations. Unknown to most of us, some of the people in ALSC, whom we connected with Malcom X Liberation University and SOBU and some other formations, had formed a Communist organization, the forerunner of the later Revolutionary Worker's League. They were in motion even further to the left, but, like myself, they were also making errors.

The most striking of all the presentations was Owusu's, because he was saying openly he was no longer a nationalist and Pan-Afrikanist, that he was an anti-imperialist struggling to learn Communist theory. Before that presentation, Carmichael had made a presentation. But the MXLU, SOBU, and RWL people were waiting for him. Stokely had been out of the country, he had stayed out of ALSC and kept his people's participation in it very marginal. There seemed to be a rivalry between Owusu and Stokely, as if Carmichael was drugged that one of his ex-disciples had jumped ship. I wondered if this was anything like the relationship Karenga and I had now.

Stokely had been questioned mercilessly by some of the RWL cadre. His "back to Africa" ideology, which he called Nkrumahism, was raked over hot hot coals, one woman calling it "a credit card ideology," referring to Stokely's many trips back and forth to Africa. But Stokely, Carmichael to the end, posed and profiled and mocked the audience. He still had partisans in the crowd, but the tide had swung toward the left. Stokely fought back but many in the audience were laughing at him.

Owusu's presentation was met with a standing ovation. Alkalimat's was the presentation that was the most clearly based on Marxist theory, and as such it was the most orderly presentation, with the most reference to consistent scientific analysis. This also was very well received, because many of us in that audience were leaning heavily in that direction.

My own presentation marched even further left, but it was still a mixed bag, still tried to square Marxism with cultural nationalism. It was so long and confused I had to skip parts of it. This convinced me, and probably several other people, that half-stepping wasn't solving anything. We had to go further. We had to quit bullshitting. If we believed that socialism, scientific socialism (as opposed to "Utopian" socialism), was the direction our people had to seek, then we should quit obstructing their progress in that direction.

For my money, nationalism was defeated at that conference at Howard in May 1974. The people on the left who had defeated nationalism did not have all their theoretical gemachts together, but they at least did provide a point of departure, a jumping-off place, and I was ready to jump off.

June of that year the Sixth Pan-African Congress was to be held in Dar es Salaam, Tanzania. It was the first Pan-African Congress designated as such held on African soil. Colonialism had kept the rest outside of Africa. Throughout the months after the Howard conference and in the organizing sessions for the "6PAC," the two-line struggle that had now appeared throughout the entire movement continuously surfaced. It was the US-Panther struggle all over, on a higher level, but the sides were just as sharply drawn.

Even in Dar, at the conference itself, Owusu and I found ourselves contending with the whole delegation of African Americans (the most independent delegation because completely nongovernmental) who maintained nationalist positions. But because of the influence of the liberation movements that were taking the most progressive positions and Tour, and Nyerere's attacks on "narrow nationalism," the left held the day in that international conference. In the end Pan-Afrikanism was redefined as "the worldwide struggle of African people against imperialism."

I had taken Obalaji, who was seven, with me to the conference. All the way over he practiced what he would say if he met Mwalimu Nyerere. Then, sure enough, we were invited to Nyerere's house, and instead of "Shikamoo, Mzee," Obalaji just stared with his mouth hung open as Mwalimu shook his little paw. The two of us had a few deliriously happy days there in the warm beautiful land of our ancestors. We would rise some mornings at seven so that we could go out the back door of our cottage, a brick replica of an African hut, and race down the beach to the cool water. You had to go that early because by 10 A.M. it was hot; by 12 noon you better not be out there or your brains would go sunny-side up.

I gave a speech at the 6PAC entitled "Revolutionary Culture and the Future of Pan-African Culture," calling for a "worldwide commitment by African people to build socialism everywhere and to take up the struggle against imperialism everywhere." The fact that both Owusu and I stood now clearly on the left, in some still largely undefined position, had been trumpeted to the four winds. But in Africa, listening to the liberation movement speakers from Frelimo, MPLA, PAC of South Africa, PAIGC, and others, I was convinced that I was moving in the correct direction. I met Walter Rodney, who was hospitalized for a minor ailment and so had missed the conference. He was teaching at the University of Dar at the time, but Owusu took me to the hospital to see him.

One shocking draggy thing was that Babu, my old friend with whom I had met and sat with Malcolm X in the Waldorf in 1965 just a month before Malcolm was murdered, had been locked up in Tanzania. To me, it was obviously the work of the CIA, the framing of Babu for the assassination of the vice president, Karume, who, like Babu, was from Zanzibar. Babu was a Marxist and the CIA had clearly not wanted him in the Tanzanian government. He had been locked up just outside Dar, where he stayed for several years without a trial.

When I asked President Nyerere about this, he told me that he thought Babu was guilty and that he was afraid to put him on trial because he feared the Zanzibaris would try to kill him. It was Babu whom those outside Africa feared most. When I had visited his home before, I remember going into his study and wondering why he had all those volumes, some forty-five of them, of Lenin lined up in his bookcases. That night he'd asked me what I thought of Cleaver and should he be allowed to come to Tanzania. (Eldridge had by then jumped his bail and fled the U.S. to Cuba, then Algeria, but had worn out his welcome in Algeria.) I told him what I thought about Cleaver, none of it complimentary.

Babu had even introduced me to Karume, at a cocktail party. Karume snubbed me and asked Babu in Swahili why he always wanted to hang around with Afro-Americans. He escorted me to countless affairs, even though he was then Minister of Economics of Tanzania, but the two of us zoomed around Dar in his car, with Babu driving. It was also Babu who was the chief moving force behind the Tanzanian Recruitment Program, which CAP pushed all over the U.S. This program called for qualified African Americans to come to Tanzania to help develop the country. It was opposed by the Tanzanian right-wing bureaucrats but the program still had gone forward. Now Babu was in jail. He was released some four years later.

And so here, too, was part of the African reality continuing to come into me. How great a trek to go from the never-never-land Africa of nationalist invention to the real thing. Though some folks can go there and still not deal with it realistically. They might go up and hang out with Idi Amin, be flown in by his special plane and feel he's a great leader because of his skin color and the favors they received—no matter the mountain of corpses flung every which way.

They might see the prehistoric backwardness of our brothers and sisters, the low level of productive forces, scenes being played out the same as they were hundreds, even thousands, of years ago, and dig it. Think it quaint and heavy and black. (Except I wish they could be stuck out in the bush when the sun disappears—not much twilight in Africa—and be searching for their way on those electric-lightless roads, or have to go to the bathroom and have to dig a trench, or have to be actually responsible for pushing back the forests and animals and ignorance and colonialism and neocolonialism. Then we would ask them again how quaint and heavy, etc.)

At the same time, it was equally clear to me that I was, we are, we African Americans are, exactly that, African Americans, and to the extent we were separated from an understanding of either the realities of Africa or our own grim present in the U.S., we were doing nothing to transform the situation. Africa itself is atomic and nuclear. Everything about it, from the blackness of its people (African Americans are light-skinned in comparison) to the absolute necessity for forward motion, means that one day there will be an upheaval on that continent that will change the world!

Along with the economic and social backwardness and political turmoil, one can see and feel atomic fires burning in Africa. It's in the people's color and faces, the electric roll of their eyes, their franticness and coolness. You feel that one day such an explosion will take place on the continent as to give the whole world more color. When all that primordial blue/blackness is reorganized on higher ground, when all that power potential and unbelievable beauty, dynamism, deep combustibility is roaring and flowing on the same track, *united* if you will, at some high level, the whole world will have taken off at a speed which can only seem incredible to us.

I could see clearly now how inextricably bound are our fates, the African and the African American, as well as our brothers and sisters in the Caribbean. We are all captured and held in backwardness by chains. Now we are, with great effort, breaking those chains and flinging them away. And though our specific situations, the particularities of our oppression and exploitation, differ to the extent that we are in different places with different conditions, there is an overall unity to our collective plight that we ignore only at our collective peril.

Though I had shed some of my naive cultural nationalist delusion about Africa, I had been rewarded with an even greater hope, which I know to be a revolutionary optimism. Knowing what is real, no matter how painful, is the only prerequisite for making real change!

Our ancient home is more beautiful than our words, but at the same time, if we are absolutely realistic and scientific, it is much more ugly as well. In the lull of the sweet air off the Indian Ocean, as I sat in the sand, contemplating the speech I was to make at 6PAC and at the same time watching my tiny son romp up and down in the warm water, happier than adults can ever be, I felt remorse at having been among the slaves taken from these shores. These motherfuckers need to be killed just because of the cold-ass weather they took us to. But then reality, again, would indict some of those African feudal lords and ladies that sold us (and who are still selling us and our brothers and sisters, the workers and peasants whose land Africa really is). Then I felt more whole, more complete, understanding perhaps the primitive nature of world society and realizing that black life must finally rise, that we cannot be kept backward and in chains, that this interlude of slavery must soon be ended, and I watched the little boy knowing that he must be readied to take up this struggle at a much higher level than his father. Knowing, also, there were African children and West Indian children who must join with the African American children, as conscious men and women, to bring our shame and humiliation to an end.

I realized, also, that the U.S. was my home. As painful and complicated as that was. I realized that the thirty million African Americans would play a major role in the transformation of black people's lives all over this planet. It was no mere truism, we lived where the head of world oppression lived and when the people of the world united to bring this giant oppressor to its knees we would be part of that contingent (of not only blacks) chosen by the accident of history to cut this thing's head off and send it rolling through the streets of North America. As the warm air lulled me, my eyes opened even wider and the child's voice was even sweeter. I loved that idea. Yeh, payback is hard, hmmm, a head rolling in the streets.

When I returned to the U.S. that idea still moved me, but I was raised up myself. I thought perhaps I had finally come of age. I was no longer a nationalist, I knew clearly that just black faces in high places could never bring the change we seek—all of us who are conscious or describe ourselves as advanced or progressive. I could see my own life and those tasks I had declared for myself with new light. I had seen Gibson and domestic "neocolonialism," I had been to Africa and seen that same boy at work over there holding the people down. It was clearer to me that only socialism could transform society, that the whole world must be at the disposal of the whole world, that all of us must benefit by each other's existence, a few billion primates of an arguably advanced species in a world dominated by insects.

Amina and I went back to Africa, to Somalia, a few months later and she discovered some of the same truths. But they were something which we had shared anyway in our widening consciousness. It was a period of deep and rapid transition, but for Amina socialism was something she had always been looking for. It was the explanation of her life, as the child of black workers, that made her own travails finally make sense.

It was the beginning leg of another journey, one that we knew would be even more rich and exciting.

Back home, it was clear now where CAP was going, at least to me. We even began to work with white groups. We organized a strike of Newark's taxi drivers, white ones included. We sat in the City Council chambers when the city government started ripping off the young people's checks in one of the federal government's summer-coolout "Youth Programs." We were working with the local Black Panthers (whose relation to the national we could never ascertain) and a mostly white Marxist group, the Revolutionary Union. The CAP cadres, students, as well as a few Panthers and RU members, were arrested in the chambers and later when they had to go to trial the prosecutor asked one little white girl from RU who had been the leadership of the takeover and the girl pointed at the Panthers and our cadres. We were working with the multinational left now, but we still had a lot to learn.

That summer, Amina organized the historic Afrikan Women's Conference in which almost one thousand women from twenty-eight states came to workshops on education, social organization, politics, health, welfare and employment, communications, and institutional development. Our left line could be seen even clearer. At our CAP general assembly in Newark, on my birthday, October 7, we declared ourselves a Marxist-Leninist organization. (The Revolutionary Communist League [MCM], which merged in 1978 with the U.S. League Revolutionary Struggle [M-L], an organization formed from I Won Kuen, a mainly Asian anti-imperialist organization, and the August 29th Movement [ATM, a largely Chicano Marxist organization].) I was a socialist, at least in name.

At forty years old, then, I was acknowledging another tremendous change in my life. In my life of changes. (And how can you play the tune, if you don't know the changes?)

Suffice it to say, this all was written some time later, as an effort at partial summation, a beginning of the "summing up." Such a summation does relieve some of the weight of those years, those comings and goings, exits and entrances. All stages in illumination and from their momentary brightness now a glow of whatever relevance, as long as it remains relevant.

At the point of removal (or exhaustion) it all can resemble a Zoom, just a Zoom, perhaps a faint roar whispering in the head and in whatever thing or process or idea that remains somehow connected to what was, even in the act of some new thing's becoming.

In 1970, Amina and I moved from Stirling Street into the fringes of the South Ward, Clinton Hill, where we still live. We paid down on a big square fortress of a stucco house which I painted red and trimmed in black, and when the seasons allow the trees to come full out, the tableau is like a not quite subtle black nationalist flag.

Here we live today, with our healthy brood of five smaller ones and the two older young women coming and going at their own order. A great many things happened after the October 7, 1974, date of our public notice to the world of our socialism. (But that is another story, which might one day be told, with whatever additions.) But we are alive and well, struggling still in the world for us and it to get better.

My wife, Amina, who can tell her own stories, and I are still very much in love, and that story itself, of a brown boy and a black girl from the blue/grey streets of the New Ark, is just in that particular focus reams and reams yet to be told.

But I leave you with this, all these words are only to be learned from. The childhood; music; blues-bottomed class distinctions: black, brown, yellow, white; HU; error farce; Village time; Harlem sojourn; home-returning black nationalist grown blood-red person—all that is like some food for thought, some sounds meant only to say, look at this, dig it, what it means, where I, and some others, been. As Monk would say, "Let's call this . . ."

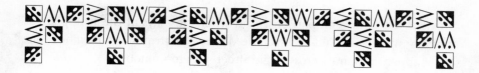

Eleven

To Sum Up

D oes anyone know actually what is life? Awkwardly said, as the awkwardly held knowledge of it "seems." I have come to as scientific an understanding of great portions of it as exist. Though that has to be deepened and there'll be even greater information come with that.

But *why* is a good question—fo' what? Naomi, an old friend of my mother would say, or her husband, Wallace—fo' what?

In some ways my own life has been a long upward series of climbing trails. Pleateaus, the amazing view, then casting gaze there's more upward, a sheer rise of dazzling rock—and the blue shining sun lit air all around. There is that begging to to go, up further. Not as ambition but the workings of a self growing into itself's identity.

I look at my son Ras sometimes and maybe think I see me then, round and brownly rosy. Eyes bulging out into the world, alive with life, whirling around like wild computers. I think I must've been like that, little and bigheaded, full of myself, intently digging my own head's noise.

"If we ever split, you better take him with you," sez Amina. "He's too much like you. I couldn't stand it!" Though they all have traces of my self and hers. But Ras, whom I stayed up all night with, plotting the historical metaphysic of his name, has such a striking physical resemblance it

447

provides the other comparisons. And when he plays at the trumpet, re-
minding me of a would-be hip little dude with an imitation-leather "gig
bag" hippety-hopping across High Street—it's too much.

And what letters does he carry? Or Oba, Shani, Amiri, Ahi (bad thing),
what letters do they carry, on their way, to where, or *wheres*, and at each
where, another letter drops in place. How life is defined. Spelled out.

The mail I carried in those big sparkling eyes, I see in theirs. Not mine,
but some I guess Amina and I helped drop in place, they carry on though
way way past that.

Like a bullet into and surrounded by the music. And Obalaji, a drummer, Ras, my horn, Shani says she wants to play violin because the rest are
too noisy. Amiri was a bass player last week, this week he's thinking percus-
sion. Music is my life—it opens me into the deeper sensitivity of the world,
what it is really about, past our worlds. That in itself was deep instruction
about the world, its shaking beauty and information, too, about myself in
it. It was social studies and aesthetic design—style and attitude. How to
hear and how to see. All that, is music; class analysis and culture delinea-
tion, grace and magic, polyrhythmic world!

And I'm still there in that, the music, always, that's me. My heroes and
life path. My story and my song.

The growing up, though, was possible, as it was, only because the music
taught me. Even the black, brown, yellow, white of the world, the snarl
and precise gibberish of class, the music explained. Its colors, when you
saw them on the street, or sitting next to you in school, "igging" you crossing the church lawn, hugged under big hats entering and exiting dark
rumbling places, those colors of my social spectrum the music had explained. I was stepping anyway.

The color code of class distinction taught me early what America was. I
had that cold training—and had but to recall it, as cold. From the soft and
dreaming to the plain out and steely.

From black and blue Belmont and Spruce to white Barringer and yellow HU, headlines in my head say fly fly up and away. To corniness and
banana extinctions. So you can end up grinning at HU, dragging a
wagonload of contradictions. Childhood, the music, spectrography of class/
caste deceit, all toted by strap wagon tied around the haid, Porgy style.

So I could blanch or become endarkened as I would, having had the
joys and lies of Amoralca pressed beneath my flesh. Aha? So this is what
thee music spake of. This is what the high dive from blues cabaret streets
into the grinning yellow of Jesus the Cool. I could march hungry, dance

dance hungry, be in it and out of it, even fantasizing with blue baby while the yellow dogs howled they knew I wasn't ready. And I never was, for death by boredom and sterility.

Yeh, I could be in HU with a Gang, again. And in the "army" with another ominous group. STOP THAT THINKING IN THERE NOW! Because despite the rope (my man thought they said *robe*) a yella shit was dropped around me back brain, I had been moved by real beauty and resisted always the rubout of its transbluesency.

And that HU, another step, another nod at me as me madre's flying machine. Not really. Just more steps for steppin'. To walk in and out, as vector of rise, getaway. Eat your way through solid rock, your head, life, society. And come out the other side and there you are somewhere (the same place) else having to do it again.

The slightly clearer reality (of the unreality) of HU was, goddammit, educational. (Custer would have said that if he was hip!) I did learn about the colored world and the colored whirl in my own life, so quickly had it spun me, flung me, away, kicking among the stars.

I was no longer a student—very suddenly—flunked out and cut loose from these last yalla apron strings. The error farce was, he says with arrows sticking out of his ass and hat, very very educational. It was like being blown away, an airplane exploding, you're flying in the air, arms flung straight out. The next thing you know some actual cracker (repeat) cracker is breathing on your nose demanding symbolic tribute.

At Barringer, I could go home. I got to get on that 9 Clifton and flee back crosstown to the polyrhythms. But that was shit, was not about any-thing on top but white shit. Very white shit. Like an official entrance into the very white. The absolute cold. And against that, to register that all of it was just me steppin' (I hoped) gettin' (perhaps) risin' (oh, no) I swore to learn. And so moved on.

Wounded, alienated, ego-crazy, subjective, slapped around, but in that punch-drunk sojourn, young boy grasping for whatever—air food love life— I actually did, on a very formal side, learn. And I think I became a little bit of a poet.

The death stare of the army blew me into art. The bland sentence so many accepted as "raisin' hell." That cheapness and easy drunken termi-nation. You had to salute your executioners. Every time you saw one.

So I was flying when I got out or when I got *got* out. These books, these hundreds of hours of contemplation, the real and mock sorrows of the young dude, the black boy, brown-skin kid with poppy eyes, they were a catapult in total, a catapulting out of that jail, I thought. I thought I was in a jail. And what was more important. More meaningful. Heavier. More heroic. Able to accept my distances and alienation. My spectrum of color understanding? Only art. And I could not paint. Art. It pushed around me. It stuck its tongue through my eyes. It sat in my mouth making acid jokes. It laughed and they thought it was me. It fought. It ran. It shivered. It screamed. That was art. I could feel myself touching it to understand. To draw out and back upon me knowing it for what it really was. Not stupidity nor homosexuality nor antilife—just sweet simple beautiful art.

I came to New York then in search of it. I thought it had something to do with intellectuals, intellectualism, white people, "classical" music, the smell of coffee downtown late fall. There were people who had told me this as well. I had inspected this landing field before being blown out of school. The people I'd met projected that. But then, later, as we ourselves were pried apart by our lives' trajectory, I could see some things I wish I'd known.

I came into New York hyped by the delusions, even pathology, of an older generation, one who when "the deal went down" scattered or sought the "primary source," Europe, like there had never been a conference in Berlin in 1884 to divide up Africa like a pie. Essentially they were still living off the elitist alienation of those folks who finally could not deal with the well-advertised grossness of the big ugly—land of the pilgrim's pride, land where my fathers died. One could not hide from one's self if one ever wanted to understand who that self actually was. And to be one's self one also had to be responsible for one's history, confront it—including the monsters and devils raging beneath its surface—and change it with real fingers and mind in the deathly reality—those stars our hope, those stripes our torment!

But living in the bubble of fantasy the not gone away, the never dawned on to be exiles, of my own generation had created—it was only another elitist removal from the bloody sidewalks of our own time. There are several hundred explanations and rationales for not dealing with reality such artists, intellectuals, poseurs have already provided to them—by institutions, commercial establishments, success and succeeders, and their own class background. Certainly when I was downtown the "mass line" was *hedonism*. The political justification the "purity of art." Yet at the asking most would whore for a pittance and not even be ashamed. A shrug would do, a purchased drink for the crowd of adulators, yearning themselves, loudly or softly, to be bought on the spot by the big pimp in the sky. God's Ho's!

My own naivete (and why belittle theirs?) helped buy my ticket into the bubble. I *did* want to create, and as I discovered that, that seemed to be enough. Except there is a persona you accept as your own. A cover and a covering. Middle-class Negroes try to buy their way into America through ignorance—like middle-class anybodies—but the oppression *has to* be *demonstrated* somehow, even unbeknownst to them. They could wear it like a badge and that might be simply the denial of its existence! Working people's lives are their awareness of it. So if I ended up for a time in a little white gang (not wholly, ever) grimacing at my own sensitivity like a special flick of agonized sunlight, that was what I had learned had translated real feeling into. It was an art-stance for, I thought, art-ing.

But I was digging, literally, my way through. Disciplines, doctrines, and personalities. There is a Tonto complex that comes with the given, a Sammy Davis/Frank Sinatra sunlight that can always be rid off into by the willing. You can be famous in America as Jackie Robinson or Paul Robeson. (You remember that collision?) You has but to remove your "e" to get "in." This is not necessarily conscious, like that, either. There are some I could name who *do* very plottingly conscious put on the mummy uniforms snickering at their wisdom and good fortune. I spotted a group, one evening, empty-ing spittoons and bedpans down their throats and calling out "of course of course " and laughing. I understood that, like the profile of Dracula's con-dominium can lurk inside you years after ye pass it. The spooky vines and shit, the wet noises. I was never wholly there. Its whiff and poot deeply frightened me. The dead things' eyes colded my song I trembled and could not laugh I was so scared—could not laugh, get to that, someone like me, who is always, always laughing.

I bought a bourgeois design. White art, my connections and accom-plices, a little fat white wife, cute as a kewpie doll full of popcorn. But that was like having your pockets and ears filled up by running near a lake. Thinking you were jogging, you know, stepping always somehow toward your heart's desire. There are children, even.

But regardless of the design inside the gourd, the world proceeds in its objective arc. You might be picking up odds and ends of it. You might be whistling the dates and certain events. You're in it anyway. I, You (singu-lar), He, She, It are—We, You (plural), They—all are in it, regardless of their specific delusion.

But I was still learning, dyed beyond my own understanding or merely completing the trajectory of ignorance I inherited as a little round colored boy from Bethany Baptist Church, Newark, New Jersey, in the reign of the yalla Lord. (Black help us!)

The desired book-success story, frozen in the middle, in the act of, because at the very moment of climax, the hero (victim) becomes conscious — sees the Lord, the path, the wheels, the grimy advertisements of extinction, pinned to the ground like Gulliver infested everywhere by flesh-eating kewpies.

But it is a whole epoch one is part of, a whole movement of life, of specific people. One is part of one's time, however that is ascertained, in whatever definition. So the doldrum '50s, the bitter FBI-McCarthy '50s, the Korean War/college days '50s, the Beatnik '50s, is also the civil rights '50s. "With all deliberate speed" did actually apply to some of us.

We began to boycott buses and form organizations, and go where we wasn't wanted or expected. We began to sit in and march. We wanted to live out ideas, involved with various disciplines and religions. We came to understand that frustration was transferable, that energy was itself valuable. That the *cool* of death, of isolation and self-imposed alienation, was not what we meant.

We, even in spite of the tight fit of an alien world, began to like ourselves better. To hear ourselves and see ourselves better. We did not hate ourselves, BeBop! We did not even hate the brown skin so many loved to touch. And the aggressive black and blue heart our childhood had given us was beating now faster than before. It threw signals to the surface in those polyrhythms. We became, at that instant, Sonny Rollins and Art Blakey, Max Roach and Clifford Brown, Horace Silver and them. Messengers of ourselves, reaching deeper.

Because even looking Dr. King in the eye we knew who he was, that brown dignified man. "Didn't *Dr.* King tell them, honey? Naaow, let them crackers do what they will. They'll never be as intelligent as that man. That Rev. Dr. Martin Luther King. No saw!"

Didn't we all know who that was. Want us to come inside the church and quit running up and down in front all round the side after them Italian Hot Dogs. "A double to go, please!"

And given that reliable, that number popping up on the board. We knew if the good doctor with that magical colored intelligenk "accent" was saying what he was saying. Hold on, Jimmy — hold on, this shit is done riz up.

What you need to embrace is yourself you yourself. "Come on now, boys, come in the church." And what was the church saying? What it always be saying. "We shall overcome!"

From Asia, Africa, Latin America, the Middle East, the Ivy League's ascension. Miles was at least as hip as JFK and Miles, though cool, would fight.

The steps reflected themselves more. The breathing was more regular. You could be whatever you wanted—that had been the direction, surrounded by models of monsters. What gangs we were in we now could begin to understand more objectively. Or at least we'd begin to stalk our own design. Our own voice. From our own sources. We could actually hear *Freedom Suite*. We knew what it meant. *Freedom Now*.

The discussions would go on everywhere. Talking to ourselves. Trying to identify ourselves, who are our friends, our enemies. Arguing with friends, and the distance that had always existed now real and perceived. Our experience must also be in the world. Otherwise who and where were we? And even on a path described in an old way from an old design, some other stuff was happening. New transmission. Though for us semiliterate intellectuals of the oppressed—trained by our people's beaters to see that the beat goes on—underdevelopment in our circles means, you shoulda known that before. Oh, if I had only known that (them, those) before!

So Malcolm X was something out of nature to us. The world speaking, for once, directly to us. Demanding clarity.

He was a path, a way, into ourselves. The black sector of the working calls come back, like on the streets in Newark, I recognized that voice and knew, like there, what was happening. That that was how that was.

A whole swirl of turnarounds hurricaned from him. The world was going through changes and that world was in us too. We had to reevaluate all we knew. There were lives in us anyway filled with dynamite. We had a blackness to us, to be sure. It was always in us, we had but to claim it. And it claimed us.

The world's a prison for black people. The most imprisoned, those who cannot dig it. There was a time when a black wind circled. The streets were tingling. Popping. It began inside the people. Inside the rearranged world. The whole earth could be bubbling, shapes changing. Changing into. Transforming. A constant. But at times there is eruption, explosion, rapid movement.

I was a child and growing through zones and degrees until I became who this was when I wrote it (even when this is a book, I'll be gone gone gone again).

The bitterness and sweetness of becoming an adult. My adolescence extended through bohemia. When Malcolm reached me I was a spindling boy. Ensconced in a life so lightly taken it could be blown away.

Echoes of warfare reached me. And of another kind of life. I was still stepping trying to go faster. At one point I grew so bitter at a world whose values became reversed. I had built a life out of casual gestures and closed moods. Out of read lies and institutional distortions. It was camping out in a lone meadow where I could say anything, disconnected from the real, and by that, be anything. Thinking that, saying that, world of fiction. (And you could get rewards for fiction riding!)

But from cool to hard bop to what come next. It's chaos! Anti-jazz! Sheets of Sound! Bullshit! Cruelty! Can it be explained in the laboratories of Zat the Rich? All that!

News came in, images. Things I did in reflection of the world, connected individuals, as all are. And even in my theoretical exposition, I was yapping, conceiving. Not just pushed by wind and invisible things. I had ideas. Conceptions. Wrote essays. Went to Cuba. Argued with colleagues about whether the world and the word were connected.

> Star avalanche.
> I thought I was finding out stuff.
> I knew I was changing.
> Life was a fiction
> A table setting
> Unromantic romanesque
> Free and easy, on the draw
> Ol' hoboes could describe it.
> I was still in college.
> And the world happened by.
> I looked at my hands, my fingers
> I stared into my
> face.
> The niggers on television
> were getting
> beaten.
> I wanted to tell
> my grandfather
> I understood
> his world.

So no matter what washed-out-blond catatonics will tell you in unreasonable recalls about rumors they heard of human beings. Don't ever believe all the Negroes Fanon, Frazier, Cabral described cannot gradually come to consciousness, cannot one day stand on instinctive (i.e., perceptive) parenthetical phrases and colors in their own speech and one day look up and feel they need to go where the air is cleaner, where they can walk down the street at peace with themselves acknowledging the blatant contradictions of this world.

There are certain petty bourgeois intellectuals and poseurs and soi-disant artists, most of whom, in the U.S., are white, who cannot understand that most people do not envy, respect, or want to be near them. Who think they are unattractive and weird. Who do not like their washed-out limp hair and slightly open mouth with just a string of saliva, in sunlight, who think they are silly-looking, square, bizarre, irrelevant, not with it, corny, mediocre. But because they are in charge of the world, they think, figure you would quit them or their buddies only under duress.

Some of Jack Kerouac's overweight catatonic graveyard-blond mistresses thought (and think) that there is some reason someone should *love* them! And figure the only reason someone can think they are square, ugly, etc. & etc., is such gone types have been brainwashed. But in truth it's the other way around (and now some of these national chauvinists scream about sexual chauvinism!). Many of these could only hook up with certain chocolate drops under the duress of white supremacy. Released or trying to be released from that and seeing things as they more nearly are, such drops would, under sudden intake of breath, say "Shit" as they stole through the windows into the cold blue night. "Shit." And, like, split. Happy. Very very happy!

The arguments and show trials, the public shootouts and private disassignations. These helped blow me into another life. Ornette Coleman asked me to write a song around that time. I never had a chance to give the song to him cause I was gone by then. It was called "I Don't Love You." Check it.

> *Whatever you've given me, whiteface glass*
> *to look through, to find another there, another*
> *what motherfucker? another bread tree mad at its*
> *sacredness, and the law of some dingaling god, cold*
> *as ice cucumbers, for the shouters and the wigglers,*
> *and what was the world to the words of slick nigger fathers, too*

> *depressed to explain why they could not appear to be men.*
> *The bread fool. The don'ts of this white hell. The crashed eyes*
> *of dead friends, standin at the bar, eyes focused on actual ugliness.*
> *I don't love you. Who is to say what that will mean. I don't*
> *love you, expressed the train, moves, and uptown days later*
> *we look up and breathe much easier*
> *I don't love you*

Blew me into another, better life. I felt. I wanted and soon I needed. I wept I was caught downtown with white people. And left. As simple as that. Like one day you got pubic hairs.

The words of black people shape the fret of historic U.S. structure. Drunk nigger. High nigger. No, the calm iron-fingered equipment operators. Who breathe these words into my life—I want to be black and clean and free.

All the frenzied discussions our Negro intellectuals had. Our people and us had been dying slaves but we like our tradition fought—and I was fighting. Learning. Fighting. No matter that the emperor weeps he has lost his trim fleet of horses. I am no kept stallion.

You are ignorant, you are less, and one day, hopefully, you know something. We are all our years in yalla training taught to desire a certain world, whose existence is imperiled always by reality. There are many in this society whose lives are fueled by unreality, who deny and hate reality. But when I left the Village, the shock of waking up to who you are and hating it proved enough to send me into an orbit that was not completely correct. All the white-hating is not necessary to love oneself. Unless you are insecure as I was. And in the blinding flash of self-search that went on in the '60s there were many of us mashed together like that. No clear ideologies, some calling themselves Muslims, some Yorubas, when we got assembled fled from wherever.

The positive aspect of all that was clear, it represented struggle, the desire for liberation. The negative was the bashing together like children. And so those structures could not last, the internal contradictions were so sharp. Like the Black Arts. Like CFUN and CAP. Like RCL. Internal contradictions, lack of science, attacks by the state.

But just like the '20s we set some further footprints on a path yet to be fully trod. Yet to be fully understood. Except it is the getting out of the prison of self-deprecation. The mind bent by oppression, such beautiful people beat into submission by ugliness. Yet there is no submission, except from the already dead. The living resist and resist. We've held that line in song and story. It'll make you weep.

Fanon laid it out how the pathological intellectuals will rush headlong, unknowing, into love of their oppressors, trying not to kill them but to be them. And discovering the trap, how they have been used, they rush again headlong, or heartlong now, into Africa of their mind. The crippled fought each other and tried to stop any health or victory even in the name of victory and resistance. There is deep sickness among oppressed people. Deep hatred of each other among the pathological. Who even while they mouth liberation are trying to kill each other so they can scramble up the ladder of the oppressor's world. Or they think they can bash the world and mash it into pieces forever and with the resulting explosion reappear as cowboys of a new world made holy by their warped desires.

So many way stations to reality. And among the middle class, black as well as white, their narrow view too often they take as the necessity of the world. All that was positive from the Black Arts will be pieced up and a lot of the stupidity, too, will go on other places, replayed because the actors have no institutions of their own from which to learn. But how to duplicate that flash of heat that we mistook for absolute reality. How to explain that breaking out of the jail of white possession, even while reinventing the same shit in blackface, had to be done. We can look back at it now and laugh. At the mistakes, the viciousness, the errors, of our struggle. But only fools, the sick, the misinformed, the white supremacy freaks, would not understand the correctness of our vault toward the real.

And the errors were not that we left that world and its sickness but that we were ever there in the first place!

When the Arts had folded for me, I could look back there too, but it was not a place one never needed to be. There are folks still there worshiping the disappeared. Some hoping what is dead will come one day—not knowing it'd come and split. We met very sinister presences and sickness, but we began to understand our own world better. Not from across the chasm reading the newspapers listening to music memorizing our childhood or fantasizing, but touching and feeling. The men the women, the sights and sounds. There was no time for drawn-out reflection, bullets smashing into the walls. A pistol in my briefcase. Confrontations every day. Yet trying to build something. And that something being held up for the bright colors to be seen in the distance and signaled further on.

That failed because we did not know enough. We were young people just out of adolescence flexing our muscles, hero-worshiping. Trying to actually fly. We loved each other and fought for each other. We learned to love black people from close up again, and we laughed a lot as well as cried and cursed. We needed each other then, in the worst way, at that time of transition. Our flag was a gold mask on a black field, divided between tragedy and comedy, the drama of our time. Or was that symbol yellow on that flag? But those times were golden not yellow. There were the terrorists of our own movement, not just the state, but the sick. But something was raised. And at the same time, the seeds of even worse mistakes were made. There's no doubt in my mind that the Black Arts Theater will be remembered even in its brief throw against the dead. Its tiny light in shadows. The victory was in the struggle the unity the raising of ourselves, our history and tradition. That is simple national consciousness, where the victims focus on the requirements of their liberation. Where a people come to see themselves in contrast to their oppressors, and their lives and laws. Where they climb back into the stream of history.

But we made the same errors Fanon and Cabral laid out, if we had but read them, understood them. Because the cultural nationalism, atavism, male chauvinism, bourgeois lies painted black, feudal dead things, blown-up nigger balloons to toy around with. I would say the Nation of Islam and the Yoruba Temple were the heaviest carriers of this, the petty bourgeois confusing fantasy again with reality. The old sickness of religion—all the traps we did not understand. Crying blackness and for all the strength and goodness of that, not understanding the normal contradictions and the specific foolishness of white-hating black nationalism. The solution is not to become the enemy in blackface, that's what one of the black intellectuals' problems was in the first place. And even hating whites, being the white-baiting black nationalist is, might seem, justifiable but it is still a supremacy game. *The solution is revolution*. We thought that then, but didn't understand what it meant, really. We thought it meant killing white folks. But it is a system that's got to be killed and it's even twisted some blacks. It's hurt all of us.

Sometimes, though, you feel you move through tragedy and shame. That you step forward in the midst of ruins and explosions. Your eyes shining. Your survival ensured somehow by the fact of the I running on that computer track between your ears, behind your eyes. You could see the Black Arts in flames months before. Even while we did our heroic work of bringing the art, the newest strongest boldest hippest most avant of the swift dark shit to the streets, you could look up at that building some nights and swear it was in flames. That it shuddered and shook wreathed in hideous screams of fire. When you looked into the eyes of some very sick nigger, who might wind up in an ice cream suit selling dope or staggering down Seventh Avenue mumbling his divinity, my brothers, or with little women never had to face a real real world playing half house in the half dark, naked and burning, you knew it was that brief youthful footstep erased by fire and a cooling unremembering rain. But what was real survived the flame.

And let the sons of the sons and the daughters of the daughters retell and evaluate it. Let us retell and evaluate it, also more quickly that we might set up more strong, more real, and go on to the actual winning of the world.

When I was driven out of New York, at this point, I did feel the world was over. It was all ruins. From the wondrous hope, the promise of first coming to Harlem. And every day it had been like seeing again, being reshown the world. Just walking that first new spring uptown was revelation, from corner to corner taking in the panorama of that community was like being refueled with long-sought *blackness*. And that itself, the mythical blackness that we pumped up full of the hopes and desires of a people, but also the delusions and illusions of a rather narrow sector among that people. What blackness was, how it could be defined. With no science. It was easy enough for dudes with robes or red weird hats, who had some words, some rituals to say, you see, this is what it was. White people ain't like this.

When the final big explosion, the separation of myself from this cauldron of confusion and desire, came about, even though I knew the stupidity, frustration, ugliness I had encountered, and was still in awe of the actual tasks, the would-be solutions had come out of my mouth so easily (way way off in another world, another life) that Newark at first was like some Elba. I remembered the first echoes of what was coming, and the moving, that rush of blood into Blood, and the array of sensuous learning, black and gold, and then that gold turned yellow, crumbled right behind my eyes. So I felt in some kind of wounded exile.

Yet as I came to retune, to take up new energy, the place of my birth stood me up in it anew. And no matter the bleak occasion I began to see yet new again, and take new spirit from that newness, new energy and courage. Because this was literally, and certainly now, Home. And if there was a blackness that was not mythical, it would be found there. And I did move toward something real and tangible. Real life, real love, practical work.

The whole sweep of the Newark return was, like anything else, educational. Busted, somehow, is how I felt. Thrown down from the clouds hard upon the ground, even though it was my own decision.

As I tried to recover from that beating, huddled close to myself like a wet dog, shivering, out my weakness. Gradually there returned a fuller sense of self. I did know some things—I had some *actual* information. It was my real home. I had roots.

From there, as I learned more and more about the place and myself there and what could be done, I started to grow again. To do the things I wanted to do again. And the myth that that political work detracted from the art is mostly just another class's view of what it all is in the first place. Certainly I became concerned with a political truth in its practical operation. Its concrete realization, and that is work. It is difficult grey stone work. But to me it was exhilarating, opening, clearing work. Like the gunfighter wounded sits somewhere practicing pulling his heat to get faster and faster.

Still I was moving through levels and levels of webs and stages and stages of steps made of different materials. I was having to find out the simplest things. To the more difficult. Learning, building. Making connections. And that whole trip was not bereft of fantasy either. That whole gunfighter fantasy. The real isolation—from an art-derived world. Although I kept working, Newark is no art colony, no panting aesthetic group. It is a grey steel and stone factory workers' town, the grim highway's end for those lovely southern men and women who came this way and mistook an "Ark" for a "York."

It was a reality less caked with the unnecessary gesture. The fantasies we stepped into had to do with our misunderstanding. As usual. The mixture of half Yorubaist, Malcolm's death-fascination Islam, bourgeois politics, black nationalism, insecurity, subjectivism, and bohemianism, still, dogged my steps. There were many of us across the country creating various weird structures. Out of the same confusion and metaphysics.

I was not as into an open metaphysics ever until going into nationalism. I could attach names and a blatant embrace of this stuff as "blackness." The feudalism, reformism, male chauvinism, all crept in or rushed in under the rubric of nationalism. Blackness. Even the apotheosis of cultural nationalism I took on because it was the best-organized form of the abstraction "blackness." Some kind of complex and funny Rube Goldberg machine of the mind.

Yet despite the downright absurdity of that trip it was still part of a long march to better understanding. To some more objective clarity. The Spirit House, the Committee for Unified Newark, the Congress of Afrikan Peoples, all have many elements to them that we still need. A theater — you know it; a black united front based on unity and struggle to fight for democracy and self-determination — of course, only it must be led by a real majority and not salesmen in cheap suits which they will switch backstage for the same thing in African. Not mediocre civil servants with cuffs. Not little-boy intellectuals serving a penance for almost whiting out. Not "Oriental" karate freaks, et cetera. Lying politicians. The numb, the dumb, the fantasized, the hiders from Afro-America. And something to consciously focus the blacks of this earth on their common attacker, of course. But not congealed in the mind-set of the above or atavists or baldhead killers or charisma students or pseudo-semi-soi-disant-aspirant-almost intellectuals or Negroes who believe Africa is a branch of Woolworth's (or the Chase Manhattan Bank).

Because then, for all your steps, our steps, we will be again where we are; if you will peer up from the book for a second and summarize the damage, the bodies, the broken hopes and lives, the still useless fantasists holding religious ceremonies in which black people's freedom is the drug of the set, for the ooooooo's and aaaaaaa's and jumping and twisting, with the same collection and the same ruthless preacher and his pitiful tastes.

I was a novice in search of blackness still and settled for a cultural/religious fiction that covered the reality of what we did, the real achievements, the actual accomplishments. It is safe to say that if we had known more, if we had known more that drift and drug. But that is a truth, if we had known more this city wouldn't be so hurting. Or we might be dead or in jail. Perhaps; that is something to consider as well. How much you are permitted to accomplish.

But I mean if all the jive and model-spaceship building I was into. . .all the. . .(denying the actuality of a life is what this is, I suppose) I'm just speculating that perhaps the fat Negro bureaucrat that squats upon our heads in this town, belching, would not be there. Because, yes, it's true. I was the drum major for that particular drum head. But, look, life is not over. The world is still here. There are still things that can be done. And I swear I do understand the world better. We will find out just how well. In words and deeds yet to be written and realitied out.

But even in that thralldom, that dumb thrall, we built some actual things, we laid out a process of learning. For the close readers. We did step through madness and bullshit. But we were not just full-of-shit tourists. We did take the city away from the lowest level, and if the next level is sickening, the task is of a higher order, and its solution is the current day's work. Are we up to it, anyone, anywhere? Of course, is the roared refrain.

That is, for all the fantasy flags and subjective flying. Stopped lives and wasted motion. I think many of us, boys and girls who grew to men and women, did come away with something of value. And when a better evaluation is given they will find something of value too.

Even now, for all those who think that "Baraka the Marxist" is just the title of a new play, the latest of the lad's interesting gambols, they must admit to movement. For myself I think that struggle and defeat finally are useful if our heads are harder, our grasp of reality firmer. I think they are.

And yet again, the clear-headed will see the striking gain I've made since I did find a woman, in the real world, whose life was connected up with mine and mine with hers before we knew anything about each other. I was going to the Bethany Baptist Church right around the corner from where Sylvia grew up. I crossed that Howard Street, back and forth Saturdays going downtown from Belmont. Or as a grocery-carrying teenager, snaking back and forth in snow and sunshine. A few years, a few blocks, away. It was just that I had to grow in a certain way, fill out in a certain way, to be where I was supposed to be at the appointed time. Because I never did know anything about love, because I was never really ready to come out of my head long enough to relate to someone else. To be in the world with another person, listening to them, touching them, holding them, making a life together with them. For all the missteps and beatings, the lies and betrayals, that was, to me, and for us, I think, a reward. We, Sylvia, now Amina, and I, can curse many things. Drains, walls, frustrations, hatreds, the normal and abnormal disappointment of developing love. Plus, there is no way that anyone can overestimate my own capacity to disappoint, to hurt, to drive away. Yet we two have been on a journey together now some sixteen years. And that in itself is the subject of another, much better book. But suffice it to say, she has been in that rush of life, she has felt that pain, she has often lamented being tied to someone whose life at times seems an abstraction. And yes, for those only recently come to consciousness about women's oppression, and who have even got some notoriety for putting down black women who were involved in struggle during the '60s because they supposedly did not know about male chauvinism, such nonsense is cruel and stupid beyond belief. And one day that story will be told from some of those women's mouths how they had to stand up under the incredible and bizarre neo-feudalist yoke of cultural nationalism. How they fought it for every inch. How they improvised and sidestepped and even threw real pots and pans to try to get free of their master the slave.

Because, fundamentally, there is no one I have ever been as close to as my wife. Not just because of that title, or that social expectation, but because we went to the university of false blackness together, even while, and at the same time, doing some real things, some important things, and most of all, even while learning some critical things about ourselves and the world.

Each one of those children is like some living loving signpost of our own journey, its defeats and its victories. While we struggled in that university of the "half world" in the world, and finally one day graduated. And also, because at each twist and turn of the world, being thrown forward and sometimes backward in ourselves and on the real sidewalks, both of us knew even more about the other, and had to understand, fight, accept what that was, and for all of it grew closer. To me, sometimes I wonder how you can really be in love with someone without such knowledge. Because at each increment, at each turn and twist, there was a drawing closer, a redefined heart, a reunderstood touch or gesture. So that we could say I knew you and loved you when you was stone crazy. I like you much better now. That is the essence of it, that as you grow you also grow more in love. Because it is a ripening—sometimes you could pity the folks who miss it and many do—that all the various stages and faces we go through, there is a time, a period, when you can become your whole self, and have another whole self with you, who would be your choice of someone to be with even before, if you were conscious. And by the time that happens, your own consciousness, you can look up and there is, indeed, someone there, who's been there and growing with you, who knows all your bullshit ways and still has made those many moves, who says, "OK, what now?" Those are both your voices at the same time!

And so the trip through metaphysical nationalism, the breakup of that camp. The conflicts with madmen and murderers, the most recent motion to Marxism. All were part of a joint journey which, meanwhile and at the same time, was most times hidden from the world, because the owners of it prefer it that way. Amina and I were raising a family, strong, beautiful, brilliant children who will be a match for all this shit, mark my words. At the same time their parents wrestled with a more primitive world.

So in comparing and measuring, in summing up, all the roads I've traveled have been the preparation, as hopefully, this present period is more

preparation. And in conversation many nights and afternoons or mornings, Amina and I run through the many changes and preparations we've
been through, even while dealing with the scabs and scarecrows, the monsters and senseless things of the present, we recall all that past we've been
through, our disguises and apprenticeships. How we loved movies and
music and black people. And how, even as the Marxists we both are, listening intently to our children's growing songs and pains, we are relieved that
we grew up to be even this close to ourselves. Unconscious, whited out,
blacked out, out in space, African clothes world, corridor of uneventful
aftermath supposed to take you out, after you miss the slam dunk which
would have ended the game, as Champion. (And I do know that Mao said
that five hundred years from now, most of what we say will seem like
children's singing!) But when you can look up and see some sophisticated
black woman, beautiful even in her forties, brown skin, close curly hair,
leg crossed perhaps, sipping something, in discussion with you or someone, anyone, about the world, and about how that world needs changing,
yes it does, be it a jazz solo or a figure of dance or the workers climbing up
the back of the world to reconstruct it all so the future will indeed be the
future. You know then your path has not been just bullshit. Just because
you had to read every book on the *New York Times Book Review* best-seller
list, you didn't know any better. Just because you had to be a white intellectual then a black nationalist even though you always had the hole card on
that class struggle, and its yellow brown and blue black contrasts that spell
out a world in this time and this place. And even though you left New
York, runned away, and built a paper house of nigger mediocre domestic
Mobutus as the postdoctoral study for the black masses, and yourself—the
fact of Amina is herself confirmation that I have not been all the way crazy,
not all the way full of shit. The fact of my lovely brown wife who is tuned
in as she is herself to what seems important to both of us, and a tall boy
with drumsticks and quoting Dr. J.'s ballet, and a big-eyed one wants to be
a leader as he plays trumpet and reads the book of practical cats, and a tiny
teeny little girl thing with her cat Sojourner Mooty-Toot who wants to play
the violin and hates nasty stuff, or the round-headed big-eyed boy who
rises at seven each morning to go through his papers and stare out the
window or sing little songs hoping to wake everybody else up, or the little
bad dude from outer space, the professional pest, who knows already he
wants to be a painter and who walked through the Metropolitan Museum
grading them dudes, all this, and our big red house, and our collective
strength and beauty and our collective intelligence and the fact, dig this,

that we are still very young!!!! That lets me know that I wasn't all the way crazy, not just bullshit mad. And even when they attack me, these agents of slowness and primitivism. Even while they try to hide pictures of me smiling or word that I am alive and well and still not crazy or pessimistic. Or hide the reality of my marriage or the identity of my wife and still publish books by catatonics trying to prove the world of catatonia is the only real world, and you was a fool to leave it, big boy. I can get happy, in spite of the frustration and racism, and attempts to kill us all. Even while they try to make it seem I am a wife beater and madman and stopped writing or stopped breathing, I can get happy anyway, like my laughter is bullets and bombs, my joy a poison gas to the haters of democracy, because despite all that, I have already survived, living not completely quietly, in fact still full of animation and almost endless energy. Still very much on the case of the place trying to turn it around and unwilling to accept no for an answer. Then that is the sharp laughter in me you hear. That runs through all of this telling despite the bad situations and backups, the stupid contexts I looked up to find myself in. The misunderstanding and mistakes. That is what you feel and hear. That I am still alive and in the company of the people I love most in the world.

So if you see us anytime, Amina and me, somewhere, myself like I look and this tall beautiful woman, maybe we are in the lobby of a theater looking at each other and laughing about something. It might just be something in the past we are laughing at, some fool or narrow escape, some sudden revelation of beauty. Understand, we are in tune with the majority, of all languages and nationalities, no matter we might look like Nick and Nora Charles in brown to some or Zora Neale and Langston to others or like a brown boy and brown girl, well dressed and sophisticated, given to irony and sudden passion, lovers of poetry and music. Make no mistake, we are serious about our lives and about our destiny, and the lives of our people and indeed of the majority of people. I guess this is what makes us dangerous, we will not die around some bullshit tip. We will not be taken out easily. In fact, we are still growing, getting stronger and more knowledgeable, and just when you get used to that, hesitate a moment and you will see a crowd of little ones surround us. That's right, they are listening for instructions, some of which they will follow, some of which they won't. They are worse than we are. And we think *we* can win!

Consider the rightness and strength of that, the easy effortless beauty. We are alive! Alive and conscious and in love! It has taken some years to reach that state of clarity and feeling. And this is but partial evidence.